SILENCING THE SELF ACROSS CULTURES

SILENCING THE SELF ACROSS CULTURES
DEPRESSION AND GENDER IN THE SOCIAL WORLD

Dana Crowley Jack
Alisha Ali

OXFORD
UNIVERSITY PRESS

OXFORD
UNIVERSITY PRESS

Oxford University Press, Inc., publishes works that further
Oxford University's objective of excellence
in research, scholarship, and education.

Oxford   New York
Auckland   Cape Town   Dar es Salaam   Hong Kong   Karachi
Kuala Lumpur   Madrid   Melbourne   Mexico City   Nairobi
New Delhi   Shanghai   Taipei   Toronto

With offices in
Argentina   Austria   Brazil   Chile   Czech Republic   France   Greece
Guatemala   Hungary   Italy   Japan   Poland   Portugal   Singapore
South Korea   Switzerland   Thailand   Turkey   Ukraine   Vietnam

Published by Oxford University Press, Inc.
198 Madison Avenue, New York, New York 10016
www.oup.com

First issued as an Oxford University Press paperback, 2012.

Oxford is a registered trademark of Oxford University Press

Library of Congress Cataloging-in-Publication Data

Silencing the self across cultures : depression and gender in the
    social world / [edited by] Dana Crowley Jack, Alisha Ali.
        p.   cm.
    Includes bibliographical references.
    ISBN: 978-0-19-539809-0 (hardcover); 978-0-19-993202-3 (paperback)
    1. Depression in women—Cross-cultural studies.   I. Jack, Dana Crowley.
    II. Ali, Alisha, 1970–
    RC537.S535   2010
    362.196' 8527—dc22

                                                                    2009035751

Printed in the United States of America
on acid-free paper

This book is dedicated, with love, to Rand,
to my children Darby and Kelsey, and to
my mother, Dorothy Beach.
Dana C. Jack

To Bruce, Talia, and Adara. And to my mother.
Alisha Ali

Acknowledgments

This book was made possible by the authors who contributed chapters, and we thank them for their central role and for their contributions. Working with Lori Handelman at Oxford University Press has been a pleasure, and we gratefully acknowledge her generous editorial help and support during this long process.

No edited book comes to completion without the help of many people. This volume benefitted immensely from David Matsumoto's review and insightful comments during its development. We also thank the seven anonymous reviewers who offered thoughtful critiques and encouragement for the ideas and shape of this volume. Thank you to Walter Lonner for his suggestions regarding the creation of this book, and to our conversations with many colleagues regarding the content of each chapter. Richard Gordon offered helpful advice regarding the internationally-authored chapters.

I (Dana Jack) received institutional support from Western Washington University and Fairhaven College of Interdisciplinary Studies through professional leave and small grants. Thank you to Carol Gilligan for her support and important insights in our discussions about silence and voice and to Joseph Trimble for his encouragement and discussion of chapters throughout the process of compiling this manuscript. A number of students at Fairhaven College helped with details of the book, especially Serina Holmstrom, Clarissa Pearce, Elizabeth Zieline, and Zoe Barnow. I thank the Fulbright Commission for the opportunity to live and teach in Nepal, an unforgettable experience that instigated this book. I am grateful for the support of members of our small writing group – Mary Cornish, Jenny Hahn, and Ara Taylor. Finally, my love and appreciation go to my family—Rand, Darby, Kelsey, and Dorothy Beach—along with new family members Juliette, Galen, and Francis. Rand has offered unfailing support and thoughtful discussions as well as editing help. I could not do any of this work without his deep understanding and good humor.

Additionally, I (Alisha Ali) wish to thank my wonderfully supportive colleagues in the Department of Applied Psychology at New York University, as well as my many doctoral students who have so generously given their time. I also thank my dear and constant friend, Maureen Fadem, for the countless hours of inspiring discussion. Lastly, thank you to my husband, Bruce, for his unfaltering love and patience, and to our two daughters, Talia and Adara, for all they have taught me.

Preface

Carol Gilligan

I remember the afternoon, the gray light, the feeling of snow. Dana Jack had come to talk about her dissertation, and we were sitting in my small office in Harvard's Schlesinger Library. We moved our chairs closer together to read through the transcripts Dana brought with her. She was studying depression in women, and she had interviewed clinically depressed women in the Pacific Northwest where she was living.

I remember the astonishment that ran through my body as I saw evidence of a first-person voice speaking in the midst of depression, an "I" saying, "I want...I know...I see...I feel...I think....I believe." Woven through the fabric of listlessness, lifelessness, helplessness, and hopelessness were signs of a self, active and present—but a self beset by a second voice, the voice of what Dana would call the "Over-Eye," an internalized observer who watched, judged, condemned, and ultimately silenced the self. In no uncertain terms, it assumed moral authority, often backed by religious sanction, addressing the self typically in second or third person, saying, "You should....one ought," and establishing how a good woman would act, what she should do. Above all, it enjoined a woman to be "selfless," to care for others and maintain relationships without speaking about or for herself. With stunning insight, Dana reframed the dynamics of depression. The exhaustion of depression reveals the energy it takes to silence the self.

In "Mourning and Melancholia," Freud attributed depression to a failure of mourning, an evasion of sadness in the face of loss. "The shadow of the object falls on the ego," he wrote. Today, depression is more commonly seen as reflecting a fault in brain chemistry, a consequence of genetic predisposition or trauma or a sequel to unfortunate life circumstances such as poverty or illness. In either case, the depressed person is rendered helpless, a victim of neurochemistry and/or fate. The mind, seen as part of the body, is treated for the most part pharmacologically. In the study of depression, serotonin reuptake inhibitors have replaced the analyst's couch.

In this light, we can appreciate the contribution of the essays collected in this volume. By listening to women and hearing the inner dialogue of depression, Dana Jack had found evidence of an active and ongoing, if losing, battle on the part of the self against the voices that would render her silent or silenced. In doing so, she picked up the moral themes in women's depression, recognizing in the voice of the Over-Eye, a culturally scripted voice. Bringing a cultural perspective to the analysis of women's depression, she also saw the bind women were caught in: To contest the voice that would silence her in the name of goodness, a woman would render herself, in its terms, selfish, bad, and wrong. Thus, she was trapped in a circle of self-condemnation; to break free meant to challenge the culture in which she was living, a framework that encompassed herself. The authors who speak in this book have done just that: challenged their native cultures by calling attention to the various ways in which they silence women, precipitating depression or causing women who resist self-silencing to struggle against feeling bad or wrong or selfish or crazy. The writing of these essays becomes a courageous act of resistance against those who would enforce or collude in women's self-silencing and thus countenance the near-epidemic rates of depression among women.

The range of cultures represented here attest to the ubiquity of pressures on women to render themselves selfless by caring for others and maintaining relationships while silencing themselves. The moral themes in women's depression expose and enforce the gender binaries and hierarchies of a patriarchal social order, where being a man means not being a woman and also being on top. To be a good woman, good wife, good mother, good daughter, good helpmate or colleague, a woman must subordinate herself to male authority and accede to the voice or the law of the fathers.

The stark implication of the self-silencing theory of women's depression is that the self does not go gently into silence. Whatever its biological substrates or sociological precipitants, depression in women is also a sign or a symptom of a woman's resistance to silencing herself. However costly or misguided, it is a resistance to the gender binaries and hierarchies of patriarchy. The etymology of the word "hierarchy," literally meaning a rule of priests, reveals the religious substrate of patriarchy, an order of living in which the *hieros*, the priest, is a *pater*, a father. The dynamics of depression thus become inseparable from the tensions between democracy and patriarchy, one grounded in equality of voice, the other privileging the voices of fathers. The resistance of the "I," the voice of the self, to the voice of the Over-Eye, the internalized voice of patriarchal authority, is a fight for voice and for relationship that is also a fight for love and democracy.

I want to pause for a moment to speak of methodology, because the exploration of depression that began with Dana listening to the voices of depressed women with an ear for the culture in which they are living is a model for how to proceed from qualitative analysis to quantitative research. With the development of the Silencing the Self Scale, it became possible to take a theory grounded in the voices of depressed women and explore its explanatory power in wider populations across a range of societies and cultures. The refinement and validation of the self-silencing theory of women's depression is among the more impressive achievements of contemporary psychological research, revealing a sophistication of method and also the power of a theory that integrates cultural perspectives in seeking to explain a major, worldwide problem in public health. It becomes a model for research that is at once experience-near or culturally thick, in Clifford Geertz's terms, and scientifically powerful in its ability to predict and explain.

At the core of the self-silencing theory of depression, the contradictions between relationship and subservience become unmistakable. Voice is integral to relationship, a sign of being present and engaged with others. Just as voice depends on resonance and as speaking depends on listening and being heard, so, too, without voice, there is no relationship, only the chimera of relationship. But as voice is grounded both in the body and in language, it roots psychology within biology and culture without reducing it to either. The counterpoint of voices in women's depression, the inner dialogue between the "I" and the Over-Eye, underscores the need for a theory of depression that encompasses not only biology but also the subjectivity of women and the power of the forces that would render them silent or silenced. The paradox at the center of the self-silencing theory of depression is that in the name of caring for others and maintaining relationships, a woman must in effect sacrifice relationship and abandon herself. Women's depression thus becomes a protest against the loss of voice and relationships, a way of saying, "I have been silenced."

Reflecting on the epidemiology of depression, Martin Seligman reminds us that during childhood, boys are more often depressed than girls. It is in adolescence that this pattern reverses, with the sharp rise in the incidence of depression among girls extending into womanhood and leading to the common observation that women are more often depressed than men—or at least are more likely to display depressive symptoms and be diagnosed as such. Depression itself with its listlessness and passivity is often seen as antithetical to masculinity. Reading Seligman, I was intrigued by his observation that whatever causes the gender flip-flop in the incidence of depression, with women becoming twice as depressed as men, it does not have its roots in girls' childhood. Something must happen to girls in adolescence, he concludes, to account for the sudden shift.

The studies of girls' development that my colleagues and I began in the 1980s offer an explanation, derived from a close listening to girls' narratives of coming of age. Approaching adolescence, girls describe a crisis of relationship as they face pressures from without and within to choose between having a voice and having relationships. As 16-year-old Iris says, reflecting on the outspokenness of younger girls, "If I were to say what I was feeling and thinking, no one would want to be with me, my voice would be too loud." Thirteen-year-old Tracy observes, "When we were 9, we were stupid." But when I say that it would never have occurred to me to use the word "stupid" since what struck me most about her and her classmates when they were 9 was how much they knew, she says, "I mean, when we were 9, we were honest." As an honest voice comes to seem or to sound stupid, girls begin to silence themselves. But they can also discern the rationale for this self-silencing, its justifications, and its adaptive value within societies or cultures where women's honest voices often sound too loud and are called stupid or crazy or bad or wrong. The dynamics of women's depression are built into the structures of patriarchy, giving rise to a tension between psychology and culture, between the desire to speak and pressures to silence oneself because, as Iris explains, "you have to have relationships."

The startling discovery made by listening to girls is that at adolescence, girls have the cognitive capacity to describe and reflect on their initiation into the codes and scripts of patriarchal womanhood. Thus, they signal the onset of dissociation: the splitting of mind from body, thought from emotion, and self from relationships, leading to a loss of voice and signs of psychological distress. Listening to girls and observing their passage from childhood to adolescence sparked the realization that the initiation into the gender codes and scripts of patriarchy bears some of the hallmarks of trauma: loss of voice, loss of memory, and consequently, loss of the ability to tell one's story accurately. Once a woman has internalized the norms and values of a patriarchal order that requires her to care for others while silencing herself, she finds herself, in the words of Jean Baker Miller, "doing good and feeling bad."

The analysis of women's depression as a manifestation of self-silencing when joined with research on girls' development suggests that women's voices may hold a key to resolving a long-standing puzzle in research on human development, a puzzle highlighted by the epidemiology of depression. The fact that boys show more signs of psychological distress during childhood, including a higher incidence of depression, can be seen to reflect their earlier initiation into the gender binaries and hierarchies of patriarchy, leading them to hide or deny the vulnerability of their bodies, to suppress emotions that imply tenderness or softness, and to construct a self that is separate from relationships. In doing so, they compromise their emotional intelligence and diminish their capacity to read the human world around them. In essence, they sacrifice relationship for hierarchy in claiming patriarchal masculinity and silence vital parts of themselves. Tenderness, relationships, and the vulnerable body become the domain of women, at once idealized and devalued, while toughness, self, and rationality are elevated and associated with masculinity.

In resisting these inner divisions, women may give voice to what men cannot say without placing their manhood in jeopardy. To the extent that women resist self-silencing, they are resisting an initiation that is costly for men as well. The study of women's depression thus highlights what is ultimately a human problem, a conflict between healthy psychological development and the culture of patriarchy with its associated ills of racism, sexism, homophobia, and other forms of intolerance. In *The Deepening Darkness: Patriarchy, Resistance, and Democracy's Future*, David Richards and I observe, "what patriarchy precludes is love between equals and thus it precludes democracy, founded on such love and the freedom of voice it encourages" (p. 19).

The signal contribution of the essays gathered here by Dana Jack and Alisha Ali is that by bringing cultural perspectives to the analysis of depression in women, they reveal the overarching framework of patriarchy. To see the framework, however, is also to reveal the possibility of shifting the frame. By joining women in their resistance to self-silencing and showing the costs of inequality, the authors of these essays link the study of depression to a call for democratic forms of living and functioning. The requisites for love—having a voice and living in relationships—are also the requisites for democracy. The fact that we, men and women alike, are born with a voice and into relationship means that we have within ourselves the capacity for love and for citizenship within democratic societies. To see depression as a sign of self-silencing is to recognize the costs of perpetuating patriarchal norms and values in all their subtle and not so subtle manifestations. The worldwide pervasiveness of depression in women is a flag, drawing attention as well to the more hidden symptoms of depression in men. My hope is that this will be the first in a series of books on depression that expose the costs of self-silencing, releasing in both women and men a voice of ethical resistance to perpetuating or justifying, in the name of morality, a history of trauma, tragedy, and violence.

References

Freud, S. (1915). Mourning and melancholia. In J. Strachey (Ed.), *The standard edition of the complete psychological works of Sigmund Freud* (Vol. 14, pp. 243–258). London: Hogarth Press.

Geertz, C. (1973). *The interpretation of cultures*. New York: Basic Books.

Gilligan, C. (1982). *In a different voice: Psychological theory and women's development.* Cambridge, MA: Harvard University Press.

Gilligan, C. (1990). Joining the resistance: Psychology, politics, girls, and women. *Michigan Quarterly Review, 29,* 501–536.

Gilligan, C. (1996). The centrality of relationship in human development: A puzzle, some evidence, and a theory. In G. Noam & K. Fischer (Eds.), *Development and vulnerability in close relationships*. Mahwah, New Jersey: Erlbaum.

Gilligan, C. (2002). *The birth of pleasure: A new map of love.* New York: Alfred A. Knopf.

Gilligan, C., & Brown, L. M. (1992). *Meeting at the crossroads: Women's psychology and girls' development.* Cambridge, MA: Harvard University Press.

Gilligan, C., & Richards, D. A. J. (2009). *The deepening darkness: Patriarchy, resistance, and democracy's future.* New York: Cambridge University Press.

Gilligan, C., Rogers, A. G., & Tolman, D. (1991). *Women, girls, and psychotherapy: Reframing resistance*. Binghamton, NY: Haworth Press.

Gilligan, C., Spencer, R., Weinberg, M. K., & Bertsch, T. (2003). On the listening guide: A voice-centered, relational method. In P. M. Camic, J. E. Rhodes, & L. Yardley (Eds.), *Qualitative research in psychology: Expanding perspectives in methodology and design*. Washington, DC: American Psychological Association.

Jack, D. C. (1991). *Silencing the self: Women and depression*. Cambridge, MA: Harvard University Press.

Jack, D. C., & Dill, D. (1992). The Silencing the Self Scale: Schemas of intimacy associated with depression in women. *Psychology of Women Quarterly, 16*, 97–106.

Miller, J. B. (1976). *Toward a new psychology of women*. Boston: Beacon Press.

Seligman, M. E. (1991). *Learned optimism*. New York: Random House.

Taylor, J. M., Gilligan, C., & Sullivan, A. (1995). *Between voice and silence: Women and girls, race and relationship*. Cambridge, MA: Harvard University Press.

Contents

Contributors

Alisha Ali, PhD, Department of Applied Psychology, New York University, New York

Jill Astbury, PhD, School of Psychology, Victoria University, Melbourne, Australia

Clelia Beltrame, BS, Center for Addictions Research and Services, School of Social Work, Boston University, Boston, Massachusetts

Guillermo Bernal, PhD, Department of Psychology, University of Puerto Rico, Centro Universitario de Servicios y Estudios Psicológicos, San Juan, Puerto Rico

Avi Besser, PhD, Department of Behavioral Sciences, Chairman, Center for Research in Personality, Life Transitions, and Stressful Life Events, Sapir College, D.N.H. of Ashkelon 79165, Israel

Laura S. Brown, PhD, Fremont Community Therapy Project, Seattle, Washington

Stephanie Cassin, PhD, Department of Psychiatry, Sunnybrook Health Sciences Centre, University of Toronto, Toronto, Ontario, Canada

Rosanna F. DeMarco, PhD, PHCNS-BC, ACRN, FAAN, William F. Connell School of Nursing, Boston College, Chestnut Hill, Massachusetts

Krystyna Drat-Ruszczak, PhD, Warsaw School of Social Psychology, Warsaw, Poland

Elaine D. Eaker, ScD, Eaker Epidemiology Enterprises, Gaithersburg, Maryland

Gordon L. Flett, PhD, Faculty of Health, York University, Toronto, Ontario, Canada

Josie Geller, PhD, Eating Disorders Program, Department of Psychiatry, University of British Columbia, Vancouver, British Columbia, Canada

Carol Gilligan, PhD, Department of Applied Psychology, New York University, New York

Richard A. Gordon, PhD, Bard College, Annandale-on-Hudson, New York

Airi Hautamäki, PhD, Swedish School of Social Science, University of Helsinki, Helsinki, Finland

Susanne Hedlund, PhD, Center for Behavioral Medicine, Roseneck Hospital, Prien am Chiemsee, Germany

Paul L. Hewitt, PhD, Department of Psychology, University of British Columbia, Vancouver, British Columbia, Canada

Bridget Hirsch, MA, Department of Counseling, Developmental, and Educational Psychology, Lynch School of Education, Boston College, Boston, Massachusetts

Dana Crowley Jack, EdD, Fairhaven College of Interdisciplinary Studies/ Western Washington University, Bellingham, Washington

Judith Jordan, PhD, Jean Baker Miller Training Institute, Lexington, Massachusetts

Margaret Kelly-Hayes, EdD, RN, FAAN, School of Medicine, Boston University, Boston, Massachusetts

Natasha S. Mauthner, PhD, Business School, University of Aberdeen, Aberdeen, Scotland

Maria I. Medved, PhD, Department of Psychology, University of Manitoba, Winnipeg, Manitoba, Canada

Sofia Neves, PhD, Departamento de Psicologia, Instituto Superior da Maia, Maia, Portugal

Guerda Nicolas, PhD, Department of Educational and Psychological Studies, University of Miami, Miami, Florida

Conceição Nogueira, PhD, Instituto de Educação e Psicologia, Universidade do Minho, Minho, Portugal

Janette Perz, PhD, Gender, Culture and Health Research Unit, School of Psychology, University of Western Sydney, Sydney, Australia

Bindu Pokharel, MA, Central Department of Rural Studies, University Campus, Tribhuvan University, Kirtipur, Nepal

María R. Scharrón-Del Río, PhD, School Counseling Program, Brooklyn College, New York

Anjoo Sikka, PhD, College of Public Service, University of Houston – Downtown, Houston, Texas

Linda Smolak, PhD, Department of Psychology, Kenyon College, Gambier, Ohio

Mary Sormanti, PhD, MSW, School of Social Work, Columbia University, New York

Suja Srikameswaran, PhD, Eating Disorders Program, Department of Psychiatry, University of British Columbia, Vancouver, British Columbia, Canada

Janet M. Stoppard, PhD, Department of Psychology, University of New Brunswick, Fredericton, New Brunswick, Canada

Usha Subba, PhD, Department of Psychology, Trichandra Multiple Campus, Tribhuvan University, Kathmandu, Nepal

Joseph E. Trimble, PhD, Department of Psychology, Western Washington University Bellingham, Washington

Jane M. Ussher, PhD, Gender, Culture and Health Research Unit, School of Psychology, University of Western Sydney, Sydney, Australia

Linda (Gratch) Vaden-Goad, PhD, School of Arts and Sciences, Western Connecticut State University, Danbury, Connecticut

Lisa K. Waldner, PhD, Department of Sociology, University of St. Thomas, St. Paul, Minnesota

Stephanie J. Woods, PhD, MSN, College of Nursing, University of Akron, Akron, Ohio

Judith Worell, PhD, Department of Education and Counseling Psychology, University of Kentucky, Lexington, Kentucky

Tanja Zoellner, PhD, Center for Behavioral Medicine, Roseneck Hospital, Prien am Chiemsee, Germany

Foreword: Silence No More

Judith Worell

I am honored and excited to share in the publication of this important volume. The editors have gathered an outstanding group of distinguished authors who present us with a range of national and international research supporting and expanding the utility of the Silencing the Self Scale (STSS). The diversity of perspectives on the culture/depression formulation is clearly enhanced by the inclusion of a single measure across research localities. Through binding together theory, assessment, and cultural awareness, we gain further access to the critical role of context in relation to women's emotional distress. Inclusion across chapters of both quantitative and qualitative approaches honors a flexibility model of research methodology that can unlock new insights on old concerns. Across the centuries of recorded history, depression has not disappeared from the human condition, and women continue to be the major recipients of its malaise. The chapters in this volume that document women's disempowerment globally can offer us further guideposts to the possibilities for change. Their messages speak to many minds and hearts, stimulating further research by opening new vistas across nationalities and cultures.

My original involvement in publication of the STSS (Jack & Dill, 1992) dates back to the time I was editor of the *Psychology of Women Quarterly* (PWQ). Due to my clinical training, practice, and research, this article carried a special historical significance for me. Since its inception in 1976, the journal served as a beacon of light that illuminated and explored the factors that influence the lives and well-being of women. It was exhilarating to be in the position of publishing high-quality articles that welcomed discussions of feminist theory and research. The articles that were published in PWQ opened doors to our knowledge and understanding of the critical role of gender, context, and a range of diverse social locations in women's lives. Although the psychology of difference was only one of many topics welcomed by the journal, I was particularly intrigued by this creative research that addressed the gender imbalance in rates of emotional distress and depression with convincing data. From my past clinical experience with women's concerns in counseling and psychotherapy, expressions of anxiety, hopelessness, and depression were among those I most frequently encountered with clients. For many clinicians, our understanding of gender dynamics was limited to a few prevailing theories that frequently tended to place blame on the woman for her concerns. In contrast, creative hypotheses and supporting data that connected client distress to broader gendered contexts were certainly a welcome addition to the journal. As this volume on the STSS so clearly articulates, the context of women's well-being or distress is reflective of the larger social milieu and cultural norms that are embedded in each particular historical time and location.

In the public arena at that time, attention to the status of women in the United States was at midstream. Federal legislation had been enacted to establish educational and employment equity, but public commitment to women's psychological health concerns lagged far behind. The importance of women's access to graduate education and professional development to research on female health cannot be underestimated. In contrast to historical invisibility or a sex-difference approach to well-being, an increased cadre of women researchers began to ask new questions about women's lives and experiences. As Barbara Wallston (1981) so eloquently wrote: "What are the questions in the psychology of women?" With this statement, she helped to reframe the research agenda away from contrived laboratory experiments toward a feminist perspective on the context of women's real lives and their "lived" experiences. For many of us, personal experiences lay the groundwork for how we proceeded with our science and what topics we chose to investigate. This was true of me as well. What was life like for women growing up before the middle of the last century? I take myself as an example.

As was typical for many young children, my early experience of gender disparities was situational and personal. In my world, girls seemed to have different rules than boys for how we dressed, how we spoke, and how we behaved at home, in school, and in public places. That boys might have a better deal than girls was also interpreted through a personal lens in particular situations related to visibility and voice. I noticed and asked questions, but seldom complained about what appeared to be the "natural order." Why did my brother have more freedom than I to go places alone? Why did the boys and men in my parents' temple sit downstairs to pray while the women and girls sat upstairs behind a screen where they remained unheard and unseen? Why did women and girls prepare, serve, and clean up after meals while boys went out to play and men sat reading the newspaper? And why was my mother reserved and apparently compliant at home but openly expressive when we were together or among her women friends? My awareness that these cultural and family rules were replicated in some form across many situations emerged only gradually. In graduate school, I continued asking questions as it became more evident that such gender divisions were trans-situational and entrenched within larger social structures. Why were there 18 men and only 2 women in my entering class? Why was the psychology department in this major university composed of 40 male but no female faculty? In those days, women students had few or no professional role models and no mentors to help them navigate the narrow halls of academia. Later experiences of exclusion were denial of faculty status in several male-only academic departments. Being the first and only woman faculty in four other institutions was affirming but also isolating. That my exclusion from the ivory tower was not personal but social and political became evident in the following years.

During the 1960s, rumblings of a revitalized women's movement broke into my silence. Invited to join a women's conscious-raising group, I discovered another world of possibilities. We read the outrageous ideas of Betty Freidan (1963) and Robin Morgan (1970), with the empowering conclusion that "the personal is political." We began to understand that the rules by which we had been living were embedded in the social, economic, and political arrangements of the larger culture. And so along with many other "foremothers," I became actively involved in what was known at the time as the Women's Liberation Movement. We were to be freed from restrictive gender-based social roles, with the attending responsibility to bring knowledge of this freedom to all women.

Of course, we know that radical change does not come easily or without a price. From many directions, both public and professional, came outrage and denial. In response to the backlash against "mouthy aggressive women libbers," I coauthored a research study on the personalities of women and men college students who supported or rejected the movement for women's legal, political, and economic equality. We were pleased to report no evidence of deviant personality for supporters on any of our measures. Instead, we found that women supporters were more autonomous (self-directed) than nonsupporters, and male supporters more cognitive and thoughtful. We presented our findings in a symposium at the American Psychological Association's annual convention that included data from psychologists, an economist, and a civil rights attorney (Worell & Worell, 1971, 1977). As some of the earliest research on this topic, the symposium attracted an overflowing audience; we knew we were on the right track.

At the same time, small groups of psychologists organized to support larger social and economic efforts. They insisted (although unsuccessfully) that state psychological associations meet only in states that had ratified the Equal Rights Amendment to the U.S. Constitution. They started their own independent organization (AWP, Association for Women in Psychology). They lobbied the American Psychological Association successfully to add a new Office of Women's Affairs, and a new APA Division (35) on the Psychology of Women. These groups breathed life and energy into many women who were yearning for professional inclusion and expression. As social scientists, we know that values and behaviors are mutually interactive; by increasing a valued activity,

commitment to the values supporting these activities can be further strengthened. And so it was for me. I became increasingly active with groups dedicated to
supporting and empowering women. The well-being of girls and women has
since directed my life efforts, a fortunate and rewarding decision.

When I served subsequently as editor of *The Psychology of Women
Quarterly*, I noted a paucity of submitted manuscripts that explored variables
related to women's psychological illness or health. It is intriguing to speculate
about the reasons for this intellectual and research void, but among them may be
the historical lack of recognition and institutional support for research on
women's health in general. Imagine my enthusiasm when I read the validation
study submitted by Dana Jack and Diana Dill on a new scale related to women's
psychological well-being, the *Silencing the Self Scale: Schemas of Intimacy
Associated with Depression in Women* (Jack & Dill, 1992). Contemporary
research on the antecedents and correlates of women's vulnerability to depression was still in its infancy. Of particular interest to me in this manuscript was
the proposed theoretical connection between how "social/gender inequality is
structured in thought to affect everyday interactions" (Jack & Dill, 1992, p. 98)
and the hypothesized cognitive schemas related to women's vulnerability to
depression. There were many other hypotheses available to account for the
gender discrepancy in the epidemiology of depression, but this article suggested
an intriguing new direction. Further, the authors tested their cognitive schema
hypothesis with a between-groups design that supported the concept of the self-
silenced voice. Needless to add, the journal published the article. I have since
recommended the STSS to a number of my doctoral students and clinical super-
visees as a useful tool for both research purposes and clinical understanding.

During the period in which women in general were facing exclusion and side-
lining, women of color and diverse cultures were even more invisible. Women
from nonmajority groups voiced concerns (and at times outrage) at their marginal status in feminist psychology, pointing to the dimensions of multiple
identity that characterize each of us as women (Landrine, 1995). Rather than
ignoring, isolating, or problematizing minority groups, a multicultural psychology movement brought group and cultural diversity from the margins to
center. The multicultural movement offered us new perspectives on the importance of considering the multiplicity and intersects of personal and social identities on women's well-being (Comas-Diaz & Greene, 1994; Robinson &
Howard-Hamilton, 2000; Worell & Remer, 2003). A significant strength of
this volume on silencing the self acknowledges and highlights the critical role of
cultural context on women's experience and expression of depression.

Since the publication of the 1992 STSS validation study, a wide range of
research has supported a number of competing hypotheses for the continued
gender discrepancy in measures of depression. Perhaps each of them deserves a
place in our consideration and possibly each of them holds some validity for
some individuals. It remains to be seen whether any of them can match the

diversity of nationalities and cultural identities encompassed by the authors included in this impressive volume.

References

Comas-Diaz, L., & Greene, B. (1994). *Women of color: Integrating ethnic and gender identities in psychotherapy.* New York: Guilford Press.

Freidan, B. (1963). *The feminine mystique.* New York: Dell.

Jack, D. C. (1991). *Silencing the self: Women and depression.* Cambridge, MA: Harvard University Press.

Jack, D. C., & Dill, D. (1992). The silencing the self scale: Schemas of intimacy associated with depression in women. *Psychology of Women, 16,* 97–106.

Landrine, H. (1995). *Bringing cultural diversity to feminist psychology: Theory, research, and practice.* Washington, DC: American Psychological Association.

Morgan, R. (1970). *Sisterhood is powerful: An anthology of writings from the women's liberation movement.* New York: Random House.

Robinson, T. L., & Howard-Hamilton, M. F. (2000). *The convergence of race, ethnicity, and gender: Multiple identities in counseling.* Upper Saddle River, NJ: Merrill.

Wallston, B. S. (1981). What are the questions in the psychology of women: A feminist approach to research. *Psychology of Women Quarterly, 5,* 597–617.

Worell, J., & Remer, P. (2003). *Feminist perspectives in therapy: Empowering diverse women* (2nd ed.). New York: Wiley.

Worell, J., & Worell, L. (1971, August). Support and opposition to the women's liberation movement. In L. Worell (Chair), *Women's liberation: Equality, legality, personality.* Symposium presented at the annual convention of the American Psychological Association, Washington, DC.

Worell, J., & Worell, L. (1977). Personality correlates in opposers and supporters of women's liberation. *Journal of Research in Personality, 11,* 10–20.

I

Setting the Stage: Social,
Biomedical, and Ethical Issues in
Understanding Women's
Depression

1

Introduction: Culture, Self-Silencing, and Depression: A Contextual-Relational Perspective

Dana C. Jack and Alisha Ali

In this volume, authors from 13 countries present new insights about women's depression. Our goal is to join the collective effort to understand the complex problem of depression and to raise new questions from international perspectives. We rely on a model called Silencing the Self (Jack, 1991, 1999), which highlights the way people think about themselves and interact in their intimate relationships, specifically around the themes of voice and silence. Contributors to this volume come from Australia, Canada, Finland, Germany, Haiti, India, Israel, Nepal, Poland, Portugal, Puerto Rico, Scotland, and the United States. Each of the authors or coauthors lives in or originates from the country under investigation and thus writes about depression and self-silencing from a position of deep cultural knowledge. Because self-silencing also has implications for prevention, self-care, and recovery from illnesses other than depression, this book also addresses such conditions as HIV/AIDS, cancer, eating disorders, and cardiovascular disease.

The idea for this collection emerged from my (Dana Jack) work as a Fulbright scholar in Nepal in 2001. I was privileged to teach in Tribhuvan University's graduate program in Women Studies and to collaborate with Nepali psychiatrists on a study of gender and depression in Kathmandu. In government outpatient clinics, I listened to clinically depressed women's and men's stories about the onset and expression of their illness. Though the cultural context was vastly different from my own, I heard familiar themes of self-silencing as they described their depression.

Nepal's society is bound together by family relationships, duty, and spiritual beliefs in a world ordered by gods and fate. Elaborate rituals and traditions organize daily life. At the same time, extreme poverty and political instability

3

shadow this beautiful, diverse mountain country. Studying depression while immersed in Nepal's complex culture led to questions that created the international focus of this volume. Does the importance for mental health of having a voice in intimate relationships vary across cultures? How do widely divergent cultural norms affect the dynamics of self-silencing and gender? Are the difficulties that lead women into self-silencing and depression similar across cultures?

In the Women Studies program, working with faculty and students who pursue gender equality for Nepal's women, I saw how women exercise far less power in society and in the family than men. Women's silence about their own needs is a basic premise of Nepal's collectivist social structure. I started to wonder, How do religion, tradition, and governmental policies affect one's experience of self in intimate relationships?

At the same time that I became absorbed with such questions, international researchers were emailing me about their work on depression. They, too, were raising questions posed by their examination of voice and silence related to depression. As their questions joined mine, it seemed that addressing self-silencing across different cultures could contribute to understanding more about the causes of depression and ways to alleviate it. What might we learn from broadening the framework of inquiry beyond the dominant models through which we have understood depression? Alisha Ali, my coeditor, added her energies to this endeavor, and the idea of this book became a reality.

I (Alisha Ali) came to this idea of a cross-cultural account of self-silencing through my work interviewing women in various parts of the Caribbean about depression, silencing, and identity. In this work, I mostly interviewed women living in impoverished conditions who lacked the material comforts that many take for granted. And yet these women did not score high on my depression measures, nor did they seem at all depressed. What protected them against depression despite their impoverished living conditions? In talking to them, I realized that they had a strong sense of self and strong voices that allowed them to express themselves freely within their immediate circle. Additionally, they did not think of themselves as particularly disadvantaged, mostly because everyone they knew lived in similar circumstances—the social comparison of "have" and "have not" was not part of their daily experience. Furthermore, the women were the social and practical leaders in their communities, so they were respected and listened to. Their collective experience of "voice" was one of self-assurance and mutual empowerment. Talking to these women and observing them in their daily lives, I began to think about voice as the embodiment of one's culture: If you're in a culture that allows you to feel that your voice matters, then you feel that you, as a person, matter. So, in thinking about self-silencing across cultures, I was curious about what other cultural settings looked like in this respect. To get a snapshot of that would require a collection of writers describing silencing, women's roles, and the meaning of voice within their respective cultures.

Silencing the Self Theory: A Brief Overview

Because studies in this edited book rely on the Silencing the Self (STS) model and its accompanying measure, the Silencing the Self Scale (STSS) (Jack & Dill, 1992), we present the model here. STS theory is based on a longitudinal study of clinically depressed women's descriptions of their experiences (Jack, 1991, 1999, 2003), including their understanding of what led up to their depression. The women detailed how they began to silence or suppress certain thoughts, feelings, and actions that they thought would contradict their partner's wishes. They did so to avoid conflict, to maintain a relationship, and/or to ensure their psychological or physical safety. They described how silencing their voices led to a loss of self and a sense of being lost in their lives. They also conveyed their shame, desperation, and anger over feelings of entrapment and self-betrayal.

Though this process feels personal to each woman, it is in fact deeply cultural. A male-centered world tells women who they are or who they should be, especially in intimate relationships. Self-silencing is prescribed by norms, values, and images dictating what women are "supposed" to be like: pleasing, unselfish, loving. As I (Dana Jack) listened to the inner dialogues of depressed women, I heard self-monitoring and negative self-evaluation in arguments between the "I" (a voice of the self) and the "Over-Eye" (the cultural, moralistic voice that condemns the self for departing from culturally prescribed "shoulds"). The imperatives of the Over-Eye regarding women's goodness are strengthened by the social reality of women's subordination—the experience of being a target of male violence, and the difficulties of financial dependence and poverty. Women's inner arguments about how they should act and feel revealed a divided self that results from self-silencing in an attempt to preserve relationships. Inwardly, they experienced anger and confusion while outwardly presenting a pleasing, compliant self trying to live up to cultural standards of a good woman in the midst of fraying relationships, violence, and lives that were falling apart.

As I followed the negative self-evaluation (words like "no good" and "worth-less") in their narratives, it became clear that women's self-judgment and behavior were guided by specific beliefs about how they should act and feel in relationships. When followed, these self-silencing relational schemas create a vulnerability to depression by directing women to defer to the needs of others, censor self-expression, repress anger, inhibit self-directed action, and judge the self against a culturally defined "good woman." In tandem with women's wider social inequality, such beliefs can keep a woman entrapped in negating situations as she blames herself for the problems she encounters.

In order to measure self-silencing, I designed the Silencing the Self Scale (Jack, 1991; Jack & Dill, 1992; Appendix A), a 31-item self-report instrument. The STSS reflects the components of relational schemas held by depressed women. The statements that comprise the scale came directly from the narratives of clinically depressed women, yet are gender neutral. Respondents endorse each statement on a 5-point scale ranging from strongly disagree to strongly agree. Four rationally derived sub-scales measure the relational schemas central to self-silencing, and each is understood as an interrelated component of the overall construct. The subscales are considered to reflect both phenomenological and behavioral aspects of self-silencing:

1. Externalized Self-Perception assesses schema regarding standards for self-judg-ment and includes the extent to which a person judges the self through external standards. For example, item #6 reflects seeing the self through others' eyes: "I tend to judge myself by how I think other people see me." The last sentence on the STSS, item #31, reads, "I never seem to measure up to the standards I set for myself." Immediately following this item, the questionnaire instructs, "If you answered the last question with a 4 or 5 [agree or strongly agree], please list up to three of the standards you feel you don't measure up to." This allows for continuing investigation concerning the standards depressed individuals use to judge the self, including gender- and culture-specific standards.

2. Care as Self-Sacrifice measures the extent to which relationships are secured by putting the needs of others ahead of the needs of the self. For example, if a woman strongly endorses item #4, "Considering my needs to be as important as those of the people I love is selfish," then that belief directs her vision of the hierarchy of needs within relationships; it guides behavior by directing how she should choose when her needs conflict with those of others she loves; and it provides a standard for negative self-judgment if she veers from its command. Further, it can arouse anger as, following its dictates, she places her needs second to those of others, yet it also commands the repression of anger by purporting a moral basis for the suppression of her own needs. It reinforces a woman's low self-esteem by affirming that she is not as worthy or important as others, and finally, it legitimizes the historical and still prevalent view of women's nature as essentially self-sacrificing and maternal (Jack, 1991, p. 123).

3. Silencing the Self assesses the tendency to inhibit self-expression and action in order to secure relationships and to avoid retaliation, possible loss, and conflict. Item #8, which is reverse-scored, reads, "When my partner's needs and feelings conflict with my own, I always state mine clearly." The items in this subscale measure both behavioral and phenomenological aspects of self-silencing, as in item #30: "I try to bury my feelings when I think they will cause trouble in my close relationship(s)."

4. Divided Self measures the extent to which a person feels a division between an outer "false" self and inner self resulting from hiding certain feelings and thoughts in an important relationship. In women, it appeared that the false self was characterized by a mode of relating through compliance to the partner's wishes, and that the feelings hidden were oppositional or angry, challenging ones, as in item #16: "Often I look happy enough on the outside, but inwardly I feel angry and rebellious."

The STSS was validated in three groups of women in radically differing settings: undergraduate women, mothers who abused drugs and were caring for young children, and a battered women's shelter group. Results demonstrated not only that STSS scores correlated with scores on the Beck Depression Inventory but also that STSS means varied with contexts in predicted ways. Participants' means in the three groups of women differed significantly from each other, with self-silencing highest among residents at battered women's shelters, intermediate among mothers who abuse drugs, and lowest among undergraduate participants. Across subsequent investigations, higher levels of self-silencing have been found to be associated with variables representing inequality, oppression, and other threats to self and relationships (Jack, Ali, & Alimchandani, 2010).

How Silencing the Self Theory Relates to Other Psychological Theories of Depression

The Silencing the Self model integrates aspects of attachment theory, relational theories, and cognitive theories of depression to explain women's vulnerability to depression. Given the impact of social disadvantage on emotional health, how might women's beliefs about how to make and maintain intimacy contribute to their vulnerability to depression? According to the attachment perspective, depression is interpersonal for both genders. Attachment theory (Bowlby, 1969, 1973, 1980) details the importance of relationships in human development and the impact that negative or insecure relationships have on functioning (see also Laurent & Powers, 2007; Mikulincer & Shaver, 2007). Confirmed by neuroscientific findings (Cacioppo, Visser, & Pickett, 2006; Cozolino, 2006), attachment theory describes that not only children but also adults have a basic, biosocial motivation to make secure, intimate connections with others. The mind is "wired for connection" (see Jordan, this volume), and throughout life, threats to relationships or social belonging set off a neural alarm network that warns of social separation (Eisenberger & Lieberman, 2004). When social relationships are threatened, the "social attachment system" (Panksepp, 1998) recruits attention and coping resources to prevent the threat of social exclusion or separation. Threats, such as relationships that are not secure or are demeaning, intensify specific attachment behaviors such as proximity seeking and reassurance seeking (Coyne, 1976; Joiner, Alfano, & Metalsky, 1992). The STS model proposes that such threats activate a set of specific attachment behaviors directed by the self-silencing relational schemas. Bowlby (1980) asserted that, in depression, "... the principal issue about which a person feels helpless is his [sic] ability to make and to maintain affectional relationships" (p. 247). From this perspective, relational disconnection and isolation are central to precipitating and maintaining depression.

Self-silencing relational schemas include a socially approved collection of "feminine attachment behaviors" (Jack, 1991) that can be described as "compliant connectedness" (p. 40). These behaviors are characterized by compulsive caretaking, pleasing others, and avoiding conflict by self-silencing. The behaviors resemble anxious attachment in their focus on the partner and in concern about securing the relationship. The self-silencing relational schemas are readily available in the culture. They are heightened in social contexts that endanger a woman or that make a woman dependent on a particular relationship for her (and her children's) economic security.

Interestingly, while stressing the social nature of mind and experience, Bowlby and many attachment theorists have overlooked the fundamental patterning of gender on consciousness and interpersonal behavior. Relational theory formulated from a feminist perspective (Gilligan, 1982; Jordan, Kaplan, Miller, Stiver, & Surrey, 1991; Miller, 1976) fills this gap, describing how women, as unequals to men, are more attuned to the quality of relationships and more likely to function as relationship "barometers" than men (Floyd & Markman, 1983). These writers stress that intimate relationships are critical for women's sense of self. Women's depression is understood as tied to the importance women place on the quality and maintenance of their relationships.

A large body of work affirms that women's gender inequality plays a significant role in their depression. Because of inequality, women experience higher exposure to social stresses known to foster depression, such as poverty, war, victimization, economic dependence, and lack of control over childbearing (Broadhead & Abas, 1998; Patel, 2001; Patel & Kleinman, 2003; Patel, Abas, Broadhead, Todd, & Reeler, 2001). Strikingly similar research findings around the world point to the importance of negative, humiliating, entrapping interpersonal events that join social stresses in precipitating women's depression (see Broadhead, Abas, Sakutukwa, Chigwanda, & Garura, 2001; Brown, 1998, 2002; Brown & Harris, 1978; Brown, Harris, & Hepworth, 1995; Kessler, 2003; Patel et al., 2001). Society affects not only a woman's power and prerogatives in relationships but also her ability to escape harmful circumstances, including psychologically damaging and/or violent relationships (Cabral & Astbury, 2000; Trivedi, Mishra, & Kendurkar, 2007). Social values and social structures, then, reinforce the notion of women's devaluation and inequality in intimate relationships.

The importance of cognitive schemas (patterns by which a person organizes and interprets experience) for vulnerability to depression has been demonstrated by numerous models, including Aaron Beck's (1987; Beck, Rush, Shaw, & Emery, 1979) extensive work and the general cognitive vulnerability-stress frameworks of Nolen-Hoeksema (1991) and Abramson, Metalsky, and Alloy (1989), updated by Hankin and Abramson (2001). Fundamentally, these models assume that an individual with a cognitive vulnerability, when confronted with a stressful event, interprets the event in a negatively biased way: utilizes dysfunctional thinking (Beck, 1984), makes negative inferences about the event (negative inferential style [Abramson et al., 1989]), or responds with a cognitive style that focuses on current negative situations and feelings (rumination rather than problem solving [Nolen-Hoeksema, 1991]). Based on evidence that cognitive, neurochemical, and affect systems are interrelated, these theories argue that certain cognitive patterns become activated in depression and structure a person's negative interpretations of experience, which also lower the person's mood and motivation.

STS theory differs from diathesis-stress models such as Beck's (1987; Beck et al., 1979) model; Blatt, Quinlan, Chevron, McDonald, and Zuroff's (1982) psychodynamic personality model; Abramson, Metalsky, and Alloy's (1989) pessimistic explanatory style model; and Nolen-Hoeksema's (1991) coping response model in two main respects. First, STS theory does not assume that self-silencing is a stable, permanent trait; instead, the theory construes self-silencing relational schemas as susceptible to the effects of variables within changing social contexts and specific relationships. Second, while diathesis-stress models largely assume a set of vulnerability factors that reside within the individual (Coyne, 1992), in STS theory, the problem is not considered to lie in an individual deficit (such as ruminative coping style [Nolen-Hoeksema, 1991]) or in a personality orientation (dependency-autonomy [Beck, 1987]). Rather, STS theory emphasizes both the importance of cognitive factors and the role of social factors, and regards them as inextricably linked and inter-active: Since establishing positive, close connections is a primary motivation throughout life, cognitive schemas about how to make and keep attachments are critical for understanding depression and are affected by social contexts, including gender.

More generally, STS theory can inform the development of a broadly integrative account of depression. Gilbert (2002) described the need for psychology to adopt a "biopsychosocial approach [that] addresses the complexity of inter-actions between different domains of functioning and argues that it is the interaction of domains that illuminate important processes" (p. 13). In depression, this interaction of domains takes the form of multiple pathways of mutual influence between psychological processes, physiology, and the social world that together determine either emotional wellness or psychological distress. We know, for instance, that during difficult times, sharing one's feelings with others stimulates the release of oxytocin, a hormone that reduces stress (Taylor et al., 2000). Similarly, silencing one's voice may interact with a range of processes known to precipitate depression, such as a negative experience of self, a threat of separation that in turn engages the attachment system, and an activation of neurobiological systems and higher order self-regulatory cognition (Eisenberger & Lieberman, 2004; Laurent & Powers, 2007; Panksepp, 1998). Because the personal, social, cognitive, and biological are interconnected, and because relational disconnection constitutes a major threat to the self, we con-sider self-silencing to be a crucial element in precipitating depression.

Men's Self-Silencing: The Puzzle of Gender

The construct of silencing the self was developed through listening to clinically depressed women. It was hypothesized to correlate with gender inequality and was presumed to be more characteristic of women than men. But from the beginning, studies have found that men usually score higher on the STSS than do women. Also, while self-silencing generally associates with women's depressive symptoms, findings among men are less consistent. Some studies of men have reported significant associations between self-silencing and depression (Duarte & Thompson, 1999; Gratch, Bassett, & Attra, 1995), while others have not (Thompson, 1995; Uebelacker, Courtnage, & Whisman, 2003). We do know, however, that while the STSS subscales replicate among women in the four studies that examine factor structure of the STSS (Cramer & Thoms, 2003; Duarte & Thompson, 1999; Remen, Chambless, & Rodebaugh, 2002; Stevens & Galvin, 1995), for men the subscale structure findings are more complex.

A greater number of studies have examined self-silencing in women than in men, but the foundational ideas that women value relationships more than men and that they quiet themselves out of inequality are challenged by the men's findings. Remembering that STSS items are gender neutral, the findings are intriguing and raise interesting questions: How does men's self-silencing relate to their greater power than women's in society? What aspects of self might they be hiding behind their silence? Are they attributing different meanings to the items on the STSS than do women? Why does men's silence also have negative psychological consequences? Investigations of such questions have included analyses of the different contexts of power out of which self-silencing occurs (Cowan, Bommersbach, & Curtis, 1995) and the different meanings and goals of self-silencing. For example, men's silence may intend to create distance, control interactions in relationships, and protect their autonomy. The precise meaning of men's self-silencing as well as its relation to depression symptoms remains unclear and is addressed in a number of the chapters in this volume (see Chapters 6, 7, 8, and 12 in particular). Taken together, the studies in this book raise a larger question about gender and silence. If gender is reproduced through enactment in social relations, does the differing use of silence by women and men play a key role in this reproduction?

More research, both qualitative and quantitative, needs to be conducted to explore men's experiences of self-silencing. It is evident that self-silencing has negative psychological consequences for both men and women. These consequences, which include an emotional distancing from others and a diminished sense of self-worth, point to the possibility that the construct of self-silencing actually transcends gender. The need for authentic connection to others is a human need, not only a "female" need, so a silencing that leads to social disconnection is detrimental for both women and men. Moreover, while the metaphor of voice has been applied almost exclusively to women's psychology, it is likely equally relevant to men's experiences. If silencing is understood to be a relational process—rather than a personality style or individual trait—then STS theory can help us to situate questions of gender not simply in the realm of either/or dichotomies, but in a more fluid domain that tells us about disempowering contexts. Such an approach can help us to achieve the goal that Cosgrove (2003) set forth in her call for psychological inquiry that is aimed at "researching gendered experience while simultaneously challenging the ontological status of both gender and experience" (p. 86).

Self-Silencing Across Cultures

Culture has a central place in this book. By the term "culture" we mean "subjective culture," defined as "a cultural group's characteristic way of perceiving its social environment" (Triandis, 1972, p. 3). Culture tells women and men different stories about their place in the world, about who they are, and about who they can and should be. Thus, in our view, gender itself is a culture. We also follow Marsella's (1988, p. 10) definition of psychological culture: "represented internally as values, beliefs, attitudes, cognitive styles, epistemologies, and consciousness patterns." Contributors in this book describe aspects of their particular external culture (Marsella, 1988) in their chapters, that is, its representation in roles and institutions.

Why would the STS theory and the STSS be suitable for use across different cultures, and how might international inquiry using this framework advance our knowledge of women's vulnerability to depression? The STSS has been used in approximately 100 published studies and approximately 18 countries, and has proven to be reliable and meaningful. The construct validity of the STSS has been affirmed by studies demonstrating correlations with hypothesized variables. For example, self-silencing has been found to correlate with "loss of self" (Drew, Heesacker, Frost, & Oelke, 2004), low self-esteem (Page, Stevens, & Galvin, 1996), diminished relationship satisfaction (Thompson, 1995), insecure attachment style (Galvin & Gillespie, 1998; Hart & Thompson, 1996), and childhood abuse (Arata & Lindman, 2002) (see also Jack et al., 2010). Together, the findings from these studies demonstrate the use of STS theory in informing our understanding of psychological processes involved in interpersonal relationships and emotional distress. This book takes these ideas and explores them across a range of cultures and countries to understand what is cultural about depression and how different cultural contexts differentially construct the experience of silencing and depression.

Though the idealized image of a "good woman" varies across cultures, a core premise is that women are unequal to men and yet responsible for the quality of relationships. Women must solve the puzzle of how to achieve intimacy within inequality. The solution presented by preceding generations of unequal marriage (and sexual) contracts (Pateman, 1988) is for women to remain quiet about inequalities in relationships and in society. In order to do so, women must exert tremendous energy against themselves to appear outwardly compliant; they must silence their voices and forgo their desire for an equal say and equal value. They sacrifice the potentialities of genuine intimacy and of self-development by adapting to what the culture sanctions as "valuable" or "normative" for women. The irony is that these actions, designed to lead to intimacy and safety, lead instead to a loss of self that both increases a woman's vulnerability to depression and decreases the possibilities of intimacy. The particular dynamics surrounding this process of loss of self are likely to differ by culture, as does the nature of the consequences facing women who do not adhere to their socially prescribed roles. Therefore, the lens of STS theory affords researchers the opportunity to engage in inquiry that exposes the dangers of inequality and oppression while at the same time exploring the process through which the social becomes the personal.

The Chapters in This Book

Authors were invited to contribute to this book because their work raised important questions and because their inclusion represented a variety of cultures, disciplines, and methods of inquiry. We looked for researchers both within and outside of the United States who had examined gender and self-silencing in order to highlight the differences in gendered patterns of self-silencing as well as differences in associations with depression. We also sought authors who could provide qualitative as well as quantitative analyses of self-silencing. In addition, we asked well-known experts from the field of psychology and beyond to add their knowledge about social factors in women's depression including human rights abuses, ethical issues related to cultural research on depression, and the use of the biomedical model. Additional experts—Carol Gilligan, Judith Worell, Laura Brown, and Judy Jordan—accepted our invitation to each write a brief introductory piece for sections of the book using their own insights and personal voice.

The chapters in Section 1, "Setting the Stage: Social, Biomedical, and Ethical Issues in Understanding Women's Depression," introduce some of the critical social issues affecting women's depression and psychological distress. This section also addresses key ethical considerations that arise in conducting research on these issues across cultures. Jill Astbury (Australia), in Chapter 2, considers how the language of "risk factors" in depression research masks massive violations of women's human rights globally, and she describes how the language in our models of depression has individualized and decontextualized women's depression. In Chapter 3, Richard Gordon (United States) discusses the impact of the biomedical model on changing conceptualizations of depression in the *Diagnostic and Statistical Manual of Mental Disorders* (American Psychiatric Association, 2000), as well as on the rise of antidepressants. Given the importance of research that examines women's depression internationally, the final chapter in Section 1, by Joseph Trimble (United States), María R. Scharrón-del Río (United States), and Guillermo Bernal (Puerto Rico), considers the ethical and methodological issues involved in such research.

Section 2 of this volume, "Self-Silencing and Depression across Cultures," contains chapters that focus on how the social world is reflected in voice and self-silencing across various countries and cultures. Tanja Zoellner and Susanne Hedland (Germany) describe sociocultural expectations that are placed on women and, using compelling examples, how German values regarding women's mothering roles may be reflected in their depression. Linda Smolak (United States) provides a broad sociocultural analysis of gendered responses on the STSS and examines some of the contextual aspects of violence and aggression that affect women's self-silencing. Dana C. Jack (United States) and Usha Subba and Bindu Pokharel (Nepal) examine how self-silencing and depression are affected in gender-specific ways by Nepal's changing social context. Airi Hautamäki (Finland) writes about the generational differences that reflect changing social values in Finland. Krystyna Drat-Ruszczak (Poland) explores the meaning of self-silencing in Polish women in light of Poland's history and images of women. Alisha Ali (United States) demonstrates the different meanings attached to self-silencing among women living in the Caribbean as compared to Caribbean immigrant women living in Canada and the United States. Sofia Neves and Conceição Nogueira (Portugal) provide a window into Portuguese history, changing values, and gender roles that affect women's self-silencing. Offering an overview of a large number of studies conducted in differing social contexts, including India, Anjoo Sikka, Linda (Gratch) Vaden-Goad, and Lisa Waldner (United States) examine the social and interpersonal factors that impinge on women's and men's authentic self-expression. In their chapter, Avi Besser (Israel) and Gordon Flett and Paul Hewitt (Canada) examine gender and personality vulnerabilities associated with depression and self-silencing. Lastly, Guerda Nicolas, Bridget Hirsch, and Clelia Beltrame (United States) provide a rich historical and cultural analysis of women's depression in Haiti, as well as the resistance to oppression mounted by Haitian women.

Section 3, "The Health Effects of Self-Silencing," considers the specific ways that silencing can affect physical health and mental health, as well as some ways of therapeutically addressing these health concerns. In the first chapter of this section, Rosanna DeMarco (United States) describes self-silencing among women in inner-city Boston who have HIV/AIDS, as well as her intervention program that centers on overcoming self-silencing. Mary Sormanti (United States) examines the effects of self-silencing on women who have young children and who are undergoing treatment for cancer, and describes how treatment programs might foster self-care for women who have been diagnosed with cancer. The chapter by Josie Geller, Suja Srikameswaran, and Stephanie Cassin (Canada) provides background on loss of voice and the possible movement toward voice for women with eating disorders. Elaine Eaker and Margaret Kelly-Hayes (United States) provide evidence from the large, prospective Framingham Offspring Study showing that women who self-silenced during marital arguments were four times more likely to die over the subsequent

10 years than were women who did not self-silence. Maria Medved (Canada) examines how women who are in support groups after myocardial heart infarction are silenced by approaches to treatment that are derived solely from men's experiences with heart disease. She presents evidence of how treatment can address self-silencing in order to facilitate women's positive coping to help them return to health. Jane Ussher and Janette Perz (Australia) analyze the purported distress associated with premenstrual symptoms and propose that such "symptoms" are in fact women's authentic expressions of the anger and dissatisfaction that they silence during the other 3 weeks of their monthly cycle. Natasha Mauthner (Scotland) presents the work of herself and others to demonstrate that women experiencing postpartum depression feel compelled to silence aspects of themselves in order to fulfill cultural expectations of motherhood. Stephanie Woods (United States) describes the associations between women's experiences of self-silencing, intimate partner violence, and physical and mental health symptoms, as well as the implications these associations have for providing responsive health care for abused women. The last chapter of this volume is a commentary and critique by Janet Stoppard with suggestions for further research.

These chapters provide broad evidence of the importance of personal agency in the lives of women experiencing physical and mental health problems. As these authors and other contributors to this book demonstrate, understanding depression and other conditions as being strongly influenced by self-silencing not only helps us to conceptualize and contextualize psychological distress but also allows us to envision the discovery and recovery of voice as a transformative step toward health and wellness.

References

Abramson, L. Y., Metalsky, G. I., & Alloy, L. B. (1989). Hopelessness depression: A theory-based subtype of depression. *Psychological Review, 96*, 358–372.

American Psychiatric Association. (2000). *Diagnostic and statistical manual of mental disorders-IV-TR*. Washington, DC.

Arata, C. M., & Lindman, L. (2002). Marriage, child abuse, and sexual revictimization. *Journal of Interpersonal Violence, 17*, 953–971.

Beck, A. T. (1984). Cognition and therapy. *Archives of General Psychiatry, 41*, 1112–1114.

Beck, A. T. (1987). Cognitive models of depression. *Journal of Cognitive Psychotherapy: An International Quarterly, 1*, 5–37.

Beck, A. T., Rush, A. J., Shaw, B. F., & Emery, G. (1979) *Cognitive therapy of depression*. New York: Guilford.

Blatt, S. J., Quinlan, D. M., Chevron, E. S., McDonald, C., & Zuroff, D. C. (1982). Dependency and self-criticism: Psychological dimensions of depression. *Journal of Counseling and Clinical Psychology, 150*, 113–124.

Bowlby, J. (1969). *Attachment and loss, vol. 1, Attachment*. New York: Basic Books.

Bowlby, J. (1973). *Attachment and loss, vol. 2, Separation: Anxiety and anger.* New York: Basic Books.

Bowlby, J. (1980). *Attachment and loss, vol. 3, Loss, sadness and depression.* New York: Basic Books.

Broadhead, J. C., & Abas, M. A. (1998). Life events, difficulties and depression among women in an urban setting in Zimbabwe. *Psychological Medicine, 28,* 29–38.

Broadhead, J., Abas, M., Sakutukwa, G. H., Chigwanda, M., & Garura, E. (2001). Social support and life events as risk factors for depression in an urban setting in Zimbabwe. *Social Psychiatry and Psychiatric Epidemiology, 36,* 115–122.

Brown, G. W. (1998). Genetic and population perspectives on life events and depression. *Social Psychiatry and Psychiatric Epidemiology, 33,* 363–372.

Brown, G. W. (2002). Social roles, context and evolution in the origins of depression. *Journal of Health and Social Behavior, 43,* 255–276.

Brown, G. W., Harris, T. O., & Hepworth, C. (1995). Loss, humiliation and entrapment among women developing depression: A patient and non-patient comparison. *Psychological Medicine, 25,* 7–21.

Brown, G. W., & Harris, T. (1978). *Social origins of depression: A study of psychiatric disorders in women.* New York: Free Press.

Cabral, M., & Astbury, J. (2000). Women's mental health: An evidence-based review. World Health Organization. Retrieved October 18, 2002, from http://whqlibdoc.who.int/hq/2000/WHO_MSD_MDP_00.1.pdf

Cacioppo, J. T., Visser, P. S., & Pickett, C. L. (Eds.). (2006). *Social neuroscience: People thinking about thinking people.* Cambridge, MA: MIT Press.

Cosgrove, L. (2003). Feminism, postmodernism, and psychological research. *Hypatia, 18,* 85–112.

Cowan, G., Bommersbach, M., & Curtis, S. R. (1995). Codependency, loss of self, and power. *Psychology of Women Quarterly, 19,* 221–236.

Coyne, J. C. (1976). Depression and the response of others. *Journal of Abnormal Psychology, 85,* 186–193.

Coyne, J. C. (1992). Cognition in depression: A paradigm in crisis. *Psychological Inquiry, 3,* 232–235.

Cozolino, L. (2006). *The neuroscience of relationships: Attachment and the developing social brain.* New York: W.W. Norton.

Cramer, K. M., & Thoms, N. (2003). Factor structure of the Silencing the Self Scale in women and men. *Personality & Individual Differences, 35,* 525–535.

Drew, S. S., Heesacker, M., Frost, H. M., & Oelke, L. E. (2004). The role of relationship loss and self-loss in women's and men's dysphoria. *Journal of Social and Personal Relationships, 21,* 381–397.

Duarte, L. M., & Thompson, J. M. (1999). Sex differences in self-silencing. *Psychological Reports, 85,* 145–161.

Eisenberger, N. I., & Lieberman, M. D. (2004). Why rejection hurts: A common neural alarm system for physical and social pain. *Trends in Cognitive Sciences, 8,* 294–300.

Floyd, F. J., & Markman, H. J. (1983). Observational biases in spousal observations: Toward a cognitive behavioral model of marriage. *Journal of Consulting and Clinical Psychology, 51,* 450–457.

Galvin, S. L., & Gillespie, D. M. (1998). *Differences in self-silencing and depression among adult attachment styles.* Poster presented at the 44th Annual Meeting of the Southeastern Psychological Association, March 26–29, -1998, Mobile, Alabama.

Gilbert, P. (2002). Understanding the biopsychosocial approach: Conceptualization. *Clinical Psychology, 14,* 13–17.

Gilligan, C. (1982). *In a different voice: Psychological theory and women's development.* Cambridge, MA: Harvard University Press.

Gratch, L. B., Bassett, M. E., & Attra, S. L. (1995). The relationship of gender and ethnicity to self silencing and depression among college students. *Psychology of Women Quarterly, 19,* 509–515.

Hankin, B. L., & Abramson, L. Y. (2001). Development of gender differences in depression: An elaborated cognitive vulnerability-transactional stress theory. *Psychological Bulletin, 127,* 773–796.

Hart, B. I., & Thompson, J. M. (1996). Gender-role characteristics and depressive symptomatology among adolescents. *Journal of Early Adolescence, 16,* 407–426.

Jack, D. C. (1991). *Silencing the self: Women and depression.* Cambridge, MA: Harvard University Press.

Jack, D. C. (1999). Silencing the self: Inner dialogues and outer realities. In T. E. Joiner & J. C. Coyne (Eds.), *The interactional nature of depression: Advances in interpersonal approaches* (pp. 221–246). Washington, DC: American Psychological Association.

Jack, D. C. (2003). The anger of hope and the anger of despair: How anger relates to women's depression. In J. Stoppard & L. McMullen (Eds.), *Situating sadness: Women and depression in social context* (pp. 62–87). New York University Press Series on Qualitative Studies in Psychology, Michelle Fine & Jeanne Marecek (Series Eds.). New York: New York University Press.

Jack, D. C., Ali, A., & Alimchandani, A. (2010). Manuscript in preparation.

Jack, D. C., & Dill, D. (1992). The Silencing the Self Scale: Schemas of intimacy associated with depression in women. *Psychology of Women Quarterly, 16,* 97–106.

Joiner, T. E., Alfano, M. S., & Metalsky, G. I. (1992). When depression breeds contempt: Reassurance seeking, self-esteem, and rejection of depressed college students by their roommates. *Journal of Abnormal Psychology, 101,* 165–173.

Jordan, J. V., Kaplan, A. G., Miller, J. B., Stiver, I. P., & Surrey, J. L. (Eds.). *Women's growth in connection.* New York: Guilford.

Kessler, R. C. (2003). Epidemiology of women and depression. *Journal of Affective Disorders, 74,* 5–13.

Laurent, H., & Powers, S. (2007). Emotion regulation in emerging adult couples: Temperament, attachment, and HPA response to conflict. *Biological Psychology, 76,* 61–71.

Marsella, A. J. (1988). Cross-cultural research on severe mental disorders: Issues and findings. *Acta Psychiatrica Scandinavica Supplementum, 344,* 7–22.

Mikulincer, M., & Shaver, P. (2007). *Attachment in adulthood: Structure, dynamics, and change.* New York: Guilford.

Miller, J. B. (1976). *Toward a new psychology of women.* Boston: Beacon Press.

Nolen-Hoeksema, S. (1991). Responses to depression and their effects on the duration of depressive episodes. *Journal of Abnormal Psychology, 100,* 569–582.

Page, J. R., Stevens, H. B., & Galvin, S. L. (1996). Relationships between depression, self-esteem, and self-silencing behavior. *Journal of Social & Clinical Psychology, 15,* 381–396.

Panksepp, J. (1998). *Affective neuroscience.* New York: Oxford University Press.

Patel, V. (2001). Cultural factors and international epidemiology. *British Medical Bulletin, 57,* 33–45.

Patel, V., Abas, M., Broadhead, J., Todd, C., & Reeler, A. (2001). Depression in developing countries: Lessons from Zimbabwe. *British Medical Journal, 322,* 482–484.

Patel, V., & Kleinman, A. (2003). Poverty and common mental disorders in developing countries. *Bulletin of the WHO, 81,* 609–615.

Pateman, C. (1988). *The sexual contract.* Stanford, CA: Stanford University Press.

Remen, A. L., Chambless, D. L., & Rodebaugh, T. L. (2002). Gender differences in the construct validity of the Silencing the Self Scale. *Psychology of Women Quarterly, 26,* 151–159.

Stevens, H. B., & Galvin, S. L. (1995). Structural findings regarding the Silencing the Self Scale. *Psychological Reports, 77,* 11–17.

Taylor, S. E., Cousino Klein, L., Lewis, B. P., Gruenwald, T. L., Gurung, R. A. R., & Updegraff J. A. (2000). Biobehavioral responses to stress in females: Tend-and-befriend, not fight-or-flight. *Psychological Review, 107,* 411–429.

Thompson, J. M. (1995). Silencing the self: Depressive symptomatology and close relationships. *Psychology of Women Quarterly, 19,* 337–353.

Triandis, H. (1972). *The analysis of subjective culture.* New York: John Wiley.

Trivedi, J. K., Mishra, M., & Kendurkar, A. (2007). Depression among women in the South-Asia region: The underlying issues. *Journal of Affective Disorders, 102,* 219–225.

Uebelacker, L. A., Courtnage, E. S., & Whisman, M. A. (2003). Correlates of depression and marital dissatisfaction: Perceptions of marital communication style. *Journal of Social and Personal Relationships, 20,* 757–769.

2

The Social Causes of Women's Depression: A Question of Rights Violated?

Jill Astbury

"The violation of any right has measurable impacts on physical, mental and social well-being; yet these health effects still remain, in large part, to be discovered and documented. Yet gradually the connection is being established."

Mann, 1999, p. 445

From the 1978 publication of *The Social Origins of Depression: A Study of Psychiatric Disorders in Women* by the British researchers George Brown and Tirril Harris, a large body of research literature has been amassed on the social factors linked to the development of depression in women. Multicountry studies reporting wide intercountry variation in rates of depression support the findings of national surveys that specific cultural arrangements, gender roles, life events, and socioeconomic and occupational factors make a significant contribution to the initiation and maintenance of depressive disorders (Brown, 1998; Patten, 2003; Ustun & Sartorius, 1995; World Health Organization [WHO], International Consortium of Psychiatric Epidemiology [ICPE], 2000).

While the social factors identified to date assist in explaining women's significantly higher rates of depression compared with men's (Brown, 1998; Brown & Harris, 1978; Brown, Harris, & Hepworth, 1995; Kessler, 2003), very little previous research on social factors has focused explicitly on human rights and framed human rights violations as a crucial social determinant of the marked gender disparity in rates of depression and other psychological disorders.

It will be argued here that the adoption of a human rights analytic framework would expand our current understanding of the social causes of depression in women and, at the same time, provide new perspectives on research, mental health promotion, and clinical treatment. A rights-based analytic approach also offers an alternative means to appraise and interpret current risk factor–based research into women's depression.

The Right to Health

The right to health is a fundamental human right and one that is explicitly identified in a number of human rights instruments. These include the Universal Declaration of Human Rights (1948), the International Convention on the Elimination of All Forms of Racial Discrimination (1965), the International Covenant on Economic, Social, and Cultural Rights (1976), the Convention on the Elimination of All Forms of Discrimination against Women (1979), and the Declaration on the Elimination of Violence against Women (1993).

Depression in Women: A Priority Public Health Issue

Depressive disorders, including major depression consisting of one or more major depressive episodes and dysthymia, constitute the most common psychological disorders experienced by women. The WHO has recognized that depression is a priority public health concern (WHO, 2001). The Global Burden of Disease (BOD) study estimates underpin the prediction that depression will be the second leading cause of disease burden in developing and developed countries by 2020. The importance of depression as a mental health concern is underlined by the fact that it accounts for the largest proportion of the burden of all mental and neurological disorders (Murray & Lopez, 1997).

The gender disparity in rates of depression, where women predominate in an approximately 2:1 ratio over men, is one of the most robust findings of psychiatric epidemiology (Astbury, 2001; Bebbington et al., 2003; Kessler, 2003, Kessler et al., 1994; Piccinelli & Homen, 1997; Weissman & Klerman, 1977). This disparity indicates an urgent need for gender-specific strategies to stem the rising tide of global disability caused by depression that is predicted for 2020.

Gendered Risk

The 1998 World Health Report stated unequivocally that "no society treats its women as well as it treats its men." Eight years after this report, the 2006 World Development Indicators revealed that:

> Unequal treatment of women - by the state, in the market and by their community and family - puts them at a disadvantage throughout their lives and stifles the development prospects of their societies. (World Bank, 2006)

Somehow this large and, in many places, continuing divide in the social treatment of women compared with men has remained something of a blind spot in the scientific imagination of psychiatric epidemiologists. Yet female gender clearly serves as a locus for many kinds of social ill treatment. According to a report prepared by Professor Fareda Banda for the United Nations human rights commissioner, Louise Arbour, women make up more than 70% of the world's poor and two-thirds of its illiterate, and own a tiny 1% of the world's titled land. For women in 53 nations, rape in marriage has not been criminalized (BBC News, 2008).

Women experience high rates of gender-based violence across the life course, beginning with selective female feticide, infanticide, childhood sexual abuse including forced child marriage, intimate partner violence, and adult sexual violence (Garcia-Moreno, Jansen, Ellsberg, Heise, & Watts, 2006; Krug, Dahlberg, Mercy, Zwi, & Lozano, 2002). According to the International Labour Office (ILO) (2005) in its report on forced labor, women and girls predominate among those trafficked for forced economic exploitation (56% women and girls compared with 44% men and boys) and are overwhelmingly at risk of being trafficking for forced commercial sexual exploitation (98% compared with 2%). The ILO (2005) estimates that 1,390,000 women and girls have been trafficked across national borders for forced commercial sexual exploitation. In war and conflict situations, sexual violence against women is used as a military tactic and has been recognized by the United Nations as organized and systematic. In June 2008, the UN Security Council approved a resolution acknowledging that sexual violence profoundly affects not only the health and safety of women but also the economic and social stability of their nations (Farley, 2008).

It is difficult to ignore the possibility that gender disparities in the rates of many psychological disorders could issue from and reliably reflect these various forms of socially condoned ill treatment.

Women predominate not only in diagnoses of depression and also in many of the disorders that commonly accompany depression, including anxiety disorders such as posttraumatic stress disorder (PTSD), panic disorder, borderline personality disorder, certain phobias, and somatization disorder. Women also predominate among the population of people with high levels of psychiatric comorbidity (three or more comorbid disorders) who suffer the highest levels of impairment (Kessler et al., 1994). The high prevalence and severe impact of depression and related disorders on women's sense of themselves, their quality of life, their relationships, and their social and occupational functioning demonstrate why depression in women deserves particular attention from researchers, policymakers, and clinicians.

The very existence of the large gender disparity in rates of depression might, in itself, be taken as prima facie evidence that women's fundamental human right to mental health was routinely violated. This gender difference first emerges in puberty (Kessler, 2003; Wade, Cairney, & Pevalin, 2002) and declines from midlife onward, although evidence on the age when the sex difference ceases to be important varies from one study and one country to another (Akhtar-Danesh & Landeen, 2007; Andrews, Hall, Teeson, & Henderson, 1999; Bebbington et al., 2003; Kessler, Foster, Webster, & House, 1992).

Although national surveys indicate that women experience significantly higher rates of depression than men during their reproductive years, this cannot be taken as unequivocal evidence of biological causation of depression in women. During these same years, a number of coexisting but nonbiological independent risk factors for depression are highly prevalent. These include the triple burden of paid work, unpaid household work, and heavy caring responsibilities and high rates of intimate partner violence and sexual violence (Astbury & Cabral, 2000; Vos et al., 2006).

Research to date on war and conflict situations indicates that there is a graded relationship between the degree of trauma experienced by victims of war and the extent and severity of their subsequent psychological symptoms. A review of research studies from Afghanistan, the Balkans, Cambodia, Chechnya, Iraq, Israel, Lebanon, Palestine, Rwanda, Sri Lanka, Somalia, and Uganda concludes that women have an increased vulnerability to the psychological consequences of war such as PTSD, anxiety, and depression (Srinivasa-Murthy & Lakshminarayana, 2006). The deliberate targeting of women and girls as objects of sexual violence during war and conflict will be discussed later, but such violence represents a common and severe source of the kind of trauma linked with common mental disorders (Srinivasa-Murthy & Lakshminarayana, 2006).

Language: Risks versus Rights

The standard public health approach to reducing the level of a negative health condition in a given population, and one that underpins BOD estimates, begins with the identification of all risk factors relevant to that condition. Ezzati, Lopez, Rodgers, Vander Hoorn, and Murray (2002) argue that it is only through reliable and comparable analysis of risks to health that effective efforts to prevent disease and injury can be developed.

The term "risk factor" is largely a product of epidemiological research. It arose out of the recognition that for many serious health conditions such as cardiovascular disease, no single cause could be identified, let alone eliminated. Instead, multiple factors, dubbed "risk factors," were found to be associated with a statistically significant increase in the risk, if not the certainty, of developing such a disease.

Many risk factors for poor health, including poor mental health, are inextricably linked with or embedded in the position a person or groups of people occupy in the social hierarchy, as evidenced by the very large research literature that has emerged since the 1980s on the social gradient in health (Stansfeld, Head, Fuhrer, Wardle, & Cattell, 2003; Stansfeld, Head, & Marmot, 1998; Townsend & Davidson, 1982; Wilkinson, 1997). This literature illustrates that those who occupy a lower position in the social hierarchy and experience protracted socioeconomic adversity have significantly higher rates of many adverse health outcomes, including depression, than those who occupy higher social positions in that hierarchy. Significant differences in health outcomes between groups occur at all points on the gradient, not just in comparisons between the lowest versus the highest points, and indicate that poverty alone is insufficient to account for them.

Through its use of the scientific language of "risk factors" or "vulnerability factors" that are "correlated" with "exposure" to "adverse" or "negative life events or experiences," existing research into the social factors that predict depression in women has unwittingly deflected our attention from the possibility that such "risk" and "vulnerability" factors might stand for something else. In particular, previously identified social risk factors for depression in women might more accurately be conceptualized as proxy variables for a range of rights violations. Moreover, if rights violations are occurring but are not being named as such because the biomedical, epidemiological terminology of "risk" serves to conceal rather than elucidate them, then it can be argued that such language is likely to be, as Mann (1999) puts it, "inapt and inept" in identifying the important forms of human suffering and injuries to human dignity that are, in fact, taking place. The inappropriateness of using the standard term "disorder" in conjunction with the suffering associated with human rights violations, as in "dignity disorder," "humiliation disorder," or "unfairness disorder," supports this assertion.

The language used by researchers and mental health professionals stakes a claim to the ownership of the intellectual or experiential territory being explored. For example, the language of psychiatry can be used to assert that much mental suffering is appropriately conceptualized as psychiatric disorder, whose causes derive primarily from biochemical alterations or malfunctioning in the brain itself. It follows from this that biochemical means will be needed to rectify the psychiatric disorder in question and that only those mental health professionals with the credentials to use these means ought to be involved in this endeavor. A model of mental illness that stresses biological causation may explain why much psychiatric discussion of human rights tends to focus on the stigma and discrimination that those with psychiatric "disorders" encounter from the wider community (Arboleda-Florez, 2001). The otherwise exemplary WHO (2001) initiative to combat stigma and discrimination, "Stop exclusion, Dare to care," also carries the implication that the primary way in which human rights violations matter in mental illness resides in the discriminatory and stigmatizing attitudes of the wider community toward those who are mentally ill. In other words, while human rights violations are certainly considered as an important consequence for those living with an existing mental illness, they are not typically entertained as a likely cause of such illness.

By contrast, a focus on human rights violations centralizes their possible role in the development of certain forms of poor mental health, such as depression. The language of rights steps beyond the terminology of scientific, neutral, decontextualized "risks" into a more political sphere. Within a rights framework, countries that are signatories to various human rights conventions that include the right to health become accountable for the health inequalities that their systems of organization and privilege, generate and sustain.

Dignity versus Humiliation

The most basic human right and one that serves as a precondition for many others is the right to dignity. The first article of the 1948 Universal Declaration of Human Rights (UDHR) asserts that:

> All human beings are born free and equal in dignity and rights. They are endowed with reason and conscience and should act towards one another in a spirit of brotherhood.

It is ironic that even while proclaiming equality, dignity, and rights for everyone, the declaration appeals to a spirit of brotherhood, oblivious to the possibility that this reflects gender bias. Several of the articles in the declaration also refer to "himself and his family" and "his rights and freedoms," and while it is true that this reflects language usage at the time the declaration was adopted and proclaimed, it is also true that the language continues to reflect gender inequalities in the enjoyment of rights today. In discussing the fact that many people live in "dignity-impugning" environments, Mann (1999) argues that an exploration of the meanings of dignity and the forms of its violation may help to uncover "a new universe of human suffering" that is detrimental to physical, mental, and social well-being.

Existing research on risk factors for depression has not been informed explicitly by a human rights approach; therefore, much of the psychological suffering deriving from human rights violations is unlikely to have been named or documented, let alone measured. The naming of different forms of human suffering logically precedes the possibility of being able to count or quantify them: "Child abuse did not exist in meaningful societal terms until it was named and then measured; nor did domestic violence" (Mann, 1999, p. 449).

Quite simply, researchers have not been moved to measure the mental health impacts for women (or men either) of the violation of their rights. These include, to name but a few from the UDHR, the right to:

- Liberty and security of person (Article 3)
- Not to be held in slavery or servitude (Article 4)

- Not to be subjected to torture or to cruel, inhuman, or degrading treatment of punishment (Article 5)
- Equality before the law … without any discrimination… (and) equal protection of the law (Article 7)
- Freedom of movement (Article 13)
- Equal rights as to marriage, during marriage, and at its dissolution (Article 16)
- Just and favorable conditions of work including equal pay for equal work (Article 23)
- A standard of living adequate for health and well-being (Article 25)

Despite the lack of explicit rights-based research regarding the development of depression in women, a number of studies do provide findings that are germane to the appraisal of the relationship between damage to dignity and/or rights violations and the subsequent experience of depression.

To support the asserted relationship between women's rights violations and the gender disparity in depression, three main types of research findings will be considered. First, I will provide a brief overview of the psychological impact of gender-based violence. The multiple forms of gender-based violence violate many of women's most basic human rights including their right to dignity, liberty, and security of person; their right to health, given the multiple negative mental health outcomes of such violence; and, in a significant number of cases, their right to life.

Second, I will focus on evidence relating to the psychological consequences of experiences or situations involving humiliation that attack human dignity. According to the Oxford dictionary, one of the meanings of "humiliate" is to injure the dignity or self-respect of a person, and while "indignity" is the antonym of "dignity," humiliation is a very closely related concept. Maintaining dignity relies to a great extent on being able to exert some control over one's person, behavior, and life. Being deprived of autonomy and control necessarily impugns dignity.

Third, I will examine the mental health impacts of unfair treatment within the workplace, focusing on interpersonal mistreatment. Emerging research in this area provides an additional line of evidence that links dignity-impugning environments and experiences with psychologically harmful outcomes and illustrates how exposure to such environments and experiences is differentially affected by gender and a subordinate position in the organizational hierarchy.

Gender-Based Violence

In April 2003, the Human Rights Commission of the UN passed a resolution expressing concern about the magnitude of the findings of the World Report on Violence and Health (Krug et al., 2002). This report noted that the lifetime prevalence of physical intimate violence reported by women, based on 48 population-based studies from around the world, ranged from 10% to 69%.

The commission acknowledged that violence is an obstacle to the full realization of the right to the highest attainable standard of health and to the enjoyment of other human rights.

Nowhere is the link between human rights violations and poor mental health for women more apparent than in the voluminous literature on the negative mental health consequences of gender-based violence (GBV). Being born female carries with it heightened "vulnerability" or "risk" of experiencing violence from an intimate or someone known to the victim, with the highest prevalence of such violence occurring in younger women.

The WHO multicountry study on women's health and domestic violence is a particularly valuable source of data (Ellsberg, Jansen, Heise, Watts, & Garcia-Moreno, 2008). It was carried out in 15 sites and 10 countries (Bangladesh, Brazil, Ethiopia, Japan, Namibia, Peru, Samoa, Serbia and Montenegro, Thailand, and the United Republic of Tanzania) between 2000 and 2003 and utilized a sample of more than 24,000 women aged between 15 and 49 years, Using standardized population-based household surveys, this study found that the lifetime prevalence of physical or sexual partner violence, or both, varied from 15% to 71% (Garcia-Moreno et al., 2006). For all settings combined, the destructive mental health impact of domestic violence is revealed very clearly. Women who reported partner violence at least once in their life compared with their nonviolated peers had an almost 3-fold increase in the odds of reporting emotional distress and suicidal thoughts (odds ratio [OR] 2.9, 95% confidence interval [CI] 2.7–3.2) and almost 4-fold increased odds of suicidal attempts (OR 3.8, 95% CI 3.3–4.5).

A large-scale U.S. study on the long-term consequences of childhood sexual abuse illustrates the compounding health effects of gender-based violence over the life course. Dube and colleagues (2005) reported that women who were sexually abused as children, compared with their nonabused counterparts, were more than twice as likely to have attempted suicide in adult life, were at a 40% increased chance of marrying an alcoholic, and had a similar increased risk of reporting current problems with their marriage.

Gender-based violence, including child sexual abuse, sexual violence in later life, and intimate partner violence, is associated with a significantly elevated risk of a range of negative mental health outcomes (Resnick, Acierno & Kilpatrick, 1997). These outcomes encompass increased rates of depression including postnatal depression and dysthymia but also anxiety, suicidality, PTSD, panic disorder and certain phobias, substance use disorder, somatization and dissociative disorder, and high levels of psychiatric comorbidity (Astbury & Cabral, 2000; Campbell, 2002; Hegarty, Gunn, Chondros, & Small, 2004). It is unlikely to be a coincidence that most of these disorders are characterized by a significant gender disparity in rates.

Women abused in both childhood and adulthood have even higher rates of many of these disorders, suggesting a graded relationship between the number of exposures to violence and the extent and severity of the negative mental health outcomes (Astbury, 1996; Chapman et al., 2004).

The deliberate exercise of coercive control by perpetrators over their female victims takes the form of physical, emotional, and sexual violence and ensures victims are socially isolated and cut off from potential avenues for psychosocial support. Men who are more controlling were reported to be more likely to be violent against their partners in the WHO multi-country study (Garcia-Moreno et al., 2006). Unlike the workplace bully who has to contend with some limitations on the scope of the bullying in time and place, the bully at home has greater scope for exercising power and control. In epidemiological terms, the "dose" and the "duration" during which the violence can be delivered are both increased.

In an Australian BOD study (Vos et al., 2006), intimate partner violence (IPV), including sexual violence, was investigated as a health "risk" factor and compared with a range of previously well-investigated health risk factors. This study found that IPV constituted a greater risk for ill-health among women aged younger than 45 years than all seven of the other major health risk factors examined. These other risk factors were the ones typically included in contemporary BOD estimates, such as high body weight; high cholesterol; high blood pressure; harmful alcohol, illicit drug, and tobacco use; and physical inactivity. IPV was associated with more than twice the risk to health as the next most important factor, illicit drug use, that contributed to less than 4% of the BOD. The largest contribution to the burden of disease associated with IPV was poor mental health. Depression, anxiety, and suicide together contributed to 73% of the total disease burden associated with IPV. Harmful health-related behaviors (tobacco, alcohol, and illicit drug use) that often co-occur with poor mental health accounted for another 22% of the disease burden attributable to IPV.

The psychological damage inextricably linked to the perpetration of gender-based violence against girls and women constitutes a critical injury to their dignity and self-respect. As noted elsewhere, violence against women, whether by their intimate partners or men not known to them, is the most prevalent and most emblematic gender-based cause of depression in women (Astbury & Cabral, 2000). Such violence encapsulates humiliation, subordination, grossly unfair treatment, and blocked escape or entrapment.

Constant denigration, subordination, and humiliation inevitably enforce a sense of inferiority, shame, and reduced self-respect and illustrate why the victim might lose her sense of self and succumb to the perpetrator's views of her worth. This damage to dignity and self is evident in the comment made by Ana Christina, a participant in Ellsberg's (1997) research in Nicaragua:

> He used to tell me, 'you're an animal, an idiot, you are worthless.' That made me feel even more stupid. I couldn't raise my head. I think I still have scars from this, and I have always been insecure. ... I would think, could it be that I really am stupid? I accepted it, because after a point... he had destroyed me by blows and psychologically. (p. 8)

One of the U.S. participants in Jack's (1991) study on women and depression speaks eloquently of the self-silencing effects of living a life of fear with an intimate partner who violently enacts his beliefs regarding male privilege and superiority, while simultaneously assigning all responsibility for that violence to his female victim:

> 'No goddamn woman is going to tell me what to do and control my life' and 'I'm going to do what I have to do here. You're going to make me have to tune you up. You want me to stomp the shit out of you.' Reactions like that, and it makes you back off. And over a period of time, like two or three years, you become accustomed to not voicing anything. (Jack, 1991, pp. 35–36)

The coercive control exercised by a violent intimate partner militates against victims being able to access social support. By contrast, if violence is disclosed to a trusted friend, relative, or health care professional, the possibilities for psychosocial support immediately increase. One study (Coker, Smith, et al., 2002), which examined the practice of screening for IPV in family practice clinics in South Carolina, reported that among women experiencing IPV, those with higher social support scores had significantly reduced risks of having poor perceived mental and physical health. The risks of anxiety for these women compared with those with low levels of social support were significantly reduced (adjusted relative risk [aRR] 0.3, 95% CI 0.2–0,4) as were their risks for depression (aRR 0.6, 95% CI 0.5–0.8), PTSD symptoms (aRR 0.5, 95% CI 0.4–0.8), and suicide attempts (aRR 0.6, 95% CI 0.4–0.9) (Coker, Davis, et al., 2002).

Besides psychosocial support, a sense of mastery, or feelings of being in control of forces that affect one's life, appears to afford protection to the mental health of pregnant women. Rodriguez and colleagues (2008), in their study of pregnant Latina women in Los Angeles, reported that the risk for depression was reduced by almost 30% in women with a greater sense of mastery. Conversely, risk increased significantly for both depression and PTSD for women with a history of trauma and IPV. Restoring feelings of being in control of the determinants of their lives is a critical task for survivors of all forms of gender-based violence. The mental health importance of being able to exercise control has also been confirmed in numerous studies of health in the workplace (Matthews & Power, 2002; Mausner-Dorsch & Eaton, 2002; Stansfeld, Head, Fuhrer, et al., 2003).

These findings illustrate that mental health interventions cannot be confined to the diagnosis and clinical treatment of psychological disorders. Such an approach fails to address the multiple instances of unfair and violent treatment that significantly predict depression and associated mental health conditions such as PTSD in women. By placing these matters outside the parameters of clinical concern, a major opportunity is missed to reduce preventable causes of depression (WHO, ICPE, 2000).

The strength of the evidence on the mental health effects of GBV mandates that competent health practice must ascertain not only whether a woman is depressed but also whether and how that depression might be associated with the violation of her dignity or other human rights, including the right to liberty and security of her person. Such violations must be identified and addressed as a matter of priority. Women are meant to have an inalienable human right to live in safety, and the mental health benefit of living in freedom from violence cannot be underestimated. In one study, the cessation of violence for women with a history of physical or sexual abuse and psychological abuse resulted in a 27% decline in the likelihood of depression; this increased to a 35% decline in women who had experienced multiple forms of abuse (Kernie, Holt, Stoner, Wolf, & Rivara, 2003).

From a rights perspective, it is little surprise that the injuries to dignity, self-worth, and self-respect caused by acts of GBV might contribute significantly to the development of so many of the psychological "disorders" in which women predominate. Women's heightened vulnerability to depressive disorder, historically the source of much perplexity for mental health researchers, might now reasonably be reframed in terms of women's increased vulnerability to human rights violations and blatantly unfair treatment in both the private sphere of the home and the public sphere of work.

Humiliation and Entrapment: The Denial of Dignity and Liberty

The early research of Brown and Harris (1978) with working-class women from Islington, London, revealed four "vulnerability" factors that increased the chances of a woman becoming depressed when she encountered a stressful life event or difficulty. These included the loss of a parent before the age of 17 years, particularly the loss of one's mother before the age of 11 years; the presence at home of three or more children younger than 14 years; a poor, nonconfiding marriage; and the lack of full- or part-time paid employment. Direct examples of rights violations such as child sexual abuse, intimate partner violence, or sexual violence in adult life were not investigated in this first study. In other words, the women's vulnerability to certain damaging experiences, precisely because they were women or girls, was not considered.

A great deal of research since Brown and Harris's groundbreaking study, in high-income countries such as the United Kingdom as well as low-income countries such as Zimbabwe (Broadhead & Abas, 1998; Brown, 1998), has confirmed the contribution that significant personal loss, lack of a confidant, heavy caring responsibilities, and lack of paid work make to the development of depression. The powerful protective role of social support in reducing the risk of depression, including postnatal depression, has also been documented (Brown, Harris, & Eales, 1996; Paykel, 1994). Other research on women in midlife has underlined the importance of a greater sense of control, less shame, and higher religious attendance in discriminating between women who experienced low levels of psychological distress and those who had high levels (Schieman, Van Gundy, & Taylor, 2001).

As a result of their ongoing investigations into the social origins of depression in women, Brown and his colleagues revised their original explanatory model as new variables were investigated. In particular, childhood sexual abuse, which did not become a legitimate, societally recognized form of human suffering and a focus of psychological research until the late 1970s (Astbury, 1996), was to prove a highly significant predictor of women's depression, including chronic depression in adult life, in the studies by this and other groups of researchers (Bifulco, Brown, & Adler, 1991; Dube et al., 2005; Mullen, Martin, Anderson, Romans, & Herbison, 1993).

By the mid-1990s, Brown and his colleagues had identified the nature and predictive importance of the characteristics of situations most likely to trigger a depressive episode. This research reiterated the importance of loss that occurred in the context of severe, disruptive, irregular life events. Loss was not confined to the loss of an actual person but encompassed the loss of an important role or a "cherished idea."

From a human rights perspective, the emergence of an abiding sense of defeat in relation to the depressogenic situation appears critical. Defeat appears to arise out of an unfavorable effort-reward ratio that is connected to the particular depressogenic situation that a woman is trying to overcome.

The chronic socioeconomic adversity characterizing the lives of women living in poverty predicts the strong likelihood of an unfavorable effort-reward ratio. In this situation, the resources needed for a life of dignity for themselves and their children remain beyond reach, regardless of the effort women living in poverty expend in jobs that pay wages below the poverty line or social security payments that do the same. The defeat and humiliation of living in such circumstances issue from and reliably reflect the effect of the violation of the social and economic rights of poor women and help to explain why their rates of depression are more than twice as high as those for women living in the most socioeconomically advantaged circumstances.

The association between poverty and depression as well as other common mental disorders in women has been reported in developing countries such as India, Chile, and Brazil (Patel, Araya, de Lima, Ludermir, & Todd, 1999); Zimbabwe (Broadhead & Abas, 1998); and South Africa (Hamad, Fernald, Karlan, & Zinman, 2008), as well as in high-income, developed countries such as the United States (Belle, 1990; Kessler, 2003).

Feelings of defeat identified among the women in the study by Brown, Harris, and Hepworth (1995) were linked, not surprisingly, to feelings of helplessness and powerlessness or loss of control. Such feelings are congruent with Seligman's (1975) view that learned helplessness resulting from lack of control over the outcome of situations was instrumental in the development of depression. Other critical characteristics of the situations that precipitated depression for the women in Brown and colleagues' (1995) study were those of humiliation and entrapment or blocked escape, especially when the situations involved significant other people, or "core ties." The researchers provide excerpts from their interviews that permit insight into the situations where participants felt humiliated and "put down": "He puts me down continually, shouting and swearing, walking out of the room if I try and discuss anything" (Brown et al., 1995, p. 17).

The central role of defeat, entrapment, and humiliation in triggering depression is evident in the relative contribution made by the characteristics of different situations to depression. Using a hierarchical rating system, nearly 75% of the situations involved entrapment or humiliation, 22% involved loss alone, and 5% concerned danger alone. The provoking severe events in almost all instances involved a core relation (Brown et al., 1995).

It is hardly surprising that the humiliation and sense of defeat implicit in being disregarded, verbally abused, and walked out on by an intimate partner whenever one tries to speak might trigger a depressive response. This constellation of characteristics can be seen to represent a display of dominance by an abusive partner that simultaneously speaks to the gendered inequality inherent in the relationship and to the continuing social subordination of women that helps to legitimate such treatment within interpersonal relationships. In this way, the very possibility that a woman might persist in her efforts to communicate when she is aware of the strong likelihood that these will meet with a punitive, demeaning response is reduced. These circumstances facilitate the "self–silencing" and consequent loss of a sense of authentic self that defined the depressed women Jack (1991) interviewed in her longitudinal study on women and depression.

The emotional distress associated with the loss of self, observable among the participants in Jack's study, indicates that this specific form of loss should be added to or perhaps integrated within the types of loss already noted in Brown, Harris, and Hepworth's (1995) study. These included loss of a person, a role, and/or a cherished idea. However, Jack's research underscores that the person who is lost can be oneself and the cherished idea that can be lost may relate to the potentials of the self that lie dormant when "women's experience of adult attachments continually intersect with issues of dominance and subordination" (Jack, 1991, p. 21). Voice and lack of or loss of voice is central here, as voice and verbal and emotional expression provide the means of sharing or shielding the self and one's cherished ideas from an intimate partner.

Maya, one of the participants in Jack's study, who had experienced two marriages characterized by IPV, exemplifies how the constriction of voice and feelings is closely linked with loss of self, self-silencing, and depression. It was not until after she was divorced and recovering from her depression that Maya experienced a return of feeling and voice:

> It felt good to cry and laugh and do all those things I hadn't done. I remember the
> first time I laughed out loud and it seemed strange to me to hear my own

laughter... and then I realized that I never laughed in my marriage. I never let anything out, but then I never felt laughter.... It really caught me by surprise because it was so loud, and I must have been so quiet all the time. I talked in a very quiet voice, more than I do now, and you could hardly - nobody heard me and I would have to repeat myself. (Jack, 1991, p. 102–103)

Feelings of humiliation might be seen as an almost inevitable response to the experience of being devalued and treated unfairly by someone of importance in the women's lives; such feelings are antithetical to the maintenance of a sense of dignity or having any control over the defeating situation.

Brown and colleagues (1995) do not conceptualize experiences of humiliation as emotional abuse or as an injury to and violation of a woman's human dignity, but they do comment on the negative congruence between the demeaning dynamic evident in the personal relationships of their depressed participants and the broader social devaluation of women: "Probably equally significant to being humiliated and devalued is what is symbolized by such atypical events in terms of a woman's life as a whole - in particular, the experience of being confirmed as marginalized and unwanted" (p. 21).

Jack's (1991) gendered analysis of the dynamic interplay between social and political factors and the personal and emotional experiences associated with depression in women extends our understanding of how the experiences of being marginalized and unwanted are linked for women to powerful gender norms and a culture of inequality that continually thwart their efforts to achieve intimacy and voice within unequal relationships.

In research and clinical practice, the psychological consequences of humiliation, marginalization, devaluation, and inequality are likely to be classified as depression, relying on the nomenclature of psychological disorder and the presence of symptoms that meet the criteria for such a diagnosis. However, as a researcher or clinician focuses on attending to the correct assignment of symptoms to a specific diagnostic category, the affronts to human dignity and the pervasive sense of demoralization from which this "mood disorder" arises can become detached from their more conspicuous, more easily classifiable symptomatic correlates. As a result, remedy and treatment are directed not toward the rectification of the humiliation and devaluation, nor to repair of the damage done to the woman's human dignity, but to the amelioration and management of what the violated woman is now perceived to carry, and is often marked and stigmatized by, namely, one or another form of mental illness. In addition, this splitting serves to obscure the social origins and social patterning of depression that sees women predominate in diagnoses of depression and focuses instead on the attributes of the depressed individual.

Work: The Psychological Effects of Unfair Treatment

According to Erik Erikson (1950), Freud's response to a question about what it took for an individual to fare well in life was simply "Lieben und arbeiten" (to love and to work).

As rates of female participation in the paid workforce increase, work has become a source of identity as well as a means to ensure physical survival for more women worldwide. Consequently, the way women and girls are treated at work, and the extent to which they are able to enjoy just and favorable conditions of work, including equal pay for equal work (UDHR, Article 23), is likely to make an increasingly significant contribution to their health and psychological well-being.

De Vogli, Ferrie, Chandola, Kivimaki, and Marmot (2007) stress the importance of fairness to health, and although multiple definitions of fairness exist, they argue that a central criterion of fairness is treating people equally in a way that is right or reasonable and positively supports their dignity and/or self-respect. Unfairness, by contrast, is a potent risk to dignity and self-respect and is hypothesized to bring about negative or stress-related reactions that lead to poor mental and physical health.

Globally, the right to equal pay for equal work remains an aspiration, not a reality. A report by the International Trade Union Confederation (ITUC, 2008) on "The Global Gender Pay Gap" found that internationally, women are disproportionately represented in low-paid and service-sector jobs. Its analysis of data from 63 countries found that, on average, women experienced pay rates that were 16.5% lower than those of their male counterparts.

Living and working in a high-income country does not provide any guarantee that this gap in pay rates will be smaller. In the United States, an analysis of census data revealed a 22% gender-based pay gap, with women, on average, earning only 78% of their male counterparts (De Navas-Walt, Proctor, & Smith, 2008). In other words, gender-based disparities in pay rates are persistent, operate as a conduit to women's higher rates of poverty compared with men's, and serve to deny many women the right to "a standard of living adequate for health and well-being" (UDHR, Article 25).

Limitations of the Current Research Base

Unequal power relationships tend to characterize the working environments of women by virtue of their overconcentration in poor-quality, low-paid jobs where they are unable to exert control over decision making (ITUC, 2008). Yet surprisingly, little research has been conducted on the psychological impact experienced by women as a result of economically inadequate work, despite its high prevalence (Lennon, 2006).

There is also a paucity of evidence on the psychological health effects of women working in "sweat shops" and other forms of poorly paid work performed in unsafe conditions as these operate outside the formal economy and in a clandestine manner, making it difficult to access evidence. As Burrow notes in the Foreword to the ITUC (2008) report:

> Hundreds of millions of women working in informal and unprotected work do not appear in any records, and many developing countries do not have the means, or in some cases the will, to keep national records on the world of work. (ITUC, 2008, p. 7)

Where Outer and Inner Worlds Meet

The treatment received and the conditions of paid work inevitably interact with the treatment and conditions women experience in their unpaid work, including housework and the care of children and others within the home. The multiplicative effects of this interaction can operate in a positive or negative manner for mental health, depending on the nature of the treatment and conditions that are experienced.

Research on women and work shows that depressive symptoms are increased by a number of different factors related to the interface between women's lives and responsibilities within and outside the workplace (Lennon, 2006). The key role of control in preserving or threatening emotional well-being is apparent in much of this research even though control, as a variable of interest, typically interacts with a number of other variables. For example, the influence that the number of children at home exerts on depressive symptoms is most marked for women with jobs that are low on control (Lennon & Rosenfield, 1992), and the difficulties associated with organizing and paying for child care have the greatest depressogenic effect for women whose jobs offer little flexibility or control (Lennon, Wasserman, & Allen, 1991). Job insecurity, signifying a lack of control, is also associated with depression (Matthews & Power, 2002), as is an unfavorable balance between the level of work demands and the level of control that can be exercised over them (Mausner-Dorsch & Eaton, 2000). Similarly, a poor reward for the effort expended has been found to predict adverse mental health outcomes among employees in the paid workforce (De Vogli et al., 2007).

Just as the ability to exercise some control over personal life circumstances reduces the likelihood of experiencing a sense of defeat in relationships with intimates (Brown et al., 1995), having agency and control in the workplace functions as a protective factor for mental health and reduces the likelihood of women experiencing depression. An analysis of data from the Canadian Community Health Survey (Blackmore et al., 2007) revealed that women with high levels of decision-making authority at work were less likely to have had major depressive episodes in the previous year than their counterparts with low decision-making authority.

Although the aforementioned research has identified a number of factors that are associated with increased rates of depression among working women, relatively little research so far, with the exception of work on sexual harassment in the workplace (Fitzgerald, 1993; Schneider, Swan, & Fitzgerald, 1997), has focused specifically on the mental health impact of being deliberately targeted for unfair interpersonal treatment within the workplace and the role of gender in this situation.

Yet such treatment probably offers the clearest examples of rights violations for individual workers. This is because, as De Vogli and colleagues (2007) observe:

> The experience of being treated unfairly seems to be connected with a threat or an attack to an individual's dignity. An important component of human dignity is determined by

the degree of respect of 'public worth' bestowed by others. Low social status is a continuous source of unfairness probably because people in subordinate positions are more likely to be disrespected or treated as inferiors by others, as well as being ignored or excluded from full participation in social life. (p. 516)

As we have seen, women as a group are highly vulnerable to occupying subordinate positions; are concentrated in lower status, lower paid jobs (ITUC, 2008); and receive unfair treatment in many other spheres of life (World Bank, 2006). This suggests that gender is a cross-cutting determinant of mental health that frequently interacts with low social position and low income and functions as a locus for unfair treatment.

Indeed, in their investigation of the relationship between unfair treatment in the workplace and the health of British civil servants in the Whitehall 11 study, De Vogli and colleagues (2007) found that female sex and having a low employment grade within the civil service increased the risk of being treated unfairly. In turn, being treated unfairly was linked significantly to many previously identified predictors of poor mental health such as a higher level of job strain and a higher effort-reward imbalance.

While not all instances of unfairness are necessarily clear violations of a person's human rights, they are likely to have a negative impact on the human dignity of those affected. Workplace bullying, a severe form of unfair treatment at work and an obvious rights violation, has been found to significantly increase the likelihood of cardiovascular disease and depression developing in both women and men. In a longitudinal study of health employees in Finland, the majority of whom were women, Kivimaki, Virtanen, and colleagues (2003) reported a bullying prevalence rate of 5% at the time of the first survey and 6% at the second survey. Workers who had experienced bullying were compared with those who had not, controlling for sex, age, and income. For the subgroup of people who experienced prolonged bullying, namely, those who reported being bullied on both occasions, there was a more than 4-fold increase in depression (OR 4.25, 95% CI 2.0–8.6). The findings of this study strongly suggest that: "Early intervention and prevention of workplace bullying may be a key factor in attempts to minimize its adverse effects on mental health" (Kivimaki, Virtanen, et al., 2003, p. 780).

Bullying affects both male and female employees, but the lack of sex-disaggregated data presented in this study means that it is impossible to tell whether men and women were affected differently by workplace bullying.

Another study on the role of inequitable treatment on psychological health does, however, focus on a female cohort. Kivimaki, Elovainio, Vahtera, Virtanen, and Stansfeld (2003) investigated the mental health impact of unfair treatment in a sample of nearly 1,800 female hospital workers. Even after adjusting in the analysis for a host of other factors that independently predict psychological well-being such as age, salary, mental distress at baseline, job control, job demands, and social support, this research demonstrated that the experience of low procedural justice produced an almost doubling of the odds of new psychiatric disorders being diagnosed in the two years that female employees were followed up. Procedural justice in this study was conceptualized as an aspect of organizational equity and defined as decision-making procedures that were consistently applied, open, and correctable and that included input from affected parties. The findings strongly suggest that inequitable treatment makes a significant and independent contribution to the likelihood of psychiatric disorders being subsequently diagnosed by a doctor for female employees who experienced unfair treatment.

Voice and the Risk of Retaliation

The role of self-silencing in the development of depression and other psychological disorders within the context of unfair treatment in the workplace is one that has received little attention from workplace researchers to date. An intriguing exception is the study by Cortina and Magley (2003), who investigated the health impacts of interpersonal mistreatment as well as what happened to employees who remained silent or vocally resisted such mistreatment. This study of 1,167 federal court employees, the majority of whom (833) were women, found that interpersonal mistreatment was very common and reported by 71% of the sample.

Their findings reveal something of a Catch 22 situation for victims of interpersonal mistreatment in the workplace. Consistent with Jack's theory that assigns a significant role to self-silencing in the development of depression, this study confirmed that there were costs to well-being—professionally, psychologically, and physically—with remaining silent in the face of mistreatment. On the other hand, there were also costs involved with speaking out against mistreatment, although retaliation was by no means automatic following the reporting of mistreatment. Around a third of the sample who were mistreated (76 of 834) did not encounter any form of retaliation victimization.

Three different forms of voice or speaking up against mistreatment were investigated by Cortina and Magley (2003), including expressing discontent to colleagues (social-support seeking), confronting the person responsible for the mistreatment, and reporting the situation to organizational authorities. All forms of voice could trigger work retaliation victimization or social retaliation victimization, but the form the retaliation took was a function of the relative power of the perpetrator to the victim in the organizational hierarchy. Victims endured more social retaliation victimization from colleagues such as being ostracized, called names, blamed, harassed, threatened, or given the "silent treatment" when they worked in lower status jobs. They also experienced greater interpersonal mistreatment if they confronted the wrongdoer about this mistreatment. By contrast, work retaliation victimization only increased as a function of confrontation, especially when powerful wrongdoers were involved.

In order to clarify the behaviors associated with the greatest level of harm, an analysis was undertaken that compared victims who remained silent with those who spoke up against mistreatment. This analysis revealed that those who restrained from speaking up and thus avoided any form of retaliation had even worse psychological and physical health outcomes than their counterparts who voiced resistance and suffered retaliation (Cortina & Magley, 2003). This finding provides strong evidence that the psychological impact of self-silencing operates as perniciously in the workplace as it does within intimate relationships.

The importance of retaliation as a form of employment discrimination resulting from a complaint of a traditional form of discrimination such as sexual harassment, age, or race is underlined by findings reported by Sincoff, Slonaker, and Wendt (2006). In an analysis of nearly 1,400 cases in the United States, they found that claims of retaliation discrimination had increased by 47% over the decade 1994–2004 and were now the second most common complaint, after race discrimination. The kind of vicious and even life-threatening retaliation that can occur was evidenced by a number of examples where sexual harassment and gender discrimination were the original forms of discrimination. Two of these follow:

> After complaining of gender harassment, a female FedEx driver's truck brakes were sabotaged and help loading her truck was denied. As a result, $3.2 million (including $2.5 million in punitive damages) was awarded. (*EEOC v. Federal Express Corp*, 2004)

> Management did not address six years of sexual harassment against a female employee. Her supervisor limited her breaks, increased her workload, yelled at her, and tried to thwart additional reports of discrimination. The jury awarded $1.4 million (including $650,000 in punitive damages), to which the judge added $174,927 in attorney fees. (*Baker v. Morrell & Co.*, 2004, as cited in Sincoff et al., 2008)

A study by Lim and Cortina (2005) of two different female populations working within a large public-sector organization provides further evidence that female gender can operate as a continuous source of unfairness. Three different forms of unfair treatment were identified and these were highly interrelated, namely, sexual harassment, gender harassment, and general incivility. A graded, inverse relationship between the number of forms of mistreatment and the level of employee well-being was observed. The findings of this study and those of Sincoff and colleagues (2006) suggest that future research in this area must take account of all forms of mistreatment that occur in the workplace, including gender-specific forms of retaliatory discrimination. Such studies must be designed in such a way that when these forms of mistreatment occur simultaneously or sequentially, their compounding negative health effects are able to be measured accurately.

Unfair treatment, whether at work or home, appears to be strongly socially patterned, reflecting the higher social position, status, and power of the perpetrator vis à vis the victim of such treatment. Marked similarities obtain between the comments of De Vogli and his colleagues, emphasizing the interconnections between an individual's sense of dignity and their social standing or public worth; the view by Brown and colleagues (1995) that a current, personal experience of humiliation and devaluation also represents or symbolize a woman's life as a whole, namely, "the experience of being confirmed as marginalized and unwanted"; Jack's research findings on inequality, self-silencing, and depression; and the quote from the 1998 World Health Report that "no society treats its women as well as it treats its men." All of these perspectives illuminate the deleterious effects of lower social status, lower public worth, and unfair treatment on the dignity and well-being of individuals and assist in clarifying how negative social or public evaluations of worth become internalized, personalized, and produce self-devaluation.

De Vogli and colleagues (2007) outline two responses to the humiliation associated with unfair treatment. One involves the inward focusing of negative emotions whereby the individual evaluates herself negatively and/or makes internal attributions of responsibility and blame for the unfair treatment. The other response is outward focused and here, the individual evaluates others and blames them for the acts of injustice:

> Inward-focused affective responses to acts of unfairness may include feelings of being devalued or insecurity about personal worth that are precursors of depression and anxiety. Outward-focused affective responses may include anger and hostility, often used as a 'face-saving strategy' to defend the loss of dignity. (p. 517)

The findings of Cortina and Magley's (2003) study clearly imply that inward-focused affective responses to unfair treatment result in worse psychological outcomes than outward responses that voice opposition to such treatment.

When Brown and colleagues' (1995) findings on the pivotal place of defeat and humiliation in interpersonal relationships in triggering depression in women are added to the societal-level forces that devalue women, engender insecurity about self-worth, and stereotype anger in women as "unfeminine," two implications emerge. One relates to the impression that no better combination of factors could be devised to constrain and reduce women's ability to exercise agency in their lives and retain dignity. The other suggests that the subordinate, unequal gendered social position that women continue to occupy vis à vis men at home and at work, including their greater vulnerability to multiple forms of gender-based violence, unfair treatment across the life course, and the very real risk of retaliation if they speak up, may prime women to engage in "inward focussed affective responses to acts of unfairness" (De Vogli et al., 2007). Such responses characterize the self-silencing behaviors of the women in Jack's (1991) study that were so closely allied to the development of depression.

Engendering the Risk of Depression

The advantages of addressing the causes of or reducing "risk factors" for poor health rather than simply treating health conditions once they arise are well documented (Ezzati et al., 2002). In the case of depression, where rates are rising in recent younger cohorts (WHO ICPE, 2000), early intervention offers the promise of being able to reduce the incidence of depression. Such interventions need to include efforts to reduce the multiple forms of unfair treatment that compromise human dignity, especially among women, who contribute disproportionately to those suffering from depression globally. This approach would have the dual benefits of simultaneously redressing multiple human rights violations and advancing women's right to the enjoyment and protection of their mental health.

Depression: A Pathoplastic Condition?

Depression may be a singular, identifiable outcome, a diagnosis made according to the criteria of the *Diagnostic and Statistical Manual of Mental Health Disorders*, fourth edition, text revision (DSM-IV-TR). But its social determinants, including the pathways through which they operate, are neither singular nor necessarily apparent where they involve human rights violations.

Different trajectories for the development of depression have been identified, and recent research has specified the types of negative or adverse events and experiences that most strongly predict depression in later life (Bifulco et al., 1991; Brown & Harris, 1975; Brown et al., 1995; Felitti et al., 1998; Kuh, Wadsworth, & Hardy, 1997). Many of these "adverse" experiences are criminal rights violations including childhood sexual and physical abuse and neglect. Furthermore, the pattern of depressive symptoms, a critical consideration in determining appropriate symptom-focused treatment, appear to vary according to the particular categories of adverse events encountered.

A recent population-based prospective, longitudinal study in the United States investigated the relationship between exposure to specific categories of adverse life events and the subsequent pattern of depressive symptoms. Keller, Neale, and Kendler (2007) recruited a sample of 4,856 individuals (53% of whom were women) who had experienced depressive symptoms in the 12 months prior to the study and followed them up on four occasions over a maximum of 12 years. Participants were asked to identify whether there was any perceived cause of their depressive symptoms, and these causes were then classified into nine different categories of adverse life events. For events associated with significant loss such as the death of loved ones and relationship break-ups, participants reported high levels of sadness, lack of pleasure, and appetite loss, and where the event was a romantic break-up, high levels of guilt.

Where the adverse events involved chronic stress and failures, increased symptoms of fatigue and hypersomnia were more apparent. For the group of participants who reported their depression came "out of the blue" and were unable to identify any specific cause, symptoms of fatigue, weight gain, and thoughts of self-harm were more dominant. The researchers concluded that depression is a pathoplastic syndrome and that the type of adverse events experienced was causally related to the particular symptom profile that developed.

This study did not report on gender differences in symptom profiles, but the strength of the findings in relation to adverse life events suggests that further exploration and elucidation of this relationship is warranted. Support for the existence of gender differences in symptom profiles does come from an analysis of data from the Canadian Community Health Survey (Romans, Tyas, Cohen, & Silverstone, 2007). Here, men and women were compared in relation to their depressive symptoms. Women were found to be significantly more likely than men to report symptoms of "increased appetite," to being "often in tears," and to be having "thoughts of death." Both this study and the one by Heller and his colleagues underline the need to carefully consider depressed symptoms in the context of women's lives as a whole.

In particular, it would be very useful to ascertain whether a different cluster of so-called symptoms resulted from exposure to various categories of unfair treatment—chronic, intermittent, and cumulative (compared with discrete negative life events) of the kind commonly experienced by women that seeks to intimidate, belittle, or exclude them. This information would assist in furthering our understanding of the mechanisms by which unfair treatment becomes transformed into psychological "symptoms" or idioms of distress and to clarify whether these overlap with or represent quite distinct symptom profiles from those already used to diagnose depression.

Conclusion

While certain experiences of unfair treatment have received significant research attention and it is well established, for example, that IPV makes a major contribution to the development of depression, anxiety, and a range of other psychological and physical health problems (Campbell, 2002; Vos et al., 2006), other violations of women's human rights await identification and investigation. As a result, there is a major gap in the literature that needs to be rectified.

Violations of women's reproductive rights, including the right to decide on the number and frequency of pregnancies, or violations that take away their economic, social, and educational rights, to name but two obvious examples, radically affect women's life chances and their likelihood of being able to maintain dignity, exercise control over their lives, and protect their emotional well-being.

The limited evidence reviewed here makes it abundantly clear that the promotion and protection of women's human's rights is as much a health issue as a rights issue; the two cannot be disentangled. However, the true magnitude and severity of the varieties of unfair, dignity-diminishing treatment that confront women on a daily basis and their as yet undocumented impacts on psychological well-being remain to be established. Rights-based research is needed to address this issue, but lucid and comprehensive guidelines to action already exist in the many UN covenants, declarations, and conventions to which governments around the world are signatories.

Without concerted action by government and nongovernment organizations and civil society to promote and protect these rights for women, the plethora of negative mental health outcomes associated with their routine violation will proliferate and compound.

References

Akhtar-Danesh, N., & Landeen, J. (2007). Relation between depression and socio-demographic factors. *International Journal of Mental Health Systems, 4,* 1–4.

Andrews, G., Hall, W., Teeson, M., & Henderson, S. (1999). *The mental health of Australia.* Canberra, Australia: Commonwealth Department of Health and Aged Care.

Arboleda-Florez, J. (2001). *Stigmatization and human rights violations* (pp. 57–72). Ministerial Round Tables, 2001, 54th World Health Assembly, Geneva, World Health Organization.

Astbury, J. (1996). *Crazy for you: The making of women's madness.* Melbourne, Australia: Oxford University Press.

Astbury, J. (2001). *Gender disparities in mental health* (pp. 73–92). Ministerial Round Tables, 2001, 54th World Health Assembly, Geneva, World Health Organization.

Astbury, J., & Cabral, M. (2000). *Women's mental health: An evidence based review.* Geneva: World Health Organization.

BBC News. (2008, April 5). *Women face bias worldwide - UN.* Retrieved August 10, 2008, from http://news.bbc.co.uk/go/pr/fr/-/2/hi/europe/7331813.stm

Bebbington, P., Dunn, G., Jenkins, R., Lewis, G., Brugha, T., Farrell, M., et al. (2003). The influence of age and sex on the prevalence of depressive conditions: Report from the National Survey of Psychiatric Morbidity. *International Review of Psychiatry, 15,* 74–83.

Belle, D. (1990). Poverty and women's mental health. *American Psychologist, 45,* 385–389.

Bifulco, A., Brown, G., & Adler, Z. (1991). Early sexual abuse and clinical depression in adult life. *British Journal of Psychiatry, 159,* 115–122.

Blackmore, E. R., Stansfeld, S. A., Weller, I., Munce, S., Zagorski, B. M., & Stewart, D. E. (2007). Major depressive episodes and work stress: Results from a national population survey. *American Journal of Public Health, 97,* 2088–2093.

Broadhead, J. C., & Abas, M. A. (1998). Life events, difficulties and depression among women in an urban setting in Zimbabwe. *Psychological Medicine, 28,* 29–38.

Brown, G. W. (1998). Genetic and population perspectives on life events and depression. *Social Psychiatry and Psychiatric Epidemiology, 33*, 363–372.

Brown, G. W., & Harris, T. (1978). *Social origins of depression: A study of psychiatric disorders in women.* New York: Free Press.

Brown, G. W., Harris, T. O., & Eales, M. J. (1996). Social factors and comorbidity of depressive and anxiety disorders. *British Journal of Psychiatry, 68*, 50–57.

Brown, G. W., Harris, T. O., & Hepworth, C. (1995). Loss, humiliation and entrapment among women developing depression: A patient and non-patient comparison. *Psychological Medicine, 25*, 7–21.

Campbell, J. C. (2002). Health consequences of intimate partner violence. *Lancet, 359*, 1331–1336.

Chapman, D. P., Whitfield, C. L., Felitti, V. J., Dube, S. R., Edwards, V. J., & Anda, R. F. (2004). Adverse childhood experiences and the risk of depressive disorders in adulthood. *Journal of Affective Disorders, 82*, 217–225.

Coker, A. L., Davis, K. E., Arias, I., Desai, S., Sanderson, M., Brandt, H. M., et al. (2002). Physical and mental health effects of intimate partner violence for men and women. *American Journal of Preventive Medicine, 23*, 260–268.

Coker, A. L., Smith, P. H., Thompson, M. P., McKeown, R. E., Bethea, L., & Davis, K. E. (2002). Social support protects against the negative effects of partner violence on mental health. *Journal of Women's Health and Gender Based Medicine, 11*, 465–476.

Cortina, L. M., & Magley, V. J. (2003). Raising voice, risking retaliation: Events following interpersonal mistreatment in the workplace. *Journal of Occupational and Health Psychology, 8*, 247–265.

De Navas-Walt, C., Proctor, B. D., & Smith J. C. (2008). *US Census Bureau, current population reports P60-235. Income, poverty and health insurance coverage in the United States: 2007.* Washington, DC: U.S. Government Printing Office.

De Vogli, R., Ferrie, J. E., Chandola, T., Kivimaki, M., & Marmot, M. (2007). Unfairness and health: Evidence from the Whitehall 11 study. *Journal of Epidemiology and Community Health, 61*, 513–518.

Dube, S. R., Anda, R. F., Whitfield, C. L., Brown, D. W., Felitti, V. J., Dong, M., et al. (2005). Long term consequences of childhood sexual abuse by gender of victim. *American Journal of Preventive Medicine, 28*, 430–438.

EEPC v. Federal Express Corporation. (2004). No 02-CV-01194 (M.C. Pa., Jury Verdict 2/24/02).

Ellsberg, M. (1997). *Candies in hell.* Licentiate thesis, Department of Epidemiology and Public Health, Umea University.

Ellsberg, M., Jansen, H. A., Heise, L., Watts, C. H., & Garcia-Moreno, C. (2008). Intimate partner violence and women's physical and mental health in the WHO multi-country study on women's health and domestic violence: An observational study. *Lancet, 371*, 1165–1172.

Erikson, E. H. (1950). *Childhood and society.* New York: W.W. Norton & Company.

Ezzati, M., Lopez, A. D., Rodgers, A., Vander Hoorn, S., & Murray, C. J. (2002). Selected major risk factors and global and regional burden of disease. *Lancet, 360*, 1347–1360.

Farley, M. (2008, June 20). U.N. deems sexual attacks a security issue. *Los Angeles Times,* p. A.3.

Felitti, V. J., Anda, R. F., Nordenburg, D., Williamson, D. F., Spitz, A. M., Edwards V., et al. (1998). Relationship of childhood abuse and household dysfunction to many of the leading causes of death in adults. The Adverse Childhood Experiences (ACE) Study. *American Journal of Preventive Medicine, 14,* 245–258.

Fitzgerald, L. F. (1993). Sexual harassment: Violence against women in the workplace. *American Psychologist, 48,* 1070–1076.

Garcia-Moreno, C., Jansen, H., Ellsberg, M., Heise, L., & Watts, C. (2006). Prevalence of intimate partner violence: Findings from the WHO multi-country study on women's health and domestic violence. *Lancet, 368,* 1260–1269.

Hamad, R., Fernald, L. C., Karlan, D. S., & Zinman, J. (2008). Social and economic correlates of depressive symptoms and perceived stress in South African adults. *Journal of Epidemiology and Community Health, 62,* 538–544.

Hegarty, K., Gunn, J., Chondros, P., & Small R. (2004). Association between depression and abuse by partners of women attending general practice: Descriptive cross-sectional survey. *British Medical Journal, 328,* 621–624.

International Labour Office. (2005). *A global alliance against forced labour. Global report under the Follow Up to the ILO Declaration on Fundamental Principles and Rights at Work.* Geneva: International Labour Office.

International Trade Union Confederation. (2008). *The global gender pay gap.* Brussels: International Trade Union Confederation.

Jack, D. C. (1991). *Silencing the self: Women and depression.* Cambridge, MA: Harvard University Press.

Keller, M. C., Neale, M. C., & Kendler, K. S. (2007). Association of different adverse life events with distinct patterns of depressive symptoms. *American Journal of Psychiatry, 164,* 1521–1529.

Kernie, M. A., Holt, V. L., Stoner, J. A., Wolf, M. E., & Rivara, F. P. (2003). Resolution of depression among victims of intimate partner violence: Is cessation of violence enough? *Violence and Victims, 18,* 115–129.

Kessler, R. C. (2003). Epidemiology of women and depression. *Journal of Affective Disorders, 74,* 5–13.

Kessler, R. C., Foster, C., Webster, P. S., & House, J. S. (1992). The relationship between age and depressive symptoms in 2 national surveys. *Psychology of Ageing, 7,* 119–126.

Kessler, R. C., McGonagle, K. A., Zhao, S., Nelson, C. B., Hughes, M., Eshleman, S., et al. (1994). Lifetime and 12-month prevalence of DSM-III-R psychiatric disorders in the United States. Results from the National Comorbidity Survey. *Archives of General Psychiatry, 51,* 8–19.

Kivimaki, M., Elovainio, M., Vahtera, J., Virtanen, M., & Stansfeld, S. A. (2003). Association between organizational inequity and incidence of psychiatric disorders in female employees. *Psychological Medicine, 33,* 319–326.

Kivimaki, M., Virtanen, M., Vartia, M., Elovainio, M., Vahtera, J., & Keltikangas-Jarvinen, L. (2003). Workplace bullying and the risk of cardiovascular disease and depression. *Occupational and Environmental Medicine, 60,* 779–783.

Krug, E. G., Dahlberg, L., Mercy, J. A., Zwi, J. A., & Lozano, R. (2002). *World report on violence and health.* Geneva: World Health Organization.

Kuh, D. L., Wadsworth, M., & Hardy, R. (1997). Women's health in midlife: The influence of the menopause, social factors and health in earlier life. *British Journal of Obstetrics and Gynaecology, 104*, 923–933.

Lennon, M. C. (2006). Women, work, and depression. In C. L. M. Keyes & S. H. Goodman (Eds.), *Women and depression: A handbook for the social, behavioural and biomedical sciences* (pp. 309–327). Cambridge: Cambridge University Press.

Lennon, M. C., & Rosenfield, S. (1992). Women and distress: The contribution of job and family conditions. *Journal of Health and Social Behavior, 33*, 316–327.

Lennon, M. C., Wasserman, G. A., & Allen, R. (1991). Relative fairness and the division of family work: The importance of options. *American Journal of Sociology, 100*, 506–531.

Lim, S., & Cortina, L. M. (2005). Interpersonal mistreatment in the workplace: The interface and impact of general incivility and sexual harassment. *Journal of Applied Psychology, 90*, 483–496.

Mann, J. M. (1999). Medicine and public health, ethics and human rights. In J. M. Mann, S. Gruskin, M. A. Grodin, & G. J. Annas (Eds.), *Health and human rights: A reader* (pp. 439–452). New York: Routledge.

Matthews, S., & Power, C. (2002). Socio-economic gradients in psychological distress: A focus on women, social roles and work-home characteristics. *Social Science and Medicine, 54*, 799–810.

Mausner-Dorsch, H., & Eaton, W. W. (2000). Psychosocial work environment and depression: Epidemiologic assessment of the demand-control model. *American Journal of Public Health, 90*, 1765–1770.

Mullen, P., Martin, J., Anderson, J., Romans, S., & Herbison, G. (1993). Childhood sexual abuse and mental health in adult life. *British Journal of Psychiatry, 163*, 721–732.

Murray, C. J., & Lopez, A. D. (1997). Global mortality, disability, and the contribution of risk factors: Global Burden of Disease Study. *Lancet, 349*, 1436–1442.

Patel, V., Araya, R., de Lima, M., Ludermir, A., & Todd, C. (1999). Women, poverty and common mental disorders in four restructuring societies. *Social Science and Medicine, 49*, 1461–1471.

Patten, S. B. (2003). Recall bias and major depression lifetime prevalence. *Social Psychiatry and Psychiatric Epidemiology, 38*, 290–296.

Paykel, E. S. (1994). Life events, social support and depression. *Acta Psychiatra Scandinavica, Supplementum, 377*, 50–58.

Piccinelli, M., & Homen, F. G. (1997). *Gender differences in the epidemiology of affective disorders and schizophrenia.* Geneva: World Health Organization.

Resnick, H. S., Acierno, R., & Kilpatrick, D. G. (1997). Health impact of interpersonal violence. 2: Medical and mental health outcomes. *Behavioral Medicine, 23*, 65–78.

Rodriguez, M. A., Heilemann, M. V., Fielder, E., Ang, A., Nevarez, F., & Mangione, C. M. (2008). Intimate partner violence, depression, and PTSD among pregnant Latina women. *Annals of Family Medicine, 6*, 44–52.

Romans, S. E., Tyas, J., Cohen, M. M., & Silverstone, T. (2007). Gender differences in the symptoms of major depressive disorder. *Journal of Nervous and Mental Disorders, 195*, 905–911.

Schieman, S., Van Gundy, K., & Taylor, J. (2001). Status, role and resource explanations for age patterns in psychological distress. *Journal of Health and Social Behavior, 42*, 80–96.

Schneider, K. T., Swan, S., & Fitzgerald, L. F. (1997). Job-related and psychological effects of sexual harassment in the workplace: Empirical evidence from two organizations. *Journal of Applied Psychology, 82*, 401–415.

Seligman, M. E. (1975). *Helplessness: On depression, development and death.* San Francisco: W.H. Freeman.

Sincoff, Z., Slonaker, W. M., & Wendt, A. C. (2008). Retaliation: The form of 21st century employment discrimination. *Business Horizons, 49*, 44–450.

Srinivasa-Murthy, R., & Lakshminarayana, R. (2006). Mental health consequences of war: A brief review of research findings. *World Psychiatry, 5*, 25–30.

Stansfeld, S. A., Head, J., Fuhrer, R., Wardle, J., & Cattell, V. (2003). Social inequalities in depressive symptoms and physical functioning in the Whitehall 11 study: Exploring a common cause explanation. *Journal of Epidemiology and Community Health, 57*, 361–367.

Stansfeld, S. A., Head, J., & Marmot, M. (1998). Explaining social class differentials in depression and well-being. *Social Psychiatry and Psychiatric Epidemiology, 33*, 1–9.

Townsend, P., & Davidson, N. (1982). *Inequalities in health: The Black report.* Harmondsworth, UK: Penguin.

Ustun, T. B., & Sartorius, N. (1995). *Psychological problems in general health care: An international study.* Chichester, UK: John Wiley & Sons.

Vos, T., Astbury, J., Piers, L., Magnus, A., Heenan, M., Stanley, L., et al. (2006). Measuring the impact of intimate partner violence on the health of women in Victoria. *Bulletin of the World Health Organization, 84*, 739–744.

Wade, T. J., Cairney, J., & Pevalin, D. J. (2002). Emergence of gender differences in depression during adolescence: National panel results from three countries. *Journal of the American Academy for Child and Adolescent Psychiatry, 41*, 190–198.

Weissman, M. M., & Klerman, G. L. (1977). Sex differences and the epidemiology of depression. *Archives of General Psychiatry, 34*, 98–111.

Wilkinson, R. (1997). Health inequalities: Relative or absolute material standards. *British Medical Journal, 314*, 591–595.

World Bank. (2006). Women in development. In *2006 World development indicators,* Washington, D.C.: Author. Retrieved August 22, 2008, from http://devdata. worldbank.org/wdi2006/contents/Section1_1_3.htm

World Health Organization. (1998). *The world health report.* Geneva: Author.

World Health Organization, International Consortium of Psychiatric Epidemiology. (2000). Cross national comparisons of mental disorders. *Bulletin of the World Health Organization, 78*, 413–426.

World Health Organization. (2001). *Mental health: New understanding, new hope. The world health report 2001.* Geneva: Author.

Drugs Don't Talk:
Do Medication and Biological
Psychiatry Contribute to
Silencing the Self?

Richard A. Gordon

This chapter will trace the sharp rise in the use of antidepressant medications over recent decades and the correlated increasingly biological view of depression. The chapter begins with a history of how antidepressant medications evolved, with the goal of showing how they started from a relatively narrow focus on depressive disorders, presumably of endogenous origin, to a later much broader purview that included the whole spectrum of mild depressive and anxiety conditions in the community. The shift of depression treatment from mental health professionals to primary care medicine, in which medication is heavily or exclusively relied on and the role of psychotherapy is minimized, will be documented. The chapter will then address powerful evidence for social factors in the origin of depression and particularly its gendered epidemiology. Particular emphasis will be placed on the work of Brown and Harris and their findings about the impact of loss, entrapment, and humiliation in the cause of depression and the role of isolation and disconnection in its maintenance. It will be argued that social understandings of the origins of depression, as well as the relevance of certain psychotherapeutic approaches, have been marginalized by the power and dominance of the ascendant biomedical discourse and practices. Implications for the treatment of depression will be explored.

The Discovery of Antidepressants and Their Biochemical Basis

Since the 1950s and '60s, the period of the discovery of antidepressant medicines and how they might work, both the professional and public view of depression and many other psychological disturbances have undergone enormous change.

From the 1930s until 1960, particularly for less severely disordered outpatients, the psychoanalytic and interpersonal views of Freud and Harry Stack Sullivan and the socially tinged perspectives of Adolf Meyer had come to dominate American psychiatry. As a result, the less severe forms of psychological disorders, moderate anxiety and depression, were understood primarily as psychosocial disturbances. These perspectives had actually become enshrined in early versions of the *Diagnostic and Statistical Manual of Mental Disorders* (American Psychiatric Association, 1952, 1968) through categories such as "depressive reaction," diagnoses that were widely applied in practice. However, the 1950s was a decade of radical breakthrough in terms of the discovery of medications (Thuillier, 1999): first, the antipsychotics (chlorpromazine, or Thorazine), then the "minor tranquillizers" (meprobromate, or Miltown), and finally the antidepressants (the monoamine oxidase [MAO] inhibitors and tricyclic antidepressants). The antidepressants were initially unheralded, for a number of reasons. First, they were seen as applying to a narrow range of depressive disorders, particularly those that were described as "melancholia" or "endogenous depression." The much larger number of typical depressions were understood as responses to environmental events or problems of character or personality. Second, and perhaps for this reason, the pharmaceutical companies were skeptical as to whether an antidepressant could ever have a sufficient market to warrant investment in its development (Healy, 1997). The excitement and huge early success of the first tranquillizers, such as Miltown, had left the impression that anxiety was a far more important mass market than depression. For all these reasons, the first presentation in 1958 about the tricyclic antidepressant imipramine in the United States by its discoverer, Roland Kuhn, was attended only by a handful of participants at a meeting of the American Psychiatric Association. It should be noted that when Kuhn labeled imipramine an antidepressant, he meant that it was a highly specific treatment for what he called "vital depression," in which the person had the kind of loss of motivation and drive, fatigue, and sapping of his/her spirits that characterizes classic melancholia (Healy, 1997). Kuhn's concept of vital depression is much more specific and narrow than the contemporary, greatly expanded meanings of depression and antidepressant (Healy, 2002).

The lack of interest in antidepressants began to change radically in the 1960s for two reasons, one commercial and the other scientific. First, the pharmaceutical company Merck overcame the skepticism that Ceiba-Geigy, who had synthesized imipramine, had had about antidepressants and synthesized a related drug, amitriptyline, to which Merck gave the brand name Elavil. Merck used a novel marketing strategy by printing 50,000 copies of a book by the pharmacologist Frank Ayd about depression that was marketed to physicians and psychiatrists (Healy, 1997). With Elavil, the era of "tricyclic antidepressants" as a generic class of drug was born, but Merck's marketing strategy gave a huge boost to the concept of depression as a disease that could be "managed" in primary care, typically without psychotherapy. It goes without saying that such a concept also promoted a radical medicalization of depression, one in which most depressions, even those formerly viewed as reactive, could be assimilated to earlier notions of "melancholia" or "endogenous depression." These rather subtle and somewhat obscure events offer a stunning demonstration of the interaction of modern psychiatric concepts with commercial and professional interests.

However, a second factor was crucial in the explosion of interest in the biology of depression, and that was the discovery of the brain mechanisms by which the antidepressants might work. In 1965, Joseph Schildkraut, a young psychiatrist who had strong interests in both psychodynamic psychotherapy and the clearly powerful new antidepressants, together with the widely respected physician researcher Seymour Kety, published a series of papers that reviewed and synthesized new research that had taken place in the previous decade on the relationship of neurotransmitters and antidepressant medicines (Schildkraut, 1965; Schildkraut & Kety, 1967). These papers, together with the simultaneous publication of a similar review by psychiatrists William Bunney and John Davis (1965), were to have an enormous impact on subsequent theorizing about psychiatric disorders. The central idea in this work was what Schildkraut called the catecholamine hypothesis, which proposed that by blocking the reuptake of norepinephrine in the central nervous system or by inhibiting the production of monoamine oxidase, the enzyme that breaks down norepinephrine, the antidepressants were correcting perhaps something like a deficiency of chemical neurotransmitters. Although Schildkraut never used the phrase in his paper, the popular idea of "chemical imbalance" can be seen as directly stemming from this idea of neurotransmitter deficiency in the brain.

Following quickly on the heels of the amine deficiency hypothesis of depression, Avid Carlsson of Sweden and Solomon Snyder of the United States formulated a dopamine hypothesis of schizophrenia based on a new understanding of the mechanisms of the phenothiazines, although in this case an excess rather than a deficiency in dopamine activity was held to be the culprit (Snyder, Banerjee, Yamamura, & Greenberg, 1974). Suddenly, through the discovery of disease-specific medications as well as advances in the understanding of how they worked, psychiatry had taken a quantum leap toward scientific respectability and credibility. Such an improvement in psychiatry's status was a welcome development for many in the field. Psychiatry had long been held in low esteem by the rest of professional medicine. Psychoanalysis, in particular, was viewed by critics not only within psychiatry but especially in the rest of medicine as a vague, prolonged, expensive treatment that had never proved its effectiveness and was poorly grounded from a traditional scientific point of view (Wilson, 1993). Yet for a number of reasons, including the powerful postwar influence of psychoanalytic ideas in the United States, psychoanalysis had risen to a dominant position within psychiatry (Hale, 1995; Wilson, 1993). By 1960, most of the prestigious psychiatry departments within U.S. medical schools were chaired by psychoanalysts. For the reasons stated earlier, however, this situation led to tremendous unease among those who felt the profession was suffering from a lack of scientific credibility.

The profession's image suffered further from the attacks of an increasingly popularized antipsychiatry movement, which generally held that psychiatry was fundamentally an oppressive profession whose ostensible function was the treatment of mental illness, but whose actual function was one of social control over society's unwanted deviants. The views and political perspectives of these thinkers were actually quite varied, but at least some of their thinking was captured in the writings of Thomas Szasz (1961). Szasz was mostly preoccupied with the avowed illegitimacy of the psychiatric use of the term "illness" or "disease." He argued that the concept of disease should be reserved to suffering that is known to be driven by underlying organic pathology. Since there were no identified pathologies underlying "mental illnesses," there was no rationale for labeling either psychotic or neurotic symptoms as illnesses. Rather, Szasz argued, most psychotic and neurotic behavior could only be described as either "deviant behaviors" that were socially undesirable or "problems in living." Although Szasz's ideas were highly influential and could be comprehended as arising in an era in which knowledge of the neurological underpinnings of psychiatric disorders was minimal, one can also understand that the new formulations of psychopharmacology could embolden those who had allegiance to a medical model of psychiatric disorder.

Given the new science of mood disorders that had resulted from the discovery of antidepressants and possible brain mechanisms of depression, the diagnosis of depression underwent some important fundamental changes in the radically revised *Diagnostic and Statistical Manual of Mental Disorders*, third edition (DSM-III), which was published in 1980—changes that subtly but powerfully emphasized the construction of depression as a medical entity (American Psychiatric Association, 1980). Although the ostensible purpose of the DSM-III was to develop a set of categories that were scientifically reliable and could provide a basis for a more scientific psychiatry, in effect, the new manual reflected the theoretical changes that were going on in the profession. In particular, the resurrection of a Kraepelinean approach to diagnosis and a marginalization of the emphasis on social and dynamic factors in the earlier versions of the manual were accentuated (Wilson, 1993). The second edition of the DSM had listed categories of neurotic depression (depressive reaction), psychotic depression, and depressive personality (American Psychiatric Association, 1968). Psychotic depression was considered to be a rare condition, most likely attributable to unknown organic factors, although the diagnosis was sometimes casually assigned to many severely depressed patients in American hospitals (Schildkraut, 2000). By far, the most common form was neurotic depression, and one can see from the use of the term "reactive" that it involved, in an essential way, the notion of a response, although perhaps irrational and inappropriately sustained, to recent or remote environmental events. Behind the dichotomy between neurotic/psychotic depression and melancholia, there was also the influential distinction between exogenous depression (of external origins) and endogenous depression (of internal origins) that was widely influential in both European and American psychiatry beginning in the 1940s.

The most important new category in the DSM-III was that of major depressive disorder (MDD), which included a mixed list of psychological (feelings of sadness, low self-esteem, excessive guilt, suicidal thoughts) and physical (loss of appetite, disrupted sleep, loss of sexual interest) symptoms. A total of nine symptoms were listed; to qualify for a diagnosis, five had to be "continuously present for at least two weeks." The DSM-III also included a category called "dysthymic disorder," which was essentially a less intense (in terms of number of symptoms) but more chronic condition. It is of considerable importance that the DSM-III essentially eliminated the idea of "reaction" (to environmental events) in its diagnostic language about depression. Horwitz and Wakefield (2007) have argued that in doing this, the DSM-III essentially obliterated the distinction between exogenous (caused by environmental events) and endogenous (caused by internal factors) depression that had been a key component of psychiatric thinking for many years. In so doing, the DSM-III and subsequent editions of the manual subtly but powerfully blurred a critical distinction. It could be argued that by eliminating environmental triggers from the discourse and by putting all symptoms, both psychological and physical, into one category with no recognition that patients with predominantly psychological symptoms and those with predominantly physical ones might be fundamentally different, the revised DSM wound up with a profoundly homogeneous and medicalized concept. If not the cause, then the DSM-III at least marked a point at which medication increasingly appeared as the first-line treatment for all depression, and reinforced and consolidated this trend with its more medicalized diagnostic concepts.

The New Biopsychiatry and the Coming of Prozac

During the 1980s, the changes in the field that had been heralded by the discovery of psychotropic medications in the 1950s and that culminated in the new diagnostic system, began to be consolidated and accelerated. New medications were being developed for obsessive-compulsive disorder and schizophrenia. Rapidly developing technologies of brain imaging were enabling neuroscientists to acquire increasingly accurate pictures of activity in various parts of the brain. Verbal psychotherapies, including evidence-based treatments such as cognitive therapy, were now increasingly and perhaps somewhat dismissively referred to as "talk therapies"; the implicit new gold standard of treatment was medication. The research on psychotherapy that did occur was mostly on shorter term behavioral or cognitive therapies. In the late 1980s, the National Institute of Mental Health (NIMH) undertook a controlled trial comparing the tricyclic antidepressants with cognitive therapy on the treatment of depression. The results were somewhat mixed, although cognitive therapy held its own in the trial and later research indicated that it may provide better protection against relapse than antidepressants (Elkin et al., 1989).

A development of huge significance in the treatment of depression was the coming to market of the drug fluoxetine, or Prozac, in 1987. In contrast with the earlier antidepressants, the chief effects of Prozac were on the neurotransmitter serotonin. Serotonergic antidepressants had been of interest in Europe since the early 1970s, but no one had succeeded in making a commercially viable and safe medication (Healy, 1997). Prozac had been a project in the works by the Eli Lilly Corporation since the 1970s. Unlike the tricyclic antidepressants, whose mechanism of norepinephrine reuptake blockade had been discovered after the fact, Prozac was designed with the goal of producing an antidepressant that specifically affected blockade of serotonin reuptake (Wong, Bymaster, & Engleman, 1995). Both the tricyclic antidepressants and the MAO inhibitors had been used rather sparingly and with caution, owing to the fact that they (especially the MAO inhibitors) had potentially severe side effects and could also be taken in overdose. However, Prozac had a far more benign side effect profile and could be used with a much larger number of patients. The potentially unpleasant or dangerous side effects of the serotonergic medications, such as the sexual side effects or, more ominously, the activation of suicidal ideation in a small number of patients, were minimized or absent in early reports on the drug (Healy, 2004). Thus, Prozac was readily adopted by primary care physicians as a drug that could be used to treat the large number of patients with depression seen in primary care. All of this coincided with the concurrent epidemiological findings in the 1980s that DSM-III "major depression" was widespread in the community, far more common than previously realized. The DSM-III criteria themselves may have contributed to the inflation of these estimates (Horwitz & Wakefield, 2007). Nevertheless, with the coming of Prozac, the era of depression as an epidemic illness that could be treated was launched (Healy, 2002).

Prozac created huge excitement in the popular press and was featured in cover stories in magazines such as *Time* and *Newsweek*. A 1990 *Newsweek* issue, with a picture of a Prozac capsule on its cover, announced "A Breakthrough Drug for Depression." A later story in the same magazine in 1994 unabashedly declared the ubiquitous magic of Prozac with the following series of rhetorical questions: "Want to boost your self-esteem, focus better on your work, tame the impulse to shop until you drop, shrug off your spouse's habit of littering the floor with underwear, overcome your shyness or keep yourself from blurting out your deepest secrets to the first stranger who comes along?... Now the same scientific insights into the brain that led to the development of Prozac are raising the prospect of nothing less than made-to-order, off-the-shelf personalities"

(Prozac: A breakthrough drug for depression, 1994). Many of the claims in this sentence appeared to reflect the ideas in Peter Kramer's surprisingly popular *Listening to Prozac*, published in 1993. Kramer's book did much to promote the idea that Prozac was far more than an antidepressant and in fact was a drug that could improve myriad "problems in living." Kramer announced that the coming of Prozac signaled a new era in medication, one in which antidepressants need not be confined to the function of remedying illness but rather have the potential to enhance performance and make people with a wide spectrum of what Freud called "ordinary unhappiness" feel and perform better. Perhaps unfortunately, Kramer called this potential use of the new psychochemicals to create "improvements" in people's general functioning and sense of well-being "cosmetic psychopharmacology." Kramer's book was on the *New York Times* bestseller list for several weeks and was soon translated into many foreign languages. The metaphor of "listening" to a drug soon became a metaphor for the radical change in psychiatric philosophy that had occurred.

The Serotonin Reuptake Inhibitors and the Broadening Use of Medication

The dramatic debut of Prozac reaped enormous sales and profits for the Eli Lilly Corporation, with sales reaching $2 billion worldwide by the early 1990s. Prozac's overwhelming success was soon followed by the development of drugs whose action on serotonin systems was similar to Prozac and whose effects on the symptoms of depression were virtually indistinguishable: Zoloft (sertraline) by Pfizer, approved by the Food and Drug Administration (FDA) in 1991, and whose sales also reached $2 billion by the mid-1990s; and Paxil (paroxetine) by Glaxo-Wellcome in 1993, which brought in $2 billion by the year 2000. Although initially designated as antidepressants, all these medications were ultimately approved by the FDA for a variety of psychiatric disorders. For example, Prozac was approved for the treatment of the eating disorder bulimia nervosa and for anxiety disorders, including panic disorder and obsessive-compulsive disorder; Zoloft for social anxiety disorder, posttraumatic stress disorder, panic disorder, obsessive-compulsive disorder, and premenstrual dysphoric disorder; and Paxil for essentially the same list. From the outset, it actually had been unclear whether these medications were fundamentally antidepressants or rather drugs that could ameliorate a spectrum of dysphoric moods, including anxiety.[1] Their labeling as antidepressants was really a matter of historical accident as well as initial marketing strategy. In fact, the "epidemic" of depression that had been elucidated by studies in the early 1990s may well have been in part a function of the creation of markets for these new medications, as has been suggested by David Healy. Rather than "antidepressant," Healy (2002) has suggested that the selective serotonin reuptake inhibitors (SSRIs) might as well have been described, with some justification, as "general serenics" (drugs that promote serenity or a general sense of well-being).

However, despite the broadening of the spectrum of conditions for which they were prescribed, the main impact of these medicines was on the treatment of depression. Insight into these effects on a practical level was yielded by a study by Olfson and colleagues (2002) of trends in depression identification and treatment. Examining two large databases (more than 30,000 people in each) in the United States, they found that over the decade from 1987 to 1997, the number of people who had been treated for depression nearly quadrupled. Those patients treated for depression were almost five times as likely to receive an antidepressant (mostly SSRIs) in 1997 than in 1987, and the number treated by physicians grew nearly 20%. Meanwhile, the number of patients who received some form of psychotherapy declined by one-third, and the percentage of people who received treatment from clinical psychologists, who generally cannot prescribe medications, declined by the same percentage. A second study by the same researchers (Olfson and Marcus, 2009) showed that from 1998 to 2005 the rate of antidepressant treatment in the United States grew from 5.84 percent of the population in 1998 to 10.12 percent in 2005 (approximately 27 million persons in 2005), an increase that held up for all age and sociodemographic groups except African Americans. The number of treated people receiving psychotherapy continued to decline significantly.

While these studies do not indicate the number of patients who received only medication treatment, the implications of an increasingly medicalized approach to depression are clear. Fueling these trends were at least three factors. First, managed care, which had by the early 1990s fairly suddenly taken hold of controlling insurance disbursements in the mental health field, from the outset saw a cost advantage in the use of antidepressants over psychotherapy. The explicit rationale for the preference was the argument that medication was evidence based, while psychotherapy, particularly longer term therapy, was not. However, it does not take a sophisticated analysis to see that even a monthly visit to a physician (which would be a higher number of visits than what is typical) and a prescription for antidepressants would be cheaper than weekly visits to a psychotherapist, even including the cost of medication.

A second and very important influence was programs initiated by national governments and supported by the pharmaceutical industry that promoted a concept of depression as a fundamentally medical disease. For example, in the United States, beginning in 1987, the federal government began a public health campaign to enhance the recognition and treatment of depression by both the public and the medical community (Regier et al., 1988). Similar programs were initiated by the 1990s in both the United Kingdom and Australia. One outcome of this initiative in North America was the development of a National Depression Screening Day. By 1997, there were more than 2,800 screening locations in the United States and Canada (Greenfield et al., 2000). One part of this initiative was a program to teach physicians to diagnose depression quickly with a symptom-oriented interview that would take approximately 10 to 15 minutes. Such a system depended heavily on using simple rating scales, closely akin to the widely used Hamilton Rating Scale of Depression. This process implied a strict illness model of depression, in which symptom relief was the primary—if not the only—goal of treatment. Such a view, of course, implies that psychotherapy is fundamentally superfluous, and it certainly would reduce such things as exploration and correction of a patient's life situation.

A final factor, which has had an enormous impact on public attitudes toward depression, was the increasingly intensive promotion of antidepressants and a brain-based view of depression to the public by the pharmaceutical industry. An FDA ruling allowing direct marketing of pharmaceuticals to consumers opened the floodgates for antidepressant advertising beginning in 1997. While these advertisements were varied in content, they inexorably promoted the idea that depression (as well as various forms of anxiety) was due to a chemical imbalance and that happiness (invariably depicted in the ads by a smiling face after treatment) could be achieved through the ingestion of the magic pills.

The explosion of interest in depression was capped by the World Health Organization's (WHO) Global Burden of Disease Study, which was published in the 1990s (Murray & Lopez, 1996). Using data from worldwide epidemiological studies and sophisticated cost analyses that involved not only health care costs but also the economic burdens of various diseases placed on society via costs such as lost productivity, the WHO study estimated that depression would be the most costly disease to society by the year 2020 worldwide. Depression had now become a "ticking time bomb," and efforts seemed more than justified to facilitate the delivery of services for the treatment of depression via primary care (Callahan & Berrios, 2005; Dawson & Tylee, 2001).

But Do Antidepressants Work?

Few would dispute that antidepressants can sometimes help people, but a more critical look at the evidence for the effectiveness of these drugs reveals some surprising findings. The first is that the double-blind placebo-controlled trials, which are the gold standard for research on medications, yield only modestly impressive results for the SSRI medications. Meta-analyses of these studies of antidepressants show that the medications produce on the whole an improvement rate of 50% to 55%, while the inactive placebo achieves an improvement of roughly 35%[2] (Greenberg, Bornstein, Zborowski, Fisher, & Greenberg, 1994). While the advantage of drug over placebo is statistically significant, it is not great in absolute terms, and some have argued from wide-ranging meta-analysis of treatment trials that the advantage only holds up for severe depression (Kirsch et al., 2008). Two further facts should be noted. First, the more precise meaning of the 50% figure is that as a group, the patients who took the active medicine achieved an average reduction of symptoms of 50%, as measured by standard symptom scales. However, this fact masks the reality that some patients may have experienced far more improvement than 50% reduction, while others may have shown little improvement. Drug studies that utilize these types of measures of improvement yield virtually no information about individual differences in treatment response. Second, the double-blind placebo-controlled trial is typically of very short duration, on the order of eight weeks. In practice, people who are prescribed antidepressants are expected to take them for several months to a period of years. Thus, the typical research trial that "proves" the effectiveness of an antidepressant poorly simulates the actual conditions under which these medicines are administered.

These weaknesses have been addressed in a recent effort to obtain a more realistic picture of how patients who are treated in actual practice respond to medication regimens. This study, called the STAR*D (Sequenced Treatment Alternatives to Relieve Depression), not only examined the initial period of response to antidepressants that is observed in pharmaceutical company–sponsored placebo trials, but also introduced further stages of treatment in which patients who did not do well in the first were either switched to different antidepressant medications, given additional medications, or provided cognitive therapy along with medication (Gaynes et al., 2008; Insel, 2006; Rush et al., 2006; Trivedi et al., 2006; Warden, Rush, Trivedi, Fava, & Wisniewski, 2007).

The complex findings from the STAR*D study, which cannot be fully addressed here, are still being published, but the results to date present a mixed picture of the success of medication-based treatments of depression. One of the most interesting is that of the some 3,800 patients who entered the study, 28% had reached full remission of their symptoms after 12 weeks. Twenty-eight percent is a modest number, and we do not know whether a trial of depression-specific psychotherapy, such as cognitive or interpersonal therapy, could produce the same level of remission in three months. A sizeable percentage of patients dropped out after the first phase of treatment. Thus, for many patients, medication alone, the treatment typically provided by primary care physicians, is obviously not enough in the real world. Other studies have examined why patients who take antidepressants either in primary care settings or from psychopharmacologists stop taking their medication (Haslam, Brown, Atkinson, & Haslam, 2005). Primary reasons offered by patients are that they cannot tolerate the side effects or they just think that the drug is not helping. Reports on these issues rarely mention a third possible factor: Many patients feel that the full complement of their real issues, such as the difficulty of coping with their life situations, is simply not being addressed in such exclusively medication-focused treatment.

In general, the experience of taking antidepressant drugs has been little studied. This is unfortunate, as the process of accepting a psychotropic medication is far more complex for some than taking a medication for a purely physical illness. Many people have profoundly ambivalent feelings about medications for an emotional illness (Karp, 1996, 2006; Stoppard & Gammel, 2003). While some eagerly adopt medications and feel enormously relieved by them, others feel that taking medication for an emotional problem, however much they may accept that it is brain based, is a sign of a loss of autonomy and personal weakness. Some psychiatrists have called such an attitude "pharmacological Puritanism," but the stubborn fact of the matter remains that many people feel that they would prefer to attempt to talk their problems through and solve them by nonchemical means. For such individuals, the simple dispensation of an antidepressant by a nonpsychiatric medical provider is a singularly unsatisfying solution (Karp, 2006).

It is difficult to make sweeping generalizations, however. In one fascinating study, chronically depressed patients were given an initial 12-week trial of either medication or cognitive therapy. Approximately half of these patients improved, and the other half remained depressed. However, when those who "failed" at the initial trial were "crossed over" to the other treatment, roughly 50% showed improvement with the treatment that they were not started on (Schatzberg et al., 2005). Whether or not a patient responds to medication or psychotherapy alone is clearly a highly individual matter.

Controversies and Advances in the Biological Model of Depression

The amine hypothesis, first formulated in the 1960s, proposes that the antidepressants work by blocking the reuptake of neurotransmitters, such as norepinephrine and serotonin, into central nervous system neurons, or in the case of the now infrequently used MAO inhibitors, by preventing the synthesis of monoamine oxidase. By the mid-1970s, the amine hypothesis had become entrenched as the core theory of the psychobiology of depression, and in a brilliant review, Akiskal and McKinney (1975) proposed that neurotransmitter deficiencies could provide the key link between psychological formulations of depression and the new understanding of the brain that was being afforded by drugs. The amine hypothesis, despite difficulties in directly demonstrating its relevance to depressed patients, has been enormously influential as a core paradigm of depression for over 40 years now. The newer "dual reuptake" antidepressants, such as Effexor and Cymbalta, are still rooted in the concept of depression as depleted amines. As suggested earlier, it has also been incorporated in the form of the idea of a "chemical imbalance" among the wider public, a notion that has been powerfully reinforced by pharmaceutical advertising. The amine hypothesis is enormously appealing, both in its simplicity and in the sense that it provides a potent metaphor for our intuitive understanding of depression as a deficiency disease: not enough good feelings, not enough pleasure, not enough motivation, not enough self-esteem, not enough decision making. The idea that such deficiencies could be reduced to low levels of neurotransmitters in the brain—particularly such "excitatory" neurotransmitters as norepinephrine (i.e., "brain adrenaline")—is almost irresistible.

But it is remarkable that to date, the research support for the amine hypothesis has been mixed at best. Valenstein (1997), and more recently Lacasse and Leo (2005) and Moncrieff and Cohen (2006), have reviewed the evidence from metabolism studies and concluded that there is virtually no consistent or direct evidence for neurotransmitter deficiencies in depressed patients. Valenstein's review suggested that studies of metabolites of neurotransmitters in the blood or spinal fluid, admittedly a very crude method for assessing levels of neurotransmitters in the brain, have found the metabolites of norepinephrine or serotonin to be low, high, or normal in depressed patients; there does not seem to be a consistent pattern, as the amine hypothesis would predict. Brain imaging studies, whose methodology has become increasingly sophisticated, may ultimately yield more precise evidence about the amine hypothesis, and some preliminary studies have been encouraging. By using radiotracers that are able to localize chemical activity in the brain more specifically, it has become possible to map the activity of neurotransmitters and related compounds more precisely in the living brain. To illustrate the potential of such methods for further illuminating the amine hypothesis, Meyer and colleagues (2006) were able to demonstrate significantly elevated levels of monoamine oxidase in several areas of the brain that are known to be relevant to depressive symptoms. This important study implies that such high levels of MAO could potentially deplete the levels of norepinephrine and serotonin in these regions, thereby lending at least indirect support to the amine hypothesis.

Despite these findings, the status of the amine hypothesis, particularly the assertion that depleted amines are the cause of depression, remains on uncertain ground. There is virtually no doubt, on the other hand, that antidepressants work by blocking the reuptake of brain amines. A more likely model of depression is that the correction of amines that is brought about by antidepressant drugs works at several levels "downstream" from the activity of norepinephrine and serotonin neurons in the brain. A more contemporary hypothesis is, for example, that improvement in the activity of norepinephrine and serotonin neurons ultimately work through a number of intermediary steps to repair stress-induced cell damage in areas such as the hippocampus (Manji, 2008).

Whatever the ultimate basis of depression on the neural level, there is little question that the "chemical imbalance" idea seems to have been vastly oversold as the cause of depression in pharmaceutical advertising and in the mind of the public. In fact, more recent pharmaceutical advertising for such drugs as Cymbalta and Abilify seem to have dispensed with the idea as a marketing tool. Recent research has been focused more on the idea that depression is rooted in dysfunctional neurocircuitry, rather than in the depletion of one or two neurochemicals. Such research, which is built on data from brain imaging studies, has yielded some intriguing hypotheses that involve such brain areas as the prefrontal cortex, the cingulated cortex, and the amygdala (Drevets, 1998). While this research has yet to yield treatments that are applicable on a large scale, considerable excitement has been generated by experimental treatments with a small number of severely depressed, treatment-resistant patients who have shown major improvements after electrical stimulation of a highly specific, small area of the cortex (the "subgenual cingulate") (Lozano et al., 2008). Again, the broad application of such treatments is in question, but it is likely that future work in the field will attempt to integrate the findings about neurocircuitry with ongoing research about pharmacology.

The Social Origins of Depression

The triumph of the biogenic model of depression is remarkable in light of the fact that it is well established that the origins of most depression are profoundly related to social factors. Social factors are undoubtedly implicated in the sharply rising rates of depression in the younger population over the past few decades, as it is highly unlikely that such changes would be caused by biological factors. The social matrix of depression is in turn exceedingly important in understanding one of the basic epidemiological facts of depression: the 2:1 ratio of women to men that suffer from depression in most parts of the world. Of course, it has been suggested many times that differences in male and female hormones may have something to do with this imbalance incidence. Changes in estrogen, for example, that occur during the postpartum period or during menopause have important possible links with such brain enzymes as monoamine oxidase and may in fact shape changes in the neurotransmitter levels of serotonin. There has been much interesting writing recently on the topic of postpartum depression, a discussion that is long overdue, as well as studies of the possible treatment with SSRIs of premenstrual dysphoria. Nevertheless, for the large numbers of women with depression, these special cases do not offer an adequate general theory of gender difference in its incidence.

The social factors that trigger depression have been established in abundant research. One very important area is that of marriage and relationships and the impact of divorce and break-up. In one study of 1,225 men and women, Bruce and Kim (1992) found that 21% of the women who reported a marital disruption over a one-year period developed severe depression, a rate three times higher than that for women who continued to be married. Interestingly, for men who experienced a marital split, 17% developed depression, a rate nearly nine times higher than those men who remained married (Fincham, Beach, Harold, & Osborne, 1997).

Relationships are not the only source of stress that leads to depression. War and its psychological impact is a powerful factor. A study by the Rand

Corporation (Alvarez, 2008) showed that some 20% of veterans returning from combat in Iraq were suffering from serious depression or posttraumatic stress disorder (these conditions are typically linked). To what extent these massive casualties of war should be attributed to the particular violence of combat in Iraq, the dislocation that soldiers feel on returning home, or relationship stress is not yet clear. The obvious fact remains: Experiences are crucial in triggering depression.

Perhaps there is no body of findings on the impact of social factors on depression in women more remarkable than the 30-year research program of the British social psychiatrist George Brown and his colleague Tyril Harris (Brown, 2002; Brown & Harris, 1978). In 1978, Brown and Harris published a critically important study, *The Social Origins of Depression*, which probably should be required reading of psychiatric residents and of any physician who treats depression, but unfortunately is not. In fact, it would be argued that if the content of current major psychiatric journals is any indication, the work of Brown and Harris and similar research has been virtually forgotten in the field (Blazer, 2005), marginalized by a collective fascination with brain mechanisms.

Studying a sample of 458 women from a working-class area of London, Brown and Harris (1978) found a very high depression rate, on the order of 15%, virtually none of whom had received any form of treatment. But more to the point, Brown and Harris had become interested in the study of what social psychiatrists call "life events," and the extent to which they precede depression. As they put it, depression in virtually all cases was "an understandable response to adversity." What they found, using rigorous interview methods, was that roughly 90% of the depressed women in their study had experienced a severely threatening life event in the year prior to the onset of their depression. The term "stressful life event" is a little bloodless, so perhaps it is better to discuss more concretely what is meant. The events in question typically led to a severe lowering of self-esteem but also, because of other circumstances in the women's lives, led them to feel that there was no escape from the situation in which they were embroiled. In a later summing up of the original and follow-up research, Brown suggests that what depressed women invariably experience is a sense of entrapment and humiliation (Brown, 2002). Instances of humiliation include such events as separation from a core partner either due to involuntary separation or voluntary leaving resulting from infidelity or abuse from the partner; the discovery of delinquency on the part of a child, such as a daughter stealing money from a mother to pay for drugs; or a criticism or put-down that threatens a core role or sense of self-esteem, for example, a mother of a hyperactive child criticized or blamed at a parent meeting.

Following the original study, Brown conducted research with a number of different populations and found essentially similar patterns in a wide variety of cultures (Brown, 2002). The social triggers of depression, along with their psychological consequences of humiliation and a sense of entrapment, were virtually ubiquitous. Important as this fundamental finding is, there is something perhaps even more revealing about Brown and Harris's research. That is, although a large percentage of women had experienced such potentially depressogenic events, only a certain number developed depression. To differentiate these groups in the original study, Brown and Harris found through systematic analysis a number of what they called vulnerability factors on the one hand and protective factors on the other. Focusing on the protective factors, any of the following made women *less* likely to develop depression following a critical event: (1) an intimate confiding relationship, usually but not always with a spouse or lover; (2) part- or full-time employment outside the home; (3) fewer than three children still at home; or (4) a serious religious commitment or involvement. On the other hand, the absence of any of these heightened a woman's risk in the face of a stressor. A review of these factors makes it quite easy to discern a pattern in these findings: The more a woman has a connection to other people outside the home, whether in the form of a confidant, a religious involvement, or work, the less likely she is to become depressed in response to a severe blow from shame-inducing and entrapping circumstances. In fact, it may be these very protective factors that enable her to overcome her sense of shame and entrapment. And the fewer of these connections and supportive relationships or involvements that she has, the more likely she is to succumb to clinical depression.

One apparent interpretation of Brown and Harris's findings regarding vulnerability is that the common factor that leads women to be vulnerable to dire stresses is isolation: being stuck with three kids at home alone, with no intimate friends to talk to, no meaningful work outside the home, and no community or religious involvement. In short, these women have been exposed to direly painful experiences, and their life circumstances are such that they lack social support and opportunity for dialogue; in effect, they are left to suffer in silence. In this context, the devastatingly low self-esteem, the hopelessness, the sadness and emptiness, and even the suicidal thoughts that are among the cardinal symptoms of depression become totally comprehensible.

And such a formulation does not preclude the analysis of depression as a biological phenomenon. Brown continually asserts that depression is a psychological response to social events that results in biological disruptions. It is clear from numerous studies that depression, whether in the form of major depressive disorder, dysthymia, or even milder episodic depression, is driven by significant genetic vulnerabilities. McGuffin, Cohen, and Knight (2007), for example, have argued that the heritability of unipolar depression may have been underestimated in the past (with heritability estimates of roughly 35%) due to research with community samples and may in fact be on the order of 75% to 80%, comparable to the heritability of bipolar disorder and schizophrenia. The work of Kenneth Kendler and colleagues has thrown light on the complex interactions of environmental events with genetic predispositions in the development of depression (Kendler, Gardner, & Prescott, 2002). Using data from the Virginia Twins study, Kendler and colleagues developed a model that indicates how genetic vulnerability can lead to depression via a number of pathways, most of these involving either early developmental or recent environmental events, including such factors as childhood sexual abuse, childhood parental loss, more recent trauma, divorce, and low social support. And critically important research by Caspi and colleagues (2003) has shown that men exposed to a traumatic event who also carried a short allele of the 5HTT serotonin promoter gene—meaning that their brains were likely to produce less serotonin under stress—were far more vulnerable to depression than those who carried two copies of the long form of the gene. This study takes us to a new level of both social and biological understanding, and is perhaps the first to give a real sense of how social events trigger a dysregulation of serotonin mostly in vulnerable individuals. It also illuminates in a particularly forceful way that the impact of social events is critical in understanding the etiology of psychiatric disorders.

The Disappearance of Gender from the Discourse about Depression

Surely one of the remarkable claims in the literature on depression is Peter Kramer's assertion in *Listening to Prozac* that Prozac can be thought of as a "feminist drug." Kramer (1993) raises this possibility in the context of two case histories in which patients had become more assertive after going on the drug. One of these, Tess, had become more of an effective manager by being able to communicate what she wanted to subordinates at work without being abrasive. A second patient, Julia, was able to become much happier in her relationship with her husband by becoming at once more assertive and less obsessively critical about "mess" in the house. Kramer asserted that Prozac was radically different from the tranquillizers of the 1950s and '60s. The tranquillizers, famously satirized as "mother's little helpers," were seen by many critics as blatantly reinforcing traditional sex roles and were therefore interpreted as further tools that supported psychiatry as an instrument of social oppression. Kramer argues that by enabling depressed women to be more assertive, Prozac (and by implication kindred drugs) works in the service of liberating women from traditional oppressive role demands and supports the aspirations of the "new woman" to be assertive, independent, and productive. Although provocative, from a social standpoint this is a rather remarkable assertion. Could a revolution in sex roles, viewed by most as only possible as the result of a historical struggle, be achieved by mass dosing with an antidepressant?

A notable but understated feature of Kramer's book was that many of the case histories he described were pharmacological consultations that he conducted while patients were seeing other therapists. Under such conditions, it is impossible to know what sort of therapeutic dialogue was going on that may have facilitated the changes that Kramer attributes to the seemingly transformative powers of Prozac. Kramer's view overall is that it is the biological change wrought by the medication that enables therapy to have its effects. This is possible, but hardly proven. It is almost certainly the case for the major mental illnesses, such as bipolar disorder. However, Kramer aims to extend the metaphor of brain-based causation to virtually the whole spectrum of human psychological problems. In another case history, he argues that a man who was always plagued by a sense of personal vagueness and poor self-esteem is, after Prozac, able to "see himself" clearly for the first time. As Kramer puts it:

> Ordinarily, we understand confidence to be a response to accomplishment, to overcoming obstacles through sustained effort. . . . Here, and in most cases I have seen the reverse was true: Medication allowed Paul to experience what had heretofore meant little to him. . . . Medication allowed him to reinterpret history – although this phrasing perhaps understates the role of the antidepressant. It might be more honest to say, 'Medication rewrites history.' Medication is like a revolution overthrowing a totalitarian editor and allowing the news to emerge in perspective. (Kramer, 1993, pp. 220–221)

Powerful medicines indeed.

On the whole, though, the relationship of the new biological psychiatry to the gender imbalance in depression has been little examined. Kramer's intriguing speculations aside, it would seem that a tacit understanding in psychopharmacology is that the SSRI drugs are essentially gender neutral. Both female and male brains are driven by serotonin, and both have the same essential neurocircuits involving the prefrontal cortex, subgenual cingulate, and amygdala. The fact that depression has a skewed epidemiology is only of incidental interest, perhaps triggered by genetic or hormonal factors or even differences in social experience. From the standpoint of pharmacology, it is of little consequence. The simple fact is that symptoms of depression are driven by underlying changes in the brain, regardless of what causes these changes. Experiential differences are of little consequence, as experience has essentially dropped out of the equation. Most practicing psychiatrists (as well as other mental health workers) know better, but such is the unwritten ideology of much contemporary biological psychiatry.

Such gender neutrality and objectivity is hardly evident in pharmaceutical advertising, however. Direct-to-consumer advertising plays a very important role, shaping public opinion about and desire for antidepressants and other medicines. While there is limited research available on this point, one study showed that for patients already taking antidepressants, the introduction of a new medication via an advertising campaign led to a dramatic increase in patient requests to change their medication (Punwani, 2005). In many instances, these requests were met. This seems unfortunate. The choice of an antidepressant should be fundamentally a medical decision, not a product of commercial manipulation of consumer preferences, as if the consumer were purchasing a new car. With regard to the gender issue, Jonathan Metzl (2002, 2003) has pointed out that advertisements for SSRIs, far from escaping the "mother's little helper bias" of the tranquillizers, continue to propagate classic gender stereotypes, although perhaps more subtly. For example, advertisements for Eli Lilly's dual-reuptake inhibitor antidepressant Cymbalta typically depict women after treatment as returning to an essentially nurturing role, whereas before they are depicted as sad, immobile, and isolated. Following medication, they are depicted as happily interacting with their children or husbands. Men, on the other hand, are typically depicted as independent after recovery: One runs alone with his dog; another just sits happily alone and smiles.[3]

Of course, pharmaceutical advertising and the concepts and biases that it propagates, however subtly, are not the same as the views of the psychiatric profession. Many psychiatrists are deeply concerned with the degree to which the pharmaceutical industry has virtually taken over their profession, or at least exerted a corrupting influence that has introduced powerful biases into the essential directions of research and treatment (Brendel, 2006; Cosgrove, Krimsky, Vijayaraghavan, & Schneider, 2006). Psychiatrists, as with most other medical professionals, are required to disclose their financial ties with industry before making presentations or in their publication of papers. In the overwhelming majority of drug-related research, such ties are typically extensive, with psychiatrists serving as consultants to very corporate entities to which their research is related. Many are on pharmaceutical giants' "speaker's bureaus" (Carlat, 2007). Of course, as one speaker at a conference commented, perhaps somewhat optimistically, a financial tie to commercial interests does not guarantee that the speaker will present biased information. To reiterate, this does not mean that the vast majority of practicing individual psychiatrists are corrupt or consumed by the contemporary biological Weltanschauung. Most are driven by a desire to help their patients get better. There has been considerable concern and embarrassment about pharmaceutical influence voiced within the American Psychiatric Association, so much so that concrete steps have been taken to reduce "industry-sponsored" symposia at its national meetings.

Drugs Don't Talk: Limitations of an Exclusive Medication Model and Alternative Discourses

Depression, as was pointed out years ago by Anthony and Bendek (1975), is an "existential" state that on a subjective, personal level involves people's responses to experiences of loss, abuse, humiliation, and entrapment. It is also a response that has physical consequences, particularly in the central nervous system, that have implications for overall physical health and behavioral functioning. Help for depression, virtually all would agree, requires intervention on many levels: psychotherapy and social support, medication, or perhaps alternative physical treatments. We know from extensive research that certain time-limited thera-pies, such as cognitive therapy or interpersonal therapy, can be highly effective in the amelioration of depression. Cognitive therapy, for example, addresses the thinking patterns of a depressed patient, particularly the negative thinking that entraps the person in a vicious cycle of despair (Beck, Rush, Shaw, & Emery, 1979). It is a generally present-focused therapy that does not require, but often does encourage, the patient to come to grips with his or her history (Young, Weinberger, & Beck, 2001). Cognitive therapy does very well when compared with drug therapies, and there is some evidence, as already pointed out, that it is even more long lasting in its effects, and especially more effective as a shield against relapse (DeRubeis et al., 2005). Interpersonal therapy (IPT) attempts to deal more directly with the social and interpersonal situations that have led to the person's difficulties (Klerman, Weissman, Rounsaville, & Chevron, 1984). Originally included as a control condition in the 1980s studies of tricyclic antidepressants, it was shown to be surprisingly effective as a treatment in its own right (Gillies, 2001; Klerman & Weissman, 1987). IPT attempts to help the person understand, come to grips with, and ultimately change the core inter-personal situations that are problematic for him or her. In light of what has been said about the social causes of depression, it should not be at all surprising that interpersonal therapy is effective.

People's access to these treatments is limited because they require experts to receive specialized training, and a lack of training in their intricacies may have an impact on their effectiveness (DeRubeis et al., 2005). This, along with factors such as cost, has led many to conclude that a primary care model is the only viable route to addressing depression on a mass level (Callahan & Berrios, 2005). But the effectiveness of cognitive and interpersonal treatments illustrates a highly important principle: recovery from depression is greatly aided when people can articulate, in the context of a therapeutic dialogue, the nature of their socially based difficulties and develop strategies to deal with them. The issue of "voice," so central in self-silencing theory, comes into play in a primary way here. Dana Jack's (1991, 1999) work has suggested the critical importance of self-silencing in the dynamics of depression, and particularly the complex way in which the internalization of social strictures on women speaking about their own sadness, coupled with the stifling aloneness of women who suffer from depression, militate against recovery.

There is little doubt that we need to greatly expand our resources to care for people with depression. Despite better rates of recognition and treatment in the industrialized countries, depression remains a condition with a high degree of stigma. Interestingly, depression in men may be more highly stigmatized than depression in women (Real, 1998). The male role, with its expectations of strength and taboo against the expression of "softer" emotions such as sadness, conflicts with the acknowledgment of problems that is needed for men to seek treatment. This dilemma has been highlighted in some recent writings about male depression (Real, 1998; Rochlen, McKelley, & Pituch, 2006). Given the debilitating nature of depression, its implications for ill health and disability, and its growing costs to society, Andrew Solomon's (2006) suggestion that we need local centers for the identification and treatment of depression, in a similar sense that we are attempting to deal with such epidemic problems as diabetes, deserves attention.

Yet the overwhelming emphasis on drug treatment as the exclusive or even primary modality for the treatment of depression, an emphasis that is actively promoted by pharmaceutical companies and supported to some degree by current psychiatric standards and emphases, does a disservice to the kind of help that people ultimately need to get well. Depression is a problem that inherently involves emotional isolation, and supportive dialogue, whether in the form of professional therapy, support groups, or a lay companionship model of helping, is a crucial component of healing. Purely pharmaceutical models of cure, as well as the correlated disease model, which views depression as a collection of symptoms driven by an underlying chemical imbalance or faulty neurocircuitry, do violence to the complex matrix of social and interpersonal factors that give rise to depression.

A fundamental consequence of the dominance of biomedical models of mental illness along with primary care models of treatment is that the opportunity for patients to come to grips with their lives in a larger way is fundamentally short-circuited. Medications are often powerfully helpful tools in treatment, but once they become the whole story, both women and men with depression are being underserved. To the extent that their causes are tied to complex forces in the social environment and that their very natures involve the totality of personality and personal experience, psychiatric illnesses are fundamentally different from other medical illness. The depression/diabetes analogy, a popular one with the pharmaceutical makers and advocates of those eager to construe psychiatric disorders in a classic public health framework, is flawed in a fundamental way. First, we have a clear definition of the physical pathology of diabetes, while no such understanding exists for depression. While it can be argued that such an understanding is only a matter of time and future research, there is a fundamental epistemological error in the analogy. While diabetes is impacted by environmental circumstances, such impacts have to do with the physical environment (e.g., the excess of carbohydrates in the diet and the lack of opportunity for exercise) and their behavioral consequences. For depression, the impact—indeed, the very nature of "environment"— is altogether different. Social and interpersonal circumstances that give rise to a sense of entrapment and humiliation can hardly be compared to an excessively carbohydrate-rich diet. The need to manage one's diet and exercise regimes as a treatment for diabetes is clear, but what type of work needs to be done to overcome a profound sense of entrapment and humiliation?

David Karp's study (2006) has shown that one of the factors that make people profoundly ambivalent about medication is the lack of social support that typically follows from treatment with medication alone. People, again both women and men, crave an opportunity to work out the complexity of their experiences with others. Such opportunities for connection may be provided by therapy, but they are hardly limited to that. Karp, for example, discusses the power of depression support groups in helping people to overcome the isolation that is such an essential part of the illness. And Brown (2002), once again, has shown the potent effect of a companion relationship on the amelioration of depression.

In a little-discussed paper, Jacqueline Sparks (2002) has suggested that it is important to recognize that the entire practice of prescribing antidepressant medication is not just a medical practice but rather sets up a particular type of discourse between the treater and the patient. Such a discourse inherently places the physician in a position of power and defines the patient as one who has a problem that lies within his or her brain. The terms of such a discourse are crucial in how they define patients' problems. Sparks argues that the impact of this medicalized discourse on adolescent psychological difficulties is particularly potent. Adolescents, in particular, seek a voice by which they can articulate their difficulties, a greater sense of personal agency and autonomy, and a connection to a wider community. Medication by itself not only may generally contribute little to these needs but also may actively work against them for some. Sparks suggests that the medical discourse about depression is particularly problematic for girls and women, given the troubled history of medical solutions for female "complaints" that are rooted in gender inequities. She provides a case history of an adolescent girl who had an unrevealed history of sexual abuse and had been offered, as a first-line treatment, multiple psychotropic medications for her problems. In refusing medication, this particular young woman sought a broader articulation of her problem both in terms of her troubled past and her relationships to those around her. Her quest was ultimately successful. As Sparks put it:

> Voices of young women are particularly prone to silencing in a world that praises female docility and privileges a male perspective. ... In the midst of forceful psychological or medical language, often in the presence of white-coated male physicians, girls may feel unable to speak their minds or resist what others propose is best of them. Without a legitimate avenue for expression of their opinion, they may find alternative, less socially acceptable means to protest restriction of their right to speak. ... Adults influenced by prevailing views of adolescents may, unwittingly, mute adolescent voices in schools, homes or clinical sites. Concentrating on managing adolescent 'acting out,' they may simply forget to ask for and listen to an adolescent girl's point of view. Lost are her ideas about what is wrong and how it might be fixed. Adolescents have been given the words and permission to 'just say no' to nonprescribed drugs. However, their own fresh perspective about the usefulness of any drugs in their lives and their own creative ideas for solving difficulties without drugs can be overshadowed when a medical script requires a medical solution. (p. 33)

Drugs in themselves are not inherently harmful and in many instances are helpful, even crucial, to recovery from depression. But the exclusive reliance on drugs as a solution to the problem of depression is profoundly problematic. We may "listen" to Prozac, but Prozac does not talk. An exclusively physical view of depression and other forms of psychological distress furthers the silencing of the self and only deepens the alienation that drives mental distress on an epidemic level to begin with.

Notes

1. Fascinating insights into the inside story of the marketing of SSRI medications have been offered by Critser (2005).
2. See, for example, Joffe et al., 1996; Greenberg et al., 1996.
3. The promotional material for Cymbalta can be viewed at the site http://www. depressionhurts.com. A newer advertisement for Cymbalta does in fact depict a man after treatment in the role of caring playfully for his children. Metzl (2002) has argued that popular narratives about Prozac have associated the drug with new female ideals of autonomy and strength. And Blum and Stracuzzi (2004) have argued that many of the new antidepressant ads associate the SSRIs with images of the new woman, independent, strong, and productive. Such cooptation of the ideals of womanhood (we suggest leaving out the term "postfeminist" because it's highly contested) in the service of marketing medications can also be understood as furthering the status quo of existing gender relationships, especially in light of the way in which the discourse of biological psychiatry undercuts discussion about the social dimensions of psychiatric symptoms.

References

Akiskal, H. S., & McKinney, W. T. (1975). Overview of recent research in depression. *Archives of General Psychiatry, 32,* 285–305.

Alvarez, L. (2008, April 18). Nearly a fifth of war veterans report mental disorders, a private study finds. *New York Times,* A1.

American Psychiatric Association. (1952). *Diagnostic and statistical manual of mental disorders.* Washington, DC: Author.

American Psychiatric Association. (1968). *Diagnostic and statistical manual of mental disorders* (2nd ed.). Washington, DC: Author.

American Psychiatric Association. (1980). *Diagnostic and statistical manual of mental disorders* (3rd ed.). Washington, DC: Author.

Anthony, E. J., & Benedek, T. (Eds.). (1975). *Depression and human existence.* Boston: Little Brown.

Beck, A. T., Rush, A. J., Shaw, B. F., & Emery, G. (1979). *Cognitive therapy of depression: A treatment manual.* New York: Guilford Press.

Begley, S. (1994, Feb 7). Beyond Prozac. *Newsweek,* pp. 36–40.

Blazer, D. (2005). *The age of melancholy: Major depression and its social origins.* New York: Routledge.

Blum, L.M. and Stracuzzi, N.F. (2004).Gender in the Prozac nation: Popular discourse and productive femininity. *Gender and Society, 18,* 269–86.

Brendel, D. H. (2006). *Healing psychiatry: Bridging the science/humanism divide*. Cambridge, MA: MIT Press.

Brown, G. W. (2002). Social roles, context and evolution in the origins of depression. *Journal of Health and Social Behavior, 43*, 255–276.

Brown, G. W., & Harris, T. O. (1978). *Social origins of depression: A study of psychiatric disorder in women*. New York: Free Press.

Bruce, M. L., & Kim, K. M. (1992). Differences in the effects of divorce on major depression in men and women. *American Journal of Psychiatry, 149*, 914–917.

Bunney, W. E., Jr., & Davis, J. M. (1965). Norepinephrine in depressive reactions: A review. *Archives of General Psychiatry, 13*, 483–494.

Callahan, C. M., & Berrios, G. E. (2005). *Reinventing depression: A history of the treatment of depression in primary care 1940-2004*. New York: Oxford University Press.

Carlat, D. (2007, November 25). Dr. drug rep. *New York Times Magazine*, 64.

Caspi, A., Sugden, K., Moffitt, T., Taylor, A., Craig, I., Harrington, H., et al. (2003). Influence of life stress on depression: Moderation by a polymorphism in the 5-HTT gene. *Science, 301*, 386–389.

Cosgrove, L., Krimsky, S., Vijayaraghavan, M., & Schneider, L. (2006). Financial ties between DSM-IV panel members and the pharmaceutical industry. *Psychotherapy and Psychosomatics, 75*, 154–160.

Critser, G. (2005). *Generation Rx: How prescription drugs are altering American lives, minds and bodies*. New York: Houghton Mifflin.

Dawson, A., & Tylee, A. (Eds.). (2001). *Depression: Social and economic time bomb*. London: BMJ Books.

DeRubeis, R. J., Hollon, S. D., Amsterdam, J. D., Shelton, R. C., Young, P., Salomon, R. M., et al. (2005). Cognitive therapy vs medications in the treatment of moderate to severe depression. *Archives of General Psychiatry, 62*, 409–416.

Drevets, W. C. (1998). Functional neuroimaging studies of depression: The anatomy of melancholia. *Annual Review of Medicine, 49*, 341–361.

Elkin, I., Shea, M. T., Watkins, J. T., Imber, S., Sotskly, S. M., Collins, J. F., et al. (1989). National institutes of mental health treatment of depression collaborative research program: General effectiveness of treatments. *Archives of General Psychiatry, 46*, 971–982.

Fincham, F. D., Beach, S. R. H., Harold, G. T., & Osborne, L. N. (1997). Marital dissatisfaction and depression: Different causal relationships for men and women. *Psychological Science, 8*, 351–357.

Gaynes, B. N., Rush, A. J., Trivedi, M. H., Wisniewski, S. R., Spencer, D., & Fava, M. (2008). The STAR*D study: Treating depression in the real world. *Cleveland Clinical Journal of Medicine, 75*, 57–76.

Gillies, L. (2001). Interpersonal therapy for depression and other disorders. In D. H. Barlow (Ed.), *Clinical handbook of psychological disorders* (pp. 309–331). New York: Guilford Press.

Greenberg, R. P., Bornstein, R. F., Zborowski, M. J., Fisher, S., & Greenberg, M. D. (1994). A metaanalysis of fluoxetine outcome in the treatment of depression. *Journal of Nervous and Mental Disease, 283*, 547–551.

Greenfield, S. F., Reizes, J. M., Muenz, L. R., Kopans, B., Kozzloff, R. C., & Jacobs, D. G. (2000). Treatment for depression following the 1996 National Depression Screening Day. *American Journal of Psychiatry, 157*, 1867–1869.

Hale, N. G. (1995). *The rise and crisis of psychoanalysis in the United States: Freud and the Americans, 1917-1985*. New York: Oxford University Press.

Haslam, C., Brown, S., Atkinson, S., & Haslam, R. (2005). Patients' experiences of medication for anxiety and depression: Effects on working life. *Family Practice, 21*, 204–212.

Healy, D. (1997). *The antidepressant era*. Cambridge, MA: Harvard University Press.

Healy, D. (2002). *The creation of psychopharmacology*. Cambridge, MA: Harvard University Press.

Healy, D. (2004). *Let them eat Prozac: The unhealthy relationship between the pharmaceutical industry and depression*. New York: New York University Press.

Horwitz, A. V., & Wakefield, J. C. (2007). *The loss of sadness: How psychiatry transformed normal sorrow into depressive disorder*. New York: Oxford University Press.

Insel, T. R. (2006). Beyond efficacy: The STAR*D trial. *American Journal of Psychiatry, 263*, 5–7.

Jack, D. C. (1991). *Silencing the self: Women and depression*. Cambridge MA: Harvard University Press.

Jack, D. C. (1999). Silencing the self: Inner dialogues and outer realities. In T. E. Joiner & J. C. Coyne (Eds.), *The interactional nature of depression: Advances in interpersonal approaches* (pp. 221–246). Washington, DC: American Psychological Association.

Joffe, R., Sokolov, S., & Streuberm, D. (1996). Antidepressant treatment of depression: A metaanalysis. *Canadian Journal of Psychiatry, 41*, 613–616.

Karp, D. A. (1996). *Speaking of sadness: Depression, disconnection and the meanings of illness*. New York: Oxford University Press.

Karp, D. A. (2006). *Is it me or my meds?* Cambridge, MA: Harvard University Press.

Kendler, K. S., Gardner, C. O., & Prescott, C. A. (2002). Towards a comprehensive developmental model for major depression in women. *American Journal of Psychiatry, 159*, 1133–1145.

Kirsch, I., Deacon, B. J., Huedo-Medina, T. B., Scoboria, A., Moore, T. J., & Johnson, B. T. (2008). Initial severity and antidepressant benefits: A meta-analysis of data submitted to the food and drug administration. *PLOS Medicine, 5*, 260–268.

Klerman, G. L., & Weissman, M. M. (1987). Interpersonal psychotherapy (IPT) and drugs in the treatment of depression. *Pharmacopsychiatry, 20*, 3–7.

Klerman, G. L., Weissman, M. M., Rounsaville, B. J., & Chevron, R. S. (1984). *Interpersonal psychotherapy of depression*. New York: Basic Books.

Kramer, P. (1993). *Listening to Prozac: A psychiatrist explores antidepressant drugs and the remaking of the self*. New York: Penguin Books.

Lacasse, J. R., & Leo, J. (2005). Serotonin and depression: A disconnect between the advertisements and the scientific literature. *PloS Medicine, 2*, 1211–1216.

Lozano, A. M., Mayberg, H. S., Giacobbe, P., Hamani, C., Craddock, R. C., & Kennedy, S. R. (2008). Subcallosal cingulated gyrus deep brain stimulation for treatment-resistant depression. *Biological Psychiatry, 64*, 461–467.

Manji, J. K. (2008). *Cellular plasticity cascades: A window into mood disorders*. Lecture at American Psychiatric Association Annual Meeting, Washington, DC.

McGuffin, P., Cohen, S., & Knight, J. (2007). Homing in on depression genes. *American Journal of Psychiatry, 164*, 195–198.

Metzl, J. (2002). Prozac and the pharmacokinetics of narrative form. *Signs, 27*, 347–380.

Metzl, J. (2003). *Prozac on the couch: Prescribing gender in the era of wonder drugs.* Durham, NC: Duke University Press.

Meyer, J. H., Ginvart, N., Boovariwala, A., Sagrati, S., Hussey, D., Garcia, A., et al. (2006). Elevated monoamines oxidase A levels in the brain: An explanation for the monoamine imbalance of major depression. *Archives of General Psychiatry, 63,* 1209–1216.

Moncrieff, J., & Cohen, D. (2006). Do antidepressants cure or create abnormal brain states? *PloS Medicine, 3,* 961–965.

Murray, C. J. L., & Lopez, A. D. (Eds.). (1996). *The global burden of disease.* Cambridge, MA: Harvard University Press.

Olfson, M., Marcus, S. C., Druss, B., Elinson, L., Tanielian, T., & Pincus, H. A. (2002). National trends in the outpatient treatment of depression. *Journal of the American Medical Association, 287,* 203–209.

Olfson, M and Marcus, S.C. (2009). National patterns in antidepressant medication treatment. *Archives of General Psychiatry, 66,* 848–856.

Prozac: A breakthrough drug for depression. (1990, March 26). *Newsweek,* p. 41ff.

Punwani, M. (2005, May). *The influence of direct-to-consumer advertising on patients' attitudes toward their psychiatric medications.* Paper presented at 2005 Annual Meeting of the American Psychiatric Association, Atlanta, Georgia.

Real, T. (1998). *I don't want to talk about it: Overcoming the secret legacy of male depression.* New York: Scribners.

Regier, D. A., Hirschfeld, R. M., Goodwin, F. K., Burke, J. F., Lazar, J. B., & Judd, L. L. (1988). The NIMH depression awareness, recognition and treatment program: Structure, aims and scientific basis. *American Journal of Psychiatry, 145,* 1351–1357.

Rochlen, A. B., McKelley, R. A., & Pituch, K. A. (2006). A preliminary examination of the "Real Men, Real Depression" campaign. *Psychology of Men and Masculinity, 7,* 1–13.

Rush, A. J., Trivedei, M. H., Wisniewski, S. R., Nierenberg, A. A., Stweart, J. W., Warden, D., et al. (2006). Acute and longer-term outcomes in depressed outpatients requiring one or several treatment steps: A STAR*D report. *American Journal of Psychiatry, 163,* 1905–1917.

Schatzberg, A. F., Rush, J., Arnow, B. A., Banks, P. L. C., Blalock, J. A., Borian, F. E., et al. (2005). Chronic depression: Medication (nefazodone) or psychotherapy (CBASP) is effective when the other is not. *Archives of General Psychiatry, 62,* 513–520.

Schildkraut, J. J. (1965). The catecholamine hypothesis of depression: A review of supporting evidence. *American Journal of Psychiatry, 122,* 509–522.

Schildkraut, J. J. (2000). The catecholamine hypothesis. In D. Healy (Ed.), *The psychopharmacologists III* (pp. 110–134). New York: Oxford University Press.

Schildkraut, J. J., & Kety, S. S. (1967). Biogenic amines and emotion. *Science, 156,* 21–30.

Snyder, S. H., Banerjee, S. P., Yamamura, H. I., & Greenberg, D. (1974). Drugs, neurotransmitters and schizophrenia. *Science, 184,* 1243–1253.

Solomon, A. (2006, November 17). Our great depression. *New York Times,* A31.

Sparks, J. A. (2002). Taking a stand: An adolescent girl's resistance to medication. *Journal of Marital and Family Therapy, 28,* 27–38.

Stoppard, J. M. & Gammel, D. J. (2003). Depressed women's treatment experiences: Exploring themes of medicalization and empowerment. In J. Stoppard & L. McMullen. (2003). *Situating sadness: Women and depression in social context* (pp. 39–61). New York: New York University Press.

Szasz, T. S. (1961). *The myth of mental illness: Foundation of a theory of personal conduct*. New York: Harper and Row.

Thuillier, J. (1999). *Ten years that changed the face of mental illness*. Malden, MA: Blackwell Science.

Trivedi, M. H., Rush, A. J., Wisniewski, S. R., Niernenberg, A. A., Warden, D., Ritz, L., et al. (2006). Evaluation of outcomes with citalopram for depression using measurement-based care in STAR*D: Implications for clinical practice. *American Journal of Psychiatry, 163*, 28–40.

Valenstein, E. (1997). *Blaming the brain: The truth about drugs and mental health*. New York: The Free Press.

Warden, D., Rush, A. J., Trivedi, M. H., Fava, M., & Wisniewski, S. R. (2007). The STAR*D Project results: A comprehensive review of findings. *Current Psychiatry Reports, 6*, 449–459.

Wilson, M. (1993). The DSM-III and the transformation of American psychiatry. *American Journal of Psychiatry, 150*, 399–410.

Wong, D. T., Bymaster, F. P., & Engleman, E. A. (1995). Prozac (fluoxetine, Lilly 110140), the first selective serotonin uptake inhibitor and an antidepressant drug: Twenty years since its first publication. *Life Sciences, 57*, 411–441.

Young, J. E., Weinberger, A. D., & Beck, A. T. (2001). Cognitive therapy for depression. In D. H. Barlow (Ed.). *Clinical handbook of psychological disorders* (pp. 264–308). New York: Guilford Press.

4

The Itinerant Researcher: Ethical and Methodological Issues in Conducting Cross-Cultural Mental Health Research

Joseph E. Trimble, María R. Scharrón-del Río, and Guillermo Bernal

I had this feeling of being violated and betrayed, then I went into shock, and then I got angry... and then I went into denial. I thought, 'oh well they don't know who I am. I was just a research subject.' After I participated in the study, I had no idea or didn't even realize what all it was going to entail in the future. And then I come to find out that all the results have been 'shared' through journal articles and publications. The realization for me was 'Oh my god, I've been abused and violated because I had no idea that they would talk about us like that. Now we've been labeled like we're just a bunch of people walking around with diseases on reservations.'

Anonymous Native American research participant (Casillas, 2006)

The unsettling and disturbing quote speaks to the core theme of this chapter—the responsible and ethical conduct of research, especially with historically disempowered and disenfranchised ethnocultural populations[1]—and the untoward effects that researchers can have on their respondents. In the past two decades, there has been a dramatic increase in mental health research conducted among ethnic, racial, and cultural groups in many parts of the world. As interest has increased, so have concerns of many cultural communities about research in general and the presence of researchers in their communities. The rising community concerns accompanied with the emergence of community-based research review committees present extraordinary complexities for researchers that are only beginning to be fully and seriously acknowledged at methodological, procedural, and conceptual levels. The most important challenge, however, is the actual responsible conduct of researchers while they are in the field and the relationship they establish with their participants (Fisher, 1999; Mohatt & Thomas, 2005; Norton & Manson, 1996).

The responsible cross-cultural study of mental health issues needs to acknowledge and address the challenges that are at the core of this juncture. In recent decades, the mental health field has witnessed a significant increase in scholarly research and position papers on ethnocultural similarities and differences in the expression and diagnosis of syndromes and illnesses. For example, Parker, Gladstone, and Chee (2001) summarized the literature on depression among Chinese communities and concluded that "the interpretation of the literature is complicated by the considerable heterogeneity among people described as 'the Chinese' and by numerous factors affecting collection of data, including issues of illness definition, sampling, and case finding; differences in help-seeking behavior; idiomatic expression of emotional distress; and the stigma of mental illness" (p. 857). In a similar vein and drawing from ethnographic interviews with European Americans, African Americans, and Puerto Ricans, Alverson and colleagues (2007) concluded that "appreciating an ethnocultural background and being alert to how it may inform individual clients' illness discourse might sensitize clinicians to the myriad qualitatively different ways that individuals understand and cope with mental illness and relate to the mental health system" (p. 1545). Both statements capture the range of intricacies associated with this field of inquiry and pose complex ethical issues.

The study of depression in women, the theme of this book, provides yet another layer of complexity. While popular and epidemiological knowledge suggest that women experience higher rates of depression (American Psychiatric Association, 1994), Colla, Buka, Harrington, and Murphy (2006) point out that depression rates differ significantly across cultural groups and postulate that social changes—including modernization, westernization, and development—may account for those differences. Reid (2002) highlights the importance of addressing the intersection of gender and culture in research. She argues that for many years, multicultural and cultural research often ignored the impact of gender and sexism within their agendas. As a consequence, the resulting discourse and research were interpreted from the dominant, male-centric perspective. Similarly, within the feminist literature, as long as the emphasis was on gender alone, the dominant ethnic/race was assumed (Reid, 2002). These statements stress the significance of the cross-cultural examination of depression in women: By focusing on the intersections of gender and culture, the voices of women within their communities are privileged over the male-centric, dominant-culture discourses. Research in this area needs to embrace the standard of "principled cultural sensitivity" (Fisher et al., 2002; Trickett & Birman, 1989; Trimble & Fisher, 2005; Trickett, Kelly, & Vincent, 1985) advocated throughout this chapter by not reproducing the historically oppressive discourses and methods that contribute to these women's experiences.

Thus, the purpose of this chapter is to raise points to encourage ethical decision making for research on depression with women from ethnocultural populations that reflect the unique historical and socio-political-cultural realities within racial and ethnic communities. A secondary objective is to highlight the connection between irresponsible research and cultural incompetence. Through the description of a real-life example, this chapter will address the epistemological, ethical, and methodological challenges that responsible researchers confront when engaging disempowered and disenfranchised persons in research with ethnocultural populations.

The need for this chapter is multifold: It emerges from the increasing distrust ethnocultural communities express toward researchers. Countless community members are intolerant and unforgiving of past research efforts for a variety of legitimate reasons; many of their suspicions and concerns derive from the cultural incompetence and insensitivity of researchers. Ideally, researchers studying different ethnocultural groups either belong to or incorporate people in their teams who belong to the culture they are studying. Herein lies one of this book's unique contributions: Each study is written by researchers who are from, and almost all of whom live in, the culture they are studying. This was not too common in cross-cultural research in the past, and is still not common enough now. Researchers should be prepared to collaborate with the communities, share results that have practical value, engage in conversations about theories and methods, and accept the conditions imposed by the communities in gaining access to respondents. Additionally, researchers must be aware of scientific, social, and political factors governing definitions of gender, race, ethnicity, and culture; understand within-group differences; and become familiar with skills in constructing culturally valid assessment instruments.

Facets of Principled Cultural Sensitivity

There are three ethical dimensions of multiculturally sensitive research: (1) applying a cultural perspective to the evaluation of research risk and benefits, (2) developing and implementing culturally respectful informed consent procedures and culturally appropriate confidentiality and disclosure policies, and (3) engaging in community and participant consultation with a standard of "principled cultural sensitivity." The concept of principled cultural sensitivity was introduced to the field of community psychology as a core component of the *ecology of lives* approach to field-based research collaboration by Trickett, Kelly, and Vincent (1985) and Trickett and Birman (1989). Briefly stated, the community psychologists maintain that principled cultural sensitivity is based on respect for those for whom research and interventions are intended and prohibits interventions that violate cultural norms. The principal goal of ecology of lives research and intervention is community development: The studies are constructed in such a way that they become a resource to the community. Unless one cares and is knowledgeable about how lives are led at the community level, such a goal would be difficult if not impossible to achieve. Additionally, the perspective emphasizes the importance of culture as a historical and contemporary aspect of the framework within which individuals appraise their situation and their options. Research from this approach underscores the community context as the stage within which individual behavior occurs (Trickett & Birman, 1989; Trickett et al., 1985).

An Unfortunate Example

Not long ago, a graduate student approached one of us with a serious concern about the contents of a recently published journal article that presented a psychiatric analysis of four women from her village.[2] The article was passed along to her by one of her classmates, who also had questions about its contents and ethical implications. The article presented a case for a unique culturally bound syndrome that closely resembled typical symptoms of depression; descriptions of the symptoms and corresponding behaviors were cast in the framework of the villagers' cultural worldviews and their historical experiences with colonialism. Although the student acknowledged the accuracy of a few of the cultural interpretations and the descriptions of the effects of colonialism on her people, she was deeply concerned that the researchers had presented enough information so that anyone familiar with the village could easily identify the respondents. Moreover, she was angry about the fact that the researchers misinterpreted the women's behavior and symptoms. She strongly maintained that the researchers failed to recognize that the behavior was completely congruent with the way her people typically express the effects of having taken on too many community and family responsibilities. From her cultural perspective, the four women were not depressed but rather were expressing their need for a time-out from domestic responsibilities. The student acknowledged that depression-like behaviors such as prolonged weeping, sadness, restlessness, loss of energy, and feelings of guilt occurred in her village when one lost a member of their extended family or loved one; the experiences are usually shared among many village members at the time of loss and in fact are expected to occur.

She sent a copy of the article to the elders in her village and asked them to comment on it as well as provide her information about the researchers. It didn't take long for her to hear back from one of the elders, who also happened to be the father of one of the women. He was deeply upset with the article's tone, inaccuracies, misrepresentations of the cultural ways of the village, and the fact that the villagers he talked to about the article were able to identify the four women. He went on to say that he wanted the student to write a letter to the authors on behalf of the village counsel and elders essentially berating and admonishing them for their mistakes as well as their whole approach to the sensitive topic. The student complied with their request, sending the letter back to the elders for their review and comment. The lengthy, somewhat jarring and direct letter eventually was sent to the authors; they never responded or acknowledged receipt of the letter. Following additional instructions from the elders, she sent the authors another letter a few months later telling them that they and any researchers from their university were no longer welcome in the village; copies were sent to the authors' departmental chair and the university's president. The president responded with a polite note indicating she would check into the complaint; the student never heard back from the university president, the chair, or any of the recipients of the letter.

This unfortunate incident illustrates several key points concerning the culturally appropriate conduct of Western research with women from ethnocultural communities, and serves as ample evidence for why more and more communities are wary of "outside" researchers who appear to place their professional and academic interests above the needs of their host communities. These outside researchers create a swarm of problems for the participants, villages, neighborhoods, and communities, and leave them to struggle with the consequences alone. This once popular and widely used safari-scholar approach to research is fading from acceptance, and one-stop data mining by these itinerant researchers is no longer acceptable. More than ever, ethnocultural community members demand that research occur in their communities under their direction and control. Researchers should be prepared to collaborate with communities, share results that have practical value, engage in conversations and discussions about theoretical concepts and methods, and accept the conditions imposed by the community in gaining access to information and respondents (Fisher et al., 2002; Trimble & Fisher, 2005).

Based on the basic principles of ecosystems and ecology of lives perspectives, the psychiatric researchers or itinerant interlopers did not fully comprehend the host community's cultural-specific lifeways and thoughtways and their influence on daily life. A background search on their credentials and research experiences suggests that they had little experience in working with ethnocultural communities of any kind, as the bulk of their research occurred in psychiatric clinics in their city and surrounding suburbs. The researchers were introduced to a village elder who was a relative from a nearby village; hence, their three-week sojourn was their first visit to the community. In effect, their research orientation was an itinerant one where context didn't seem to matter to them.

Sections of the publication indicate that the researchers had little knowledge of the history of the village, including its struggles with colonialism, missionaries, the presence of miners and loggers, and the nature of the village's relationship with government agencies, including the politics associated with their relationship with the village. Moreover, some of the article's historical statements and descriptions of their linguistic and cultural background were incorrect and misleading. In addition, the gender dynamics within the village were not researched or described, and there was a complete lack of awareness about the gender and power relations between the researchers and the women interviewed. It is no surprise, then, that this research on women from this village had the effect of further disempowering and pathologizing them, thus reproducing the oppressive gender and racial dynamics from the researchers' culture.

Finally, this case incident will provide other examples of the researchers' gender and culturally insensitive improprieties and blunders in subsequent sections of the chapter. But there is one incident that bears mention as it serves to reinforce the point that the researchers' interests were self-serving and that explorations into the deep cultural meaning of the villagers' lifeways and thoughtways were not valued. The researchers were observing one of their participants one afternoon as she responded to a series of psychological tests, and from all indications, she appeared to be acting out classic depression symptoms. Hoping to get a construct or term in the village's indigenous language that captures a description of a culturally bound syndrome, one of the researchers turned to a nearby villager—a man, not a woman—and asked him if there were words or phrases they had in their language to describe her illness or sickness. The man thought for a moment and then told them what it was; the researchers had him repeat the phrase while they tape-recorded it and wrote it down phonetically. The researchers used the phrase in their journal article as an example of an exotic culturally bound syndrome that was frequently used by the villagers to describe depression. Unfortunately, the researchers never asked for a literal translation of the phrase; otherwise, they might not have reported it: the villager's phrase translates to mean "she's not being herself today."

Roots of the Itinerant Research Orientation

Anti-oppressive research involves making explicit the political practices of creating knowledge. It means making a commitment to the people you are working with personally and professionally in order to mutually foster conditions for social justice and research. It is about paying attention to, and shifting, how power relations work in and through the processes of doing research. (Potts & Brown, 2005, p. 255)

To avoid replicating the abuses of the itinerant researcher approach, it is crucial to examine the epistemological assumptions that underlie the ethical behaviors and methodological choices in research. The itinerant researcher is guided by the assumptions and traditions of the Western positivist paradigm in modern science, what Linda Smith (2005) calls the Western "discourse of discovery." The researcher objectifies the subjects of research; research participants become this exotic object that the researcher travels to visit and, once in their presence, submits to examination via various instruments. The itinerant research orientation assumes that the results and the "truth" to be obtained will appear because of the methodology used, regardless of the subjective qualities of the researcher and his or her relation to the participants and community. Researchers who work from this approach reproduce the patterns of oppression and exploitation that these ethnocultural communities have endured both throughout their history and currently.

Morin (1984) enumerates 13 principles that correspond to the paradigm of simplification from which conventional, Western science approaches its objects of inquiry. These include the principles of disjunction, reductionism, and one-dimensionality; the elimination of what is historical and contextual; and the incapacity to concede autonomy to the objects of inquiry (Morin, 1984). We examine these principles and assumptions to illustrate ethical and responsible research with ethnocultural populations.

Decontextualized Knowledge

The principle of disjunction privileges objectivity over subjectivity. In order to objectively observe, research entrenched in this paradigm assumes that the isolation of the object of inquiry from its surroundings or context is necessary. The paradigm of simplification also presupposes that the knowledge of the object is equal to the knowledge of its parts (reductionism). As a result, the interactions between the parts and the interactions between the object of inquiry and its context are obliterated, making the knowledge derived from it one-dimensional. Martín-Baró and Blanco Abarca (1998) refer to this principle as the partialization ("parcialización") of human experience within positivist science, denoting both how it pertains to only a part of the phenomena studied and how it manifests as a bias privileging only certain parts and dimensions. Barnhardt and Kawagley (2005), in their discussion of indigenous knowledge systems, have also characterized Western science and education as privileging compartmentalized and decontextualized knowledge. This approach often clashes with the worldview of the communities that the research and knowledge are trying to describe.

The researcher who assumes the conventional, Western scientific approach strives to be detached and removed from the object of study and from the results of his or her study. This detachment starkly contrasts with one of the aforementioned requirements of principled cultural sensitivity: *caring* how lives are lived at the community level. From this perspective, a detached researcher is not a culturally competent researcher.

Elimination of History

Martín-Baró and Blanco Abarca's (1998) psychosocial approach, particularly their writings about the psychology of liberation, critiques what they call Western science's ahistorical reductionism. When mental health researchers fail to acknowledge and consider the his(her)stories of the relationships between many ethnocultural populations and biomedical research, their attempts at earning the communities' trust are likely to be perceived as deceitful and insincere. The legacies of the Tuskegee study in the African American community, the early oral contraceptive trials in Puerto Rico, and the large-scale coerced sterilization of Native

American and Puerto Rican women, among many others, have served to highlight the role of research as a tool of colonization and oppression (Smith, 2005). Any research done within ethnocultural and historically oppressed communities starts where the last one left off. Part of acknowledging the communities' histories often includes repairing relationships and making amends for past abuses.

Autonomy and Self-Determination of Participants

> If researchers consider expertise to be lodged primarily with other PhDs who have been socialized in the language and logic of our theories and methods, to what extent does social research align itself primarily with dominant discourses, ignoring the expertise of those who suffer most? (Fine, 2006, p. 95)

> The dominant white culture is killing us slowly with its ignorance. By taking away our self-determination, it has made us weak and empty. (Anzaldúa, 1999, p. 108)

Itinerant researchers are not concerned with the importance of self-determination in the communities they study. For many ethnocultural and indigenous scholars, recognizing autonomy in the populations they are researching includes questioning Western science's epistemic privilege: that is, the primacy of the knowledge gathered by "scientific means" over all other ways of acquiring and producing knowledge. In many cases, this questioning translates into "centering the margins" (Hill, Muñoz, & Correia, 2007): addressing the communities' issues from a framework of "self determination, decolonization, and social justice" (Smith, 1999, p. 4). To work from this paradigm, the researcher must privilege the validity of the knowledge of ethnocultural populations.

Within mental health research, centering the research agenda from a framework of self-determination entails recognizing a community's right to have control over how psychological health and maladjustment are defined, assessed, and addressed within their own contexts (Hill, 2005). In addition, responsible informed consent procedures need to promote the autonomy and self-determination of these communities: Informed consent should safeguard the populations under study from exploitation (Snyder & Barnett, 2006). In our case example, the women were not aware that their information would be shared and disclosed (i.e., published); this puts into question the validity of the informed consent procedures of the study. Moreover, the itinerant researchers imposed their own perceptions and judgments on what constituted pathology in the women of the tribe; the only intent of addressing the community's knowledge about the women's situation was to fit it into the researchers' particular perspective.

Ethical Challenges in Cross-Cultural Research

The growing intensity of grievances of people from countless ethnocultural communities worldwide captured the attention of researchers and their respective professional associations. Flowing largely from the scandalous accounts of the infamous Tuskegee Syphilis Study, the U.S. government—principally through what now is the National Institutes of Health—advocated and enacted strict ethical research guidelines. In the 1979 Belmont Report, the principles of autonomy, beneficence, and justice were identified as the moral ideals to which all research ethics should aspire. These principles formed the basis of federal regulations and scientific codes of conduct that require investigators to design studies that protect against harm by adequately minimizing research risks, maximizing potential research benefits, protecting confidentiality, and ensuring that participation is voluntary (Fisher et al., 2002; Mohatt & Thomas, 2005; U.S. Department of Health and Human Services, 2001).

The American Psychological Association's (APA) *Ethical Principles of Psychologists and Code of Conduct* (APA, 1992) and the *Guidelines on multicultural education, training, research, practice, and organizational change for psychologists* (APA, 2002) direct psychologists to conduct research ethically and competently. The APA's *Guidelines for Research in Ethnic Minority Communities* (Council of National Psychological Associations for the Advancement of Ethnic Minority Interests, 2000) stress the importance of involving community members in the design, implementation, analysis, and interpretation of all research. Additionally, in the APA's *Guidelines on Multicultural Education, Training, Research, Practice, and Organizational Change for Psychologists*, "[c]ulturally sensitive psychological researchers are encouraged to recognize the importance of conducting culture-centered and ethical psychological research among persons from ethnic, linguistic, and racial minority backgrounds" (APA, 2002, p. 40).

Responding to the clarion call for a stance on ethical research principles from their membership, in 2002, the International Union of Psychological Science (IUPsyS) convened an ad hoc committee to identify, develop, and submit a universal declaration of ethical guidelines. The committee was directed to identify principles and values that would provide a common moral framework for psychologists worldwide and would guide the development of distinctive standards appropriate for different cultural groups and their settings. In 2005, the committee acknowledged an exceptionally important standard when they stated:

> Respect for the dignity and worth of human beings is expressed in different ways in different communities and cultures. It is important to acknowledge and respect such differences. On the other hand, it also is important that all communities and cultures adhere to moral values that respect and protect their members both individually and collectively.... The continuity of lives and cultures over time connects people today with the cultures of past generations and the need to nurture future generations. As such, respect for the dignity and worth of all human beings also includes moral consideration of and respect for cultural communities. (Universal Declaration of Ethical Principles for Psychologists, n.d.)

The emphasis of the Universal Declaration of Ethical Principles for Psychologists[3] on morality is in keeping with the fundamental ethical principle that one "should do no harm" when it comes to the conduct of research of any kind. Framing ethical principles and guidelines to include "moral considerations" is an indispensable condition for guiding research ventures.

The voices of Canada's Aboriginal people guided the publication and release of "a set of principles to assist in developing ethical codes for the conduct of research internal to the Aboriginal community or with external partners" (Castellano, 2004, p. 98). Eight principles are laid out calling for the appropriate and enforceable protection of Aboriginal people's interest in research ventures, highlighting the rights of Aboriginal people as the true owners of the information they provide for researchers and the researchers' obligation to consider in their research plans the Aboriginal people's struggles for self-determination. Similarly, in a document titled *Values and Ethics: Guidelines for Ethical Conduct in Aboriginal and Torres Strait Islander Health Research*, released by Australia's National Health and Medical Research Council (2003) and written in collaboration with Aboriginal and Torres Island representatives, the authors point out that "[t]he construction of ethical relationships between Aboriginal and Torres Strait Islander Peoples on the one hand and the research community on the other must take into account the principles and values of Aboriginal and Torres Strait Islander cultures" (p. 3). The report goes on to describe a variety of ways Australia's Aboriginal and Torres Strait Island people can work collaboratively with academic researchers to achieve mutual goals.

Evaluating Research Risks and Benefits from a Cultural Perspective

The general rules of scientific conduct embodied in professional codes of conduct provide critical yet incomplete guidance for identifying and resolving the complex ethical challenges inherent in research involving ethnocultural populations. Investigators engaged in the critical task of generating information on which psychological services, public opinion, and policies for ethnocultural groups will be based are thus faced with the formidable responsibility of ensuring their procedures are scientifically sound, culturally valid, and morally just.

Modern Western science promotes a science of alienation. In this form of science, both researcher and participant are alienated from the product of the study. The quest for answers often does not produce immediate applicable results but joins the larger body of knowledge for future development and use. In graduate school, we are encouraged to study a lofty or new area and concentrate on publishing the results in journal articles that will be accessible to the academic and scientific community; typically, this does not make results available or applicable to the studied communities. This lack of immediacy and applicability of the studies' results to the communities is often antithetical to the quest for knowledge in other cultures and worldviews.

Ethics in psychology, both in the clinical and research practices, should be anchored by liberating practices (Martín-Baró & Blanco Abarca, 1998; Smith, 2005). As researchers, if we are not part of the community that we are to research, a commitment to liberating praxis means being aware of your positions of power in relation to the community; knowing the history of the community and its struggles and dynamics of oppression; contributing to and respecting the right to self-determination; and striving to not reproduce the oppressive and exploitative patterns that the community has experienced in its history.

Amalio Blanco Abarca (in the prologue to Martín-Baró & Blanco Abarca, 1998) highlights the "commitment with the well-being" of the disempowered and disenfranchised communities that is inherent to Martín-Baró's psychosocial approach. This commitment goes beyond the principle of beneficence: Doing "good" within psychology entails a commitment to being personally and socially self-reflective and self-aware (committed to concientization) and to incorporate these reflections in our theoretical, clinical, and research practices.

Moral Persuasions and Value Orientations

Close compliance with professional ethical principles and standards begins with the personal moral persuasion of researchers: It requires them to reflect on their actions and their corresponding cognitive-emotional foundation. The assessment of morality can be construed as a rational process; thus, the assessment of whether or not one's research approach "will do no harm" should lead to logical decisions in favor of protecting the rights of study participants. Unfortunately, some researchers take a more self-serving approach where their needs, aspirations, and desires overshadow those of their host communities. This approach—likely rationalized by the researcher—is the foremost reason for the problems ethno-cultural communities have had historically and continue to experience with outside researchers. Self-serving researchers may believe they can mask their selfish intentions, but they may be deceiving themselves to believe they will go unnoticed. The prominent cultural anthropologist Ward Goodenough reminds us:

> The principle that underlies problems of ethics is respecting the humanity of others as one would have others respect one's own. If field [researchers] genuinely feel such respect for others, they are not likely to get into serious trouble. But if they do not feel such respect, then no matter how scrupulously they follow the letter of the written codes of professional ethics, or follow the recommended procedures of field (research) manuals, they will betray themselves all along the line in the little things. (1980, p. 52)

Echoing Trimble and Mohatt, we take pause to ask, "what does it mean to be an ethical person when conducting research with [women from] ethnocultural communities?" (Trimble & Mohatt, 2005, p. 327). In addition to the personal challenges to researchers that these authors' question summons, communities also will want to know what kind of person they will be working with. If researchers don't closely follow and live by a set of principled virtuous ethics such as prudence, integrity, respectfulness, benevolence, and reverence (Trimble & Mohatt, 2005), at some point they will slowly alienate their hosts and may be asked to leave. Furthermore, it is vital that researchers become aware of their own gender dynamics and how they are reproduced in the research process and in interactions with women from ethnocultural communities.

Methodological Challenges

Alvidrez and Areán (2002) highlight the importance of doing research that results in improved accessibility and quality of services (i.e., effectiveness research) when engaging in mental health research with ethnocultural populations that have limited access to health and mental health services. One of the ways to improve the quality of services is by culturally adapting interventions to make them more acceptable, to improve their fit with ethnocultural groups, and to increase their utility in real-world settings. For example, in preparation for launching efficacy[4] and effectiveness[5] studies with Puerto Rican adolescents, a framework was developed (Bernal, Bonilla, & Bellido, 1995; Bernal & Sáez-Santiago, 2006) to culturally adapt or culturally center evidence-based interventions. The framework serves as a methodological tool and includes eight elements or dimensions that must be considered in the adaptation process in order to augment the ecological validity of an intervention (i.e., language, persons, metaphors, content, concepts, goals, methods, and context). The assumption is that an intervention is likely to be more effective when it is congruent with the culture and context of the person. Yet, how ethnicity and culture play a role in the treatment process and how interventions may need to be adapted to meet the needs of diverse individuals is still a challenge for the field (Bernal, 2006). It is also a challenge to develop evidence-based, culturally centered interventions (Bernal & Sáez-Santiago, 2006) beyond the one-size-fits-all approach (Bernal Jiménez-Chaffy, & Domenech Rodriguez, 2009).

As an example of how the gap between passive "subjects" and distant "experimenters" can be bridged—moving us more toward a science of intervention that is participatory and culturally informed—participants in two initial efficacy trials of cognitive-behavioral therapy and interpersonal psychotherapy with depressed adolescents (Rosselló & Bernal, 1999; Rosselló, Bernal, & Rivera-Medina, 2008) were invited to focus groups to learn about their experiences. Former participants and their parents became consultants to the investigators: The adolescents offered suggestions on making manual-based interventions more flexible and the parents (primarily mothers) asked for tools for dealing with their children's depression. As a result, treatments were modified and a psychoeducational intervention for parents was designed, which was presented to other groups of parents for feedback on its relevance, feasibility, and utility.

Engaging ethnocultural populations from principled cultural sensitivity is akin to promoting community ownership of the entire research endeavor and, ultimately, to respecting members' autonomy and right to self-determination. From its very beginning, during the identification of the issues to be studied, throughout the recruitment process, the informed consent procedures, the study implementation, the ongoing monitoring of ethical and cultural issues, and the interpretation and application of the results for the sustainable benefit of the community, responsible researchers must privilege and honor the communities' priorities to foster and repair the trust that has historically been betrayed by the itinerant approach (Alvidrez & Areán, 2002). Alvidrez and Areán advocate for having a presence in the community prior to the study and maintaining it after data collection to ensure a beneficial impact to the population. This presence is marked by the building and nurturing of relationships with the community characterized by respect; recognition of the communities' values, needs, and priorities; and sustained involvement (Smith, 2005). Researchers must be reliable, innovative, committed to the work, and trusted and respected by the community, and must represent a source of help (Nama & Swartz, 2002).

Culturally Respectful and Responsible Informed Consent Procedures

For an informed consent procedure to be valid, participants need to be able to understand the information provided, give consent freely and voluntarily, and be competent to give consent (Barnett, Wise, Johnson-Greene, & Bucky, 2007; Gross, 2001). When doing research with ethnocultural populations, the first two conditions present important ethical considerations. Itinerant researchers forget that our notion of "science" and "research" is bound by culture. Therefore, in order to responsibly request informed consent, it is of utmost importance to reveal the assumptions within this process that we often take for granted. This includes how and who to ask for consent, how to explain and distinguish research from treatment, and the power dynamics involved in the intersections of culture, gender, educational level, and socioeconomic status.

In our first example, the actions and conduct of the itinerant interlopers violated at least one of the ethical and moral principles embedded in their professional association and in the village's codes and standards for virtuous behavior. The ethics codes of the psychiatric and psychological associations highlight the important of safeguarding confidentiality in both research and practice as "[c]onfidentiality is essential to psychiatric treatment" (American Psychiatric Association, 2006, p. 7). The four women described in our unfortunate example were given pseudonyms to protect their anonymity; however, most of the villagers knew their true identities, and it also turns out that frequent visitors to the village knew the four women by name after they read the article. Clearly, the researchers did not comprehend the meaning of anonymity from the villager's worldview; otherwise, this lamentable incident could have been prevented. As a result, the professional membership of the researchers to the American Psychiatric Association was jeopardized after an ethical complaint was filed by an anonymous member.

In addition to the ethical obligation, the researchers were obliged to collect informed consent forms from all participants as required by U.S. federal guidelines and institutional review boards (Berg, Appelbaum, Lidz, & Parker, 2001; Faden & Beauchamp, 1986). Regrettably, the participants in our example had little or no idea what a human subjects consent form was or meant. Nonetheless, because the researchers were doctors, participants unwittingly signed them without fully understanding the reason behind the request. Thus, informed consent was not truly obtained. Commitment to the well-being of a community needs to include the will and resources to carry out ethical and scientifically sound research; this includes regarding informed consent as a process, not an outcome, and going to great lengths to obtain it. This is an enterprise that may take more time and resources than what is commonly perceived (Adams et al., 2007).

Typically, problems arise when community participants are invited to participate in a study where they may be giving away certain rights and responsibilities that may not be known at the study's outset; in effect, when they sign a consent form, they may not fully comprehend the binding implication of their signature. For example, after learning that blood samples were being used for purposes other than what was stated in consent forms, the Havasupai Tribe of Arizona filed a $52 million lawsuit against Arizona State University and the Arizona Board of Regents (Hendricks, 2004).[6] In retrospect, in our case example, villagers and the study participants had no idea the researchers were going to publish analytic case studies of those who were ostensibly experiencing depression. Similarly, the Havasupai participants had no idea their blood samples would be for anything else but to study the correlates of diabetes. Instead, they were used in studies related to inbreeding, schizophrenia, and human migration theories (Hendricks, 2004).

Even when the possibility of using the data collected in further studies is clearly outlined and discussed during the informed consent process, the history of exploitative research practices and the lack of immediate benefits for the community can make participants weary and suspicious (Molyneux, Wassenaar, Peshu, & Marsh, 2005). Disempowered and disenfranchised communities are asked for a leap of faith in favor of the researchers. Despite histories of exploitation, misinterpretation, and data mining in their communities by itinerant researchers, they are asked to trust and give of themselves without knowing how their participation will be used in the future. These situations represent instances of biocolonialism. Hawthorne (2007) contends that "colonial theft [has been] extended to human anatomy" (p. 318) to the extent that biological material from ethnocultural groups is being used without their knowledge and consent for the academic and/or economic profit of itinerant researchers and/or other institutions (i.e., DNA racial profiling) and in the absence of any gain for the ethnocultural communities.

There are various language issues that are relevant to ethical informed consent procedures. In composing consent forms for use in field research, researchers often use unfamiliar scientific jargon and odd sentence and paragraph construction; these, along with a lack of understanding of what happens if they refuse to sign, contribute to a lack of informed consent (Trimble & Fisher, 2005). In addition, most consent forms have been verified to be an average of three grades higher than the reading level of the typical study participant (Brainard, 2003). The conduct of ethical research demands that informed consent procedures be presented in language that is understandable, which may require having additional versions of consent forms in the participants' native language. Nevertheless, when consent forms are translated into other languages, the English meaning of terms and sentences does not always accurately translate into words and sentences found and used in the language of the participants. Some researchers have experienced interpretation difficulties with participants who are not literate or whose reading comprehension levels are too low to understand consent forms (Gostin, 1995).

A similar dilemma occurs when participants mistakenly believe that signing an informed consent form terminates their right to withdraw from a study or question procedures or postexperimental reaction (Fisher, 2002). Interestingly, in our example only 3 of the 20 village participants who signed the consent form had a high school diploma. Although all participants were bilingual and could read the consent forms (in English), 16 of them preferred to use their native language in conversations. None complained about signing the consent form, but the majority felt it wasn't necessary because they didn't believe the doctors would intentionally harm them.

Cultural values and norms involving self and other public avowal can present problems for research institutions and professional associations concerning the maintenance of anonymity and confidentiality in research studies. Self and other public avowal—public declaration of one's name, family background, kin relationships, and tribal or village affiliation—is important to numerous American Indians and Alaska Natives. Mohatt and Thomas (2005) recount a circumstance involving confidentiality and consent forms in which the worldviews of the local university's institutional review board (IRB) and the potential participants from Alaska Native villages clashed. The IRB denied the request for approval of the study's research methods and consent forms because the potential participants were asked whether they wanted to be publicly identified and have the accounts of their experiences with sobriety published with their names included. After the research team informed certain village Native elders about the IRB decision as well as the possibility of purging the raw data after five years, the elders protested, stating "that they could not imagine why they would tell their story if it would not be shared with others and would be destroyed" (Mohatt & Thomas, 2005, p. 104). The research team provided information to the IRB members about the village's values and norms concerning personal name and family acknowledgment as well as the complaints from the elders. After much debate, the IRB agreed to the use of multiple consent forms that provided the participants various levels of confidentiality to choose from.

Informed Consent of Treatment Research in Ethnocultural Populations

The challenges and issues regarding informed consent in research with ethnocultural populations apply both to discovery-oriented research and hypothesis-testing research (Bernal & Scharrón-del Río, 2001). Nevertheless, hypothesis-testing research, such as efficacy and effectiveness research for interventions, incorporates yet another level of informed consent: treatment. Ethical codes include informed consent stipulations for both research and treatment; however, for participants in underserved communities, the distinctions between these two may not seem clear-cut.

Within treatment research, additional issues regarding the process of signing for consent arise. While Western science assumes that informed consent is an individual decision, collectivist cultures may favor group or family decision-making processes (Kaljevic & VandeCreek, 2006; Shaibu, 2007). Moreover, if the potential participant is a woman, she may need to consult with her husband or other men in her family (Molyneux et al., 2005; Shaibu, 2007).

In their article about community voices and informed consent in developing countries, Molyneux and colleagues (2005) described the discussion groups facilitated with community members in a rural part of Kenya where a large biomedical research unit was based. These authors report that while some participants were not concerned about the signing of the consent forms, others (in particular, those who had declined to participate in research) had mixed feelings and views about this process. In cultures where oral traditions are highly valued, researchers insisting on the act of signing for written consent (which privileges the written word over the spoken word) can make the participants "suspicious" (Shaibu, 2007). According to Alvidrez and Areán (2002), the misuse of research to justify oppression and discrimination against ethnic and cultural minorities along with the exploitation suffered by these groups under the pretext of research fuel their distrust toward research endeavors. Moreover, their histories of oppression and exploitation often undermine their ability to attribute "benign or beneficent motives" to researchers (Alvidrez & Areán, 2002, p. 104). These instances highlight the cultural clash of values and practices that can take place between the ethnocultural communities and the inflexible application of Western research institutional practices. When IRB expectations and policies are intended to be acritically applied to research with ethnocultural communities, the research ethics invoked are "much more about institutional and professional regulations and codes of conduct than it is about the needs, aspirations, or worldviews of 'marginalized and vulnerable' communities" (Smith, 2005, p. 96).

If research takes place within a clinical setting or involves providing treatment or resources in a severely underserved community, potential research participants may worry about the repercussions of refusing consent (Molyneux et al., 2005). Participants may worry that their future care will be of lesser quality, that they will be labeled as difficult or problematic, and that their relationship with the clinics and service providers will be damaged. The fear of losing access to the few available treatment resources may seem like opening the door to life-threatening repercussions.

An indispensable part of informed consent is that the person becomes a research participant voluntarily and freely (Snyder & Barnett, 2006). For a severely underserved population, the choice of participation may entitle choosing the research treatment versus no treatment; this is not much of a choice. The ethical and responsible researcher needs to be aware of the inequities and disparities (in access to and availability of quality care) that characterize the community's health system when conducting research with women from underserved groups (Alvidrez & Areán, 2002).

Barnett and colleagues (2007) note that court rulings have dictated that in addition to including the risks and benefits associated with participation in a treatment study, potential participants must be informed of the risks associated with refusing treatment and offered "reasonably available alternatives" —with their respective risks and benefits—during the informed consent procedure. Therefore, in order for informed consent to be valid and fully voluntary, participants must have another option for treatment. In severely underserved groups, other options for treatment may be scarce or nonexistent.

The issue of the "reasonably available" treatment option goes to the heart of ethical issues in designing both efficacy and effectiveness research. Randomized clinical trials are the gold standard for demonstrating causality. To establish efficacy, the ideal is to have a no treatment, placebo, or control group to increase the likelihood of detecting a treatment effect. The ethical ideal would lead one to design studies in which all treatment conditions include effective treatments, or in the case of a no treatment condition, reasonable treatment options are available so that the decision to participate is fully voluntary. We offer two examples from the third author's experience.

In a study of intergenerational family therapy with methadone maintenance patients in the San Francisco Bay Area, predominantly ethnocultural patients were randomized to either a manual-based family therapy or to didactic family psychoeducation. The investigators believed that the design itself was both ethical and more rigorous than having opted for a no-treatment control. However, there were consequences to this decision: A treatment effect could not be demonstrated convincingly since both conditions appeared to be beneficial in various measures of outcome. At the time, the criterion for publication was having demonstrated an effect and thus the outcome paper was never actually published.

In a second study that focused on psychological treatments for depressed adolescents (Rosselló & Bernal, 1999), the issue of design and ethics was revisited. Here the investigators opted for contrasting two treatments that had empirical support in the field: cognitive-behavioral therapy and interpersonal psychotherapy. Although the use of a no-treatment control group was scientifically justified (there was no evidence on the efficacy of these interventions in Puerto Rico), it was clear to the investigators that there were no "reasonable available" treatment options for adolescents, particularly poor adolescents.[7] Given the earlier experience without a no-treatment control group, the research team opted for explaining to potential participants that they had a 33% chance of not getting treatment for three months, but made a commitment to offer the treatment of choice after the waiting period. There are consequences to this option: The costs of the study increase and there can be no meaningful comparisons at the subsequent follow-up between treatment and control conditions. In sum, there are always trade-offs in considering designs that are responsive to both ethics and culture. Ethical issues of ensuring reasonably available treatment options to ethnocultural groups have important implications for the design of studies when treatment is not available and when what is available is unreasonable.

Ethical and Responsible Mental Health Research with Ethnocultural Populations

Kim, Park, and Park (2000) identify three approaches to cross-cultural research: universalist, contextual, and integrationist. The universalist approach, from which the itinerant researcher operates, represents the traditional epistemology of psychology and science, where the goal is to discover existing universal truths. Within this approach, the influence of culture is minimized, ignored, and often pathologized. The contextual approach, on the other hand, emphasizes the importance of understanding the participants from their own frame of reference. Kim, Park, and Park (2000) suggest that indigenous psychologies emerged as a "worldwide reaction" to the pressing need to decry the universalist assumptions and the effects of research from this perspective: "Although existing psychological theories and concepts are assumed to be objective, value free, and universal, in reality they are deeply enmeshed with Euro-American values. . . . As such, they can be characterized as imposed etics or pseudoetics, not true universals" (p. 64).

The integrationist approach proposes the integration of the knowledge and methods produced by both the "cross-cultural testing of psychological theories" and the indigenous psychologies (Kim et al., 2000). While there is no given formula or model to guide this integration (Hill, Pace, & Robbins, in press), research efforts from this approach must reflect a commitment to the autonomy and self-determination of the involved communities. Integrationist researchers must engage ethnocultural groups from a standard of principled cultural sensitivity. Martín-Baró and Blanco Abarca (1998) call for a revision of the assumptions and principles that guide our psychological methods and concepts. This revision, they advocate, should proceed from a place of commitment to action that reflects the needs and priorities of disenfranchised communities, and not from the comforts of our offices in the ivory tower. Research among disempowered communities should not be a mere academic exercise, but responsive to the immediacy of communities' realities and needs.

If in the process of doing research the participants and/or the community feel alienated, enraged, estranged, victimized, exploited, and misunderstood, who is the research serving? How can we genuinely advocate for doing research in communities if the process is victimizing in itself and the results and benefits of engaging in such exercise will not be immediately available for them? As such, our research with women from ethnocultural populations should not reproduce the patterns of exploitation and oppression based on race, gender, and/or culture that have historically existed. Let us recognize research as an intervention in itself, one that will have various effects in the participants and the community in which it is done.

Notes

1. An ethnocultural community is a group of people that share similarities stemming from their ethnic, racial, and/or cultural background. Throughout this chapter, we use the term "ethnocultural communities" to refer to nondominant groups that have been historically marginalized.
2. All descriptions and narratives concerning the case example are factual. To protect the anonymity of the village and the women, the sequence of events has been modified and some incidents have been condensed. This case example, its ethical implications, and the effects of the itinerant researchers' transgressions on the women and their community have not been published elsewhere prior to this chapter.
3. This Universal Declaration represents a collaborative effort of the IUPsyS, the International Association of Applied Psychology (IAAP), and the International Association for Cross-Cultural Psychology (IACCP).
4. An efficacy study aims to determine whether an intervention can cause significant benefits in a controlled environment (experimental conditions) (Nelson & Steele,

2006); an example of this kind of study is a randomized clinical trial, in which an intervention group is compared to a control group.

5. An effectiveness study assesses whether an intervention will work and provide benefits in actual clinical or real-life settings (Nelson & Steele, 2006).

6. A Maricopa Arizona County Superior Court judge dismissed the case in May 2007 on a legal technicality.

7. The waiting period to get an appointment in the public mental health system was about four months and the available treatment was almost exclusively pharmacological.

References

Adams, V., Miller, S., Craig, S., Sonam, Nyima, Droyoung, Le, P. V., & Varner, M. (2007). Informed consent in cross-cultural perspective: Clinical research in the Tibetan autonomous region, PRC. *Culture, Medicine & Psychiatry, 31,* 445–472.

Alverson, H. S., Drake, R. E., Carpenter-Song, E. A., Chu, E., Ritsma, M., & Smith, B. (2007). Ethnocultural variations in mental illness discourse: Some implications for building therapeutic alliances. *Psychiatric Services, 58,* 1541–1546.

Alvidrez, J., & Areán, P. A. (2002). Psychosocial treatment research with ethnic minority populations: Ethical considerations in conducting clinical trials. *Ethics & Behavior, 12,* 103–116.

American Psychiatric Association. (1994). *Diagnostic and statistical manual of mental disorders (DSM-IV)* (4th ed.). Washington, DC: Author.

American Psychiatric Association. (2006). *The principles of medical ethics with annotations especially applicable to psychiatry.* Arlington, VA: Author.

American Psychological Association. (1992). *Ethical principles of psychologists and code of conduct.* Washington, DC: Author.

American Psychological Association. (2002). *Guidelines on multicultural education, training, research, practice, and organizational change for psychologists.* Washington, DC: Author.

Anzaldúa, G. (1999). *Borderlands/La frontera: The new mestiza* (2nd ed.). San Francisco, CA: Aunt Lute Books.

Barnett, J. E., Wise, E. H., Johnson-Greene, D., & Bucky, S. F. (2007). Informed consent: Too much of a good thing or not enough? *Professional Psychology: Research and Practice, 38,* 179–186.

Barnhardt, R., & Kawagley, A. O. (2005). Indigenous knowledge systems and Alaska: Native ways of knowing. *Anthropology & Education Quarterly, 36,* 8–23.

Belmont Report. (1979). *Ethical principles and guidelines for the protection of human subjects research.* Washington, DC: U.S. Department of Health, Education, & Welfare.

Berg, J. W., Appelbaum, P. S., Lidz, C. W., & Parker, L. S. (2001). *Informed consent: Legal theory and clinical practice.* New York: Oxford University Press.

Bernal, G. (2006). Intervention development and cultural adaptation research with diverse families. *Family Process, 45,* 143–151.

Bernal, G., Bonilla, J., & Bellido, C. (1995). Ecological validity and cultural sensitivity for outcome research: Issues for the cultural adaptation and development of psychosocial treatments with Hispanics. *Journal of Abnormal Child Psychology, 23,* 67–82.

Bernal, G., Jiménez-Chafey, M.I., & Domenech Rodríguez, M.M. (2009). Cultural adaptation of evidence-based treatments for ethno-cultural youth. *Professional Psychology: Research and Practice, 40,* 361–368.

Bernal, G., & Sáez-Santiago, E. (2006). Culturally centered psychosocial interventions. *Journal of Community Psychology, 34,* 121–132.

Bernal, G., & Scharrón-del Río, M. R. (2001) Are empirically supported treatments (EST) valid for ethnic minorities? *Cultural Diversity and Ethnic Minority Psychology, 7,* 328–342.

Brainard, J. (2003, January 17). Study finds research consent forms difficult to comprehend. *Chronicle of Higher Education,* p. A21.

Casillas, D. M. (2006). *Evolving research approaches in tribal communities: A community empowerment training.* Unpublished master's thesis, University of South Dakota, Vermillion, SD.

Castellano, M. B. (2004). Ethics of aboriginal research. *Journal of Aboriginal Health, 1,* 98–114.

Colla, J., Buka, S., Harrington, D., & Murphy, J. M. (2006). Depression and modernization. *Social Psychiatry & Psychiatric Epidemiology, 41,* 271–279.

Council of National Psychological Associations for the Advancement of Ethnic Minority Interests. (2000). *Guidelines for research in ethnic minority communities.* Washington, DC: American Psychological Association.

Faden, R. R., & Beauchamp, T. L. (1986). *A history and theory of informed consent.* New York: Oxford University Press.

Fine, M. (2006). Bearing witness: Methods for researching oppression and resistance—A textbook for critical research. *Social Justice Research, 19,* 83–108.

Fisher, C. B. (1999). *Relational ethics and research with vulnerable populations. Reports on research involving persons with mental disorders that may affect decision making capacity* (Vol. 2, pp. 29–49). Rockville, MD: Commissioned Papers by the National Bioethics Advisory Commission.

Fisher, C. B. (2002). Participant consultation: Ethical insights into parental permission and confidentiality procedures for policy relevant research with youth. In R. M. Lerner, F. Jacobs, & D. Wertlieb (Eds.), *Handbook of applied developmental science* (Vol. 4, pp. 371–396). Thousand Oaks, CA: Sage.

Fisher, C. B., Hoagwood, K., Boyce, C., Duster, T., Frank, D. A., Grisso, T., et al. (2002). Research ethics for mental health science involving ethnic minority children and youths. *American Psychologist, 57,* 1024–1040.

Goodenough, W. H. (1980). Ethnographic field techniques. In H. C. Triandis & J. W. Berry (Eds.), *Handbook of cross-cultural psychology. Methodology* (Vol. 2, pp. 39–55). Boston: Allyn & Bacon.

Gostin, L. O. (1995). Informed consent, cultural sensitivity, and respect for persons. *Journal of the American Medical Association, 274,* 844–845.

Gross, B. H. (2001). Informed consent. *Annals of the American Psychotherapy Association, 4,* 24–24.

Hawthorne, S. (2007). Land, bodies, and knowledge: Biocolonialism of plants, indigenous peoples, women, and people with disabilities. *Signs, 32,* 314–323.

Hendricks, L. (2004, February 28). Havasupai file $25M suit vs. ASU. *Arizona Daily Sun*, p. A1.

Hill, J. S. (2005). *Decolonizing personality assessment: An examination of the Minnesota Multiphasic Personality Inventory – 2*. Unpublished doctoral dissertation, University of Oklahoma, OK.

Hill, J. S., Muñoz, V. I., & Correia, M. (2007). *Still centering the margins: Assimilation, pressure, resistance, and transformation in psychology education*. Paper Presentation to the AERA Annual Meeting, Chicago, IL.

Hill, J. S., Pace, T. M., & Robbins, R. R. (in press). Decolonizing personality assessment and honoring Indigenous voices: A critical examination of the MMPI-2. *Cultural Diversity and Ethnic Minority Psychology*.

Kaljevic, T., & VandeCreek, L. (2006). Cultural considerations of informed consent. *Psychotherapy Bulletin, 41*, 43–46.

Kim, U., Park, Y., & Park, D. (2000). The challenge of cross-cultural psychology: The role of the indigenous psychologies. *Journal of Cross-Cultural Psychology, 31*, 63–75.

Martín-Baró, I., & Blanco Abarca, A. (1998). *Psicología de la liberación*. Madrid: Editorial Trotta.

Mohatt, G. V., & Thomas, L. R. (2005). "I wonder, why would you do it that way?" Ethical dilemmas in doing participatory research with Alaska Native communities. In J. E. Trimble & C. B. Fisher (Eds.), *Handbook of ethical and responsible research with ethnocultural populations and communities* (pp. 93–115). Thousand Oaks, CA: Sage.

Molyneux, C. S., Wassenaar, D. R., Peshu, N., & Marsh, K. (2005). 'Even if they ask you to stand by a tree all day, you will have to do it (laughter). . .!' Community voices on the notion and practice of informed consent for biomedical research in developing countries. *Social Science & Medicine, 61*, 443–454.

Morin, E. (1984). *Ciencia con consciencia*. Barcelona: Anthropos.

Nama, N., & Swartz, L. (2002). Ethical and social dilemmas in community-based controlled trials in situations of poverty: A view from a South African project. *Journal of Community & Applied Social Psychology, 12*, 286–297.

National Health and Medical Research Council (NHMRC). (2003). *Values and ethics: guidelines for ethical conduct in Aboriginal and Torres Strait Islander health research*. Canbera, Australia: Author.

Nelson, T. D., & Steele, R. G. (2006). Beyond efficacy and effectiveness: A multifaceted approach to treatment evaluation. *Professional Psychology: Research and Practice, 37*, 389–397.

Norton, I. M., & Manson, S. M. (1996). Research in American Indian and Alaska Native communities: Navigating the cultural universe of values and process. *Journal of Consulting and Clinical Psychology, 64*, 856–860.

Parker, G., Gladstone, G., & Chee, K. T. (2001). Depression in the planet's largest ethnic group: The Chinese. *American Journal of Psychiatry, 158*, 857–864.

Potts, K., & Brown, L. A. (2005). Becoming an anti-oppressive researcher. In L. A. Brown & S. Strega (Eds.), *Research as resistance: Critical, indigenous and anti-oppressive approaches* (p. 303). Toronto: Canadian Scholars' Press.

Reid, P. T. (2002). Multicultural psychology: Bringing together gender and ethnicity. *Cultural Diversity and Ethnic Minority Psychology, 8*(2), 103–114.

Rosselló, J., & Bernal, G. (1999). The efficacy of cognitive-behavioral and interpersonal treatments for depression in Puerto Rican adolescents. *Journal of Consulting and Clinical Psychology, 67*, 734–745.

Rosselló, J., Bernal, G., & Rivera-Medina, C. (2008). Individual and group CBT and IPT for Puerto Rican adolescents with depressive symptoms. *Cultural Diversity and Ethnic Minority Psychology, 14*, 234–245.

Shaibu, S. (2007). Ethical and cultural considerations in informed consent in Botswana. *Nursing Ethics, 14*, 503–509.

Smith, L. T. (1999). *Decolonizing methodologies: Research and indigenous peoples.* New York: Zed Books.

Smith, L. T. (2005). On tricky ground: Researching the Native in the age of uncertainty. In N. K. Denzin & Y. S. Lincoln (Eds.), *Handbook of qualitative research* (3rd ed., pp. 85–107). Thousand Oaks, CA: Sage.

Snyder, T. A., & Barnett, J. E. (2006). Informed consent and the process of psychotherapy. *Psychotherapy Bulletin, 41*, 37–42.

Trickett, E. J., & Birman, D. (1989). Taking ecology seriously: A community development approach to individually-based interventions. In L. Bond, & B. Compas (Eds.), *Primary prevention and promotion in the schools* (pp. 361–390). Newbury Park, CA: Sage.

Trickett, E. J., Kelly, J. G., & Vincent, T. A. (1985). The spirit of ecological inquiry in community research. In E. Susskind & D. Klein (Eds.), *Community research: Methods, paradigms, and applications.* New York: Praeger.

Trimble, J. E., & Fisher, C. B. (Eds.). (2005). *Handbook of ethical and responsible research with ethnocultural populations and communities.* Thousand Oaks, CA: Sage.

Trimble, J. E., & Mohatt, G. V. (2005). Coda: The virtuous and responsible researcher in another culture. In J. E. Trimble & C. B. Fisher (Eds.), *Handbook of ethical and responsible research with ethnocultural populations and communities* (pp. 325–334). Thousand Oaks, CA: Sage.

Universal Declaration of Ethical Principles for Psychologists. (n.d.). Retrieved October 14, 2009, from the International Union of Psychological Science Web site: http://www.am.org/iupsys.

U.S. Department of Health and Human Services. (1991, revised 2001, August). *Title 45 public welfare, part 46, code of federal regulations, Protection of human subjects.* Washington, DC: Author.

II

Self-Silencing and Depression Across Cultures

Introduction

On the Critical Importance of Relationships for Women's Well-Being

Judith Jordan

Women's desire for connection with others, often portrayed as a sign of their "weakness"—that they are too needy and too dependent—is being viewed in a new light. The ways in which women take responsibility for and encourage growth in children, among friends, and in primary pairings are increasingly understood as making essential contributions to the human community. They are also being reframed as signs of strength (Gilligan, 1982; Miller, 1976). As several chapters in this section demonstrate, various pathways to connection can serve to foster women's growth, interpersonal development, and overall health.

Until the 1980s, mainstream Western psychological theory failed to accurately represent the psychology of women. Based on studies of men, psychological maturity was portrayed by characteristics such as separation, autonomy, independence, and the capacity for logical thought. According to these standards, women had fallen short (Broverman, Broverman, Clarkson, Rosenkrantz, & Vogel, 1970; Comstock, 2005). They were viewed as too emotional, irrational, overly sensitive, and too contextual. In the field of psychology, this led to pathologizing women in gender-biased ways (Caplan & Cosgrove, 2004; Kaplan, 1983). In *Toward a New Psychology of Women*, Jean Baker Miller (1976) challenged existing trends that saw women's need for relationships as a sign of deficiency. Miller began to reframe relational traits such as empathy, participating in the growth of others, caring, and compassion as signs of strength and as essential for the well-being of all human beings.

Miller's work arose from clinical settings where she observed that women were misunderstood by existing theory; she suggested it was time for people to listen to women to find out from them what they valued, how they grew, and what concerned them. Miller and subsequently Miller's colleagues at the Stone Center (Jordan, Kaplan, Miller, Stiver, & Surrey, 1991) noted that relationships are at the center of women's lives. Relational-Cultural Theory (RCT), developed at the Stone Center by Miller, Jordan, Stiver, and Surrey (Jordan, 1997; Jordan, Kaplan, Miller, Stiver, & Surrey, 1991; Jordan, Walker, & Hartling, 2004; Miller & Stiver, 1997), is a value-laden, justice-oriented theory. It strongly asserts the importance of relationships to women and to men. But it acknowledges that women have borne the major responsibility for the forming and maintaining of relationships. It also points to the ways in which the unequal distribution of power distorts relationships and leads to chronic disconnections and disempowerment around race, sexual orientation, class, and other stratifying social factors. It seeks to rewrite psychological theory, moving from a separate-self psychology to a relational psychology.

At the same time that the Relational-Cultural Theorists were reworking an understanding of the psychology of women, Carol Gilligan was developing a similar picture of women's development (Gilligan, 1982). In an academic setting, her research on moral development created an understanding of the ethic of care, long seen as associated with women and therefore considered as less developed than an ethic of "rights." Using the metaphor of voice, rather than self, Gilligan also emphasized the importance of listening to women's experiences and finding the ways they lost voice and confidence. Gilligan, too, worked with colleagues in developing her theory (Brown, 1998; Jack, 1991; Ward, 2000). Both Gilligan's and Miller's groups were coming to similar conclusions: People grow through and toward relationships throughout the lifespan (Jordan, 1986).

The usual trajectory of psychological development prevalent in dominant theories emphasized movement toward independence, characterized by an attitude of, "You're born alone and you die alone." Psychodynamic theorists emphasized that psychic structure is internalized and then is supposed to operate "independent of context." Thus, Freud (1957) addressed the process of creating ego where id was, and Kohut (1984) spoke of the importance of developing internal structures to regulate self-cohesion and self-esteem. In the ideal developmental paths envisioned by these systems, self-esteem regulation should be internalized; moral judgments should be dictated by a system of rights; the "self" is made safe by building solid boundaries and gaining power over others; and mature functioning is characterized by independence and the capacity to engage in competitive and aggressive action motivated by self-interest. The notions of separation, autonomy, and competition conveniently supported (and emanated from) the values of the twentieth-century capitalist, hyperindividualistic culture of the United States. Social psychologists have noted that in the United States, psychological theories put a much higher premium on the separate self than in any other culture (Markus & Kitayama, 1991). Characteristic of these approaches, the value systems influencing the theory building were kept invisible and the mantle of scientific objectivity clouded their contextuality.

Despite surrounding contexts that tend to devalue the importance of connection, women around the world are the carriers for the well-being of relationships. Their very sense of who they are is formed in and grows through relationships. Motherhood is a defining achievement for many women, and almost universally women are the primary caretakers for children, often attempting to protect them from famine, wars, and other violations. Their relationships with partners, male or female, are often at the core of their sense of who they are (Miller & Stiver, 1997). Friendships play a vital role in women's lives: Sanchez-Hucles (2003) notes that within women's friendships, "women receive validation, liberation, empowerment, and a greater sense of their own worth and ability to be self-determining in spite of societal pressures" (p. 120).

There is a need not only to enjoy the benefits of relationships for oneself but also to contribute to the well-being of others—a need for mutuality. While other developmental models acknowledge the importance of "attachment," this is largely viewed as a one-way process: We are seen as needing "supplies" from others (Bowlby, 1988; Goleman, 2006), we need others to serve as a secure base (Bowlby, 1988), or we use them as mirroring self-objects (Kohut, 1984). In fact, there are increasing data that we have a need to participate in the growth of others as much as we need to be beneficiaries of others' interest in us. In growth-fostering relationships, both people grow and are changed (Jordan, 1986). Neurological data now confirm that mutuality occurs at a neurobiological level (Goleman, 2006; Schore, 1994). The emphasis on mutuality and on the power of the larger social context to shape individual development constitute two of the major differences between Relational-Cultural Theory and other attachment-oriented or relational paradigms.

All relationships are characterized by disconnections and misunderstandings. When these disconnections are addressed in the relationship, when the more powerful person specifically and empathically responds to the person who is hurt, stronger connections are forged. When, however, the more powerful person is unresponsive or responds negatively with anger, denial, or humiliating and violating actions, the disconnection becomes chronic. The injured person feels she cannot bring her full experience into the relationship and begins to keep more and more of herself out of the relationship. Authenticity suffers and the mutuality of the relationship is altered. Over time, the person begins to develop strategies of disconnection, keeping more and more of her authentic responses hidden and out of the relationship. Sometimes this turns into shame and a sense of being deeply flawed. It always involves a sense of isolation and a loss of voice.

The disempowerment, silencing, and suffering that goes with the isolation of chronic disconnection is a core source of human suffering. What Miller (1976) called "condemned isolation" can set in, which is a state of feeling outside the human community, unacceptable, immobilized, and self-blaming. It is akin to a profound feeling of shame in which we feel others cannot possibly respond empathically to us (Jordan, 1989). Relationships are drained of their vitality and a pervasive sense of aloneness takes over. Condemned isolation occurs at both the individual level and the social level. Groups marginalized by shaming, nonresponsiveness, and stratification suffer in their sense of unworthiness and disempowerment. The systematic use of shaming and isolation is a powerful form of social control, whether by abusing partners or dominant societal groups. "Isolation is the glue that holds oppression in place" (Laing, 1998).

When RCT theorists speak of the necessity of mutually empathic connection in people's lives, they are not just referring to the "feel good" relationships of warm and cozy friendships or partnering. They are also referring to the relationships that connect us across difference. "Good conflict" in relationships is celebrated, where people can represent and learn from difference. Miller suggested that anger is a vital part of authentic relationships and growth; it is, in fact, around the negotiation of difference that the most powerful growth occurs. Dana Jack has similarly looked at the ways in which anger restores connection and silencing anger can take one to the disconnection of inauthenticity, what she calls "false self" and depression (1991, 1999, 2003).

Growth-fostering relationships are not always harmonious: Robust connection depends on developing patterns of "good conflict," which, for women, is complicated. The dominant culture does not welcome protest or expression of difference from the nondominants; women are not supposed to be angry. Miller (1976) suggested that they are given the cultural role of "quintessential accommodators." I remember in my own professional training, I was seen as a "nice," empathic therapist. But some supervisors suggested I needed to "get in touch with my aggression." Many years later, as a staff member at this same training institution and an outspoken feminist critic of many of its practices, I was described by one of these same supervisors as, "What an angry woman!" Too much or too little, it's very hard to "do anger" correctly if you're a woman. But anger is essential to addressing injuries and working toward personal and social justice.

RCT points to the need for social justice, where differences are not stratified and punished but where people stretch to meet one another and grow around the difference they find. RCT supports people in staying authentically connected to their own experience as they respond to another's experience. Movement toward mutually respectful relationships is movement away from oppressive and destructive connections. In fact, growth-fostering relationships lead to an experience of what Miller and Stiver (1997) called "the five good things": zest, clarity, a sense of worth, productivity, and a desire for more connection. Mutual empathy and mutual empowerment contribute to the development of these qualities.

When feminist psychologists first began to articulate a new psychology of women, by women and for women, many of their early formulations were met with derision. "Bedrock" principles of psychological development had determined that individuals grow toward self-sufficiency, independence, stronger intrapsychic structure, and less dependence on others (Broverman et al., 1970; Pollack, 1998), characteristics that were valued in the wider society.

Recent research has begun to erode the traditional view of separateness and to provide data supporting the contentions of these early relational pioneers.

Resnick and colleagues' (1997) study of 12,000 adolescents demonstrated that the single most important factor in preventing suicide, substance abuse, and violence in teenagers, across demographics, was having a good relationship with one adult. Shelly Taylor and colleagues (2000), experts in stress research, began a revision of our understanding of reactions to stress that has had great impact. Looking at the "bedrock" theory of "fight or flight" in response to stress, Taylor noticed that almost all of these data were collected on male organisms: male albino rats, macaque monkeys, and humans. When these stress studies were replicated using female organisms, quite a different pattern emerged. The females congregated and reached out to one another in the face of stress (depending on species it could be, for example, grooming or phoning a friend). Taylor called this the "tend and befriend" response to stress. These data strongly supported the call from both Miller and Gilligan to listen to and learn from girls, women, and even female rats! And it revealed the gender biases nestling deep in even the most trusted and "objective" of theories.

The most recent validation of the power of relationships in people's lives comes from the field of neuroscience. The newest neurobiology data have made abundantly clear that relationships literally shape one's brain and are essential for human growth and well-being. The brain is hardwired to connect; we are born with strong empathic potential (Schore, 1994; Siegel, 1999). We are wired to feel pain when we are socially excluded; in fact, the anticipation of social exclusion leads to a firing in the anterior cingulate, the area of the brain that registers both physical and social pain. Being left out, being marginalized personally or as part of a social group is experienced as real pain (Eisenberger & Lieberman, 2004). In addition to helping us understand the pain of individual isolation, this work helps us appreciate the suffering that occurs with social marginalization and oppression.

Growth-fostering human connection is the sustenance of psychological development. New studies underscore that psychological development involves mutuality: Our brains grow in mutually empathic exchanges (Schore, 1994). Mirror neurons underlie empathic responsiveness to one another. Mirror neurons are designed to fire in response to others. The early research indicated that when monkeys observed other monkeys grasping a cup, the exact same pathways of neurons lit up in the observing and observed monkeys. In humans, mirror neurons likely function to lead us to "feel with" another person, to tear up when we see them cry, to respond in kind to their responses. In empathic engagement between two people, both people's brains are being sculpted and changed. For example, when functional magnetic resonance images are done of people engaged in empathic interactions, there is mutual firing and mutual growth in the social centers of the brain (Goleman, 2006). Both people are affected and grow. No doubt when people are treated respectfully and empathically in terms of social identity, growth is encouraged, whereas exclusion and scorn create debilitating disconnections and disempowerment. Ultimately, abusive treatment and neglect kill off brain neurons. Studies document the pruning (loss) of neurons in response to abuse or neglect (Banks, 2000; Goleman, 2006). Taken together, these findings demonstrate that our neurobiology predisposes us to responsive, empathic engagement with others (Cozolino, 2006).

Maureen Walker (personal communication) often asks this question of any theory: "Who tells the story and who does the telling serve?" Let's name our values, take responsibility for them, and allow people to see how they influence our theory. Our culture pays lip service to relationships but continues to trivialize the profound importance of connections in people's lives. The field of psychology has contributed to this practice in its overemphasis on independence and separation and its tendency to characterize the desire for closeness as a regressive need. In fact, our desire for connection and our ability to evolve in the direction of true mutuality in relationships is based on complex human motivation and capabilities. In putting relationships, not self, at the center, we move beyond the typical paradigms of altruism versus egoism:

> Both people contribute to, and both are sustained by, grow in, and depend on the relationship. People do not just come together to 'give' or 'take' or trade off dependencies. They create relationships together to which they both contribute and in which they both can grow. At its best, this kind of relationship goes beyond the duality of self and other and describes true community and relational interdependence. (Jordan, 1986, p. 4)

Personally, I believe that the world, filled with fear and hostilities, is finding that the old paradigm of separation, competition, and gaining power over others in order to find safety simply isn't working. We are hardwired to connect; we are ultimately deeply interdependent. But our social conditioning toward separation and independence puts us at odds with our very biology. This creates profound stress. To disavow our inevitable vulnerability is to distort human experience. In honoring connections—our real need for one another—and in valuing the development of kindness, compassion, and profound respect, we create hope. The more we can spread the message of the power of connection, the more safe the world will be. And the more we will all find creative and life-affirming voices and action.

References

Banks, A. (2000). PTSD: *Post-traumatic stress disorder: Relationship and brain chemistry. Project report, No. 8.* Wellesley, MA: Stone Center Working Paper Series.

Bowlby, J. (1988). *A secure base.* New York: Basic Books.

Broverman, I. K., Broverman, D. M., Clarkson, F. E., Rosenkrantz, P. S., & Vogel, S. R. (1970). Sex role stereotypes and clinical judgments of mental health. *Journal of Consulting and Clinical Psychology, 34,* 1–7.

Brown, L. M. (1998). *Raising their voices: The politics of girls' anger.* Cambridge, MA: Harvard University Press.

Caplan, P., & Cosgrove, L. (2004). *Bias in psychiatric diagnosis.* New York: Jason Aronson.

Comstock, D. (Ed.). (2005). *Diversity and development: Critical contexts that shape our lives and relationships.* Belmont, CA: Brooks/Cole.

Cozolino, L. (2006). *The neuroscience of human relationships: Attachment and the developing social brain.* New York: W.W. Norton.

Eisenberger, N., & Lieberman, M. (2004). Why rejection hurts: A common neural alarm system for physical and social pain. *Trends in Cognitive Sciences, 8,* 294–300.

Freud, S. (1957). The future prospects of psychoanalytic therapy. In J. Strachey (Ed.), *The standard edition of the complete psychological works of Sigmund Freud* (Vol. 2, pp. 139–152). London: Howarth Press.

Gilligan, C. (1982). *In a different voice: Psychological theory and women's development.* Cambridge, MA: Harvard University Press.

Goleman, D. (2006). *Social intelligence: The new science of human relationships.* New York: Bantam Books.

Jack, D. C. (1991). *Silencing the self: Women and depression.* Cambridge, MA: Harvard University Press.

Jack, D. C. (1999). *Behind the mask: Destruction and creativity in women's aggression.* Cambridge, MA: Harvard University Press.

Jack, D. C. (2003). The anger of hope and the anger of despair: How anger relates to women's depression. In J. M. Stoppard & L. M. McMullen (Eds.), *Situating sadness: Women and depression in social context.* New York: New York University Press.

Jordan, J. V. (1986). *The meaning of mutuality. Work in progress, No 23.* Wellesley, MA: Stone Center Working Paper Series.

Jordan, J. V. (1989). *Relational development: Therapeutic implications of empathy and shame. Work in progress, No 39.* Wellesley, MA: Stone Center Working Paper Series.

Jordan, J. V. (Ed.). (1997). *Women's growth in diversity.* New York: Guilford.

Jordan, J. V., Kaplan, A., Miller, J. B., Stiver, I., & Surrey, J. (1991). *Women's growth in connection.* New York: Guilford.

Jordan, J. V., Walker, M., & Hartling, L. (Eds.). (2004) *The complexity of connection: Writings from the Stone Center's Jean Baker Miller Training Institute.* New York: Guilford.

Kaplan, M. (1983). A woman's view of DSM-III. *American Psychologist, 38,* 786–792.

Kohut, H. (1984). *How does analysis cure?* Chicago: University of Chicago Press.

Laing, K. (1998). *In pursuit of parity: Teachers as liberators.* Katalyst Workshop Held at the World Trade Center, Boston, MA.

Markus, H. R., & Kitayama, S. (1991). Culture and the self: Implications for cognition, emotion, and motivation. *Psychological Review, 96,* 224–235.

Miller, J. B. (1976). *Toward a new psychology of women.* Boston: Beacon Press.

Miller, J. B., & Stiver, I. (1997). *The healing connection: How women form relationships in therapy and in life.* Boston: Beacon Press.

Pollack, W. (1998). *Real boys: Rescuing our sons from the myths of boyhood.* New York: Random House.

Resnick, M., Bearman, S., Blum, R., Bauman, K., Harris, K., James, J., et al. (1997). Protecting adolescents from harm: Findings from the national longitudinal study on adolescent health. *Journal of the American Medical Association, 278,* 226–236.

Sanchez-Hucles, J. (2003). Intimate relationships. In L. Slater, J. H. Daniels, & A. Banks (Eds.), *The complete guide to mental health for women*. Boston: Beacon Press.

Schore, A. (1994). *Affect regulation and the origin of the self: The neurobiology of emotional development*. Hillsdale, NJ: Erlbaum.

Siegel, D. J. (1999). *The developing mind: How relationships and the brain interact to shape who we are*. New York: Guilford Press.

Taylor, S., Klein, L., Lewis, B., Gruenwald, T., Guring, R., & Updegraff, J. (2000). Biobehavioral responses to stress in females: Tend-and-befriend, not fight-or-flight. *Psychological Review, 107*, 411–429.

Ward, J. (2000). *The skin we're in: Teaching our children to be emotionally strong, socially smart, spiritually connected*. New York: The Free Press.

5

Women's Self-Silencing and Depression in the Socio-cultural Context of Germany

Tanja Zoellner and Susanne Hedlund

Women's Depression Rates in Germany

Depression rates in Germany are comparable to depression rates in other Western developed nations, especially the United States, with lifetime prevalence estimates ranging from 9% (Wittchen, Essau, van Zerssen, Krieg, & Zaudig, 1992) to almost 15% (Jacobi et al., 2004) for the general population. Despite variations in lifetime prevalence estimates for major depression across countries in different studies (Jacobi et al., 2005), the 2:1 female-to-male sex ratio is strikingly consistent cross-culturally (e.g., Gater et al., 1998; Kessler, McGonagle, Nelson, et al., 1994), including Germany (Jacobi et al., 2004).

Until recently, prevalence estimates of mental disorders in Germany could only be extrapolated from various smaller and regionally limited studies (Fichter, 1990; Wittchen & van Zerssen, 1987; Wittchen, Müller, & Storz, 1998). These studies have suggested lifetime prevalence rates of 8% to 10% for men and 20% to 26% for women in Germany's adult population. However, recently, the first nationally representative survey of mental disorders in Germany assessing the prevalence of mental disorders by employing a fully structured and standardized instrument (the Munich-Composite International Diagnostic Interview [M-CIDI]) has been conducted: the Mental Health Supplement of the German National Health Interview and Examination Survey (GHS-MHS) (Jacobi et al., 2002; Wittchen, Nelson, & Lachner, 1998). For the first time, the GHS-MHS provides reliable lifetime and 12-month prevalence estimates.

The core survey was based on a stratified, nationally representative sample of 130 sites all over Germany and was administered to a total of over 7,000 individuals aged 18 to 79 years (Jacobi, 2003). Results revealed that 17.3% of the population (women: 23.5%; men: 11.1%) met criteria for any unipolar depressive disorder defined as any major depressive disorder and/or dysthymic disorder at least once during their life course. Moreover, 10.9% were diagnosed as having had any unipolar depressive disorder in the past 12 months (women: 14.2%; men: 7.6%). Clinically significant depressive symptoms were even more widespread: 25% of the population reported having experienced lifetime depressive symptoms—nearly one-third (31.7%) of the female and 18.4% of the male population. A comparison of the genders revealed that the sex ratio of 2:1 (women to men) applies only to single episodes of major depressive disorder, with lifetime prevalences of 12.3% for women and 6.3% for men. Lifetime prevalences for dysthymic disorder were 5.8% for women and 3.3% for men. Gender differences became even larger for recurrent major depressive disorder: 8.4% of the female population compared to 2.7% of the male population have suffered from recurrent major depressive disorder during their lifetime. These prevalence rates are similar to data reported from the Netherlands (Bijl, Ravelli, & van Zerssen, 1998) and the United States (Kessler, McGonagle, Zhao, et al., 1994; Kessler et al., 2003), all studies using comparable designs and instruments (Jacobi, 2003). Due to the lack of reliable empirical data for earlier time periods in Germany and elsewhere, it remains unknown whether depression rates for women have risen, declined, or stayed the same in the last decades, which makes it hard to link sociocultural changes to potential changes in depression rates.

The Sociocultural Context for Women in Germany

By and large, Germany as a modern Western European country is comparable to other industrialized countries with regard to the development of women's roles and rights in society. Starting in the 1970s, the women's movement successfully began addressing gender inequalities in German society such as abortion rights, women's access to education, and violence against women. The movement has raised awareness of women's equal rights in all personal and societal affairs. Nowadays, girls and young women can take their equal status and equal access to all societal opportunities for granted. Feminist theory is not deemed necessary anymore and is not discussed widely. However, most people would agree that gender equality has not yet been reached fully. Probably comparable to movements in the United States, there has been a recent setback in the sense of a growing tendency to subscribe to neo-bourgeois values. Popular journalists propose a return to traditional gender roles where women get back to their "original and natural" abilities of caring for others full time in order to stabilize and even "save" society. At the same time, however, many modern women and men voice egalitarian attitudes emphasizing equal chances and widely overlapping characteristics and strengths of the sexes. Popular and successful women nowadays represent a new, self-assured, positive, and life-affirming feminism (Dorn, 2006).

Social norms regarding gender roles and influencing women's self-silencing behavior have also changed over the generations. Starting with the feminist movement in the 1970s, there is now a culturally shared "egalitarian" norm of relationship and family formation (Huinink & Mayer, 1995) with an ideal "to talk about everything" in an intimate relationship. Sociological studies show, however, that there is still a great gap between the ideal and reality (Seidenspinner & Keddi, 1994). Germany compares negatively with countries such as France, Finland, or Denmark regarding speed of societal change and persistence of conservative attitudes toward women, especially toward working mothers, facts that are reflected by specific societal and legal conditions in Germany.

For example, until 1977, there was a legally prescribed role division between husband and wife in marriage, with the wife being responsible for leading the household and the husband for earning the family income. Simultaneously, a husband could prevent his wife from taking paid employment (Federal Ministry for Youth, Family Affairs, Women, & Health, 1989). Brückner (2004) showed how the institutional environment and social policy in Germany have maintained and even produced gender inequalities originating from gender biases in the labor market and from the traditional division of labor in families. The single (male) breadwinner family model still constitutes the implicit normative basis for the social security, tax, and health insurance systems. "Part of the generosity of the public pension, welfare and insurance system lies in the fact that entitlements extend to any dependents a worker may have. Public health insurance covers a nonworking spouse and children at no additional cost" (Brückner, 2004, p. 22), and unemployment benefits take dependents into account. In contrast, a second wage in the family is taxed very high. This explains why, "unless a woman has a high wage, it may simply be not worth the trouble to go work when the net gain for the family is negligible" (p. 25). Despite these discouraging structural conditions for married women to be employed, most women without children go to work outside the home.

The public recognition of women as equals, the normality of women's employment, and their almost equal educational status stand in sharp contrast to the sluggish change in social reality, especially in regard to working mothers. The structural conditions for parenthood and family life have only partially changed. The scarcity of day care centers for younger children and less than full-time kindergarten and school schedules make it hard or sometimes impossible to combine work commitment with child rearing (Huinink & Mayer, 1995). In consequence, the birth of the first child still leads in most cases to a comeback of the traditional family with the conventional labor division between the sexes: Men have a family; women live family. Fathers continue to pursue long-term occupational goals, whereas mothers are simply expected to sacrifice their career opportunities in order to take care of their children (Rerrich, 1988) and—in "logical" consequence—of their husbands and households (Ratzenböck, 1990).

After several years at home, women typically cannot reach higher positions anymore and German women tend to be employed only part time as long as children live at home. Few women in their late 40s or older are then able to gain full-time employment commensurate with their level of education. German husbands—with few exceptions—have so far shown little inclination to contribute a major, or even equal, share of housework and child care (Huinink & Mayer, 1995). This leads to the paradox that in Germany, we have one of the highest rates of highly educated women in Europe but one of the lowest employment rates for mothers: Only about 50% of mothers are employed part or full time (Eichhorst & Thode, 2002). Thus, half of German mothers automatically fulfill the criteria for one of the four main vulnerability factors for depression (Brown & Harris, 1978), that is, the lack of full- or part-time employment. One could call this a socially expected self-silencing with the implicit understanding that the mother sacrifices her wishes and hopes for her own life in favor of rearing the children. One would also expect that a second vulnerability factor—the presence at home of three or more children under the age of 14—applies to many German women. However, in spite of the ideal of motherhood, Germany has one of the lowest birth rates in Europe and very few women have three or more children.

Huinink and Mayer (1995) characterize women's dilemma in Germany as follows:

> Young women in Germany are confronted with hard choices between commitment to work and commitment to children.... If they commit themselves more to their family and children, they face losses in economic independence and old-age security. If they commit themselves more to work, they face lower incomes and shorter careers than men and they still have to deal with strong social norms favouring motherhood. (p. 195)

On the other hand, recent changes in family politics under chancellor Angela Merkel focus on improving the compatibility of paid employment and family care by supporting mothers to work outside the home even when they have small children. One important measure is the increase in the amount of day care centers for children under age 3. The country is split in this regard: The more progressive Germans consider this development timely for a country that wants to foster equal opportunity; more conservative Germans, on the other hand, evoke the destruction of the nuclear family and fear that mothers will be forced to have their children brought up by strangers. This skepticism toward nonparental care is probably rooted in the particular German version of idealization of motherhood.

Idealization of Motherhood

Even young women have internalized a particularly German ideal of the mother that is rooted deeply in German history (Vinken, 2002). It constitutes an unquestioned cultural intuition that the full-time presence of the mother at home during the first years of life is the indispensable precondition for raising emotionally healthy children. It seems self-evident in the culture that young children would be at a disadvantage if they were cared for by strangers most of the day or even by the father. There is a strong moral prejudice against putting children below age 3 into institutionalized care. At least until the children have reached age 3, mothers simply are expected to stay at home if at all possible. Women seem to accept this model willingly, but the suspicion of self-silencing with regard to hopes and dreams in the occupational realm definitely arises. Conversely, mothers of small children who work full time or even part time are considered bad mothers and confronted with the reproach of neglecting their children and being selfish. A Scandinavian female professional with a $3\frac{1}{2}$-year-old child returning to work full time was repeatedly asked by other mothers: "Don't you feel like a 'Rabenmutter' (raven-mother, very bad mother)?"—an expression that is missing from other European languages. A Turkish lawyer, Seyran A., a working mother of a 1-year-old daughter, talks about her impression of many German mothers: "As soon as the child is born, their lives are turned upside-down, they give up everything they have achieved for themselves, just to be with their children exclusively" (Dorn, 2006, p. 105, translated T.Z.). The difficult societal conditions for combining work with child rearing and the ideal of motherhood make being a full-time working mother of young children simply inconceivable. The ideal of motherhood, which is based on the ideal of self-sacrifice for one's children, is reflected in many young women's way of "planning" their career. The occupational counselor Utal Glaubitz observed that graduating girls who prepare to go to the university are preoccupied with the question of how to combine their work with family duties later on (Dorn, 2006). This is also a sign of women's self-silencing: They begin by putting their occupational interests second in order to comply with implicit societal demands regarding their role in the family.

Research has not addressed yet in what ways and to what extent the German obsession with a certain form of motherhood and its consequences for a woman's life course have affected rates of women's depression. However, doubts about being a good, caring mother constitute a frequent theme of depressed women who have children and who work outside the home.

Self-Silencing in Depressive, Agoraphobic, and Healthy Women

This section presents the main and relevant results of a quantitative, cross-sectional questionnaire study on self-silencing in German women (Zoellner, 1999). The study investigated self-silencing, attachment styles, fear of abandonment, comfort with closeness, and marital satisfaction, comparing clinically depressed women with clinically agoraphobic and healthy women. To our knowledge, it constitutes the first study on self-silencing behavior in Germany. The main aims were to confirm the relationship between women's self-silencing and depressive symptoms in a German sample and to test the specificity of self-silencing behavior for depression rather than for overall psychopathology in women.

The depressive group was recruited solely from inpatient hospitals and had been diagnosed as having a major depressive disorder (single episode or recurrent) by licensed psychotherapists. The agoraphobic group was recruited in part from inpatient hospitals and in part from a self-help organization and fulfilled the *Diagnostic and Statistical Manual of Mental Disorders*, fourth edition (DSM-IV), criteria for agoraphobia with or without panic disorder according to the Panic and Agoraphobia Scale (PAS; German version by Bandelow, 1997). The healthy sample was a convenience sample. Demographically, healthy and depressive women were more similar to each other than to the agoraphobic women. Mean ages were 48 (depressed), 46 (healthy), and 32 (agoraphobic), $SD = $ 7 to 10 years. All healthy women, most depressive women, but only one-third of agoraphobic women were married; the others lived in a cohabiting partnership. Mean relationship duration was about 20 years for depressive and healthy women and 8.5 years for agoraphobic women. The majority of women in all the three samples were employed (68% to 82%). Most depressed and most healthy women (85% to 90%) had children (one to three) compared to only 30% of agoraphobic women. The differences in number of children, relationship status, and relationship duration between agoraphobic women and the other two samples are probably due to an age artifact.

Results revealed highly elevated self-silencing scores for depressed women ($n = 19$) in the overall Silencing the Self Scale (STSS, German version by Zoellner, 1999; $M = 100.6$) that were comparable to those found in the sample of battered women by Jack and Dill (1992; $M = 99.9$). In contrast, healthy women ($n = 22$) had the lowest self-silencing scores ($M = 71.6$) and agoraphobic women ($n = 17$) scored in between ($M = 83.8$) (see Table 5.1). All group differences were highly significant.

To test the specificity of self-silencing for depression in women, it was necessary to compare depressive women with another clinical control group. The agoraphobic female sample was an obvious clinical control group and a rather hard test for the specificity of self-silencing for depression because there are sociocultural hypotheses on the emergence of agoraphobia in women that also stress traditional female role norms and traditional relationship arrangements as causative factors for the emergence of female agoraphobia (Kleiner & Marshall, 1985; Vandereycken, 1983). Therefore, elevated scores in self-silencing for agoraphobic women compared to healthy women were expected. An investigation of the subscales of the STSS detected interesting differences between the samples concerning the specificity of self-silencing for depression. Figure 5.1 shows that depressed women showed significantly higher scores in all

Table 5.1 Group Means and Group Comparisons in STSS Sum and Subscales

	Group				Group Comparisons			
	D	A	H		All	D vs. A	D vs. H	A vs. H
n	19	17	22		58	36	41	39
STSS Sum								
M	100.6	83.8	71.6	X^2	22.1***	—	—	—
SD	22	15.1	12.2	z	—	-2.4*	-4.***	-3.1*
Externalized Self-Perception								
M	19.6	20.9	14.0	X^2	20.7***	—	—	—
SD	5.8	4.0	3.8	z	—	-0.9	-3.5**	-4.2***
Care as Self-Sacrifice								
M	29.1	21.1	23.5	X^2	12.6**	—	—	—
SD	6.9	5.2	5.0	z	—	-3.2**	-2.6**	-1.4
Silencing the Self								
M	29.2	21.8	20.1	X^2	17.9***	—	—	—
SD	6.9	6.0	4.3	z	—	-3.1**	-4.0***	-0.9
Divided Self								
M	22.9	19.5	14.0	X^2	20.3***	—	—	—
SD	6.3	4.6	5.0	z	—	-1.7	-4.0***	-3.3**

Note: Due to the small sample size, the Bonferroni-corrected Kruskal-Wallis-test (X^2) as a nonparametric analysis of variance method was used for group comparisons. Mann-Whitney-U-tests (z) for specific group comparisons were used in an exploratory manner. D = depressive sample; A = agoraphobic sample; H = healthy sample.
* $p < 0.05$; ** $p < 0.01$; *** $p < 0.001$.

four subscales of the STSS compared to healthy women and significantly higher scores in the subscales Silencing the Self and Care as Self-Sacrifice compared to agoraphobic women (for statistical information, see Table 5.1).

In contrast, for agoraphobic women, only a high Externalized Self-Perception and, to a lesser degree, a Sense of a Divided Self were descriptive for this sample and led to an elevated overall STSS score compared to healthy women. In the core self-silencing subscales (i.e., Care as Self-Sacrifice and Silencing the Self), however, agoraphobic women showed relatively low scores, similar to healthy women. It seems as if the STSS measured significant clinical aspects of the experience for women with agoraphobia such as comparing oneself with outer standards and the feeling of a divided outer and inner self without tapping a self-silencing behavior in intimate relationships. Like healthy women, they did not show a behavior toward their partner that would be described as self-silencing. They neither thought that care means self-sacrifice nor did they try to inhibit their own emotions, thoughts, and behaviors in order to avoid conflict.

Qualitative data drawn from answers to the last STSS item that asked participants to list standards that they do not live up to (but wished to do so) further stressed the difference in the dynamics in agoraphobic women compared to

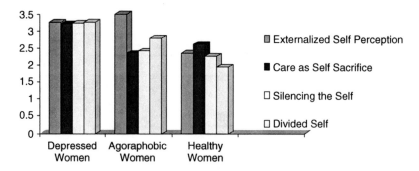

Figure 5.1 Differences in STSS subscales between the three samples.
Note: Subscale means were divided by number of their items for comparison reasons.

depressed women. The majority of agoraphobic women listed traditionally more "masculine" self-referring standards of independence, self-assurance, autonomy, perfectionism, good looks, education, and employment. They said, for example, I want "to be more independent, free and tolerant," "to be myself, articulate my opinion, lead the life I want to live," "to be thin, work without fear and be more stress resistant" (Zoellner, 1999, p. 69). Thus, sociocultural hypotheses on the traditional female role and traditional relationship arrangements as causative factors for the development of agoraphobia in women are not supported by these results.

Depressed women more often articulated standards of the good woman and wife that they thought they could not live up to. For example, one woman wrote, "I cannot satisfy my husband with my household work but I want to," another one said she wanted "to be a good woman and to have a good marriage," and another woman wrote, "I cannot be a good cook and housewife; I am not a good wife and I am not understanding enough" (p. 69). The answers of the depressed participants mirror the pressure on German women to fulfill a traditional female role model in addition to being a modern woman. The degree to which German women of today are still judged by how they fulfill their roles as wives and mothers is reflected in the depressed women's concerns and self-perceptions. Depressed women in general—including the participants of the study—feel guilty because they have not been able to function fully anymore in the household or family due to their depression. Most women in the study worked part time, so that they had to live with a tension between the ideal of motherhood and the reality of being a working mother; this seems to have created strong inner conflicts in particular for the depressed women in the study, who reacted with feelings of guilt.

The sample of psychologically healthy women seemed to cope better with the tensions between the ideal of motherhood and the reality of being a working mother: They did not describe standards that they would not be able to meet. The data do not permit causal reasoning with regard to depression and conflicts between work, family, and the ideal of motherhood. We cannot, at this point, decide whether these inner conflicts contribute to the development of depression or whether the content of rumination and guilt feelings in depressed women simply reflect gender-specific sociocultural norms.

These female voices also reveal the different concerns of depressed and agoraphobic women. Agoraphobic women raise concerns in regard to values of being strong and self-assured and having their own opinion, whereas depressed women more often raise relational concerns about their roles as caregivers and wives. The difference in values between depressed and agoraphobic women cannot be due to a cohort effect between the two samples (more individualistic values in the younger generation, i.e., in the agoraphobic women) as one could suppose, because the healthy female sample with the lowest self-silencing scores were as middle-aged as the depressed sample. However, the differences in the depressed and the agoraphobic sample may, in great part, be due to age differences that covary with differences in marital status, relationship duration, and number of children. On the other hand, 30% of the agoraphobic women had children and 30% were married, but none of them raised concerns about not fulfilling the "female role." The quantitative and few qualitative results, thus, confirm the specificity of two self-silencing subscales for female depression in Germany.

According to Jack (1991), a woman's self-silencing behavior in intimate relationships is not only influenced by socially prescribed gender roles but also motivated by an insecure attachment to her male partner and fear of a relationship break-up if she does not adhere to the image of the "good woman." Attachment theory claims that the quality of early mother attachment creates an internalized working model about self and self-in-relation, which later will influence partner relationships strongly: "There is a strong causal relationship between an individual's experience with his parents and his later capacity to make affectional bonds..." (Bowlby, 1987, p. 58). Longitudinal studies have supported this hypothesis of the influence of early attachment experiences on later adult cognitive representations of intimate relationships (e.g., Grossmann, Grossmann, Winter, & Zimmermann, 2002). The attachment style can be classified along the dimensions of Fear of Abandonment and Comfort with Closeness and Dependence so that three insecure and one secure attachment styles arise (Hazan & Shaver, 1990). Most probably, those insecurely attached women with strong fear of abandonment tend to show self-silencing behavior in intimate relationships because they have developed the belief that they are not loved for their own sake but have to meet the partner's expectations to a very high degree in order to maintain the relationship. To test this hypothesis, attachment styles (German version by Doll, Mentz, & Witte, 1995) and the attachment dimensions of Fear of Abandonment and Comfort with Closeness and Dependence (Adult Attachment Scale, German version by Friedlmeier, 1994) were also assessed.

As expected, healthy women's marriages resembled, in the majority of cases, a secure adult attachment, whereas most depressed and agoraphobic women's intimate relationships mirrored an insecure (either anxious-ambivalent or anxious-avoidant) attachment style. Results in the two attachment dimensions, that is, Fear of Abandonment and Comfort with Closeness and Dependence, confirmed these findings. Healthy women showed little fear of abandonment and a high level of comfort with closeness toward their husbands. In contrast, depressed women as well as agoraphobic women attained significantly higher scores in the Fear of Abandonment and significantly lower scores in Comfort with Closeness and Dependence dimensions, with no significant differences between the two clinical samples. Results of the correlational analyses corroborated Jack's propositions about the relation between self-silencing, relationship variables, and depth of depression as measured by the Beck Depression Inventory (BDI; German version by Hautzinger, Bailer, Worall, & Keller, 1994). In the overall sample, self-silencing was highly positively correlated with fear of abandonment ($r = .46$, $p < .01$) and with depth of depression ($r = .64$, $p < .01$). Relationship satisfaction as measured by the relationship assessment scale (RAS, German version by Sander & Boecker, 1993) correlated highly negatively with the STSS ($r = -.55$, $p < .01$).

In summary, results of this research project comparing self-silencing in depressed, agoraphobic, and healthy women supported propositions made by Jack's self-silencing theory with respect to depressed women (Jack, 1991). For the agoraphobic women, the elevated scores in overall self-silencing were solely due to highly elevated scores in only two subscales (Externalized Self Perception and Divided Self) and point to a different dynamic in agoraphobic women's relationship difficulties: They seem to be struggling with becoming more autonomous and strive for more independence rather than trying to fulfill sex role norms of the good woman. In contrast, results of the study suggest that self-silencing behavior is quite frequent in depressed women's intimate relationships and is related to an attachment style that is characterized by fear of abandonment and discomfort with closeness and dependence. The behaviors measured by two of four subscales that denote the core of the self-silencing concept, that is, Silencing the Self and Care as Self-Sacrifice, seem to be specific to women with depression.

Clinical Experience with Depressed Women

The results on depressed women's high level of self-silencing and the differing cognitive pattern in agoraphobic women correspond to our clinical experience as psychotherapists. In depressed women, self-silencing behavior is almost always present. The typical dynamics are as follows: Childhood experiences of not being heard, of needs or concerns not being taken as important, and of feelings of not being taken seriously result in a deep sense of insecurity. In consequence, as adults, these women typically hold back their innermost feelings and try to hide how small, miserable, and hurt they feel deeply inside. Due to early experiences of actual rejection when showing their innermost feelings, they also fear rejection as adults when speaking their minds. These women fear disregard or abandonment if the other person would get to know her "bad or weak real self." This notion is rooted in attachment theory and research. Bowlby (1988a) describes this process of internalization:

> The working models a child builds of his mother and her ways of communicating and behaving towards him, and a comparable model of his father, together with the complementary models of himself in interaction with each, are being built by a child during the first few years of his life and, it is postulated, soon become established as influential cognitive structures (Main, Kaplan, and Cassidy, 1985). The forms they take, the evidence reviewed strongly suggests, are based on the child's real-life experience of day-to-day interactions with his parents. Subsequently the models of himself that he builds reflect also the images that his parents have of him, images that are communicated not only by how each treats him but by what each *says* to him.... This means that the patterns of interaction to which the models lead, having become habitual, generalized, and largely unconscious, persist in a more or less uncorrected and unchanged state even when the individual in later life is dealing with persons who treat him in ways entirely unlike those that his parents adopted when he was a child. (pp. 129–130)

In order to get at least acknowledgment, attention, and possibly even love, women with this internalized self-representation try to live up to other people's expectations. They often try to present an outer self of a strong, functioning, nice, pleasing, uncomplicated, happy woman because they think that this is the way to get what they are longing for. Furthermore, by using such an externalized self-perception, they condemn their "weak inner self" and try to deny it, even to themselves. This leads to a split between an outer and an inner self (divided self). Care as self-sacrifice often takes on the meaning of caring more for other people's feelings and needs than for one's own. Behavior is not driven by one's own needs, aims, feelings, and limits but is guided by the concern whether or not the other person might feel hurt. Depressed women often wish to learn how to set limits but "without hurting someone else." This self-silencing behavior is usually not confined to the partner or husband but has become a generalized way of making contact. Typically, depressed women are afraid of appearing selfish and egoistic when putting their own needs first and making their own person important in their lives.

Furthermore, self-silencing interfaces with the sociocultural context in as far as German women still have to live up to unspoken social standards of a "good woman." Although German women are encouraged to pursue careers and take on paid employment—unless they have small children—their "success in life" is still judged by whether or not they have managed to get married or live in a long-term relationship, whether or not they have children, and how they fulfill their roles as wives and mothers. In terms of social judgment, it is still more important for women to have "success" in private life than in the workplace; for men it is still the other way around. The degree to which German women of today are still judged by how they fulfill their "female role" is reflected in depressed women's content of rumination, self-perceptions, and feelings of guilt.

Typically, depressed women feel guilty because they have not been able to function fully anymore in the household or family due to their depression. Or, working mothers—even single mothers—feel guilty because they have taken up paid employment and leave their children with a stranger. Depressed single women feel like failures because they have not managed to (ever) find a husband or partner and feel as if they are worth less than others because they are single. And in fact, there is quite some social pressure on single women over about the age of 35 to find a husband or, at least, a male partner. Single women of that age or older often have to face negative social judgments such as "there is something wrong with her" or "she is too complicated, too picky, or too egoistic." It is still true for many parts of the country that a woman's social prestige increases at the moment she gets married. For German men, in contrast, there is much less social pressure with regard to marriage, children, or intimate relationships. Surely, there might be some social judgment on single men over age 45 approximately, but it is far less derogative and it does not diminish his overall social prestige. Consequently, depressed men are usually not concerned with their "failure to find a wife" but seem to be more concerned with their failure or inadequate functioning in the workplace.

In clinical practice, women's depression and self-silencing behaviors are intertwined. The aforementioned study cannot address the causal status of the concept of self-silencing due to its cross-sectional design. Thus, it is not clear whether self-silencing behavior leads to the development of a clinically significant depressive disorder, whether self-silencing resembles accompanying symptoms of being depressed, or whether there are other confounding third factors that influence both depression and self-silencing behavior. One potential important third factor influencing both self-silencing behavior and depression seems to be the role of violence, partner violence as well as experiences of childhood maltreatment or abuse. In fact, two depressed participants of the aforementioned study came up to the first author after filling out the questionnaires and told her about their experiences of domestic violence with their current husbands. It seemed as if they wanted to let her know about the background and influencing factors of their depression.

We consider that partner violence plays a great role in producing self-silencing behavior as well as depression. In an ongoing atmosphere of domestic violence and under chronic threat, a behavior of self-silencing can be regarded as a seemingly or at least initially useful adaptive strategy to avoid further acts of violence. Due to the experience that one wrong word or an objection leads to another violent attack, the woman tries to "make it right" and "be a good woman." This effort might or might not be driven by the societal myth that a good woman can transform a man with her love and the delegation of responsibility for the success of the marriage or relationship to the female partner (Firle, Hoeltje, & Nini, 1996; Jack, 1991). In any case, it seems as if the behaviors of self-silencing and care as self-sacrifice in the context of violence do not necessarily mirror a woman's conviction concerning internalized social imperatives but can simply be regarded as protective strategies with survival value in the context of a violent relationship. Moreover, when the cycle of violence continues, the woman must develop a kind of a divided self so that more self-assertive aspects of her personality will be dissociated, thus allowing her to remain in this threatening and dangerous relationship. The experience of physical violence most often goes along with psychological violence such as degradation, name calling, threatening, controlling, and questioning the woman's inner experience. This chronically undermines a woman's sense of self and self-worth and produces a deep insecurity about one's own perceptions. A person who is deeply insecure and does not trust her own feelings, perceptions, and experiences must measure herself against outer standards because inner standards are not available or are not trusted. Therefore, a behavior that could be considered an externalized self-perception might be a consequence of being battered as well as a sign of a deep-seated insecurity.

We have outlined how the experience of partner violence can lead to behaviors similar to the behaviors of self-silencing. However, self-silencing is motivated by societal norms of "being a good woman and a good wife," whereas in the case of violence, self-silencing can be regarded as a survival behavior. The result might be the same: depression. Partner violence probably leads to self-silencing behavior as well as depression, and self-silencing behavior favors the development of a depressive disorder. In fact, the role of violence for the development of psychiatric disorders including depression has recently received growing attention.

Partner Violence and Depression

In a meta-analysis on intimate partner violence as a risk factor for psychiatric disorders, the weighted mean prevalence of depression among battered women was 48% across 18 studies (Golding, 1999). The weighted mean odds ratio was 3.80, representing a strong association by epidemiological criteria. Golding (1999) further showed that depression was associated with temporal proximity to battering and that severity and duration of violence were associated with prevalence or severity of depression, thus providing evidence for a dose-response relationship. Altogether, results of the 18 studies gave credibility to a causal role of partner violence in the development of female depression and also other psychiatric disorders such as posttraumatic stress disorder.

The prevalence of violence against women by their intimate partners is alarmingly high worldwide, as also in Germany. Until recently, conservative estimates suggested that one in five to one in seven women in Germany have experienced physical or sexual violence by a current or former partner (Schröttle, 1999, as cited in Federal Ministry for Family Affairs, Senior Citizens, Women, and Youth [FMFSWY], 2004). The first nationally representative survey of violence against women in Germany with data from over 10,000 women, however, found that at least 25% of women have experienced physical or sexual violence by an intimate partner at least once in their lifetimes (FMFSWY, 2004). Two-thirds of the women having experienced partner violence have sustained physical injuries. For many women, violence is not an exceptional singular experience: From all women having experienced physical or sexual violence by an intimate partner, only 28% reported about 1 violent incidence, 17.5% about 2 to 3, almost 15% about 4 to 10, 11% about 10 to 20, almost 6% about 20 to 40, and 12% even more incidences. The German prevalence rates are very similar to the ones found in the Netherlands, Great Britain, and Sweden of 23% to 28%.

In regard to women's self-silencing behavior, psychological violence in intimate relationships as another form of power imbalance between the sexes is also of great interest. The national survey cited previously found psychological violence and control by the male partner to be present in every seventh intimate relationship. Psychological violence was defined as behaviors such as controlling social contacts, money, or mail; ignoring the partner; disrespecting the woman's opinions or wishes; disparaging the partner in public; blaming the partner; and threatening to damage or take away important things. Not surprisingly, there was a significant association between psychological violence and physical violence in intimate relationships.

Furthermore, physical and sexual partner violence and the degree of sharing household chores were significantly and negatively associated. Overall, in only 47% of all intimate relationships were household chores equally distributed between the partners. In violent relationships, however, the distribution of household chores was even more unequal than in nonviolent relationships. Violence results in psychological difficulties for most women: In a large sample of over 3,400 women in violent relationships (psychological, physical, or sexual violence), up to 70% in each subgroup suffered from a reduced sense of self-worth, chronic rumination, depressive mood, sleeping disorders, difficulties with concentration, and rage (FMFSWY, 2004).

Early Experiences of Violence and Later Depression

In Germany, 13% of women were victims of sexual violence before the age of 16 when applying the legal definition of sexual violence (FMFSWY, 2004). The legal definition of sexual violence encompasses forcing, or the attempt to force, someone to have sexual intercourse with penis or other objects; forcing intimate touch or petting on someone; forcing unwanted intimate sexual practices on someone; and forcing someone to watch pornographic movies or material and then enacting it (FMFSWY, 2004). Not only current experiences of violence such as partner violence but also earlier victimizations have been held responsible for women's higher rates of depression and other psychiatric disorders. For example, the National Women's Study (Saunders, Kilpatrick, Hanson, Resnick, & Walker, 1999, as cited in Nolen-Hoeksema, 2002) found for the United States that women who had been victims of completed rape in childhood had a lifetime prevalence of depression of 52% compared to 27% in nonvictimized women. Similar results come from the Epidemiological Catchment Area Study, which found a 2.4-fold increased risk of depression for women who had become victims of rape during childhood or adulthood (Burnam et al., as cited in Nolen-Hoeksema, 2002). "Cutler and Nolen-Hoeksema (1991) estimated that as much as 35% of the gender difference in adult depression could be accounted for by the higher incidence of assault of girls relative to boys" (Nolen-Hoekema, 2002, p. 500). How can the association between violence during childhood and later depression be explained? What are the psychological processes that mediate this association?

Research shows that childhood abuse, and especially more severe forms of childhood sexual abuse, raises the risk for the development of adult psychiatric disorder by a factor of at least 2 to 3 (e.g., Kendler et al., 2000). In addition, we suppose that there is also a specific process for the development of depression in adulthood in women with a history of childhood abuse. We hypothesize that early experiences of violence (sexual, physical, or emotional) can lead to a failure to trust one's own perceptions and values and act accordingly. This poor sense of self arises because the girl repeatedly experiences that her feelings, boundaries, and needs are not respected. As a consequence, she learns to attend to the caregiver's feelings, moods, and needs instead of her own as a survival strategy because she is dependent on the caregiver and needs to ensure the attachment (Bowlby, 1988b). In the same realm, Herman (1992) states: "All of the abused child's psychological adaptations serve the fundamental purpose of preserving her primary attachment to her parents in the face of daily evidence of their malice, helplessness, or indifference" (p. 102). Also, because the child is treated badly, she develops a deep sense of unworthiness and badness (Herman, 1992, pp. 98–107) along with a self-critical and derogatory internal voice. One can regard this "internal voice" (cognitive-emotional self-schema) as a form of "internalized violence against the self." The person treats herself as badly as her parents or other important caregivers have treated her in childhood. Low self-esteem, a sense of being bad and unworthy, and little practice in knowing and caring for one's own needs, feelings, and personal boundaries make a person dependent on other people's approval for her sense of self-worth and sources of comfort (Herman, 1992, pp. 98–107). Therefore, in order to get approval, she will try to please other people and try to adhere to others'—her family's or societal—expectations of her as a woman:

> This malignant sense of inner badness is often camouflaged by the abused child's persistent attempts to be good. In the effort to placate her abusers, the child victim often becomes a superb performer. She attempts to do whatever is required of her. She may become an empathic caretaker for her parents, an efficient housekeeper, an academic achiever, a model of social conformity. (Herman, 1992, p. 105)

Apparently, the experience of childhood abuse promotes later self-silencing behavior mediated by a poor sense of self and in combination with societal imperatives of being a "good woman" because such a person is particularly dependent on approval from others.

Ms P

To illustrate these ideas, we present a brief clinical case of a 32-year-old woman with recurrent and severe depressive disorder and posttraumatic stress disorder due to several incidences of severe physical violence by her father against her and the family when she was a child (6 to 10 years). She underwent inpatient psychotherapeutic treatment for several weeks. Like many other depressed female patients, Ms P tried to live up to other people's expectations, especially to the ones of her close family and friends. She tried to be exceedingly helpful and never established adequate boundaries, thus disregarding her own needs. She was convinced that this was the only way to receive at least acceptance and liking from others. She did not consider herself to be worthy of acceptance, liking, or love without doing something for others. Speaking her mind or setting boundaries was fraught with intense fear of rejection. In addition, she hid her feelings and needs when she thought others would find them inappropriate. In social contexts, she took care to present a nice, caring, knowledgeable, and rather compliant person. The idea of putting her own needs first seemed to be egoistic to her, which was the worst she would have wanted to become. Ms P showed many behaviors and cognitions that could be described as facets of self-silencing.

Ms P had at first tried to hide her extremely critical and self-debasing inner voice even from her therapist, lest she might be a "bad and inappropriate patient," unable to use cognitive restructuring techniques effectively. This fear was a result of earlier therapy experiences. Only the direct exploration of this old, negative inner voice brought about a turning point in treating this depression. After allowing those negative and self-derogating cognitions and concurrent emotions of shame and self-hate to come to the surface, typical statements such as "you are bad, you are lazy, you are fat and disgusting, you are a complete failure, you failed in your career, you are not normal" were written down. Reading the sentences now produced an emotional distancing effect, and Ms P realized that they represented almost completely the voice of her father. Feeling the pain about having turned the father's disdain and violence toward herself mobilized healthy resources such as self-soothing capacities. Together with the emerging anger against her father, they helped her regain her sense of self and establish a more gentle, appreciating, and accepting inner voice and more appropriate attitudes toward herself. In time, she overcame the self-silencing behavior, spoke her mind more frequently, became able to set limits, and ceased pleasing others all the time. Instead, she attended more to her own needs. To our knowledge, she has not suffered a depressive relapse in over two years—a fact that can be considered very meaningful in light of more than 10 depressive episodes before coming to our hospital.

Conclusion

We have outlined the sociocultural context for today's women in Germany that resembles in large part the experience of women in other Western or European countries. As in other modern societies, German women—until they become mothers—have equal opportunities, are generally encouraged to pursue careers, and usually share with their male partners an egalitarian model of their intimate relationship. Due to the particular German version of the ideal of motherhood and the social, political, and economic environment that favors the single-breadwinner model, women's lives seem to turn upside down with the first child. Compared to other European countries such as Sweden or France, there seem to be higher obstacles for women in Germany to pursue their career and their interests after becoming mothers. Also, as in many, even the so-called progressive, Western cultures, the social judgment of women's achievements hinges to a large degree on their fulfillment of the female role—whether they have managed to find a long-term partner and to have children. Through these mechanisms, the self-silencing of women in Germany in the areas of professional achievement, building a career, and at the same time enjoying an equal social standing while also having a family is culturally and socially encouraged.

Furthermore, we strongly believe that the influence of early experiences of violence and current partner violence on the development of self-silencing behavior, depression, and other psychiatric disorders is still highly underestimated and therefore also neglected by scholars. Violence in the family against children and women apparently constitutes a worldwide problem and is by far not specific to Germany. On the contrary, the issue of family violence nowadays is an acknowledged problem in Germany that has gained increased public attention. There exists a sociopolitical determination to change the situation of children and women and there is a clear condemnation of family violence.

Moreover, as we have mentioned earlier, there has been a major recent change in the political agenda under the first female German chancellor, Angela Merkel, regarding opportunities for women (and men) to combine paid employment with family care. German women are now encouraged to work outside the home even when they have small children. Thus, the sociocultural context forming women's experiences and self-silencing behavior is changing in favor of a more broadly defined female self-realization.

References

Bandelow, B. (1997). *Panik- und Agoraphobie-Skala (Panic and Agoraphobia Scale, PAS)*. Testmappe. Göttingen: Hogrefe.

Bijl, R. V., Ravelli, A., & van Zerssen, G. (1998). Prevalence of psychiatric disorders in the general population: Results of the Netherlands Mental Health Survey and Incidence Study (NEMESIS). *Social Psychiatry and Psychiatric Epidemiology, 33,* 587–595.

Bowlby, J. (1987). Attachment. In R. L. Gregory (Ed.), *The Oxford companion to the mind* (pp. 57–59). Oxford: Oxford University Press.

Bowlby, J. (1988a). Lecture 7: The role of attachment in personality development. In J. Bowlby (Ed.), *A secure base: Parent-child attachment and healthy human development* (pp. 119–136). New York: Basic Books.

Bowlby, J. (1988b). Lecture 5: Violence in the family. In J. Bowlby (Ed.). *A secure base: Parent-child attachment and healthy human development* (pp. 77–98). New York: Basic Books.

Brown, G. W., & Harris, T. (1978). *Social origins of depression: A study of psychiatric disorder in women.* London: Tavistock.

Brückner, H. (2004). *Gender inequality in the life course: Social change and stability in West Germany 1975-1995.* New York: Aldine de Gruyter.

Doll, J., Mentz, M., & Witte, E. H. (1995). Zur Theory der vier Bindungsstile: Messprobleme und Korrelate dreier integrierter Verhaltenssysteme (The theory of the four attachment styles: Measurement issues and correlates of three integrated behavior systems). *Zeitschrift für Sozialpsychologie, 26,* 148–159.

Dorn, T. (2006). *Die neue F-Klasse. Wie die Zukunft von Frauen gemacht wird (The new f-class. How women shape the future).* Munich: Piper.

Eichhorst, W., & Thode, E. (2002). *Vereinbarkeit von Familiy und Beruf (Combining family and work commitment).* Gütersloh, Germany: Bertelsmann Stiftung.

Federal Ministry for Family Affairs, Senior Citizens, Women, and Youth (FMFSWY). (2004). *Lebenssituation, Sicherheit und Gesundheit von Frauen in Deutschland. Eine repräsentative Untersuchung zu Gewalt gegen Frauen in Deutschland*

(Life situation, safety, and health of women in Germany. A representative inquiry on violence against women in Germany). Berlin, Germany: Government Printing Office.

Federal Ministry for Youth, Family Affairs, Women, and Health. (1989). Frauen in der Bundesrepublik Deutschland (Women in the Federal Republic of Germany). Bonn, Germany: Government Printing Office.

Fichter, M. (1990). Verlauf psychischer Erkrankungen in der Bevölkerung (The course of psychiatric disorders in the population). Berlin: Springer.

Firle, M., Hoeltje, B., & Nini, M. (1996). Gewalt in Ehe und Partnerschaft (Violence in marriage and intimate relationships). Report by the Federal Ministry for Family Affairs, Senior Citizens, Women, and Youth. Bonn, Germany: Government Printing Office.

Friedlmeier, W. (1994). Fragebogen zu Sozialen Beziehungen (German version of the Adult Attachment Scale). Unpublished manuscript, University of Konstanz, Germany.

Gater, R., Tansella, M., Korten, A., Tiemens, B. G., Mavreas, V. G., & Olatawura, M. O. (1998). Sex differences in the prevalence and detection of depressive and anxiety disorders in the general health care settings – Report from the World Health Organization collaborative study on Psychological Problems in General Health Care. Archives of General Psychiatry, 55, 405–413.

Golding, J. M. (1999). Intimate partner violence as a risk factor for mental disorders: A meta-analysis. Journal of Family Violence, 14, 99–132.

Grossmann, K. E., Grossmann, K., Winter, M., & Zimmermann, P. (2002). Bindungsbeziehungen und Bewertungen von Partnerschaft (Attachment relations and representations of intimate relationships). In K. H. Brisch, K. E. Grossmann, K. Grossmann, & L. Köhler (Eds.), Bindung und Seelische Entwicklungswege (Attachment and psychological developmental paths) (pp. 125–164). Stuttgart, Germany: Klett-Cotta.

Hautzinger, M., Bailer, M., Worall, H., & Keller, F. (1994). Beck-Depressionsinventar (BDI) Testhandbuch (Beck Depression Inventory). Bern, Switzerland: Huber.

Hazan, C., & Shaver, P. (1990). Love and work: An attachment-theoretical perspective. Journal of Personality and Social Psychology, 59, 270–280.

Herman, J. (1992). Trauma and recovery. The aftermath of violence: From domestic abuse to political terror. New York: Basic Books.

Huinink, J., & Mayer, K. U. (1995). Gender, social inequality, and family formation in West Germany. In K. Oppenheim Mason & A.-M. Jensen (Eds.), Gender and family change in industrialized countries (pp. 168–199). New York: Oxford Press.

Jack, D. C. (1991). Silencing the self: Women and depression. Cambridge: Harvard Press.

Jack, D. C., & Dill, D. (1992). The Silencing the Self Scale: Schemas of intimacy associated with depression in women. Psychology of Women Quarterly, 16, 97–106.

Jacobi, F. (2003). Diagnosing mental disorders in epidemiological studies: The German Health Interview and Examination Survey and its Mental Health Supplement (GHS-MHS) as an example of standardized data collection with clinical features. Along with a report on: Epidemiology of depressive disorders in a nationally representative population sample in Germany: Prevalence, comorbidity, sociodemographic correlates, impairment, and treatment rates. Master's thesis for MSc in Affective Neuroscience, University of Maastricht.

Jacobi, F., Rosi, S., Faravelli, C., Goodwin, R., Arbabzadeh-Bouchez, S., & Lépine, J. P. (2005). The epidemiology of mood disorders. In E. J. L. Griez, C. Faravelli, D. J. Nutt, & J. Zohar (Eds.), *Mood disorders: Clinical management and research issues* (pp. 3–34). London: Wiley.

Jacobi, F., Wittchen, H. U., Hölting, C., Höfler, M., Müller, N., Pfister, H., et al. (2004). Prevalence, comorbidity and correlates of mental disorders in the general population: Results from the German Health Interview and Examination Survey (GHS). *Psychological Medicine, 34*, 597–611.

Jacobi, F., Wittchen, H. U., Müller, N., Hölting, C., Sommer, S., Höfler, M., & Pfister, H. (2002). Estimating the prevalence of mental and somatic disorders in the community: Aims and methods of the German National Health Interview and Examination Survey. *International Journal of Methods in Psychiatric Research, 11*, 1–18.

Kendler, K. S., Bulik, C. M., Silberg, J. Hettema, J. M., Myers, J., & Prescott, C. A. (2000). Childhood sexual abuse and adult psychiatric and substance use disorders in women. An Epidemiological and Cotwin control analysis. *Archives of General Psychiatry, 57*, 953–959.

Kessler, R. C., Berglund, P., Demler, O. J. R., Koretz, D., Merikangas, K. R., Rush, A. J., et al. (2003). The epidemiology of major depressive disorder: Results from the National Comorbidity Survey Replication (NCS-R). *Journal of the American Medical Association, 289*, 3095–3105.

Kessler, R. C., McGonagle, K. A., Nelson, C. B., Hughes, M., Swartz, M., & Blazer, D. G. (1994). Sex and depression in the National Comorbidity Survey 2. Cohort effects. *Journal of Affective Disorders, 30*, 15–26.

Kessler, R. C., McGonagle, K. A., Zhao, S., Nelson, C. B., Hughes, M., Eshleman, S., et al. (1994). Lifetime and 12-month prevalence of DSM-III-R psychiatric disorders in the United States: Results from the National Comorbidity Survey. *Archives of General Psychiatry, 51*, 8–19.

Kleiner, L., & Marshall, W. L. (1985). Relationship difficulties and agoraphobia. *Clinical Psychology Review, 5*, 581–595.

Nolen-Hoeksema, S. (2002). Gender differences in depression. In I. H. Gotlieb & C. L. Hammen (Eds.), *Handbook of depression* (pp. 492–509). New York: Guilford.

Ratzenböck, G. (1990). Mutterliebe. Bemerkungen zur gesellschaftlichen konstruierten Verknüpfung von Mutterliebe und Familie (Motherlove. Remarks about a socially constructed combination of motherlove and family). In M. Bernold, A. Ellmeier, J. Gehmcher, E. Hornung, G. Ratzenböck, & B. Wirthensohn (Eds.), *Familie: Arbeitsplatz oder Ort des Glücks? (Family: Workplace or place of happiness?)* (pp. 19–49). Vienna, Austria: Picus.

Rerrich, M. S. (1988). *Balanceakt Familie: Zwischen alten Leitbildern und neuen Lebensformen (Family as a balancing act: Between old concepts and new forms of living).* Freiburg, Germany: Lambertus.

Sander, J., & Boecker, S. (1993). Die Deutsche Form der Relationship Assessment Scale (RAS): Eine kurze Skala zur Messung der Zufriedenheit in Partnerschaft (German version of the Relationship Assessment Scale). *Diagnostica, 39*, 55–62.

Seidenspinner, G., & Keddi, B. (1994). Partnerschaft – Frauensichten, Männersichten (Intimate relationships – Women's and men's views). In G. Seidenspinner (Ed.), *Frau sein in Deutschland (Being a woman in Germany)* (pp. 63–81). Munich: DJI.

Vandereycken, W. (1983). Agoraphobia and marital relationship: Theory, treatment, and research. *Clinical Psychology Review, 3*, 317–338.

Vinken, B. (2002). *Die deutsche Mutter. Der lange Schatten eines Mythos (The German mother. The long shadow of a myth)*. Munich: Piper.

Wittchen, H. U., Essau, C. A., van Zerssen, D., Krieg, J. C., & Zaudig, M. (1992). Lifetime and six-month prevalence of mental disorders in the Munich follow-up study. *European Archives of Psychiatry and Clinical Neuroscience, 241*, 247–258.

Wittchen, H. U., Müller, N., & Storz, S. (1998). Psychische Störungen: Häufigkeit, psychosoziale Beeinträchtigungen und Zusammnehänge zu körperlichen Erkrankungen (Psychiatric disorders: Their frequency, psychosocial impairment and relationship with somatic diseases). *Das Gesundheitswesen, 60*(Sonderheft 2), 95–100.

Wittchen, H. U., Nelson, C. B., & Lachner, G. (1998). Prevalence of mental disorders and psychosocial impairments in adolescents and young adults. *Psychological Medicine, 28*, 109–126.

Wittchen, H. U., & van Zerrsen, D. (Eds.). (1987). *Verläufe behandelter und unbehandelter Depressionen and Angststörungen – eine klinisch-psychiatrisch und epidemiologische Verlaufsuntersuchung (Course of treated and untreated depression and anxiety disorders – a clinical, psychiatric and epidemiological long-term study)*. Berlin: Springer.

Zoellner, T. (1999). *Self-silencing und Bindungsstile bei depressiven, agoraphoben und gesunden Frauen (Self-silencing and attachment styles in depressed, agoraphobic, and healthy women)*. Unpublished master's thesis, University of Konstanz, Germany.

6

Gender as Culture: The Meanings of Self-Silencing in Women and Men

Linda Smolak

Self-silencing was originally conceptualized as a female problem. The underlying idea was that, beginning sometime in early adolescence, many girls began to suppress their own identities, to self-silence, in order to develop and maintain relationships (e.g., Brown & Gilligan, 1992; Gilligan, 1982; Jack, 1991). Furthermore, Jack (1991) explicitly linked self-silencing to the higher rate of depression among women. Both Jack (Jack & Dill, 1992) and Harter (Harter, Waters, Whitesell, & Kastelic, 1998) developed scales to measure self-silencing (or, phrased more positively, voice). Empirical studies comparing genders on these measures have yielded surprising findings: Typically there are no gender differences in mean scores on these measures. Indeed, sometimes men seem to demonstrate more self-silencing than women do (e.g., Duarte & Thompson, 1999; Gratch, Bassett, & Attra, 1995; Haemmerlie, Montgomery, Williams, & Winborn, 2001; Harter et al., 1998; Page, Stevens, & Galvin, 1996; Spratt, Sherman, & Gilroy, 1998). Furthermore, contrary to Jack's (1991) theory, the correlations between self-silencing and depression are often similar for men and women (e.g., Duarte & Thompson, 1999; Smolak & Munstertieger, 2002; Uebelacker, Courtnage, & Whisman, 2003).

There are several possible explanations for the similarities between women and men on measures of self-silencing. First, perhaps the theory is incorrect. Perhaps men are at least as likely as women to suppress their own wishes and needs in order to maintain intimate relationships. Second, perhaps there are methodological problems with either the measures or the samples routinely used in these studies. Third, it may be that the meaning of self-silencing differs for men and women, rendering the similarities in mean scores somewhat misleading. While female self-silencing seems to be related to culturally sanctioned power-lessness, male "self-silencing" may reflect the masculinity norm of emotional restraint. Finally, women may be so enculturated with the importance of being "nice" and subservient in relationships (e.g., Mahalik et al., 2005) that they may underestimate their own self-silencing. Men, on the other hand, socialized to expect to be dominant in relationships, might overestimate their own self-silencing and the amount they have sacrificed for the relationship.

The overarching purpose of this chapter is to explore these possible explanations of the unexpected similarity in women's and men's mean scores on the self-silencing measures, with a special focus on how culture might affect both the level and the self-awareness of voice. More specifically, this chapter aims to do three things: (1) briefly review the findings concerning gendered performance on the measures, including an analysis of the commonly employed measures and samples; (2) consider other areas in which men and women appear to be similar if one does not explore the process and context underlying the behavior; and (3) present hypotheses describing gendered pathways to the similar mean responses on voice measures. It is, then, my contention that the similarities between men and women on the self-silencing measures may mask important gender differences in the development and effects of voice. Once we examine the potential causes and effects of self-silencing, it becomes evident that we need more research to illuminate the possibly differential development of voice in men and women.

How Gendered Are the Responses on Self-Silencing Measures?

The Silencing the Self Scale (STSS; Jack & Dill, 1992) and the Saying What I Think Around Others scale (SWIT; Harter et al., 1998) are both designed to measure voice but have substantially different foci. The STSS includes both psychological and interpersonal processes in self-silencing, particularly those that might be related to depression, and socially dictated self-silencing behaviors. Jack (1991) and Jack and Dill (1992) argued that these processes or schemas were gender specific. They focused on the women's relationship schemas as influences on self-silencing behavior, which, in turn, contributed to lower self-esteem and increased the risk of depression. The STSS has four subscales: Externalized Self-Perception (e.g., "I tend to judge myself by how I think other people see me"), Care as Self-Sacrifice (e.g., "Caring means putting the other person's needs in front of my own"), Silencing the Self (e.g., "I don't speak my feelings in an intimate relationship when I know they will cause disagreement"), and Divided Self (e.g., "Often I look happy enough on the outside, but inwardly I feel angry and rebellious"). A total score can be calculated or one can use the subscales. However, since the subscales are conceptualized as interrelated and covarying components of self-silencing, the use of only one or two subscales may result in incomplete information about not only overall voice but also the subscales that are employed (Jack, 1999).

As the title of the SWIT (Harter et al., 1998) suggests, the SWIT focuses on one of the behavioral aspects of voice (i.e., being able to express thoughts and opinions to others). People with "voice" have "authentic" rather than "false" selves (Harter et al., 1998). The SWIT is designed for use with high school and college students. It consists of a set of five questions (e.g., "Some people are able to let their parents know what's important to them") asked about various contexts (e.g., parents, female students/classmates, male students/classmates, female friends, male friends, close friends, and professors/teachers). The idea here is that voice is socially determined and hence susceptible to contextual cues and influences. Voice is conceptualized as context specific, varying from one setting/audience to another. While sociocultural determinants are crucial in the theory underlying the STSS, the desire to preserve relationships and not express anger is a more pervasive role expectation in the STSS than in the SWIT. Because the SWIT assumes behaviors are context specific, no total scores are calculated. Thus, it is possible to have voice, and hence authenticity, in one context but not in another (Harter et al., 1998).

The scales do appear to measure somewhat different constructs, with only small to moderate correlations among the STSS and SWIT subscales (Smolak & Munstertieger, 2002). Despite the differences between the scales, research on gender differences has yielded similar results. Both indicate that women do not generally show less "voice" than men do. When the STSS is used, it is actually fairly common for men to score higher than women do (i.e., show less voice) on the Care as Self-Sacrifice subscale (e.g., Cramer & Thoms, 2003; Duarte & Thompson, 1999; Page et al., 1996; Smolak & Munstertieger, 2002; Thompson, Whiffen, & Aube, 2001) and the total STSS scores (Cramer & Thoms, 2003; Duarte & Thompson, 1999; Gratch et al., 1995; Remen, Chambless, & Rodebaugh, 2002; Thompson, 1995; Uebelacker et al., 2003). There is no STSS subscale on which women routinely show higher levels of self-silencing than men do.

On the SWIT, adolescent girls may show more voice than boys do with female classmates and close friends (Harter et al., 1998). Similarly, among college students, women may show more voice with female students, while men show more voice with male students (Smolak & Munstertieger, 2002).

Two measures that may be related to the STSS and the SWIT deserve some mention. Tolman and Porche (2000) have developed the Adolescent Femininity Ideology Scale (AFIS). One subscale of the AFIS is the Inauthentic Self in Relationships, a scale that is correlated with both self-esteem and depression. This scale has not been used with boys. However, the scale does indicate the continued theoretical assumption that voice is a problem for girls.

The Objectified Body Consciousness Scale (OBC; McKinley & Hyde, 1996) includes a Surveillance subscale. This scale measures the tendency to monitor one's body, viewing it as an outsider might. This is similar conceptually to the Externalized Self-Perception subscale of the STSS. There is a version of the OBC, including the Surveillance subscale, for preadolescents and adolescents (Lindberg, Hyde, & McKinley, 2006).

The Surveillance scale of the OBC has been used much more frequently with women than with men. However, when both genders have been included in a sample, it has generally been the case that girls and women have higher scores than boys and men do (e.g., Grabe, Hyde, & Lindberg, 2007; Lindberg et al., 2006; McKinley, 1998; Tiggemann & Kuring, 2004). It is noteworthy that this gender difference is evident even in preadolescents (Lindberg et al., 2006). Furthermore, pubertal development is positively correlated with surveillance in girls but not boys (Lindberg et al., 2006), suggesting that a more adult-like female body is more of a liability than an adult-like male body is. This may be one reason that at least certain aspects of female self-silencing begin to emerge in adolescence.

Another recent study of "voice" in children did not use a survey instrument. Bassen and Lamb (2006) examined positive affiliation, negative affiliation, and assertiveness in 7th and 10th graders. They found that girls were not clearly less assertive than boys (Bassen & Lamb, 2006). Assertiveness, while related to voice, is not synonymous with it. It is noteworthy that, consistent with the relational theory underlying the self-silencing measure (Jack, 1992), older girls in this sample were more positively affiliative (e.g., interested in being agreeable, likeable, and wanting to please) and less negatively affiliative (e.g., hurtful or insensitive in relationships) than older boys were.

Gender and Factor Structure in the STSS

Originally, the factors of the STSS were derived based on theory rather than factor analysis (Jack & Dill, 1992). At least three studies have examined the validity of the proposed factor structure in samples of women and men (Cramer & Thoms, 2003; Duarte & Thompson, 1999; Remen et al., 2002). All three studies find that Jack and Dill's four-factor structure is roughly appropriate for women. But two of the studies report that Jack's model does not fit the men's data. For example, Remen and colleagues (2002) reported a four-factor solution for men. Three of these factors, Silencing the Self, Care as Self-Sacrifice, and Externalized Self-Perception, overlapped with the women's factors. However, a factor that Remen and colleagues (2002) labeled "autonomy/concealment" emerged in place of the Divided Self subscale. This scale seems "largely inconsistent with Jack's concept of self-silencing" (Remen et al., 2002, p. 154). It seems to capture a person's intent to put one's own needs ahead of others while maintaining self-sufficiency. Items on this factor also seem to represent hiding undesirable components of one's personality from others.

Cramer and Thoms (2003) identified the expected four factors for women but a three-factor solution for men. The three factors were labeled as Self-Silencing, Divided/Externalized Self, and Care as Self-Sacrifice. The second factor in their study overlaps some with the autonomy/concealment factor found by Remen and colleagues (2002), but the two factors are more different than similar.

Thus, it appears that Jack's (1991) theoretically derived factors apply to women. They do not clearly fit men's data. Indeed, a factor structure that consistently fits male data has yet to be identified. Remen and colleagues (2002) further examined the convergent and discriminant validity of both the factors and the total STSS scores. They found that men's data did not as consistently follow hypothesized relationships as women's did. Most notably, they had hypothesized that avoidant attachment would be an effective indicator of discriminant validity and would not be correlated with STSS scores. This was true for women. But for men, there were significant relationships between avoidant attachment and STSS scores. Most notably, the Autonomy/ Concealment factor was moderately ($r = .39$) correlated with avoidant attachment. In fact, autonomy/concealment was more strongly correlated with avoidant than anxious/ambivalent attachment, contrary to hypotheses and the reverse of the women's pattern. Apparently not only the factor structure but also the meaning of the factors differed between the two genders (Remen et al., 2002). Similarly, although Duarte and Thompson (1999) found similar factor structures for women and men, there was a significant correlation between the Care as Self-Sacrifice and the Divided Self STSS subscales for women but not for men. Duarte and Thompson (1999) suggest that this difference may indicate that self-sacrifice to care for others may more negatively impact the self-definition of women than men.

The findings of Remen and colleagues (2002) and Duarte and Thompson (1999) may indicate a different process or at least perception of self-silencing in women than in men. Both results suggest that men may be reporting self-silencing that occurs as an outcome of emotional restraint, not wanting to demonstrate distress because it is "unmanly" to do so, while women may actually be sacrificing some component of self in order to maintain a relationship through their self-silencing.

Gender Differences in Correlates of Self-Silencing

Several studies have shown that women's and men's scores on the STSS are similarly correlated with concurrent measures of psychopathology and self-esteem (e.g., Duarte & Thompson, 1999; Gratch et al., 1995; Haemmerlie et al., 2001; Page et al., 1996; Spratt et al., 1998; Uebelacker et al., 2003). For example, Smolak and Munstertieger (2002), Uebelacker and colleagues (2003), and Duarte and Thompson (1999) found that the STSS was as related to depression in men as it was in women. Page and colleagues (1996) reported that there were not significant gender differences on the STSS, but they did find significant gender X Externalized Self-Perception and gender X Care as Self-Sacrifice interactions, with a marginally significant ($p < .07$) gender X Divided

Self interaction with the subscales predicting depression more effectively for men than for women, after self-esteem was controlled. These findings focusing on depression are potentially important because the STSS was originally formulated for use with depressed women.

However, there are several questions to be raised about these findings. First, the majority of these studies are done with European American college students. Interestingly, several of these studies find no gender differences in depression in their samples (e.g., Haemmerlie et al., 2001; Page et al., 1996; Thompson et al., 2001). These findings are consistent with other studies of depression in undergraduates that report no gender difference or even a higher rate of depression in men than in women (Grant et al., 2002). Nonetheless, the lack of gender differences in depression raises the possibility that these samples are not representative and that the "typical" relationships between gender and self-silencing are different from what emerged in these samples. For example, given the frequently documented correlation between depression and self-silencing, we might expect that a group of women who is unusually low on depression will also be unusually low on self-silencing. Conversely, men who are particularly high on depression may also be higher than average on self-silencing. Either situation could result in an unexpected finding of no gender difference in self-silencing.

Some correlates of self-silencing do show gender differences. Smolak and Munstertieger (2002) reported several differences in the relationships between the STSS and measures of eating problems. STSS-Externalizing was more strongly related to binge eating in women compared to men, accounting for more than twice the variance in the women's data. Three emotional eating subscales were significantly related to SWIT and STSS subscales for women but not for men. Thompson (1995) reported that, in a community sample of adults, the STSS total score was significantly more correlated with depression in women than in men. This finding is particularly interesting given the failure to find gender differences in the correlation between the STSS and depression in college samples (e.g., Duarte & Thompson, 1999; Smolak & Munsterteiger, 2002).

Furthermore, Thompson (1995) reported that the STSS was significantly, negatively correlated with women's adjustment in their marriage and with their report of their husbands' adjustment. Among men, these relationships were not significant. Uebelacker and colleagues (2003) reported that self-silencing mediated the relationship between martial dissatisfaction and depression in women. This relationship could not even be examined in men because marital dissatisfaction and depression were not correlated in men. Thus, as predicted by self-silencing theories, there do appear to be gender differences in the meaning of self-silencing within the context of relationships.

Furthermore, self-silencing is related to gender role. Smolak and Munstertieger (2002) reported that both men and women who scored higher on masculinity showed more voice on both the STSS and the SWIT. This was true on most of the STSS and SWIT subscales, with the exception of the SWIT-Female Students measure. On the other hand, femininity was less frequently correlated with the STSS and SWIT subscales but, when it was, higher femininity was associated with less voice. The interesting exception was that, for men, higher femininity was associated with lower self-silencing on the Care as Self-Sacrifice subscale. Traditionally masculine students, on the other hand, simply engage in less self-silencing. Thus, the culturally defined roles for men and women may be a source of self-silencing.

Harter and colleagues (1998) examined mean differences in SWIT scores between girls who were rated as feminine or androgynous in public (male classmates, teachers) versus private contexts (parents and close friends). They found that feminine girls demonstrated lower levels of voice in public places as compared to private places but there was no such difference for androgynous girls. On the other hand, masculine boys tended to show higher levels of voice than did androgynous boys, though this was only true in the context of male classmates. Again, then, traditional gender roles may encourage voice in males while discouraging voice in females.

Witte and Sherman (2002) correlated scales measuring feminist identity with the STSS. They reported that college women's scores on Passive Acceptance of feminine roles and Revelation, a measure of knowledge about sexism, each were positively correlated with STSS total scores as well as the Externalized Self-Perception, Silencing the Self, and Divided Self subscales. Thus, high scores on these two scales, measuring the lowest levels of feminist identity, are associated with greater loss of voice. On the other hand, the scale assessing the highest level of feminist identity, Synthesis, was negatively correlated with the Silencing the Self subscale. If scores on the Beck Depression Inventory were controlled, then only the Passive Acceptance correlations continued to be significant. Thus, it appears that high traditional femininity is a risk factor for high self-silencing. Furthermore, feminist identity may serve as a protective factor, perhaps by reducing the likelihood of depression.

Summary

The research on gender and self-silencing is complex and, perhaps, confusing. Men often seem to be *more* self-silenced than women do (e.g., Cramer & Thoms, 2003; Duarte & Thompson, 1999; Page et al., 1996; Smolak & Munstertieger, 2002; Thompson et al., 2001). Furthermore, some studies do demonstrate similar relationships between self-silencing scores and other behaviors and attitudes, including depression and self-esteem for both women and men (e.g., Duarte & Thompson, 1999; Smolak & Munstertieger, 2002). In addition, some studies (e.g., Duarte & Thompson, 1999) document the psychometric reliability and validity of the scales for each gender. These results would seem to suggest that STSS and SWIT do indeed measure the same construct in females and males.

However, there are also several findings that indicate that STSS and SWIT scores relate to other attitudes and behaviors differently in men and women (e.g., Smolak & Munstertieger, 2002; Thompson, 1995; Uebelacker et al., 2003). Furthermore, limited research indicates that gender role, including the development of feminist identity, is related to STSS and SWIT scores (Harter et al., 1998; Smolak & Munstertieger, 2002; Witte & Sherman, 2002). In general, traditional femininity (as measured, e.g., by the Bem Sex Roles Inventory [BSRI], Bem, 1974) is associated with less voice, while masculinity is associated with greater voice. This raises the possibility that some subset of women, that is, those who adopt the culturally Euro-American–sanctioned definition of womanhood and so are low on masculinity and high on femininity (a combination that is less likely to occur among men), are at risk for a loss of voice. This might be particularly likely for those adolescent girls who are experiencing gender intensification, that is, increased pressure to adopt more feminine and less masculine behaviors and attitudes (Galambos, Almeida, & Petersen, 1990). It may be that if we move beyond college samples to those that have a higher proportion of such girls and women, we would find more gender differences in voice. This seems particularly possible given that several of the college samples show other unusual patterns (e.g., no gender difference in depression). Prospective research examining temporal precedence of voice, depression, and gender roles would be particularly useful. Research using samples from cultures and ethnic groups that embrace gender roles that differ from those of European American college students would also be of great value in disentangling the meaning of male and female responses to the STSS and SWIT.

In addition, it is possible that differences in the perception of SWIT and STSS items artificially create gender similarities. Men and women may answer the questions in the same way but for different reasons. Duarte and Thompson's (1999) findings of different relationships among the STSS subscales for men and women raise this possibility. So do the findings on gender differences in the relationship of the voice scales to other behaviors (e.g., eating disorders). The studies that find different factor structures for the STSS in males versus females (e.g., Remen et al., 2002) also support this argument. Finally, the failure to find strong relationships between SWIT and STSS scores (Smolak & Munstertieger, 2002) raises the possibility that at least one of them is not truly tapping voice.

In sum, there is a variety of evidence to suggest that the meaning of voice, as measured by the SWIT and STSS, may differ for men and women. If we assume that the measures are valid, how radical is this argument? Are there other behaviors where men and women appear to be equivalent on a survey measure and yet, in reality, are not really reporting on the same experience? If there is, and especially if that behavior is potentially related to self-silencing, then it bolsters the argument that men's and women's voice scores have different meanings.

Gender and Sexual Harassment

People frequently think of sexual harassment as a "women's" problem. For example, it is more likely to be covered in Psychology of Women textbooks than in texts for other psychology courses. Yet, when researchers survey students, there is typically little or no gender difference in reports of sexual harassment (American Association of University Women [AAUW], 2001; Hill & Silva, 2006; Murnen & Smolak, 2000). Sometimes boys actually report more sexual harassment than girls do (e.g., Lindberg et al., 2006). For example, in a survey of over 2,000 college students, 62% of the women and 61% of the men reported sexual harassment experiences. Slightly more women (35%) than men (29%) reported experiences with physical harassment (e.g., being grabbed or touched) (Hill & Silva, 2006). In a survey of 2,064 8th through 11th graders, 83% of the girls and 79% of the boys reported sexual harassment experiences (AAUW, 2001). A survey of 10- to 12-year-olds found that boys were somewhat more likely than girls to report sexual harassment ($p < .10$) (Lindberg et al., 2006). In an interview study of third- to fifth-grade children, boys reported a greater variety of sexual harassment episodes than girls did, though the difference was not significant (Murnen & Smolak, 2000). Thus, as in the self-silencing literature, there is a seemingly anomalous set of findings: A putatively "female" experience actually occurs with comparable frequency in males.

However, as I have argued for self-silencing, there is also evidence that sexual harassment means something different to boys/men and girls/women. Murnen and Smolak (2000) found that the total number of types of sexual harassment was correlated with global self-esteem, social self-esteem, and the weight-shape dimension of the Body Esteem Scale for girls but not for boys. Furthermore, boys and girls reacted differently to sexual harassment. Children were asked how child victims of sexual harassment, as described in 11 scenarios, would react to the incidents. Girls were significantly more likely than boys to report that girls would be "scared" by sexual harassment. Indeed, 57.5% of the girls compared to only 17% of the boys said children would be scared as a reaction to at least 1 of the 11 presented scenarios. Girls who thought that victims would be frightened also reported lower body esteem than girls who did not. There were not enough boys who claimed boys would be scared to do a comparable analysis. In addition, girls who claimed they did not know how the victims would feel, a response that may be indicative of self-silencing (Brown & Gilligan, 1992), had lower body esteem and weight-shape dimension scores of the Body Esteem Scale. These girls also had significantly lower social self-esteem and lower global esteem. Other than a trend for the correlation between boys' saying "don't know" and social self-esteem ($p < .10$), none of these relationships was significant for boys.

Similarly, the AAUW's surveys of college students and adolescents (AAUW, 2001; Hill & Silva, 2006) suggest that men and women have different reactions to and understandings of sexual harassment experiences. In the AAUW surveys, students were reporting on their own experiences. Again, the evidence suggests that women are more negatively affected by sexual harassment than men are. For example, while 35% of the women felt less sure of themselves after sexual harassment, only 16% of men reported less self-confidence. Behaviors were also more affected in women than in men. More women stayed away from particular buildings or places on campus (27% vs. 11%) and more women found it hard to study or pay attention in class (16% vs. 8%).

Similarly, among 8th to 11th graders, girls are more likely than boys to feel self-conscious (44% vs. 19%) and less confident (32% vs. 16%) because of harassment episodes. Girls are also more likely than boys (30% vs. 18%) to stop talking in class because of sexual harassment (AAUW, 2001). Boys who engage in harassing acts think they are being funny (Hill & Silva, 2006; Kowalski, 2000). This underscores the completely different perspective boys and men and girls and women adopt in relation to sexual harassment: Girls and women are frightened and self-conscious, while boys and men find it amusing.

What all of this suggests is that girls are more dramatically affected by harassment. They report more distress. They are more likely to change their behavior. And harassment may be more related to various aspects of self-esteem in girls than in boys. There are not empirical data that clearly establish why girls and women might be more negatively affected than boys and men are. However, it is possible that the pervasive societal context that portrays boys as sexually powerful and girls as victims contributes to differences in sexual harassment as well as to self-silencing.

Sexual terrorism theory (Sheffield, 1995) suggests that sexual violence serves a social purpose, that is, to enforce the inferior status of women in society. Sexual violence includes sexual harassment and pornography as well as rape and child sexual abuse. These forms of violence keep women from moving around freely, since the incidents and attacks are, as the word "terrorism" implies, random and unexpected. Any woman who is any age or ethnicity could be a victim no matter what the time of day or the place. Furthermore, such acts keep women "in line," reminding them to be "seen and not heard." Within this theory, things like sexual harassment and pornography are frightening to women because they serve as reminders of the possibility of rape and assault. Girls and women learn to ignore or live with the harassment (e.g., Magley, 2002), to not express their true feelings about the harassment.

Sexual violence, including harassment, often requires that women turn to men to protect them. Although it is men who create the risk to women, the patriarchal power structure does not provide women with other options. Women must try to maintain relationships with men, a position that opens the door to self-silencing. Thus, the feminine gender role focuses on being nice and attractive, while the masculine role emphasizes aggressiveness and muscularity (e.g., Grogan & Richards, 2002; Mahalik et al., 2003; Mahalik et al., 2005).

Being nice makes women seem less threatening and more likeable, but it is at the cost of status (e.g., Matschiner & Murnen, 1999). In this sense, male-to-female sexual harassment reproduces gender roles and maintains the relative statuses of men and women. Indeed, sexual terrorism theory argues that the culture provides propaganda, in the form of media images and pornography, that reinforces these relationships (Bordo, 1993; Sheffield, 1995).

Sexual harassment is also related to objectification. Objectification refers to the tendency of American culture to treat women's bodies as objects to be looked at and enjoyed by other people. More specifically, women are supposed to look a certain way in order to satisfy the sexual interests of men, including men whom the women do not know (Fredrickson & Roberts, 1997). Men's bodies, on the other hand, are primarily agentic and functional. They are supposed to do things, while women are just decorative and available for men's sexual gratification. This gives men permission to sexually harass and, again, encourages women to be passive, compliant—and silent.

Objectification has several negative implications (Fredrickson & Roberts, 1997; McKinley & Hyde, 1996). Among them is the tendency to self-objectify. This means that women internalize the gaze of "the other" and judge whether they meet the criteria of attractiveness and femininity. They engage in "self-surveillance," monitoring their appearance and behavior. It is noteworthy that women engaging in self-surveillance judge themselves using other people's standards and so lose the ability to read cues from their own bodies (McKinley & Hyde, 1996). Self-surveillance, then, shares a "loss of self" with self-silencing, particularly with the "externalized self-perception" component of self-silencing.

Summary

Sexual harassment reflects the gender roles of men and women in relationships. Men, apparently, are expected to not only look at women but also to comment on, touch, and otherwise assume the availability of women. Women are supposed to want to look good for men. These gender roles also raise issues of control. There are questions of who can control whom and who may say what. Modern gender roles continue to have implications for the motivation for behavior in relationships—women should be interested in appearing as sexual objects for men and being invested in romantic relationships (Mahalik et al., 2005). The relationship of these attitudes, as well as the ubiquitous experience of sexual harassment and other gender violence, may contribute to gender differences in the development of voice.

Different Meanings of Self-Silencing

Part of the experience of being a girl or woman is being the object of men's desires. Girls learn at an early age that it is important to be attractive, that this is a socially sanctioned pathway to success (e.g., Murnen, Smolak, Mills, & Good, 2003). Thus, women are more invested in their appearance than men are, in terms of time, effort, and relationship to self-definition (e.g., Mahalik et al., 2005; Smolak & Murnen, 2007). This investment in appearance, and the accompanying self-surveillance to monitor one's achievement of the cultural norm (Fredrickson & Roberts, 1997; McKinley & Hyde, 1996), does not include an active or agentic component. Rather, it is men who are the "doers," while women are mainly objects. These cultural definitions of the meaning of men's and women's bodies form the context within which women's self-silencing develops.

In addition, women have some reason to be afraid of men. Cultural norms, sometimes termed "rape supportive rules" (Anderson, Simpson-Taylor, & Hermann, 2004), permit and perhaps encourage boys and men in certain situations to commit sexual violence against girls and women. Sexual harassment is a reminder to women that sexual violence could be visited upon them at any time (Sheffield, 1995). A significant minority of girls and women are victims of sexual or physical violence, a large enough group so that all women know others who have been victimized. Again, this serves as a reminder of the possibility of violence at the hands of men. These are specific experiences that may contribute to self-silencing in women.

Women's roles may also require them to be "nicer" than men are (Mahalik et al., 2005). Again, this may be related to women's objectification in the culture as well as to women's desire to placate men to avoid violence. The latter may be particularly operative in public situations (Harter et al., 1998) or in situations of domestic violence (Jack & Dill, 1992).

Thus, women have different "lived experiences" than men do and these may contribute to gender differences in self-silencing. At least three cultural forces may contribute to women's self-silencing in public settings and in relationships. First, there is the cultural definition of women's bodies as passive, while men are defined as active. This further implies that women are not particularly intelligent and that their role is to be "seen and not heard." Not surprisingly, then, men are more likely to interrupt conversations in order to control them (Athenstaedt, Haas, & Schwab, 2004) and women who are too assertive and active are judged as less likeable and less attractive (e.g., Carli, 1990; Matschiner & Murnen, 1999). Since attractive women are more successful both in their careers and in social relationships (Smolak & Murnen, 2004), girls learn at a young age to work on their looks and be careful what they say.

The second force is sexual violence. Part of the purpose of sexual violence, including sexual harassment, is to silence women (Sheffield, 1995). Sexual violence is rooted in the ideologies of sexism and patriarchy and hence acts to strengthen these societal constructs (Sheffield, 1995). Many girls and women are, indeed, silent in the face of sexual harassment. For example, in one sample of working women, about 74% coped with sexual harassment by avoiding the situation, 72% detached themselves from the harassment, and nearly 70% simply endured the harassment (Magley, 2002). A significant number of women do not report more severe gender violence, including rape and spousal abuse (e.g., Koss, 1993). This is at least partly because women, having been socialized in the same culture as men are, harbor some acceptance of rape supportive rules (Anderson et al., 2004). When women decide against reporting harassment or rape, for example, they are to some extent complying with their role as victims and men's role as "sexual terrorists" (Sheffield, 1995). Thus, despite anger or frustration, women do not stand up for themselves. Such socialization also may be part of self-silencing.

The third force is the expectation that girls and women will be "nice" (Mahalik et al., 2005) and will avoid being "negative" in relationships (Bassen & Lamb, 2006). This broad cultural value means that girls and women may more faithfully adhere to the adage to "say something nice or don't say anything at all," again particularly in their relationships with men. The fact that men hold more power in society contributes to this interest in developing and maintaining noncontentious relationships.

Thus, in women, self-silencing is hypothesized to represent an attempt to fill a gender role marked by passivity, body shame, fear and vulnerability, and niceness. As has been emphasized, gender roles are *culturally* defined. Therefore, it is possible that these influences, and indeed perhaps self-silencing itself, are culturally specific phenomena. The vast majority of self-silencing research has been conducted on predominantly or exclusively European American samples. Not all cultures, including not all U.S. ethnic groups, require girls to be "nice" (Brown & Grande, 2005). African American girls do not appear to be as dissatisfied with their bodies as are girls from other U.S. ethnic groups (including European Americans; (Grabe & Hyde, 2006). African American girls also have higher self-esteem in several realms, including athletics, physical appearance, and social self-concepts, than European American girls do (Malanchuk & Eccles, 2006).

On the other hand, although the participants in Brown and Grande's (2005, p. 241) study identify "not wanting to be angry or to evoke others' anger" and hence lack of voice as a "White quality," Gratch and colleagues (1995) found that Asian/Asian Americans had higher scores on the STSS than did other U.S. ethnic groups (African Americans, Caucasians, Hispanics) who did not differ from each other. Thus, much more research is needed to understand the specific sociocultural roots and expression of self-silencing.

In U.S. culture, passivity, body shame, and "niceness" are not primary characteristics of the male gender role (Mahalik et al., 2003). For example, several studies have demonstrated that, even in early adolescence, boys and men report substantially less body shame than girls and women do (e.g., Grabe et al., 2007; Lindberg et al., 2006). These characteristics therefore cannot account for men's average self-silencing scores, which are often equal to or higher than women's.

Men's Self-Silencing

Some men are indeed victims of sexual violence. Those men may follow a similar pathway to self-silencing as women do. However, there is no reason to believe that more men than women experience sexual violence. Thus, these factors cannot explain why samples of men, especially college men, in the United States report mean levels of self-silencing greater than or equal to those of women.

One possibility is that when men say they don't express their feelings or that they try to behave as others expect, they are enacting components of the male gender role. Specifically, men are expected to control their emotions, demonstrate self-reliance, take risks, and exert power over women (e.g., Mahalik et al., 2003). Men do demonstrate these characteristics more frequently than women do (Mahalik et al., 2003). For example, men are less likely to display their emotions than women are (e.g., Kring & Gordon, 1998); thus, they may "self-silence" in terms of emotional displays in order to conform to the male gender stereotype. They also may feel compelled to act self-reliant or take risks, even when they would prefer to be less "in charge." Again, men may often feel that they are "giving up" something in order to play the male role in adult relationships. This possibility is underscored by research documenting an STSS factor for men that emphasizes autonomy, another masculine characteristic (Remen et al., 2002), as well as by the lack of a relationship between the STSS subscales of Silencing the Self and Divided Self in men (Duarte & Thompson, 1999).

In general, research indicates that masculine characteristics, in both men and women, are associated with better mental health than are feminine characteristics (e.g., Murnen & Smolak, 1997). However, most such studies measure masculinity in terms of assertiveness and dominance. When one looks specifically at risk taking, it appears to be associated with somatization. Somatization disorders may be viewed as physical manifestations of unexpressed emotions, including anxiety. Dominance is also correlated with somatization, while self-reliance is positively related to depression (Mahalik et al., 2003). These correlations suggest a psychologically dangerous suppression of emotional expression and one's own preferences in the service of gender. The direct relationship of these characteristics to self-silencing has not been assessed.

The most important difference between male self-silencing and female self-silencing is that the former is not clearly related to culturally sanctioned powerlessness. The male gender role holds some danger for men, but it does not put them in a low-status position in society. While the surface behavior of men and women may look similar, the deep structure of the behaviors and the developmental pathways to self-silencing differ.

Conclusion

There are numerous reasons to believe that the lack of a gender difference on self-silencing measures does not imply that men and women are truly similar on these dimensions. But, before we can definitively argue this or the basis for the differences, several questions require additional research.

First, the generalizability of the finding of no differences needs to be established. Most of the research is with European American college students. It may be that college men are especially tuned in to gender roles and are careful to not look "too traditional" in completing questionnaires. Or there may be developmental differences in men's and women's responses. Jack and Dill (1992) found that battered women and new mothers had higher self-silencing scores than college women did. It is possible that men at different stages of development or in different contexts will differ from college students.

Second, the validity of the measures with both genders needs more attention. Although both the SWIT and the STSS appear to have adequate validity by most measures, they are not substantially correlated with one another. They do not appear to be measuring the same thing. We need clearer information on what each assesses in order to properly interpret gender similarities and differences. The documented differences in factor structure in the STSS (e.g., Remen et al., 2002) make this interpretative task even more difficult. It may be necessary to conduct qualitative, interview studies with men, of the sort Jack (1991) did with women in developing the STSS, in order to ascertain what self-silencing behaviors mean to men.

If methodological issues can be resolved, we then need to move on to prospective research that can help establish male and female pathways to self-silencing. Such research must include a careful examination of gender role and its contribution to self-silencing. Gender role assessment should include the "lived experiences" of being female (such as sexual harassment) and male (such as pressure to engage in high-risk or even illegal behavior) as well as attitudinal components. Attention must also be given to definitions of gender roles in different cultures and ethnic groups in order to more fully understand what components of gender role and voice are related.

The question of whether there are gender differences in the meaning or development of self-silencing is crucial to understanding the outcomes of self-silencing. Ultimately, these differences may help to explain gender differences in depression, anxiety, and eating disorders. Self-silencing in girls appears early in adolescence. The combination of early onset of self-silencing and pathological outcomes of loss of voice should make these research questions a top priority.

References

American Association of University Women (AAUW). (2001). *Hostile hallways: Bullying, teasing, and sexual harassment in schools.* Washington, DC: AAUW Educational Foundation.

Anderson, V., Simpson-Taylor, D., & Hermann, D. (2004). Gender, age, and rape supportive rules. *Sex Roles, 50,* 77–90.

Athenstaedt, U., Haas, E., & Schwab, S. (2004). Gender role self-concept and gender-typed communication behavior in mixed-sex and same-sex dyads. *Sex Roles, 50,* 37–52.

Bassen, L., & Lamb, M. (2006). Gender differences in adolescents' self-concepts of assertiveness and affiliation. *European Journal of Developmental Psychology, 3,* 71–94.

Bem, S. L. (1974). The measurement of psychological androgyny. *Journal of Consulting and Clinical Psychology, 42,* 155–162.

Bordo, S. (1993). *Unbearable weight: Feminism, Western culture, and the body.* Berkeley, CA: University of California Press.

Brown, L., & Gilligan, C. (1992). *Meeting at the crossroads: Women's psychology and girls' development.* Cambridge, MA: Harvard University Press.

Brown, L., & Grande, S. (2005). Border crossing—Border patrolling: Race, gender, and the politics of sisterhood. In P. Bettis & N. Adams (Eds.), *Geographies of girlhood: Identities in-between* (pp. 231–252). Mahwah, NJ: Lawrence Erlbaum.

Carli, L. (1990). Gender, language, and influence. *Journal of Personality and Social Psychology, 59,* 941–951.

Cramer, K., & Thoms, N. (2003). Factor structure of the Silencing the Self Scale in women and men. *Personality and Individual Differences, 35,* 525–535.

Duarte, L., & Thompson, J. (1999). Sex differences in self-silencing. *Psychological Reports, 85,* 145–161.

Fredrickson, B., & Roberts, T. (1997). Objectification theory: Toward understanding women's lived experiences and mental health risks. *Psychology of Women Quarterly, 21,* 173–206.

Galambos, N., Almeida, D., & Petersen, A. (1990). Masculinity, femininity, and sex role attitudes in early adolescence: Exploring gender intensification. *Child Development, 61,* 1905–1914.

Gilligan, C. (1982). *In a different voice: Psychological theory and women's development.* Cambridge, MA: Harvard University Press.

Grabe, S., & Hyde, J. S. (2006). Ethnicity and body dissatisfaction among women in the United States: A meta-analysis. *Psychological Bulletin, 132,* 622–640.

Grabe, S., Hyde, J. S., & Lindberg, S. (2007). Body objectification and depression in adolescents: The role of gender, shame and rumination. *Psychology of Women Quarterly, 31,* 164–175.

Grant, K., Marsh, P., Syniar, G., Williams, M., Addlesperger, E., Kinzler, M., et al. (2002). Gender differences in rates of depression among undergraduates: Measurement matters. *Journal of Adolescence, 25,* 613–617.

Gratch, L. V., Bassett, M., & Attra, S. (1995). The relationship of gender and ethnicity to self-silencing and depression. *Psychology of Women Quarterly, 19,* 509–515.

Grogan, S., & Richards, H. (2002). Body image: Focus groups with boys and men. *Men and Masculinities, 4,* 219–232.

Haemmerlie, F., Montgomery, R., Williams, A., & Winborn, K. (2001). Silencing the self in college settings and adjustment. *Psychological Reports, 88*, 587–594.

Harter, S., Waters, P., Whitesell, N., & Kastelic, D. (1998). Level of voice among female and male high school students: Relational context, support, and gender orientation. *Developmental Psychology, 34*, 892–901.

Hill, C., & Silva, E. (2006). *Drawing the line: Sexual harassment on campus.* Washington, DC: AAUW Educational Foundation. (Available at www.aauw.org.)

Jack, D. C. (1991). *Silencing the self: Women and depression.* Cambridge, MA: Harvard University Press.

Jack, D. C. (1999). Silencing the self: Inner dialogues and outer realities. In T. E. Joiner & J. C. Coyne (Eds.), *The interactional nature of depression: Advances in interpersonal approaches* (pp. 221–246). Washington, DC: American Psychological Association.

Jack, D. C., & Dill, D. (1992). The Silencing the Self Scale: Schemas of intimacy associated with depression in women. *Psychology of Women Quarterly, 16*, 97–106.

Koss, M. (1993). Detecting the scope of rape: A review of prevalence research methods. *Journal of Interpersonal Violence, 8*, 98–122.

Kowalski, R. (2000). "I was only kidding!": Victims' and perpetrators' perceptions of teasing. *Personality and Social Psychology Bulletin, 26*, 231–241.

Kring, A., & Gordon, A. (1998). Sex differences in emotion: Expression, experience, and physiology. *Journal of Personality and Social Psychology, 74*, 686–703.

Lindberg, S., Hyde, J. S., & McKinley, N. (2006). A measure of objectified body consciousness for preadolescent and adolescent youth. *Psychology of Women Quarterly, 30*, 65–76.

Magley, V. J. (2002). Coping with sexual harassment: Reconceptualizing women's resistance. *Journal of Personality and Social Psychology, 83*, 930–946.

Mahalik, J. R., Locke, B., Ludlow, L., Diemer, M., Scott, R., Gottfried, M., et al. (2003). Development of the Conformity to Masculine Norms Inventory. *Psychology of Men and Masculinity, 4*, 3–25.

Mahalik, J. R., Mooray, E. B. Coonerty-Femiano, A., Ludlow, L. H., Slattery, S. M., & Smiler, A. (2005). Development of the conformity to feminine norms inventory. *Sex Roles, 52*, 417–435.

Malanchuk, O., & Eccles, J. (2006). Self-esteem. In J. Worell & C. Goodheart (Eds.), *Handbook of girls' and women's psychological health* (pp. 149–156). New York: Oxford University Press.

Matschiner, M., & Murnen, S. K. (1999). Hyperfemininity and influence. *Psychology of Women Quarterly, 23*, 631–642.

McKinley, N. M. (1998). Gender differences in undergraduates' body esteem: The mediating effect of objectified body consciousness and actual/ideal weight discrepancy. *Sex Roles, 39*, 113–123.

McKinley, N. M., & Hyde, J. S. (1996). The Objectified Body Consciousness Scale: Self-objectification, body shame, and disordered eating. *Psychology of Women Quarterly, 22*, 623–636.

Murnen, S., & Smolak, L. (1997). Femininity, masculinity, and eating disorders: A meta-analytic approach. *International Journal of Eating Disorders, 22*, 231–242.

Murnen, S., & Smolak, L. (2000). The experience of sexual harassment among grade-school students: Early socialization of female subordination. *Sex Roles, 43*, 1–17.

Murnen, S. K., Smolak, L., Mills, J. A., & Good, L. (2003). Thin, sexy women and strong, muscular men: Grade-school children's responses to objectified images of women and men. *Sex Roles, 49,* 427–437.

Page, J., Stevens, H., & Galvin, S. (1996). Relationship between depression, self-esteem and self-silencing behavior. *Journal of Social and Clinical Psychology, 15,* 381–396.

Remen, A., Chambless, D., & Rodebaugh, T. (2002). Gender differences in the construct validity of the Silencing the Self Scale. *Psychology of Women Quarterly, 26,* 151–159.

Sheffield, C. (1995). Sexual terrorism. In J. Freeman (Ed.), *Women: A feminist perspective* (5th ed., pp. 1–21). Mountain View, CA: Mayfield Press.

Smolak, L., & Munstertieger, B. (2002). The relationship of gender and voice to depression and eating disorders. *Psychology of Women Quarterly, 26,* 234–241.

Smolak, L., & Murnen, S. K. (2004). Feminist perspectives on eating problems. In J. K. Thompson (Ed.), *Handbook of eating disorders and obesity* (pp. 590–606). New York: Wiley.

Smolak, L., & Murnen, S. K. (2007). Feminism and body image. In V. Swami & A. Furnham (Eds.), *The body beautiful: Evolutionary and socio-cultural perspectives* (pp. 236–258). London: Palgrave Macmillan.

Spratt, C., Sherman, M., & Gilroy, F. (1998). Silencing the self and sex as predictors of achievement motivation. *Psychological Reports, 82,* 259–263.

Thompson, J. (1995). Silencing the self: Depressive symptomatology and close relationships. *Psychology of Women Quarterly, 19,* 337–353.

Thompson, J., Whiffen, V., & Aube, J. (2001). Does self-silencing link perceptions of care from parents and partners with depressive symptoms? *Journal of Social and Personal Relationships, 18,* 503–516.

Tiggemann, M., & Kuring, J. (2004). The role of body objectification in disordered eating and depressed mood. *British Journal of Clinical Psychology, 43,* 299–311.

Tolman, D., & Porche, M. (2000). The Adolescent Femininity Ideology Scale: Development and validation of a new measure for girls. *Psychology of Women Quarterly, 24,* 35–376.

Uebelacker, L., Courtnage, E., & Whisman, M. (2003). Correlates of depression and marital dissatisfaction: Perceptions of marital communication style. *Journal of Social and Personal Relationships, 20,* 757–769.

Witte, T., & Sherman, M. (2002). Silencing the self and feminist identity development. *Psychological Reports, 90,* 1075–1083.

7

"I Don't Express My Feelings to Anyone": How Self-Silencing Relates to Gender and Depression in Nepal

Dana C. Jack, Bindu Pokharel, and Usha Subba

The following excerpt comes from a young woman seeking treatment at a government outpatient mental health clinic in Kathmandu, Nepal. She has just been diagnosed with major depressive episode by a Nepali psychiatrist and is describing what she thinks has caused her symptoms:

> I feel like I may die any time. They [family] treat me very bad, they scold me all the time. Especially my sister-in-law who does not love me or like me at all. My sister-in-law looks for chances to put me down, and most of the time she criticizes me. She even encourages my mother to scold me. She always poisons the ear of my mother. I don't express my feelings to anyone, I keep it inside me. (Age 18, unmarried, living in a joint family, Hindu, Chhetri caste[1])

In this chapter, drawing on interviews, focus groups, and quantitative findings from three studies in Kathmandu, Nepal, we explore the question, does self-silencing associate with depression in a collectivist culture very different from Western, industrialized countries?

In traditional Nepali society, people's lives are tightly ruled by gender roles, religion, and necessity. The culture is rich and diverse, with approximately 59 ethnic groups and more than 60 different languages, strong communities, and deep, long-standing traditions. Approximately 80% of Nepal's people are Hindu. Within this group, laws and social practices reinforce a strong patriarchal system with women's subordination embedded in the family structure, legal system, workplace, health care system, and religion. Women are expected to accept their inequality in society and in intimate relationships: Pursuing one's own goals is superseded by a collectivist emphasis on the family welfare and serving the needs of family members. Valued personal traits include "sacrifice for the common good and maintaining harmonious relationships with close others" (Oyserman, Coon, & Kemmelmeier, 2002, p. 5), part of a collectivist orientation. Thus, self-silencing and self-sacrificing harmonize with cultural prescriptions for being a "good woman." Men carry the power within the family and the responsibility to provide financial resources, make major decisions, and keep family cohesion. Masculinity, especially in Hindu society, means being strong and not revealing sorrow or weakness to others; it also requires enforcing family members' conformance with tradition and family values.

Though Nepal's model of a "good woman" varies among ethnic groups, among the Hindu it is most influenced by the Brahmanical cultural ideal of the "good woman" (Bennett, 1983; Skinner & Holland, 1998).[2] The idealized Nepali good woman marries young and becomes a daughter-in-law and wife who is hard working, faithful, devoted to her husband, and focused on keeping harmony among family members. The bride, who moves into the husband's extended family's home, is viewed as an "outsider" who serves his immediate family members' needs and demands through clearly prescribed rules and restrictions on her behavior. Early on, a girl is socialized into accepting and enacting her *karma* (duty) as the prime virtue of a Hindu woman. Trained since childhood to put her family first and ignore her own wishes, she is obedient and helpful to her mother-in-law and other members of her husband's family. With the birth of sons, she acquires the central identity of Hindu women—that of a respected mother, "a good woman with a good fate" (Skinner & Holland, 1998, p. 92). Finally, she becomes a mother-in-law (the woman with the highest status within the family) and oversees the lives of her daughters-in-law. In old age, she is economically and emotionally dependent on her family.

This ideal of a good woman is lived out with expectations that it will lead to security, a sense of belonging and self-esteem within a harmonious extended family. Romantic love is not necessarily anticipated, particularly within arranged marriages in which women care for husbands and in-laws out of duty and tradition. Those whom a woman serves are expected to fulfill certain responsibilities for her welfare. Traditions and family and community pressures reinforce the ideal of the good woman, while long-standing social practices continue to restrict women's freedoms even though laws increasing women's equality have recently been enacted. Sons are considered to have economic, social, or religious value; daughters are often regarded as an economic liability because of the dowry system that still exists among most Hindu Nepalese (Fikree & Pasha, 2006). Within some quarters of Kathmandu, these values are strongly challenged by Westernization. But among hill, mountain, and Terai villages, where there is no electricity or media, and where approximately 90% of the population lives (Bal, Pokharel, Ojha, Pradhan, & Chapagain, 2004), few alternatives to traditionalism are available.

Before considering depression in Nepal, we offer a brief sketch of the broader social context in which it occurs. Nearly 40% of people in Nepal have incomes of less than $1 a day; the average per capita income is U.S. $260, making Nepal the poorest country in South Asia, and the 12th poorest country in the world (World Bank, 2006). Women's health and social standing are very poor relative to men's. During 2001, women's adult literacy rate was 26% compared to a rate of 62% among men (EarthTrends, 2003). Women's lack of schooling and work opportunities, other than unpaid agricultural, give few alternatives to early marriage and childbearing. In 2001, 56% of rural women were married by 18, 25% before 16, and 71% by age 20 (Chow, Thapa, & Achmad, 2001). Nepal's low Gender Empowerment Measure of 0.385 (United Nations Development Programme [UNDP], 2001) clearly indicates women's marginalized status relative to men in economic, political, and professional spheres. Trafficking of girls and women was estimated in 1995 to affect approximately 5,000 to 7,000 females between the ages of 10 and 20, and carries disastrous consequences for victims' physical and mental health (Human Rights Watch, 1995).

While the social power and possibilities for men may be better than those for women, poverty affects men's abilities to adequately support their families, with many men having to work outside Nepal, where they are often abused and cheated in host countries. The Maoist insurgency from 1996 to 2006 resulted in approximately 13,000 deaths and large numbers of internally displaced people (Human Rights Watch, 2007).

Mental health in Nepal is a largely neglected area and faces numerous barriers to improvement, including social stigma, inadequate resources such as personnel and health facilities, and a virtual absence of formal mental health services in isolated rural areas, where approximately 90% of the population lives (Bal et al., 2004). No epidemiological data on Nepal's rates of mental illness, including depression and suicide, have been published. Most of Nepal's people depend on traditional ways of understanding and treating mental problems, primarily turning to traditional healers. Long-standing cultural practices and even some laws discriminate against those with mental problems. For example, the husbands of women who are considered "mad" (the local slang for mentally troubled, which includes severe depression) can divorce or marry a second wife (Bal et al., 2004), and families can withhold portions of land from a member considered mad (Pach, 1998). In Nepal, depression manifests most often through physical symptoms including persistent headaches, weakness, and bodily pain, a pattern of symptom expression similar to that found in many Asian societies that stigmatize mental illness (Lauber & Rossler, 2007): Physical complaints serve as the idiom for depression (Kleinman & Good, 1996). There is no Nepalese word for depression equivalent to the Western concept. The closest term is "dukkha," which means suffering.

Background of the Studies

In 2000–2001, thanks to the Fulbright program in Nepal, the first author was privileged to teach in Tribhuvan University's graduate program in Women

Studies and to collaborate with Nepali colleagues on studies designed to examine the cultural relevance of self-silencing and its relationship to depression and gender. Prior to using the Silencing the Self Scale (STSS, Jack & Dill, 1992) in Nepal, the conceptual equivalence of STSS items and their meaning were adapted to Nepalese culture and language through the translation monitoring process (Van Ommeren et al., 2001) that includes translation by Nepali colleagues, back-translation, four focus groups with literate and nonliterate women in Kathmandu to ensure relevance and clarity of concepts, and psychometric studies.

Two-week test-retest reliability of the finalized adapted STSS was established with a group of 95 master's students at Tribhuvan University. Scale alpha for the 39 women was .79; for the 56 men it was .69. Convergent validity was established by predicted correlation with major depression as measured by the Composite International Diagnostic Interview (CIDI), Section E 2.1 (World Health Organization, 1997) that assessed point prevalence of depression. Correlations of the STSS and the CIDI were as follows: women: $n = 39$, .56, $p < .001$; men: $n = 56$; .28, $p < .05$.

Next, working with Nepalese psychiatrists from Tribhuvan University Teaching Hospital and Patan Mental Hospital, we explored the question, how does culture affect depression and self-silencing.[3] Women and men seeking help at the only two government outpatient mental health clinics in Kathmandu, if diagnosed with unipolar major depressive disorder (according to the *Diagnostic and Statistical Manual of Mental Disorders*, fourth edition [DSM IV]) by Nepali psychiatrists, were asked by the interviewers if they wanted to participate in an in-depth interview exploring what they thought was causing their distress. All the participants were assured that participation was voluntary and that no identifying information would appear in reports, nor would their personal details be revealed to clinic staff.

After informed consent was explained, interviewers asked participants to respond to the following: (1) demographic questions; (2) a semi-structured interview, which had been reviewed by the participating psychiatrists, pilot tested, and revised before use in the study; (3) the CIDI that assessed point prevalence of depression[4]; and (4) a shortened version of the STSS (containing representative items from each of the four subscales: #2 through 9, 15, 16, 19, 25, 29, and 31) (see Jack & Van Ommeren, 2007, for details). We shortened the STSS since all questions on the CIDI depression section had to be included and giving both instruments in full, verbally to nonliterate participants, would have been too demanding of their time. The interview lasted from one to two hours.[5]

The consecutive sample consisted of 34 women and 62 men. Women participants in the outpatient clinics study ranged in age from 18 to 68, with a mean age of 37; men's ages ranged from 15 to 73, with mean of 30. Fifty-seven percent of women were nonliterate compared to 11% of men, and only 3% of women and 16% of men had attended college. The larger number of men than women seeking help at the clinics reflects the Nepalese practice of spending family resources more willingly on male members than female, and men's freedom and financial ability to seek help themselves without family consent.

Psychiatrists' diagnoses of major depression corresponded with the point prevalence measure of DSM-IV depression (CIDI, WHO, 1997) for women (97%) and for men (95%). Cronbach alpha for male outpatient participants using the shortened STSS was .696; women's was .674. Means on the shortened STSS were not significantly different for women ($M = 47.68$; SD, 8.12) and men ($M = 47.26$; SD, 8.73), $t(94) = .23$, ns. The correlation of total depression symptoms on the CIDI, Section E, and STSS scores among the outpatient participants were as follows: women: $n = 34$, .23, $p < .05$; men: $n = 62$, .48, $p < .001$.

Because the STSS correlated with the CIDI among the male students in the validation study and depressed male outpatients, we decided to conduct focus groups to explore the meanings each gender attributed to items selected from the STSS. Announcements in undergraduate classes at Tribhuvan University, Kathmandu, Nepal, requested volunteers to fill out three questionnaires and engage in focus group discussion of "things about yourself and your experiences." Students were advised that their participation in groups would take approximately two hours and were also offered a payment of Rs 100 (approximately $1.50). One hundred students responded to the invitation: 50 women and 50 men. Coauthors Bindu Pokharel and Usha Subba[6] led 11 focus groups, 5 composed of women only (2 groups of 8 women, 3 groups of 10 women), 5 of men only (2 groups of 8 men, 3 groups of 10 men), and one group with 4 male and 4 female participants between September 2002 and July 2003 (see Jack, Kim, Pokharel, & Subba, 2010).

Participants completed a demographic form, the STSS, and the CIDI, Section E, and then discussed specific items from each of the STSS subscales. In this chapter we report their discussions of items 8, 16, 29, and 31, which had been among those administered to the clinic participants: #2 through 9, 15, 16, 19, 29, and 31.

The women comprise an elite and unusual group compared to most women within Nepalese society. Relative to the larger population (within their age group), the overall enrollment of women in higher education was 3% in 2001, compared to 8% of men (Women in Development Network [WIDN], 2007).[7] Compared to the female outpatient participants, most of whom were nonliterate, these undergraduates were gaining new images of their possibilities through education. Thus, the focus groups offer a brief glimpse of how their relational schemas, measured by the STSS, are affected as traditional female role requirements collide with new personal opportunities. For the young men, education also offers opportunities and yet, in 2002–2003, when the focus groups occurred, men's prospects were being negatively affected by the social upheaval and turmoil during the Maoist conflict. Thus, men found themselves responsible for economic provision for families at a time when their chances for employment and career were severely limited.

Overall, male participants were older (mean age 25.98) than females (mean age 24.26). Women and men did not significantly differ on the following: marital and parental status, type of family (50% of women and 40% of men lived in joint families), religion (all women and 90% of men described themselves as Hindu), and income, with most reporting "average" income.

Cronbach alpha among women in the focus groups was $\alpha = .792$; for men it was $\alpha = .561$. Levels of self-silencing did not significantly differ for women and men, nor did women and men score differently on any of the items discussed in the focus groups (#8, 16, 29, and 31). Unlike findings in most depression studies, more men ($n = 12$) scored as experiencing major depressive episode by the CIDI than women ($n = 9$). For women only did self-silencing correlate with depression symptoms (.315, $p < .05$); the correlation among men was .187, ns. Finally, we compared means of the shortened version of the STSS used with outpatients with a similar calculated score for focus group participants and found significantly higher levels of self-silencing among the depressed outpatients relative to focus group participants both overall and by gender.

Listening to Self-Silencing in Nepal: Depression, Life Contexts, and Cultural Patterns

As depressed Nepali women and men describe the factors they think created their distress, women's narratives powerfully reveal the impact of gender inequality on their lives.[8] While both women (70%) and men (50%) most frequently describe problems in their relationships, 40% of women pointed to problematic relationships with their spouse, while 18% of men did. Thirty-five percent of women identified problems in relation to in-laws, while none of the men did. It is not surprising that women, but not men, report problematic in-law relations because the women live with their in-laws while their husbands are treated royally when they visit their wife's parents.

The outpatient women describe marital relationships of financial dependence, roles that require them to serve men and in-laws, physical and sexual abuse, truncated educational and occupational opportunities, and, for many, early marriages or widowhood that bring severe difficulties. For example, 60% of the women who considered their symptoms as caused by problems in their relationships described being beaten by husbands, while 8.8% said they were being beaten by in-laws. In 79% of women's interviews, relationship and economic problems overlapped; their narratives reveal that economic dependency made them unable to leave an entrapping relational situation (see Jack & Van Ommeren, 2007, for details). These factors not only contribute to women's feeling of a precarious existence but also encourage self-silencing as a survival strategy to avoid dire emotional, physical, and economic consequences from more powerful men and in-laws.

The high rate of familial violence reported by female outpatient participants is not unusual in Nepal, where more than one-third of women of all age cohorts have experienced violence against them in their homes (Bal et al., 2004; Paudel, 2007). The linkage between violence against women and depression is well established by studies in many cultures; yet, in Nepal, there is a "cultural silence on violence in the family" (Paudel, 2007, p. 217). Being a victim of battering is a known precipitant of depression and other health problems in women (see Astbury, Chapter 2).

Depressed male outpatients listed inadequate income (50%) on a par with relationship problems as causing their symptoms (50%). Problems with work overlapped with income concerns in almost every instance. Men also described health problems as causes of their distress. The details of the men's family problems will be presented in the examples that follow.

What does self-silencing sound like among these Nepali women and men diagnosed with major depression in the outpatient study? Given their difficult social and material life circumstances, does the self-silencing construct add any explanatory power for understanding precipitants of their depression? We will draw on interviews from depressed outpatients and focus group undergraduates to illustrate similarities and differences on the four subscales of the STSS: Care as Self-Sacrifice, Silencing the Self, Divided Self, and Externalized Self-Perception. (For a full explanation of the subscales, see Chapter 1.) The relational schemas represented by these subscales reinforce each other so that as one aspect is strengthened, it heightens the other three. Subscales are intended to capture the phenomenology of depression and have no specific order of importance (Jack & Dill, 1992). For example, the more a woman perceives herself through others' eyes (Externalized Self-Perception), the more she may feel a requirement to engage in self-sacrificing behaviors that are part of the female "good woman" role (Care as Self-Sacrifice); silence her own desires, voice, and feelings (Silencing the Self); and outwardly comply with others' expectations while inwardly resisting or rebelling (Divided Self). In U.S. studies, the dynamic of silencing the self contributes to a fall in self-esteem and feelings of a loss of self, and associates with depression across a wide range of studies (see Chapter 1). The four subscales are neither discrete nor mutually excusive; thus, the following examples will contain aspects of more than one schema.

Care as Self-Sacrifice: Examples from Outpatients Diagnosed as Depressed

This construct reflects the "good woman" morality of selflessness that was central in the narratives of depressed women in the United States (Jack, 1991, 1999). Placing the needs of others before the self as a moral demand and as a required behavior reveals one way social subordination is internalized: A woman considers her needs and wishes as less deserving than those of others for whom she cares. This rule of subservient "goodness," when continually followed, both reflects and lowers one's value and negatively affects self-esteem. What occurs in Nepal, when care as self-sacrifice is demanded of women through strong cultural traditions?

In the depressed outpatient women's accounts,[9] self-sacrifice is a constant in their lives, yet they receive none of the expected returns for this caring behavior. They describe that putting others first occurs within negative relationships that are characterized as disconnected, debasing, emotionally abusive, and/or violent.

Explaining the troubles and hostility in her family, Sarmila, age 42, from a small village outside Kathmandu, expresses resentment that her self-sacrifice has not brought expected benefits within the family. She describes herself as the daughter-in-law in a family of six with average income, a Hindu of the Chhetri caste, and nonliterate. Her STSS (short form) score was 42, less than one standard deviation below the outpatient women's mean of 47.68.

> I was the one who found wives for my brothers-in-law. Because the responsibility was on me for all household things, I did not attend to my own happiness at all. Once the in-laws were married, all our family was scattered. I had to take care of all the festivals, and now I continue to be responsible for taking care of my relatives because my sisters-in-law do not do anything. I feel that I never get anything back when I give to others. I cannot talk to my husband because he has heart problems. Women have to stay and sacrifice for men. My in-laws dominate my children, saying bad things about them and to them, and my in-laws hate me. My husband has a second wife.

After 29 years within her husband's family, Sarmila finds herself isolated among in-laws who do not value her long-term contribution to their welfare. Though she has followed the traditional life path and behaviors of a good Nepali woman, Sarmila has not experienced any positive returns. Instead, she feels disconnected and isolated by the family's hostility, even that her in-laws hate her.

Married at 13 and completely dependent on this family, Sarmila has hidden her feelings behind outward compliance and self-sacrificing, "good woman" behaviors. But the litany of injustices in her narrative shows that Sarmila is clearly angry and resentful. She describes her current symptoms as precipitated by her family's increasing animosity toward her children's future. It appears as if Sarmila could endure her own maltreatment and disconnection, but not when it extends to her son or daughter. The family (including her husband) dismisses her daughter's future marriage as unimportant, as unworthy of the family's resources or obligations: "My in-laws dominate my children and say that my daughter will do a 'flying marriage' [go off with any man without a formal marriage ceremony] so they do not need to arrange one." Also, her sister-in-law is now turning against her son, saying that he will inherit none of the family property. Her family's insulting refusals to help arrange a suitable marriage for her daughter and their hostility to her son's inheritance signal that her children's positive future is severely jeopardized. Her family is not fulfilling their duty to care for its members, leaving her self-sacrifice unrewarded, her children excluded, and her security in old age threatened.

Sarmila has little power within the family to influence these events that are central to her life. Being reflected as marginal and valueless to her family threatens her interdependent sense of self, a self that is part of and depends on the extended family. It also threatens her self-esteem which is based on the regard of others, particularly within the collective "we" of the family[10]. Saying that she "speaks to no one about my troubles," Sarmila's distress becomes so overwhelming that she takes the unusual step of seeking outside help at the clinic. Doing so reflects the depth of her alienation from family as well as her despair.

Men's outpatient narratives provide examples of the care as self-sacrifice construct that sound very different from women's. To understand, we must look through the frame of the "good man" as pictured in Nepal. This idealized image contains specific standards by which a man often measures his success or failure: providing for the family, achieving status in the community, and exercising family leadership. Traditional masculinity, especially in Hindu society, requires hiding weakness and vulnerability. It also requires competition and assertion in wider society, depending on one's caste. Describing what caused their symptoms, men in the outpatient study primarily detail tension around the roles they are expected to perform, a lack of respect from their family, or being distressed by family members' nonconforming behavior that threatens family reputation.

In addition to different norms of goodness that direct their self-evaluation and feelings of despair, men and women have different power and prerogatives in Nepali society. Men are less subject to the will of others and have greater personal freedom than women, but they bear the major responsibility for the family's survival. For men in Nepal, "responsibility for the family's survival" is a more accurate name than "care as self-sacrifice" for the relational schema that directs their self-sacrificing behavior. Men often must sacrifice their own goals and desires to provide for the family. Yet, in Nepal as in many countries, providing economically for the family affirms and supports men's dominance. Conversely, the inability to provide adequately for the family can threaten a man's sense of masculine identity and his feelings of worth. The following example reveals the interconnections among these aspects of male identity, self-sacrifice, and self-silencing.

Krishna, age 28, Hindu, of the Chhetri caste, is married with two daughters and lives in a joint family of 11 in a small village in far eastern Nepal. He is the second son. His STSS (short form) score is 61, roughly one and a half standard deviations above the male mean (47.26).

> We men have goals in our life. But since I left school I could not reach the level of my friends. My older brother used to stay away from the village because he was a government jobholder. All of the family workload is borne by me. Because of this I was down. I felt low. I started worrying about it. Finally it got worse. Yesterday...I had a severe headache. I had difficulty in breathing. Friends took me to the hospital and the doctors told me to go to mental hospital.

Krishna also describes his self-silencing and psychological despair.

> Recently I am not confident. I think about too much. I hide things. I can't think of any new plan. It's not seen that I am suffering from sickness while I am with friends. It worries me very much. When angry at times I am violent; I beat people then later I regret it. I feel I will die. It's really hard to show people how bad my suffering is. I want to talk but I don't. It is really hard to control my brain.

Summing up the primary reason for his symptoms, he says, "I am not to be able to be as good as others."

Krishna begins with the central issue that repeats through his interview: He cannot reach his goals and, comparing himself to others, he feels inferior. Because he left school at 16 to marry for love rather than wait for his family to arrange a marriage, his brother and friends have surpassed him in status and options. They have jobs and income and live away from the village, visible aspects of male success. He is sacrificing his own goals to bear "all of the family workload," which makes him feel trapped. Anxiety and hopelessness accompany his inability to think of a new plan to improve his life. Krishna feels his responsibility to the family intensely, yet also yearns to chart his own path as his brother and friends have done. Caught between these two incompatible aims, he becomes seriously depressed.

Guided by a masculine script, Krishna does not reveal his vulnerability to anyone; instead, he self-silences. He also describes the behaviors of a "divided self" as he presents an outwardly normal self to others while hiding his suffering. His isolation and disconnection only reinforce his humiliation and despair. In accord with cultural norms for men's emotional expression prevalent in Nepal and many other countries (Moller-Leimkuhler, 2003), he expresses depression through anger and violence. Self-silencing furthers his disconnection, increases his anxiety over his conflicts, lowers confidence, and creates a trap of self-imposed isolation: "I want to talk but I don't." The distress that brings Krishna to the clinic is so intense that he feels like he "will die."

The relational schemas that direct Sarmila's and Krishna's behaviors are clearly shaped by cultural pressures regarding gendered behaviors in Nepal. They take opposite form in the two preceding examples. Sarmila experiences despair when fulfilling the expected role of self-sacrifice does not bring emotional closeness, security, and belonging within the family. Her social powerlessness leaves few alternatives for her life. Though Krishna has social power, he carries the male role responsibility to provide for his family. His distress arises from the incompatibility of his desires to pursue his more individualistic, personal goals as they directly conflict with his family responsibilities. His self-sacrifice comes through providing his labor for their survival. His feelings of conflict and unhappiness as he fulfills this cultural requirement lead to anguish, which he hides by self-silencing.

Care as Self-Sacrifice: Examples from Undergraduate Focus Groups

In the undergraduate focus groups, married women's discussions of care as self-sacrifice[11] were filled with descriptions of putting husbands and their husbands' families first, while unmarried participants focused on fathers and brothers. Unlike the depressed female outpatients, most undergraduate participants critiqued the model of selflessness expected of women, yet they are participants as well as observers of the behaviors they describe: "Our culture and society always demands that we should play a certain role of sacrificing ourselves to please men in every sphere of life as mother, wife and daughter who provides love and security to men." Their critical assessment highlights the rapid changes occurring in Kathmandu as women experience their own personal aspirations. Nevertheless, the relational schema that one should be selfless, that is, pleasing, compliant, and putting others' needs first, maintains a strong grip on their thoughts and actions.

The following quotes from focus groups participants had wide consensus:

"One should act especially to please her own husband because, by nature, men rule over women's freedom and constrict their desires."

"Women always sacrifice their interest and desires to keep their relationship and tolerate everything to some extent because our society does not allow us to go live alone separate from the family. The family and children are everything in the life of women."

"Women are always tolerating events and demands of their husbands and family members because of their maternal home. The husband's family always accuses the daughter-in-law's parents and relatives if she makes any mistake; they will disrespect her parents."

"We give priority to our husband's happiness to maintain conjugal life. We learn such behavior from mothers and sisters in law who always give husbands first priority. Before marriage, parents teach their daughters to give more care and love to the family where she is going to marry than to the family of origin. It is one of the good traits of the ideal daughter in law that one should follow to keep joint family atmosphere good."

Undergraduate men also emphasize the importance of families and family harmony in their lives; however, their self-sacrifice is not based on pleasing but on respect for hierarchy in the family. The majority in each focus group agreed that "they all try their best to keep their family happy" and make sacrifices for the elders in the family, primarily parents. For example, "I am studying just to please my parents. I wanted to work in a business but because of my family I am doing a degree." "I married the girl chosen by my parents even though I did not want to get married at the time." "My plans were to go into the army but because of my parents I am studying economics."

These young men also discussed the responsibility they bear for the family: "Being the eldest son, I am responsible for the happiness of each family member of the home, fulfilling their needs and providing security." "They [men] are the source of happiness of their family – their life–partner and others." Some men explicitly disagreed with the requirement for self-sacrifice: "It is necessary to have self-esteem, and act like a man. Society doesn't demand that we sacrifice our interests and will for the sake of others' happiness."

While women's examples reveal that they self-sacrifice for men, men's examples show that they expect their wife's or future wife's adjustment to the man's home and his wishes:

"It is not necessary to act in a special way to please my life partner. She is also a part of the family and should blend into the home atmosphere, take care of herself, and not be demanding of me to treat her differently."

"When my wife wants something, it is difficult. I try to manage the situation by being neutral, trying not to please nor rebuke her." Other men agreed, saying, "If we please our wives, other members of the [joint] family will be angry with us and say, 'I am henpecked [joitingre].''

A married man said he will agree with his wife to please her only after evaluating her wishes in light of acceptability to society and his family norms: "If she [wife] wants to wear a skirt instead of a traditional sari or kurta surwal, I cannot give permission to her." This statement gained wide agreement in his focus group.

Thus, while both women and men stress the importance of maintaining family harmony, they do so in very different ways—women by sacrificing their "interests and desires" to men who have social power, men by reinforcing the family hierarchy through obedience to elders and expectations of conformance from wives. Among undergraduate men, as in the depressed men's example, "care as self-sacrifice" does not capture the flavor of the schema that directs their behavior in relationships. Rather, the phrase "responsibility for the family" also more accurately encompasses their descriptions.

Silencing the Self and Divided Self: Examples from Outpatients Diagnosed as Depressed

The Silencing the Self schema directs a person to keep "unacceptable" thoughts out of expression in intimate relationships. Divided Self represents a person's presentation of an outer self that does not correspond with inner thoughts and experiences. While the person outwardly complies with expected behaviors, inwardly, he or she often feels angry and rebellious (Jack, 1991, 2003). How do these concepts sound in interviews with depressed Nepali women and men and in the focus groups, where the cultural requirement to maintain family harmony would seem to encourage self-silencing and the experience of a divided self?

The following example shows how silencing the self interlocks with the experience of a divided self in depression. Sushma is 35, Hindu, of the Chhetri caste, and lives in Kathmandu. She has never attended school and is nonliterate. Her STSS score is 49, less than one standard deviation above the women's outpatient mean. An arranged marriage at 15 to a husband who was 30 has severely curtailed her options. She says that she came to the hospital on her own for symptoms of "sleep disturbance, I am easily irritated, have a heaviness of my head—I feel some movement inside my head, appetite loss, and fearfulness. While walking on the road I become afraid." When asked what she thinks has caused her symptoms, she responds:

> When I got out [of the hospital], my husband beat me as I was unable to do house chores, and my husband never loved me. I have three children but he still beats me when he is drunk. My husband is the main cause of my illness. Because of him I am ill. He never cared about me, he does whatever he wants. He doesn't listen to me. Every night he is drunk and he tries to manipulate my children saying 'Your mother will leave you one day.' There are five people in my family and we all live in one rented room. We have to cook and sleep in the same room. My husband is an electrician, my children study, so the economic condition is very bad.

Sushma illustrates themes common to the depressed participants: arranged marriage at a young age to an older man, economic dependence on her husband, and marital violence with few options for escape. She feels isolated and power-less in a nuclear family without possible help from an extended family or other women within a village. Her feelings accurately reflect these factors and, together with her gender inequality, powerfully affect her agency.

Sushma states, "I do not share anything with anyone else." She despairs at her children's response to their father's negative talk about her: "It is very painful as I took care of them for all this time and now I see distrust in their eyes. They behave differently, they don't listen to me." Prior to this, Sushma's children had been a source of positive connection and intimacy. Now she fears that love and support from her children—which is also women's economic insurance—is being stolen by her husband. Women who are alone do not fare well in Nepali society. Lacking resources, education, or extended family, her choices are limited.

Telling her story for the first time, Sushma does not blame herself for her situation nor does she feel any personal responsibility for her husband's beha-vior: She did not make the choice of whom to marry and has little influence over her husband. She has fulfilled all the demands of her role, including bearing two sons and making the best of a bad marriage. She protests her unlucky fate: "I feel like I am the unluckiest person because my husband does not love me and now my children are changing." In fact, arranged marriage is an uncertain fate for women in Nepal, with no guarantee of a good man or kind in-laws. Not only can a husband be a drunkard but he can also hoard or squander scarce resources.

Sushma's interview also reveals her divided self: "I do not have good relationship with my husband. In front of others I act as if nothing is wrong but really things are very bad." Sushma follows the norm of hiding family troubles when with others. But inwardly, she is angry at her husband who "never loved me," "never cared about me," "does whatever he wants," "doesn't listen to me," and "beats me." Sushma is not passive or submissive in accepting her misfortune. As she sees distrust in her children's eyes, Sushma's sense of doom and betrayal increases, leading her to take a major step of resistance to her unlucky fate. She seeks outside help. Though a violent marriage may have forced her to self-silence and appear outwardly compliant, her inner anger and despair propel her into action. Realistically, however, Nepal has few long-term solutions for women who are impoverished and nonliterate and who courageously move out of abusive marriages. Sushma may choose to risk the dangers of the street rather than the ongoing humiliation and pain of her marriage when paired with losing her children's love.

Men's self-silencing is not associated with inequality, financial dependency, and/or fear of the partner, recurring themes in Nepali women's interviews. Rather, it most often pairs with a desire to hide one's shame and fear, and to maintain dominance through presenting an image of strength. While women outwardly present compliance and subservience as part of a divided self, men outwardly present their power, that is, their invulnerability, while silencing feelings that may appear "weak."

The strongest reason for self-silencing among men is not their vulnerability in relationships but their fear and humiliation due to perceived failures to live up to the demands of the male role. The example from Prakash, age 38, married with two children, no formal schooling but literacy, is emblematic. His (short form) STSS score of 47 is close to the male outpatient mean.

> I know I am sick, I am here for treatment. I am scared to become mad. I went to other hospitals and they told me to come here to mental hospital. I feel like I am losing myself, my memory power is going down. I am not able to work and if I don't work I won't be able to make my family happy. I have headaches. . . . I feel like I will die very soon or I won't be able to work ever in my life. I always think about my children. My children ask me for school fees and my wife asks for money to buy household things at that time if I don't have any money, I get angry. I don't tell anything to anyone or they might go and tell others and laugh at me. They won't help me at all, I know that very well so it is a waste to tell them about my problems.

Prakash first sketches the terrain of his inner world, a realm where he feels "scared," that he is "losing myself," and where he feels he "will die." He hides these vulnerable feelings of anxiety and pain, fearing humiliation and ridicule if they become known. His self-silencing leads to a divided self, with an outer self fashioned to appear strong to hide his inner fear. When his wife asks for money, Prakash quickly hides his shame and inadequacy behind a mask of anger. Prakash also fears the stigma that accompanies "madness" in Nepali society, which may explain why he first went to hospitals that have no mental health clinics. He worries about his children's futures, wanting to pay for their education as insurance for their success and well-being. Prakash's self-silencing and deeply divided self lead him to suffer in isolation, cut off from the care and concern that he might receive from his family.

Like Prakash, depressed male outpatients are more self-blaming than are the depressed female participants. Perhaps because men have more freedom and power to make choices and pursue their goals, they are relatively more individualistic than Nepali women and thus feel more responsible for their successes and failures. Because a man's failure in his provider role affects the family negatively, it also can threaten a man's interdependent sense of self as well as his masculine identity that rests on his achievements, status, and social comparison. Even though the origins of men's self-silencing and the aspects of self they hide differ from those of women, their silence nevertheless furthers disconnection and associates with depression.

Silencing the Self and Divided Self: Examples from Undergraduate Focus Groups

In each focus group, women spoke about how men's dominance affects their self-silencing and leads them to behave outwardly in ways that don't reflect their inner self. The quotes below illustrate the interlocking nature of self-silencing and divided self[12]:

> "Because men are the ones that govern women's desire and interests, we always keep silent even though the situation is very terrible sometimes." A number of the female focus group participants said that not addressing their own interests or saying their feelings makes them feel *ukus mukus*, "suffocated inside the heart."
>
> "I talked with my husband about stopping studies as I do not want to continue, but my husband became angry about it; from then on I never talked about my studies with him. I am continuing my studies because of my husband's wishes."
>
> "I am adjusting to living in a joint family and not saying what I think because they blame 'educated' women for the break-up of the family. When we get higher education, we face the stereotype that our in-laws believe it is difficult to make an educated woman obey; the image is that once women become educated, they become selfish."

One woman lucidly summed up the tension between her inner and outer realities: "Our culture and society always demands that we should play a certain role of sacrificing ourselves to please men in every sphere of life as mother, wife and daughter who provides love and security to men. Sometimes I play a fake role to maintain family happiness and peace though it hurts me very badly." Enacting a pretense of outer compliance exacts an inner cost, dividing her experience of self. She can describe what she is doing and why. This awareness likely derives from education, which gives her the freedom of an unsilenced voice of critique at the university, while, at home, she mutes her voice and complies with expectations about her behavior. Gender is actively (re)produced through purposely self-silencing and following prescribed "good woman" behaviors.

These undergraduates actively negotiate the ideologies defining good Hindu women, including the social practices, meanings, and practical conditions of being a wife, mother, and student. For example, one student said, "It is very difficult to make my husband go out for an outing to minimize boredom. But slowly and gradually, I have convinced him and have been able to keep my own interests intact, but it took a lot of effort and time. I did this because it is culturally prohibited and impossible to go out alone after marriage." This young woman subverted existing limitations on women's freedom but stays within traditional confines, working toward a solution in which she could keep her interests alive but not invite criticism or social disapproval. Her example illuminates how women exercise their agency to create a path, without breaking relationships, between their desires and interests and the social structures that constrain them.

Men's discussion of self-silencing provides a picture that agrees with women's emphasis on keeping family harmony, but sharply diverges in terms of how and when one does so. For example, across focus groups, most men said that they must silence their opposing voice toward parents and other senior family members: "We must consent and can't argue. It is the way of keeping peace and harmony in the family; otherwise it will ruin the family life." But others qualified the preceding statement, commenting that silencing one's will is only required in trifling matters: "We need to compromise in order to maintain relationships, and compromise is okay for small things. It should not be against your nature and will; otherwise that relationship can be broken at any time." Other men thought they did not need to moderate self-expression: "We can express ourselves freely...because we are the son, or the male."

Men agreed that they can only show a certain kind of feeling, and not reveal their vulnerability: "A Nepali saying is 'never show your sorrows to others.' It gives more trouble to you than it makes you happy." They describe suppressing vulnerable feelings rather than expressing them. Some agreed with one man's comment, "Sometimes I take alcohol to make myself able to reveal thoughts that are not acceptable in front of family members so that they will think I am drunk and not in a normal state and that's why I talk so freely. It is a kind of strategy to speak out loud to feel free of tension." In other words, alcohol frees the tongue to speak about feelings that are ordinarily disallowed.

In discussing the STSS item denoting divided self, a number of men thought that "if we try to suppress feelings, it will burst out in anger which takes away the peace of the home. It is impossible to act to please others. It is better to confront a situation directly and make adjustments." Further, some groups agreed that "sometimes we hide personal weakness and feelings to be good in front of the others." Men also used the term *ukus mucus* in Nepali, saying that while trying to suppress the thoughts and feelings "it starts a pain in my chest." Many men said that "we can't reveal our inner feelings easily," with one participant reporting, "I don't have the vocabulary to make them easily expressed in a proper way."

Externalized Self-Perception: Examples from Outpatients Diagnosed as Depressed

This concept reflects an experience of self and self-judgment that are based on cultural standards and the opinions of significant others. In a collectivist culture, where individuals are more attuned from the outset to "see the self through others' eyes," what meaning might this concept have in relation to depression?[13]

The fall in self-esteem, present in Nepali depressed participants' interviews, appeared to be located in an experience of self that is embedded in relationships and in the regard of others. This experience of self has been labeled by Roland (1991, p. 225) as a "we-self" rather than an "I-self"[14] more characteristic in Western individualist countries. While the loss of self-esteem occurs in depression across cultures, in the U.S., it appears most often to derive from a failure to measure up to one's own, internalized standards. The more individualistic the sense of self, the more the guilt over a "failure" since the individual is accountable, through whatever choices have been made, for creating something of the self. In Nepal, a person's choices are strongly determined by others in the family and by "fate."

Depressed women and men clearly locate the "feeling about what I should be" in their ability to fulfill cultural and family expectations. In Nepal, *laj*, the term most often translated as shame, arises from violations of expected behaviors. For Hindu women, shame accrues when departing from behaviors of the Brahmanical cultural model of the "good woman," especially regarding violations of sexual restraint and modesty (Bennett, 1983; Galvin, 2006; McHugh, 2001; Skinner & Holland, 1998). These values, reflecting the "eyes" of the culture, are experienced as an "Over-Eye" (Jack, 1991), which keeps the self in line with cultural standards and directs ongoing self-judgment and behavior. For example, the restrictions on women's physical movement, self-expression, and sexuality are internalized and work as a form of self-inhibition and self-surveillance. For men, shame arises when one has fallen short of expectations attached to the idealized "good man," such as an inability to provide economically for the family, revealing one's weaknesses or vulnerability, or incidents of obvious disrespect from others (Skinner, Pach, & Holland, 1998).

Meena, age 22, who has completed a year of college, was brought to the clinic by her parents. Her STSS (short form) score was 48, less than one standard deviation above the female outpatient mean. She met with the interviewer by herself. In response to why she came for treatment, she said, "When I think of the past I am afraid of the future. For the past one and a half months I like to be alone, and do not want to talk to anyone." After this, Meena answered only yes or no to questions until the end of the interview, when she described the events she felt were causing her symptoms:

> When I was 16, I was in love with a man and had an affair for five years. My boyfriend and I had sex many times. [Interviewer: 'Why did you have a sexual relationship with him before marriage?'] He used to love me so much and we were about to marry, so in this situation, sex did not seem such a big thing. But a year ago, he left me and married someone else. I asked him why and he said, 'I don't need you any more. I got what I wanted from you – I needed a pass-time girl, so I loved you and passed a happy time with you, and now I don't need you because someone else is in my life and she is my wife.' I could not eat anything for two days and just kept on crying and crying.... I started staying alone in my room and stopped talking to anyone. Even today my parents do not know the reason behind my illness.

Assuming she would marry her boyfriend, Meena violated Nepalese norms that good Hindu women abstain from sex until marriage (even the interviewer asks why she would do so). Suddenly, this man's humiliating words undercut her own vision of their past love's reality and her own value. His abandonment holds more than a loss of love—it threatens her identity and her future. If others, including her parents, learn of her sexual relationship, it will be hard for them to arrange a good marriage because she has been "spoiled." Hindu women in Nepal who deviate from the life path of the good woman are considered problematic and are punished in a variety of ways (Skinner & Holland, 1998, p. 93).

Reduced to nothing more than a "pass-time girl" by the man who held her future, Meena can no longer view her sexual actions as justified by love and future marriage. She had risked flouting cultural standards to choose her own partner and enact her desire. But this rebellion has come to a tragic end. Through whose eyes, through what values, does she now see and judge herself? Struggling over how to interpret herself or envision her future, she, in fact, grapples with her identity as a good or bad woman in Nepal.

Meena's example also highlights how women fear punishment for sexual transgressions while men do not: Four of the outpatient men described their relations with prostitutes, while one described his sexual assault of a young adolescent girl. The last question of the interview asks, "How do you feel about the interview, and do you have any other comments or questions for us?" Meena replied, "I feel relief but I feel afraid even now because I don't know what is going to happen next." Self-silencing increases Meena's isolation: Alone in her psychological as well as physical room, she fears her future. It is possible that Meena felt better after the interview with the young Nepali female interviewer who was warm and understanding. We do not know what happened with Meena, as she was from a remote district that required days of travel to Kathmandu. She was prescribed amitriptyline and told to return in two weeks. She never returned.

Depressed men's narratives were filled with the feeling of "what I should be is not what I am." Men locate the gap between the "should be" and the reality of their lives by measuring themselves against the societal standards of traditional masculinity. As they describe it, this requires being both the primary wage earner and dominance in marriage and the family. In the following example, we can see how this model operates when traditional roles are violated and the wife is the primary wage earner.

Bal, 28, is Hindu, Chhetri caste, and married with one son. He lives in a joint family of 10 in Kathmandu, and has completed primary school. He is the oldest son, and reports that there is not enough food for his family. Bal describes the symptoms for which he seeks treatment: "I feel heaviness on my head, sometimes my vision is blurry and I can't identify the person." He says, "I cannot work, I cannot share things with anyone, I have to bear whatever people say to me." His STSS score is 45, two points below the male outpatient mean. Asked "Are there difficulties at home that are causing problems?" Bal responds:

> I can't stand my wife. I become irritated whenever I see my wife. I want to fight with my wife. I lose my temper at small things. I am always discussing this with my friends. They tease me and make jokes because my wife works and earns more than I do. She is running the family with her money. I become angry when people say that 'you are living on your wife's money.'... I don't know why I get so irritated whenever I see my wife. I feel she is my enemy. I have inferiority complex. I feel like my wife tries to dominate me so I beat her. I am always worried about what my family thinks of me because I cannot work and my wife is earning for us. I sometimes feel trapped and regret why did I get married. That is why I am ill....
> I don't share my things with anyone. I wish I could work like other people. When I'm angry I go out, I don't talk to anyone. I beat my wife and son.

Bal clearly sees and judges himself through others' eyes as he describes his despair. His friends' barbed teasing defines his disgrace while their jokes convey a cultural requirement. As the oldest son, his duty is to provide the family income and he has failed. Providing the family's income is a clear standard by which others—as well as himself—measure his success and failure. The double bind—that he and his family need his wife's income but her income humiliates him—sustains his feeling of being trapped. To ward off the negative judgment, both from himself and others, Bal turns his wife into the enemy and his humiliation into rage and hostility, beating his wife and son in order to reassert his power and control. In Nepali society as well as in many countries, men learn that anger and aggressiveness are ways to express psychological pain, particularly against women (Moller-Leimkuhler, 2003). Cut loose from his moorings in masculinity and experiencing a loss of face with others, Bal's self-esteem plummets into an "inferiority complex."

Externalized Self-Perception: Examples from Undergraduate Focus Groups

Undergraduate women in the focus groups agreed with the statement (#31) from the Externalized Self-Perception subscale that "my feeling about what I should be is not what I am." Their statements to follow reveal that they see and judge themselves from two clashing perspectives: Traditional role requirements compete with new possibilities of achievement. Married women across a number of groups agreed that "Our roles as wives, mothers and daughters-in-law are obstacles to our academic advancement." One participant said, "I'm satisfied with my married life but still when I think about my career and compare with my unmarried friends, I feel that I've lagged behind." They also said, "Household responsibilities come to mind at the time of study." Other representative comments include: "Women are always deprived of family as well as social support for our career development." "Being the eldest daughter, I have to hold the responsibility for the family and do not have time to think for myself." These conflicts surrounding the feeling of "what I should be" reveal that new opportunities create possibilities and problems for identity and self-judgment as university women try to fulfill competing standards.

The standards men use to see and judge themselves came up strongly as they discussed the sentence "my feeling about what I should be is not what I am." Their discussions turned quickly to the social obstacles that kept them from pursuing their sense of what they should be or want to be. These obstacles kept them from regarding themselves and their futures positively. Nepal's political chaos and the social disruption from the Maoist insurgency have brought new pressures on these men. Their concerns included being financially dependent on their families, worry that their future prospects are slim because of the social disruption caused by the Maoist insurgency, concern that they would never be able to financially provide for their family, and that they were not recognized in society and might never be. They also frequently identified social problems that they feared hindered their future opportunities, such as the poor quality of the educational system, disappointment with the university, inadequate English classes, and a failure to be admitted to the department they wanted, as well as other concerns. Male students identified problems with civic society three times more often than did female students, not surprising since men's lives take place in the public arena, whereas women's lives are still mostly confined to the home (Jack et al., 2010).

When undergraduate men described their feeling that they are not the person they should be, their blame was not self-directed but placed on the political situation, the poor educational system, a civil society that is in upheaval, and the socioeconomic context that offers few career opportunities. However, some of the focus group members blamed themselves for being incompetent in studies, not finding work, or a lack of aggression and initiative in pursuit of their goals.

Concluding Observations and Further Questions

The exploratory studies of women and men presented in this chapter confirm the relevance of the self-silencing construct for understanding depression in Nepal. The situations that women regard as precipitating their distress involve disruption, violence, or problems in a core relationship. These circumstances are characterized by loss, humiliation, entrapment, social inequality, and a lack of viable options in order to exercise choice and control. These Nepal findings offer a useful cross-cultural comparison corroborating known precipitants of women's depression identified by other studies in South Asia (Trivedi, Mishra, & Kendurkar, 2007) and elsewhere in the world (Broadhead & Abas, 1998; Broadhead, Abas, Sakutukwa, Chigwanda, & Garura, 2001; Brown, 2002; Brown & Harris, 1978; Cabral & Astbury, 2000; Kessler, 2003). They also call attention to the effects of inequality and violence on women's lives (see Astbury, Chapter 2) and support the vital importance of social action to address these known factors that affect women's depression.

Numerous studies in the West identify the absence of a confiding relationship as a vulnerability factor for women's depression (see, for example, Brown, Harris, & Hepworth, 1995). While in Nepalese society, as in other South Asian countries, the majority of people do not usually discuss personal, physical, or mental problems outside the family, most people have at least one confidant—usually a family member (Rodrigues, Patel, Jaswal, & de Souza, 2003). Research in India, the country with a culture most similar to Nepal's Hindu society, also identified a woman's keeping feelings to herself as a central factor in postpartum depression (Rodrigues et al., 2003). Most of the depressed women in Nepal describe isolated disconnection within their families, without a confidant, in a cultural context where one's well-being and even survival are rooted in familial relationships.

Self-silencing adds an important dimension to these known precipitants. Depression is an illness of disconnection. Interpersonal events that precipitate depression are characterized by their threat of social disconnection as well as the ongoing, stressful experience of living in intimate relationships that are demeaning, conflictual, threatening, and nonconfiding. The very act of hiding feelings from others affirms to the self that what is being concealed is unacceptable or dangerous. Self-silencing, which is elicited and also reinforced by negative relational events, furthers disconnection from others as well as from one's self. It heightens the impact of adverse circumstances through increasing a person's isolation, exacerbating the psychological impact of difficult ongoing situations. Threats of isolation from the family (to survival itself) if one communicates unacceptable feelings creates a difficult bind that can activate the pathways of mutual influence among psychological, biological, and social processes that together precipitate depression.

Most people who live in social adversity do not develop a depressive disorder (Trivedi et al., 2007). While each person in the outpatient study identified specific stressors that he or she considered to cause their symptoms, the vast majority also pointed to vigilant, isolating silence as a core factor. Importantly, self-silencing is a relational action, not an individual trait or a cognitive style, but rather a negotiation of self in relationship. It follows lines of social power and expected gendered behaviors with the goal of insuring safety and/or closeness. However, self-silencing reduces the possibility of a close, confiding relationship within which one can share life's problems while it also creates an inner dynamic of loss of self, lowered self-esteem, and inner division. Is it possible that self-silencing is one of the processes that mediates the relationship between social adversity and depression?

For example, self-silencing might mediate between social adversity and depression through its effect on the self. With India, Nepal shares a collectivist emphasis on the family with an interdependent sense of self. Even though, as attachment and feminist theorists have emphasized, the self is inherently relational and motivated toward connection, culture affects the experience of self, emotions, and behaviors (Oyserman et al., 2002). More research within collectivist cultures would help our understanding of how the construct of self-silencing may affect vulnerability to depression in ways that may differ from more individualist cultures. In addition, social factors such as caste, arranged marriage, and education may strongly affect self-silencing and depression within these cultures. The Nepal studies lay the groundwork for such further research, including an examination of the role of self-silencing as a mediator between adverse social events and depression.

Analysis of the depressed men's interviews and focus group discussions revealed that the motivations and goals of their self-silencing differed from those of women. For the depressed men, hiding vulnerability through self-silencing in compliance with demands of "masculinity" associates with depression, while it also protects and reproduces men's position of dominance. Men's feeling of "what I should be" clusters around different attributes of self than does women's. As a group, Nepali men enjoy different levels of material and social power than women and face different demands to fulfill their roles: self-assertion rather than self-sacrifice, dominance rather than submission. As a result, their images of relatedness—how to make and maintain relationships—differ from women's in the "shoulds" that direct behavior and self-judgment. Their moral beliefs about a "good man," embedded in their relational schemas, direct their self-silencing and restrict their willingness to reveal difficult feelings. From depressed Nepali men's interviews, it is clear that their self-silencing holds negative psychological consequences of increasing isolation and diminished self-worth.

In the focus groups, women and men scored similarly on the STSS, yet discussions of specific items within the groups revealed that each gender attributed different meanings to the items, underscoring the need for a foundational study of self-silencing in men. STSS mean scores among Nepali students are sharply higher than scores reported for white undergraduates in the United

States, possibly because collectivist values of self-restraint and harmonizing in relationships do not conflict with self-silencing. As well, the marked gender inequality and strongly delineated gender roles may heighten self-silencing in Nepal and, thus, endorsement of scale items. In Western cultures, self-silencing conflicts with the individualist emphasis on self-development and self-expression, which may curb agreement with scale items.

Silencing the self theory rests on the assumption that the self is relational, that relationships have profound effects on our biological mechanisms, our minds, and on all aspects of functioning (see Schore, 2003; Siegel, 2001). Depression, too, most often appears to be social/interpersonal in origin and effect. Emotional experience and regulation, as revealed in these interviews from Nepal, are not individual processes, but rather interpersonal ones that unfold within specific social/relational contexts, influencing and influenced by biopsychosocial factors. Accordingly, self-silencing is not considered a "response set" of passivity, a stable personality factor, or a form of inadequate coping with difficult circumstances. Rather, the relational schemas that direct self-silencing in women and men are shaped by the objective realities of their lives as well as by the social mentalities within cultures. These schemas affect the most important aspects of their lives: how to connect within important relationships and how to be a valued "good" woman or man in society.

Gender, in Nepal as elsewhere, profoundly affects how one can be a "self in intimate relationship," what a person may voice, and what must remain unspoken. Depressed women and men in Nepal describe that maintaining family and important relationships is a core value. Even though the self-silencing relational schemas that direct their behavior differ by gender, for both, hiding tormenting feelings and vital aspects of self in order to sustain important bonds plays a central role in precipitating depression.

Notes

1. The Hindu caste system is complex and important in Nepal. In this research, the "untouchable" castes were very few in number and we did not analyze STSS scores in relation to caste. For an overview of caste, see Pradhan and Shrestha (2005).
2. The Hindu epic, the *Ramayana* from the 3rd century BC, supplies this ideal through the example of Sita, who undergoes one sacrifice after another for her husband, Lord Rama. The story is known in its broad outlines by almost all Nepali Hindus.
3. Vidaya Sharma, MD, of Tribhuvan University Teaching Hospital; Nirakar Shrestha, MD, former director of Patan Mental Hospital, the only government mental hospital in Kathmandu; and Mark Van Ommeren, PhD and Bhogendra Sharma, MD, of the Center for the Victims of Torture (CVICT), were collaborators. Without their expertise and help, the work would not have been possible.
4. The CIDI has been translated into Nepali and utilized in a study among Nepali-speaking Bhutanese refugees (Van Ommeren et al., 1999; Van Ommeren et al., 2001). Questions from this measure were asked verbally by trained Nepalese

interviewers. The CIDI assesses DSM-IV depression as a binary variable (*present/not present*) and point prevalence indicates a diagnosis based on the presence of symptoms within the past two weeks.

5. Interviewers had been trained in qualitative interviewing by Dana Jack and in administering the CIDI, Section E, by Mark Van Ommeren. Interviews and the instruments were administered verbally in a private room in the clinic. Interviews were not tape recorded, since such equipment is unfamiliar to many. Interview notes were written out after interviews and translated into English by the interviewers.

6. Bindu Pokharel, PhD, was on the faculty at Women Studies, and now teaches in the Department of Rural Development. Usha Subba was teaching in the Psychology Department at Tribhuvan University.

7. The tertiary gross enrollment ratio is defined as enrollment at third level, regardless of age, expressed as a percentage of the population in the theoretical school-age group corresponding to this level of education. The women's share of tertiary enrollment refers to the percentage of students enrolled in tertiary education who are female (United Nations Statistical Division, 2004).

8. Written interviews were typed and imported into Ethnograph software, which allows systematic analysis of themes. Five students were trained to code interviews; the following analysis results from the codings.

9. In all outpatient examples that follow, each participant has been diagnosed as depressed by Nepali psychiatrists and also has scored as depressed on the CIDI. All of the examples that follow come from Hindu outpatient participants, and all names are fictitious.

10. While women in the United States also experience a relational self, the "we-self" regard in Nepal appears to be based much more within family relationships. In the United States, it appears more based on the quality of the intimate marital relationship and/or on the "successful" individual self based on one's achievements.

11. The English version reads, "In a close relationship I don't usually care what we do, as long as the other person is happy," while the Nepali translation says, "Often I don't take care of my own happiness if it gives happiness to my loved ones."

12. The Nepali version of item #8 reads, "When my life-partner's needs and feelings conflict with my own, I will tell him or her clearly" (reverse-scored, Nepali translation), and item #16 reads, "On the outside I am looking happy but on the inside, I am seething" (Nepali translation).

13. Item #31, one of the items in the Externalized Self-Perception subscale, reads in English: "I never seem to measure up to the standards I set for myself." While the English sentence clearly locates the standards within the person, even as individually chosen, the Nepali translation is more ambiguous regarding the location of the standards: "My feeling about what I should be is not what I am." The Nepalese translation appears to be more collectivist in orientation, with "what I should be" located not so specifically within the self as self-chosen standards.

14. Roland (1991) describes the "we-self" as follows: "...the inner representational world of Indians is much more organized around images of 'we,' 'our,' 'us'; or around an 'I' that is always relational to a 'you,' usually in one or another kind of hierarchical relationship. This is in contrast, for instance, with the American highly individualistic sense of 'I' and 'me,' with its inherent duality between 'I' and 'you,' the

'you' frequently being implicitly a more or less equal other in egalitarian relationships or even hierarchical ones" (cites omitted, p. 225).

References

Bal, S. K., Pokharel, A., Ojha, S. P., Pradhan, S. N., & Chapagain, G. (2004). Nepal mental health country profile. *International Review of Psychiatry, 16*, 142–149.

Bennett, L. (1983). *Dangerous wives and sacred sisters: Social and symbolic roles of women in Nepal.* New York: Columbia University Press.

Broadhead, J. C., & Abas, M. A. (1998). Life events, difficulties and depression among women in an urban setting in Zimbabwe. *Psychological Medicine, 28*, 29–38.

Broadhead, J., Abas, M., Sakutukwa, G. H., Chigwanda, M., & Garura, E. (2001). Social support and life events as risk factors for depression in an urban setting in Zimbabwe. *Social Psychiatry and Psychiatric Epidemiology, 36*, 115–122.

Brown, G. W. (2002). Social roles, context and evolution in the origins of depression. *Journal of Health and Social Behavior, 43*, 255–276.

Brown, G. W., & Harris, T. O. (1978). *Social origins of depression: A study of psychiatric disorder in women.* New York: Free Press.

Brown, G. W., Harris, T. O., & Hepworth, C. (1995). Loss and depression: a patient and non-patient comparison. *Psychological Medicine, 25*, 7–21.

Cabral, M., & Astbury, J. (2000). *Women's mental health: An evidence-based review.* World Health Organization. Retrieved October 18, 2002, from http://whqlibdoc. who.int/hq/2000/WHO_MSD_MDP_00.1.pdf

Chow, M. K., Thapa, S., & Achmad, S. I. (2001). Surveys show persistence of teenage marriage and childbearing in Indonesia and Nepal. *East-West Center Population and Health Studies, 58*, 1–4. Retrieved November 14, 2008, from http://www2. eastwestcenter.org/pop/misc/p&p-58.pdf

EarthTrends. (2003). *Population, health, and human well-being – Nepal.* World Resources Institute. Retrieved March 25, 2005, from http://earthtrends.wri.org/ pdf_library/country_profiles/pop_cou_524.pdf

Fikree, F. F., & Pasha, O. (2006). Role of gender in health disparity: The South Asian context. *British Medical Journal, 328*, 823–826.

Galvin, K. (2006). *Forbidden red: Widowhood in urban Nepal.* Spokane, WA: Washington State University Press.

Human Rights Watch. (1995). *Rape for profit: Trafficking of Nepali girls and women to Indian brothels.* Retrieved July 17, 2003, from http://www.hrw.org/sites/default/ files/reports/india957.pdf

Human Rights Watch. (2007). *Children in the ranks: The Maoists' use of child soldiers in Nepal.* Retrieved March 19, 2008, from http://www.hrw.org/reports/2007/ nepal0207/3.htm

Jack, D. C. (1991). *Silencing the self: Women and depression.* Cambridge, MA: Harvard University Press.

Jack, D. C. (1999). Silencing the self: Inner dialogues and outer realities. In T. E. Joiner & J. C. Coyne (Eds.), *The interactional nature of depression: Advances in interpersonal approaches* (pp. 221–246). Washington, DC: American Psychological Association.

Jack, D. C. (2003). The anger of hope and the anger of despair: How anger relates to women's depression. In J. Stoppard & L. McMullen (Eds.), *Situating sadness: Women and depression in social context* (pp. 62–87). New York University Press Series on Qualitative Studies in Psychology, Michelle Fine & Jeanne Marecek (Series Eds.). New York: New York University Press.

Jack, D. C., & Dill, D. (1992). The Silencing the Self Scale: Schemas of intimacy associated with depression in women. *Psychology of Women Quarterly, 16,* 97–106.

Jack, D. C., Kim, J., Pokharel, B., & Subba, U. (2010). *Self-silencing and depression among undergraduates in Nepal.* Manuscript submitted for publication.

Jack, D. C., & Van Ommeren, M. (2007). Depression in Nepalese women: Tradition, changing roles, and public health policy. In V. M. Moghadam (Ed.), *From patriarchy to empowerment* (pp. 243–257). Syracuse, NY: Syracuse University Press.

Kessler, R. C. (2003). Epidemiology of women and depression. *Journal of Affective Disorders, 74,* 5–13.

Kleinman, A., & Good, B. (1996). *Culture and depression.* Berkeley, CA: University of California Press.

Lauber, C., & Rossler, W. (2007). Stigma towards people with mental illness in developing countries in Asia. *International Review of Psychiatry, 19,* 157–178.

McHugh, E. (2001). *Love and honor in the Himalayas: Coming to know another culture.* Philadelphia: University of Pennsylvania Press.

Moller-Leimkuhler, A. M. (2003). The gender gap in suicide and premature death or: Why are men so vulnerable? *European Archives of Psychiatry in Clinical Neuroscience, 253,* 1–8.

Oyserman, D., Coon, H. M., & Kemmelmeier, M. (2002). Rethinking individualism and collectivism: Evaluation of theoretical assumptions and meta-analyses. *Psychological Bulletin, 128,* 3–72.

Pach, A. (1998). Narrative constructions of madness in a Hindu village in Nepal. In D. Skinner, A. Pach III, & D. Holland (Eds.), *Selves in time and place: Identities, experience, and history in Nepal* (pp. 111–128). New York: Rowman & Littlefield.

Paudel, G. S. (2007). Domestic violence against women in Nepal. *Gender, Technology and Development, 11,* 199–233. Retrieved October 7, 2008, from http://gtd.sagepub.com

Pradhan, R., & Shrestha, A. (2005). *Ethnic and caste diversity: Implications for diversity.* Working Paper Series No. 4, Asian Development Bank, Nepal Resident Mission. Retrieved October 14, 2007, from http://www.adb.org/Documents/Papers/NRM/wp4.pdf

Rodrigues, M., Patel, V., Jaswal, S., & de Souza, N. (2003). Listening to mothers: Qualitative studies on motherhood and depression from Goa, India. *Social Science and Medicine, 57,* 1797–1806.

Roland, A. (1991). *In search of self in India and Japan: Toward a cross-cultural psychology.* Princeton, NJ: Princeton University Press.

Schore, A. N. (2003). *Affect dysregulation and disorders of the self.* New York: WW Norton.

Siegel, D. J. (2001). *The developing mind: How relationships and the brain interact to shape who we are.* New York: Guilford Press.

Skinner, D., & Holland, D. (1998). Contested selves, contested femininities: Selves and society in process. In D. Skinner, A. Pach III, & D. Holland (Eds.), *Selves in time and place: Identities, experience, and history in Nepal* (pp. 87–110). New York: Rowman & Littlefield.

Skinner, D., Pach III, A., & Holland, D. (Eds.). (1998). *Selves in time and place: Identities, experience, and history in Nepal.* New York: Rowman & Littlefield.

Trivedi, J. K., Mishra, M., & Kendurkar, A. (2007). Depression among women in the South-Asia region: The underlying issues. *Journal of Affective Disorders, 102,* 219–225.

United Nations Development Programme. (2001). *Nepal human development report 2001.* Retrieved February 14, 2002, from http://www.adb.org/Documents/Papers/NRM/wp4.pdf

United Nations Statistical Division. (2004). *Technical notes.* Retrieved on November 14, 2008, from http://www.focusintl.com/education4.htm#TECH

Van Ommeren, M., deJong, J., Sharma, B., Komproe, I., Thapa, S. B., Jakaju, R., et al. (2001). Psychiatric disorders among tortured Bhutanese refugees. *Archives of General Psychiatry, 58*(5), 475–482.

Van Ommeren, M., Sharma, B., Thapa, S., Makaju, R., Prasain, D., Bhattari, R., et al. (1999). Preparing instruments for transcultural research: Use of a Translation Monitoring Form with Nepali-speaking Bhutanese refugees. *Transcultural Psychiatry, 36,* 285–301.

Women in Development Network. (2007). *Adult literacy rates in Nepal 2001.* Retrieved November 14, 2008, from http://www.focusintl.com/education1.htm

World Bank. (2006). *Poverty reduction in South Asia: Poverty in Nepal.* Retrieved January 18, 2009, from http://web.worldbank.org/WBSITE/EXTERNAL/COUNTRIES/SOUTHASIAEXT/EXTSAREGTOPPOVRED/0,contentMDK:20574069~menuPK:493447~pagePK:34004173~piPK:34003707~theSitePK:493441,00.html

World Health Organization. (1997). *Composite International Diagnostic Interview* (Section E, Core Version 2.1). Geneva: World Health Organization.

8

Silencing the Self across Generations and Gender in Finland

Airi Hautamäki

The "Strong Woman" Tradition in Finland

In this chapter, I explore the question, has the early individualization of Finnish women, which has its deep roots in the hard-working peasant woman working as an equal, side by side with her husband, been reflected in their attitudes about self-silencing in relationship? By the term "individualization," I refer to a woman's ability to differentiate or develop a sense of distinctiveness from the family (Björnberg, 1992; Hautamäki, A., 2000), based on taking part in the labor force and economic independence. Thus, the individualization of women implies that women take part in the labor market as working individuals in their own right, and not only as representatives of their family or husband (Bjerrum Nielsen & Rudberg, 1994). First, I will explore historical and social factors that have affected the individualization of women in Finland, child-rearing practices and their effects on women and men, and depression and suicide in Finland. Then, through presenting the findings from a series of studies, I examine the central issue of this chapter: how and whether self-silencing differs between gender and generation in Finland.

In Finland, the early individualization of women as working individuals was rooted in the old rural community. In fact, a matriarchal tradition appears in the national epic of Finland, named Kalevala (Lönnrot, 1981). There, the Matron of the North (*Pohjolan emäntä*) sends men to war and to work. In this early epic, men may serve women, and women may go hunting in the woods alongside men. Before World War II, Finland was a poor, predominantly agricultural, sparsely populated country, living off its forests. In the old Finnish rural community, families did not have enough money to keep mothers out of work. Finnish women worked full time along with men on the small farms, which rendered

175

the Finnish woman her traditional identity of persistence, stamina, and strength. The process of swift urbanization in Finland began during World War II, when Finnish women entered the public arena and the workplaces outside the home. Finnish society has developed from a rural to a predominantly urban, knowledge-based society within the last half of the twentieth century. Finland differs from the other Western countries in the timing, speed, and intensity of this transition (Ingold, 1997).

The entry of women into the labor markets depended on the building up of the Nordic welfare state: public maternal welfare clinics, maternal leaves, from 1978 the right to share parental leaves, and public day care for working parents. The maternal leave (four months) is followed by the parental leave, which lasts six months. The parental leave can be taken by either the mother or the father. In addition, fathers can take between 1 and 18 days of paternity leave in order to look after their baby at home together with the mother, and paternity allowance is paid during the leave to the father. The amount of the maternity, paternity, and parental allowances is linked to earnings, with a minimum rate of EUR 22.04 per day for each allowance.

Traditionally, there has been a weak male breadwinner model in Finland; that is, the father has not been strong in offering economic welfare, and the role of the woman is both that of a mother and a worker (Garcia-Ramon & Monk, 1996). In the 1950s, about 51% of mothers worked outside home, and not more than 8% of those worked part time (Westman, 2000). The Nordic welfare state, providing public day care for all children, has made possible that in 1996, 91% of women worked outside the home, mostly full time. Since the 1970s, working outside the home in a full-time job has been the standard solution for Finnish women whose husbands do not provide enough economic support.

Because of the long maternal leaves, 94% of children younger than 1 year are taken care of at home. In 1996, only 22% of children younger than 3 years were in public day care. In contrast, 63% of the 3- to 6-year olds were in public day care. The number of children in Finland taking part in public day care corresponds to the average European level (Hautamäki, A., 2000). Along with maternal employment, parents also have come to share the household work, and fathers often take considerable responsibility for care of their children. In the 1990s, the idea of a negotiation of a new kind of gender contract on the family level was initiated by progressive social scientists, the aim of which would be a new kind of fatherhood. Both parents would be equally responsible for the care of their young children and domestic duties (Karisto, Takala, & Haapola, 1998). Currently, negotiations around the gender contract proceed, not only on the family level, but also on state and municipal levels. The historically early entrance of Finnish fathers into caretaking for their infants has been supported by encouraging paternal leaves by the federal government in Finland, that is, that fathers should use the parental leaves to the same extent as mothers do. Even though there has been a distinct move from the traditional, complementary gender roles toward equal and similar gender roles, still only a small part of Finnish fathers use their possibility to take the parental leave.

In contrast to the other Nordic countries, part-time labor has not been common in Finland. The special efforts (e.g., public day care) made in Finland to facilitate women's labor force participation are currently reflected in a high percentage (80.6%) of dual-earner couples. The length of the workweek among these couples is relatively long, 77.4 hours per week (Jacobs & Gerson, 2004). In an international comparison between 10 countries, Finland has the highest ratio of wives' to husbands' hours of paid work among dual-earner couples. Finnish women have, in fact, achieved the highest level of equality in paid working time. Working women contribute with 92% as many hours on the job as do their spouses. Married American women (36.4 hours) rank second only to Finnish women (37.2 hours) per week in the length of the average workweek (Jacobs & Gerson, 2004). Even if there also are more extensive public investments in day care for young children in Finland, Jacobs and Gerson (2004) conclude that there is a price of gender equality. The double burden working women carry includes substantial time pressures in dual-earner families.

It is not surprising that Finnish women have been considered strong. Legally they have equal rights to men in society. Finnish women were, in fact, the first in Europe to gain the right to vote at the state level in parliamentary elections, as early as 1906. However, gender is a structure according to which power still is distributed in the Finnish working life, in both a horizontal and vertical way (Haavio-Mannila, 1987). Men often occupy the leading top positions, women the more subordinate ones, and the labor market is segregated according gender; that is, men are more often found in technology, natural science, and administration, while women are more employed in humanities, education, and public health care and child care.

Is one result of the historically early individualization and emancipation of Finnish women that the Finnish cultural context differs from other cultural contexts in the demand for appeasing behaviors measured by the Silencing the Self Scale (STSS)? Do Finnish women feel that they have a voice of their own, that is, that their silencing the self schemas are less pronounced?

Attachment Patterns and Depression in Finland

Not only are social expectations about behavior in relationships considered to affect the level of self-silencing, but also individuals' models of attachment carry strong importance in terms of their potential to affect self-silencing beliefs and behaviors. The child's experiences with the caregiver, particularly the protective availability of the caregiver, are encoded into the child's memory systems as internal working models of self in relationships to others (Bowlby, 1973; Hautamäki, A., Hautamäki, L., Maliniemi-Piispanen, & Neuvonen, 2008).

The working models guide perception, interpretation, and behavior in close relationships. Operating outside awareness, they influence expectations and behavior in later close relationships (Crowell & Treboux, 1995). Three attachment patterns have been found to exist reliably across cultures: secure, avoidant, and ambivalent-resistant attachment (Ainsworth, Blehar, Waters, & Wall, 1978; Van IJzendoorn & Sagi, 1999).

A securely attached child has sensitive parents, and he or she has learned to seek and to receive protection and comfort when needed. Securely attached children have learned to express feelings openly, because they have developed trust in the protective availability of caregivers (Ainsworth et al., 1978). Finnish culture has a smaller proportion of securely attached persons (Crittenden, 2000; Hautamäki, A., Hautamäki, L., Neuvonen, Maliniemi-Piispanen, in press) than found in other countries (Van IJzendoorn & Sagi, 1999); the most frequent attachment pattern among healthy Finnish toddlers is avoidant, that is, dismissing of feeling (Moilanen, Kunelius, Tirkkonen, & Crittenden, 2000). This dismissive or avoidant attachment pattern is also predominant in the adult population, particularly among men, according to studies hitherto conducted in Finland (Hautamäki, A., et al., 2008; Männikkö, 2001).

Avoidant children have been reinforced in a predictably negative way for display of affect, particularly fear, desire for comfort, and anger. Their working models of attachment are organized cognitively to inhibit affect and to seek predictable outcomes. Avoidant children learn to organize their attachment-related responses by deactivating their attachment system via minimizing their emotional displays (e.g., their eye contact with the caregiver) and by taking an early responsibility for regulating their affect. For an avoidant or dismissive adult, defense against processing affective information, such as by numbing of affect, is effectively organized (Crittenden, 2006). A person characterized by a more dismissive attachment style dismisses his or her own feelings and tends to look at things through the eyes of his or her parents (and later, significant others), and to deactivate the attachment system by diverting attention to other, less affectively arousing issues (Crittenden, 2006).

The affects dismissed in an avoidant or dismissive attachment pattern are anger, fear, and desire for comfort. The dismissive attachment style is linked to the following prototypic attachment self-report statement in the Relationship Questionnaire (Bartholomew & Horowitz, 1991): "I am comfortable without close emotional relationships. It is very important to me to feel independent and self-sufficient, and I prefer not to depend on others or have others depend on me."

Independence and self-reliance have been demanded in rural contexts in order to survive the hard winters and economic hardships, particularly in the scarcely populated areas in Finland (Crittenden, 2000). According to Crittenden (2000), parents of avoidant (Type A1-2) children offer sufficient protection against real danger, but less comfort in daily hassles. The time and place for direct communication and sharing of feelings have been restricted in the hard rural everyday life. Parents have tended to respond to the child's affect (anger, fear, pleas for comfort) when it has signaled real danger, but consistently have rejected what seemed to be "unnecessary" affect, when the parents thought that the child actually was safe. By taking the perspective of the significant other, the child learns to inhibit these "unnecessary" affects, and becomes independent early in regard to his or her affective self-regulation. An individual with a dismissive attachment style may feel obliged to take into account and adjust to the perspective of significant others, even at the cost of his or her own feelings (Crittenden, 2006). Thus, a dismissive attachment style is based on cognitive self-schemas that include dismissing the self and one's own feelings by taking one-sidedly the perspective of the significant other in close relationships. Some parallels may be drawn to silencing the self schemas, particularly in terms of what Jack and Dill (1992) call "externalized self-perception."

Crittenden (2000) proposes that the Finns represent an industrious population with a homogenous culture that emphasizes self-reliance, predictability, and hard work more than fun or happiness. But the same avoidant strategy, dismissing of feelings, with which Finns have learned to protect themselves from the invariant risks of the long, cold winters and a difficult geopolitical position in relation to mighty neighbors may create specific psychological risks, that is, disorders related to the inhibition of affect (Crittenden, 2000, p. 372): "Thus, depression and its ultimate expression, suicide, were the dangers of both the over-inhibition of negative affect and unrestrained negative affect." Particularly, a very strong and consistent inhibition of affect may increase the risk of sudden intrusions of affects (i.e., the individual is flooded with feelings that he or she is not prepared to cope with). For example, violence may be acted out in a state of intoxication with alcohol.

Finland has high male suicide mortality, among the highest in Europe, especially among young Finnish men (Diekstra & Gulbinat, 1993; Lester, 1997; Lönnqvist, Henriksson, Isometsä, Marttunen, & Heikkinen, 2003). Currently, suicide is the most common cause of death among Finnish men aged 20 to 34 (Pesonen, 2006), and Finnish men commit suicide four times more often than Finnish women. Fifteen percent of Finnish men have been thinking about suicide, compared to 9% of Finnish women (Pesonen, 2006). Alcohol dependence, heavy drinking in combination with alcohol intoxication, increases the risk of suicide in Finland (Poikolainen, 1995). The prevalence of alcohol dependence has been more frequent among men (7%) than among women (2%), based on data collected from a nationally representative sample of 8,028 people (Pirkola et al., 2004). Since the 1990s, Finnish women have, however, increased their consumption of alcohol, which may show up in the increase of suicidal behavior in the next decades to come. In fact, alcohol-positive suicides among women increased during 1987–1996 in Finland (Pesonen, 2006).

Since the beginning of the 1990s, some preventive efforts regarding suicide have been taken (e.g., alerting health personnel to the early signs of self-destructiveness, improving health care services and antidepressant medication, and increasing the cooperation between health authorities, social workers, and the police) (Pesonen, 2006). In the last 15 years, there has, in fact, been a slight decline in the trend of suicidal behavior in Finland, particularly among men.

Depressive mood and major depressive episodes have, however, been more prevalent among women (Isometsä, Aro, & Aro, 1997; Kessler, 2003). These differences in rates of depression between men and women seem to hold even if there are methodological differences in regard to design and sampling (Rytsälä, 2006). The prevalence of an episode of major depression during the past 12 months was more common among women (7%) than among men (4%) in Finland, based on symptom data collected from a nationally representative sample of 8,028 people utilizing the World Health Organization's Composite International Diagnostic Interview (Pirkola et al., 2004). The Finnish results concerning the gender gap seem consistent with those obtained in Western European countries and North America (Marecek, 2006). Women were more active in seeking help for their problems than men (Lester, 1995), the prevalence of the use of mental health services was more common among women (7%) than men (4%), and use was most common in the age group 45 to 54 years (Pirkola et al., 2004). The prevalence of antidepressant use in adults rose from 3.6% to 7.3% between the years of 1994 and 2003; in men, it rose from 2.7% to 5.4%, and in women, from 4.5% to 9.1%. Thus, the increase in antidepressant use from 1994 to 2003 doubled for both Finnish men and women (Sihvo et al., 2006). However, the relative increase was greatest among young adults, with a similar trend for men and women.

Studies of Self-Silencing, Depression, and Attachment in Finland

According to theory, silencing the self is responsive to the demands of the social context for certain behaviors of women. Thus, silencing the self should differ in accordance with the historical changes of the cultural context, that is, the progress of the individualization of women (Bjerrum Nielsen & Rudberg, 1994; Hautamäki, A., 2000). Silencing the self, then, may lessen as women become more equal to men economically and through the psychological process of individualization within the family.

In order to explore the relationship of self-silencing to individualization, gender, and depression, I conducted the following studies. The psychometric properties of the STSS were assessed in three low-risk samples in Finland. Participants included undergraduate students from two universities in Finland in order to assess how endorsing silencing the self schemas were related to depression among young men and women. The third study attempted to measure the differences in self-silencing schemas and attachment styles among women of two generations: mothers and their adult daughters, as well as a small number of the daughters' spouses. These participants were part of a study focusing on transmission of attachment across three generations, from grandmother to grandchild (Hautamäki, A., et al., 2008). Because of the small numbers of participants, the three studies are more exploratory than confirmatory.

The first study occurred at the University of Joensuu in Eastern Finland. The STSS (translated into Finnish by the author) and the Beck Depression Inventory (BDI) (Beck, Steer, & Garbin, 1988) were administered to 30 female psychology undergraduates and 31 male computing science students. Female participants' mean age was 25.5 years ($SD = 7.38$); male participants' age mean was 23.2 ($SD = 3.55$). Internal consistency of the STSS and the subscales was found to be acceptable (Nielsen, 1999), as reported in Table 8.1.

In the second study, 70 female social science undergraduates and 51 male social science undergraduates at the University of Helsinki in Finland's capital city completed the same instruments, the STSS and the BDI. The female mean age was 22.7 years ($SD = 4.4$); males' was 23.2 ($SD = 2.9$). Internal consistency of the STSS and the subscales was also found to be acceptable (see Table 8.1) (Sigfrids, 2008).

The third study consisted of a low-risk sample of mothers and their adult daughters, part of a larger examination that focused on the transmission of attachment across three generations (Hautamäki, A., et al., 2008). The sample could be considered a community sample, as the participants were enrolled through the local maternity guidance offices visited by all the expectant mothers from the respective areas. Criteria for inclusion were that the married or cohabiting couple was expecting their first child, the expectant mother was at least 18 years old, and the maternal grandmother agreed to participate in the study. The health care nurses gave all the visiting expectant mothers a written presentation of the follow-up study, inviting them to participate. Enrollment in the study was voluntary.

Thirty-three mothers and 34 adult daughters responded to the STSS; additionally, a subsample of husbands of the adult daughters also completed the STSS ($n = 20$). Mothers, their adult daughters, and their adult daughters' husbands also completed the self-report Relationship Questionnaire on attachment styles (Bartholomew & Horowitz, 1991) based on Bartholomew's (1990) four-category model of adult attachment. The respondents reported their degree of correspondence to four attachment styles: secure, dismissing/avoidant, preoccupied/ambivalent-resistant, and fearful, using a 4-point Likert-type scale.[1] Prototypic descriptions of the four attachment styles were treated as continuous variables. As a forced-choice approach was not used, the respondents could not be classified into attachment styles.

Additionally, mothers and their adult daughters completed the Identity Structure Analysis (ISA) (Weinreich, 1980, 1986), a measure that analyzes individuals' construals of their gender identity based on their endorsement of culturally

Table 8.1 Descriptive Statistics and Internal Consistency of the Silencing the Self Scale (STSS), Subscales, and Total Scores for Three Groups

STSS	n	M	SD	Cronbach alpha
Study 1				
Female undergraduates	30			
1.Silencing the Self		17.23	4.83	0.80
2.Externalized Self-Perception		13.50	4.42	0.77
3.Care as Self-Sacrifice		22.23	4.52	0.66
4.Divided Self		12.53	4.08	0.74
TOTAL		*65.50*	*12.57*	*0.84*
Male undergraduates	31			
1.Silencing the Self		22.06	4.88	0.71
2.Externalized Self-Perception		14.90	4.21	0.67
3.Care as Self-Sacrifice		24.06	4.73	0.57
4.Divided Self		16.48	4.03	0.56
TOTAL		*77.52*	*10.39*	*0.68*
Study 2				
Female undergraduates	70			
1.Silencing the Self		19.72	5.63	0.78
2.Externalized Self-Perception		15.87	4.86	0.74
3.Care as Self-Sacrifice		22.66	5.33	0.66
4.Divided Self		14.24	5.37	0.81
TOTAL		*72.05*	*14.94*	*0.85*
Male undergraduates	51			
1.Silencing the Self		22.72	4.25	0.56
2.Externalized Self-Perception		15.47	4.41	0.72
3.Care as Self-Sacrifice		24.00	4.34	0.53
4.Divided Self		16.11	5.69	0.84
TOTAL		*78.83*	*12.47*	*0.79*
Study 3				
Mothers	33			
1.Silencing the Self		23.13	6.15	0.79
2.Externalized Self-Perception		13.41	4.21	0.68
3.Care as Self-Sacrifice		25.91	5.46	0.65
4.Divided Self		14.25	4.53	0.78
TOTAL		*76.69*	*15.05*	*0.86*
Adult daughters	34			
1.Silencing the Self		15.25	3.50	0.79
2.Externalized Self-Perception		12.00	3.26	0.68
3.Care as Self-Sacrifice		23.53	5.12	0.65
4.Divided Self		9.03	1.75	0.78
TOTAL		*60.41*	*8.37*	*0.86*
Their husbands	20			
1.Silencing the Self		21.70	6.80	0.85
2.Externalized Self-Perception		12.95	4.33	0.73
3.Care as Self-Sacrifice		24.80	6.06	0.76
4.Divided Self		11.20	2.38	0.49
TOTAL		*70.65*	*16.35*	*0.90*

determined values and belief systems. Respondents were asked to check on a scale of zero to seven which position best reflected their views in relation to constructs such as "ambitious – not at all ambitious," "acts and thinks independently – lets other people guide oneself," "strong – weak," "dominant – submissive," "caring – mainly takes care of one's own business," "intelligent – less intelligent," "self-sacrificing – does not sacrifice one's own need because of the child," "always available for the child – not always available for one's child," etc. (Perander, 2005; Wager, 1998). In this study, the aim was to explore how these two generations of women construed their feminine identity based on the ISA.

The age of the mothers ranged from 39 to 73 ($M = 56$); the age of their adult daughters ranged from 19 to 35 ($M = 28$). The age of the husbands ranged from 19 to 42 ($M = 31$). The educational level of the adult daughters was high (74% had qualified for university studies, significantly higher than that of their mothers, 27% of whom had qualified for university studies), and also slightly higher than that of their spouses (43% had qualified for university studies) (Hautamäki, A., et al., 2008). The internal consistency (alpha) of the STSS and the subscales were examined separately for the women and men. Alphas on subscales are satisfactory except for subscale 2, Care as Self-Sacrifice (for women), and subscale 4, Divided Self (for men) (see Table 8.1).

Regarding construct validity, in the first study, female students' BDI scores correlated significantly ($r = .53, p < .01$) with their total STSS scores, as well as with the subscales Divided Self ($r = .64, p < .01$) and Externalized Self-Perception ($r = .60, p < .01$). Even if male students endorsed the STSS significantly stronger than female students, their STSS scores did not correlate significantly with the level of depression measured by the BDI. For men, only Externalized Self-Perception correlated significantly ($r = .57, p < .01$) with the level of depression as measured by the BDI. The female students' BDI scores ($M = 4.50$) did not differ significantly from that of the male students ($M = 6.45$).

In the second study, female students' BDI scores correlated significantly ($r = .51$, $p < .01$) with their total STSS scores, as well as with the subscales Divided Self ($r = .56, p < .01$) and Externalized Self-Perception ($r = .52, p < .01$). Also in this study, male students endorsed the STSS significantly stronger than female students. In contrast to the earlier study, their STSS scores correlated significantly with their BDI scores ($r = .48, p < .01$). Even the subscales Externalized Self-Perception ($r = .55, p < .01$) and Divided Self ($r = .52, p < .01$), correlated significantly with the level of depression as measured by the BDI, which was similar to the female participants. The female students' BDI scores ($M = 8.06$) did not differ significantly from that of the male students ($M = 7.52$).

In sum, the STSS and its subscales were reliable for both the Finnish female and male undergraduate studies, with the lowest reliability demonstrated by the Care as Self-Sacrifice subscale, that is, to put the needs of others before the self to secure attachments. This may reflect the new cultural model that accompanies the individualization of women in which self-denial is gradually being replaced by the ideal of self-fulfilment. Also, young women safeguard their autonomy and explore different options when they plan their lives (Björnberg, 1992). It is no longer a question of "either-or," either you are living for your loved ones or you live as an independent working woman. Instead, is more like "both-and." It is self-evident to combine both motherhood and work, living for others and for yourself, all at the same time. Oechsle and Zoll (1992, p. 53) conclude that this "doppelter Lebensentwurf" (i.e., subjective life planning that takes both family and employment into account) is the new normative model of female biography. The question is *how* one should combine living for others and living for one's own self-fulfilment. The life planning of Finnish women includes both options, and the Finnish welfare state has assisted in building up support systems for combining motherhood with active participation in working life. Apparently, the subscale Care as Self-Sacrifice does not interpret correctly the complex cognitive schemas of the Finnish female participants. Young Finnish women do not think that taking care of others would exclude possibilities to choose one's individual life style. One can, and should, do both.

Whereas the construct validity of the STSS for use with women was supported through the significant correlations with the BDI, evidence for men was mixed. Among the University of Helsinki social science undergraduates, the STSS correlated significantly with the BDI both for women and men, and these correlations did not differ significantly by gender (see also Gratch, Bassett, & Attra, 1995). In the second study, the female and male students were more similar to each other in terms of university programs studied (i.e., social sciences) than at the University of Joensuu study, in which female psychology undergraduates were compared with male computer science undergraduates. The latter group of young men may have been more stereotypically masculine, in the Finnish avoidant way, not reporting and even denying experiences of negative emotion (see Stapley & Haviland, 1989). Norms of masculinity in subgroups of men in European and American societies still put pressure on men to be detached, cool, and tough, as it were, to "bite the bullet" (Marecek, 2006).

As the participants in these studies were university students, the distributions of the BDI values were skewed to the lower range and their variation was very small. Very few BDI values fell into the clinical range. Apparently, the undergraduate participants in these studies pose limits regarding the extent to which results may be generalized. Possibly, studies of clinically depressed individuals would result in even clearer connections between the STSS and the BDI. Studies of low-risk populations may not suffice to address links between the STSS and depression, though, in Finland, these studies have demonstrated the reliability of the STSS scale and construct.

The STSS means of the undergraduates in the first and the second study in Finland were in general lower than means of undergraduates in comparable studies in the United States and Canada (Carr, Gilroy, & Sherman, 1996; Cramer & Thoms, 2003; Haemmerlie, Montgomery, Williams, & Winborn,

2001; Jack & Dill, 1992; Smolak & Munstertieger, 2002). This was true for both women and men.

STSS across Two Generations: Mothers and Their Adult Daughters and Spouses

In the mothers and daughters and their spouses study, the means of the STSS scores were lower for the younger, daughter generation of Finnish women than those of comparable studies of 155 Canadians in cohabiting relationships (Thompson, 1995), of 155 married Americans (Uebelacker, Courtnage, & Whisman, 2003), and of a community sample of 109 women and 89 men (Thompson, Whiffen, & Aube, 2001). Even though the samples have been small in Finland, and the Finnish studies therefore are more exploratory than confirmatory, the studies of younger women in Finland find lower self-silencing. This may reflect the early individualization of Finnish women as working individuals who toiled alongside their husbands in the old rural community. Additionally, the educational level of the women was significantly related to the total level of the STSS, $F(2,63) = 4.85$, $p < .011$; to the Care as Self-Sacrifice subscale, $F(2,63) = 4.21$, $p < .019$; and to the Silencing the Self subscale, $F(2,63) = 4.10$, $p < .021$: The lower the educational level, the higher the STSS. The two generations of women differed significantly on the STSS total score, $t(64) = 5.38$, $p < .000$; and on the subscales Silencing the Self, $t(64) = 5.85$, $p > .000$, and Divided Self, $t(64) = 6.11$, $p < .000$. After controlling for educational level, the results were the same: The mother generation had significantly higher STSS scores than their adult daughters. Particularly, Divided Self and Silencing the Self subscale scores decreased from one generation to the next, while Care as Self-Sacrifice and Externalized Self-Perception subscales remained similar from one generation to the next.

These changes on Divided Self and Silencing the Self subscales may be interpreted as generational effects, that is, that young women thought they were entitled to a voice of their own, which reflected changing gender norms and the individualization of modern working women in Finland. Their responsiveness to self did not, however, exclude responsiveness to significant others; the scores of Externalized Self-Perception and Care as Self-Sacrifice were similar to those of their mothers. Thus, the young women appeared to express the new cultural ideal of self-fulfilment (Björnberg, 1992), according to which taking care of others did not exclude self-fulfilment. But even if the silencing the self schemas of the mother generation differed significantly from those of their adult daughters, neither group, in their construals of their gender identity, stressed the traditional caring femininity of self-sacrifice. In their constructions of their gender identity (ISA; Weinreich, 1980), both generations valued strength, acting and thinking independently, and intelligence more than caring availability (e.g., being self-sacrificing, always available for one's child). There were no significant intergenerational differences in regard to these dimensions (Perander, 2005). Thus, even if the adult daughters silenced themselves less than their mothers did, both generations of women, independent of age, valued strength and autonomy more than caring availability in regard to their child. It is not probable that the daughter generation, even when they become older and perhaps more similar to their mothers, would lose their voice, taking into account both the long-standing ideal of the strong Finnish woman and the new cultural model of self-fulfilment.

STSS across Gender

Similar to other published studies but contrary to expectation (see Chapter 6, this volume), men scored significantly higher than women on the STSS in the three samples. In study 1, men scored significantly higher than women on the STSS ($t = -4.08$, $df = 59$, $p < .000$), particularly the two subscales Silencing the Self ($t = -3.88$, $df = 59$, $p < .000$) and Divided Self ($t = 3.80$, $df = 59$, $p < .000$). In study 2, men scored significantly higher than women on the STSS ($t = -2.53$, $df = 109$, $p < .013$), particularly the subscale Silencing the Self ($t = -3.30$, $df = 116$, $p < .001$). In study 3, men scored significantly higher than women on the STSS ($t = -3.02$, $df = 52$, $p < .004$) and the two subscales Silencing the Self ($t = -4.14$, $df = 52$, $p < .000$) and Divided Self ($t = -3.85$, $df = 52$, $p < .000$). The results are the same when controlling for the educational level of the spouses. These findings are consistent with Cramer and Thoms's (2003), Gratch and colleagues' (1995), Smolak and Munstertieger's (2002), and Thompson's (1995) results for men on the STSS.

Still, the means for the Finnish men on the STSS in the three studies were much lower than those for comparable studies of male undergraduates and men from community samples in the U.S. and Canadian studies reported earlier in this chapter. Even though both the United States and Finland are individualistic societies (Schaffer, 2006), they may differ in equality. As one of the Nordic welfare states, Finland is an egalitarian society in which equality is the founding and pervasive value. All individuals are considered equal in status, with the same rights. According to Schaffer (2006), the United States accepts the principle of social hierarchy with stress on competition and personal status. Combining Triandis's (1995) vertical versus horizontal classification of societies with the individualistic versus collectivistic distinction, the United States may be considered an individualistic and a vertical society (Schaffer, 2006), and Finland an individualistic and a horizontal society (in regard to the equality of education, see Hautamäki, J., et al., 2008). Perhaps the norms of masculinity for men in Finland, because of the generally accepted equality claim, put less pressure on men to be detached, cool, and tough. Additionally, the historically early entrance of fathers in Finland into the caretaking of their infants, supported also by the federal government's encouragement of paternal leaves, has increased expectations of more nurturing, emotionally more expressive fatherhood.

STSS and Self-Reported Attachment Style:
The Generational Study

Self-rated dismissing, preoccupied, and fearful attachment styles (Bartholomew & Horowitz, 1991) correlated significantly with the scores on the STSS for men and women, which is consistent with Silencing the Self Theory and our predictions.

For men, the total STSS correlated significantly only with a self-reported preoccupied attachment style ($r = .53$, $df = 19$, $p < .02$) as did subscales Externalized Self-Perception ($r = .55$, $df = 19$, $p < .01$) and Divided Self ($r = .55$, $df = 19$, $p < .01$): "I want to be completely emotionally intimate with others, but I often find that others are reluctant to get as close as I would like. I am uncomfortable being without close relationships, but I sometimes worry that others don't value me as much as I value them" (Bartholomew & Horowitz, 1991). Of the fathers, 57% reported that the secure attachment style described them well or very well. The corresponding percentages for the fearful attachment style were 14%, for the dismissive attachment style 9%, and for the preoccupied attachment style 9%.

In the group of older and younger women, 64% reported that the secure attachment style described them well or very well. As expected, secure attachment did not correlate significantly with the STSS. Eighteen percent of the women reported that the fearful attachment style described them well or very well and corresponded to their functioning in current close relationships: "I am somewhat uncomfortable getting close to others. I want emotionally close relationships, but I find it difficult to trust others completely or to depend on them. I sometimes worry that I will be hurt if I allow myself to become too close with others" (Bartholomew & Horowitz, 1991). The corresponding percentages were 3% for the dismissive attachment style and 11% for the preoccupied attachment style among women. For women, a fearful attachment style correlated significantly with the total STSS ($r = .47$, $df = 65$, $p > .000$), the subscale Silencing the Self ($r = .53$, $df = 65$, $p < .000$), and the subscale Divided Self ($r = .46$, $df = 65$, $p < .000$). A dismissive attachment style correlated significantly with the Divided Self subscale ($r = .37$, $df = 65$, $p < .002$) and the total STSS ($r = .25$, $df = 65$, $p < .04$). Also, a self-rated preoccupied attachment style correlated significantly with the total STSS ($r = .27$, $df = 65$, $p < .03$), the Externalized Self-Perception subscale ($r = .26$, $df = 65$, $p < .03$), and Silencing the Self subscale ($r = .27$, $df = 65$, $p < .03$).

An attachment style that was more atypical to one's gender, for women, the dismissive, for men, the preoccupied, appeared to be related to reporting silencing the self. Earlier findings (Bartholomew & Horowitz, 1991; Brennan & Morris, 1997) indicate that men perceive themselves as more dismissing and women as more preoccupied and fearful in their romantic relationships, consistent with Chodorow's (1978) distinction between the female relational self and the male separated self. One explanation is based on cultural stereotypes concerning male and female behavior: Men tend to present themselves as avoidant of closeness and dismissing feelings, and women tend to present themselves as more clingy and anxious (Feeney & Noller, 1996). For women, a self-reported dismissive or fearful attachment style was significantly related to the STSS, that is, what Jack (1991) described as "compliant relatedness." As data were correlational, they do not allow for causal statements concerning STSS variance and attachment style. A dismissive individual may, however, be more prone to take the perspective of the significant other, even at the cost of losing touch with his or her own feelings (Crittenden, 2006).

For men, in the third study, the preoccupied attachment style, atypical to their gender, appeared to be connected to compliant relatedness. Traditionally, preoccupied or anxious/ambivalent attachment has been connected to insecurity, emotional dependency, and clinging in love relationships (Hindy & Schwartz, 1994). Rooted in low self-esteem, it stems from a fear that the loved one is not available enough and results in a perpetual questioning of the partner's affections, coupled with coercive pressures for continued availability. An obsessive preoccupation may emerge with the romantic partner's responsiveness, parallel with feelings that the partner is reluctant to commit and insufficiently attentive (Hazan & Shaver, 1994).

The Individualization of the Finnish Woman: Narrative Examples

Results from the generational study may be discussed in terms of the cultural heritage transmitted across generations regarding how to cope with the necessities of survival characterizing the old Finnish rural way of life, that is, trying to cope through persistent hard work during the long, cold winters in combination with economic hardships (Hautamäki, A., et al., 2008). The mother generation in this study had been born before, during, or immediately after World War II, and some of them had even experienced the hardships, sufferings, and losses connected to the Winter War and Continuation War (Hautamäki, A. & Coleman, P. G., 2001). In the Finnish countryside, the work just had to be done in a predictable way in harsh living conditions. Committed to the cultural model of the Protestant ethic in its secularized version (Weber, 1978), hard work and self-denial were the supreme values for the older generation in this study. During their childhood in the 1940s and the '50s, they had experienced authoritarian forms of child rearing in combination with unresponsive parenting

(Hautamäki, A., 2000), which had created conditions for the development of avoidant or dismissive attachment (Hautamäki A., et al., in press). Many representatives of the older generation stated that they had tried to give their children a better life, for example, by encouraging them to make use of all the educational opportunities that the egalitarian educational system in Finland offered.

Among the older, the mother, generation, only 25% were securely attached, as assessed by the Adult Attachment Interview (AAI; Hautamäki, A. et al., in press). The narrative selections that follow are from the third study and are based on the closing, integrative questions from the Adult Attachment Interviews. In these questions, respondents are asked to assess the impact of their early experiences on their current functioning in close relationships, for example: "Any setbacks, something that has hindered your development?" "What did you learn from your parents?" "What would you like your child to learn from you, being your child?" In what follows, narratives of different generations represent mother-daughter pairs.

A pervasive theme among the older women interviewed with the AAI was a lack of self-worth, that is, positive self-regard or global self-esteem (Dutton & Brown, 1997). The first narrative was selected as an exemplar or prototypic description in which the respondent succinctly analyzed the impact of unresponsive parenting on her feelings of self-worth. The AAI attachment classification, the self-report attachment style, and the STSS score are reported. The quotations were translated into English by the present author. The BDI was not completed by this sample.

1. A 55-year-old mother of one child, working as a secretary, described the authoritarian and unresponsive rural child upbringing in the 1940s in Finland when answering the AAI question, "How do think your childhood experiences have affected your adult personality? Are there any aspects of your childhood that you think were a setback or hindered your development?": "In any case, one did not develop any kind of self-confidence. Because one never got any kind of feedback, if one had done something well or right. One never got any kind of praise. Instead only more was demanded." According to the interviewee, this created a lack of positive self-regard and self-worth in her relationships with other people, including her own child, in regard to what to permit the child to do and what not to do. To the interviewer's question: "How has this impacted your adult life?" the respondent answered: "Just until the last years. Now perhaps in the last five years, maybe it's an exaggeration, perhaps in the last three years, one has at last been reconciled with oneself." Note the interviewee's distancing way of speaking about herself in the third person, dismissing herself and her feelings.

In the Adult Attachment Interview, the respondent got the classification of avoidant, Type A2 classification (Crittenden, 2006). However, in her reflections in hindsight, the respondent expressed some emerging insight concerning the impact of unresponsive parenting. In the self-report Relationship Questionnaire, she gave herself the value of 2 (describes my view a little) to *all* four prototypic attachment style descriptions. According to a Finnish study using the Relationship Questionnaire, the tendency to rate one's attachment style with several attachment descriptions indicated a lower psychosocial functioning (i.e., weaker self-esteem and depression) and a less adaptive personality (Männikkö, 2001). The respondent's STSS score was 80, less than one standard deviation above the mean of the middle-aged female group ($M = 76.69, SD = 15.05$).

2. Her 26-year-old daughter studied at the university and responded to the question: "In what way do you think you are similar to your mother?" as follows: "Perhaps a little like that ... that you, in advance, before something happens you worry about it, somewhat unnecessarily. But she takes, in fact, care and worries much more than I do. . . . But sometimes you think that one would not always need to think and worry about everything [the respondent mimicked her mother, sighing deeply, like a very worried person, and went on talking, in her mother's worried voice]: 'As this is not quite good ... whatever will become of that?' And so I won't worry and ... Mother has always sort of been of a worrying kind. . . . Even if she has, when getting older, learned a little that she isn't that sort of a worrying kind any longer, she won't unnecessarily, particularly not in advance worry, but still . . . . She always did that before, but I only wait and [laughing] see, does the heaven really fall down on me or not!"

This adult daughter described her mother as worrying about everything in advance and trying to take care of everything, but herself as an easy-going person. She also presented herself as more temperamental than did her mother: "Well, I immediately become enraged if the kitchen is sloppy, but after that it's over very quickly. And, in that way, I perhaps express these ... opinions, even somewhat sharply at times [a disarming laugh]." As the interviewer asked: "You described yourself as 'open, talkative, and extravert.' Could you please tell me about a situation?" the interviewee responded: "Well, yes, I am like that ... among my friends . . . . We are that kind of female friends, that they are all that kind of very talkative. I may be that kind of ... may even seek the attention, like to be in the focus of attention . . . . There, if our opinion should be stated, then I am the one articulating it. That I am even pushed to do that: 'Well, you state it, as you are capable of expressing it.'" She described herself as capable of asserting herself, as much more assertive than her mother, and also as very capable of expressing her views. She even told about an episode in which she had advised and encouraged her mother to be more assertive in conflict situations at her job.

In the self-report Relationship Questionnaire test, she gave the value of 3 (describes my view well) to the secure attachment style description: "It is relatively easy for me to become emotionally close to others. I am comfortable depending on others and having others depend on me. I don't worry about being alone or having others not to accept me." Additionally, she gave herself the value of 2 (describes my view a little) to the preoccupied attachment style description. In the AAI, she got the preoccupied, Type C1-2 classification

(Crittenden, 2006).[2] The respondent's STSS score was 68, one standard deviation above the mean of the of group adult daughters ($M = 60.41$, $SD = 8.37$).

3. The difficulty of being honest when not allowed to express affect (e.g., anger, fear, or pleas for comfort) was stressed by a 42-year-old mother of five children, a farmer's wife, who took care of the cattle: "Concerning honesty, as one did not dare to tell [the parents, AH], if something had happened. Even if honesty was stressed, you would not dare, you got the feeling that you would get spanked anyway!" But the interviewee said that she had tried to do better with her own children: "They tell me whatever has happened.... Even my son in the primary grade, when he came from school, said: 'They will phone you from school.' I said: 'What did you do?' 'I went through the window, that's what they will phone you about.' When he opened the door, he immediately told me what had happened."

In the AAI, this participant was classified as "earned secure" (Pearson, Cohn, Cowan, & Pape Cowan, 1994). In contrast to "continuous secures," who have experienced sufficient comfort and protection in their early attachment relationships, earned secures have been able to develop a coherent perspective on their negative, early attachment relationships. Consequently, they are less prone to re-enact poor parenting practices with their own children (Lichtenstein Phelps, Belsky, & Crnic, 1998), they have overcome distressing childhood experiences, and they have been able to break the intergenerational cycle of malevolent parenting (Roisman, Padron, Sroufe, & Egeland, 2002). Earned secures also seem able to maintain their adaptive and flexible parenting under stress (Lichtenstein Phelps et al., 1998).

During her adult life, the interviewee seemed to have reorganized from an insecure attachment pattern into earned secure. Gradually, she had developed a coherent, nuanced view on her adverse early attachment relationships (i.e., a father abusing alcohol and, at times, beating up his wife). She could analyze, in a humorous way, how it had left her with a tendency still to see herself through the eyes of other people, trying to measure up to their standards. For this reason, she felt happy to have offered her children the possibility to honestly express their feelings, often perceived as negative.

However, even if earned secures are able to discuss their early distressing experiences in a coherent and nuanced way during the AAI, they still may be at a greater risk for depressive symptomatology in adulthood (Pearson et al., 1994). Many earned secures have high-quality adult romantic relationships (Roisman et al., 2002), which may have offered new ways of seeing and experiencing themselves during their adult years. The respondent said that when she met her spouse the first time, she recognized his "kind eyes." She described her relationship to her husband as very supportive in terms of "helpful to her," "taking care of her," "cheerful and easy-going," "honest," and "loyal." She offered the following episode for "cheerful and easy-going": "Then as I have the inclination that I occasionally wake up at nights and I start ruminating about things that have happened during the day, ... he, once in the morning, when I told him that, said: 'You should have woken me up, so we could have ruminated together!'" Thus, the respondent expressed an inclination to ruminate about past things, but also the possibility to share her worries with her husband. Additionally, she exemplified how kindly helpful her husband was: "He is observant, so to say, if you are there doing your work, and if he sees any kind of need for help, you don't have even to ask him, there he comes running. In the same way, if somebody asks, he immediately goes helping, you are not feeling like: 'Could I ask him or not?' but he is already there, devoid of all pretense, helping."

The respondent's STSS score was 55, which is more than one standard deviation below the mean of the mother generation in study 3. But the respondent's age was 42 years, at the low end of the age distribution of the mother generation, and far below the mean age of 56.

4. Her 20-year-old daughter, studying at the university, told the interviewer about her trusting relationship to her newly wed husband when answering the question: "Now, as an adult, what do you do, when you are upset?": "I go to Peter and ... crawl in his lap surely [laughing] there also, that no ... just as regressive as before." (Note the respondent's dysfluent speech around her desire for comfort and slight dismissal of it, which is typical of a more reserved person.) She answered the question: "You said that your relationship was 'equal'?" as follows: "Well, at least I feel that ultimately we have so similar, to some degree, goals and dreams, and things like that. ... There are, so to say, no conflicts. ... Perhaps Peter is even more flexible that I feel ... there are, so to say, no power struggles. I feel that I have my own peace [laughing]—you do not need to adapt yourself much." Her answer to the question: "You said that you have a 'confidential' relationship with your husband?" was as follows: "Yeah! That you can tell everything that springs up in your mind and ... you don't have to be afraid of how the other will react and, in that way, even from your past you can tell all that you want." Thus, the respondent described her trustful relationship to her husband in which she could spontaneously express herself and also share her negative feelings.

In the self-report Relationship Questionnaire, she thought that the secure attachment style described her very well, and that the insecure attachment style descriptions did not correspond to her functioning in close relationships. In the AAI, the respondent got the classification of reserved secure, Type B1-2. The respondent's STSS score was 66, less than one standard deviation above the mean of the daughter generation in study 3 ($M = 60.41$, $SD = 8.37$).

Silencing the Self among Finnish Women: Reviving Ophelia?

Results from these exploratory studies may be discussed in terms of the historically early individualization and emancipation of Finnish women. The Finnish cultural context differs from other cultural contexts in the demand of behaviors measured by the STSS. The tradition of women's labor force participation and the importance of their education in Finland are more established than in other Western countries. The traditionally equal position of Finnish women to men has decreased the demands of compliant connectedness, that is, the appeasing behaviors, inhibition of self-expression, and compulsive caregiving as measured by the STSS. In the generational study, silencing the self decreased significantly from middle-aged and elderly mothers to their adult daughters, with the older generation scoring significantly higher on the STSS than their adult daughters. Particularly, divided self and silencing the self decreased from one generation to the next, while care as self-sacrifice and externalized self-perception remained similar from one generation to the next.

As previously argued, one possible interpretation is that the young women thought they were entitled to a voice of their own (Gilligan, 1982). Their responsiveness to self did not, however, exclude responsiveness to significant others; that is, externalized self-perception and care as self-sacrifice were similar to those of their mothers. The younger women experienced themselves as both connected and self-determined at the same time (Bjerrum Nielsen & Rudberg, 1994; Harter, 1999); they appeared to follow the solution proposed by Chodorow's (1978) call for gender balance in childcare, as expressed by Westkott (1998, p. 397): "Chodorow's androgynous golden mean of individuated but affiliated mothers and fathers nurturing the next generation of balanced children was nevertheless dependent primarily upon a change in male behavior." It is up to men to put an end to the gender imbalance by engaging in nurturing activities in the domestic sphere.

Currently, Finnish fathers are involved in the primary caretaking of their young children (Moilanen et al., 2000). Today, in an increasing number of families, it is no longer given by tradition how to share the domestic chores and caretaking responsibilities. Instead, it is a result of negotiations between the spouses. Young and more educated fathers are more involved in child care and housework than older and less educated fathers. Highly educated women with a career considered to be of the same importance as that of their husbands have husbands who really did their fair share of the work at home (Moxnes, 1992). The lower self-silencing scores of Finnish men relative to U.S. results may indicate an increasing freedom of expressing feelings connected to a new kind of expectation of nurturing fatherhood, fathers functioning along with mothers as primary caretakers of even their young children (Johansson, 2000). As Moxnes (1992) concludes in regard to Norwegian women, an essential factor in these family negotiations is the woman's bargaining power—her status in terms of education and occupation. The high level of education and full-time work in the younger female age cohorts in Finland guarantee economic independence and bargaining power for women in their negotiations with their husbands about the distribution of household tasks and the caretaking responsibility of the children.

While young women try to live according to the new cultural model of self-fulfillment (Björnberg, 1992) connected to the "doppelter Lebensentwurf"

(Occhsle & Zoll, 1992), not all men seem to accept a more equal division of reproductive labor. The increased divorce rates, when women try to balance the demands
of motherhood and employment while children are young, may point to spousal
conflicts in regard to equally sharing caretaking responsibilities and domestic tasks.

But even if the silencing the self schemas of the mother generation differed
significantly from those of their adult daughters, their images and ideals of
femininity did not differ. Neither generation, in their constructions of their
gender identity as measured by the ISA (Weinreich, 1980), stressed the traditional
caring femininity of self-sacrifice. In their constructions of identity, both generations of women valued autonomy, strength, and intelligence more highly than self-
sacrifice or being always available for their child. Thus, their images of femininity
were not restricted to motherhood. The results agreed with Wager's (1998) study
using the ISA concerning constructions of femininity in academic women in
Finland. The academic women endorsed autonomy as one of their central
values, and were ambivalent in regard to values dealing with care for others,
including self-sacrifice, that is, values associated with traditional femininity and
silencing the self schemas. In the present study, both generations of women seemed
to transcend what Benjamin (1990) has characterized as the normative image of
motherhood bound to the traditional gender division of labor: ". . . the ideal of a
mother who provides symbiosis and then separation 'on demand' must be
replaced by the mother who also moves under her own steam" (p. 476).

In Finland, women have, in fact, been moving under their own steam because
of the long and well-established tradition of women's labor force participation
and education. The low level of STSS scores of younger women relative to U.S.
scores may be interpreted against this background. The differences between the
two generations of Finnish women in silencing the self schemas may, however,
be related to the change in the cultural model, where the ethos of self-denial,
hard work, and the responsibility for other persons is replaced by an ethos of
self-fulfilment, coupled with sole responsibility for oneself (Björnberg, 1992).
The idea of self as an identity project (Giddens, 1991) implies the continuous
commitment of developing oneself through work and education (Hautamäki, A.,
2000), and is closely intertwined with the progress of individualization.

Inconsistent with Silencing the Self Theory, but consistent with other studies
(Cramer & Thoms, 2003; Gratch et al., 1995; Thompson, 1995), Finnish men in
the three samples scored significantly higher than women on the STSS. In one of
three samples studied in Finland, even the correlations between endorsing self-
silencing schemas and depression did not differ by gender (see also Gratch et al.,
1995, and Chapter 6, this volume). This raises the question, are there, in fact,
gender differences in the cognitive schemas activated by the scale items? Remen,
Chambless, and Robebaugh (2002) conclude that their study provided some
support for the validity of the four subscales of the STSS for women and for the
interpretation that women's cognitive self-silencing schemas are intended to
maintain relationships. For men, a new factor emerged in the factor analysis,

"Autonomy/Concealment," which did not reflect any of Jack and Dill's (1992) subscales. Remen and colleagues (2002) suggest that the STSS, for men, may tap a motive to avoid intimacy and close relationships that limit their autonomy and self-determination. Thus, for men, the scale may tap motives not to secure greater intimacy but to endorse autonomy and to hide some aspects of the self from one's partner in order to secure self-determination. The interpretation is consistent with Chodorow's (1978) view on the genesis of gender identity: ". . . the basic feminine sense of self is connected to the world, the basic masculine sense of self is separate" (p. 169). Thus, both sexes utilize the self-silencing schema, but perhaps for different purposes in close relationships. Further research should tap the question of why and how men and women use self-silencing schemas in their close relationships (Cramer & Thoms, 2003).

The fact that the Finnish men scored significantly higher on the STSS than women may be connected to the predominant avoidant or dismissive attachment style in Finland, particularly for men (Hautamäki, A., et al., 2008; Männikkö, 2001), according to which it is important both to avoid intimacy and to endorse one's self-determination. An avoidant individual has learned to dismiss his own affects. In order to do so, he maintains a sufficient distance in relationships, deactivating his attachment system. There is a discomfort with intimacy because it may activate the attachment system and arouse the dismissed affect.

Avoidant or dismissive attachment may result both from parental unresponsiveness and control. In Finland, an unresponsive parent is much more frequent than a controlling one (Hautamäki, A. et al., in press; Kemppinen, 2007). Distant parenting, quietness, and independence have been valued in Finland (Keller et al., 2004; Kemppinen, 2007). With an unresponsive parent, the child is not, however, pressed to safeguard his autonomy to the same extent as with a controlling, intrusive parent. In fact, as early independence is expected by the unresponsive parent, the child may have to work to maintain his relationship to the caregiver in order to keep the emotional connection going. Thus, a special feature of Finnish avoidant attachment may be that the developing child learns not only to endorse his autonomy but also to maintain his relationship to the caregiver by not expressing affects that may be perceived as negative.

The avoidant strategy, dismissing one's feelings in order to secure both the relationship to loved ones and one's autonomy, may, however, create specific psychological risks. These may include disorders related to the overinhibition of affect, as well as sudden intrusions of the forbidden affects that the individual has neither learned to cope with nor adequately handle. The intruded affects of anger and desire for comfort are seen in an unregulated form in connection with the use of alcohol, for example, and violent acts; the abuse of alcohol is also related to suicidal behavior. Maybe Finnish women, in the process of achieving gender balance and more equal gender roles, have been able more rapidly to grasp the new opportunities provided by societal change. Currently, the educational level of Finnish women excels that of Finnish men in all age cohorts except the 60+ age cohorts. The high level of education in the younger female age cohorts guarantees their economic independence; currently, most divorce processes of married couples are initiated by the female partner. Men seem to have been slower to adjust to the rapid changes in the gender role expectations, and are currently attempting to catch up and seize the new opportunities—but not without some difficulty (Johansson, 2000). As Harter (1999) succinctly puts it, "Reviving Ophelia" (Pipher, 1994) is a valuable goal. But Hamlet is also suffering from a lack of voice—at least in the Finnish, gendered scene of intimate relationships.

Notes

1. Bartholomew (1990) designed the self-report measure for the purpose of studies that cannot use the Adult Attachment Interview (Hesse, 1999) because it requires an extensive face-to-face interview. The theoretical rational for four, rather than three, attachment patterns was the distinction between the two working models of self, and of others, presumed to underlie the attachment styles. Secure attachment was assumed to be based on a positive model of both self (self as worthy of love) and of others (others as available and caring), whereas the fearful attachment style was based on a negative model of both self (self as unworthy of love) and of others (others as distant and rejecting) (Bartholomew, 1990). The dimensions of self and others presumed to underlie the attachment styles have been validated in subsequent studies (Bartholomew & Horowitz, 1991; Griffin & Bartholomew, 1994).

2. As the AAI and self-rating scales assess different phenomena, the first focusing on an individual's ways of processing attachment-relevant information, the other on the self description an individual is able to access, the concordance of the two assessments has been found to be negligible. Self-report inventories have not been related to the AAI assessments (Hesse, 1999). The AAI is a semistructured interview focusing on an individual's description and evaluation of early attachment relationships and their effects on current functioning in close relationships. The classification of the transcript primarily depends on the form in which the story is told, especially the degree of coherence of discourse and mind in regard to attachment-related issues (Hesse, 1999). By analyzing the coherence of the discourse using complex criteria, trained coders are able to assign transcripts to the Ainsworth-based categories. The greater an individual's capacity is to integrate attachment-relevant information from different, also less conscious nonverbal memory systems, the greater the coherence of mind is considered to be (Crittenden, 2006). The self-report method only taps those ways of relating in current romantic attachment relationships to which an individual has conscious access.

References

Ainsworth, M. D. S., Blehar, M. C., Waters, E., & Wall, S. (1978). *Patterns of attachment: A psychological study of the Strange Situation.* Hillsdale, NJ: Lawrence Erlbaum.

Bartholomew, K. (1990). Avoidance of intimacy: An attachment perspective. *Journal of Social and Personal Relationships, 7,* 147–178.

Bartholomew, K., & Horowitz, L. M. (1991). Attachment styles among young adults: A test of a four-category model. *Journal of Personality and Social Psychology, 61,* 226–244.

Beck, A., Steer, R. A., & Garbin, M. G. (1988). Psychometric properties of the Beck Depression Inventory: Twenty-five years of evaluation. *Clinical Psychology Review, 8,* 77–100.

Benjamin, J. (1990). The alienation of desire: Women's masochism and ideal love. In C. Zanardi (Ed.), *Essential papers on the psychology of women.* New York, London: New York University Press.

Bjerrum Nielsen, H., & Rudberg, M. (1994). *Psychological gender and modernity.* Oslo, Copenhagen, Stockholm: Scandinavian University Press.

Björnberg, U. (Ed.). (1992). *European parents in the 1990s: Contradictions and comparisons.* London: Transactions Publishers.

Bowlby, J. (1973). *Attachment and loss. vol. II: Separation.* Harmondsworth, UK: Penguin Books.

Brennan, K. A., & Morris, K. A. (1997). Attachment styles, self-esteem, and patterns of seeking feedback from romantic partners. *Personality and Social Psychology Bulletin, 23,* 23–31.

Carr, J. G., Gilroy, F. D., & Sherman M. F. (1996). Silencing the self and depression among women: The moderating role of race. *Psychology of Women Quarterly, 20,* 375–392.

Chodorow, N. J. (1978). *Reproduction of mothering.* Berkeley, CA: University of California Press.

Cramer, K. M., & Thoms, N. (2003). Factor structure of the Silencing the Self Scale in women and men. *Personality and Individual Differences, 35,* 525–535.

Crittenden, P. M. (2000). A dynamic-maturational exploration of the meaning of security and adaptation. Empirical, cultural, and theoretical considerations. In P. M. Crittenden & A. H. Claussen (Eds.), *The organization of attachment relationships. Maturation, culture and context* (pp. 358–416). Cambridge, New York: Cambridge University Press.

Crittenden, P. M. (2006). A dynamic-maturational model of attachment. *Australian and New Zealand Journal of Family Therapy, 27,* 105–115.

Crowell, J. A., & Treboux, D. (1995). A review of adult attachment measures: Implications for theory and research. *Social Development, 4,* 294–327.

Diekstra, R. F. W., & Gulbinat, W. (1993). The epidemiology of suicidal behavior: A review of three continents. *World Health Statistics Quarterly, 46,* 52–68.

Dutton, K. A., & Brown, J. D. (1997). Global self-esteem and specific self-views as determinants of people's reactions to success and failure. *Journal of Social and Personality Psychology, 73,* 139–148.

Feeney, J., & Noller, P. (1996). *Adult attachment.* Thousand Oaks, CA: Sage Publications.

Garcia-Ramon, M. D., & Monk, J. (1996). *Women of the European Union. The politics of work and daily life.* London, New York: Routledge.

Giddens, A. (1991). *Modernity and self-identity: Self and society in late modern age.* Cambridge, UK: Polity Press.

Gilligan, C. (1982). *In a different voice: Psychological theory and women's development.* Cambridge, MA: Harvard University Press.

Gratch, L., Bassett, M. E., & Attra, S. L. (1995). The relationship of gender and ethnicity to self-silencing and depression among college students. *Psychology of Women Quarterly, 19,* 509–515.

Griffin, D., & Bartholomew, K. (1994). Models of the self and other: Fundamental dimensions underlying measures of adult attachment. *Journal of Personality and Social Psychology, 67,* 430–445.

Haavio-Mannila, E. (1987). Kohti vertailevaa pohjoismaista valtiotieteellistä naistutkimusta. In A. Saarinen, E. Hänninen-Salmelin, & M. Keränen (Eds.), *Naiset ja valta.* Tutkijaliitto. Jyväskylä: Gummerus.

Haemmerlie, F. M., Montgomery, R. L., Williams, A., & Winborn, K.A. (2001). Silencing the self in college settings and adjustment. *Psychological Reports, 88,* 587–594.

Harter, S. (1999). *The construction of the self: A developmental perspective.* New York, London: Guilford.

Hautamäki, A. (2000). The matrix of relationships in the late modern family in the Nordic countries: A haven in a heartless world, a disturbed nest or a secure base? In A. Hautamäki (Ed.), *Emergent trends in early childhood education – Towards an ecological and psychohistorical analysis of quality* (pp. 33–121). Research Report 216. Helsinki, Finland: University of Helsinki, Department of Teacher Education.

Hautamäki, A., & Coleman, P. G. (2001). Explanation for low prevalence of PTSD among older Finnish war veterans: Social solidarity and continued significance given to wartime sufferings. *Aging & Mental Health, 5*(2), 165–174.

Hautamäki, A., Hautamäki, L., Neuvonen, L., & Maliniemi-Piispanen, S. (in press). Transmission of attachment across three generations. *European Journal of Developmental Psychology, 6.*

Hautamäki, A., Hautamäki, L., Maliniemi-Piispanen, S., & Neuvonen, L. (2008). Kiintymyssuhteen välittyminen kolmessa sukupolvessa – äidinäitien paluu? (The transmission of attachment across three generations – the return of grannies?) *Psykologia, 6,* 421–442.

Hautamäki, J., Harjunen, E., Hautamäki, A., Karjalainen, T. Kupiainen, S., Laaksonen, S., et al. (2008). *PISA 06 Finland. Analyses, reflections and explanations.* Helsinki, Finland: Publications 2008:44. Ministry of Education.

Hazan, C., & Shaver, P. R. (1994). Attachment as an organizational framework for research on close relationships. *Psychological Inquiry, 5,* 1–22.

Hesse, E. (1999). The Adult Attachment Interview. Historical and current perspectives. In J. Cassidy & P. R. Shaver (Eds.), *Handbook of attachment. Theory, research, and clinical applications* (pp. 395–433). New York, London: The Guilford Press.

Hindy, C. G., & Schwarz, J. C. (1994). Anxious romantic attachment in adult relationships. In M. B. Sperling & W. H. Berman (Eds.), *Attachment in adults: Clinical and developmental perspectives* (pp. 179–203). New York: The Guilford Press.

Ingold, T. (1997). Finland in the new Europe. People, community and society. *EAGLE Street, Newsletter of the Finnish Institute in London, No. 4.*

Isometsä, E., Aro, S., & Aro, H. (1997). Depression in Finland: A computer assisted telephone interview study. *Acta Psychiatrica Scandinavica, 96*, 122–128.

Jack, D. C. (1991). *Silencing the self: Women and depression.* Cambridge, MA: Harvard University Press.

Jack, D. C., & Dill, D. (1992). The Silencing the Self Scale: Schemas of intimacy associated with depression in women. *Psychology of Women Quarterly, 16*, 97–106.

Jacobs, J. A., & Gerson, K. (2004). *The time divide: Work, family and gender inequality.* Cambridge, MA: Harvard University Press.

Johansson, T. (2000). *Det första könet? Mansforskning som ett reflektivt projekt.* Lund, Sweden: Studentlitteratur.

Karisto, A., Takala, P., & Haapola, I. (1998). *Matkalla nykyaikaan: Elintason, elämäntavan ja sosiaalipolitiikan muutos Suomessa.* Porvoo, Finland: WSOY.

Keller, H., Yovsi, R., Borke, J., Kärtner, J., Jensen, H., & Papligoura, Z. (2004). Developmental consequences of early parenting experiences: Self organization and self regulation in three cultural communities. *Child Development, 75*, 1745–1760.

Kemppinen, K. (2007). *Maternal sensitivity: Continuity and related risk factors.* Kuopio University Publications D., Medical Sciences, 412. University of Kuopio, Finland.

Kessler, R. C. (2003). Epidemiology of women and depression. *Journal of Affective Disorders, 74*, 5–13.

Lester, D. (1995). Preventing suicide in women and men. *Crisis, 16*, 79–84.

Lester, D. (1997). Suicide in an international perspective. *Suicide Life Threatening Behavior, 27*, 104–111.

Lichtenstein Phelps, J., Belsky, J., & Crnic, K. (1998). Earned security, daily stress, and parenting: A comparison of five alternative models. *Development and Psychopathology, 10*, 21–38.

Lönnqvist, J., Henriksson, M., Isometsä, E., Marttunen, M., & Heikkinen, M. (2003). Itsetuhokäyttäytyminen ja itsemurhat. In J. Lönnqvist, M. Heikkinen, & M. Henriksson (Eds.), *Psykiatria* (pp. 589–603). Hämeenlinna, Finland: Duodecim.

Lönnrot, E. (1981). *Kalevala.* (Original work published 1835.) Porvoo, Finland: WSOY.

Männikkö, K. (2001). *Adult attachment styles. A person-oriented approach.* University of Jyväskylä, Finland: Jyväskylä Studies in Education, Psychology and Social Research, 185.

Marecek, J. (2006). Social suffering, gender and women's depression. In C. L. M. Keyes & S. H. Goodman (Eds.), *Women and depression: A handbook for the social, behavioral, and biomedical sciences* (pp. 283–308). Cambridge: Cambridge University Press.

Moilanen, I., Kunelius, A., Tirkkonen, T., & Crittenden, P. M. (2000). Attachment in Finnish twins. In P. M. Crittenden & A. H. Claussen (Eds.), *The organization of attachment relationships: Maturation, culture and context* (pp. 125–140). Cambridge: Cambridge University Press.

Moxnes, K. (1992). Changes in family patterns – changes in parenting? A change toward a more or less equal sharing between parents? In U. Björnberg (Ed.), *European parents in the 1990s: Contradictions and comparisons* (pp. 211–228). London: Transaction Publishers.

Nielsen, M. (1999). *Itsensä vaientaminen ja depression – sukupuolierot suomalaisilla yliopisto-opiskelijoilla.* University of Joensuu, Department of Psychology, unpublished master's thesis.

Oechsle, M., & Zoll, R. (1992). Young people and their ideas on parenthood. In U. Björnberg (Ed.), *European parents in the 1990s: Contradictions and comparisons* (pp. 45–58). London: Transactions Publishers.

Pearson, J. L., Cohn, D. A., Cowan, P. A., & Pape Cowan, C. (1994). Earned- and continuous-security in adult attachment: Relation to depressive symptomatology and parenting style. *Development and Psychopathology, 6,* 359–373.

Perander, H. (2005). *Konstruktion av den kvinnliga könsidentiteten – en tvågenerationsstudie.* University of Helsinki, Department of Social Psychology, unpublished master's thesis.

Pesonen, T. (2006). *Trends in suicidality in Eastern Finland, 1988-1997.* Kuopio University Publications D., Medical Sciences, 392. University of Kuopio, Finland.

Pipher, M. (1994). *Reviving Ophelia: Saving the selves of adolescent girls.* New York: Ballantine.

Pirkola, S., Lönnqvist, J., et al. (2004). Psychological symptoms and mental disorders. In A. Aromaa & S. Koskinen (Eds.), *Health and functional capacity in Finland: Baseline results of the Health 2000 Health Examination Survey.* Publications of the National Public Health Institute, B12/2004. Finland, Helsinki: National Public Health Institute.

Poikolainen, K. (1995). Alcohol and mortality: A review. *Journal of Clinical Epidemiology, 48,* 455–465.

Remen, A. L., Chambless, D. L., & Rodebaugh, T. L. (2002). Gender differences in the construct validity of the Silencing the Self Scale. *Psychology of Women Quarterly, 26,* 151–159.

Roisman, G. I., Padron, E., Sroufe, A., & Egeland, B. (2002). Earned secure attachment status in retrospect and prospect. *Child Development, 73,* 1204–1219.

Rytsälä, H. (2006). *Functional and work disability and treatment received by patients with major depressive disorder.* Helsinki, Finland: Publications of the National Public Health Institute, A9/2006. National Public Health Institute.

Schaffer, H. R. (2006). *Key concepts in developmental psychology.* London: Sage.

Sigfrids, J. (2008). *Att tysta ner sig själv och depression – en studie i könsskillnader bland universitetsstuderande kvinnor och män.* University of Helsinki, Department of Social Psychology, unpublished master's thesis.

Sihvo, S., Sevon, T., Haukka, J., Hemminki, E., Keskimäki, I., Lumme, S., et al. (2006). Incidence and prevalence of antidepressant use in the adults in Finland, 1994-2003. *European Journal of Public Health, 16,* 216.

Smolak, L., & Munstertieger, B. F. (2002). The relationship of gender and voice to depression and eating disorders. *Psychology of Women Quarterly, 26,* 234–241.

Stapley, J. C., & Haviland, J. M. (1989). Beyond depression: Gender differences in normal adolescents' emotional experiences. *Sex Roles, 20,* 295–308.

Thompson, J. M. (1995). Silencing the self: Depressive symptomatology and close relationships. *Psychology of Women Quarterly, 19,* 337–353.

Thompson, J. M., Whiffen, V. E., & Aube, J. A. (2001). Does self-silencing link perceptions of care from parents and partners with depressive symptoms? *Journal of Social and Personal Relationships, 18,* 503–516.

Triandis, H. C. (1995). *Individualism and collectivism.* Boulder, CO: Westview Press.

Uebelacker, L. A., Courtnage, E. S., & Whisman, M. A. (2003). Correlates of depression and marital dissatisfaction: Perceptions of marital communication style. *Journal of Social and Personal Relationships, 20,* 757–769.

Van IJzendoorn, M. H., & Sagi, A. (1999). Cross-cultural patterns of attachment: Universal and contextual dimensions. In J. Cassidy & P. R. Shaver (Eds.), *Handbook of attachment: Theory, research, and clinical applications* (pp. 713–734). New York, London: Guilford Press.

Wager, M. (1998). Women or researchers? The identities of academic women. *Feminism & Psychology, 8,* 236–244.

Weber, M. (1978). *Den protestantiska etiken och kapitalismens anda.* (Original work published 1904.) Borgholm, Sweden: Argos.

Weinreich, P. (1980). *Manual for identity exploration using personal constructs.* Research Paper No. 1. Centre for Research in Ethnic Relations, University of Warwick, UK.

Weinreich, P. (1986). The operationalization of identity theory in racial and ethnic relations. In J. Rex & D. Mason (Eds.), *Theories of race and ethnic relations.* Cambridge: Cambridge University Press.

Westkott, M. (1998). Female relationality and the idealized self. In B. McVicker Clinchy & J. K. Norem (Eds.), *The gender and psychology reader* (pp. 396–406). New York, London: New York University Press.

Westman, A. L. (2000). *Under the Northern lights: The reflection of gender on the career of women managers in Finnish municipalities.* Publications in Social Sciences, No. 43. University of Joensuu, Finland.

9

The Meaning of Self-Silencing in Polish Women

Krystyna Drat-Ruszczak

At the core of Jack's self-silencing concept is an idea arising from theories of the relational self that considers attaining a sense of basic human connectedness to be the goal of development. Feminist theorists generally contend that interpersonal intimacy is a profound organizer of female experience (Chodorow, 1978; Gilligan, 1982; Jack, 1991). The question of gender differences in orientation toward others has repeatedly drawn researchers' attention. For example, Marcus and Kitayama (1991), Clancy and Dollinger (1993), and Niedenthal and Beike (1997) have argued that women tend to maintain connectedness, while men prefer a more individualistic orientation.

More recently, Shelley Taylor and colleagues (2000) have proposed a biobehavioral model of female responses to stress. The model assumes that female responses are characterized by a pattern that is labeled "tend-and-befriend," whereas the classic "fight-or-flight" model is regarded as characteristic of men. The "tend-and-befriend" pattern means that women respond to stress by tending (i.e., nurturing offspring, exhibiting behaviors that protect them from harm) and by befriending (i.e., affiliating with social groups to reduce risk). In particular, the "tending" pattern appears in "*quieting* and caring for offspring, and *blending into the environments*" (italics added), whereas the patterns of "befriending" translate into the creation of networks of associations for the exchange of resources and responsibilities that provide protection for the woman and her offspring under stressful conditions (Taylor et al., 2000, p. 412). According to the model, the basis for the tend-and-befriend pattern of responses is a neuroendocrine mechanism of releasing the oxytocin hormone and its modulation by estrogen. Together with endogenous opioid mechanisms, these hormones influence maternal affiliative and nursing behaviors, calming women under stress conditions.

The model assumes that women have typically borne a greater role in the care of young offspring than men and that they typically play the primary role in bringing the offspring to maturity. The criterion of adaptiveness of women's behavior (as well as nonhuman species) is biological: The tend-and-befriend responses are those that increase the likelihood that mother and child will survive without jeopardizing their health. The model does not make any assumptions about the social roles of women. As the authors have stressed, the model "should not be construed to imply that women should be mothers or … by virtue of these mechanisms will be good mothers" (Taylor et al., 2000, p. 423). It should be emphasized that though biobehavioral, the "tend-and-befriend" model does not exclude the sociocultural approach, but rather enriches and supports it. In fact, the authors state that their model concerns a so-called "central tendency," and thus, due to the flexibility of human behavior, the individual "tend-and-befriend" responses will vary across cultures, social roles, and personality factors.

The tend-and-befriend model provides us with a biobehavioral point of view from which to view self-silencing theory, presenting the opportunity to consider at least some self-silencing behaviors as adaptive, that is, not necessarily resulting in depression and damaging of women's self. The criterion of adaptiveness of tend-and-befriend responses on the biological level is clear—bringing healthy offspring to maturity. The criteria of well adjusted on the psychological level are far more complex. One criterion appears to be the level of individual well-being. But another criterion seems also to be achieving a coherence of inner personality while also fulfilling social roles within one's society. On the adaptive dimension, the silencing the self pattern is clearly situated on the poorer adjusted pole, while tend-and-befriend responses fall on the well-adjusted, healthy end of the spectrum. Yet it is conceivable that the more self-silencing behaviors shift into the tending and befriending direction, the more they may move toward the healthy and adaptive pole.

Therefore, it would be important to determine which cultural, social, and dispositional factors, and by what means, interact with and influence women's self-silencing behavior. Which factors determine whether a woman's tend-and-befriend pattern reveals either healthy "quiet and caring" behaviors with strong socioemotional bonds or, in contrast, a clear self-silencing style of relational behavior with a sense of loss of self in relationships and with depressive symptoms? The main aim of this chapter is to engage the question, can self-silencing, considered here as a style of regulating the self in relationships, be seen as an effective psychological response to pressures prescribed on a biological level and to social expectations prescribed by gender stereotypes within Polish society? Self-silencing may perform an adaptive function in a person's relational life by ensuring the protection and raising of a woman's children, but on the other hand, research so far confirms that self-silencing does not associate with psychological health. Moreover, as Jack (1991, 1999b; Jack & Dill, 1992) has argued, self-silencing consists of four dimensions, measured by the subscales. Are all the subscale dimensions similar in their measure of maladaptiveness, resulting in depression and loss of self, or are some related to more adaptive relational as well as individual well-being? Does each subscale convey a similar meaning?

In accordance with our intention of examining the dimensions of self-silencing utilizing the subscales, it would be useful to determine which cultural, social, and dispositional factors interact with and influence each of the self-silencing components. What constellation of those factors leads either to functional, socially adaptive behaviors with strong relational ties or, on the contrary, causes a distortion of the self, experienced as a sense of loss of self in relationships and depressive symptoms? I use "adaptability" to mean women's abilities to adapt themselves on a psychological level to the biological tasks postulated by the "tend-and-befriend" model as well as to social demands deriving from gender stereotypes. The latter seem to arise from and reinforce biological differences between sexes and serve as a filter through which women view their position in the social world. By "adaptive" I mean a style of self and relationship regulation by which women cope with these double biological and social pressures.

Due to the idea of possible compatibility of demands on social and biological levels, I begin with an analysis of Polish-specific gender stereotypes, including sociocultural circumstances specific to Polish women, and then present findings from three empirical studies to explore the questions mentioned earlier. I begin by asking, what are the historical and sociocultural determinants of women's situation in Poland, and which are likely to prescribe self-silencing for women?

In Which Ways Do Gender Stereotypes Prescribe Self-Silencing for Women?

The roles and social status of women in Poland have been influenced by at least three major historical and sociocultural circumstances. The first one is derived from the fact that the dominant religion in Poland is Catholicism with its widely practiced cult of the Virgin Mary, mother of God. This has resulted in a high positive evaluation of communal virtues such as concern and caring for others, and in the high symbolical value of the traditional role of the mother (Środa, 2002).

The second circumstance results from the long-lasting (over 200-year-old) tradition of independence movements in Poland, which offset women's leading subservient domestic lives. A woman's duty was to raise her children in the patriotic spirit, to take care of the household, and to be brave during her spouse's absence from home. These circumstances have added an agentic and assertive feature to the social role prescribed for women.

Finally, the third important circumstance stems from four decades of a socialist system established after World War II. Women's professional activation en masse, though caused by political decisions beyond their reach, amplified women's active role, especially in the family. Women were now made responsible for the "organization" of basic material goods, a task they fulfilled often with a certain feeling of pride and satisfaction.

Thus, the stereotype of a woman's role was shaped both by a religion strongly emphasizing traditional values and by those national and ideological movements that were supporting active and agentic values, primarily supporting her responsibility for her family's well-being. This resulted in a common stereotype of the "Matka-Polka," (the "Polish mother"), by some sociologists labeled a *managerial matriarchy* (Titkow & Domanski, 1995, p. 15). The meaning of the word "managerial" here is slightly different than in common use of the term "manage." Due to numerous anticipated adversities, success is not guaranteed. Thus, on the one hand the Polish mother is resourceful, obliged to find a remedy for all troubles. On the other hand, however, she bears adversities humbly and silently, praying to God (or to the Holy Mother), hoping for the reverse of bad fortune. To put it another way, the "managerial matriarchy" phrase conveys a mixture of obligation to overcome troubles and the duty to accept them and to suffer without complaining. In Poland, women aren't socially perceived as weak or unable to take any responsibility for their actions. On the contrary, it is believed that they are strong enough to manage, to deal with difficult situations, and to withstand them in humble and silent ways. Second, in the Polish stereotype, the emphasis is shifted from the relationship between the couple to the mother-child connection: A complex task of offspring protection is emphasized. Whereas in both stereotypes a woman is expected to care for harmony in family relationships, in Polish tradition, due to historical conditions, a man is shifted to the background as a shadowy figure of Saint Joseph in the prototype configuration of the Holy Family.[1]

The relationship of a woman with her husband could formally be in accordance with the patriarchal tradition, but she often acts as an informal head of family, exerting influence on the course of events. Thus, a woman would formally ask for her spouse's opinion, but at the same time, she would know when and how to ask for it in order to get acceptance and approval for *her* plans and *her* intentions. However, most of her plans and her intentions are not individual but communal ones—linked with her children, who are treated as a symbolic extension of a woman's self through relationship (Aron, Aron, & Smollan, 1992). As Mira Marody (1993) has summarized: "Polish women have a tendency to subordinate their own individual development to family goals, which they try to achieve by using private methods and tricks" (p. 864).

It seems that the stereotype of Polish mother as a "good mother," who never surrenders and even while suffering does not lose spirit but smiles, closely fits Taylor's idea of tend-and-befriend female behavior. First, the stereotype recommends behaviors predicted by Taylor's model of "high maternal investment": nurturing and caring for children as an obligatory activity. Second, but crucially important, is that the "good mother" stereotype, like the tend-and-befriend pattern, works under threatening conditions. The threatening ideology derives from the Polish history of struggles for independence; however, it has roots in religion, too. Some conservative, religious circles in Poland still maintain a climate of threatening tension, finding a liberal ideology a menace to traditional or national values, especially to the traditional family.

The Polish mother stereotype also prescribes silencing the self in many situations as described earlier: with the husband, to act in accordance with the patriarchal tradition, to elevate family goals over her own, for the good of children, and so on. In these ways, we can see how silencing the self also fits with the tend-and-befriend notion. Self-silencing may function as a mode of social survival and adaptation in specific contexts. In an evolutionary sense, survival (whether it be biological or social) under perilous circumstance sometimes requires adaptive behaviors that are self-preserving while at the same time somewhat damaging to an organism's state of well-being. Thus, perhaps the social adaptation of self-silencing, while not ideal from a personal empowerment point of view, can be viewed as a necessary accommodation to culturally prescribed demands in this Polish context.

Empirical Evidence for the "Polish Mother" Stereotype

The content of the Polish mother stereotype is clearly visible in women's values and activities such as (1) their hierarchy of values, (2) their attribution of responsibility for their fortune, and (3) their preferred coping behaviors. Data from the Polish General Social Survey (Czapinski & Panek, 2005) reflect patterns that reveal how the stereotype may be affecting large numbers of Polish women:

1. Among the hierarchy of values, *health* is first for both women and men, while women ranked *successful marriage* second, closely followed by *children* and next, by *job* and *money*. For men, *children* are ranked fifth after *job* and *money*.
2. Women's attribution of responsibility is even more interesting. They attribute responsibility for their fortune to *themselves* (58%) and *Providence* (49%), whereas men attribute their fortune mostly to *authorities* (63%), then to *Providence* (43%), and to *themselves* (39%) last.
3. More than twice as many women as men pray to God for help in a difficult situation (47% and 19%, respectively). These forms of coping do not exclude goal-oriented behavior, but this latter solution is more frequently declared by men (56%) than women (46%). Fifty-three percent of women attend church four or more times monthly, while 40% of men do so. However, both prayer and church attendance are more frequent among inhabitants of small towns and rural areas, and both increase with age.

In general, Czapinski and Panek's (2005) data suggest that the stereotype of the Polish mother may be stronger in rural areas/small towns and among older women.

How the Transformation of the Polish Sociopolitical System Has Influenced Well-Being in Women

An important factor known to affect the level of well-being is one's socioeconomic status. In Poland, this status is influenced by consequences following the collapse of communism and sociopolitical and economic system changes after 1989. The conditions of Poles' lives were fundamentally altered by this event.[2] The transition to democracy and especially to a market economy has required changes in the entire social order, but these changes have not been accompanied by radical changes in social mentality. During the previous regime, Polish society learned that individual activity is either undesirable or futile. Especially workers in state industrial as well as agricultural sectors who were mostly uneducated and older were not aware of new demands and opportunities deriving from the transition. They still believed in the protective role of the state and in the egalitarian distribution of goods. Individual success during the social transformation required a person to be active, ready to take economic risks, and aware that state providence was no longer prevailing. Therefore, the change from a socialist system was associated with numerous new and highly stressful phenomena. For these reasons, certain characteristics of women's roles such as an individualistic career orientation as well as awareness of one's individual rights, established for years in Western culture, still are relatively fresh and controversial in Poland.

According to relevant studies (Czapinski & Panek, 2005), not all people have experienced equally the benefits and disadvantages of these sociopolitical changes. Those who have benefited are young people with a good education, living mainly in large towns and cities; those who suffered from the changes are older, have a lower education, and live in rural areas or small towns. The disproportion between the development opportunities of winners and losers resulting from the sociopolitical changes is constantly rising.

Are Polish Women Winners or Losers in the Sociopolitical Transformation?

Czapinski and Panek's (2005) data reveal that women compared to men must overcome many more barriers and display much more determination to achieve a winner's position socioeconomically. This determination is a privilege of young women: Their educational aspirations are markedly higher than those of men. In the 20 to 24 age group, significantly more women than men go to primary school: 63% versus 52% in towns and cities and 59% versus 42% in rural areas, respectively. However, education still does not protect them against unequal earnings nor against the risk of unemployment: 43% of women compared to 53% of men are unemployed, and as many as 42% of unemployed women looked for a job two years or longer; for men the figure is 24%.

Finally, women reported depression more frequently than men. Studies conducted systematically since 1992 by Czapinski (1993; Czapinski & Panek, 2005) show the unchanging level of depression in Poland during the last 10 years. In their studies of representative samples in Poland, women scored significantly higher than men on a shortened version of the Beck Depression Inventory measure [$M = 5.19$ vs. 4.01, respectively, $F(1,8818) = 233.72$, $p < .000$].[3] Women also self-report somatic stress symptoms more often (21% of women and 13% of men) and unwanted loneliness (26% of women and 18% of men). Age increases the risk for all these components of distress, while education protects against them. It should be emphasized, however, that women in Poland do not report that they are unhappy. On the contrary, 68% of them declare having a sense of happiness and as many as 69% the will to live.

To conclude, the aforementioned data concerning the consequences of the sociopolitical transformation suggest that the well-being of women in Poland might be strongly related to their economic position, determined by education, employment, and dwelling place. The data also suggest that a crucial factor regarding self-silencing behavior among women might be age. The older generation, maturing before systemic social changes, seems to retain the basic features of the "Polish mother" stereotype, while it is possible that the young women would be more individualistic, more self-oriented than the generation of their mothers. Moreover, young women's behavior seems to be guided more by popular culture and media stereotypes than by the traditional pattern of the woman's role. Thus, the self-silencing pattern might be a less significant phenomenon among younger women.

It seems that because of Poland's specific sociocultural background, the dimensions of self-silencing might vary on their association with other variables and thus on their meaning in Poland as compared to other countries. My studies have explored whether the dimensions of self-silencing identified by Jack and Dill (1992) are different or similar in Poland than in published studies from other countries. These four dimensions have been measured by subscales of the Silencing the Self Scale (STSS): (1) Externalized Self-Perception (judging oneself by external, societal standards), (2) Care as Self-Sacrifice (considering others' needs and feelings as more important than one's own), (3) Silencing the Self (inhibiting self-expression), and (4) Divided Self (inner division resulting from presenting a "false" outer self). Three studies that investigated the relation of specific social factors to dimensions of self-silencing in Polish women are described in the following sections.

The Studies

Predictions and Overview

The first study presents the Polish version of the STSS. In the second, examining the construct validity of the Polish version of the measure, I was particularly concerned whether the STSS dimensions (as measured by the subscales) might be predicted by different attachment styles. The third study was conducted on a differentiated community sample to determine whether self-esteem and social support were significant predictors of self-silencing dimensions, and whether the STSS subscales would significantly predict several aspects of well-being.

I expected particularly that those dimensions of self-silencing that are predicted by attachment styles that denote relationship engagement may facilitate successful dealing with the biological task of bringing up one's children and would not be dysfunctional. Therefore, they might not necessarily be associated with depression in Polish women. The active component of the "Polish mother" stereotype, which reflects an active coping attitude, provides an additional rationale to consider an adaptive aspect of women's self-silencing behavior. Again, by adaptive, I mean a form of coping that serves as an effective way both to fulfill the pressures on the biological level (Taylor et al., 2000) and to meet social expectations that are fixed in the previously described Polish gender stereotype. Adaptation, in this sense, would be evidenced by a lack of indicators of negative well-being and with the presence of at least a few indicators of positive well-being.

Polish Adaptation of the Silencing the Self Scale

A series of studies were conducted to adapt the STSS to Polish and to check whether the adapted scale was reliable and valid. A key question was whether the Polish version of the STSS retains the four-factor structure of the American original as well as its other psychometric qualities. The initial pool of the 31 items of the original STSS was translated into Polish[4] and then back-translation was carried out by two independent native speakers. The results were then checked for possible shifts in meaning and a second round of translation into Polish followed.

The study was conducted on a sample of 221 female undergraduates of the University of Gdańsk ranging in age from 19 to 30 years ($M = 23$, $SD = 2$). The participants followed a course in personality psychology and an introduction to clinical psychology. They filled out the scale included in a larger packet of several personality questionnaires. An initial principal components analysis was performed and four factors were selected for further consideration. The oblimin rotation (with Kaiser normalization) was applied. However, the solution obtained was not satisfying, primarily because the reliability of the Care as Self-sacrifice subscale, consisting of six original items only, was less than acceptable ($\alpha = .56$). After deleting from further analysis all 9 items of which the Care as Self-Sacrifice subscale originally consisted and 2 additional unreliable items from other subscales, we submitted the remaining 20 items to oblimin rotation. The resulting three factors accounted for 48% of variance and were similar to the Jack (1991) subscales: (1) Divided Self (seven items), (2) Externalized

Self-Perception (six items), and (3) Silencing the Self (seven items). The remaining sentences constituting three scales retain the essential meaning of the Silencing the Self construct.[5]

The structure of the shortened 20-item Polish version of the STSS was examined in two community samples in order to check whether the three-factor structure of the STSS replicated over different samples. The first nonclinical sample served as a control group in several studies (not presented here) of bulimic and codependent women. This sample was composed of 152 women with no history of eating disorders or alcohol abuse in their families. The age of participants varied from 19 to 61 years ($M = 30$, $SD = 10.78$). The second sample included 231 women (for detailed characteristics of this sample see below, Antecendents and Consequences of Self Silencing). Factor analyses performed on the results of these two community samples showed replicability of the three-factor structure. In each sample, the alpha values satisfactorily confirmed the internal consistency of three STSS subscales as found in Poland.

It is hard to say why the reliability of the original Care as Self-Sacrifice subscale appeared so low. As Jack and Dill (1992) observed, this subscale also had the lowest, although acceptable, internal consistency in the American undergraduate sample. Perhaps intercultural differences in item meaning were responsible for the fact that in Polish samples the items constituting the original Care as Self-Sacrifice did not emerge as a robust subscale underlaid by a single factor.

Attachment Styles as Predictors of Self-Silencing

I was interested to examine relations between self-silencing and theoretically overlapping concepts. In light of the basic assumptions of Jack (1991) and Chodorow (1978) concerning female intimacy experiences, I decided to explore John Bowlby (1980) and Mary Ainsworth's (1989) concept of attachment styles. The concepts cast theoretical light on the idea of silencing the self and allow examination of the question posed earlier: Can self-silencing be an adaptive response in certain social contexts, particularly in terms of the meaning of adaptation described by the tend-and-befriend model, for example, as in "blending into environments"? An adaptive response may not always be immediately beneficial; the question is, do some subscales of the Silencing the Self Scale measure aspects of behavior and self-experience that are more harmful than others? Do the behaviors measured by the Silencing the Self subscale allow a woman to fulfill the Polish stereotype of the good mother and also to successfully raise her children without the same negative psychological consequences that are found with dividing the self or judging and evaluating the self through others' eyes?

The major premise of attachment theory is that early interactions with attachment figures form a critical base for later perceptions and expectations (so-called "models") of the self and others. These models shape an individual's beliefs regarding whether the self is worthy of love and support or not, and whether others are trustworthy and available or, on the contrary, unreliable and rejecting (Bowlby, 1980). I have used Bartholomew and Horowitz's (1991) four-category model of adult attachment to assess the following four patterns of attachment: secure, preoccupied, dismissing, and fearful. *Secure* individuals have a sense of worthiness coupled with the expectation that other people are accepting and responsive. *Preoccupied* individuals are identified by a negative model of the self but a positive model of others. They strive for self-acceptance by gaining the acceptance of valued others. *Fearful-avoidant* individuals have a negative view of others and a negative view of the self. By avoiding close involvement with others, they protect themselves against anticipated rejection. Finally, *dismissing-avoidant* individuals have a negative model of others but maintain a positive self-image. By defensively denying the importance of close relationships, they try to maintain a sense of independence and invulnerability.

Both theory and the narratives of self-silencing women as well as their depressive symptoms presented in Jack's work lead us to predict that self-silencing behavior would associate with a negative model of the self resulting in high dependence (reliance) on others. The tend-and-befriend perspective leads us to hypothesize that for relatively successful dealing with the task of "bringing the offspring to maturity," a positive model of others may be critical. Such a positive model guarantees an approach orientation essential to create, maintain, and utilize the social group in order to manage stressful conditions. Whereas evidently a secure attachment style is a precondition of fully adapted behavior from the tend-and-befriend perspective, a preoccupied attachment style might be considered as a base for developing relatively more adaptive behavior than the fearful or dismissive attachment styles. Both these latter two are characterized by a negative model of others and thus both share a pattern of avoidance. Accordingly, I hypothesized that the Silencing the Self subscale would be predicted by a preoccupied style, corresponding with women's tendency to go along with others.

I administered Bartholomew and Horowitz's (1991) Relationship Questionnaire self-report measure to 192 undergraduate women (drawn from the undergraduate sample). This measure consists of four short paragraphs describing the four attachment styles. The respondents were asked to rate the degree to which they resemble each of the four styles on a 7-point scale.

A regression analysis was performed with the three self-silencing subscales as dependent variables and the styles of attachment as independent variables. The results (the beta coefficients) are presented in Table 9.1.

As can be seen, none of the self-silencing dimensions was positively predicted by secure attachment. On the contrary, the secure style was negatively associated with scores on the Externalized Self-Perception and Silencing the Self subscales.

Table 9.1 Silencing the Self Subscales as Predicted by Model of Attachment Styles

Positive (+) or Negative (−) Model		Attachment Styles as Predictors	Externalized Self-Perception		Silencing the Self		Divided Self	
			β	R^2	β	R^2	β	R^2
Of Other (Avoidance)	Of Self (Dependence)							
+	+	Secure	−.31**		−.17*		−.13	
+	−	Preoccupied	.09		.18*		.17*	
−	−	Fearful	.02		.04		.15†	
−	+	Dismissing	−.10		.11		.17*	
				.14		.10		.14

Note: On left side are basic dimensions of model of attachment styles adapted from Bartholomew and Horowitz (1991, p. 227). High avoidance is implied by negative model of other and high dependence is implied by negative model of self.
Three separate regressions were conducted, one for each subscale of STSS.
$^{\dagger} p < .10$; $^{*} p < .05$; $^{**} p < .001$.

The latter dimension, however, was also positively associated with preoccupied attachment, a style that does not avoid relationships but focuses on them with a "too great" intensity and anxiety. Such a result indicates that women high on the Silencing the Self subscale are ready to rely on other people; however, this tendency seems not to be warm and nurturant, as in the case of secure attachment.

As Bartholomew and Horowitz (1991) have shown, preoccupied subjects are also dominating in relationships (i.e., trying to preserve their level of safety by a vigilant, controlling interpersonal style). The preoccupied attachment style predicts high scores on both the Silencing the Self and the Divided Self dimensions. However, Divided Self was also predicted by a dismissing attachment style and (although marginally) by a fearful style. Thus, the Divided Self dimension appeared to reflect a more complicated relational style as it revealed an ambivalence (i.e., approach-avoidant tendency) in social relations. The women high on Divided Self are likely to suffer from serious difficulties in becoming close to and relying on others. They also may be dependent on the one hand and striving to be independent on the other. The contradictory approach-avoidant tendencies as well as the ambivalent model of self may lead to a warm-dominant, cold-hostile, and even cold-passive behavior at times. Such behavior suggests a high level of personal and social insecurity; therefore, the Divided Self dimension seems to present a disorganized relational style, not an adaptive one.

Among subscales, Externalized Self-Perception had the strongest negative relationship with secure attachment, and thus appeared to reflect relational behavior guided by a negative model of the self and of the others. Such a pattern is associated more often with depression (e.g., Kobak, Sudler, & Gamble, 1991) and, presumably, with a constricted relational self.

To sum up, although all three dimensions of self-silencing (as adapted in Poland) are based on one theoretical construct, they seem to involve different styles of regulating the self in relationships. It is likely that they also represent differing adaptations within one's relationships, with some being possibly less harmful and/or associated with more positive outcomes than others.

Based on engagement in relationship as a precondition for dealing with the "biological" task of safe-raising children, the study suggests that the Silencing the Self dimension may indicate better adaptation to this task than the other two dimensions of the scale. Broader determinants of self-silencing as well as broader consequences are examined in the next study in order to confirm this line of reasoning and to expand the psychological meaning of each dimension.

Antecedents and Consequences of Self-Silencing

I designed this third study to explore the meaning of women's self-silencing in Poland in the context of those psychological variables that should most strongly affect it. I examined both the antecedents (such as self-esteem and social support) and consequences (indicators of well-being) of self-silencing. I considered both these directions of relations within a broader sociocultural context and controlled for such basic sociodemographic variables as age, education, place of living, employment, and marital status.

Self-esteem and social support would seem to play a key role in women's self-silencing. Self-esteem is a central trait, in the sense that it is one of the most important of the self-concepts and affects many other elements (Baumeister, 2000). The self-concept of people with low self-esteem appears to be confused, unstable, uncertain, and, as Baumeister (2000) has noticed, "full of gaps" (p. 11). People low in self-worth are oriented mainly toward self-protection. They are ready for self-enhancement only when their safety is externally ensured (Wood, Giordano-Beech, Taylor, Michela, & Gaus, 1994). As my study of attachment styles has shown, the low self-esteem of self-silencing women seems to be an important mechanism of developing and maintaining such a behavior.

The benefits of social support to psychological and physical functioning appear to be well established. The availability of social support buffers people against the ill effects of stress (Cohen, Sherrod, & Clark, 1986). Studies also have demonstrated that women have wider and more intimate social networks than men and they also experience greater benefits from their social network interactions (Gurung, Taylor, & Seeman, 2003; Turner, 1994).

Additional factors that I considered would influence self-silencing overall are age and education level. Age determines the kinds of influences that a cohort of women was exposed to while they were growing up. Education level is also important because it has been demonstrated that women's educational and occupational behaviors can translate into higher status for women in general (Twenge, 2001). Employment, though, as Twenge (2001) argues, increases the status of a woman only when her job is a prestigious one. In Poland, the possibility of gaining education and finding an attractive and prestigious job is highly determined by the place of inhabitance. Compared to the other nations, Polish citizens move relatively rarely. Those women with education have probably already found a job in larger cities or abroad; the rate of employment emigration is extremely high. At the end of 2007, the rate was 2.27 million, of which more than 50% were women (GUS, 2008). Those who stay and live in the country or in small towns are more likely influenced by the stereotype of a traditional gender role. To conclude, it seems likely that older age in women, their lower education, and the fact of living in a village should significantly increase the overall level of self-silencing. This would be due to their significantly lower internal resources that derive from these important social factors.

Regarding the consequences of the differing dimensions of self-silencing measured by the subscales, I examined some broader components of psychological health, operationalized in terms of (1) low level of depression, (2) low level of psychosomatic stress, and (3) high level of subjective well-being. I predicted that the Silencing the Self dimension would reveal a better adaptation, that is, fewer negative psychological consequences, than the other two subscales. I expected that it would be related not only to general satisfaction with life but also especially to particular satisfaction with relational (communal) aspects of living (i.e., to the satisfaction with children and home, with one's partner, and with one's confidant and friend). On the other hand, agentic satisfaction concerning satisfaction with achievements, income, education, and work seems associated more with an individualistic than interdependent oriented self. Therefore, I predicted that agentic satisfaction would not be as closely associated with any of the self-silencing dimensions as would communal satisfaction.

The study was conducted on a community sample of 231 participants (women only) who varied by age (17 to 67 years; $M = 32.5$ years, $SD = 11$ years). Self-esteem was measured by the 10-item Rosenberg (1965) Self-Esteem Inventory. The Berliner Social Support Scales were used (BSSS; Łuszczynska, Kowalska, Mazurkiewicz, & Schwarzer, 2006; Schulz & Schwarzer, 2003) to determine participants' experience of support. The BSSS includes separate measures of the following: (1) support seeking and support receiving, which served to calculate the index of support balance; and (2) close person support. Depression symptoms were determined by the Beck Depression Inventory (BDI; Beck, 1967). In this study, scores ranged from 0 to 49 ($M = 7.84$, $SD = 7.49$, a $= .88$). A measure of somatic stress symptoms (such as severe headaches, strong pain in the chest) was derived from the module of the General Social Survey used in systematic studies of the quality of life of Poles (Czapinski & Panek, 2005).

Participants also completed two reliable and valid subjective well-being scales: (1) Cantril's Self-Anchoring Ladder measure of overall life satisfaction

Table 9.2 Self-Esteem, Support Balance, and Close Person's Support as Predictors of Silencing the Self Subscales

Predictors	Externalized Self-Perception			Silencing the Self			Divided Self		
	β	R^2	ΔR^2	β	R^2	ΔR^2	β	R^2	ΔR^2
Step 1									
Age	.12			.37***			.19†		
Education	−.21**			−.19**			−.17*		
Town-city	−.08			−.15*			.04		
Employment	−.03			−.04			.03		
Marital status	−.05			−.11			−.08		
		.05	.09*		.15	.18***		.02	.05
Step 2									
Self-esteem	−.48***			−.26***			−.34***		
Support balance[a]	−.22**			−.12			−.09		
Close person's support	−.05			−.07			−.22***		
		.31	.26***		.26	.12***		.23	.22***

Note: Three separate regressions were conducted, one for each subscale of the Silencing the Self Scale.
[a] The correlation between support balance and close person's support was not significant ($r = 0.12$).
† $p < .10$; * $p < .05$; ** $p < .01$; *** $p < .001$.

(Cantril, 1965) and (2) the Satisfaction with Various Aspects of Life, derived from the module of the General Social Survey (Czapinski & Panek, 2005).

To examine the relationship between self-esteem, social support, and self-silencing as well as to control the sociodemographic variables, two hierarchical multiple regression analyses were carried out on each subscale of the STSS as a dependent variable. Age, education, place of living, employment, and marital status were entered as predictors at step 1, followed by self-esteem, support balance, and close person's support, entered at step 2.

As can be seen in Table 9.2, the analysis revealed three significant predictors of Externalized Self-Perception: low self-esteem, low education, and low support balance. Interestingly enough, the Divided Self subscale appeared to have almost the same predictors, although poor support from a close person contributed instead of poor social support. This suggests that in the case of women high on the Divided Self subscale, the missing support is related to their troubled close relationships rather than to the gaps in their wider social network. Age also predicted the Divided Self subscale, though marginally. Low self-esteem and poor social or close person's support together explained 26% of the variance of Externalized Self-Perception and 22% of Divided Self after controlling for age, education, place of living, employment, and marital status.

This pattern was slightly different for the Silencing the Self subscale. First of all, age appeared to be a significant and strong predictor, explaining 18% of the variance already at step 1. Second, for this subscale, the place of living appeared as a smaller but significant predictor, which suggests that women who live in villages or towns are higher on the Silencing the Self subscale than those who reside in cities. Third, only low self-esteem, but not lack of support, predicted the score of this scale at step 2, explaining 26% of its variance. Low education together with low self-esteem were significant predictors of all three self-silencing subscales.

Regarding the consequences of self-silencing, Tables 9.3 and 9.4 show results of regression analyses performed on well-being components as dependent variables with STSS subscales as independent predictors.

Interestingly, the contribution of each subscale varied over the specific components of well-being, which suggests that the three subscales differ in their psychological consequences and meaning (see also Jack, 1999b). The Externalized Self-Perception subscale appeared to be a significant predictor of a high level of depression ($\beta = .27$) and low satisfaction with life ($\beta = -.23$). Both these well-being indexes were also predicted by the Divided Self subscale ($\beta = .22$; $\beta = -.15$). The Divided Self subscale additionally predicted high levels of somatic stress symptoms ($\beta = .26$). On the contrary, the Silencing the Self subscale was not related to any of these components of well-being (see Table 9.3).

The relations of subscales to communal satisfaction support the argument being developed here. The Silencing the Self subscale significantly predicted satisfaction with children and home ($\beta = .31$) and (although marginally) satisfaction with the intimate partner ($\beta = .15$). On the contrary, the Divided Self subscale was a significant, strong predictor of dissatisfaction with the partner ($\beta = -.48$) and with confidant and friend ($\beta = -.32$). Dissatisfaction with one's partner explained the highest portion of variance (16%) in the Divided Self subscale. Externalized Self-Perception was related neither to satisfaction nor to

Table 9.3 Silencing the Self Subscales as Predictors of Subjective Well-Being Components: Depression, Somatic Symptoms of Stress, and Global Satisfaction with Life

Predictors	Depression		Stress Symptoms		Satisfaction with Life	
	β	R^2	β	R^2	β	R^2
Externalized Self-Perception	.27**		.06		−.23**	
Silencing the Self	−.09		−.07		−.07	
Divided Self	.22*		.26**		−.15†	
		.13		.05		.08

Note: Three separate regressions were conducted, one for each index of well-being.
† $p < .10$; * $p < .05$; ** $p < .01$.

Table 9.4 Silencing the Self Subscales as Predictors of Communal and Agentic Satisfaction of Subjective Well- Being Components

	Communal Satisfaction					Agentic Satisfaction	
	Children & Home[a]		Partner[b]		Confidants & Friends		Achievement, Finances, Education, Work
Predictors	β	R^2	β	R^2	β	R^2	β	R^2
Externalized Self-Perception	−.14		.10		−.02		−.20*	
Silencing the Self	.31**		.15†		.09		−.07	
Divided Self	−.09		−.48***		−.32***		−.06	
		.05		.13		.06		.06

Note: Four separate regressions were conducted, one for each communal satisfaction and one for agentic satisfaction.
[a] For having children only. [b]For having a partner/husband only.
*p < .05; **p < .01; ***p < .001.

dissatisfaction with close relationship; however, this subscale predicted dissatisfaction with achievement, finances, education, and work ($\beta = -.17$), which are labelled jointly as "agentic satisfaction."

Summing up the results of this study, all the dimensions of self-silencing were affected by poor education and low self-esteem. In addition, each dimension was predicted by slightly different constellations of personal and/or environmental factors and each contributed more or less differently to predict various aspects of well-being. A high score on the Externalized Self-Perception subscale was most strongly related to low self-esteem and poor social support. This dimension was also related to depression and unhappiness with life; however, it was not associated with any indexes of communal (relational) life. On the contrary, unhappiness in relationships was the most salient feature of the women high on the Divided Self dimension. Consistently, this subscale was determined by poor support from a close person and predicted all the three negative indicators of well-being: depression, somatic stress symptoms, and dissatisfaction with life (marginally).

Quite another picture of women's well-being was revealed by the Silencing the Self subscale. First, women's relational satisfaction, particularly with children and home, was revealed, and was marginally extended to the partner. Consistently, the dimension was related neither to depression nor to somatic stress symptoms, and revealed no significant relationships with either agentic satisfaction with life or with the variable "confidants and friends." Neither social nor kin support contributed to the prediction of this dimension, and only a marginal imbalance between the required and received social support was revealed. Second, older age and living in the country or small towns were additional demographic and social characteristics of high scores on the Silencing the Self subscale.

Clearly, these three dimensions of self-silencing reflect different styles of relational functioning and different forms of adaptation to social reality.

Do the Dimensions of Self-Silencing Reflect Adaptive Styles?

Given that the dimensions of self-silencing reflect styles of regulating the self in relationships, let's consider whether the Silencing the Self dimension presents a "good enough" adaptation to the biological tend-and-befriend pattern that increases the likelihood that mother and child will survive, and a simultaneous adaptation to the gender stereotypes prevalent in Poland. Do our findings confirm our hypothesis that this dimension reflects a better adaptation with fewer negative consequences than the other two? To answer this question, we should take into account the meaning of "well-adapted style" and its goals. Viewing the results from the adaptation perspective, the Silencing the Self style may be considered well matched to the Polish gender stereotype. First of all, the older age of women associated with this style argues for such a matching. As mentioned in the introduction, age determines the influences a cohort of women was exposed to while they were growing up. Older women have experienced all the impact of the "classical" Polish stereotype of "Polish mother" and learned it well. As I described earlier, this stereotype makes a woman the main person responsible for caretaking of children and shifts a man to the background. As if carefully following this prescription, the women high in the self-silencing subscale reported happiness with children, marginally extending their satisfaction to the partner. Moreover, the stereotype obliges a woman to carry out her duty and to be happy regardless of any difficult conditions or even against any difficulties. A heroic attitude is particularly praised and complaints are not socially acceptable. Again, as the stereotype prescribes, the women were "silent" about themselves and revealed neither depression nor dissatisfaction. Thus, this style has shown the pattern of response that fully fits the cultural patterns and social expectations for women's traditional behavior in Poland.

Does this pattern indicate a healthy response or merely a "silent" one and thus is not actually effective? In our study, the women did not show any sources of satisfaction other than communal ones. The results revealed, however, that two environmental conditions promoted this style, namely, poor education and residence in the country. As the analysis of the current economic situation of people in Poland has revealed, a significant number of the women, especially those who are older, with low education, and living in rural areas or small towns, are evidently the "losers" in the sociopolitical transformation process and they are now in a more unfavorable position than before. Thus, we may conclude that women who endorse the self-silencing dimension, whereas being unable to benefit from transformation, at least succeeded in engagement in family. Focusing on the offspring is an aspect of women's biological response to stress as described by the tend-and-befriend theory (Taylor et al., 2000). Even though the greater preoccupation of these women with relationships than with the self results in their limited access to their own inner state (as the "silent zone" has shown), the Silencing the Self dimension still seems to be more well-adapted for psychological health than dividing the self or judging the self through others' eyes. A self-silencing style harmonizes with women's current resources and their current living conditions and provides a strong source of their feeling at least some pride and pleasure instead of frustration, depression, and distress. It may be taken for granted that despite the environmental and social changes, some women might rather preserve their well-learned adaptive style, well matched to the traditional system of values, than to try to modify it.

Both other styles, Externalized Self-Perception and Divided Self, as they associate with depression and dissatisfaction with life, are evidently dysfunctional. However, the Externalized Self-Perception dimension also revealed a "silent zone" concerning the whole communal area, as if women were keeping their emotions about relationships dampened. Even their poor support balance was related to the wider social network, not to their close relationships. Indicating depressive symptoms without reporting any relational troubles resembles the defense mechanism of displacement, with suffering redirected away from relationships to the self. One may say that the troublesome self is experienced as less dangerous than any troubles with relationships. The insecure attachment strongly related to this style seems to reflect the women's inhibition in relationships and thus, their constricted self.

Finally, the Divided Self dimension revealed another strong pattern of responses relating both to the self and relationships. The women documented by Jack's studies (1991) openly reported relational unhappiness as well as depression and somatic symptoms. Even though their close relationships appeared as highly disorganized, they showed high access to their own emotions. Their troublesome relations seem a potential source of their depression and somatic symptoms. Disclosing high unhappiness with a partner, as well as with friends, they are likely to feel lonely and despairing but also, as Jack (1999a) has demonstrated, angry about all their relationships. As my study indicated, the styles of attachment related to this dimension reflect the women's ambivalent feelings and contradictory relational behaviors: going toward and away from others. Thus, the Divided Self style as a way of coping with relationships seems to be motivated both by a greater readiness of women to engage in relationships and by readiness to leave them and withdraw. Each solution results in dissatisfaction: with self and with relationship.

Also important is that low education and low self-esteem jointly determine the high scores on all of the subscales, suggesting a reciprocal relationship between these two factors. Low self-esteem may inhibit women's motivation to enter or return to school and to improve their education level. Additionally, low education can decrease the range of opportunities for enhancing self-esteem. Thus, both factors impact each other, limiting a potential for setting individual goals; both work for maintaining and reinforcing women's overall self-silencing. As shown in the analysis of education in Poland, most younger women are studying, while after age 35, women's educational activity disappears. Thus, social conditions favor mainly the younger women and appear to somewhat protect them against developing a self-silencing pattern.

Taking into account all the determinants of the self-silencing dimensions and viewing them once more from biological, sociocultural, and personal perspectives, the Silencing the Self dimension appeared to be more directly shaped by the gender stereotype of the Polish mother than the other two. The relative psychological effectiveness of this style results from its fitting into specific social conditions on the one hand and specific women's resources on the other. The specific social conditions include a rural place of living that limits the women's educational possibilities. The specific women's resources appear to be their older age and low self-esteem. Both social conditions and resources favor the women's relying upon the traditional cultural patterns and upon self-silencing.

The two other dimensions, Externalized Self-Perception and Divided Self, revealed ineffective, dysfunctional ways of coping with relationships. We may speculate that especially the Externalized Self-Perception style is highly influenced by that aspect of the Polish cultural gender pattern that prescribes to hide one's relational troubles. The extremely low self-esteem of these women together with poor social support codetermine and reinforce this style. Both of the styles (Externalized Self-Perception and Divided Self), however, are ineffective in following the tend-and-befriend pattern. They do not lead to a gain in environmental or emotional support, leaving women with low emotional security. Implicitly or explicitly, both are associated with severe disturbance of women's relational self. Both confirm the prediction of Jack's theory of self-silencing as a model of women's depression. Findings regarding the Silencing the Self subscale, as revealed in the Polish study, do not contradict Jack's model: Self-silencing appeared to be effective and adaptive enough for older Polish women during a specific socioeconomic and political transition period in Poland.

Conclusions

The most important finding of this study is that all three dimensions (i.e., Silencing the Self, Externalized Self–Perception, and Divided Self) of the self-silencing construct are associated differently with well-being, stress, and attachment styles. Evidently, the self-silencing of women as the theoretical concept measured by Jack's STSS is not a simple, homogenous phenomenon. Each of the dimensions of self-silencing appeared to be involved with specific individual and sociocultural determinants in slightly different ways. Thus, the results of the study argue for distinguishing different psychological mechanisms within the whole phenomenon called silencing the self, as Jack has argued (Jack, 1999b; Jack & Dill, 1992), as well as for considering them in specific sociocultural contexts.

The finding that specific contexts can shape an individual's self-perceptions, emotions, and behaviors can be seen as directly related to Taylor and colleagues' (2000) "tend-and-befriend" model, especially in its emphasis on how this bio-behavioral "central tendency" may be shaped in the face of threats. The social perils of disapproval, rejection, conflict, or loss of relationship can constitute very real threats that may lead a woman to silence aspects of herself simply as a means of social survival. Further, as Taylor and colleagues (2000) argue, "blending into the environments" may be occurring as a way to avoid negating attention. In the case of older Polish women with low education, blending into the stereotype of the "Polish mother" through engaging in self-silencing may offer some safety and sense of personal fulfillment in rearing children and fulfilling communal goals. This happens especially in difficult socioeconomic conditions and seems to be a well-known way of existence, deeply rooted in culture, ensuring a dignity to women instead of humiliation and fear. Therefore, positive well-being, concerning the satisfaction with children, is achieved when a self-silencing style harmonizes with the biological imperatives carried in the tend-and-befriend pattern and at the same time is supported by the content of the sociocultural gender stereotype. Most important, however, the specific external circumstances are needed to support and facilitate this style, as well as some inner, individual factors. Living in a small town or in the country, older age, low education, and low self-esteem together support the solution, making self-silencing relatively personally effective, or "effective enough."

This research therefore points to the need for further investigation regarding how specific social contexts, political and economic changes, gender roles, and status of women relate to the dimensions of self-silencing, including how the consequences of self-silencing might vary across cultures. For example, previous research in Western countries has found that women who experience violence from intimate partners score highest in self-silencing (see also Chapters 1, 11, and 22, this volume), and describe that they use silence as a strategy of safety in dangerous relationships (Jack, 1991). In my research in Poland, women's silence seems to be used as a strategy of safety more against external difficulties and stress than against oppressive relationships within a family. Perhaps this is a reason that their self-silencing did not appear psychologically and/or somatically damaging. Finally, given the findings of my research, it would be important to gain further evidence on the mutual/interacting relationship between the biological and cultural prescriptions for women's self-silencing behaviors.

Notes

1. This stereotype is widespread in Polish martyrdom literature and widely exists in the social consciousness. For example, in the Polish version of the Christmas carol "Silent Night," the Holy Mother is alone and smiling, watching the Holy Baby in the crib, while in the American or German versions the phrase "Holy Family" is used.
2. For details, see Geremek (1999), de Zavala Golec & Skarzynska (2006).
3. These estimates were computed from the raw data of three national sample surveys (2000, 2003, 2005), which can be found at http://www.diagnoza.com. The shortened version of the BDI, which is used by Czapinski (1993; Czapinski & Panek, 2005) consisted of items N, O, P, Q, R, T, and U of the original Beck Inventory.
4. I wish to thank Sylwia Kot, who initiated translation work on the Polish version of the STSS.
5. The three factors resulting from oblimin rotation were as follows: The first recovered six items of the original version of the Divided Self subscale (5, 13, 17, 19, 21, 25) and one from the Silencing the Self subscale (8). The second consisted of five items recovered from the Externalized Self-Perception subscale (6, 7, 23, 28, 31) and one from the Silencing the Self subscale (30). Finally, the third factor recovered from the Silencing the Self subscale consisted of seven out of nine original items (2, 8, 14, 15, 18, 20, 26). All three factors accounted for 48% of variance.

   The internal consistency of the Divided Self, Externalized Self-Perception, and Silencing the Self subscales was acceptable (α = .82, .71, and .81, respectively, and .89 for the total scale). There was a moderate correlation between the Divided Self and Externalized Self-Perception subscales (.50) and a slightly stronger one between the Divided Self and the Silencing the Self subscale (.64), and the relation between Externalized Self-Perception and Silencing the Self was r = .55.

   A subset (n = 87) of our sample completed the STSS scale again three to four weeks later. The test-retest correlations for Divided Self, Externalized Self-Perception, and Silencing the Self subscales were .69, .77, and .83 respectively, showing a substantial stability over a one-month period.

References

Ainsworth, M. D. S. (1989). Attachments beyond infancy. *American Psychologist, 144,* 709–716.

Aron, A., Aron, E. N., & Smollan, D. (1992). Inclusion of other in the self scale and the structure of interpersonal closeness. *Journal of Personality and Social Psychology, 63,* 596–612.

Bartholomew, K., & Horowitz, L. M. (1991). Attachment styles among young adults: A test of a four-category model. *Journal of Personality and Social Psychology, 61,* 226–244.

Baumeister, R. F. (2000). Ego depletion and the self's executive function. In A. Tesser, R. B. Felson, & J. M. Suls (Eds.), *Psychological perspectives on self and identity* (pp. 9–34). Washington, DC: American Psychological Association.

Beck, A. (1967). *Depression: clinical, experimental, and theoretical aspects.* New York: Harper & Row.

Bowlby, J. (1980). *Attachment and loss: Sadness and depression.* New York: Basic Books.

Cantril, H. (1965). *The patterns of humans' concerns.* New Brunswick, NJ: Rutgers University Press.

Chodorow, N. (1978). *The reproduction of mothering: Psychoanalysis and the sociology of gender.* Berkeley, CA: University of California Press.

Clancy, S. M., & Dollinger, S. J. (1993). Photographic description of the self: Gender and age differences in social connectedness. *Sex Roles, 29,* 477–495.

Cohen, S., Sherrod, D. R., & Clark, M. S. (1986). Social skills and the stress-protective role of social support. *Journal of Personality and Social Psychology, 50,* 963–973.

Czapinski, J. (1993). Polski Generalny Sondaż Dobrostanu Psychicznego: Badania panelowe 1991 i 1993 – struktura danych i podstawowe statystyki (Polish general well-being survey: Panel researches 1991 and 1993 – structure of data and basic statistics). Warszawa: Polskie Towarzystwo Psychologiczne (Polish Psychological Association).

Czapinski, J., & Panek, T. (2005). *Diagnoza spoŁeczna 2005 (Social Diagnosis 2005. Objective and subjective quality of life in Poland).* Warszawa: Wyższa Szkoła Finansów i Zarządzania. Rada Monitoringu Społeczengo (University of Finance and Management. The Council for Social Monitoring). Retrieved November 9, 2006, from http://www.diagnoza.com

De Zavala Golec, A., Skarzynska, K. (Eds.). (2006). *Understanding social change: Political psychology in Poland.* Hauppage, NY: Nova Science Publishers.

Geremek, B. (1999). The transformation of Central Europe. *Journal of Democracy, 10,* 1–115.

Gilligan, C. (1982). *In a different voice: Psychological theory and women's development.* Cambridge, MA: Harvard University Press.

Gurung, R. A. R., Taylor, S. E., & Seeman, T. E. (2003). Accounting for changes in social support among married older adults: Insights from MacArthur studies of successful aging. *Psychology and Aging, 18,* 487–496.

GUS. (2008). *Informacja o rozmiarach i kierunkach emigracji z Polski w latach 2004 – 2007.* Główny Urząd Statystyczny. Departament Badań Demograficznych. Materiał na konferencję prasową w dniu 25 lipca 2008. (Central Statistical Office, Department of Demographic Research. *An information about an extent and directions of emigration from Poland in the years 2004-2007.* Material on the press conference on July 25, 2008). Retrieved August 20, 2008, from http://www.stat.gov.pl

Jack, D. C. (1991). *Silencing the self: Women and depression.* Cambridge, MA: Harvard University Press.

Jack, D. C. (1999a). *Behind the mask: Destruction and creativity in women's aggression.* Cambridge, MA: Harvard University Press.

Jack, D. C. (1999b). Silencing the self: Inner dialogues and outer realities. In T. E. Joiner & J. C. Coyne (Eds.), *The interactional nature of depression: Advances in interpersonal approaches* (pp. 221–246). Washington, DC: American Psychological Association.

Jack, D. C., & Dill, D. (1992). The Silencing the Self Scale: Schemas of intimacy associated with depression in women. *Psychology of Women Quarterly, 16,* 97–106.

Kobak, R. R., Sudler, N., & Gamble, W. (1991). Attachment and depressive symptoms during adolescence: A developmental pathways analysis. *Development and Psychopathology, 3,* 461–474.

Łuszczyńska, A., Kowalska, M., Mazurkiewicz, M., & Schwarzer, R. (2006). Berlińskie Skale Wsparcia Społecznego (BSSS): Wyniki wstępnych badań nad adaptacją skal i ich własnościami psychometrycznymi. (Berlin Social Support Scales [BSSS]: Polish version of BSSS and preliminary results on its psychometric properties). *Studia Psychologiczne (Psychological Studies), 44*, 17–27.

Marcus, H. R., & Kitayama, S. (1991). Culture and the self: Implications for cognition, emotion, and motivation. *Psychological Review, 98*, 224–253.

Marody, M. (1993). Why I am not a feminist: Some remarks on the problem of gender identity in the United States and Poland. *Social Research, 60*, 853–864.

Niedenthal, P. M., & Beike, D. R. (1997). Interrelated and isolated self-conceptions. *Personality and Social Psychology Review, 1*, 106–128.

Rosenberg, M. (Ed.). (1965). *Society and the adolescent self-image*. Princeton, NJ: Princeton University Press.

Shulz, U., & Schwarzer, R. (2003). Soziale Unterstützung bei der Krankhaitsbewältigung: Die Berliner Social Support Skalen (BSSS). *Diagnostica, 49*, 73–82.

Środa, M. (2002). Być kobietą w Polsce [To be a woman in Poland] Conference *Polki w Unii Europejskiej* [Polish women in European Union]. *Warszawa, 6–7*, 11.

Taylor, S. E., Cousino Klein, L., Lewis, B. P., Gruenwald, T. L., Gurung, R. A. R., & Updegraff J. A. (2000). Biobehavioral responses to stress in females: Tend-and-befriend, not fight-or-flight. *Psychological Review, 107*, 411–429.

Titkow, A., & Domanski, H. (1995). *Co to znaczy być kobietą w Polsce [What doesn't mean to be a woman in Poland]*. Warszawa: Instytut Filozofii i Socjologii PAN [Institute of Philosophy and Sociology of Polish Academy of Science].

Turner, H. A. (1994). Gender and social support: Taking the bad with the good? *Sex Roles, 30*, 521–541.

Twenge, J. M. (2001). Changes in women's assertiveness in response to status and roles: A cross-temporal meta-analysis, 1931-1993. *Journal of Personality and Social Psychology, 81*, 133–145.

Wood, J. F., Giordano-Beech, M., Taylor, K. L., Michela, J. L., & Gaus, V. (1994). Strategies of social comparison among people with low self-esteem: Self-protection and self-enhancement, *Journal of Personality and Social Psychology, 67*, 713–731.

10

Exploring the Immigrant Experience through Self-Silencing Theory and the Full-Frame Approach: The Case of Caribbean Immigrant Women in Canada and the United States

Alisha Ali

The concept of silencing the self is grounded in the notion that the social world can shape one's behavior and one's self-perceptions in ways that precipitate a gradual alienation between the private self and the public self (Jack, 1991). Because the social world is constituted by the broader cultural milieu in which an individual and groups of individuals reside, silencing the self theory can be a powerful tool in examining the interface between self and culture. The theory can further be used to explore the process of transitioning from one culture to another, a process embodied in the immigrant experience. In this chapter, I describe the role of self-silencing in a particular type of immigrant experience: that of women who have emigrated from the English-speaking Caribbean to Canada or the United States. The basis for this discussion is a series of focus groups that were conducted in Toronto and New York City in which Caribbean immigrant women talked about the idea of self-silencing within the context of their lives as immigrant women. Through a comparison of the focus group findings from the Canadian immigrant sample and the American immigrant sample, it is possible to detect phenomenological differences in the role that self-silencing plays in adapting to the cultural context in the United States in contrast to the cultural adaptation described by the immigrant women in Canada. I contend that these differences, which I outline in this chapter, emerge from differing meanings and constructions around race, identity, and selfhood between these two host countries.

My interest in conducting focus groups with Caribbean immigrant women around the concept of self-silencing stemmed from the findings of a series of studies in which my colleague, Brenda Toner, and I investigated self-silencing, depression, and related constructs in women living in the Caribbean (including women living in Jamaica, Barbados, and Trinidad and Tobago) and in Caribbean Canadian women (i.e., immigrant women of Caribbean descent living in Canada). In the first of these studies, we found that the Caribbean Canadian women scored higher on the Silencing the Self Scale (STSS) and on the Beck Depression Inventory (BDI) than did the women living in the Caribbean (Ali & Toner, 2001). We further found that the women living in the Caribbean reported deriving meaning in their lives primarily from friendships, family, and relationships, whereas the Caribbean Canadian women were more likely to report deriving meaning from individual pursuits and careers. In another study, we examined the experiences of emotional abuse among Caribbean women and Caribbean Canadian women. In that study, we found that the Caribbean Canadian women were more likely than the Caribbean women to cite institutional and systemic causes for their abuse than were the women living in the Caribbean (Ali & Toner, 2005).

In a subsequent study (Ali, 2008), interviews were conducted with Caribbean immigrant women living in Canada and the United States to examine their encounters with racism in their host countries. This study used a version of the contextual rating system originally developed by Brown and Harris (1978) to collect data on life stress and adapted to focus on particular domains of stressors (Ali, Oatley, & Toner, 1999). Among the findings from this study were the following: (1) in the overall sample, nearly one-third of the immigrant women reported at least one first-hand encounter with racism since immigrating to their host country; (2) the majority of these encounters occurred in workplace settings; and (3) in participants' descriptions of the effects of racism on their emotional well-being, the most commonly reported effects included self-directed blame and a loss of a sense of one's self-worth.

Taken together, the findings from these studies raised several questions, including the following: How might immigration and adaptation to Canada or the United States influence self-silencing among women from the Caribbean? What is the relationship between self-silencing and systemic racism in the experiences of Caribbean immigrant women in Canada and the United States? And, more broadly, what can the interplay between self-silencing, racism, and emotional distress tell us about the immigrant experience? All of these questions are embedded in an assumption that aspects of a host culture create a social experience for immigrant women in which emotional well-being can be compromised through prolonged acculturative stress. To directly investigate this phenomenon, it is necessary to examine the experiences of women who have lived in the Caribbean and then immigrated to Canada or the United States. From a methodological point of view, such examination would have to involve either longitudinal research (i.e., following women through the premigration and postmigration periods) or retrospective research that allowed women to reflect on both their premigration selves and their postmigration selves. The present study involved the latter design in an attempt to encourage the active voices of immigrant women in capturing the social and relational intricacies at play in the immigration process.

Acculturative stress experienced by immigrant women is likely influenced by contradictions in the value systems between one's country of origin and the host country (Henry, 1994; Javed, 1995). Both Canada and the United States are generally understood to embrace a value system that fosters independence and individualism. However, Caribbean theorists have written that Caribbean culture is difficult to categorize with respect to notions of collectivism and individualism (Barriteau, 1998; Sutton, 1974). The implications of Caribbean culture in the context of psychological experiences of independence and interdependence are therefore not easily identified. On the one hand, the Caribbean region has a history of collectivist influences emerging largely from kinship structures that emphasize communal action and group-oriented activity (Senior, 1991). On the other hand, there is a recognized presence of forces of self-assertion and individual rights arising from various anticolonialist struggles (Beckles, 1992). Some theorists speculate that such self-assertion is particularly evident among Caribbean women, stating that there is a widely acknowledged notion of the "strong Caribbean woman" (Brodber, 1982). This stereotype may persist in North America as well as in the Caribbean. However, immigrant women are also typically considered to occupy a disempowered social position in North American society (Javed, 1995; Raghavan, Sherman, Stiles, Roberts, & Stamper, 2008), so there may be contradictory stereotypes at play in the lives of Caribbean immigrant women in North America.

Given the cultural complexities inherent in this work, the research I present in this chapter was designed to contribute to the growing knowledge base of findings pertaining to the interconnected content domains of immigration, culture, and psychological well-being. This research was also designed to extend the application of self-silencing theory into research on immigration. There were two general aims in this research. The first was to explore the role that self-silencing theory might play in helping us to understand the immigrant experience among Caribbean Canadian and Caribbean American women. The second, more theoretically complicated aim was to examine the self-silencing construct itself and how the cultural context might shape a woman's experience of self-silencing. Jack (1991) has described self-silencing as being context-dependent. If self-silencing depends on context, then the same woman can report different levels of self-silencing in different contexts. In this study, each of the women has resided in two different cultural contexts (her country of origin in the Caribbean and her host country—either Canada or the United States), and the women were asked to share their insights on the differing contexts with respect to their first-hand experiences of self-silencing.

Because this study was directed in part at examining the context-dependent nature of self-silencing, it was necessary to adopt an overall theoretical approach that recognized the crucial role of context and environment. To this end, the development of this study was informed by the *full-frame approach* (Goodman & Smyth, in press; Smyth, Goodman, & Glenn, 2006). The full-frame approach is an orientation that frames women's experiences through the consideration of such factors as personal history, social history, and ethnicity. According to this approach, we cannot understand conditions such as physical illness and psychological distress without including an analysis of the social and material factors that create and perpetuate these conditions. For women who are marginalized by multiple interacting forms of oppression (including racism, gender discrimination, and economic disadvantage), this approach encourages a conceptualization of the factors *surrounding* the phenomenon or condition under study rather than a sole focus on the problem itself (Smyth et al., 2006). The full-frame approach uses a set of principles aimed at identifying both the constraints and the resources that together structure women's lived experiences. These principles include an emphasis on understanding the interplay between the external and internal worlds and a focus on the centrality of relationships and role definitions in influencing women's well-being. Another tenet of this approach is the belief that women—and indeed all people—are most able to achieve emotional wellness when they are encouraged to both reflect on their personal histories (e.g., their upbringing, experiences of trauma, the development of personal strengths) and play an active role in telling their personal narratives of what they've experienced and what they hope for the future. This telling or "framing" of personal narratives usually involves participation in support groups where women share their stories with other women and describe their past experiences as well as their most important personal goals.

The full-frame approach has been used by practitioners to inform the development of social services that are responsive to the needs of diverse populations of women; it has generally not been used in formulating research questions or research methods. However, the method of inquiry adopted in the research I describe here was designed to fulfill the full-frame principles as a means not only of capturing the lived experience of the immigrant women in the focus groups but also of understanding the connections between their experiences and their need for authentic self-expression in navigating a host culture. Therefore, as I describe next, the present study was designed to be an integration of inquiry into the context-specific nature of immigrant women's sense of self and examination of the cultural construction of silencing.

The Present Study

In this study, focus groups were conducted in Toronto and New York with Caribbean immigrant women. Five focus groups (ranging from five to eight participants) were conducted in Toronto, and five focus groups (ranging from five to seven participants) were conducted in New York City. These focus groups were highly structured and began with a specific script. After participants were welcomed to the group and signed a consent form, they were each handed a copy of the STSS with the items grouped by subscale. For instance, for the Care as Self-Sacrifice subscale, all items within that subscale were presented under the heading "Item Group One" (the actual subscale names—e.g., Care as Self-Sacrifice—were never presented to the participants). Participants were then asked to read all items in Item Group One, and were verbally instructed as follows: "After reading all statements in Item Group One, please think about how those thoughts and ideas relate to your life back in the Caribbean and about how those thoughts and ideas relate to your life here in—[Canada/the United States]. Then, as a group, we'll discuss the similarities and differences you've thought of. Please feel free to use the pens and paper provided to write down notes on your thoughts as you read the statements." The first subscale was then discussed by the group until no new information appeared to emerge. At that point, participants were asked to read the statements in Item Group Two (the second subscale of items) and were provided with the same verbal instructions to discuss that group of items. The focus group continued until the fourth and final group of items was discussed. The focus groups lasted approximately 60 to 90 minutes, and were each recorded and directly transcribed.

The participants in this study were women between the ages of 27 and 59 who had emigrated within the last 10 years from the English-speaking Caribbean to either the United States ($n = 34$) or Canada ($n = 31$). Their countries of origin were Jamaica, St. Vincent, Guyana, Barbados, or Trinidad and Tobago. Seventy-eight percent of the women were of African descent and 22% were of Indian descent. The Canadian sample was recruited from the Toronto area, and the U.S. sample was recruited from New York City. Seventy-nine percent of the Canadian sample and 68% of the U.S. sample worked outside of the home. Participants were recruited through advertisements in community centers, local newspapers, and college campuses. In order to take part in the study, a woman must have immigrated directly to her host country (either Canada or the United States) from the Caribbean at least five years prior to the interview, must have been age 18 or older when she immigrated, and must have lived continuously in their host country since arriving (with periods of living abroad not exceeding six months at a time).

In analyzing the focus group data, the data from the Canadian sample and the data from the U.S. sample were examined separately. The focus group transcripts were coded using the qualitative data analysis strategy described by Strauss and Corbin (1998). The analysis was conducted in three distinct stages with two coders in each stage. In the first stage, each coder read all transcripts and the two coders together compiled a list of all themes that emerged from their readings. This resulted in a list of 33 themes for the Canadian sample and 27 themes for the U.S. sample. In the second stage, the coders grouped together all themes that shared similar content. This grouping led to a list of 9 categories in the Canadian sample and 11 categories in the U.S. sample. In the final stage, the categories were examined and thematic groupings were derived by formulating broader conceptual themes composed of three to four categories each. In each of the two samples in this study (i.e., the Canadian sample and the U.S. sample), three of these broad themes were derived. To follow are the findings within each of these themes, beginning with the themes from the Canadian sample and followed by the American sample.

Focus Group Themes

Caribbean Canadian Women

Social Expectations of Women

While the general consensus across the focus groups was that women appear to have more equality overall in Canada—especially in the workplace—the theme of gender relations also captured the impression that women in Canada are most highly praised for trying to "have it all" by raising a family and simultaneously pursuing a career. In the Caribbean, on the other hand, the participants felt there was a greater emphasis on the woman's role in the home. In one focus group, when discussing the items from the Care as Self-Sacrifice subscale, a participant stated the following:

> The idea of caring for another person is an important idea in both places, but the West Indian ideal is someone who keeps a good home, while here it is like the woman makes her husband look good if she is also successful like him: then together they look like a successful couple. The man and the woman are supposed to be more similar to each other here [in Canada] but also here you're supposed to seem successful and give up what you want if what you most want is to be with your children and keep a good home. So then you have to go against the way you were raised.

In another focus group, when the participants were discussing the items from the Divided Self subscale, the discussion also turned to the notion of male/female differences in expected roles. Participants in these focus groups frequently described the expectation that, in Canada, women are assumed to be more emotional than men but are not expected to show all of their emotions openly. As one participant described:

> When I read this part "inwardly I feel angry and rebellious" [STSS item #16], it makes me think of a woman who has been told she shouldn't ever be angry. When I was growing up, we always saw my mother saying to my aunts or to my father or to anyone what she was angry about. I think talking about it is important if you feel

anger. But here you have to be more lady-like or you are not a desirable woman. It's true what someone said a few minutes ago. What did you say? [turns to another participant] Here it's more repressed? Yes, repressed. If you're angry, just be angry, that's what I say.

In both of these quotes, it appears that the participants feel there is something inauthentic about the ways that women are expected to act in Canadian society. The perception that Caribbean society more readily embraces the idea of a woman as primarily being a homemaker, while at the same time expecting women to express their anger, is in keeping with the apparent contradictions described by theorists: It seems that Caribbean society supports the traditional role of the woman but also supports her self-expression and even expects that she will express her anger. However, the contradiction that was discussed in the focus groups was the contrast they saw in Canada between the supposed ideal of individualism (as one participant stated, "Canadians and Americans are the same in thinking they are individual persons first and group members second") and the reality that women in Canada are not expected to show anger. As I will discuss later, participants in the American sample described a similar dynamic at play in the United States.

Family Ties

A theme that appeared frequently in all of the Canadian focus groups was the theme of differences between Canada and the Caribbean with respect to the role of family. This theme most often arose during the discussion of items from the Care as Self-Sacrifice subscale. The role of the mother was described as self-sacrificing in Canadian culture and in Caribbean culture. However, the participants described differences between the two cultures with respect to the context surrounding self-sacrifice. The words of this participant described a view expressed by many:

> Yes, in Jamaica the wife, the mother is to think about the children and the family first and doesn't have much time to think about "What do I want?" But the mother there is the middle of everything, the center. The home is nothing without the mother – and the grandmother – there. But you come to this country and you try to teach your children the reason that you do so much for them with the schooling, the chances for a better life, but here the center in these families is the father. The father is the one who matters outside and inside of the family. So here you have to forget about what mattered most to your mother and her mother, you have to be like other families. But you lose the idea that the mother knows what is best for the family and the mother takes the lead in doing what is best - and your children, they lose that too.

These sentiments are noteworthy in light of the previous quantitative findings that Caribbean Canadian immigrant women scored higher on self-silencing compared to women living in the Caribbean (Ali & Toner, 2001). Perhaps the process of emigrating from the Caribbean to Canada involves a change in role wherein women are expected to silence their anger (as described in the previous section) and also to relinquish their role as head of the household. In another focus group, this theme was present in a Trinidadian woman's description of her relationship with her sons:

> Back home [in Trinidad] my young son and my older son would listen to me and I would feel I could talk to them and they would want to do what I wanted them to do. But here, you are a mother as a job, not as part of what keeps the family together. Our older boy, when we were back home, he would always come home first before seeing his friends and not just be with them all the time. But now both boys are with their friends all the time. Part of this also is that it seems fine to people here that the father is away working two jobs and away from the family. So now I don't have him to talk to at home, and when he at home he tired or he sleeping all the time. So I don't tell him what I feel, or that I feel lonely. Like missing my sisters back home, I tell them on the phone I miss them, but here there's no one to tell that to.

The isolation of the immigrant experience, in this instance, is coupled with the loss of role of the mother as being connected to her family, and of the family members providing mutual support. The silencing that occurs in this context relates to the literal loss of a listener, be it one's children or one's partner. Henry (1994) has described the immigrant experience as one of giving up familial closeness for the sake of material striving. The construct of self-silencing can help us to understand the emotional sacrifice involved in that process. Because many immigrant parents choose to leave their countries of origin to provide a better life for their children, they make a deliberate choice to put their own needs second. But the need for emotional closeness is a fundamental need driven by the primacy of relational connection in human experience. The theme that follows is a reflection of the centrality of this connection in mental health and wellness.

Loss of Self

In the previous quantitative study (Ali & Toner, 2001), women who had immigrated to Canada from the Caribbean reported higher scores on the Beck Depression Inventory relative to women living in the Caribbean. The possibility that the immigrant experience can compromise one's emotional well-being is reflected in the theme of loss of self. In comparing Canada to the Caribbean on the items of the STSS, the women in the focus groups frequently commented on how they felt different about themselves and related to people differently in Canada than they did in their country of origin. As one participant described:

> You don't realize until you're somewhere different how much you were used to being around people you had always known. We could shout out the window to our neighbor, and we had been neighbors with them since my great-grandparents were alive. Here [in Canada], everything is locked up and people are inside most of the

time, and you can have a whole day where you don't see anyone you know. So that means you start feeling lonely. When that started for me, I felt sad and lonely; then I felt how back home I would just feel happy and be happy being around people I knew. After my first months here [in Canada], I would sometimes cry. I was not the same happy person. Without people to be happy with, you can't really feel happy.

A participant in another focus group described a similar feeling of loss of sense of self, which began shortly after her marriage to a Canadian man who was considerably older than she was:

> I came here on my own to go to nursing school. I didn't have much money and I married a White Canadian man even though he was eleven years older than me and I had known him shorter than one year. We stayed married for nearly four years. He never met any of my family from Guyana and never wanted to travel there to meet my parents. He didn't like how I talked because of my accent, and I started to see how I must seem to him – like I was not smart and like I was low-class. It made it so I could not relate to him and he couldn't relate to me. So yes, I did feel that "never seeming to measure up" [from STSS item #31].

It may be that the loss of self experienced by immigrant women is tied to the fact that the process of self-definition involves understanding oneself through connection to others. When a woman feels no authentic connection to her partner, her sense of self suffers. This problem is likely even more pronounced for immigrant women who additionally feel that they are surrounded by strangers in their host country.

Caribbean American Women

Gender Relations

This theme was very similar in content to the theme from the Canadian sample called "Social Expectations of Women." The women in the American focus groups generally agreed that men and women were more similar to each other in the United States than in the Caribbean. The consensus was that American women have to maintain a certain workplace persona that involves not expressing their emotions. For example, in discussing the items from the Silencing the Self subscale of the STSS, one of the participants stated the following:

> I feel I don't fit in much here [in the U.S.] because I seem loud. In America, people think that women are all into women's rights and standing up for yourself. That's true, and I think American women, especially women who work, do act like men – they do because they have to if they want respect. But the difference here is that women *also* have to be demure and soft-spoken, like they're one person at work and another person in their marriage. West Indian women can be loud and speak what we think, but we don't act like men, [we don't act] like we haven't got emotions.

Another participant described marked differences between the Caribbean and the United States with respect to dating and male-female relationships:

> It's like going on a date here [in the U.S.] is like a job interview. The woman has to be poised and serious and see if the man has a good enough job and enough money. I don't like the dating here. I have to pretend that what the man thinks is more important than what I think. When I was dating in Jamaica, I usually knew the person's family or some of his friends before dating him, so there was more comfort between us. Now I go on dates with American men – White, Black, or whatever – and I have to listen to everything about them and they don't want to know about me. Like what I think or feel doesn't matter.

For these immigrant women, there is a contrast between how they were expected to behave in the Caribbean and the expectations they face in the United States. They point to the apparent contradiction that women in the United States have equal rights and yet have to be a silent audience to men. The immigrant experience itself may influence the dynamic described by these women as well: Resistance to acting "demure" and to not speaking one's feelings is a challenge if, in your country of origin, you were expected to embrace self-expression and were largely around familiar people with whom you could speak your mind.

Externalized Self-Perception

A striking difference between the Canadian and American focus groups pertained to the discussions of the items from the Externalized Self-Perception subscale. While the discussion of these items was generally brief in the Canadian focus groups and did not reveal many notable differences between Caribbean and Canadian society, the American focus groups showed that the participants viewed the notion of externalized self-perception to be central to women's experiences in the United States, and especially to the experiences of immigrant women. One participant explained the difference between her experience in the United States and her home country of Jamaica as follows:

> American women have like a list of things that they have to be all the time: have the right clothes, look like you have money, look younger than you are. And you're not supposed to be happy until you have those. It's different from back home [in the Caribbean] where lots of people don't have much but people don't care so much about that. You don't do the "judging myself by how other people see me" [from STSS item #6] because people already know you and you know them and it's OK. In America, even if someone is your friend, you still have to impress them with how you look and what you've got.

The theme of externalized self-perception was also evident when the focus group participants discussed their interpersonal relationships. As one participant stated:

> I've had two long-term relationships with American men. I think what happens when you're different from other people because of your color or because of how you talk, you start to see yourself like an outsider and you feel self-conscious. That's what "I tend to

judge myself" [from STSS item #6] feels like to me. It means like with my ex-boyfriend I was supposed to feel grateful that I was dating an American who was born here because the only job I can get is as a part-time aide. So I was judgmental of myself – and I still am now – and he was judging me all that time. You can't have a real relationship that way.

The idea of judging oneself by the standards of the host country (i.e., American society) was prevalent within this theme and seemed to function in tandem with unequal dynamics in intimate relationships, especially for women who described relationships with men who were "White" and/or "American."

Race and Racial Discrimination

The theme of race and racial discrimination was the theme that most deeply separated the focus group findings from Canada and those from the United States. In the Canadian focus groups, race and color were mentioned frequently; however, racism and racial discrimination were discussed more often and in more detail in the U.S. focus groups. The following statement typifies the sentiments that were expressed:

In Trinidad, there is a racial problem but it isn't about who is White and who is not White the way it is here [in the U.S.]. In Trinidad, whether you are Indian or Black you don't feel that you are worse than anyone else. Here I think anyone who is not White feels worse and people look down on you. I've felt that when I was trying to find a job. A woman interviewing me asked if I could communicate well in English over the phone for a phone marketing job. I said English was my only language. She said to me that people in this country hang up the phone right away if they hear someone who talks like me. That definitely made me doubt what kind of job I could do and what people here would think I couldn't do. So, this one [points to STSS questionnaire] "When I make decisions, other people's thoughts and opinions influence me more than my own thoughts and opinions" [STSS item #23]; I would never had said that back home, but now for me that is true.

Some of the women in the American focus groups commented not on their first-hand experiences with racism but on the overall racism that is present in American society. These comments frequently involved comparisons between the United States and the Caribbean, such as this description:

I think a big difference between Black women who grow up here [in the U.S.] and Black West Indian women is that here they grow up from the beginning being told they are like "second-class citizens," everything around them tells them they're not as good because they're not White. I think that makes you timid. So yes, I can see how they can think things like "Caring means putting the other person's needs in front of my own" [STSS item #3]. That's how you would think if you think other people are more important than you.

Statements such as this describe a sort of "immunity" that immigrant women of color may have due to an upbringing in a culture that is not directly White dominant.

These descriptions also demonstrate a marked difference between the role of race and racism in American society and the dynamics that may surround race in the Caribbean.

Integrating Self-Silencing Theory and the Full-Frame Approach

Examining the findings from this study and from the previous quantitative studies of self-silencing in Caribbean immigrant women, it is apparent that there is some connection between the cultural adaptation of immigration and the development of self-silencing thoughts and behaviors. Clearly, the social isolation and disconnection that are common for new immigrants can influence a woman's sense of self. Additionally, for the Caribbean American women in particular, there can be feelings of alienation and diminished self-worth precipitated by encounters with racism, or even by the knowledge that one now resides in a racist society. The goal of this research, in adopting the full-frame approach, was to bring a new perspective to exploring the context-dependent nature of self-silencing. The context can be seen as the *frame* or, in other words, as the environment or setting that frames a woman's experiences, actions, and self-perception. So, what do these findings tell us about the factors that frame women's self-silencing?

Two key ideas emerge from these findings regarding the ways in which self-silencing is framed or is dependent on context. One involves a difference or distinction that appeared *within* the overall group of focus group participants (i.e., in both the U.S. and Canadian samples), and the other is a difference *between* the U.S. and Canadian samples. The first difference pertains to the women's comparisons of Caribbean culture and American/Canadian culture and the extent to which they reported being personally affected by the cultural differences they observed with respect to self-silencing. For the most part, the women in all of the focus groups described Caribbean expectations of women as less consistent with the notion of self-silencing and Canadian/American society as contributing to self-silencing in women. For instance, in one of the Canadian focus groups, after reading a set of items on the STSS, one woman stated, "West Indian women just don't act that way. They don't think something and not state it." However, not all of the women reported silencing themselves more after immigrating than they did back home in the Caribbean. There was, in several of the focus groups, a notable divide in which some participants reported that their self-perceptions and self-silencing behavior changed after immigrating while some participants did not report such changes.

This distinction raises the question, what differentiates women who self-silence more after immigrating from those who do not? Protective factors around self-silencing can be identified through research that is similar to the research on factors that protect women against depression. For example, in their research on women's depression, Brown and Harris (1978) found that most episodes of depression were preceded by major life stress. However, they also found that most women who experienced major life stress did not become depressed. The most important protective factor they identified was having a trusted confidant to speak to and feel connected to. The presence of a confidant may be especially crucial for immigrant women because they can easily become socially isolated. Several women in the focus groups described the importance of the emotional support they received from talking on the phone to loved ones in their countries of origin. It is possible that such support can be a protective buffer against self-silencing.

The key difference *between* the U.S. and Canadian samples that emerged from the focus group findings pertains to racism. In the U.S. focus groups, there was a distinct sense that being "American" means being White and that people of color are understood to be of lesser stature in American society. This sense may relate in part to the notion that American identity is homogenous and tied to race, whereas Canadian "identity" is a far more vague concept (Ali, 2006). The findings around race suggest that part of the frame, or context, of self-silencing is the inequality associated with racism.

Jack's (1991) theory is predicated in part on the assumption that social inequality between men and women is a contributing factor in women's depression. However, racial inequality is also socially disempowering and can compromise one's sense of self. For immigrant women of color, racism may be more salient a challenge than gender inequality. If Silencing the Self Theory is to continue its viability and applicability as a theory of depression in women, it must carry explanatory power in capturing the full frame of women's oppression. Because the effects of racism on women's well-being can best be understood from an integrative perspective that includes both social and psychological elements, the use of Silencing the Self Theory and the full-frame approach is relevant and appropriate. In future work, this combined perspective can be applied in research aimed at further understanding how racial discrimination influences changes in role, identity, and self-expression in immigrant women. This integrative stance can also guide research that informs the development of more responsive and effective services to meet the needs of women who immigrate to Canada and the United States.

References

Ali, A. (2006). Identity as contested space: A Canadian vantage on an epistemological challenge. *Feminism & Psychology, 16*, 345–349.

Ali, A. (2008). Examining the effects of racism on the emotional well-being of Caribbean immigrant women: An integration of feminist and phenomenological approaches. In C. Raghavan, A. Edwards, & K. Vaz (Eds.), *Benefiting by design: Women of color in feminist psychological research and practice* (pp. 129–142). Newcastle, UK: Cambridge Scholars Press.

Ali, A., Oatley, K., & Toner, B. B. (1999). Emotional abuse as a precipitating factor for depression in women. *Journal of Emotional Abuse, 1,* 1–13.

Ali, A., & Toner, B. B. (2001). Symptoms of depression among Caribbean women and Caribbean-Canadian women: An investigation of self-silencing and domains of meaning. *Psychology of Women Quarterly, 25,* 175–180.

Ali, A., & Toner, B. B. (2005). A cross-cultural investigation of emotional abuse in Caribbean women and Caribbean-Canadian women. *Journal of Emotional Abuse, 5,* 125–140.

Barriteau, V. E. (1998). Liberal ideology and contradictions in Caribbean gender systems. In C. Barrow (Ed.), *Caribbean portraits* (pp. 346–356). Kingston, Jamaica: Ian Randle Publishers.

Beckles, H. M. (1992). Kalingo (Carib) resistance to Europe colonisation of the Caribbean. *Caribbean Quarterly, 38,* 1–14.

Brodber, A. (1982). *Perceptions of Caribbean women: Toward the documentation of stereotypes.* Bridgetown, Barbados: Institute of Social and Economic Research.

Brown, G. W., & Harris, T. O. (1978). *Social origins of depression: A study of psychiatric disorder in women.* London: Tavistock.

Goodman, L., & Smyth, K. F. (in press). Social justice for marginalized women: Multicultural and feminist roots of the full frame approach to social services. In M. Constantine (Ed.), *Social justice and empowerment initiatives in psychology and education.* New York: Teachers College Press.

Henry, F. (1994). *The Caribbean diaspora in Toronto: Learning to live with racism.* Toronto: University of Toronto Press.

Jack, D. C. (1991). *Silencing the self: Women and depression.* Cambridge, MA: Harvard University Press.

Javed, N. S. (1995). Salience of loss and marginality: Life themes of "immigrant women of color" in Canada. In J. Adleman & G. Enguidanos (Eds.), *Racism in the lives of women: Testimony, theory, and guides to anti-racist practice* (pp. 13–22). Binghamton, NY: Harrington Park Press.

Raghavan, C., Sherman, J., Stiles, C., Roberts, O., & Stamper, S. (2008). Doing gender: Parental beliefs about gender identity in Asian-Indian immigrant families. In C. Raghavan, A. Edwards, & K. Vaz (Eds.), *Benefiting by design: Women of color in feminist psychological research and practice* (pp. 143–158). Newcastle, UK: Cambridge Scholars Press.

Senior, O. (1991). *Working miracles: Women's lives in the English-speaking Caribbean.* Bloomington, IN: Indiana University Press.

Smyth, K. F., Goodman, L., & Glenn, C. (2006). The full frame approach: A new response to marginalized women left behind by specialized services. *American Journal of Orthopsychiatry, 76,* 489–502.

Strauss, A., & Corbin, J. (1998). *Basics of qualitative research* (2nd ed.). Thousand Oaks, CA: Sage.

Sutton, C. (1974). Cultural duality in the Caribbean. *Caribbean Studies, 14,* 96–101.

11

Deconstructing Gendered Discourses of Love, Power, and Violence in Intimate Relationships: Portuguese Women's Experiences

Sofia Neves and Conceição Nogueira

The aim of this chapter is to discuss the importance of the self- silencing construct in the foundation and perpetuation of gendered discourses about love, power, and violence in heterosexual intimate relationships. This construct can be materialized in the construction of meanings around close relationships. Drawing upon our research findings on self-silencing in various groups of Portuguese women, we argue that women's silence is linked to cultural norms and a strict gender hierarchy. Within these culturally constructed imperatives, institutionalized power structures serve to define the expression of self-sacrificing love as a *natural* characteristic of women. This expression is additionally assumed to extend to the provision of care to others. Men, on the other hand, are presumed to *naturally* inhabit a position of authority. This essentialist vision restricts women's self-determination and provides men with the social licence to employ physical, psychological, and sexual violence.

This chapter explores feminist approaches to understanding the psychological consequences of these gendered inequalities. Our analysis emphasizes the relationship between strict cultural dictates around intimacy and women's tendency to experience an absence of autonomy and voice. By reconfiguring some key concepts originally viewed as being part of human nature, it is possible to counteract these socialized tendencies. The result of this critical exercise gives feminist researchers and clinicians effective opportunities to develop new means of empowering women.

Being a Woman in Portugal

Portugal lived under an autocratic regime until 1974 when, due to the intervention of the Armed Forces Movement (a group of rebel officers who opposed the regime), democracy was restored. The Carnations Revolution, or the April 25 Revolution, was a military-social process that intended to end 40 years of dictatorship established by António de Oliveira Salazar, the politician that implemented in the country the New State ("Estado Novo") and forced people to believe that Portugal should remain proudly alone. After the Revolution, António Spínola, president of the Junta of National Salvation ("Junta de Salvação Nacional)," was elected to be the president of the Portuguese Republic, a position he occupied from May 15, 1974, until September 20 of the same year (when he was replaced by Costa Gomes). One year later, a constituent assembly was chosen, for the first time, by universal suffrage and elaborated the constitution of the Portuguese Republic, where the Portuguese Republic is described as a Democratic state. This constitution of 1976 was considered the most egalitarian in Europe.

In fact, the revolution that gave liberty back to the Portuguese was a milestone in the establishment of fundamental rights, particularly in the case of women, in so much as it established, for instance, women's right to vote and access to the bar, the diplomatic service, and all positions in local government. As Ferreira notes (1998), women saw their social status change in important areas, such as (1) the right of access to any and all professions; (2) the right to vote; (3) husbands were no longer allowed to read their wives' mail, nor refuse to allow them to leave the country; (4) maternity leave was extended to a 90-day period; (5) equality in all areas was recognized by the constitution; and (6) a new civil code was approved in which the figure of the "head of the family" disappeared. As a result of the historical transformations in the Portuguese society, the expansion of the Portuguese scientific community in the last 20 years has been partly achieved through women's contributions (Amâncio & Ávila, 1995), in the sense that they have made a great effort to progress in academic careers, as shown by the significant number of women who have obtained their PhDs and qualifications since the 1980s (OCT/MCT, 2001).

The spring of 1974 undoubtedly inaugurated in Portugal a period of rapid modernization in terms of economic, social, and cultural development,[1] but this did not produce the implementation of an effective equality between the sexes. As Amâncio and Oliveira (2006) emphasized, the formal recognition of rights did not change the previous gender ideology.

According to Women Watch (1997):

Equality between men and women is a fundamental principle of Portuguese law and common law. However, neither constitutional guarantees of equality, nor the presence of statutory measures for women in the job market have been sufficient to achieve equality between men and women. Although there have been significant changes in gender relations in the last few years - such as the growing participation of women in the labour market, their resulting economic independence, and the increase in women's participation in secondary school levels and higher education - these changes have not yet been translated into a global improvement of laws concerning women, nor in women's exercise and enjoyment of full citizenship. (para. 1–2)

Recent surveys pointed out that gender inequalities are not perceived as indicators of social inequality in Portugal and that women's rights do not seem to be a major priority (Nielson, 2003). The latest census of the population carried out in 2001 shows that women represent more than half of the Portuguese population, around 52.63%. The specific mode of participating in social, economic, and family life; their average lower wages; their greater job insecurity; and the concomitant weaker social welfare due to a more irregular participation in the economic activity (Comissão para a Cidadania e Igualdade de Género [CIG], 2009) make them the face of poverty, leading some authors to characterize poverty in Portugal, as is the case in other countries, as being feminine (Perista, 1999).

The economic inequality of Portuguese women is clarified when we analyze the several factors that at various levels contribute to this situation. As far as the health conditions are concerned, for instance, gender inequalities are so glaring that Portugal approved in January 2007 in the 120th session of the executive council of the World Health Organization (WHO) various resolutions that aimed to introduce precisely these gender specificities in all areas of health care policies. In particular, the resolution "Gender, Women and Health" proposes to increase knowledge and evidence on how sex differences and gender inequalities impact on specific health problems and health services. 20% of portuguese population suffers from depression (Ministério da Saúde de Portugal, 2009), and circulatory diseases are the most important cause of death, especially among women (Instituto Nacional de Estatística, 2006).

The fragility of Portuguese women's position is also conditioned by the high rate of criminality that affects them. In Portugal, the high figures of domestic violence outline a worrying scenario that has been increasingly clarified due to the changes in the Portuguese penal code in 2000. Until then, the crime of domestic violence was not public, resting only on the victim's decision to press charges. Due to this, many violent occurrences remained unreported, and therefore were not included in the official statistics. In the last decade, Portuguese society has developed a series of political and legal directives in order to raise citizens' awareness of home criminality and domestic violence.

A pioneering study carried out in Portugal with 1,000 women, entitled "Violence Against Women" (Lourenço, Lisboa, & Pais, 1997), concludes that the domestic context is referred to by women as the most common place in which they have been victims of violence (43%). Among the various types of violence exerted, psychological violence stands out the most, representing 76.4% of these cases, followed by physical and sexual violence, which present similar figures (10.6%). As far as physical violence is concerned, "the age groups of 35-44 years old (16%) and those who are 65 or older (15.2%) present the highest incidence in terms of women who may be the object of violence" (Lourenço et al., 1997, p. 35).

In the year 2008, a Associação Portuguesa de Apoio à Vítima (APAV) registered 18669 crime occurrences. Among these, 90% were domestic violence crimes.

Approximately 30.9% of the situations of domestic violence imply psychological violence and 27.1% physical violence. Approximately 90% of the victims were women, 34.6% were aged between 26 and 45 years, and more than half were married.

In 2004, the women's group União de Mulheres Alternativa e Resposta (UMAR; Group of Women's Alternatives and Answers) created an observatory of murdered women (Observatório de Mulheres Assassinadas), an organization that aims to register and analyze homicide cases of women killed by their intimate partners in Portugal.

In 2009, almost 30 women had been victims of homicide by their partners, and since 2004, 201 women were killed by their partners in our country (UMAR, 2009).

Even if all indicators point to the fact that being a woman in Portugal may correspond to an experience of great vulnerability, some recent studies suggest that gender roles are undergoing some change, which may help the future of Portuguese women, especially younger women who might experience more equality with men than at present.

In 2002, Portugal took part, under the coordination of Karin Wall (Instituto de Ciências Sociais-Universidade de Lisboa) and Lígia Amâncio (Instituto Superior de Ciências do Trabalho e da Empresa) in the International Social Survey Programme, a continuous program of cross-national collaboration on social science surveys. The study was dedicated to the theme of family and gender; used a sample of 1,092 subjects, 520 men and 572 women, aged over 18 and residing in the continental Portugal; and had as major objectives to understand (1) the attitudes of Portuguese men and women concerning gender roles in the family (in waged and nonwaged labor), (2) the attitudes of Portuguese men and women concerning the organization of family life, and (3) the attitudes of Portuguese men and women concerning gender roles and the organization of family life according to gender.

According to Wall and Amâncio (2007), the data concerning attitudes on family division of gender roles indicate that the Portuguese maintain less conservative attitudes on the division of paid/unpaid labor while holding very conservative views on issues concerning the impact of women's employment on maternal care and family life.

Concerning the organization of the couple's life, there were both clearly modernist attitudes regarding the setup of the couple and on divorce as well as more conservative views relative to the centrality of the child and to parenting. Finally, as regards the attitudes of Portuguese men and women concerning gender roles and the organization of family life according to gender, it was evident that differences arose mainly around the following issues: the feminine role (81.2% Portuguese women believe that the best way for a woman to ensure her independence is by having a job; only 69.1% of men corroborate this), the male role in the domestic context, the centrality of marriage (more important for the "happiness" of men than for the "happiness" of women), and the relation between marriage and parenting, a relation increasingly more valued by men.

As noted by Torres (2001), changes in Portugal follow a particular rhythm when compared to those in other countries. Torres finds that "one knows, in any case, that some atavisms remain, are renewed and even traditions are re-invented, in a mixture often hard to perceive" (p. 1).

Self-Silencing, Love, Power, and Violence in Portuguese Women's Voices

Of the wide range of research projects on gender difference and its relationship with intimacy, the subject of the self and of its formation through relational and social contact with others, namely, through intimate love relationships, has been considered of great interest.[2] The search for evidence that could confirm that men and women presumably form their selves based on different expectations as well as distinct social and cultural roles signaled an important stage in the research on the constitution of the self in light of gender issues. As Rudberg and Nielson (2005) point out, a significant number of social and cultural researchers have emphasized the way people use cultural concepts to organize their social world and to constitute themselves and others in meaningful ways. According to this perspective, the self is seen as a social product whose construction depends on culturally rooted visions of what it is to be a man or a woman. The ways in which male and female identity develop and the specific issues individuals face at different developmental phases can be assumed to play a role in how gender is understood and expressed as part of one's identity (Fivush & Buckner, 2003). Researchers working from a social constructionist perspective reject the essentialist vision that the world is made of underlying structures (e.g., psychological traits), defending instead the notion that all knowledge is constantly negotiated through social interaction (Burr, 2003; Nogueira, Neves, & Barbosa, 2005). Adopting a constructionist vision of the self, many researchers underline an alleged propensity of women to construct their selves out of their involvement in intimate relationships (Jack, 1991), valuing it more or less positively according to the quality of those relationships.

The articulation of relationships among love, power, and violence undertaken by feminist movements does not separate the analysis of the propensity of women to, in light of sociocultural demands underlying the feminine condition, relegate their personal needs in favor of taking care of others and of maintaining their relationships of intimacy and thus silencing their voices. Silencing the self, also known as "loss of voice," has been increasingly recognized over recent years by feminist psychologists and social scientists as a significant threat to healthy development.

Silencing the Self Theory (Jack, 1991) suggests that cognitive schemas related to the creation and maintenance of intimate and safe relationships lead women into silencing certain thoughts, feelings, and actions, instigating a decrease in their self-esteem and a perception of the loss of the self (Jack & Dill, 1992). This theory sustains the view that women form their concept of the self based on their participation in close, intimate, and genuine relationships with significant people and that whenever the maintenance of those relationships is in some way at risk, women's self-esteem and their sense of personal identity are seriously compromised. Consequently, the attempt to build and sustain relationships of intimacy may give rise to a set of distorted cognitive schemas, including pathological ones, known as self-silencing. When developing these cognitive schemas, women are doing no more than preserving the durability of their intimate relationships, silencing their personal needs, and overestimating the needs of those who are significant to them (Ali et al., 2000). Self-silencing seems to increase as women accommodate cultural schemas associated with traditionally feminine roles, which prompts self-silencing behavior such as the repression of one's feelings (Jack, 1991). This behavior emphasizes the uneven character of relationships as well as consolidates women's status of subjection in intimate relationships.

This issue becomes more relevant in societies where traditionally gender differences are ostensibly observed. Many researchers have associated social inequality with high rates of female depression (WHO, International Consortium of Psychiatric Epidemiology [ICPE], 2000), highlighting the fact that the status they have been subjected to (a status of submission and absence of power) places them in a situation of great emotional and physical vulnerability that has severe consequences for their quality of life. Self-silencing also portrays a process by which women apparently lose awareness of their own feelings and of what is really important for them as individuals. The sacrifice of autonomy so as to preserve the love relationship generates a cycle of dependence, which, allied with the cycle of vulnerability, motivates a clear weakening of the ability to make decisions that benefit the self.

To consider self-silencing as a result of instituted social practices and discourses and conceive of it in its political dimension represents an interesting challenge. Taking into account that self-silencing reveals a tendency toward the annihilation of personal needs in favor of the satisfaction of the partner's needs, it seems logical to analyze this construct in the sphere of violent intimate relationships, where questions of male supremacy, within a logic of control and domain, act to mute victims' voices. If there is a culturally determined tendency for women to silence themselves in intimate relationships in situations of violence, this tendency will certainly become more evident. Within this line of thought, our understanding is that in cases of violence within intimate relationships, self-silencing is a reflection of the absence of women's power. A study carried out in Portugal in 2003 (Lisboa, Carmo, Vicente, & Nóvoa, 2003), relating to the socioeconomical costs of violence against women, gives an account of the high psychological costs resulting from this problem. About one-fifth of the 445 women in this investigation needed to see a psychologist or psychiatrist due to some mental disorder: 49% of these women admitted that they did so as a result of the violent situation they experienced. Depressive patterns rank clearly in evidence in this search for therapeutic help; they are associated with a perception of loss of identity, personal annihilation, and incapacity. These characteristics are compatible with the emotional frame of the self-silencing construct.

Bearing in mind the social fragility of women in Portugal already characterized here, we were interested to know whether the level of self-silencing among Portuguese women might reflect the imposition of a culture still based on patriarchal values, where violence against women has ample ground for affirmation. Theoretically, it makes sense that patriarchal values may sustain a *feminine condition of self-silencing*, closely connected to inequality and social oppression. We would expect to find this among women who are involved in abusive, unequal relationships. However, at the same time in Portuguese society, some women and men also hold less conservative values regarding gender roles and women's prerogatives in relationships (Wall & Amâncio, 2007). Younger women and men in universities might reflect these less conservative values in lower self-silencing scores.

In order to understand the importance of the self-silencing construct in the foundation and perpetuation of gendered discourses about love, power, and violence in heterosexual intimate relationships, and also to understand how self-silencing can be materialized in the construction of meanings around close relationships, we developed an exploratory research project[3] with different groups of Portuguese women, using the Silencing the Self Scale[4] (Jack & Dill, 1992) and another assessment tool, the Discourses about Intimacy: Self-Reflection Questionnaire (Neves & Nogueira, 2003).[5]

The decision to study the importance of the self-silencing construct in the foundation and perpetuation of gendered discourses about love, power, and violence in heterosexual intimate relationships was not arbitrary. The first author's clinical experience of therapeutic intervention with women who are victims of violence in intimate relationships served as a basis for this research. The enunciation of love as an argument for the maintenance of violent relationships and of experiences of power imbalances in intimate relationships as well as the tendency for self-silencing are recurrent in the life history of women who were victims of violence in intimate relationships. This corroborates the evidence presented by the literature on the subject. Towns and Adams (2000), in their analysis of the discourses of romantic love of women who were victims of violence in intimate relationships, showed how cultural constructions of what should be a perfect partner entrap women in these nets of violence (Boonzaier & De La Rey, 2003).

This study was carried out in Portugal with 450 women university students, whose average age was 25 years old, and with 11 women who were users of victim support services and victims of violence in intimate relationships, whose average age was 44 years old. All the women involved in this research agreed to participate after having been informed of the objectives that guide it. The instruments for data gathering were used simultaneously with an instruction sheet as well as a form for personal data. These instruments were filled out anonymously. In the students' case, these instruments were filled out in the classroom context, in the presence of teachers, and in the victims' case, they were carried out in their respective services for victim support, in the presence of psychologists.

The geographical location of the institutions of higher education where the study with university students was carried out was the north of Portugal (Braga, Porto, Viana do Castelo). Higher education courses stereotypically related to the female sex (nursing, social services, education, psychology, sociology) were selected with the objective of using programs with the highest number of women. The institutions for support of women who were victims of violence, from which the sample of 11 women was collected, are situated in the region of Braga and Porto.

This research aimed to achieve the following two general objectives: (1) analyze the intimate experiences of university students and of women who were victims of violence in intimate relationships in light of indicators such as love, power, violence, self-silencing, and equality; and (2) create a space for self-reflection on the dynamics involved in the sphere of intimacy of each of these groups of women, students, and victims, so as to increase their awareness of their satisfaction or dissatisfaction regarding their love relationships.

As qualitative and quantitative methods were used in this research, we followed a triangulation approach of data analysis. The statistics program SPSS 11.0 was used to analyze quantitative data, whereas qualitative data (comprised of the written responses to the sentences proposed) were examined through critical discourse analysis, that is, through detecting "patterns of meaning which organize the various symbolic systems human beings inhabit, and which are necessary for us to make sense to each other" (Parker, 1999, p. 3). A cultural discourse has an important role in the reproduction of dominance, because it reflects the relations between discourse structures and power structures (Dijk, 1993). Our analysis was made through the identification of those relations in the women's sentences. From the discourse analytical perspective, we read the sentences as social and cultural products, constructed in the interaction with the power structures. The meanings and the concepts used by women have, in this way, a symbolic reference that we tried to recognize in our data analysis. This recognition allowed us to categorize the information collected into patterns of meanings.

In this study, the analysis of data showed that equality in intimate relationships is experienced differently by women who are university students and by women who are victims of violence in intimate relationships. Indeed, the former identify equality as an emergent characteristic in their relationships, whereas the latter recognize the nonexistence of this feature in their relationships with their partners. Even though there is little evidence of violence in intimate relationships in the group of women who are university students (only 14 admitted this fact when questioned about partner violence in the questionnaire), in the cases where they are also victims of violence, their tendency to construct egalitarian relationships diminishes substantially. This confirms the close relationship between violence and inequality.

The sample of cases of violence in intimate relationships is based on the 35 to 45 age group, since this is the age bracket that national statistics indicate as the most vulnerable to victimization (or at least this is the time in their lives when women decide to make public their situation as victims).

Our findings substantiate the idea that women in violent intimate relationships experience an absence of power; such participants in our study stress that they have less power in their relationships. The absence of power is displayed particularly in the restriction on their personal freedom, which is clearly associated with the self-silencing construct. Jack and Dill (1992) found that violence in intimate relationships corresponded with elevated levels of self-silencing, as evidenced in three distinct groups of women: university students ($n = 63$, $M = 78.4$), mothers who took drugs during pregnancy ($n = 270$, $M = 81.8$), and victims of violence who were residents in shelters ($n = 140$, $M = 99.9$). In our study, the levels of self-silencing in the Portuguese university women ($M = 70.39$) were lower than any of the means reported by Jack and Dill (1992). However, we found the levels of self-silencing in the victims of violence ($M = 86.4$) to be higher than the levels in the Portuguese university women ($M = 70.39$).

This finding confirms our expectation of an association between violence in intimate relationships and self-silencing. Given this association, it would also be expected that the university women's reflections on love and intimacy would differ from those of the victims of violence. Therefore, we analyzed the discourses of love of the two samples separately. The analysis of the women's discourses indicates that the university students present three types of possible discourses of love: discourses of romantic love, discourses of reality love, and discourses of confluent love. The coexistence of various ways of defining and conceptualizing love represent what has been socially associated with this construct, demarcating collective and shared assertions of signification.

The various contents appearing in the texts produced by the women were grouped according to their meaning. This grouping provided the identification of the three types of thematic discursive categories of love.

The first type of discourse, labeled discourses of romantic love, includes a set of three subdiscourses: *love as essence, passionate love*, and *unidirectional love*. Given their conservative and traditional characteristics, these discourses appear to be those where a greater self-silencing of the women occurs, in so much as they incorporate the ideas of selfless care for the other, implying a nonsatisfaction of the woman's personal needs. Studies in this area indicate that these subdiscourses are typical of women who hold traditional views of love and intimacy. This set includes the discourses of the three discursive typologies that bear the stamp of the romanticism characteristic of love, which makes it indispensable to human existence (it is the essence of life, as some women affirmed). In this view, love is a process that guarantees happiness on earth; it is an altered physical and psychological state whose structure is unilateral, with no demands of reciprocity.

This idea of *love as essence* occupies a sovereign position in people's lives. It is based on the idea of one giving without expecting anything in return (which makes it a unilateral rather than a bilateral process). It necessarily implies an attitude of self-sacrifice in relation to others and in relation to one's own needs, but it is also necessary to one's personal and social realization. Such an idea has accompanied for decades the discourses of the ideal "female condition," in which the portentous apology for the affectionate and caring female role has propagated the philosophy that women should be relegated to the so-called domestic sphere. The following phrases from different undergraduate participants exemplify this tendency: "An indescribable feeling and indispensable in a person's life. It's the reason why it is worth living in this world"; "Love is the essence of life. To be happy you only need to love, and this implies everything, even sacrifice"; "The reason why I live. Love is something that I can't explain, because it's the most noble feeling of life" "The best of life. Without love I think I couldn't survive."

The discourse of *passionate love* highlights the experiences of physiological activation that, according to some authors, are responsible for a sort of individual torpor, such as that pointed out by Berscheid and Walster (1974), Ortega y Gasset (2002), Sternberg (1998), and Hendrick and Hendrick (1992). This enamoring process, which inebriates feelings and emotions, gives rise to a set of reactions that seem to escape personal control. This idea that love is uncontrollable and entrancing conveys the belief that autonomy and independence are limited when individuals fall in love, making them act, from our perspective, in a dysfunctional manner. In these circumstances, love is described by women in our study as a "state of trance" or "a burning flame." In the case of these women, for whom romantic love means the love of loving others (and less self-love) and abnegation of one's individuality, this dysfunctionality can become problematic in the sense that it can be a risk factor leading to submission. When the absence of rationality in love relationships makes one incapable of making decisions and of safeguarding one's physical and cognitive-emotional state, it can constitute a state of high emotional dependency, consigning women to a subordinate condition.

The discourses of *unidirectional love* can be perceived in the following phrases, where love is: "total delivery, feeling well with another person"; "always want the good of your partner, fight for his well-being, friendship, trust, complicity, intimacy, passion, all together and mixed up"; "sharing, one single journey with common objectives. It is to give without having anything in return"; "to be OK with someone forgetting that you might have another way of being happy"; "to want that the partner be happy." Romantic love emerges, then, as a fundamental condition for human happiness, as something irrational and irascible, as passionate love, endorsing women's belief in a poeticized and idealized love experience, similar to a "fairy tale."

The polar opposite of romantic love has been defined in the so-called discourses of reality love. In this second typology, love emerges under the cover of a language of truth, in which it is simultaneously perceived as positive and negative. It is a love that refers to the constraints and limitations it creates, in a discourse made up of many strands. From this perspective, love as a concept loses the fascination and transcendent character of romantic love and assumes a realistic intent. Examples of discourses of reality love follow: "before anything a state of mind that may lead to either positive or negative psychological states when unrequited or exacerbated, for instance the consequences of exaggerated jealousy. It is a fact that love influences even our health"; "something wonderful, makes me feel complete, desired, loved, wanted. Love is an indescribable feeling, very personal and which each one feels in one's own way. For me it is necessary to live. On the other hand, it has its negative aspect, in terms of submission and in situations of rows or numbness, if there wasn't so much love, this would be more bearable"; "learn how to be patient. Love is a difficult thing, easy and difficult at the same time"; "a huge confusion of feelings"; "something that completes persons, that makes them happier, but also that can bring them more worries."

Finally, the last category of love discourses is that of confluent love, in accordance with Giddens's (2001) construct of the term. In this approach, equality, construction, and sharing prevail as central values and thus love is no longer a unilateral phenomenon. Like Anália Torres's (2001) conceptualization of constructed love, this type of discourse represents the development of relationships of intimacy based on the strengthening of a process that involves two people, in which both share responsibilities, rights, and duties. Even though these are not the discourses of the majority of our participants, they are clearly visible in our university students' responses, demonstrating that equality increasingly governs their construction of intimacy in love relationships. For the women who adopt these discourses, love is "a feeling shared between two people that love, help and above all respect each other. In love, or say in a relationship, one should not try to change either partner, but help them"; "knowing how to share feelings with the other. Love is living in harmony between two people, even if there are differences, knowing how to harmonize them, understanding each other mutually and accepting those differences"; "a total giving where there are no inequalities"; "to share, to give, to be accomplices"; "a feeling of fulfillment"; "to feel that the other person likes me and I like him too. To share feelings, emotions without fear."

The discourses of love used by women who were victims of violence display a language marked by the violence they experienced. Indeed, it can be inferred that, even though some of them still have a positive perception of love, their view of the construct is extremely realistic in so far as they also contemplate its negative aspects. Thus, this perspective resembles the discourses of reality love identified in the analysis of the texts by university women students. The notion of love assumes various forms and denominations for these women, though it is clearly understood that all these definitions of love are permeated with their abusive experiences. For these women, love is "something I don't have in my life, but deep down I believe exists"; "what links us to someone. What makes us have children and a life in common"; "some rubbish that only comes in novels and soaps. But I believe it exists"; "it's important. I can't describe it, but is special. When we love we think with the heart, not with the head. That's why we allow ourselves to be humiliated"; "the biggest of all feelings in a million of sins."

Deconstructing Gendered Discourses within Feminist Practices: Conclusions

As well as giving voice to women, this research attempted to understand to what extent collectively shared gendered discourses contribute to sustaining discourses on love, power, and violence in heterosexual relationships of intimacy as well as how self-silencing is materialized in the construction of meanings about gendered intimacy. It sought to analyze whether love, power, and violence discourses that continue to exist in heterosexual relationships of intimacy are or are not gendered discourses, that is, discourses that promote the traditional division of female and male roles and, consequently, that influence differentially the intimate experiences of women and men. On the other hand, it also aspired to understand whether self-silencing itself reflects an expression of institutionalized power structures that serve to define the expression of self-sacrificing love as a natural characteristic of women. Having in mind feminist theoretical and epistemological orientations (necessarily engaged in the analysis of how societal practices construct the gender order[6]), the conceptualization of intimacy came to include elements associated with gendered power relationships. In this study, one can detect the emergence of a *new sentimental order*, adopting an expression originally used by Bernadette Bawin-Legros (2004) to illustrate the contradiction of contemporary love—it seems that there is a hope for a fusion between people (what Giddens [2001] called the "pure relationship") but at the same time there is a growing need for self-actualization, which might lead to a growing need for equality though still subject to the *old* gender order. As Bawin-Legros (2004) argues, the postmodern values that support the new sentimental order make possible the appearance of a form of love that requires the ongoing negotiation of autonomy and unity, freedom and commitment, and fusion and individualization (Budgeon & Roseneil, 2004).

The relationship between violence in intimate relationships, absence of power, experiences of inequality, romantic love, and self-silencing is an unavoidable fact that emerges from the analysis developed in this chapter The feminist conceptualization that underlies this relationship contemplates an acceptance that the patriarchal structures and gender orders that shape them continue to influence contemporary experiences of intimacy.

The results of our study indicate, however, that Portuguese society is, perhaps, in a transition phase. The patriarchal structures and gender orders affect the way women conceive their sense of intimacy and live their love experiences, but attitudes among younger and university-educated people are presently less traditional and less conservative. Wall and Amâncio (2007) also found similar changing attitudes through their International Social Survey Programme. This ongoing change is probably due to the social and legislative transformations that Portugal instigated in the last decades. The establishment of a progressive constitution that guarantees women's civil rights and equality, the massive presence of young women in university contexts, the public criminalization of domestic violence, and, more recently, in 2007, the decriminalization of abortion are some of the examples that might explain this tendency of younger women to express lower levels of self-silencing when compared with U.S. samples.

Those who are involved in psychological interventions with women who were victims of violence easily realize the multiple traps in which their lives are entangled. Structural traps are laid at several stages of their lives, from which it is very difficult to escape and which become recurrent experiences of absence of power to make choices and decisions. Self-silencing is frequently a compulsory choice that women have to make as a means to preserve their own safety and identity. Traditional psychological therapies carry responsibility for the increase in these experiences of enclosure and disempowerment because they have unreflectively intensified women's absence of power (Carlson, 1997). The tendency to privilege medical approaches and to consider and treat women as incomplete human beings, emphasizing their deficits and not promoting their strengths (Crawford & Marecek, 1989; Crawford & Unger, 2000), led psychology to be extremely inadequate in terms of the application of its practices and theories to women, especially in therapeutic settings. The sexist propensity of psychological science, which is extensive in Portugal,[7] has been largely documented and recognized in the literature. In our opinion, the insertion of notions of equality and equal rights in the sphere of therapeutic relationships, together with the reorganization of their ability to face the challenges of coresponsibility in the processes of intervention they participate in, is one way of restoring women's power.

Sesan and Katzman (1998) affirmed that feminist therapies contribute to women's empowerment through an increase of self-awareness resulting from the establishment of egalitarian therapeutic relationships, the valorization of women's potential, and the patients' involvement in social change (Seu & Heenan, 1998). In this way, feminist therapies act against therapeutic work proposed by traditional therapies, which concentrate their action on the reduction of the patients' symptoms. This challenge should then consider not just the symptoms but rather the contextual conditions in which such symptoms are developed. It should also make the treatment viable by focusing on the areas of strengthening and resiliency (White, Russo, & Travis, 2001) and not only on the curative aspect.

Feminist therapists believe in their patients' capacity to act proactively in their own environments (Enns, 1997), transforming and informing them with new meanings. From our perspective, this is the great potential of feminist therapies in psychology. These are oriented not just toward the use of a cluster of clinical techniques applied to effect behavioral changes or to alleviate symptoms but, above all, to empower women. So as to help women break unequal power cycles in their relationships with the male sex, therapists should analyze their political perspectives on sexist, discriminatory, and inequality dynamics and realize to what extent the political, economic, and social system contributes to patriarchal oppression (O'Neil & Egan, 1992). Psychology, on the other hand, should revise its practices and theoretical approaches. It's estimated that in Portugal there are 10,000 psychologists (Machado, Lourenço, Pinheiro, & Silva, 2004). The place of critical feminist psychology lags behind in becoming part of the prevailing discourse of psychology, though the courses of intervention proposed by psychological science are less narrow (Nogueira, Saavedra, & Neves, 2006). The dominant discourse in Portuguese psychology still remains the positivist one. It was only after the Carnations Revolution that the social sciences (and psychology particularly) as well as feminist reflection (Amâncio, 1994, 2002) were acknowledged in the Portuguese universities. This late arrival entailed a "passover" of the institutional period of women's studies in universities, which typically happened elsewhere in the 1970s but which has never taken place in Portuguese universities. Therefore, the debates around the women's studies/gender studies or feminist studies have never existed in Portugal, specifically inside psychology.

The possibility of framing our research within a wider and more comprehensive movement of social change is, thus, a challenge. It is indeed a strategic challenge that makes us rethink the importance of the therapeutic relationships we establish and in which we deconstruct our own power hierarchy (Neves & Nogueira, 2003, 2004). Psychology has been prodigal in creating power hierarchies between social groups through the theories and practices developed in the course of its history. In the specific case of women, this question of creating power hierarchies acquires particular relevance in the sense that psychology has contributed in a notorious way to promote their invisibility in and for science. It is therefore the right time for those involved in science to review their positions.

Feminist psychology designates a strategic space between feminism and psychology (Burman, 1998; Nogueira, 2001). Perceiving science as frankly influenced by the social, political, and cultural structures of a given time and space means admitting that it is composed of ideological textures (Nogueira et al., 2006). Only in this way will we be truly capable of pursuing the objective of social change and, thus, promote the deconstruction of gendered discourses on love, power, and violence, struggling in this way against the tendency toward self-silencing and its implications for women's physical and psychological health.

Notes

1. Some indicators report the economic, social, and cultural development of the Portuguese society, in particular, the reduction of the child mortality rate and the increase of mean life expectancy (Carrilho & Magalhaes, 2000).
2. The interest of psychology in the nature of the self goes back to the emergence of science itself in the nineteenth century, when introspective methods seemed to be the most appropriate ones in the exploration and understanding of this construct (cf. Gonçalves [1995]). Since then, there have been many perspectives on the self in psychology. These have ranged from essentialist approaches, which conceive of the self as a unique, individual, and private structure, to narrative and social approaches, which perceive the self to be a product of social interaction and, in this way, as a construction susceptible to change. This diversity has made it an object of study "which remains as one of those imponderables that we do not totally comprehend" (Forgas, Williams & Hippel 2002, p. 2). In any case, these more recent approaches have become more visible in social psychology in the last few years and theoretical production and empirical research in this area have also been widely diffused.
3. This research is part of first author's PhD thesis: The (De)Construction of Gendered Discourses about Love, Power and Violence in Intimate Relationships: Feminist Methodologies in Critical Social Psychology (2005), published in 2008.
4. The Silencing the Self Scale was translated to Portuguese language and back-translated; the understanding and meaning of items were tested by a group of women from different social backgrounds and ages.
5. The production of this inquiry through questionnaire was based on a previous study undertaken with a group of women who were victims of violence in intimate relationships. This instrument is composed of two parts. The first part presents 23 optional items, in a Likert scale from 1 to 5, which assess the areas of equality, power, violence, and silencing (some items are intended to explore in more detail some of the questions posed in the Silencing the Self Scale). The second part of this tool is composed of sentences that refer to the meaning given to some concepts or actions. The participants complete the sentences by writing what they think about the issues proposed. This task intends to promote the reflection about meaning specifically around the constructs of love, power, and violence and their articulation with gender questions.

6. Gender order is an expression created by Connell (1987, 1995) to designate the institutionalized gender practices that guide the social reproduction of inequality.
7. To explore this issue please consult Nogueira and colleagues (2006).

References

Ali, A., Toner, B., Stuckless, N., Gallop, R., Diamant, N., Gould, M., et al. (2000). Emotional abuse, self-blame and self-silencing in women irritable bowel syndrome. *Psychosomatic Medicine, 62*, 76–82.

Amâncio, L. (1994). *Masculino e Feminino: A Construção Social da Diferença*. Porto, Portugal: Edições Afrontamento.

Amâncio, L. (2002). O género na Psicologia Social em Portugal. Perspectivas actuais e desenvolvimentos futuros. *Ex aequo - Revista da Associação Portuguesa de Estudos sobre as Mulheres, 6*, 55–75.

Amâncio, L., & Ávila, P. (1995). Gender in science. In J. Correia (Org.), *A comunidade Científica Portuguesa nos finais do século XX* (pp. 135–162). Oeiras, Portugal: CELTA.

Amâncio, L., & Oliveira, J. M. (2006). Men as individuals, women as a sexed category: Implications of symbolic asymmetry for feminist practice and feminist psychology. *Feminism & Psychology, 16*, 35–43.

Associação Portuguesa de Apoio à Vítima (APAV). (2008). *Relatório Estatístico*. Retrieved December 14, 2009, from http://www.apav.pt/portal/pdf/APAV_Totais_Nacionais_2008.pdf

Bawin-Legros, B. (2004). Intimacy and the new sentimental order. *Current Sociology, 52*, 241–250.

Berscheid, E., & Walster, E. (1974). A little bit of love. In T. Huston (Ed.), *Foundations of interpersonal attraction* (pp. 355–381). New York: Academic Press.

Boonzaier, F., & De La Rey, C. (2003). "He's a man, and I'm a woman:" Cultural constructions of masculinity and femininity in South Africa women's narratives of violence. *Violence Against Women, 9*, 1003–1029.

Budgeon, S., & Roseneil, S. (2004). Editors' introduction: Beyond the conventional family. *Current Sociology, 52*, 127–134.

Burman, E. (Ed.). (1998). *Deconstructing feminist psychology*. London: Sage.

Burr, V. (2003). *Social constructionism*. London: Routledge.

Carlson, B. (1997). A stress and coping approach to intervention with abused women. *Family Relations, 46*, 291–299.

Carrilho, M. J., & Magalhaes, G. (2000). *Fertility and family surveys in countries of the ECE region. Standard country report: Portugal*. New York, Geneva: United Nations.

Comissão para a Cidadania e Igualdade de Género (CIG). (2009). *Situação económica*. Retrieved May 1, 2009, from http://www.cig.gov.pt/

Connell, R. (1987). *Gender and power*. Stanford, CA: Stanford University Press.

Connell, R. (1995). *Masculinities*. CA: University of California Press.

Connell, R. (1995). *Masculinities*. Berkeley, CA: University of California Press.

Crawford, M., & Marecek, J. (1989). Psychology reconstructs the female: 1968-1988. *Psychology of Women Quarterly, 13*, 47–165.

Crawford, M., & Unger, R. (2000). *Women and gender: A feminist psychology*. Boston: McGraw-Hill.

Dijk, T. (1993). Principles of critical discourse analysis. *Discourse and Society, 4*, 249–283.

Enns, C. Z. (1997). *Feminist theories and feminist psychotherapies: Origins, themes, and variations*. New York: Haworth Press.

Ferreira, V. (1998). Engendering Portugal: Social change, state politics and women's mobilization. In A. Costa Pinto (Ed.), *Modern Portugal* (pp. 162–188). Palo Alto, CA: Society for the Promotion of Science and Scholarship.

Fivush, R., & Buckner, J. (2003). Creating gender and identity through autobiographical narratives. In R. Fivush & C. Haden (Eds.), *Autobiographical memory and the construction of a narrative self: Developmental and cultural perspectives* (pp. 149–168). Mahwah, NJ: Lawrence Erlbaum Associates.

Forgas, J., Williams, K., & Hippel, W. (2003). Responding to social world. Explicit and implicit processes in social judgments. In J. Forgas, K. Williams, & W. Hippel (Eds.), *Social judgments: Implicit and explicit processes* (pp. 1–22). Cambridge: Cambridge University Press.

Giddens, A. (2001). *Transformações da intimidade: Sexualidade, amor e erotismo nas sociedades modernas*. Oeiras, Portugal: Celta Editora.

Gonçalves, M. (1995). *Auto-Conhecimento e Acesso Instrospectivo. Do self reificado ao self narrativo*. Braga, Portugal: Instituto de Educação e Psicologia, Universidade do Minho.

Hendrick, S., & Hendrick, C. (1992). *Romantic love*. Newbury Park, CA: Sage.

Instituto Nacional de Estatística (INE). (2006). *Men and women in Portugal*. Lisboa, Portugal: Instituto Nacional de Estatística.

International Social Survey Programme. (2005, January). Family and gender survey. *Resumo Geral*. Oral presentation at VII Seminário de Apresentação e Discussão de Resultados das Atitudes Sociais dos Portugueses. Instituto de Ciências Sociais, Lisboa, Portugal. Retrieved May 2, 2007, from http://www.ics.ul.pt/asp/papers_issp/Resumogeral.pdf

Jack, D. C. (1991). *Silencing the self: Women and depression*. Cambridge, MA: Harvard University Press.

Jack, D. C., & Dill, D. (1992). The Silencing the Self Scale: Schemas of intimacy associated with depression in women. *Psychology of Women Quarterly, 16*, 97--106.

Lisboa, M., Carmo, I., Vicente, L., & Nóvoa, A. (2003). *Os Custos Sociais e Económicos da Violência contra as Mulheres. Síntese dos Resultados do Inquérito Nacional de 2002*. Lisboa, Portugal: CIDM.

Lourenço, N., Lisboa, M., & Pais, E. (1997). Violência contra as Mulheres. *Cadernos Condição Feminina*. Lisboa, Portugal: Comissão para a Igualdade e para os Direitos das Mulheres.

Machado, A., Lourenço, O., Pinheiro, A., & Silva, C. (2004). As duas faces de Janus da Psicologia em Portugal. *Análise Psicológica, 2*, 319–333.

Ministério da Saúde de Portugal. (2009). Depressão. Retrieved January 6, 2010, from http://www.portaldasaude.pt/portal/conteudos/enciclopedia+da+saude/saude+mental/depressao.htm

Neves, S. (2008). *Amor, poder e violências na intimidade: Os caminhos entrecruzados do pessoal e do político*. Coimbra, Portugal: Quarteto.

Neves, S., & Nogueira, C. (2003). A psicologia feminista e a violência contra as mulheres na intimidade: A (re)construção dos espaços terapêuticos. *Psicologia e Sociedade, 15,* 43–64.

Neves, S., & Nogueira, C. (2004). Terapias feministas, intervenção psicológica e violências na intimidade: Uma leitura feminista crítica. *Psychologica, 36,* 15–32.

Nielson, H. (2003). *One of the boys? Doing gender in Scouting.* Geneva: World Organization of the Scout Movement.

Nogueira, C. (2001). *Um novo olhar sobre as relações sociais de género.* Lisboa, Portugal: FCG-FCT.

Nogueira, C., Neves, S., & Barbosa, C. (2005). Fundamentos construcionistas sociais e críticos para o estudo do género. *Psicologia: Teoria, Inve stigação e Prática, 10,* 195–209.

Nogueira, C., Saavedra, L., & Neves, S. (2006). Critical (feminist) psychology in Portugal: Will it be possible? *Annual Critical Review, 5,* 136–147 Retrieved April 23, 2007, from http://www.discourseunit.com/arcp/5.htm

OCT/MCT. (2001). *Women and science: Review of the situation in Portugal.* Retrieved April 23, 2007, from http://www.oces.mctes.pt//docs/relatorios/50648/files/women-nationalreportportugal.pdf

O'Neil, J., & Egan, J. (1992). Abuses of power against women: Sexism, gender role conflict, and psychological violence. In E. Cook (Ed.), *Women, relationships, and power: Implications for counseling.* Alexandria, VA: ACA Press.

Ortega y Gasset, G. (2002). *Estudos sobre o Amor.* Lisboa, Portugal: Relógio D'Água.

Parker, I. (1999). Varieties of discourse and analysis. In I. Parker and the Bolton Discourse Network (Eds.), *Critical textwork: An introduction to varieties of discourse and analysis.* Buckingham, UK: Open University Press.

Perista, H. (Coord.). (1999). Os *usos do tempo e o valor do trabalho – Uma questão de género.* Lisboa, Portugal: DEPP/CIDES.

Portuguese Association for Victim Support (APAV). (2006). *Estatísticas: Totais Nacionais 2006.* Retrieved April 9, 2007, from http://www.apav.pt/portal/pdf/totais_nacionais_2006.pdf Rudberg, M., & Nielson, H. (2005). Potential spaces - Subjectivities and gender in a generational perspective. *Feminism & Psychology, 15,* 127–148.

Sesan, R. & Katzman, M. A. (1998). Empowerment and the eating disordered client: Differentiation within feminist therapy in Heenan, C., & Seu, B., (Eds.). *Feminisms and psychotherapies.* (pp. 78–95). New York: Sage Publications.

Seu, B., & Heenan, C. (1998). *Feminism & psychotherapy: Reflections on contemporary theories and practices.* London: Sage.

Sternberg, R. (1998). *Cupid's arrow: The course of love through time.* Cambridge: Cambridge University Press.

Torres, A. (2001). *Sociologia do casamento.* Oeiras, Portugal: Celta.

Towns, A., & Adams, P. (2000). "If I really loved him enough, he would be okay": Women's accounts of male partner violence. *Violence Against Women, 6,* 558–585.

União de Mulheres Alternativa e Resposta (UMAR). (2009). *Observatório de mulheres assassinadas.* Retrieved January, 2010, from http://www.umarfeminismos.org/observatorioviol/estatisticas2009.html

Wall, K., & Amâncio, L. (2007). *Família e género em Portugal e na Europa.* Lisboa, Portugal: Imprensa das Ciências Sociais.

White, J. W., Russo, N. F., & Travis, C. B. (2001). Feminism and the decade of behavior. *Psychology of Women Quarterly, 25,* 267–279.

Women Watch. (1997). *National action plan:* Portugal (Translation of the Resolution of the Council of Ministers no. 49/97). Retrieved May 8, 2007, from http://www.un.org/womenwatch/confer/beijing/national/portnap.htm

World Health Organization, International Consortium of Psychiatric Epidemiology. (2000). Cross-national comparisons of mental disorders. *Bulletin of the World Health Organization, 78,* 413–426.

12

Authentic Self-Expression:
Gender, Ethnicity, and Culture

Anjoo Sikka, Linda (Gratch) Vaden-Goad, and Lisa K. Waldner

It has been a long-standing assumption in psychology that having voice and being authentic are necessary goals for healthy developmental growth and progress. Without authenticity and voice, one might face life, as suggested by Erikson (1968), stagnating in conflicts of identity and be destined to be withdrawn, depressed, and unready to exercise the resourcefulness required for true intimacy. Jack (1991) presents a theory that explains the link between lack of voice in intimate relationships (self-silencing) and depression among women. She posits that women's feelings of competence and well-being emerge from the quality of relationships, for which they feel responsible. Silencing the self results from the need to maintain attachment and security within the context of the lower power, disadvantaged status, and financial insecurity women face in the larger society. The resultant sense of a divided self, lack of authenticity, negative views of self, perceptions that one never really "measures up," and a negative view of the future can push women into depression.

Our interest was in the portability of the construct of self-silencing across a range of contexts and cultures. We conducted several studies with colleagues to further explore the complex phenomenon of self-silencing and its proposed correlates of depression, self-esteem, relationship adjustment, role taking, conflict tactics, and social class. In addition, we tested the construct of self-silencing with men and women across diverse contexts, ethnicities, and sexual orientations. Participant samples in these studies include urban college students who are African American, Asian American, Caucasian, and Hispanic; community samples of young club-going singles and female dancers; urbanites in Western India; Pakistani and Indian women immigrants to America with arranged marriages; and community samples of gays, lesbians, and heterosexuals in committed relationships.

Our findings were multidimensional. In the following sections, we summarize these findings and draw an expanded view of self-silencing. We have grouped the findings from these studies into separate categories: (1) gender and ethnicity; (2) gender, sexual orientation, and violence; (3) gender and high-risk behaviors; and (4) factor structure of self-silencing.

Gender and Ethnicity

In the first of a series of studies that examined the role of ethnicity in the Silencing the Self Scale (STSS) and depression scores, Gratch (now, Vaden-Goad), Attra, and Bassett (1994), explored the ways in which young (mean age = 24.49 years), single male and female undergraduate students from diverse ethnic backgrounds practice self-silencing. Based on Jack's (1991) initial work with depressed women, the expectation was that women would have higher self-silencing scores than men, given that women often are in relationships of inequality and end up fulfilling the nurturing imperative (that a women cares for others, often silencing her negative feelings in order to serve and nurture selflessly) (Gilligan, 1982). Two hundred participants (84.5% single, 87% without children, average age = 24.49 years) were surveyed with a demographic questionnaire, the STSS, and the Beck Depression Inventory (BDI) (Beck & Steer, 1987). Women's and men's self-silencing scores were not significantly different ($M = 81.85, SD = 13.64$ for men; $M = 79.69, SD = 18.62$ for women). Ethnic differences in self-silencing scores were evident, with Asian/Asian Americans'[1] self-silencing scores being significantly higher ($M = 93.84, SD = 17.33, n = 50$) than all the other ethnic groups (African Americans: $M = 72.62, SD = 14.75, n = 50$; Caucasians: $M = 77.36, SD = 18.82, n = 50$; Hispanics: $M = 79.26, SD = 14.97, n = 50$) [$F_{(3,192)} = 15.30, p < .0001$]. Asian/Asian Americans had significantly higher depression scores than African Americans ($M = 11.62$ and 7.70, respectively) [$F_{(3,192)} = 3.18, p < .025$], though no other differences were statistically significant for the variable of depression. The correlation between the STSS and BDI for the whole sample was .4926 ($p < .0001$), suggesting a moderate, positive relationship between these two variables. Similar correlations were also apparent among Asian/Asian Americans ($r = .57, p < .0001$), Caucasians ($r = .61, p < .0001$), and Hispanics ($r = .50, p < .0002$). The correlation between depression and the STSS among African Americans was not significant ($r = .10$). In this first study, our initial explanation for lack of significant differences between self-silencing scores for men and women was in terms of men not having the language to express emotions or refraining from speaking to maintain power or avoid a conflict.

In a follow-up study, self-silencing and depression were examined in 604 men and women of diverse ethnic backgrounds (African American, Asian/Asian American, Caucasian, and Hispanic). Extending Jack's arguments that women's roles lead them toward self-silencing in relationships, Gratch, Bassett, and Attra (1995) hypothesized that women would have higher self-silencing scores and that the correlation between self-silencing and depression would differ between men and women. In addition, the authors sought to investigate the levels of self-silencing in different ethnic groups with the expectation that self-silencing would differ depending on the inequalities afforded men and women, gender role expectations, and norms. Men ($n = 289$) and women ($n = 315$) from four ethnic groups—African American ($n = 146$), Asian/Asian American ($n = 127$), Caucasian ($n = 163$), and Hispanic ($n = 168$)—were offered course credit or restaurant coupons to participate in this study. Most students were single (87%), young adults ($M = 24.20$ years), and did not have children (87%). Participants were administered a demographic questionnaire, the STSS, and the BDI (in that order). Results revealed that (1) men ($M = 84.55$, $SD = 15.77$) had significantly higher self-silencing scores than women ($M = 77.48$, $SD = 18.12$), [$F_{(1,596)} = 27.14$, $p < .01$]; and (2) Asians/Asian Americans had significantly higher self-silencing scores ($M = 88.23$, $SD = 15.61$) than any of the other represented groups: Hispanics ($M = 80.39$, $SD = 16.52$), Caucasians ($M = 78.44$, $SD = 17.21$), and African Americans ($M = 77.72$, $SD = 18.33$) [$F_{(3,596)} = 10.70$, $p < .01$]. An additional finding was that women had significantly higher depression scores ($M = 9.87$, $SD = 8.70$) than men ($M = 8.73$, $SD = 7.39$) [$F_{(1,596)} = 3.06$, $p < .041$]; and Asians/Asian Americans had significantly higher depression scores ($M = 10.82$, $SD = 9.02$) than Caucasians ($M = 7.99$, $SD = 7.82$) [$F_{(3,596)} = 3.04$, $p < .029$]. The correlations between self-silencing and depression scores were moderate, ranging from .32 to .63 ($p < .01$; see Table 12.1). Though each of these correlations was significant and was the lowest among the Asians/Asian Americans, any statistically significant differences in correlations were only evident between Caucasian ($r = .38$) and African American ($r = .63$) women [$z_{(77,74)} = 2.09$, $p < .05$].

We hypothesize that lower correlations between self-silencing and depression scores among Asians/Asian Americans are due to primacy of the collective self (rather than the individual self), which may have a less detrimental effect from self-silencing. In addition, significantly higher self-silencing scores among Asians/Asian Americans could perhaps be explained by socialization in a culture that is highly collectivistic, with emphasis on the value of hierarchy (due to factors such as age, social status), harmony, order, suffering, and perseverance (Hsu, 1970, 1971; Kitano, 1988; Shon & Ja, 1982; Sue, 1981; Triandis et al., 1986). Specifically, norms that center around care as self-sacrifice, an explicitly communicated emphasis on others' perceptions of them and, to some extent, the value of suffering as representing "goodness," may be possible reasons for these higher self-silencing scores among Asians/Asian Americans.

To further explore the high self-silencing scores of Asians/Asian Americans, we conducted a study with an urban university sample of Indian men ($n = 54$) and women ($n = 83$) in India (Gratch et al., 1996). Approximately 31% of the sample was married, with 65% single and 2% each divorced and widowed. The STSS, BDI, Rosenberg Self-Esteem Scale (RSE) (Rosenberg, 1979), and Locke

Table 12.1 Mean and Standard Deviations of Self-Silencing, Depression, and Correlations by Gender and Ethnicity

Ethnicity	Gender	STSS	Depression	BDI
African American	Males			
1		74.36 (10.60)	7.08 (6.43)	
2		81.87 (16.91)	8.13 (6.66)	.50*
African American	Females			
1		70.88 (18.05)	8.32 (8.40)	
2		74.00 (18.85)	10.97 (9.28)	.63*
Asian/Asian American	Males			
1		91.32 (14.46)	12.60 (9.06)	
2		91.23 (13.96)	10.03 (7.86)	.32*
Asian/Asian American	Females			
1		96.36 (19.77)	10.64 (8.93)	
2		84.93 (16.73)	11.68 (10.14)	.41*
3		81.41 (12.49)	3.88 (3.57)	.26 (ns)
Caucasian	Males			
1		79.08 (13.81)	6.24 (5.18)	
2		80.49 (15.52)	7.20 (6.87)	.42*
Caucasian	Females			
1		75.64 (22.94)	9.28 (8.18)	
2		76.30 (18.66)	8.82 (8.67)	.38*
Hispanic	Males			
1		82.64 (15.68)	8.08 (6.18)	
2		85.69 (14.58)	9.88 (7.89)	.45*
Hispanic	Females			
1		75.88 (13.71	7.96 (7.05)	
2		76.51 (16.85)	8.73 (6.96)	.59*
General (across ethnic groups)	Males			
4		77.90 (12.99)	10.50 (13.59)	NA
5		75.76 (17.93)		.56**
	Females			
4		74.20 (17.16)	11.90 (10.55)	.45*
5		69.90 (16.16)		.41*

1, Gratch, Attra, & Bassett (1994).
2, Gratch, Bassett, & Attra (1995).
3, Gratch (unpublished research on Indian and Pakistani women in arranged marriages).
4, Gratch et al. (1997).
5, Gratch et al. (1998).
*$p < .01$; **$p < .001$.

Short Marital Adjustment Scale (SMAT) (Locke & Wallace, 1959) were administered to explore the functioning of self-silencing in this setting. The SMAT has an internal consistency (Cronbach's alpha) of .84 and assesses overall marital happiness as well as specific aspects of marital life (e.g., finances, conflicts, commonality of interests, sexual compatibility). This scale has been used with Western (Burley, 1995) and non-Western couples (Chen et al., 2007). Freeston and Piechaty (1997) re-examined the validity of this instrument and found it to be relevant for a broadly based definition of adjustment. The selection of the SMAT to measure relationship adjustment was predicated upon the assumption that self-silencing is debilitating to relationships. The expected finding was that individuals with high self-silencing scores would have poorer relationship adjustment. In addition, we expected that individuals who often judge themselves by others' (imagined) perceptions of them would be vulnerable to negative self-evaluation and self-doubt that would result in lower measured self-esteem on the RSE.

Our earlier findings (Gratch et al., 1995) of low correlations between self-silencing and depression among Asians/Asian Americans were substantiated. The correlation was statistically significant, positive, and low ($r = .24$, $p < .02$) for the combined sample, but was not statistically significant for the separate samples of men and women. Surprisingly, there was no significant difference between men and women in their STSS (men: $M = 87.48$, $SD = 10.9$; women: $M = 86.80$, $SD = 14.61$) or BDI scores, though both scores were higher in the Indian sample (STSS $M = 87.08$, $SD = 13.18$; BDI $M = 10.44$, $SD = 10.83$) than the U.S. samples of Asians/Asian Americans (Gratch et al., 1995). Correlations between depression and self-silencing scores were significantly higher in Asian/Asian American samples (i.e., $r = .35$) than in the Indian sample (i.e., $r = .24$) ($z_r = 2.69$, $p < .05$), suggesting, perhaps, a higher prominence of the individualist self in western Asian/Asian American samples and of a collective self in the Indian sample.

Individuals with a high degree of individualism (and resultant prominence of the individualist self) may see self-silencing as the repression of one's authenticity and as a deterrent to one's self-actualization. This may result in significant negative consequences for their sense of control over their own lives and may lead to feelings of depression. In talking about the collective and individualist self, however, Oyserman (1993) cautions against the assumption that individualism and collectivism are two extremes of the same scale and suggests that these may be two different dimensions. Lending support to this conceptualization, Gaetner, Sekikides, and Graetz (1999) report that members of certain ethnic minority groups (African Americans, Asian/Asian Americans, and Latinos) score higher on measures of collectivism than Anglo Americans, yet also score as high as Anglos on measures of individualism. They propose that threats to the individual self often result in an increased preference for self-definition in terms of the collective self for that situation, reducing the negative repercussions of threats to self.

In the Indian sample, self-esteem was also found to have a low, but statistically significant correlation with self-silencing—higher self-esteem being associated with lower STSS scores ($r = .31$) and better relationship adjustment (SMAT) ($r = -.52$). Self-silencing and relationship adjustment were not significantly correlated, though the observed correlation was low and negative ($r = -.24$), suggesting that success of a marital relationship may be perceived to be outside of one's own control (i.e., extended family members). A majority of the married respondents reported having "arranged marriages." The lack of significant differences between men and women in terms of self-silencing and its correlates may be explained by a smaller sample size, the urbanicity of the sample (where social structures may often be overridden by the demands of urban life—commuting, maintaining a dual income for the family) and westernization, the educational level (high) of the sample, and institutionalization of support for women in this university sample in terms of tuition waivers for women attending college. Finally, the STSS was administered in English. Significant differences were apparent as a result of caste/class status—people who belong to the "protected" class (as designated by the Indian government) had scores that were significantly higher than those of the nonprotected class in three areas: self-silencing (93.56 vs. 85.26), depression (16.17 vs. 9.15), and self-esteem (21.17 vs. 18.44—higher scores represent lower self-esteem). Relationship adjustment was not significantly correlated with the STSS, contrary to what would be predicted from Silencing the Self Theory. It is possible that different definitions and expectations of relationships are not congruent with those represented by the SMAT and that the quality of marital relationships plays a less important role in one's definition of self and related variables, particularly when the responsibility for maintaining a marriage is perceived to be a collective/social responsibility.

In order to examine how self-silencing operates within an arranged marriage, 17 immigrant Indian and Pakistani women (average age = 37 years, $SD = 12.34$ years) residing in the United States, whose marriages had been arranged (number of years of marriage ranged between 1 and 45 years, $M = 15.12$ years, $SD = 12.90$ years), participated in a study examining the relationship between self-silencing and depression scores. The correlation between self-silencing and depression holds true to those found in our other studies with Asians and Asian Americans ($r = .263$). However, statistical significance was not achieved, likely due to a low sample size. Similar to the findings from the study with urbanites in India ($-.24$), we found a nonsignificant correlation between self-silencing and relationship adjustment scores ($r = -.351$, not significant), lending further credence to the notion that marital happiness might not be central to Indian and Pakistani women's definition of self. In addition, the correlation between years of marriage and self-silencing scores was found to be .216 and not statistically significant. Mean scores were as follows: STSS = 81.41 ($SD = 12.49$); SMAT = 113.71 ($SD = 26.42$); BDI = 3.88 ($SD = 3.57$).

Questions addressed in future research with Indian and Pakistani men and women could help tease out the underlying patterns that might explain the low depression, high SMAT, and moderate STSS scores. For example, how do men's and women's levels of self-silencing change with increasing years in a relationship? How do Indian and Pakistani men and women resolve/deal with conflicts in a relationship? Are the SMAT and the STSS culturally appropriate for use in India and Pakistan without translation and cultural adaptation?

In an effort to examine the hypothesis that maintenance of the marriage could be perceived as a collective responsibility, we asked this sample of Indian and Pakistani women several questions about the input of parents and elders in choosing the marriage partner and in the event of a divorce or separation. On a 5-point scale (1 = no input; 5 = very high input), respondents gave their parents an average score of 3.691, themselves an average score of 4.206, and their spouses (who are male) an average score of 4.412. This supported our hypothesis that selecting a marital partner and making a decision to separate or divorce is a family responsibility. However, reflecting the patriarchal nature of this culture, higher ratings for input in decisions for marriage and divorce were given to the male spouse. A composite variable "arranged marriage" was derived by averaging responses to questions about the amount of input parents and elders had in arranging the marriage of the respondents. The degree to which a marriage was "arranged" correlated significantly with depression scores ($r = -.652$, $p = .005$); that is, the higher the degree of "arrangement" of marriage, the lower the depression scores. This relationship, combined with the low correlation of self-silencing scores with depression scores, suggests that collective responsibility for arranging and maintaining the marriage mediates the relationship between self-silencing and depression scores. This hypothesis warrants further exploration in research studies.

It is noteworthy that the differences in self-silencing scores of men and women consistently did not match our expectations because men had higher self-silencing scores than women. However, we believed that these counterintuitive findings were due to different ways in which men and women used self-silencing and that these differences might be a function of the fact that most research participants were single. One hypothesis is that men may believe that women have more power in the precommitment phase of the relationship, and hence may silence aspects of themselves with the aim of winning over a mate (Gratch, 1995).

Women may indeed have more power in the precommitment phase to the extent that they may be less interested because they take longer than men to develop romantic feelings or to fall in love. Previous research on heterosexual dating relationships has established that men tend to fall in love more quickly than women (Rubin, Peplau, & Hill, 1981). Waller's "principle of least interest" maintains that the person least interested in the relationship has more power (Waller, 1937). This suggests that in relationships where the level of romantic feelings is unequal, the person who is more "in love" will have less power.

In order to further explore the nature of self-silencing among men and women and each ethnicity represented in previous studies, a qualitative study using focus group methodology was conducted. Twenty-four men and 24 women were recruited to participate in focus groups consisting of six individuals each.

Groups were segregated by gender and ethnicity (African American, Asian/Asian American, Caucasian, Hispanic) and were given three items from each subscale (Divided Self [DS], Silencing the Self [STS], Externalized Self-Perception [EXP], and Care as Self-Sacrifice [CSS]). The focus group discussions were led by a discussion leader (a university student) who also matched them in terms of gender and ethnicity. Our interest was in hearing how the people were thinking of the items, and of what kinds of scenarios from their own lives were brought to mind by the items. Gender differences emerged in discussions in response to three of the items that were discussed: Item #2 (STS Subscale): "I don't speak my feelings in an intimate relationship when I know they will cause disagreement"; Item #5 (DS Subscale): "I find it is harder to be myself when I am in a close relationship than when I am on my own"; and Item #20 (CSS Subscale): "When it looks as though certain of my needs can't be met in a relationship, I usually realize that they weren't very important anyway." On the following sections, we include some general conclusions and exemplars of personal statements for each conclusion (Gratch, 1996).

Pertaining to items 2 and 5, patterns of timing of self-silencing emerged as differing for men and women. A female participant, Pat, stated that she began to "lose" herself at the moment of marriage, further emphasizing that she became unable to be herself or cause disagreement once she was married. Perhaps becoming more enmeshed in the culture's female role encouraged her in the direction of silencing herself to nurture the relationship.

> It became immediate when we began to walk down the aisle. It was as if there was a sudden, abrupt change here all of a sudden. I was not allowed to speak my feelings. . . . I began to question my own feelings. What I'm feeling—is it justified or unjustified? I soon got to the point where I didn't trust my own judgment enough to be able to determine if I had a valid reason to be upset about something. (Pat, Caucasian)

Beth (Caucasian) said, "peacekeeping is our job," and Alicia (Hispanic) stated, "It's in our culture—we're not supposed to talk back to them," emphasizing the subservient role of women, in addition to the roles of peacekeeper and caretaker of relationships.

Men spoke of silencing certain aspects of their selves early in the relationship as a function of their guardedness in the precommitment phase of the relationship, or hiding certain feelings and thoughts to move the relationship to another level.

> I do keep some things to myself no matter who the person is. There are so many different stages of a close relationship that I have been in. For instance, when I first meet the person, I'm not going to be myself completely because I have so many reservations about what could happen. Altogether, I was interpreting this to mean 'after I had gotten past all that' because it says 'in a close relationship.' Later on, I'm very open and I just share. I don't think I hold back at all. . . . If I get to that stage I'm pretty much free to express myself. I don't really hold back. (Robert, Caucasian)

This comment exemplifies the functional role of self-silencing as being that of seeking commitment by presenting a more "acceptable" self to the potential partner. A comment by two other male participants sums up this argument:

> You should act a certain way that is going to be pleasing and satisfying to them during the gelling process. (Damon, Hispanic)
>
> I think I am better able to be myself when I am married in a close relationship than when I was single or a bachelor, because when you're single, you try to impress. It's like the predator after the game: you're sleek, you're sly; you're trying to move in on the attack. Once I had gotten married, I was able to sit back and open myself, and express all my feelings. (Jack, Caucasian)

Glenn, an African American male, describes the silence of a female partner in the relationship:

> You get to know a lot about each other. You know when she's not saying something, you can pick it up. It must have been our anniversary or it must have been that ring I forgot to get her. If you know you're friends, you won't have that problem.

In response to Item #20 ("When it looks as though certain of my needs can't be met in a relationship, I usually realize that they weren't very important anyway."), important differences due to gender and ethnicity emerged, though any conclusions regarding the latter should be made with considerable caution because of the small sample size. The overarching conclusion was that men viewed relationships as a means to fulfill their needs, whereas women's thoughts about relationships involved postponing, negating, or negotiating their needs. Excerpts from focus groups follow:

> My needs are just as important as his are. We have to try to compromise, try to agree to do certain things. And if the person doesn't do certain things, and if the person doesn't like it, I think that he or she should still do it to please the other. And it has to work both ways. Otherwise, I don't think our relationship would really work. (Maria, Hispanic)
>
> I think in a relationship we should—if it's a really good relationship, a serious relationship—you should speak up what you feel. Even though, in reality in my relationship, I don't." (When the moderator emphasized that the item was about her personal relationship, she elaborated). "I don't do that. Not usually.... I usually keep quiet. I just pretend most of the time. But inside my heart, no way." (Debbie, Asian)
>
> I dislike people thinking you have to forfeit you own needs and to the other person's—help the other person because you're supposed to care for them. If they [needs] are not being met in a relationship, what are you still in it for.... If most of them aren't being met, then you're with the wrong person. That's how I feel. (Bernadette, African American)

The views of men in response to this question were substantially different. Jim (Caucasian) said, "If my needs aren't met in a relationship, I meet them somewhere else."

Dean (Caucasian) agreed:

> I can't imagine that if you had a need that was important to you that wasn't met, that you would decide it wasn't important just because it couldn't be met. It should be met . . . exactly because the other person wants those needs to be met.

Marco (Hispanic) expressed similar ideas: "If they are my needs, I'm entitled to have them; I'm entitled to express them; I'm entitled to pursue them." Glenn, African American, added:

> If [my needs are not met], then the relationship is a problem—it will dissolve anyway. It is a two-sided thing. If she's open to communication, then she's willing to say, 'OK, then I understand that you need this that I haven't been able to give you.' If she doesn't come half way, then she doesn't want you anyway.

Whereas the dominant theme in men's comments was that if needs are not met, there is really no reason for the relationship to continue, women's responses were more complex. They agree that relationships are need-meeting structures, but they intimate that their own needs are not met. This, of course, is the very basis for women's self-silencing in contexts of inequality, as described by Jack (1991). A notable exception is apparent in the comments of African American men and women, where the emphasis is still on communication and negotiation, though voicing may not result in listening, as exemplified by the following quotes:

> I've been with my boyfriend for 2 years and he does the same thing. If I say something . . . or, 'did you hear me?' [he'll say] 'Uh-Huh,' then he'll say, 'Oooh!' And I'll say, 'Are you watching the game?' [he'll say] 'No, I heard you. . . . See, I was, I was uh uh uh. I've got to go; let me call you right back.' Then he'll call me back and start talking about something else. (Tammy, African American)
>
> He's not listening. He hears what I say, but he's not listening effectively. . . . He doesn't listen to what I say. And when he does say something, he doesn't communicate well. (Michelle, African American)

The function of relationships as need-meeting structures warrants further examination. That is, whose needs are more likely to be met in a marital relationship? Further analysis of the comments in this focus group resulted in emergence of two intimacy concepts: (1) focused intimacy concept—a belief that *all* the individual's needs should be met by the relationship, which would include comments that emphasize that both partners' needs should be met equally, or the needs of the dominant partner should be met; and (2) diffuse intimacy concept—a belief that the relationship should meet some of the intimacy needs of the individuals, but one may look outside for some of the needs to be met (e.g., saving a day to go to the movies with friends) (Reiss, Anderson, & Sponaugle, 1980). We hypothesize that self-silencing is heightened and more damaging in relationships typified by inequality in the context of focused intimacy beliefs about relationships (where a dominant partner's needs take precedence).

The findings from the diverse group of studies summarized in this section suggest some general conclusions and implications for future research. First, the relationship between the STSS and depression, self-esteem, and relationship adjustment were in the directions expected, though these relationships varied by ethnic group (see Table 12.1). STSS scores, in general, were higher among South Asians and Asians/Asian Americans, and among men in all ethnic groups (with the exception of Study 1, where Asian/Asian American women had higher self-silencing scores than Asian/Asian American men). We explain the higher STSS scores in (1) ethnic minority groups in terms of their collectivist orientation and (2) men in terms of lacking the language of self-expression, and their seeking power or control of a situation in the precommitment phase of a relationship. It is possible that the Silencing the Self model is more applicable to those whose "individual" selves are more prominent and where the responsibility for maintaining a relationship is assigned to individuals of lower status. In addition, in cultures where intimate relationships do not serve as the sole source of addressing one's intimacy needs, the association of self-silencing with depression may be lower. Jack (1991) also suggests that women's self-silencing to maintain relationships may also stem from insecurity. Some support for this notion may be obtained from the fact that, among Asian/Asian American women in our studies, the lowest STSS and depression scores occurred among married Indian and Pakistani women residing in the United States. It is possible that the South Asian women's sense of security in a marriage is enhanced by cultural norms and expectations that assign responsibility for arranging marriages and preventing dissolution of a marriage to parents as well as to the individual.

Future research in this area should further explore the prominence of an individual or collective self as a contextual factor in explaining the relationships between STSS and other variables. Could it be possible that the Silencing the Self model is most applicable to individuals with subordinate status and with more prominent individual (vs. collective) selves? Another area worth exploring is the presence of differences in STSS and BDI scores due to social class status but not gender in the Indian society. Interviews and in-depth studies that investigate the perceptions of members of the lower caste and resultant self-silencing and depression could explore the usefulness of the Silencing the Self model in terms of "social silencing" of marginalized groups. We also consider that information on the subscales of self-silencing for ethnic groups would be very valuable, including focus group interviews with representatives from these groups to explore the different reasons and ways in which they self-silence.

Gender, Sexual Orientation, and Violence

To further examine the construct of self-silencing and its correlates, we hypothesized that how individuals "use voice" in relationships may play a role in mediating conflict. Those failing to constructively communicate their thoughts and feelings to intimate partners because of choice, caring, lack of skillfulness, inhibition, or all of the above, may create a relationship context where one or both partners resolve conflict using physical violence. In such relationships, both individuals suffer from inadequate communication and the lack of intimacy, as well as from violence.

Past research has suggested that women and men practice self-silencing for different reasons. Specifically, men use silence or withdrawing as a tactic to maintain power in relationships (Gottman, 1994; Levenson & Gottman, 1985; Noller, 1993; Thompson, 1997), while women use silence to keep relationships and by appearing passive and compliant to the perceived wishes and needs of another (Jack, 1991). We were curious about how the different strategic uses of silence may interact with conflict and, specifically, with the use of physical violence. Furthermore, we aimed to understand how other social, psychological, or relational factors are related to self-silencing. These other factors include the need for interpersonal control, strategies for resolving conflicts in relationships, the ability to take the role of the other, relationship adjustment, commitment, depression, and sexual orientation.

An ethnically diverse community sample of gays, lesbians, and heterosexuals in Houston, Texas, was recruited ($n = 113$) to participate in this study. Respondents were recruited from two sites, an urban university campus and a grocery store in a predominately gay district (Gratch et al., 1998). Tests of comparability revealed that there were no differences between the community and student samples on any of the measurement instruments, so the samples were combined.

Sixty-three men and 50 women who self-identified as being involved in a committed relationship, with the majority married or living with a partner (77%), volunteered to participate in this study. Of these respondents, the average relationship length was 6.56 years ($SD = 8.46$) and the average age of the sample was 38.13 years ($SD = 12.77$). The ethnic/racial composition of the sample was predominately Caucasian (76.1%), with the rest identifying as Hispanic (14.2%), African American (3.5%), or other (6.2%). Other sample characteristics include a high rate of full-time employment (80%) and mean incomes between $30,000 and $40,000 per year (in 1998). A majority of the sample described themselves as heterosexual (55.4%), with the rest identifying as homosexual (43.7%) or bisexual (0.9%).

Besides the STSS, respondents completed the Conflict Tactics Scale (CTS), which consists of a list of tactics one might use to resolve conflict in relationships (Straus, 1979). There are three subscales: a three-item *Reasoning Scale*, a six-item *Verbal Aggression Scale*, and an eight-item *Violence Scale*. Respondents indicated the number of times they and their partners used these tactics over the past year. Additional measurement tools included a five-item commitment scale, with higher scores suggesting a greater level of commitment (Rusbult, 1983); the

SMAT, with higher scores indicating more adjustment (Locke & Wallace, 1959); an interpersonal control scale (ICS); and a role-taking scale (RTS) (Stets, 1992). The ICS measures whether or not respondents perceive themselves as asserting a high degree of control over their intimate partners. The RTS measures the degree that respondents perceive themselves as having the ability to understand the position or perspective of others. Finally, the BDI (Beck & Steer, 1987) was used to measure depressive symptoms in this sample.

Relative to self-silencing, gender, and other related scales, there are general results suggesting that men ($M = 75.76, SD = 17.93$) are more self-silencing than women ($M = 69.90, SD = 16.16$) [$t(108) = 1.77, p < .04$, one-tail test], and this is accompanied by correlational evidence that suggests that those men who are high self-silencers also are (1) less able to take the role of the other ($r = .48, p < .0001$) and (2) more depressed ($r = .56, p < .0001$). Women's results are some-what different. Consistent with other findings (Uebelacker, Courtnage, & Whisman, 2003), women who are high self-silencers are (1) less likely to feel that their relationships are well adjusted ($r = -.79, p < .0001$) and (2) more likely to be depressed ($r = .41, p < .0041$). No other general gender differences were found for the other scales.

To examine the potential relationship between self-silencing and violence, we dichotomized the latter: If a person perpetrated (or experienced) one or more acts of violence (as measured by the CTS), he or she was classified as violent (or having experienced violence). Men classified as perpetrators are more depressed ($M = 11.38, SD = 9.09$) than those who are not ($M = 4.58, SD = 3.75$), [$t(13.1) = -2.64, p < .02$]. Perpetrators also used more interpersonal control ($M = 21.08, SD = 7.37$) than non-violent men ($M = 16.04, SD = 4.91$), [$t(13.4) = -2.25, p < .04$] and have less ability ($M = 13.69, SD = 3.77$) to take the role of the other ($M = 11.33, SD = 2.49$), [$t(14.9) = -2.14, p < .05$]. Victimized men when compared to nonvictims show no differences on any of these measures.

For women, there was no relationship between self-silencing and the perpetration of relationship violence. Furthermore, perpetrating relationship violence was unrelated to any of the measurement scales. In contrast, women who experience partner violence are more silent ($M = 82.60, SD = 10.81$) than those who do not ($M = 65.89, SD = 15.43$), [$t(45) = -3.32, p < .0025$]. Those who report partner violence are also more depressed ($M = 13, SD = 10.01$) than those who do not ($M = 6, SD = 4.03$), [$t(98) = -2.17, p < .05$]. Self-silencing was also examined to compare individuals by their self-rated sexual orientation. No differences were found between homosexuals and heterosexuals in the use of self-silencing.

Women who have experienced partner violence are both more depressed and self-silenced. Self-silencing may be a strategy that women use to protect them-selves from physical violence; they may be afraid to voice concerns and feelings lest these revelations lead to conflict. Given the association between levels of self-silencing and physical violence, this strategy is not entirely successful. As we noted earlier, for women there is a negative correlation between self-silencing and relationship adjustment, lending further credence to the view that self-silencing is associated with less healthy relationships for women. The lack of a relationship between self-silencing and violence for men suggests that men do not need to use this strategy as a means of reducing the likelihood of physical violence, yet the relationship between higher levels of self-silencing and the inability to take the role of the other suggests that relationships are negatively impacted regardless of why self-silencing occurs.

In general, the findings of this study substantiated our belief that self-silencing is an indicator of poorer adjustment and quality of relationships. Furthermore, we found evidence supporting differences in reasons for self-silencing among men and women. Though the relationship between depression and STSS scores was evident in both male and female respondent groups, other correlates were different for men and women. Men who were high self-silencers were less able to take the role of the other, while women who were high self-silencers were more dissatisfied with their relationships. The finding among women is congruent with Jack's Silencing the Self Theory, which posits the development of a relational self in women with primacy given to maintaining relationships. The finding of lower ability to take the role of others as a correlate of higher self-silencing suggests that men may lack the perspective in addition to the language to express themselves in a relationship. Future research in this area could explore the temporal pattern of self-silencing and victimization from abuse. Does self-silencing precede abuse or vice versa? Based on multiple variables that tap into the quality, dynamics, and nature of relationships on the one hand and self-silencing on the other hand, research on subtypes of self-silencers could shed additional light on this complex phenomenon.

Gender and High-Risk Behaviors

In a related program of research, Gratch and colleagues (1997) incorporated HIV transmission risk and prevention strategies used by high-risk populations into the general framework of the STSS and its correlates. From past research, it was evident that high levels of knowledge of HIV transmission and prevention strategies do not predict safer sex practices such as condom use (Krahe & Reiss, 1995). Since utilization of AIDS prevention strategies requires assertion of one's voice in interpersonal settings, we hypothesized that the degree to which one inhibits self-expression within intimate relationships (self-silencing) may be a predictor of condom use or other HIV infection prevention strategies. Placing others' needs before one's own is a critical element of the self-silencing construct (as measured by the Care as Self-Sacrifice subscale). Our assumption was that individuals who self-silence in intimate relationships would fail to use HIV infection prevention strategies because the latter requires assertion of one's will. So, the question became, "to what degree might men's and women's self-silencing reflect an inability to adequately protect themselves from the threat of AIDS?"

To explore this question in a community sample (Houston, Texas) of female exotic dancers and young club-going singles ($n = 101$), we administered the following scales: the STSS (Jack & Dill, 1992), BDI (Beck & Steer, 1987), AIDS Risk Questionnaire (which measured the extent to which the respondents had placed themselves at risk for contracting HIV), AIDS Behavior Questionnaire (strategies used to avoid placing themselves at risk—e.g., carrying condoms, refraining from having sex for fear of getting AIDS), and Perceived Barriers to AIDS-Protective Behaviors (perceptions that there would be negative consequences if the respondent tried to use AIDS-protective strategies) (Gielen, Faden, O'Campo, Kass, & Anderson, 1994). The majority of the individuals were Caucasian (80.4%) and single (91%). Participants were recruited in two waves: (1) club-going men and women were approached in nightclubs and bars and were given questionnaire packets (after signing informed consent forms) to be mailed back in a self-addressed envelope; (2) exotic female dancers were recruited through a process of snowball sampling, where several dancers were contacted and asked to share questionnaire packets with others with whom they worked.

While the dancers were expected to have the most difficulty with risk and the use of health-protective strategies, we found no significant differences in mean scores for any of the variables except for perceived barriers to using AIDS-protective behaviors, with the club-going men reporting a significantly higher level of perceived barriers [$F_{(2,83)} = 3.54, p < .03$], particularly when compared to dancers (perceived barriers by men: $M = 8.7, SD = 4.25$; perceived barriers by dancers: $M = 5.54, SD = 2.15$). STSS scores of club-going men ($M = 77.90$, $SD = 12.99$), club-going women ($M = 74.20, SD = 17.16$), and dancers were similar ($M = 73.8, SD = 15.18$). The correlation between the STSS and BDI was statistically significant for the total sample ($r = .29, p < .01$) and among club-going women ($r = .45, p < .01$). However, as far as the correlation between STSS and AIDS-related variables are concerned, we found that STSS and BDI scores were significantly correlated with higher levels of perceived barriers to using AIDS-protective behaviors among men only (STSS and Barriers, $r = .43, p = .02$; BDI and Barriers, $r = .69, p < .001$). Thus, men who were high self-silencers or had higher depression scores perceived more barriers to using AIDS-protective behaviors.

As suggested by our previous research, we feel that men tend to withhold their thoughts and feelings in order to establish order and control (i.e., a strategic use of self-silencing) (also see Smolak, Chapter 6). Since previous research suggests that men's self-silencing occurs more frequently in precommitment phases of relationships (Gratch et al., 1995), we conclude that men's self-silencing during the precommitment phase coincides with the period of highest risk for HIV transmission. Findings from this same research (Gratch et al., 1995) suggest that women tend to self-silence more during or after commitment in relationships, which is when they may experience feelings of unequal power, fear of loneliness, or role constraint. Given the significant correlation (though low) between the STSS and BDI for the entire sample and for club-going women, and the high correlation between men's STSS and BDI on the one hand and perceived barriers to using AIDS-protective behaviors on the other, we believe that self-silencing is detrimental to one's psychological as well as physical well-being. Specifically, we feel that physical well-being may be threatened by perceived lack of voice and assertion in using AIDS-protective behaviors among men who are in the pre-commitment phase of a relationship. Research by DeMarco (see Chapter 15) and Jacobs and Thomlison (2009) has further illuminated the relationship of self-silencing to HIV/AIDS vulnerability and prevention strategies.

The Factor Structure of the STSS

The finding that men are higher in self-silencing than women appears contrary to feminist developmental theory (Gilligan, 1982; Jack, 1991; Miller, 1976), which suggests that within intimate relationships, women are more likely to use silence to maintain intimacy and closeness because of gender-based power differentials and social inequality. Earlier we noted that past research has found either no differences between men and women on their STSS scores (Cowan, Bommersbach, & Curtis, 1995; Gratch et al., 1994, 1996, 1997) or counter-intuitive findings, with men's average self-silencing scores higher than those of women (Gratch et al., 1995; Thompson, 1995; Smolak, Chapter 6). To explore gender differences, we conducted a factor analysis of the STSS, using data collected in a previous study (Gratch, Bassett, & Attra, 1995) with an ethnically diverse group of undergraduate students ($n = 604$) (Gratch, 1997). This sample was almost evenly split between men ($n = 289$) and women ($n = 315$). The ethnic composition of the sample was divided between African American (24.4%), Asian American (20.9%), Caucasian (26.7%), and Hispanic (28%).

The STSS is composed of four rationally derived subscales: (1) Externalized Self-Perception (EXP), (2) Care as Self-Sacrifice (CSS), (3) Silencing the Self (STS), and (4) Divided Self (DS). These subscales have been found to be highly reliable and intercorrelated (Jack & Dill, 1992).

Based on past research (Gratch et al., 1995) and Jack's Silencing the Self Theory (1991), we assumed that the Divided Self subscale would be the most salient for women and the Silencing the Self subscale most prominent for men. Several studies and the original theory provide guidance for understanding these differences. First, men may be more self-silencing because self-disclosure within an intimate relationship may be more difficult for those with masculine gender-role identities (Eisler & Blalock, 1991) and so men may not have developed a language to describe or discuss emotional feelings (Balswick, 1988; Doyle, 1983; Rabinowitz & Cochran, 1994) or may feel uncomfortable disclosing vulnerabilities (Luria, Friedman, & Rose, 1987). Second, men may use self-silencing as an active strategy for maintaining power and influence within intimate relationships (Gottman, 1994; Levenson & Gottman, 1985; Noller, 1993; Thompson, 1997). For example, men may tend to "stonewall" by changing the topic, only minimally participating in the conversation, or, on the more extreme side, remaining silent or walking away from the conversation. Uebelacker and colleagues (2003) report that it is far more common for both husbands and wives to report the use of a wife-demand husband-withdraw communication strategy than the husband-demand wife-withdraw strategy. The use of silence as a means of control is consistent with Thompson (1997), who also found that the STS subscale is more tactical in nature for men than for women.

Principal components extraction with varimax rotation was used in two initial runs with the 31 STSS items to estimate the number of factors from eigenvalues. In these initial runs, the maximum number of factors with eigenvalues greater than one was nine for men and eight for women. With the help of scree plots, breaks in the relative sizes of (and differences between) eigenvalues were identified in each analysis. These breaks suggest that the optimal solution when including 21 items was three factors for both men and women. This analysis was followed with an orthogonal rotation with the criterion for item inclusion set at .30. Any item loading on more than one factor was placed with the factor representing its highest loading. Two items were dropped (1 and 11) because they did not load for either men or women. Several different rotation and extraction decisions were tried, with the final solution using oblique rotation with the extraction of four factors. There are important gender differences in the ordering of the factors. For men, Factor 1 is the Silencing the Self factor accounting for approximately 21.79% of the variance. Factor 2 is Externalized Self-Perception (nine items, 7.3% of the estimated variance). Care as Self-Sacrifice is the third factor (six items, 5.94% of the variance) followed by factor 4, Divided Self (five items, 4.45% variance). Interestingly, the women's and men's factor orders were reversed. Factor 1 for women is Divided Self (eight items, 26.05% variance). Factor 2 is Care as Self-Sacrifice (eight items, 8.16% variance). Factor 3 is Externalized Self-Perception (seven items, 5.55% of the variance), followed by factor 4, Silencing the Self (five items, 4.75%).

The factor structure for women in this analysis reveals more importance for the Divided Self subscale. This is in complete contrast for men, where this factor was the least significant. Also, the Divided Self subscale was more significantly correlated with higher levels of depression in women than men ($z_r = 2.84$, $df = 310, 286$, $p < .05$, two-tailed). According to Jack (1991), the need to create a divided self arises because women are often the subordinate in unequal intimate relationships. As a survival strategy, women may develop more dualistic personalities by silencing feelings that are unacceptable by the larger culture and their intimate partners. Voice is given only to feelings that portray compliance and acceptability. Women present a public "illusion of intimacy" (Jack, 1991, p. 49), which stresses being loving, thoughtful, happy, giving, and selfless. Having a "divided self" in a relationship is problematic as there is no place for authenticity or expressing conflict, anger, or aspects of personality that conflict with more traditional, selfless expectations. When negative feelings arise and are judged by the self or others to be unacceptable, women hide these feelings until they erupt in anger, which results in guilt and a new cycle of self-silencing (Jack, 1991). Thompson (1997) also found that higher levels on the Divided Self subscale are associated with lessened feelings of intimacy.

The items themselves that comprise the two factors of greatest importance in this analysis lend further support for the growing distinction between men's and women's versions of self-silencing. The items comprising the Silencing the Self subscale seem to represent a more situational or strategic (vs. a personal) perspective. For example, Item 30, "I try to bury my feelings when I think they will cause trouble in my close relationship(s)," and Item 14, "Instead of risking confrontations in close relationships, I would rather not rock the boat," can both be interpreted as a way to avoid conflict and maintain power. Conversely, the Divided Self factor reveals a more personal perspective. Examples include Items 25, "I feel that my partner does not know my real self," and 17, "In order for my partner to love me, I cannot reveal certain things about myself to him/her." These items have less to do with making tactical decisions to be silent and more to do with the need to hide unacceptable aspects of the self.

Taken together, the factor analysis findings suggest both practical and theoretical directions for working with and studying men and women in relationships. For example, given the connection for men between "situationally" not speaking up and depression—regardless of the underlying reasons for not speaking up—perhaps therapists might develop strategies for men that more strongly encourage "talk" as part of treatment and provide men with the necessary tools for such communication. Men also need to be made aware of the possibility that their use of silence and withdrawal may be an attempt to control and maintain power over their female partner. For women, strategies that enable them to "cross the divide" and bring their authentic concerns and identities back in sync with their more public self might be helpful, particularly if accompanied with interventions targeted at the family or the intimate other.

Conclusions

In our studies of self-silencing in various contexts of relationships and ethnicity, we found that high STSS scores were usually related to different negative psychological outcomes in men and women, with culture/ethnicity moderating this relationship. Higher self-silencing scores were not consistently related to depression among single men, though in a sample of men in committed relationships, they were related to lower ability to take the role of the other and higher depression scores. In a sample of women (primarily Caucasian), relationship adjustment was highly correlated with self-silencing, where lower relationship adjustment was associated with higher self-silencing scores. Depression and self-silencing among women were also correlated (in the low-to-medium range), supporting Jack's findings in the validation study of the STSS (Jack & Dill, 1992). This information combined with the results of the factor structure of the STSS with men and women warrant the conclusion that men and women self-silence for different reasons. Women are socialized to take on the role of nurturer of relationships and define themselves through these relationships. It makes sense that quality of relationships feature heavily in their self-silencing (as demonstrated by the primacy of the Divided Self subscale and the higher correlations between marital adjustment and self-silencing). Men's self-silencing, on the other hand, appears to be utilized to avoid conflict or to appease the other, perhaps also as a result of a lower confidence in their ability to express themselves or not having the language to do so. It is also possible that men self-silence to retain power or to maintain connection. It is apparent however, that in general, self-silencing is not healthy—for both men and women. It also suggests pathways for therapeutic intervention when self-silencing exists in conjunction with depression and lower marital adjustment.

Through studies with ethnically different groups, we note that the correlation between depression and self-silencing varies between .32 and .79. Due to the diversity of samples included in this study (in terms of gender, marital status, ethnicity, and sexual orientation), it is difficult to ascertain an overarching pattern of correlations. Perhaps the nature of self-silencing is a critical consideration in determining the relationship between self-silencing and depression. We have hypothesized, and to some extent confirmed, that men and women refrain from exercising voice in intimate relationships for different reasons.

It is also possible that cultural values that emphasize the norm of the self in relation to others (harmony, collectivism, care for others, self-sacrifice) may moderate the relationship between self-silencing and depression. In fact, self-silencing may be a socially sanctioned behavior, though not necessarily healthy, and hence may not be perceived as emerging out of a sense of powerlessness or helplessness (also see Drat-Ruszczak, Chapter 9). It might also be possible that the collectivist nature of a society serves as a protective factor for women and men who self-silence at a high level by allowing them to attribute negative threats to self to their collective self, breaking the link between self-silencing and depression even in situations where the individuals are in positions of subordination. In addition, concern for others' perceptions and externalized self-perception may exist at a higher level in these groups (particularly among Indians). It is noteworthy that depression and self-silencing scores were high in the Indian samples, but the correlation between these two scores was low. We suggest that the root causes of self-silencing and depression are separate in that self-silencing may arise from a socially sanctioned response in a highly hierarchical society, whereas depression may emerge from a range of interacting social, psychological, and biological factors. Also, a fatalistic orientation (prevalent in India) has been found to increase psychological distress (Ross, Mirowsky, & Cockerham, 1983).

Another trend apparent from the research we report is that men and women may self-silence at different points in a relationship, with men silencing in the early part of the relationship (precommitment phase) followed by voice postcommitment; and women silencing more in the latter part of the relationship, after the point of commitment, with voice earlier in the relationship. People's beliefs about relationships and their function (and resultant expectations of a relationship) may also contribute to self-silencing if there is a socially sanctioned inequality where one partner's needs take precedence over the other's. Given that men's self-silencing scores are as high or higher than women's self-silencing scores, it is also possible that men silence more than women throughout the relationship but the reasons for silence may change. Men may use silence in the precommitment phase as a means to try to avoid self-disclosure and gain the upper hand in a relationship when women may initially have more power. In the postcommitment phase, silence may be used to maintain power or exercise emotional restraint (see Smolak, Chapter 6). The primacy of the Silencing the Self factor among men (as opposed to the Divided Self factor being the most salient for women) lends credence to this argument.

In examining self-silencing scores of single, club-going men and women and exotic dancers, average self-silencing scores are not significantly different; however, there is a link between self-silencing and perceived barriers to AIDS-protective behaviors for single, club-going men only. Thus, we feel that self-silencing also seems to function as a risk factor for AIDS-protective behaviors among men, further emphasizing the need to provide men with strategies to aid self-expression. In addition, self-silencing is a function of status factors where individuals in subordinate relationships report higher levels (as demonstrated by the higher STSS scores among members of a lower caste in India).

We note that self-silencing is possibly also influenced by expectations of a relationship. We hypothesize that it is the most damaging in relationships where there are high levels of inequality and a focused intimacy concept; self-silencing is possibly not as high or as damaging in relationships typified by a more diffuse notion of intimacy or the expectation that it is acceptable to have some needs met outside of the primary relationship. It is also possible, as noted in the study with Indian and Pakistani women in arranged marriages, that a view of marital partner selection and dissolution of the marital relationship as being a collective responsibility absolves the self of the damaging effects of failure of relationships, threats of such failure, and the sole responsibility of maintaining the relationship.

Since self-silencing among women (as initially proposed by Jack, 1991) results from women being placed in subordinate roles and expectations to achieve and maintain harmonious relationships in a society that values indivi- duation and independence, it is important to acknowledge that the nature of self- silencing may be impacted by immediate, situational factors *and* by the larger society's values and norms. Further research that investigates self-silencing in cultural and immediate, situational contexts are warranted, particularly with implications for psychological interventions.

Note

1. Participants self-identified as belonging to this ethnic group. Though a heterogeneous group including people of Chinese, Taiwanese, Korean, Japanese, and South Asian origin, some elements of cultural heritage (e.g., collectivism, high regard for authority) may be common among Asians/Asian Americans.

References

Balswick, J. O. (1988). *The inexpressive male.* Lexington, MA: D.C. Heath.

Beck, A. T., & Steer, R. (1987). *The Beck Depression Inventory.* San Antonio, TX: The Psychological Corporation.

Burley, K. A. (1995). Family variables as mediators of the relationship between work- family conflict and marital adjustment among dual-career men and women. *Journal of Social Psychology, 135*(4), 483–497.

Chen, Zi, Nao, T., Uji, M., Hiramura, H., Shikai, N., Fujihara, S., & Kitamura, T. (2007). The role of personalities in the marital adjustment of Japanese couples. *Social Behavior and Personality, 35*(4), 561–572.

Cowan, G., Bommersbach, M., & Curtis, S. R. (1995). Codependency, loss of self, and power. *Psychology of Women Quarterly, 20,* 375–392.

Doyle, J. A. (1983). *The male experience* (2nd ed.). Dubuque, IA: William C. Brown Company.

Eisler, R., & Blalock, J. (1991). Masculine gender role stress: Implications for the assess- ment of men. *Clinical Psychology Review, 11,* 45–60.

Erikson, E. (1968). *Identity, youth, and crisis.* New York: Norton.

Freeston, M. H., & Piechaty, M. (1997). Reconsiderations of the Locke-Wallace Marital Adjustment Test: Is it still relevant for the 1990s? *Psychological Reports, 81*(2), 419–434.

Gaetner, L., Sekikides, C., & Graetz, K. (1999). In search of self-definition: Motivational primacy of the individual self, motivational primacy of the collective self, or con- textual primacy? *Journal of Personality and Social Psychology, 76*(1), 5–18.

Gielen, A., Faden, R. R., O'Campo, P., Kass, N., & Anderson, J. (1994). Women's protective sexual behaviors: A test of the Health Belief Model. *AIDS Education and Prevention, 6,* 1–11.

Gilligan, C. (1982). *In a different voice: Psychological theory and women's development.* Cambridge, MA: Harvard University Press.

Gottman, J. (1994). *Why marriages succeed or fail.* New York: Simon & Schuster.

Gratch, L. V. (1995, August). The importance of diversity in understanding the complex construct of self-silencing. In D. Jack (Chair), *Self-silencing and depression across diverse racial and cultural groups.* Symposium conducted at the annual meeting of the American Psychological Association, New York, NY.

Gratch, L. V. (1996). *Self-silencing in intimate relationships: Focused interviews by gender and ethnicity.* Unpublished transcripts, University of Houston-Downtown.

Gratch, L. V. (1997, May). The vitality of self-silencing as a portable construct: From intimacy to the workplace. In L. Gratch (Chair), *To become oneself with others: Ten years of research on self-silencing and depression.* Symposium presented the annual meeting of the American Psychological Society, Washington, DC.

Gratch, L. V., Attra, S. L., & Bassett, M. E. (1994, June). *The effects of gender and ethnicity on self-silencing and depression.* Paper presented at the annual meeting of the American Psychological Society, Washington, DC.

Gratch, L. V., Bassett, M. E., & Attra, S. L. (1995). The relationship of gender and ethnicity on self-silencing and depression among college students. *Psychology of Women Quarterly, 19,* 509–515.

Gratch, L. V., Bassett, M., Azar, G., Ferguson, D., Haidar, L., Hale, S., et al. (1995, June). *Understanding "voice" in relationships: Interpretive differences in self-silencing by males and females.* Paper presented at the annual meeting of the American Psychological Society, New York, NY.

Gratch, L. V., Sikka, A., Waldner-Haugrud, L., Murff, W., Hudges, J., Lane, E., et al. (1996, July). *Self-silencing, depression, self-esteem and relationship adjustment among urbanites in India.* Paper presented at the annual meeting of the American Psychological Society, San Francisco, CA.

Gratch, L. V., Waldner, L., Hudgens, J., Coats, K., Freeman, M. D., Muff, W., et al. (1998, May). *Communication and conflict with intimate partners: Self-silencing and the Conflict Tactics Scales.* Paper presented at the annual meeting of the American Psychological Society, Washington, DC.

Gratch, L. V., Waldner, L., Murff, W., Benites, J. C., Hudgens, J., Simpson, G., et al. (1997, May). *Self-silencing, AIDS and intimacy issues: Dancers and young singles on the "Richmond Strip."* Paper presented at the annual meeting of the American Psychological Society, Washington, DC.

Hsu, F. L. K. (1970). *Americans and Chinese.* New York: Doubleday.

Hsu, F. L. K. (1971). Psychosocial homeostasis and jen: Conceptual tools for advancing psychological anthropology. *American Anthropologist, 73,* 23–44.

Jack, D. C. (1991). *Silencing the self: Women and depression.* Cambridge, MA: Harvard University Press.

Jack, D. C., & Dill, D. (1992). The Silencing the Self Scale: Schemas of intimacy associated with depression in women. *Psychology of Women Quarterly, 16,* 97–106.

Jacobs, R. J., & Thomlison, B. (2009). Self-silencing and age as risk factors for sexually acquired HIV in midlife and older women. *Journal of Aging and Health, 21*(1), 102–128.

Kitano, H. L. (1988). The Japanese American family. In D. H. Mindel, R. W. Habenstein, & R. Wright, Jr. (Eds.), *Ethnic families in America* (3rd ed., pp. 258–275). Englewood Cliffs, NJ: Prentice Hall.

Krahe, B., & Reiss, C. (1995). Predicting intentions of AIDS preventative behavior among adolescents. *Journal of Applied Social Psychology, 25,* 2118–2140.

Levenson, R. W., & Gottman, J. (1985). Physiological and affective predictors of change in relationship satisfaction. *Journal of Personality and Social Psychology, 49,* 85–94.

Locke, H. J., & Wallace, K. M. (1959). Short marital-adjustment and prediction tests: Their reliability and validity. *Marriage and Family Living, 21*(3), 251–255.

Luria, Z., Friedman, S., & Rose, M. D. (1987). *Human sexuality.* New York: John Wiley & Sons.

Miller, J. B. (1976). *Toward a new psychology of women.* Boston: Beacon Press.

Noller, P. (1993). Gender and emotional communication in marriage: Different cultures or different social power? *Journal of Language and Social Psychology, 12,* 132–152.

Oyserman, D. (1993). The lens of personhood: Viewing the self and others in a multicultural society. *Journal of Personality and Social Psychology, 65*(5), 993–1009.

Rabinowitz, F. E., & Cochran, S. V. (1994). *Man alive: A primer of men's issues.* Pacific Grove, CA: Brooks/Cole Publishing Company.

Reiss, I. L., Anderson, R. E., & Sponaugle, G. C. (1980). A multivariate model of the determinants of extramarital sexual permissiveness. *Journal of Marriage and the Family, 42,* 395–411.

Rosenberg, M. (1979). *Conceiving the self.* New York: Basic Books.

Ross, C. E., Mirowsky, J., & Cockerham, W. C. (1983). Social class, Mexican culture, and fatalism: Their effects on psychological distress. *American Journal of Community Psychology, 11*(4), 383–399.

Rubin, Z., Peplau, L. A., & Hill, C. T. (1981). Loving and leaving: Sex differences in romantic attachments. *Sex Roles, 7,* 821–835.

Rusbult, C. E. (1983). A longitudinal test of the investment model: The development (and deterioration) of satisfaction and commitment in heterosexual involvements. *Journal of Personality and Social Psychology, 45,* 101–117.

Shon, S. P., & Ja, D. Y. (1982). Asian families. In M. McGoldrick, J. K. Pearce, & J. Giordano (Eds.), *Ethnicity and family therapy* (pp. 208–229). New York: Guilford Press.

Sue, D. W. (1981). *Counseling the culturally different: Theory and practice.* New York: Wiley.

Stets, J. E. (1992). Interactive processes in dating aggression: A national study. *Journal of Marriage and Family, 54,* 165–177.

Straus, M. A. (1979). Measuring intrafamily conflict and violence: The Conflict Tactics (CT) Scales. *Journal of Marriage and Family, 41,* 75–88.

Thompson, J. M. (1995). Silencing the self: Depressive symptomatology and close relationships. *Psychology of Women Quarterly, 19,* 337–353.

Thompson, J. M. (1997, June). *Silencing the Self, individual and relationship functioning in a community sample of heterosexual couples.* Paper presented at the annual meeting of the American Psychological Society, Washington, DC.

Triandis, H. C., Bontempo, R., Betancourt, H., Bond, M., Leung, K., Brenes, A., et al. (1986). The measurement of etic aspects of individualism and collectivism across cultures. *Australian Journal of Psychology, 38,* 257–267.

Uebelacker, L. A., Courtnage, E. S., & Whisman, M. A. (2003). Correlates of depression and marital dissatisfaction: Perceptions of marital communication style. *Journal of Social and Personal Relationships, 20,* 757–769.

Waller, W. (1937). The rating and dating complex. *American Sociological Review, 2,* 727–734.

13

Silencing the Self and Personality Vulnerabilities Associated with Depression

Avi Besser, Gordon L. Flett, and Paul L. Hewitt

In this chapter, we examine how personality factors associated with depression relate with self-silencing, a contextual perspective that focuses on interpersonal factors, with the following two main goals. First, we present the argument that there are many reasons why people engage in self-silencing, and these reasons reflect personality vulnerability factors associated with depression that also happen to be associated with self-silencing. While Jack (1991, 1999a) argues that a person self-silences to maintain existing interpersonal relationships, we contend that self-silencing can be motivated by many goals and objectives. Second, we outline our current work on self-silencing and personality vulnerability factors associated with depression. We argue that self-silencing is not only associated with a tendency to be depressed but also with some core personality traits associated with depressive vulnerability. Moreover, we argue that self-silencing combines with these personality factors, either as a mediating or a moderating factor, to increase the risk for elevated levels of psychological distress.

The three main personality factors we will focus on are dependency, self-criticism, and perfectionism. The main motive for self-silencing among people with high levels of dependency and neediness is the desire to maintain relationships. However, self-evaluative concerns also play a significant role and contribute to self-silencing tendencies. People with high levels of self-criticism may silence the self because they are self-punitive and feel a sense of shame about aspects of their character and behavior. Similarly, perfectionistic people may self-silence because they are fearful of making mistakes and of the consequences of making mistakes. They may also engage in self-silencing because they are overly invested in publicly presenting an image of perfection.

Although dependency, self-criticism, and perfectionism are distinguishable orientations, they have certain factors in common that should contribute to a shared tendency toward silencing the self. While it is recognized, generally, that dependent individuals will make extreme sacrifices to gain the love and approval of others, research indicates that self-criticism and perfectionism are also associated with concerns about losing the approval of other people (Hewitt & Flett, 1991; Luthar & Blatt, 1993). It is also possible for self-criticism and perfectionism to be evident in the interpersonal sphere—people may be self-critical because of inadequate behavior in social situations and people may be highly invested in meeting the perfectionistic expectations of other people and in trying to portray themselves in public as flawless (see Hewitt et al., 2003). It is our awareness of the interpersonal aspect of each of the constructs that has contributed to our interest in conducting a research program on the role of these personality factors in how new mothers adjust to the transition to parenthood and the associated relationship challenges and role demands. Clearly, all of the personality factors considered in this chapter have a clear interpersonal component.

In what follows, we describe each of the personality constructs mentioned previously in more detail, with a particular emphasis on how each is conceptualized and how each is relevant to an understanding of silencing the self. We summarize research conducted in our laboratories on personality and silencing the self and outline the implications of the associations between self-silencing and personality vulnerabilities. Finally, we conclude by discussing the negative emotional, interpersonal, and health consequences for people who self-silence and who are characterized by these personality vulnerability factors. In particular, we analyze the associations among self-silencing, personality vulnerabilities, and stress, and present the argument that people with vulnerable personalities who also engage in self-silencing may suffer from chronic and destructive forms of stress that may result, ultimately, in health problems.

Dependency and Self-Criticism: The Anaclitic and Introjective Orientations

Research on personality and depression has been a predominant theme in the personality literature (see Flett, Hewitt, Endler, & Bagby, 1995). While earlier work focused extensively on attributional style and depression, more recent work has focused on constructs such as self-criticism, dependency, perfectionism, optimism-pessimism, and reassurance seeking. The dimensions of dependency and self-criticism were introduced and described at length by Blatt (1974, 2004). Dependency is a reflection of an anaclitic orientation that involves a preoccupation with other people and a need to keep them in close proximity. A high level of dependency is derived from an insecure attachment style (see

Levy, Blatt, & Shaver, 1998; Zuroff & Fitzpatrick, 1995). In contrast, self-criticism is a reflection of an introjective orientation that involves an evaluative focus on achieving personal goals and working toward standards in an autonomous fashion (see Blatt, Quinlan, Chevron, McDonald, & Zuroff, 1982). However, the essence of this construct is a highly punitive, evaluative response to the self when standards are not achieved and expectations are not met. Blatt and Blass (1996) stated that the self-critical orientation reflects a need for self-definition and development of a sense of personal identity, while the dependent orientation reflects a need for relatedness and association with other people.

Blatt and colleagues defined a theory of personality involving the dimensions of dependency and self-criticism (Blatt, 1990; Blatt, Cornell, & Eshkol, 1993; Blatt et al., 1982). This theory is consistent with the long tradition that contrasts other and self-directedness as two basic modalities of human experience. Blatt and colleagues suggested also that the adequate coordination between interpersonal relatedness and self-definition might reduce stress and lead to physical and psychological well-being (Blatt et al., 1993). According to this model, normal development is characterized by a dialectic interweaving of other and self-directedness, leading to a flexible balancing of the characteristic capacities involved in these two processes (Helgeson, 1994). These two processes evolve in an interactive, reciprocally balanced, dialectic process from birth through senescence (Blatt, 1974, 1990, 1995; Blatt & Blass, 1996). This model assumes that individual differences in the relative emphasis on each of these processes delineate two personality styles—self-criticism and dependency—each with favored modes of cognition and coping strategies. An overemphasis on self-critical or dependency motives results in dysfunctional attitudes and is assumed to constitute vulnerability to depression.

Extensive empirical research has found a strong positive association between self-criticism and depression and a less robust but still significant association between dependency and depression (Besser, 2004; Besser & Priel, 2003a,b, 2005a,b; Besser, Priel, Flett, & Wiznitzer, 2007; Nietzel & Harris, 1990; Priel & Besser, 1999, 2000), and this general pattern of findings has continued to emerge in recent years. However, two important caveats about the stronger association between self-criticism and depression need to be noted. First, the decidedly less robust association between dependency and depression is due, in part, to the fact that the dependency construct includes an adaptive component that reflects establishing a healthy connectedness to other people. That is, dependency appears to include both vulnerability and resilience components (Blatt, Zohar, Quinlan, Zuroff, & Mongrain, 1995; Rude & Burnham, 1995). It is the vulnerability component of dependency that should be most relevant to silencing the self. Second, recent data suggest that self-criticism and dependency interact so that people characterized jointly by these two orientations are particularly at risk for depression (see Mongrain & Leather, 2006).

Silencing the self is believed to be especially likely to occur in relationship contexts (see Jack, 1999a). It is important to note that an extensive and growing body of research also highlights the relevance of both self-criticism and dependency in relationship outcomes and relationship processes (for a review, see Blatt, 2004). This research suggests that both dependency and self-criticism undermine relationship satisfaction, but for very different reasons (e.g., Whiffen & Aube, 1999). While the excessive need for reassurance of people high in dependency may alienate their partners, self-critical people have a hostile interpersonal style that leads others to reject them (Mongrain, Lubbers, & Struthers, 2004). The main point for our purposes is that self-silencing, dependency, and self-criticism are all relevant to behaviors, events, and processes that occur in relationships, and this points to the possibility that these constructs may be interrelated.

Silencing the Self, Dependency, and Self-Criticism

Given this description, what is the link between silencing the self and both dependency and self-criticism? And why should there be an association? If viewed from a conceptual perspective, the case for linking self-silencing and dependency seems rather obvious. Indeed, in a previous paper, Whiffen and Aube (1999) discussed self-silencing within the context of dependency and neediness and postulated that women high in dependency and interpersonal neediness are likely to engage in self-silencing behavior in order to further their relationship goals. Whiffen (2007) has gone on to suggest that many women suffer from "a secret sadness" that is rooted deeply in maladaptive relationship patterns. The notion of a "secret sadness" follows from Blatt and Zuroff's (1992) statement that "dependent individuals rely intensely on others to provide and maintain a sense of well-being, and therefore have great difficulty expressing anger for fear of losing the need gratification that others can provide" (p. 528). The unwillingness or inability to express anger is a central characteristic of women who engage in self-silencing (see Jack, 2001).

But why should self-criticism be linked with self-silencing? People high in self-silencing have been described as hearing self-condemning, harsh voices in their heads (e.g., Jack, 1999a), almost as if they have internalized unrealistic societal values that are being used as a guide for self-evaluation. Intuitively, it seems natural that people who are unsure of themselves and feel negatively toward themselves would keep their deficiencies, concerns, and true feelings to themselves, especially if they have unfulfilled desires for social approval and recognition for positive accomplishments and clear successes. We would also suggest that one reason why self-criticism and self-silencing are associated is that there is a reciprocal association between these variables. Initially, self-critical people will silence themselves, but this act of self-negation, in turn, should foster additional feelings of self-reproach and reductions in self-esteem, and this gets reflected in an increasingly negative personal identity.

Existing evidence points to a link between self-criticism and self-silencing. For instance, Jack (1999a) provided descriptive case examples of self-critical individuals who engage in self-silencing behavior. A possible link between self-criticism and self-silencing is also indicated by research showing that self-critical individuals are characterized by low levels of frankness and that they tend to avoid self-disclosure (Wiseman, 1997). Self-critical people tend to pursue self-presentational goals that revolve around making a positive impression on other people and concerns about portraying certain emotional states (see Mongrain & Zuroff, 1995). Finally, both self-criticism and dependency have been associated with an ambivalence regarding emotional expression (Mongrain & Zuroff, 1994); perhaps this ambivalence is a by-product of the self-silencing process.

Initial data on this topic were reported by Besser, Flett, and Davis (2003). We examined the associations among self-criticism, dependency, self-silencing, loneliness, and depression in a sample of 167 university students, including a significant subset of participants who were currently in dating relationships. Dependency and self-criticism were assessed with the Depressive Experiences Questionnaire (DEQ; Blatt, D'Afflitti, & Quinlan, 1976). We found that individuals with high levels of dependency tended to be characterized by silencing the self and this finding held regardless of whether the individuals were or were not in a current relationship, and regardless of levels of depressive symptoms as measured by the Center for Epidemiological Studies Depression Scale (CES-D; Radloff, 1977). Our analyses involving self-criticism provided evidence consistent with case descriptions of self-silencing people characterized by excessive self-criticism (see Jack, 1999a). Higher levels of self-criticism were associated with self-silencing regardless of relationship status. These data signify that many people with elevated self-criticism are characterized by high sensitivity to external feedback and may be aware of conflicting aspects of the public self versus the private self, so one protective approach they adopt is to engage in self-silencing behavior in an attempt to maintain or improve their relationships. However, as noted, self-silencing is also evident among self-critical individuals who are not even in a current relationship. In general, these data are consistent with the results of a daily monitoring study that showed that self-critical individuals make fewer requests for social support and have a general style that distances them from other people (see Mongrain, 1998).

New research in our laboratories continues to explore the association between self-silencing and both dependency and self-criticism. As can be seen in Table 13.1, the initial results of a new study conducted on 227 university students from York University are very much in keeping with our previous results (Flett, Besser, & Hewitt, 2009).

Overall levels of silencing the self were associated with both self-criticism ($r = .49$) and dependency ($r = .37$). Self-criticism was associated significantly

Table 13.1 Correlations between Self-Silencing and Personality Measures

| Measures | Total | Self-Silencing Measures | | | |
		External	Care	Self-Silence	Divided Self
Self-criticism	.49	.58	.29	.33	.48
Dependency	.37	.46	.47	.21	.14
Self-oriented perf	.01	.09	.01	−.02	.04
Other-oriented perf	−.01	.05	−.11	−.08	.12
Socially prescribed perf	.27	.29	.10	.21	.31
Perfectionism cognitions	.40	.49	.32	.22	.34
PSP-promotion	.26	.31	.10	.19	.24
PSP-avoid imperfect	.28	.35	.22	.20	.19
PSP-avoid disclosing	.31	.26	.11	.28	.34
High standards	.09	.13	.02	.04	.09
Concern over mistakes	.36	.39	.23	.26	.30
Doubts about actions	.33	.38	.22	.25	.28
Parental expectations	.14	.07	.09	.12	.13
Parental criticism	.23	.21	.12	.21	.26
Shame	.38	.45	.22	.30	.32
Neg social interactions	.35	.33	.25	.34	.37
Daily hassles	.45	.44	.41	.30	.34
Depression	.45	.41	.30	.34	.47

Note: $p < .01$ when r is .18 or greater. Based on $n = 227$ students (157 women, 70 men). The following abbreviations were used: self-oriented perf (self-oriented perfectionism); other-oriented perf (other-oriented perfectionism); socially prescribed perf (socially prescribed perfectionism); PSP-promotion (perfectionistic self-promotion); PSP-avoid imperfect (the need to avoid appearing imperfect); PSP-avoid disclosing (the need to avoid disclosing imperfections); and neg social interactions (negative social interactions).

with all four Silencing the Self Scale (STSS; Jack & Dill, 1991) subscales, with the strongest association being between self-criticism and an externalized view of the self. The four subscales are Externalized Self-Perception, Care as Self-Sacrifice, Silencing the Self, and Divided Self (i.e., the public self does not reflect the true self). Dependency was correlated significantly with three of the four STSS subscales; the only subscale not associated with dependency was Divided Self.

Given the link between self-silencing and self-criticism, it is not surprising that self-silencing and self-blame are related. Ali and colleagues (2000) found a very strong association between self-silencing and self-blame among women with irritable bowel syndrome. A history of emotional abuse during adulthood was also associated with self-silencing and self-blame. This scale included items assessing various forms of emotional maltreatment, including being denigrated, insulted, and humiliated.

In our new study of self-criticism and dependency, we also included a self-report measure of shame, in line with Jack's (1999a) observations about the relevance of shame in self-silencing. Specifically, we administered the Experience of Shame Scale (ESS) by Andrews, Qian, and Valentine (2002). This 25-item measure assesses characterological shame, behavioral shame, and bodily shame. Shame and self-criticism both involve negative self-evaluation, but shame involves a sweeping judgment of the total self (i.e., a global attribution) along with the sense that others are aware of this shamefulness. Shame is also similar to factors and processes presumed to underscore self-silencing because people who experience shame are cognizant of self-discrepancies and feel they are not meeting ideal standards (Tangney, Niedenthal, Covert, & Barlow, 1998), as we discuss in greater detail later. Jack (1999a) noted that self-silencing stems, in part, from comparing the self to harsh, idealistic standards.

Our current results involving shame and self-silencing are also displayed in Table 13.1. As might be expected, ESS scores were associated with total self-silencing and with scores on all four STSS subscales. Andrews and colleagues (2002) found that shame predicted susceptibility to depression in a longitudinal investigation, so it follows that individuals who self-silence and are character-ized by shame are also at risk for substantial and persistent distress.

Comparative analyses suggest that shame and self-criticism have comparable associations with indices of distress, and that shame, self-criticism, and dependency are intercorrelated (see Flett et al., 2009). However, the results of a regression analysis predicting overall self-silencing scores indicate that these measures are not redundant with each other. Significant unique variance in self-silencing is predicted by shame, self-criticism, and dependency, and we regard this as evidence of the unique aspects of the link between shame and self-silencing.

We now turn to a description of perfectionism and its association with self-silencing. Perfectionism is a construct that has been linked with self-criticism, both conceptually and empirically (see Blatt, 1995). Given the link between self-criticism and self-silencing, it follows that perfectionism may also be associated with self-silencing. This possibility is explored in the next segment of this chapter.

Perfectionism: A Multidimensional Construct

A focus on the attainment of high standards is a continuing theme in research on personality and depression. Extensive research has explored the role of individual differences in perfectionism (Cox & Enns, 2003; Hewitt & Flett, 1991). This research indicates that certain dimensions of perfectionism may be associated not only with concurrent depressive symptoms but also with the chronicity and persistence of depressive symptoms (Cox & Enns, 2003; Hewitt, Flett, Ediger, Norton, & Flynn, 1998). Research with the Multidimensional Perfectionism Scale (MPS; Hewitt & Flett, 1991) has focused on three dimensions: self-oriented perfectionism (i.e., exceedingly high personal standards), other-oriented perfec-tionism (i.e., demanding perfection from others), and socially prescribed perfectionism (i.e., a pressure to be perfect imposed on the self). Socially pre-scribed perfectionism has shown a consistent association with depression (see Flett & Hewitt, 2002; Flett, Besser, & Hewitt, 2005).

Another highly relevant perspective for understanding depression involves individual differences in self-silencing. The construct of self-silencing was hypothesized by Jack (1991) to account for the preponderance of depression among women. However, subsequent research has shown that self-silencing is relevant for both women and men (Thompson, 1995). People high in self-silencing are self-sacrificing individuals who keep their distress to themselves in an attempt to maintain or improve interpersonal relationships. Their distress often takes the form of unexpressed anger (see Jack, 1999a, 2001). People high in self-silencing conceal their true feelings out of desires to maintain relation-ships and obtain the approval of significant others.

A link between perfectionism and self-silencing follows from Jack's (1999a) observation that the standards used for self-evaluation are central to an under-standing of self-silencing behavior. Jack suggested that a sense of inferiority and self-reproach stems from the idealistic standards that the self-silencer uses to judge the self. The standards themselves have a social aspect because they reflect social dictates and a sense of being obliged to act in a socially approved of manner and to achieve prescribed goals. Unfortunately, for self-silencing indi-viduals, this focus on ideals and being perfect as the accepted standard should make them susceptible to dysphoria when they perceive a substantial gap between the actual self and the goal of being perfect.

Jack (1999a) provided a series of compelling case examples of distressed people who clearly exhibited perfectionistic characteristics and who engaged in self-silencing. These people appear to suffer from the "tyranny of the shoulds" described by Horney (1950) and by Ellis (2002), and they seem to be character-ized jointly by elements of both socially prescribed perfectionism and self-oriented perfectionism. For instance, a physician named Carol described the perfectionistic pressures inherent in the "Supermom syndrome." Specifically, she noted that:

> You can't be Supermom and can't do it all, and yet we all have this image that we can, and we measure ourselves by the standards of our mothers in terms of raising kids. You know, I feel guilty when I'm not there with the warm milk and cookies and when I'm not putting every Band-Aid on. And then I'm guilty because I'm not enough of a spouse for my husband, and I'm guilty because I'm not doing an adequate job professionally and never quite getting it right. (Jack, 1999a, p. 233)

Carol responded to these pressures by presenting as a picture of a person who apparently acquiesced to these demands while silencing the self.

Jack (1999a) also reported the case of a male physician named Dan. This doctor revealed his tendency toward self-silencing by engaging in workaholic and perfectionistic tendencies that were in accordance with social obligations and expectations. He was described as suffering from a litany of shoulds that were rooted, in part, in an externalized self-perception and "acquiescence to unrealistic standards" (p. 239).

Our analysis of the various perfectionism dimensions indicates that self-silencing is particularly relevant to socially prescribed perfectionism, given the tendency for socially prescribed perfectionists to need approval and to strive to please others (Hewitt & Flett, 1991, 2004). These people feel that perfectionistic demands have been imposed on them. This sense of being treated unfairly should foster a sense of resentment that is akin to the anger of self-silencing women described by Jack (2001). Also, socially prescribed perfectionism is associated with passive, indirect responses to life problems in a manner that is reminiscent of self-silencing (Hewitt & Flett, 2002). A link between socially prescribed perfectionism and self-silencing can be inferred from results of a study of dating students (see Flett, Hewitt, Shapiro, & Rayman, 2003). This study showed that socially prescribed perfectionism was associated with low scores on a measure of "voice." Voicing one's concerns is one way of responding to dissatisfaction in interpersonal relationships.

Research on Silencing the Self and Perfectionism

The initial study of perfectionism and self-silencing was conducted by Geller, Cockell, Hewitt, Goldner, and Flett (2000). They administered the MPS and the STSS to 21 anorexic patients, 21 women with other psychiatric disorders, and 21 normal control participants. Geller and colleagues (2000) examined the correlations for the total sample by collapsing across the groups. These analyses showed that both self-oriented and socially prescribed perfectionism were associated robustly with all STSS measures (r's ranging from .55 to .77). However, there is a need to re-examine the magnitude of the associations between silencing the self and trait perfectionism in another sample given that the extreme scores among the group of anorexic patients likely inflated the magnitude of these correlations.

The associations among perfectionism and silencing the self in college students were explored by Flett, Besser, Hewitt, and Davis (2007). A sample of 202 university students completed the MPS (Hewitt & Flett, 1991, 2004), the STSS, and Radloff's (1977) CES-D Scale. The results showed that self-oriented perfectionism was not associated significantly with overall scale scores, but there was a significant association between self-oriented perfectionism and the Silencing the Self subscale. The main finding that emerged was that socially prescribed perfectionism was associated significantly with the overall scale score ($r = .32$) and with all four STSS subscales, with correlations ranging from .19 to .42. Additional analyses tested the possibility that self-silencing may mediate or moderate the association between socially prescribed perfectionism and depression. Indeed, we found that depression was elevated among socially prescribed perfectionists who were also high in self-silencing. These data are described in more detail in a subsequent segment of this chapter.

Recently, we have re-examined the association between perfectionism and silencing the self as part of the study mentioned earlier that also included indices of dependency and self-criticism. This newer investigation is unique in that it examined perfectionism and silencing the self from a more comprehensive perspective. Specifically, this study included four different measures of perfectionism: (1) Hewitt and Flett's (1991) MPS; (2) the MPS (Frost, Marten, Lahart, & Rosenblate, 1990); (3) the Perfectionism Cognitions Inventory (PCI; Flett, Hewitt, Blankstein, & Gray, 1998); and (4) the Perfectionistic Self-Presentation Scale (Hewitt et al., 2003). We will focus initially on the results involving trait levels of self-oriented, other-oriented, and socially prescribed perfectionism. The pattern of correlations obtained in this study was very much in keeping with the findings obtained by Flett and colleagues (2007). As can be seen in Table 13.1, self-oriented and other-oriented perfectionism were not associated significantly with silencing the self. However, socially prescribed perfectionism had a modest but significant association with overall scale scores. It was also associated with three of the four STSS subscales with the strongest associations being with subscales assessing Externalized Self-Perception and Divided Self.

While these data are interesting and certainly fit with our conceptualization of how trait perfectionism and silencing the self should be associated, many of the findings obtained with the other perfectionism dimensions included in this study were more robust in a statistical sense, and they seem particularly meaningful from a theoretical perspective. First, consider the results obtained with the Frost MPS (see Table 13.1). Frost and colleagues (1990) developed a multifactor measure that assesses aspects of perfectionism directed toward the self (high personal standards, doubts about actions, and concern over mistakes) and two aspects of perfectionism that reflect the perceived presence of parental demands on the self (i.e., high parental expectations and parental criticism). Historically, research has established that concern over mistakes and doubts about actions are the two dimensions linked most consistently with psychological distress, and experimental work has focused on the negative reactions of people high in concern over mistakes once a mistake has been made (for a review, see Frost & DiBartolo, 2002).

As can be seen in Table 13.1, both concern over mistakes and doubts about actions were associated significantly with silencing the self. A smaller but still significant association was also found between silencing the self and high parental criticism. The link with concern over mistakes suggests that for some people, their self-silencing is motivated by the desire to avoid making mistakes and the consequences of these mistakes. The nature of these consequences can vary substantially as a function of the individual's interpersonal context. If we were assessing the battered women who were included in the research described originally by Jack and Dill (1992), these women were exceptionally high in silencing the self. Undoubtedly their focus would be on fears about making a mistake (or being perceived as making a mistake) that would then provide a misguided, self-serving rationale for their abusive partner to engage in further mistreatment. However, the current findings were derived from a sample of university students. A significant proportion of these students indicated that they have experienced maltreatment during childhood, and this accounts, in part, for the obtained association. However, other students have not been maltreated and the link between silencing the self and concern over mistakes simply reflects fears of failure and their great sensitivity to failure feedback and the self-esteem implications of being imperfect.

Past theory and research have focused on self-silencing in the romantic relationship context. A study by Thompson, Whiffen, and Aube (2001) found that self-silencing was associated with perceiving the partner as critical and intolerant, and both of these factors were associated with greater depression. In this context, they posited that self-silencing is a form of interpersonal coping. However, our results with the Frost MPS showed that other forms of criticism such as perceived parental criticism are also linked with self-silencing. One important direction for future research is to examine self-silencing in children and adolescents. Clearly, children and adolescents who desire parental approval but resent perfectionistic pressures being put on them are in a cognitive and emotional bind that is akin to the conflict described by Horney (1950): When children are not able to express their anger toward parental figures, it becomes repressed and creates basic hostility and basic anxiety. The hostility must remain repressed and perhaps gets directed inward at the self.

Self-Silencing and Perfectionistic Automatic Thoughts

Table 13.1 also includes information about the association between self-silencing and perfectionism cognitions. It is important to assess perfectionism cognitions and self-statements because there have been extensive writings on the internal dialogues of self-silencing individuals and how the internal dialogue fails to be expressed (Jack, 1999a,b, 2001). The PCI (Flett et al., 1998) is an attempt to assess automatic thoughts about the need to be perfect and cognitive rumination over mistakes and imperfections that characterize perfectionists who can't help thinking about mistakes. The PCI is based on the premise that perfectionists who sense a discrepancy between their actual self and the ideal self or their actual level of goal attainment and high ideals will tend to experience automatic thoughts that reflect perfectionistic themes (Besser, Flett, & Hewitt, 2004; see Flett et al., 1998). It is believed that perfectionists with high levels of perfectionism cognitions are especially susceptible to negative affect in the form of depression about failure to attain perfection in the past, as well as in the form of anxiety about the likelihood of failing to attain perfection in the future.

The PCI has a range of item content that reflects the frequency of direct thoughts about the need to be perfect, as well as thoughts of an individual's cognitive awareness of his or her imperfections. Several thoughts on the PCI such as "I should be perfect," "I should never make the same mistake twice," and "I must be efficient at all times" are very much in keeping with general observations by Albert Ellis (2002) about perfectionism and irrational thinking. Much of the automatic thought content comes in the forms of "shoulds" and "oughts" that reflect a pressure to live up to real or imagined expectations.

As can be seen in Table 13.1, the PCI was correlated with overall silencing the self scores ($r = .40$), and it was also associated with all four subscales. Secondary analyses of these data suggest that PCI predicts unique variance in self-silencing in hierarchical regression analyses, over and above the variance attributable to trait perfectionism (Nepon, Flett, Besser, & Hewitt, 2009). Thus, the internal dialogue of some self-silencing individuals is focused on the need to be perfect and an awareness of not measuring up to extreme perfectionistic ideals. As noted by Ellis (2002), the ultimate question here is why has perfectionism attained such an irrational importance to the extent that the quest for perfection can dominate cognitive processes and be ruminated about over and over? While the family may play a significant role in the development of perfectionism, we must also acknowledge cultural pressures and messages that emphasize the need to be perfect in general and to be perfect in specific life domains (e.g., perfect physical appearance) in order to be regarded as a worthwhile individual who is desired by other people.

Silencing the Self and Perfectionistic Self-Presentation

Horney (1950) stated that when it comes to emotional displays, neurotic perfectionists tend to display friendliness toward others because there is a palpable sense that they *should* be friendly out of a prescribed need to be obedient and devoted to others. This observation by Horney predated the more recent discovery of a facet of the perfectionism construct known as perfectionistic self-presentation; it is this facet that seems most relevant to silencing the self. Perfectionistic self-presentation is based on the premise that certain perfectionists are highly invested in covering up their mistakes and are preoccupied with trying to present themselves as perfect (i.e., self-promotion) or defensively minimizing the number of mistakes that are on display for others to see.

A need to present a perfect self is implicated in the accounts that were obtained by Stephens (1987) as part of her investigation of 50 adult female suicide attempters. Consider the following excerpt:

> My mother wanted me to be perfect, strong, able to take care of any kind of problem that came forth. It was a burden to me because I couldn't show her how truly things bothered me. I had to be this super daughter that never got upset and never cracked or anything and it was a really *hard* thing. She put out, 'Oh, my

daughter's never given me any trouble. She's a *perfect* daughter; she's always been a *perfect* daughter.' I didn't want to be perfect. I wasn't strong; I was crumbling inside. I wasn't perfect. (Stephens, 1987, p. 114)

This excerpt highlights the fact that socially prescribed perfectionism and the need to appear perfect can be linked inextricably for many people. In this particular instance, the need to present a façade stemmed from maternal expectations.

Hewitt and colleagues (2003) hypothesized that there are stable individual differences in the tendency to engage in perfectionistic self-presentation and that there are three components to perfectionistic self-presentation. The Perfectionistic Self-Presentation Scale (PSPS, Hewitt et al., 2003) was developed to assess three aspects of perfectionistic self-presentation—namely, perfectionistic self-promotion, an unwillingness to display imperfections, and an unwillingness to disclose imperfections to others. This third dimension involves avoidance of personal communications about issues that could reveal the perfectionist's flaws.

Initial research indicates that perfectionistic self-presentation is indeed a multidimensional construct (Hewitt et al., 2003). Although perfectionistic self-presentation is correlated significantly with trait perfectionism, a perfectionistic self-presentational style still predicts unique variance in psychological distress after taking into account the variance attributable to perfectionism as assessed by the respective Multidimensional Perfectionism Scales. Other research with the PSPS indicates that perfectionistic self-presentation is associated with low levels of appearance self-esteem (Hewitt, Flett, & Ediger, 1995) and relationship difficulties in married couples (Flett, Hewitt, Shapiro, & Rayman, 2003; Habke, Hewitt, & Flett, 1999). Elevations in perfectionistic self-presentation are also correlated with facets of the anxiety sensitivity construct, including a fear of expressing publicly observable symptoms of anxiety (Flett, Greene, & Hewitt, 2004).

There is little doubt that self-silencing individuals engage in perfectionistic self-presentation. Jack (1999a), in fact, suggested that while women may look passive and compliant, it actually takes a great deal of effort to consciously self-monitor and inhibit the self in order to project this image. It is even more difficult when the image being presented is one that emphasizes flawlessness.

Accumulating evidence is in keeping with the proposed association between self-silencing and perfectionistic self-presentation. Indeed, Geller and colleagues (2000) found evidence of a robust link between perfectionistic self-presentation and silencing the self, but we felt that the select nature of their clinical sample pointed to a need to re-examine this issue. Accordingly, the PSPS was included in our new study conducted with university students (see Nepon et al., 2009). The results are shown in Table 13.1. Note that all three PSPS facets were associated with the STSS Silencing the Self subscale, with the strongest association being between self-silencing and the need to avoid disclosing imperfections to others.

This association has particular implications in therapy and counseling contexts because it is unlikely that perfectionistic self-silencers would be willing to reveal their true concerns and past mistakes and shortcomings, if they even sought help in the first place. The help-seeking process can be regarded as a process that involves threats to self-esteem because inadequacies and imperfections will have to be revealed to others (for a related discussion, see Hewitt & Flett, 2007).

Our most recent work has been focused more extensively on this link between self-silencing and perfectionistic self-presentation. The purpose of these investigations was to not only extend our findings but also examine the generalizability of the obtained associations because the data described thus far were obtained entirely from Canadian university students. Our recent work conducted in Israel attests to the generalizability of these findings, briefly outlined next.

A recent experimental study was conducted to examine the extent to which individual differences are associated with upset after experiencing a public humiliation (Besser, Flett, & Hewitt, 2009b). Our interest in humiliation stems not only because of its potential relevance to self-presentational concerns and self-silencing but also from evidence indicating that humiliation is a potent interpersonal stressor that elicits profound depressive reactions (see Brown, Harris, & Hepworth, 1995; Farmer & McGuffin, 2003). It was our expectation that perfectionistic self-presenters high in self-silencing would be especially distressed in such a situation. A sample of 150 students in Israel completed a battery of personality measures and reported their affective reactions to a hypothetical scenario (i.e., learning while with other people that the news has been made public that one's partner has been unfaithful). This focus on hypothetical scenarios is in keeping with eliciting feelings of shame and guilt by having people respond to hypothetical scenarios listed on measures such as the Test of Self-Conscious Affect (Tangney, Wagner, & Gramzow, 1989), which assesses emotions such as shame and guilt. Analyses of our data have confirmed that perfectionistic self-presenters, relative to those low in perfectionistic self-presentation, do indeed report stronger distress reactions. Self-silencing was not associated with stronger distress reactions. However, in keeping with the investigation by Flett and colleagues (2007), strong associations were found between self-silencing and perfectionistic self-presentation. This pattern of findings suggests that those people who are prone to distress following humiliation will be likely to "suffer in silence" and not express their distress to others.

Another new study with data collected in Israel examines perfectionism, self-silencing, depression, and marital adjustment in married couples (Besser, Flett, & Hewitt, 2009a). Both perfectionism and self-silencing have been implicated separately in prior research on poor functioning in relationships (see Haring, Hewitt, & Flett, 2003; Harper & Welsh, 2007). A unique aspect of this new study conducted with 72 couples is that each participant provided self-reports of self-silencing and depression and they also rated their partner's degree of self-silencing and depression. Initial analyses have confirmed that

Table 13.2 Correlations between Self-Silencing and Perfectionistic Self-Presentation

		Self-Silencing Measures			
Measures	Total	External	Care	Self-Silence	Divided Self
PSP-promotion	.25**	.25*	.08	.21*	.24**
PSP-avoid imperfect	.34**	.38*	.13	.28**	.25**
PSP-avoid disclosing	.37**	.27*	.13	.36**	.33**

Note: *$p < .05$; **$p < .01$. Based on $n = 144$ respondents. The following abbreviations were used: PSP-promotion (perfectionistic self-promotion); PSP-avoid imperfect (the need to avoid appearing imperfect); and PSP-avoid disclosing (the need to avoid disclosing imperfections).

both perfectionistic self-presentation and self-silencing associated significantly with self-reported depression and reduced marital satisfaction. In addition, as can be seen in Table 13.2, perfectionistic self-presentation and self-silencing are correlated significantly. The magnitude of the correlations across the four STSS factors is quite comparable to the magnitude of correlations reported in Table 13.1.

Personality Vulnerabilities and Depression: Self-Silencing as a Moderator or Mediator

In a previous review paper, Flett and colleagues (1995) issued a call for research that tests the extent to which established risk factors combine within an individual such that the confluence of factors is linked with elevated levels of distress. It follows logically that someone who is characterized by high levels of self-criticism, dependency, and perfectionism should tend to have greater distress than the person who has high self-criticism but not elevated levels of the other two personality factors. By the same token, it follows that people characterized jointly by personality vulnerabilities and a relatively high level of self-silencing will experience greater levels of dysphoria (i.e., the moderational hypothesis). A moderator is present when one variable (i.e., an independent variable) is moderated or influenced by the level of another variable (i.e., the moderator); these variables combine and interact to have a joint influence on the level of another variable.[1]

It is just as possible that one of the ways that personality vulnerabilities translate into elevated levels of dysphoria is through the already established association that these personality vulnerability factors have with silencing the self (i.e., the mediational hypothesis). A mediator is when an association exists between two other variables because of their mutual link with an intervening variable, which is known as the mediator.

We have evaluated both of these possibilities in our initial investigations in this area. Specifically, the Flett and colleagues' (2007) study with self-silencing and the Hewitt and Flett MPS also evaluated whether the association between perfectionism and depression is moderated or mediated by self-silencing. In particular, we tested whether socially prescribed perfectionism interacts with elevated self-silencing to produce elevated levels of depression and the related possibility that self-silencing mediates the link between socially prescribed perfectionism and depression. We observed that at the conceptual level, the "silencing the self" construct has several components and features that are relevant to socially prescribed perfectionism and that ought to combine with socially prescribed perfectionism to produce elevated depression. In general, self-silencing is believed to contribute to a "loss of self" that is linked with depression (see Drew, Heesacker, Frost, & Oelke, 2004), and this loss of self should be particularly deleterious for socially prescribed perfectionists who feel hopeless to achieve the standards imposed on them. Also, certain aspects of the silencing the self construct should be particularly damaging for socially prescribed perfectionists. Most notably, individuals with a high socially prescribed perfectionism who also tend to judge themselves by external standards should be at risk because the impact of their inability to meet expectations is magnified.

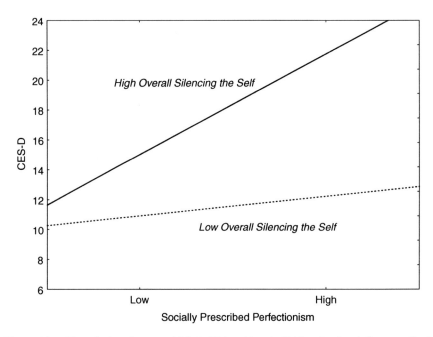

Figure 13.1 The relations between high (+SD) and low (−SD) levels of socially prescribed perfectionism and depressive symptoms for high (+SD) and low (−SD) levels of overall Silencing the Self.

The main findings of interest that emerged from our statistical tests of the hypothesized moderational effect(s) are summarized in Figures 13.1 and 13.2.

It was found that overall self-silencing did indeed interact with socially prescribed perfectionism to predict increased distress. Further analyses of self-silencing in terms of the individual STSS subscales found that it was the Externalized Self-Perception factor that combined with socially prescribed perfectionism to produce elevated levels of depressive symptoms. This follows in that a tendency to judge the self by external standards should magnify the salience and impact of socially prescribed perfectionism on personal functioning.

Other tests supported the mediation hypothesis. The notion that self-silencing is a mediator of the link between socially prescribed perfectionism and depression is in keeping with coping models that suggest that a maladaptive response to stressful circumstances mediates or moderates the link between perfectionism and depression (Flett, Besser, & Hewitt, 2005; see Hewitt & Flett, 2002). In the present instance, the tendency for socially prescribed perfectionists to be high in self-silencing would constitute an ineffective way of responding to interpersonal conflict and stress, and this tendency to silence the self could, in turn, contribute

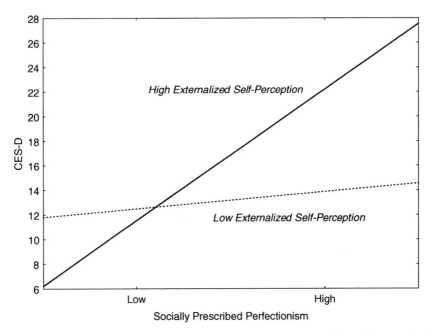

Figure 13.2 The relations between high (+SD) and low (−SD) levels of socially prescribed perfectionism and depressive symptoms for high (+SD) and low (−SD) levels of Externalized Self-Perception subscale.

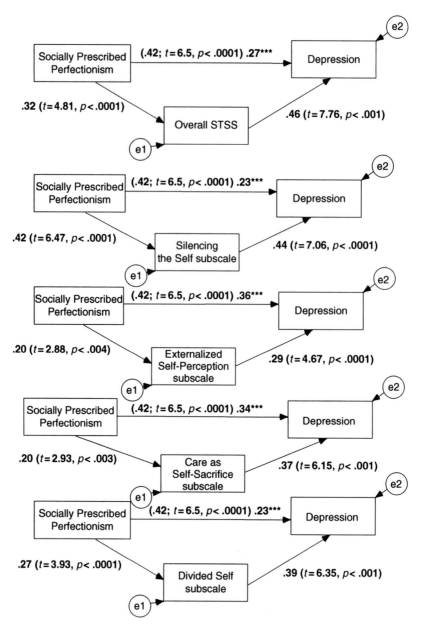

Figure 13.3 Direct and indirect associations between socially prescribed perfectionism and depression and the mediating role of STSS and STSS subscales.
Note: Bolded estimates are significant regression coefficient βs. Numbers in parentheses are βs before STSS scores were entered into the model. Small circles represent residual variances, and unidirectional arrows depict hypothesized associations.

to depression. A mediational model is also suggested to the extent that self-silencing does indeed involve a loss of sense of self and a negative self-view, which, in turn, should be related to depression.

What did the mediational tests reveal? The results of these analyses are summarized in Figure 13.3. First, the mediational analyses showed that all facets of the self-silencing construct partially but significantly mediated the link between socially prescribed perfectionism and depression. Thus, some of the dysphoria reported by socially prescribed perfectionists is due to the tendency for socially prescribed perfectionism to be associated with various aspects of self-silencing.

Collectively, these data highlight the need to consider the interplay between self-silencing and personality vulnerability factors when predicting levels of psychological stress. As indicated by Hewitt and Flett (2002), perfectionists can respond with maladaptive coping responses or adaptive coping responses when confronted with stressful, challenging circumstances. Self-silencing in this situation can be a form of avoidance that may seem adaptive but actually perpetuates elevated psychological distress. Clearly, this possibility merits further investigation in longitudinal research.

In addition, research should consider other factors of potential importance that are common to the various personality vulnerability factors. One important direction is to incorporate individual differences in rumination; parenthetically, both rumination and self-silencing were suggested as factors that contribute to the gender difference in depression. Rumination has been linked empirically with self-criticism, dependency, and perfectionism (for a review, see Nolen-Hoeksema, Wisco, & Lybubomirsky, 2008). Rumination is also associated with shame (Orth, Berking, & Burkhardt, 2006), and has also been linked with silencing the self (Hart & Thompson, 1996). The tendency to brood should keep current and previous inadequacies, mistakes, and humiliations active cognitively and highly salient for the distress-prone individual, and this should contribute to prolonged depression while the vulnerable individual continues to engage in self-silencing.

Personality Vulnerabilities, Silencing the Self, and Stress

The next segment of this chapter explores the significance, both theoretical and practical, of a possible association between silencing the self and stress. Although several authors have provided accounts that suggest that people high in self-silencing are exposed to elevated levels of stress, our survey of the literature revealed few empirical attempts to examine stress and self-silencing. The primary exception is a study of life stress and self-silencing in unipolar depression by Ali, Oatley, and Toner (2002). Stress and the contextual meaning of stress were assessed in this study via semistructured interviews. Ali and colleagues (2002) confirmed that there was an association between self-silencing and depression in this clinical sample, and they found higher levels of self-silencing among women with relational stressors. Finally, an exploratory phase of this research showed that women with lower levels of self-silencing at the beginning of treatment showed greater reductions in depressive symptoms over time, relative to women with high levels of self-silencing prior to treatment.

Dependency, self-criticism, and perfectionism have all been linked consistently with stress, and there have been tests of the congruency hypothesis (i.e., achievement-based factors such as self-criticism and perfectionism will interact with the experience of achievement stressors to produce depression, while interpersonally based factors such as dependency will interact with the experience of interpersonal stressors to produce depression). Overall support for the congruency hypothesis has been mixed at best, but there is no doubt that there is a consistent association between these personality factors and stress.

The finding of an association between self-silencing and relational stress reported by Ali and colleagues (2002) fits nicely with past research in our laboratories on a particular form of stress. Specifically, we have focused on stress in the form of frequent negative social interactions. Negative social interactions have a substantial and negative impact on emotional reactions and thought processes, especially when the negative social interaction involves a conflict important with a significant other. Several researchers have reported a link between negative social interactions and reports of psychological distress (e.g., Bolger, DeLongis, Kessler, & Schilling, 1989; Rook, 1984; Sandler & Barrera, 1984). For instance, Bolger and colleagues (1989) had subjects complete diary accounts and provide mood ratings over a six-week period. Analyses established that interpersonal conflicts were the most upsetting stressors and these stressors accounted for over 80% of the variance in daily mood ratings.

Flett, Hewitt, Garshowitz, and Martin (1997) found in a sample of students that higher depression symptom scores were correlated significantly with the frequency of negative social interactions and with socially prescribed perfectionism, sociotropy, and autonomy. Additional results indicated that the frequency of negative social interactions accounted for unique variance in depressive symptoms over and above the variance predicted by personality traits, but it did not interact with these personality traits to predict unique variance in depressive symptoms. It was also found that the reported frequency of negative social interactions was correlated positively with socially prescribed perfectionism, sociotropy, and autonomy, especially among women.

Because self-silencing and interpersonal stress are seemingly associated, and frequent negative social interactions are linked with a perfectionistic orientation, we examined self-silencing, personality, and interpersonal stress by including the Inventory of Negative Social Interactions (INSI; Lakey, Tardiff, & Drew, 1994) along with the other measures listed in Table 13.1. Lakey and colleagues (1994) developed the INSI to assess the frequency of negative social interactions. It can be seen in Table 13.1 that negative social interactions were associated with overall levels of self-silencing as well as elevated scores on all four STSS subscales.

We also included a measure of daily hassles that was created specifically by Kohn and his colleagues for use with university students (see Kohn, Lafreniere, & Gurevich, 1990). This measure taps various factors that students may experience on a daily basis including a social mistreatment factor. Past research has established that daily life hassles represent a chronic and destructive form of stress that seems to have a greater negative impact on well-being than does the experience of major life events (see Blankstein & Flett, 1992, for a discussion). In this instance, it can be seen in Table 13.1 that self-silencing was also associated with daily hassles.

These findings combine to suggest that people who have vulnerable personalities and who tend to engage in self-silencing are exposed to highly deleterious forms of stress. Daily interpersonal events that involve negative social interactions are bound to have a profound influence on these individuals, both in the short term in terms of distress and ruminating over upsetting events and in the long term in terms of exacting a significant toll through health consequences. There is growing evidence of the benefits of coping via emotional expression (Stanton et al., 2002), yet here we are describing individuals who have a tendency to be highly stressed and to react strongly to stress yet being unwilling or unable to express the stress, distress, and concerns to others. Clearly, these individuals should benefit greatly from stress counseling and other treatment interventions designed to encourage them to express themselves and seek out the support of other people.

Personality and Self-Silencing in Women Versus Men

The final segment of this chapter briefly considers the issue of whether the link between personality vulnerabilities and self-silencing is equally applicable to women and men. At present, systematic research on personality and self-silencing has not been conducted, so little is known about possible gender differences in the relevance and the associations that self-silencing have with personality constructs such as dependency, self-criticism, and perfectionism. Most existing research has been conducted with university student samples, and this reliance on student samples could possibly obscure gender differences; male university students may have more homogenous experiences than other people as a result of the common components of the student role and associated lifestyle. Thus, given the paucity of data, any observations here about gender differences are admittedly speculative.

This caution notwithstanding, it is important to highlight some key issues and provide suggestions for future research. Our new study on self-silencing in couples yielded little evidence of gender differences, so it is quite possible that there are more similarities between women and men than differences when it comes to the personality and self-silencing link. Nevertheless, it is quite possible that differences are expressed and experienced in different roles and interpersonal spheres (e.g., see Mauthner, Chapter 21).

Conclusion

Although Jack (1999a) has noted correctly that self-silencing is distinct from personality traits because self-silencing can fluctuate according to current relationship outcomes and issues, the current chapter indicates that self-silencing is linked clearly with dispositional personality traits associated with vulnerability to depression. Our review established that dependency, self-criticism, and various dimensions of perfectionism are all linked significantly with silencing the self. Moreover, there is some evidence indicating that self-silencing acts as a mediator or moderator in the association between personality and depression. One way of interpreting the mediational results is that self-silencing is one of the highly maladaptive responses of vulnerable individuals who are clearly very high in interpersonal sensitivity and responsiveness to negative interpersonal interactions and associated stressors. Although much of our analysis focused on self-silencing adults in interpersonal relationships, the association between self-silencing and personality vulnerability suggests that self-silencing is perhaps a long-lasting style that may be detectable among vulnerable children and adolescents. Regardless of whether this turns out to be true, as determined by future research, it is most certainly the case that there is the potential for great risk and distress among self-silencing people who are also characterized by personality vulnerabilities. In general, our analysis highlights the need for continuing vigilance among clinicians, counselors, and educators and society as a whole because certain people are particularly vulnerable and they may seem to be functioning well even though they are suffering in silence.

Note

1. In this instance, we use the term "mediator" to refer to a variable Z (i.e., silencing the self) that accounts for the effect of a predictor variable X (i.e., trait personality vulnerabilities) on a criterion variable Y (i.e., loneliness), and we use the term "moderator" to refer to a variable Z (i.e., silencing the self) that qualifies the effect of a predictor variable X (i.e., trait personality vulnerabilities) on a criterion variable Y (i.e., depression) (Baron & Kenny, 1986).

References

Ali, A., Oatley, K., & Toner, B. B. (2002). Life stress, self-silencing, and domains of meaning in unipolar depression: An investigation of an outpatient sample of women. *Journal of Social and Clinical Psychology, 21*, 669–685.

Ali, A., Toner, B. B., Stuckless, N., Gallop, R., Diamant, N. E., Gould, M. I., et al. (2000). Emotional abuse, self-blame, and self-silencing in women with irritable bowel syndrome. *Psychosomatic Medicine, 62*, 76–82.

Andrews, B., Qian, M., & Valentine, J. D. (2002). Predicting depressive symptoms with a new measure of shame: The Experience of Shame Scale. *British Journal of Clinical Psychology, 41*, 29–42.

Baron, R. M., & Kenny, D. A. (1986). The moderator-mediator variable distinction in social psychological research: Conceptual, strategic and statistical considerations. *Journal of Personality and Social Psychology, 51*, 1173–1182.

Besser, A. (2004). Self- and best-friend assessments of personality vulnerability and defenses in the prediction of depression. *Social Behavior and Personality, 32*, 559–594.

Besser, A., Flett, G. L., & Davis, R. A. (2003). Self-criticism, dependency, silencing the self, and loneliness: A test of a mediational model. *Personality and Individual Differences, 35*, 1735–1752.

Besser, A., Flett, G. L., & Hewitt, P. L. (2004). Perfectionism, cognition, and affect in response to performance failure vs. success. *Journal of Rational-Emotive and Cognitive-Behavior Therapy, 22*, 301–328.

Besser, A., Flett, G. L., & Hewitt, P. L. (2009a). Perfectionism and self-silencing in relationship adjustment and distress in couples. Manuscript in preparation.

Besser, A., Flett, G. L., & Hewitt, P. L. (2009b). Perfectionistic self-presentation, self-silencing, and distress in response to humiliation. Manuscript in preparation.

Besser, A., & Priel, B. (2003a). A multisource approach to self-critical vulnerability to depression: The moderating role of attachment. *Journal of Personality, 71*, 515–556.

Besser, A., & Priel, B. (2003b). Trait vulnerability and coping strategies in the transition to motherhood. *Current Psychology, 22*, 57–72.

Besser, A., & Priel, B. (2005a). The apple does not fall far from the tree: Attachment styles and personality vulnerabilities to depression in three generations of women. *Personality and Social Psychology Bulletin, 31*, 1052–1073.

Besser, A., & Priel, B. (2005b). Interpersonal relatedness and self-definition in late adulthood depression: Personality predispositions, and protective factors. *Social Behavior and Personality, 33*, 351–382.

Besser, A., Priel, B., Flett, G. L., & Wiznitzer, A. (2007). Linear and nonlinear models of vulnerability to depression: Personality and postpartum depression in a high risk population. *Individual Differences Research, 5*, 1–29.

Blankstein, K. R., & Flett, G. L. (1992). Specificity in the assessment of daily hassles: Life stress, locus of control, and adjustment in college students. *Canadian Journal of Behavioural Science, 24*, 382–398.

Blatt, S. J. (1974). Levels of object representation in anaclitic and introjective depression. *The Psychoanalytic Study of the Child, 24*, 107–157.

Blatt, S. J. (1990). Interpersonal relatedness and self-definition: Two personality configurations and their implications for psychopathology and psychotherapy.

In J. L. Singer (Ed.), *Repression and dissociation* (pp. 299–335). Chicago: University of Chicago Press.

Blatt, S. J. (1995). The destructiveness of perfectionism: Implications for the treatment of depression. *American Psychologist, 50,* 1003–1020.

Blatt, S. J. (2004). *Experiences of depression: Theoretical, clinical, and research perspectives.* Washington, DC: American Psychological Association.

Blatt, S. J., & Blass, R. (1996). Relatedness and self-definition: A dialectic model of personality development. In G. G. Noam & K. W. Fischer (Eds.), *Development and vulnerabilities in close relationships* (pp. 309–338). Hillsdale, NJ: Erlbaum.

Blatt, S. J., Cornell, C. E., & Eshkol, E. (1993). Personality style, differential vulnerability and clinical course in immunological and cardiovascular disease. *Clinical Psychology Review, 13,* 421–450.

Blatt, S. J., D'Afflitti, J. P., & Quinlan, D. M. (1976). Experiences of depression in normal young adults. *Journal of Abnormal Psychology, 85,* 383–389.

Blatt, S. J., Quinlan, D. M., Chevron, E. S., McDonald, C., & Zuroff, D. C. (1982). Dependency and self-criticism: Psychological dimensions of depression. *Journal of Counseling and Clinical Psychology, 150,* 113–124.

Blatt, S. J., Zohar, A. H., Quinlan, D. M., Zuroff, D. C., & Mongrain, M. (1995). Subscales within the dependency factor of the Depressive Experiences Questionnaire. *Journal of Personality Assessment, 64,* 319–339.

Blatt, S. J., & Zuroff, D. C. (1992). Interpersonal relatedness and self-definition: Two prototypes for depression. *Clinical Psychology Review, 12,* 527–562.

Bolger, N., DeLongis, A., Kessler, R. C., & Schilling, E. A. (1989). Effects of daily stress on mood. *Journal of Personality and Social Psychology, 57,* 808–818.

Brown, G. W., Harris, T. O., & Hepworth, C. (1995). Loss, humiliation, and entrapment among women developing depression: A patient and non-patient comparison. *Psychological Medicine, 25,* 7–21.

Cox, B. J., & Enns, M. W. (2003). Relative stability of dimensions of perfectionism in depression. *Canadian Journal of Behavioural Science, 35,* 124–132.

Drew, S. S., Heesacker, M., Frost, H. M., & Oelke, L. E. (2004). The role of relationship loss and self-loss in women's and men's dysphoria. *Journal of Social and Personal Relationships, 21,* 381–397.

Ellis, A. (2002). The role of irrational beliefs in perfectionism. In G. L. Flett & P. L. Hewitt (Eds.), *Perfectionism: Theory, research, and treatment* (pp. 217–229). Washington, DC: American Psychological Association.

Farmer, A. E., & McGuffin, P. (2003). Humiliation, loss and other types of life events and difficulties: A comparison of depressed subjects, healthy controls, and their siblings. *Psychological Medicine, 33,* 1169–1175.

Flett, G. L., Besser, A., & Hewitt, P. L. (2005). Perfectionism, ego defense styles, and depression: A comparison of self-reports versus informant ratings. *Journal of Personality, 73,* 1355–1396.

Flett, G. L., Besser, A., & Hewitt, P. L. (2009). Personality vulnerabilities, shame, and self-silencing in psychological distress. Manuscript in preparation.

Flett, G. L., Besser, A., Hewitt, P. L., & Davis, R. A. (2007). Perfectionism, silencing the self, and depression. *Personality and Individual Differences, 43,* 1211–1222.

Flett, G. L., Greene, A., & Hewitt, P. L. (2004). Dimensions of perfectionism and anxiety sensitivity. *Journal of Rational-Emotive and Cognitive-Behavior Therapy, 22,* 39–57.

Flett, G. L., & Hewitt, P. L. (2002). *Perfectionism: Theory, research, and treatment.* Washington, DC: American Psychological Association.

Flett, G. L., Hewitt P. L., Blankstein K. R., & Gray L. (1998). Psychological distress and the frequency of perfectionistic thinking. *Journal of Personality and Social Psychology, 75,* 1363–1381.

Flett, G. L., Hewitt, P. L., Endler, N. S., & Bagby, R. M. (1995). Conceptualization and assessment of personality factors in depression. *European Journal of Personality, 9,* 309–350.

Flett, G. L., Hewitt, P. L., Garshowitz, M., & Martin, T. R. (1997). Personality, negative social interactions, and depressive symptoms. *Canadian Journal of Behavioural Science, 29,* 28–37.

Flett, G. L., Hewitt, P. L., Shapiro, B., & Rayman, J. (2003). Perfectionism, beliefs, and adjustment in dating relationships. In N. J. Pallone (Ed.), *Love, romance, sexual attraction: Research perspectives from current psychology* (pp. 31–60). New Brunswick, NJ: Transaction Publishers.

Frost, R. O., & DiBartolo, P. M. (2002). Perfectionism, anxiety, and obsessive-compulsive disorder. In G. L. Flett & P. L. Hewitt (Eds.), *Perfectionism: Theory, research, and treatment* (pp. 341–371). Washington, DC: American Psychological Association Press.

Frost, R. O., Marten, P., Lahart, C., & Rosenblate, R. (1990). The dimensions of perfectionism. *Cognitive Therapy and Research, 14,* 449–468.

Geller, J., Cockell, S. J., Hewitt, P. L., Goldner, E. M., & Flett, G. L. (2000). Inhibited expression of negative emotions and interpersonal orientation in anorexia nervosa. *International Journal of Eating Disorders, 28,* 8–19.

Habke, A. M., Hewitt, P. L., & Flett, G. L. (1999). Perfectionism and sexual satisfaction in intimate relationships. *Journal of Psychopathology and Behavior Assessment, 21,* 307–322.

Haring, M., Hewitt, P. L., & Flett, G. L. (2003). Perfectionism, coping, and quality of intimate relationships. *Journal of Marriage and the Family, 65,* 143–158.

Harper, M. S., & Welsh, D. P. (2007). Keeping quiet: Self-silencing and its association with relational and individual functioning among adolescent romantic couples. *Journal of Social and Personal Relationships, 24,* 99–116.

Hart, B. I., & Thompson, J. M. (1996). Gender role characteristics and depressive symptomatology among adolescents. *Journal of Early Adolescence, 16,* 407–426.

Helgeson, V. S. (1994). Relation of agency and communion to well-being: Evidence and potential explanations. *Psychological Bulletin, 116,* 412–428.

Hewitt, P. L., & Flett, G. L. (1991). Perfectionism in the self and social contexts: Conceptualization, assessment, and association with psychopathology. *Journal of Personality and Social Psychology, 60,* 456–470.

Hewitt, P. L., & Flett, G. L. (2002). Perfectionism and stress in psychopathology. In G. L. Flett & P. L. Hewitt (Eds.), *Perfectionism: Theory, research, and treatment* (pp. 255–284). Washington, DC: American Psychological Association Press.

Hewitt, P. L., & Flett, G. L. (2004). *Multidimensional Perfectionism Scale: Technical manual.* Toronto: Multi-Health Systems Inc.

Hewitt, P. L., & Flett, G. L. (2007). When does conscientiousness become perfectionism? *Current Psychiatry, 6*, 49–60.

Hewitt, P. L., Flett, G. L., & Ediger, E. (1995). Perfectionism, coping, and depression symptomatology in a clinical sample. *International Journal of Eating Disorders, 18*, 317–326.

Hewitt, P. L., Flett, G. L., Ediger, E., Norton, R., & Flynn, C. (1998). Perfectionism chronic and state symptoms of depression. *Canadian Journal of Behavioural Sciences, 30*, 234–242.

Hewitt, P. L., Flett, G. L., Sherry, S. B., Habke, M., Parkin, M., Lam, R. W., et al. (2003). The interpersonal expression of perfection: Perfectionistic self-presentation and psychological distress. *Journal of Personality and Social Psychology, 84*, 1303–1325.

Horney, K. (1950). *Neurosis and human growth: The struggle toward self-realization.* London: W.W. Norton & Company.

Jack, D. C. (1991). *Silencing the self.* Cambridge, MA: Harvard University Press.

Jack, D. C. (1999a). Silencing the self: Inner dialogues and outer realities. In T. Joiner & J. C. Coyne (Eds.), *The interactional nature of depression* (pp. 221–246). Washington, DC: American Psychological Association.

Jack, D. C. (1999b). Ways of listening to depressed women in qualitative research: Interview techniques and analyses. *Canadian Psychology, 40*, 91–101.

Jack, D. C. (2001). Understanding women's anger: A description of relational patterns. *Health Care for Women International, 22*, 385–400.

Jack, D. C., & Dill, D. (1992). The Silencing the Self Scale: Schemas of intimacy associated with depression in women. *Psychology of Women Quarterly, 16*, 97–106.

Kohn, P. M., Lafreniere, K., & Gurevich, M. (1990). The inventory of college students' recent life experiences: A decontaminated hassles scale for a special population. *Journal of Behavioral Medicine, 13*, 619–630.

Lakey, B., Tardiff, T. A., & Drew, J. B. (1994). Negative social interactions: Assessment and relations to social support, cognition, and psychological distress. *Journal of Social and Clinical Psychology, 13*, 42–62.

Levy, K. N., Blatt, S. J., & Shaver, P. R. (1998). Attachment styles and parental representations. *Journal of Personality and Social Psychology, 74*, 407–419.

Luthar, S. S., & Blatt, S. J. (1993). Dependent and self-critical depressive experiences among inner-city adolescents. *Journal of Personality, 61*, 365–386.

Mongrain, M. (1998). Parental representations and support-seeking behaviors related to dependency and self-criticism. *Journal of Personality, 66*, 151–173.

Mongrain, M., & Leather, F. (2006). Immature dependence and self-criticism predict the recurrence of major depression. *Journal of Clinical Psychology, 62*, 705–713.

Mongrain, M., Lubbers, R., & Struthers, W. (2004). The power of love: Mediation of rejection in roommate relationships of dependents and self-critics. *Personality and Social Psychology Bulletin, 30*, 94–105.

Mongrain, M., & Zuroff, D. C. (1994). Ambivalence over emotional expression and negative life events: Mediators of depressive symptoms in dependent and self-critical individuals. *Personality and Individual Differences, 16*, 447–458.

Mongrain, M., & Zuroff, D. C. (1995). Motivational and affective correlates of dependency and self-criticism. *Personality and Individual Differences, 18*, 347–354.

Nepon, T. B., Flett, G. L., Besser, A., & Hewitt, P. L. (2009, June). *Perfectionistic self-presentation and perfectionism cognitions in silencing the self.* Poster presented at the annual meeting of the Canadian Psychological Association, Montreal, Quebec.

Nietzel, M. T., & Harris, M. J. (1990). Relationship of dependency and achievement/autonomy to depression. *Clinical Psychology Review, 10*, 279–297.

Nolen-Hoeksema, S., Wisco, B. E., & Lyubomirsky, S. (2008). Rethinking rumination. *Perspectives on Psychological Science, 3*, 400–424.

Orth, U., Berking, M., & Burkhardt, S. (2006). Self-conscious emotions and depression: Rumination explains why shame but not guilt is maladaptive. *Personality and Social Psychology Bulletin, 32*, 1608–1619.

Priel, B., & Besser, A. (1999). Vulnerability to postpartum depressive symptomatology: Dependency, self-criticism and the moderating role of antenatal attachment. *Journal of Social and Clinical Psychology, 18*, 240–253.

Priel, B., & Besser, A. (2000). Dependency and self-criticism among first-time mothers: The roles of global and specific support. *Journal of Social and Clinical Psychology, 19*, 437–450.

Radloff, L. (1977). The CES-D Scale: A self-report depression scale for research in the general population. *Applied Psychological Measurement, 1*, 385–401.

Rook, K. (1984). The negative side of social interaction: Impact on psychological well-being. *Journal of Personality and Social Psychology, 46*, 1097–1108.

Rude, S. S., & Burnham, B. L. (1995). Connectedness and neediness: Factors of the DEQ and SAS Dependency scales. *Cognitive Therapy and Research, 19*, 323–340.

Sandler, I. N., & Barrera, M., Jr. (1984). Toward a multidimensional approach to assessing the effects of social support. *American Journal of Community Psychology, 12*, 37–52.

Stanton, A. L., Danoff-Burg, S., Cameron, C. L., Bishop, M., Collins, C. A., Kirk, S. B., et al. (2002). Emotionally expressive coping predicts psychological and physical adjustment to breast cancer. *Journal of Consulting and Clinical Psychology, 65*, 875–882.

Stephens, B. J. (1987). Cheap thrills and humble pie: The adolescence of female suicide attempters. *Suicide and Life-Threatening Behavior, 17*, 107–118.

Tangney, J. P., Niedenthal, P. M., Covert, M. V., & Barlow, D. H. (1998). Are shame and guilt related to distinct self-discrepancies? A test of Higgins' (1987) hypotheses. *Journal of Personality and Social Psychology, 75*, 256–268.

Tangney, J. P., Wagner, P. E., & Gramzow, R. (1989). *The test of self-conscious affect.* Fairfax, VA: George Mason University.

Thompson, J. M. (1995). Silencing the self: Depressive symptomatology and close relationships. *Psychology of Women Quarterly, 19*, 337–353.

Thompson, J. M., Whiffen, V. E., & Aube, J. A. (2001). Does self-silencing link perceptions of care from parents and partners with depressive symptoms? *Journal of Social and Personal Relationships, 18*, 503–516.

Whiffen, V. (2007). *A secret sadness: The hidden relationship patterns that make women depressed.* Oakland, CA: New Harbinger Publications.

Whiffen, V., & Aube, J. (1999). Personality, interpersonal context, and depression in couples. *Journal of Social and Personal Relationships, 16,* 369–383.

Wiseman, H. (1997). Interpersonal relatedness and self-definition to the experience of loneliness during the transition to university. *Personal Relationships, 4,* 285–298.

Zuroff, D. C., & Fitzpatrick, D. (1995). Depressive personality styles: Implications for adult attachment. *Personality and Individual Differences, 18,* 253–365.

14

Sociopolitical, Gender, and Cultural Factors in the Conceptualization and Treatment of Depression among Haitian Women

Guerda Nicolas, Bridget Hirsch, and Clelia Beltrame

The important roles that culture and gender play in the manifestation and treatment of mental illness have been well documented (Burns & Mahalik, 2007; Kleinman & Kleinman, 1985; Mahalik, Burns, & Syzdek, 2007; Sue & Zane, 1987). Although researchers are beginning to address these issues for some ethnic and cultural groups such as African Americans (Miranda, 2000), Latinos (Bernal & Scharron del Río, 2001), and Asians (Sue, Arredondo, & McDavis, 1992), relatively little is known about Black Caribbeans. Similar to other ethnic groups, the Black Caribbean community is heterogeneous, composed of many distinctive cultural groups located in various regions of the Caribbean islands. In this chapter, we present a summary of the sociopolitical and gender role factors, as well as the health beliefs and conceptualization of illness among Haitian women. We continue by offering an examination of how these factors intersect and influence the perception of depression among Haitian women. Finally, using the Multicultural Competency Model (MCC; Arredondo et al., 1996) as a framework (Sue et al., 1982, 1992), we illustrate the link between culture and depression for Haitian women.

Sociopolitical History and Gender Factors

Although phenotypically similar to other Black Americans (Desrosier & St. Fleurose, 2002; Rowlands, 1979; Turnier, 2000), Haitians are undeniably distinct from African Americans with regard to many elements of culture such as beliefs, language, food, politics, history, and methods of arrival to the United States (Huff & Kline, 1999; Zephir, 1996). As noted by Hopp and Herring (1999), Haitians' health beliefs and cultural practices significantly differ from those of African Americans by individual factors, such as "...degree of acculturation, country of origin, education level, socioeconomic level, and the time of freedom historically" (p. 219). Through an examination of the historical role of Haitian women in the social and political events of the country, researchers and service providers may gain important insight that can aid in the understanding of the client as well as how best to foster her well-being.

Sociopolitical Factors

As depicted in most history texts, in 1492, Christopher Columbus occupied the island of Hispaniola for Spain and built the first settlement on Haiti's north coast. In 1697, through the Treaty of Ryswick, the island was divided into two parts, with the French controlling Saint Dominique and the Spaniards controlling Santo Domingo. For more than 100 years and at the height of slavery, Saint Dominique became an important territory to France, supplying it with the island's natural resources such as sugar, rum, coffee, and cotton. As a result, France enslaved over 500,000 people, mostly from western Africa, to the island in order to continue its mass production of these commodities. However, from 1791 to 1803, a slave rebellion, led by Boukman and commanded by Toussaint Louverture, was launched against the colonists and the Napoleon army. Through many battles, including the Battle of Vertieres in 1803 (commonly known as the slaves' ultimate victory against the French), Haiti—or *Ayiti* in Creole (meaning "mountainous country')—became the second independent state in the Western Hemisphere, and the first free Black republic in the world.

Gender Factors

In addition to Haiti's sociopolitical history, the literature on gender roles is an invaluable source of information in understanding Haitian women's unique experience with depression. This section is a summary of the historical and current literature on gender roles for Haitian women.

Through a historical examination of Haitian struggles to achieve the independence of their country, it is evident that Haitian women played a pivotal role in the eradication of slavery not only in Haiti but also in the Western Hemisphere (Laurent, 2003). Their role and impact are apparent through the description of historical figures such as *Ezili Danto*, known for her spiritual presence and power behind the many Haitian women who victoriously fought with Toussaint, Petion, and Dessalines in creating the first independent Black republic in the world; *Anacaona*, who refused to be enslaved and fought for the liberty of Haitians to her death; *Manbo Cecile Fatiman*, a Haitian priestess who participated in the well-known ceremony known as Bwa Kayiman with Boukman in 1791 (during which time Haitians decided that freedom was essential for their survival); and many more. Through a review of these women's stories, we learned of their courage in combat during the revolution and of their tireless efforts to obtain voting rights for women before any other country in the Western Hemisphere. The legacies of these women are passed on through oral history of the people as well as through literature. For example, Danticat's (2005) book entitled *Anacaona: Golden Flower, Haiti* and the art exhibit on Ezili Danto at the American Museum of Natural History keep their work alive. These women serve as role models for girls and women in the country and abroad, and their legacy plays a pivotal role in the development of many grassroots activism organizations in Haiti and in the United States (Charles, 1995).

The impact that migration and transnational processes have had on Haitian women is another factor that helped to shape and reshape not only Haitian women's political identities but also the current political landscape of the country itself (Gammage, 2004). Gammage (2004) argues that the "feminization of agriculture and the displacement of male income earners from the countryside has changed economic roles and may have contributed to the emergence of rural women as a political force" (p. 761). Haitian women's participation in the creation and implementation of local and national grassroots organizations has helped the fight for equal rights and equitable distribution of resources, and overall for the "formation of contemporary Haitian civil society and the moves toward democratization" (Gammage, 2004, p. 762). These grassroots and historical events had an everlasting impact on the roles of Haitian men and women on the island and abroad.

The Development of the Haitian Women's Movement

Despite the active involvement of Haitian women in Haiti's independence, it was not until 1934 that the first Haitian women's organization, *Ligue Feminine d'Action Sociale* (Women's League for Social Action), was formed. Created by an elite group of middle- and upper-class professional and intellectual Haitian women, this organization played an important political role in the country for 25 years. The central focus of this organization was to obtain legal rights in the areas of equality for married women, including access to education and suffrage for all women in the country. Through this association, Haitian women were able to gain the right to vote and attend universities by the end of 1950s (Charles, 1995). With their successes, however, came many tribulations: Many members of the league were victims of torture, rape, and death under the presidency of Francois Duvalier (1957–1971) and his son Jean-Claude (1971–1986).

The torture and arrest of Yvonne Hakim Rimpel in 1958, one of the founders of the league and a prominent journalist, led to a protest by 36 of its members calling for an investigation in Rimpel's case (Zéphir, 1991). The league was subsequently driven to silence for many years. The 1970s marked the re-establishment of a few professional Haitian women's groups in Haiti and the simultaneous establishment of a Haitian women's movement both in the United States and Canada. In fact, by the 1980s, the women's movement emerged and helped to reshape Haitian society into a more egalitarian and democratic mindset. With the demise of Duvalier's dictatorship in 1986, many Haitian women activists returned to Haiti and assisted in the creation of new organizations such as *Solidarité Fanm Ayisyen* (SOFA, Haitian Women's Solidarity), *Klinik Sante Fanm* (Women's Health Clinic), Committee to Defend Working Women's Rights (KODDFF, in Kreyó), and *Kay Fanm* (Women's House) (Charles, 1995). Currently, both in Haiti and in the Diaspora, Haitian women are continuing the legacy of the many women warriors of the past in improving the lives of Haitian women. Individuals such as Ginette Apollon (director of the Women's Commission of the Confédération des Travailleurs Haitiens [CTH] and president of the health workers union affiliate of the CTH) and Rea Dol (cofounder and director of the Society of Providence United for the Development of Petionville [SOPUDEP] and coordinator of a federation of women's organizations that focuses on women's rights, education, economic empowerment, and social justice) are examples of the noted grassroots women who continue to fight against social, political, and educational inequalities of women in Haiti and in the Diaspora (Bell, 2001; Donaldson, 2008). Despite the high rate of poverty, health issues, and political turmoil, Haitian women have courageously adapted to their extensive history of fighting for equal rights by coming together collectively as a group to promote social change and equality.

Influence of the Haitian Women's Movement on Gender Roles

The evolution and growth of the Haitian women's movements led to a redefining of women's roles, power, and identity in Haiti and abroad (Charles, 1995; Fuller, 1999). Haiti is a country that, "in any of its dimensions, simply cannot be considered without recognition of the role and significance of women and their activities" (Gammage, 2004). Haitian women have many responsibilities from household tasks to agricultural tasks. For example, many Haitian women are often found alongside Haitian men planning and harvesting crops and raising livestock. Furthermore, Haitian women are employed in a variety of settings such as schools, hospitals, community organizations, and factories, to name a few. Although historically Haiti has been dominated by male figures and the institutional power still resides with men on the island, over 70% of rural households are headed by women (Edmond, Randolph, & Guyliane, 2007). In fact, some authors have referred to Haiti as "matrifocal," highlighting the economic and social power of the men and the accountability and responsibility of women for children's' welfare (Colin & Paperwalla, 1996, 2003; Laguerre, 1981, 1984). Thus, women are often referred to as the backbone of the family in Haitian culture. For example, the well-known author Edwidge Danticat (1994) observed in her book *Breath, Eyes, and Memory* that "Only a mountain can crush a Haitian woman." The quote "*Fam se poto mitan*" (women are the center post), a common Haitian proverb, epitomizes the role of Haitian women in Haiti. In fact, a recent film entitled *Poto Mitan: Haitian Women Pilars of the Global Economy* depicts the current story of Haitian women's struggle, courage, resistance, and democracy. Today, the perception of gender roles are continuing to shift in Haiti with the occupation of Haitian women in prominent positions, such as the interim president Ertha Pascal-Trouillot (1990–1991), the prime minister Claudette Werleigh (1995–1996), and more recently the election of Michelle Pierre-Louis (2008) as the new prime minister of the country. The election of Haitian women in prominent political positions both in Haiti and in the Diaspora (e.g., three-term election of Marie St. Fleur in Massachusetts) signals that the imprints of Haitian women are visible today and will no doubt continue to shift the roles of women in the culture.

Cultural Factors

The sociopolitical history and evolution of gender roles in Haiti are integral parts of the cultural identity of Haitians. The link between culture and mental health has been well documented by many researchers (Bernal & Scharron del Rio, 2001; Trimble & Fisher, 2006). However, it is only recently that a focus on culture and mental health for Haitians was undertaken (Nicolas et al., 2007). In an effort to understand the association between culture and depression for Haitian women, a summary of the cultural health beliefs of Haitians is provided followed by an examination of the cultural aspects of depression among Haitian women. This section concludes with an application of a multicultural framework in integrating culture and mental health for this population.

Cultural Health Beliefs and Conceptualization of Illnesses among Haitians

In the Haitian community, being in "good health" is associated with one's ability to maintain internal equilibrium between *cho* (hot) and *fret* (cold). In order for an individual to achieve balance, the person must pray, eat well, give attention to personal hygiene, and have good spiritual habits (Colin & Paperwalla, 1996; Kirkpatrick & Cobb, 1990). Characteristics such as being strong, having good color, being plump, and being free from pain all promote good health among individuals. In order to develop and maintain these characteristics, a person must eat right, sleep right, keep warm, exercise, and keep clean (Laguerre, 1984;

Miller, 2000). As a result, the development of any illness is viewed as an assault to the body through many different etiologies.

Among Haitians, illness (mental or physical) often occurs in several chronological stages (Angel & Guarnaccia, 1989). Regardless of the severity of the illness, a progression of symptom reporting will be observed among Haitian clients. An illness often begins with the person reporting *Kom pa bon* ("I do not feel well"), which does not lead to the development of any serious symptoms. This is followed by a decrease in activity, confinement to home, and the person reporting *moin malad* ("I am sick"). In the next stage, the person may report *moin malad anpil* ("I am very sick"), which is associated with an increased severity of symptoms accompanied by confinement to bed. The last stage in the development of the illness is a sense of hopelessness about ever getting better, during which time the person will report *moin pap refe* ("I am dying") (Angel & Guarnaccia, 1989; Laguerre, 1984).

In addition to Haitians' unique conceptualization of illness, the Haitian culture has significant spiritual beliefs that are the cornerstone of the culture (Miller, 2000). For example cultural healing rituals such as Voodoo ceremony (performed by a Hougan or Mambo) and the use of herbs (such as root sarsaparilla and senna) are common practices to alleviate physical and psychological ailments of individuals. The following excerpt from Prince (2005), an herbal doctor, provides an example of the practice of folk medicine among Haitians:

> I treat people with digestive problems, acid stomach, gas, constipation and sexual problems. I treat fevers, and colds, and aches. I have medicine, which cleans and purifies the blood. I treat children who aren't growing well, or who are being persecuted by evil spirits. In addition, we always make sure that the sick person gets the best possible care from a medical doctor, and sometimes the doctor works together with me. I work with people who have chronic illnesses, including diabetes, hypertension, and HIV/AIDS. While I cannot cure these diseases, there is much that can be done to help a person live a longer, healthier life. (p. 2)

Consequently, it is important that mental health professionals do not dismiss a report of "I do not feel well" as not warranting immediate attention or care. It is essential that providers probe for further information about the symptoms in order to determine if immediate follow-up is necessary (Holcomb, Parsons, Giger, & Davidhizar, 1996). Also, an appreciation and welcoming of these cultural spiritual beliefs is essential in working with Haitian clients (Miller, 2000).

Depression among Haitian Women

Depression is a universal phenomenon, yet the experience of it is largely impacted by one's native culture, social and political history, and individual experiences. Although there is no documented research linking the sociopolitical history of Haiti to the psychological well-being of its people, it is likely to have an impact on the experiences of individuals. In fact, scholars have argued, "depression is always influenced by social and political dimensions" (NiCarthy, 2004, p. 22). While depression cannot be reduced to sociopolitical factors alone, it must not be fully understood from an individual perspective. In fact, Turnier (2000) attributes the roots of depressive symptoms among Haitian women to historical events that they experienced in Haiti. The cultural gender norms, the historical participation of Haitian women in the independence of the country, and their continuous involvement in activism for equality of women on the island as well as abroad must be integrated in the assessment of depression among these women. Considering the uniqueness of the culture coupled with the ever-increasing number of Haitians settling in the United States, it seems imperative for researchers and clinicians to increase their awareness, knowledge, and skills in understanding the interconnection between culture and the manifestation and treatment of mental illnesses such as depression, specifically among Haitian women (Nicolas et al., 2007).

Research findings on the mental health of ethnic minorities further emphasize the need for understanding and considering cultural factors and call attention to limitations of current research, which may not take these factors into consideration. For example, international studies have found higher diagnoses of schizophrenia among Black Caribbeans compared to Whites (Jackson et al., 2004). However, researchers caution that this could be due to lack of consideration of cultural backgrounds (Blazer, Kessler, McGonagle, & Swartz, 1994). Nevertheless, it was found that Black Caribbean women have depressive disorders at higher rates than White women in the United States and they were less likely to seek mental health help (Brown, Schulberg, & Madonia, 1996; Joe, 2005). Studies of large populations in the United States demonstrate the lack of attention that has been paid to the mental health of ethnic minority populations, and research seems to have established that Black immigrants in the United States have higher rates of mental health problems than nonimmigrant populations in the United States (Jackson et al., 2004).

To date, there are no epidemiological depression studies in Haiti or in the United States on the prevalence or rate of depression among Haitians by any categories (e.g., gender, age). Existing literature on depression among Haitian women is based largely on clinical observation data, which suggest that depression can take many different forms and that current westernized categories as well as ways of assessing depression among these women may not be culturally relevant (Nicolas, DeSilva, Grey, & Gonzalez-Eastep, 2006; Nicolas et al., 2007; Turnier, 2000). For example, Nicolas and colleagues (2007) have identified three distinctive types of depression in a sample of Haitian women: *Douluer de Corps* (pain in the body), which is often described by symptoms such as feelings of weakness (*faiblesse*) and faintness; *Soulagement par Dieu* (relief through God), which is often associated with specific difficulties in one's life;

and *Lutte sons Victoire* (fighting a winless battle), which often is painted as a very bleak generalized picture of the individual's life. These categories are consistent with what other clinical researchers have noted among Haitians in other countries, such as Canada (Turnier, 2000). Unfortunately, there is no empirical research on the depression rate of Haitian women and the few related writings that exist attempt to integrate their symptoms into the framework of Western mental illness, which does not take into account the culture of the population (Azaunce, 1995; Bevilacqua, 1980; Sargant, 1967). To date, Gustafson (1989) and Nicolas and colleagues (2007) have written the only articles on depression among Haitians from a cultural perspective. Given the role that culture plays in the manifestation of depression among Haitians, a conceptual framework is needed in order to integrate sociopolitical, gender, and cultural factors in the assessment and treatment of depression for this population.

The Multicultural Competency Model and Depression among Haitian Women

Although significant research has focused on the importance of integrating culture in the diagnosis and treatment of mental health issues among ethnic minority women, these concepts and models are not easily applied across different cultural groups. In addition, the American Psychological Association (APA) has called for practitioners to develop competency in multicultural counseling as an effort to ensure that clients are receiving culturally relevant services (APA, 1991). Explicit in this recommendation is a recognition that culture needs to play a fundamental role in the assessment and treatment of individuals from diverse cultural backgrounds (Pedersen, 1988). Among the many cultural models, the Multicultural Competency Model (Arredondo et al., 1996; Sue et al., 1982, 1992) is the most accepted model that is used in the areas of training, supervision, and teaching in the field of psychology (Pope-Davis, Liu, Toporek, & Brittan-Powell, 2001). Importantly, it provides a three stage developmental approach in working culturally with ethnically diverse clients (Delgado-Romero, Galván, Maschino, & Rowland, 2005). Although some researchers have questioned the empirical foundation of this model (Constantine & Ladany, 2001; Ponterotto, Fuertes, & Chen, 2000), the general principles of the model can serve as a foundation for researchers and clinicians in how to increase their multicultural understanding of ethnically diverse individuals. Despite the inherent differences in the sociopolitical histories and contexts of various cultural groups, ethnically diverse individuals share the experience of the power, social construction, and socialization that often operates within various systems (i.e., family, school, and work; Sue et al., 1982). In this section of the chapter, we provide a description of each of the stages of the tripartite MCC model with illustrations of its applicability through examples from the Haitian culture.

Stage one. The first stage of the MCC model, *cultural awareness*, focuses on the awareness of the researcher and/or clinician's viewpoint, culture, and biases in conjunction with the person's viewpoint from another, unfamiliar culture as well as assumptions that may arise from the difference between these points of contact (Pedersen, 1988). Sue and colleagues (1998) noted that "culturally skilled therapists are aware of how their own cultural background and experiences, attitudes, values, and biases influence psychological processes" (p. 38). This stage of the model urges researchers and clinicians to examine their cultural beliefs and any biases that might be held about other cultural groups in order to reduce the risk of alienating or stigmatizing the beliefs of individuals (Pedersen, 1988).

As previously highlighted in this chapter, the health beliefs and practices of Haitians differ from the Western perspective on the etiology of mental and physical illness. In utilizing stage one of the MCC model, one might ask oneself, "What were my initial reactions to the summary about Haitian cultural beliefs? How are these beliefs similar or different from my own beliefs about health as a researcher or clinician? How would I react to hearing about these beliefs?" These are among the many questions that one can ask in an attempt to become aware of one's own cultural viewpoint in comparison to that of another cultural group. Through an evaluation of these and other questions, an individual can begin working through his or her cultural assumptions and biases. Furthermore, through such a process, an individual can begin to increase his or her cultural knowledge about individuals from diverse ethnic backgrounds.

Stage two. The second stage of the MCC model is *enhanced knowledge* about the views of clients as well as an understanding of the function and influence of historical, social, and political events within that culture that may have impacted the behaviors and attitudes of individuals within that culture (Sue et al., 1998). According to Sue and colleagues (1998), "culturally skilled therapists should familiarize themselves with relevant research and the latest findings regarding mental health and mental disorders of various ethnic and racial groups. They should actively seek out educational experiences that enrich their knowledge, understanding, and cross-cultural skills" (p. 40). In order to utilize the most effective assessments, interventions, and treatments, it is imperative to be familiar with the risk and protective factors associated with the specific culture with which one is working. Being knowledgeable about the sociopolitical history and gender roles of Haitian women will enable one to recognize significant risk and protective factors for this specific population. Researchers argue that an examination of the risk factors associated with mental health concerns among Haitian women must take into account factors such as race, gender and gender roles, poverty, violence, and stigma (Lawless, 1986; Portes & Rumbaut, 2001a). Specifically, existing literature on Haitian women suggest that Haitian women's risks for negative health issues may be due in part to their sociopolitical history, economic conditions, and geographical location (DeSantis & Thomas, 1990;

Desrosiers & St. Fleurose, 2002; Kessler & McLeod, 1984; Neuman, 1986; Pierce & Elisme, 2001; Rowlands, 1979). In addition, stressors associated with acculturation and migration patterns (Pape et al., 1986) must be taken into account as additional risk factors for members of the Diaspora. Specifically, an examination of the different levels of acculturation (Rudmin, 2003) as well as the various factors associated with acculturative stress (i.e., physical and social isolation, shifts in gender roles, language, challenges in maintaining one's culture) may elucidate important information regarding the mental health of Haitian women. Although the risk factors for Haitian women's mental health are abundant (Lawless, 1986; Pape et al., 1986; Portes & Rumbaut, 2001b), there are many resources that can serve as protective factors for Haitian women. These include religious beliefs (Nicolas, Desilva, Prater, & Bronkoski, 2009), strong family connections (Nicolas et al., 2007), and a rich oral storytelling tradition. Danticat (1996) summarizes this oral tradition well in her book *Krik? Krak!*, stating, "I took to the past to Haiti—hoping that the extraordinary female storytellers I grew up with—the ones that have passed on—will choose to tell their stories through my voice" (Casey, 1995, pp. 525–526). In her book, Danticat presents the legacies and visions of Haitian women through narratives of mothers and daughters whose personal tragedies have contributed to the formation of communities in Haiti. Through a cultural knowledge of the strengths of Haitians as depicted in art, literature, and research, service providers and researchers will be better equipped in addressing the psychological well-being of Haitians in Haiti and abroad.

Stage three. The last stage of the MCC model, *cultural skills*, is the ability to integrate knowledge and awareness in the development and implementation of services in a culturally sensitive manner (Sue et al., 1998). In addition to addressing the enhancement of cultural knowledge and awareness about ethnically diverse clients, this stage highlights and questions the expertise of researchers and service providers in delivering effective services to ethnically diverse clients. Sue and colleagues (1998) suggest that "the culturally skilled psychologist or therapist has knowledge of models of minority and majority identity, and understands how these models relate to the therapy relationship and the therapy process" (p. 41). For example, research on self-silencing theory by Ali, Oatley, and Toner (2002) fount that women in individual psychotherapy who scored high on self-silencing at the beginning of therapy had less positive therapeutic outcomes from their therapy compared to women who had scored low on self-silencing. This indicates that self-silencing may be a barrier to successful therapy and therefore, in the MCC model, attempts should be made to bridge the gap between client and therapist and enhancing clients' expression of their authentic self. With respect to stressors associated with discrimination, research has shown that an increase in perceived societal and systemic discrimination from Caucasians resulted in significant increases of being diagnosed with major depressive disorder, conduct disorder, and oppositional defiant disorder among African American and Caribbean adolescents living in the United States (Portes, Kyle, & Eaton, 1992). In a study comparing Caribbean women in living in Canada to those living in the Caribbean, Ali and Toner (2001) found higher reporting of self-silencing and levels of depressive symptoms among the Caribbean Canadian women. They postulate that discrimination may be one factor that contributes to lower emotional well-being among Caribbean women who had immigrated to Canada. The results of these studies demonstrate the importance of incorporating cultural sensitivity into mental health services and programs for ethnically diverse individuals. Given the cultural influence in the manifestation and expression of depression symptoms, the types of interventions and the strategies for delivery of services are likely also to be influenced by the culture of the individual offering treatment. This is especially true considering that mental illness is not an area that is well accepted in the Haitian culture (Colin & Papperwalla, 1996), and thus Haitians often underutilize mental health services (Portes et al., 1992). In Haiti, mental illnesses often remain untreated unless they are connected to some significant social disruption for the individual (Colin & Papperwalla, 2003). Consequently, due to the stigma associated with mental illness in Haitian culture, an individual who is suffering from depression symptoms may not admit to it (Colin & Papperwalla, 1996). A Haitian who seeks care from a biomedical practitioner such as a psychiatrist may not think he or she was treated unless there was evidence that a physical exam was done. Given the paucity of intervention research on Haitians in general, especially Haitian women, it is imperative not only that risk and protective factors are recognized but also that there is an understanding of the existing barriers to services when providing mental health treatment to this population.

Barriers to Services

Similar to other ethnic minority groups in the United States, Haitian women encounter many barriers that impact their access to services within the United States. These barriers include institutional racism, prejudice and racism against Haitians, low literacy rate, lack of acculturation, and limited English language proficiency (Albertini & Barsky, 2003; Metayer, Jean-Louis, & Madison, 2004; Pape et al., 1986; Pierce & Elisme, 2001; World Health Organization, 2005). For example, the 1996 Immigration Act in the United States, requiring financial independence from the government as a prerequisite for citizenship qualification, serves as a barrier for new immigrants in need of services (Aparicio & Kretsedemas, 2003). In addition, this citizenship is directly connected to obtaining health insurance coverage, which is another significant barrier for many immigrant groups, including Haitians, in the United States (Coreil, Lauzardo, & Heurtelou, 2004; Lillie-Blanton & Hudman, 2001). Additionally, insurance coverage in the United States is directly linked to access as it reduces the financial barriers often associated with receiving medical care (Guendelman, Scauffler, & Pearl, 2001; Penchansky & Thomas, 1981; Rhoades, Brown, & Vistnes, 1998). To effectively address the mental health needs of Haitians in the United States, mental health workers and community members must take a closer look at these barriers and the development of intervention strategies to prevent or eliminate them.

Access to Mental Health Treatment in Haiti

In Haiti, the health care system consist of mainly three sections: (1) the public sector (Ministry of Public Health and Population and Ministry of Social Affairs), (2) the private for-profit section (private practice professionals), and (3) the nonprofit sectors (nongovernmental organizations [NGOs]). According to Pan American Health Organization (PAHO) reports, there are total of 371 health posts, 217 health centers, and 49 hospitals in the Haiti. However, it is estimated that more than 40% of the population, especially those in rural areas, uses traditional folk remedies for health problems. Although in 1996 the Ministry of Health introduced a health policy that would grant access to health care to all Haitian residents, the political instability in the country has derailed these efforts. To date, Haiti has no organized structure health care system and only a fraction of the residents have access to any form of health care services. The majority of individuals in Haiti rely on public and NGO-established organizations for health services where they must pay a minimal fee based on their income and family size (PAHO, 2007).

Physical health is the main priority of health officials in Haiti; only two government institutions focus on mental health in Port-au-Prince, the capital of the country. Thus, most Haitians are neither familiar with nor seek services from the mental health care system. In fact, the mental health governmental systems in Haiti are greatly stigmatized and often seen as places for individuals who have "lost" their minds. The compounded effect of the stigma associated with mental health, risk factors, barriers to services, and the lack of available mental health intervention data on Haitians has prompted several authors (Desrosier & St. Fleurose, 2002; Miller, 2000; Nicolas et al., 2006) to offer specific recommendations in providing mental health services to Haitians in a culturally responsive manner.

In Haiti and in the United States, understanding how Haitian clients perceive and make meaning of their symptoms must be the first step in addressing the mental health needs of these clients. In order to obtain this understanding, it needs to be understood that the way a client perceives the symptoms may have implications for service utilization and adherence to treatment. Such a process calls for a shift in the traditional assessment method in understanding the mental health issues of clients from different ethnic and racial backgrounds. Asking Haitian clients questions such as, "How do you think these symptoms came about?" "What meaning do you make of them?" and "Why do you think that these things are happening to you now?" may allow the clinicians to gain a greater understanding of clients' perceptions and experiences of their symptoms.

Conclusions

The information presented in this chapter highlights some key areas (i.e., sociopolitical, gender, and cultural health beliefs) that practitioners and researchers must take into account when working with Black Caribbean populations. Cultural differences play an important role in the manifestation of mental health issues, as exemplified among Haitian women (Nicolas et al., 2006). Although some attempts have been made through research to understand how cultural beliefs impact the perception of mental illness, much more research is needed in this area for Haitian women.

The importance of multicultural competencies summarized in this chapter calls for an integration of awareness and knowledge of the various cultural contexts in which individuals operate and for the development of strategies to effectively integrate cultural knowledge into services and research with ethnically diverse individuals or groups (APA, 1991). In this chapter, we provide a summary of the three main components of the MCC model using Haitians as an exemplar for how to apply this model to a cultural group. Specifically, in the chapter we illustrate how researchers and service providers can enhance their awareness, knowledge, and skill sets within the historical, sociopolitical, and gender contexts of Haitian women.

Depression exists around the world; however, we must recognize that ways of understanding the illness, expression of symptoms, and help-seeking patterns vary across and within different cultural groups. In addition, it is evident not only that differences in racial categorizations need to be taken into consideration but also that differences in socialization, culture, and belief systems within the same ethnic group need to be accounted for. Thus, the information presented here reinforces the message expressed by many cross-cultural researchers that culture matters (Nicolas et al., 2006; Trimble & Fisher, 2006; U.S. Department of Health and Human Services, 2001) and must be taken into account when conducting research with ethnic and immigrant groups. Given their cultural background, we recommend that Haitian clients be active agents in treatment planning in order to develop a sense of connection to the process (Desrosier & St. Fleurose, 2002). This will be consistent with clients' active participation in cultural ritual healing ceremonies (DeSantis & Thomas, 1990; Gustafson, 1989).

Haiti has a rich historical, sociopolitical, and gender role history that is an integral part of the culture and thus of the background of individuals who originate from within that culture. Enhancing awareness, understanding, and appreciation of these factors will lead to more engagement and connection with Haitian women and more effective treatment interventions, and will promote culturally relevant research.

References

Albertini, V. L., & Barsky, A. E. (2003). *Extension of CARE to the Haitian Community.* Retrieved February 17, 2008, from http://www.brhpc.org/dbsite/brhpc/editor/tbl Publications_FileObject_bv.asp?key=1131.

Ali, A., Oatley, K., & Toner, B. B. (2002). Life stress, self-silencing and domains of meaning in unipolar depression: An investigation of an outpatient sample of women. *Journal of Social and Clinical Psychology, 21,* 669–685.

Ali, A. & Toner, B. B. (2001). Symptoms of depression among Caribbean women and Caribbean-Canadian women: An investigation of self-silencing and domains of meaning. *Psychology of Women Quarterly, 25,* 175–180.

American Psychological Association. (1991). *Guidelines for providers of psychological services to ethnic, linguistic, and culturally diverse populations.* Washington, DC: APA Press.

Angel, R., & Guarnaccia, P. (1989). Mind, body and culture: Somatization among Hispanics. *Social Science and Medicine, 28,* 1229–1238.

Aparicio, A., & Kretsedemas, P. (2003). Haitian immigrants and welfare services in Miami-Dade County. *Florida Scholar Practitioner Team.* Retrieved March 18, 2005, from: http://www.wkkf.org/Pubs/Devolution/ FloridaSPReportHaitianImmigrants_00331_03706.pdf

Arredondo, P., Toporek, R., Brown, S. P., Jones, J., Locke, D. C., Sanchez, J., et al. (1996). Operationalization of the multicultural counseling competencies. *Journal of Multicultural Counseling & Development, 24,* 42–78.

Azaunce, M. (1995). Is it schizophrenia or spirit possession? *Journal of Social Distress and the Homeless, 4,* 255–263.

Bell, B. (2001). *Walking on fire: Haitian women's stories of survival and resistance.* Ithaca, NY: Cornell University Press.

Bernal, G., & Scharron del Río, M. R. (2001). Are empirically supported treatments valid for ethnic minorities? Toward an alternative approach for treatment research. *Journal of Cultural Diversity and Ethnic Minority Psychology, 7,* 328–342.

Bevilacqua, J. (1980). Voodoo: Myth or mental illness? *Journal of Psychiatric Nursing and Mental Health Services, 18,* 17–23.

Blazer, D. G., Kessler, R. C., McGonagle, K. A., & Swartz, M. S. (1994). The prevalence and distribution of major depression in a national community sample: The National Comorbidity Survey. *American Journal of Psychiatry, 151,* 979–986.

Brown, C., Schulberg, H., & Madonia, M. (1996). Clinical presentations of major depression by African Americans and Whites in primary medical care practice. *Journal of Affective Disorders, 41,* 181–191.

Burns, S. M., & Mahalik, J. R. (2007). Understanding how masculine gender scripts may contribute to men's adjustment following treatment for prostate cancer. *American Journal of Men's Health, 1*(4), 250–261.

Casey, E. (1995). Remembering Haiti. *Callaloo, 18,* 524–528.

Charles, C. (1995). Gender and politics in contemporary Haiti: The duvalierist state, transnationalism, and the emergence of a new feminism (1980–1990). *Feminist Studies, 21,* 135–164.

Colin, J. M., & Paperwalla, G. (1996). Haitians. In J. G. Lipson, S. L. Dibble, & P. A. Minarik (Eds.), *Culture & nursing care: A pocket guide* (pp. 139–154). San Francisco, CA: University of California, Nursing Press.

Colin, J. M., & Paperwalla, G. (2003). People of Haitian heritage. In L. D. Purnell & B. J. Paulanka (Eds.), *Transcultural health care: A culturally competent approach* (pp. 70–84). Philadelphia: F.A. Davis Company.

Constantine, M. G., & Ladany, N. (2001). New visions for defining and assessing multicultural counseling competence. In J. G. Ponterotto, J. M. Casas, L. A. Suzuki, & C. M. Alexander (Eds.), *Handbook of multicultural counseling* (2nd ed., pp. 257–310). Thousand Oaks, CA: Sage.

Coreil, J., Lauzardo, M., & Heurtelou, M. (2004). Cultural feasibility assessment of tuberculosis prevention among persons of Haitian origin in south Florida. *Journal of Immigrant Health, 6*, 63–69.

Danticat, E. (1994). *Breath, eyes, memory.* New York: Soho Press.

Danticat, E. (1996). *Krik? Krak!* New York: Vintage Books.

Danticat, E. (2005). *Anacaona: Golden flower, Haiti, 1490 (The royal diaries).* New York: Scholastic, Inc.

Delgado-Romero, E. A., Galván, N., Maschino, P., & Rowland, M. (2005). Race and ethnicity in empirical counseling and counseling psychology research: A 10-year review. *The Counseling Psychologist, 33*, 419–448.

DeSantis, L., & Thomas, J. T. (1990). The immigrant Haitian mother: Transcultural nursing perspective on preventive health care for children. *Journal of Transcultural Nursing, 2*, 2–15.

Desrosier, A., & St. Fleurose, S. (2002). Treating Haitian patients: Key cultural aspects. *American Journal of Psychotherapy, 56*, 508–522.

Donaldson, S. V. (2008). Recovering Haiti: Silence, history and trauma. In E. Danticat's (Ed.), *Breath, eyes, memory.* Paper presented at the annual meeting of the American Studies Association. Retrieved February 4, 2009, from http://www.allacademic. com/meta/p114261_index.html

Edmond, Y. M., Randolph, S. M., & Guylaine, R. L. (2007). The lakou system: A cultural, ecological analysis of mothering in rural Haiti. *Journal of Pan African Studies, 2*, 19–32.

Fuller, A. (1999). Challenging violence: Haitian women unite women's rights and human rights. *Association of Concerned African Scholars Bulletin: Women and War, 55/56*, 39–48.

Gammage, S. (2004). Exercising exit, voice and loyalty: A gender perspective on transnationalism in Haiti. *Development and Change, 35*, 743–771.

Guendelman, S., Scauffler, H. H., & Pearl, M. (2001). Unfriendly shores: How immigrant children fare in the U.S. health system. *Health Affairs, 20*, 257–266.

Gustafson, M. B. (1989). Western voodoo: Health care to Haitian refugees. *Journal of Psychosocial Nursing, 27*, 22–25.

Holcomb, L. O., Parsons, L. C., Giger, J. N., & Davidhizar, R. (1996). Haitian Americans: Implications for nursing care. *Journal of Community Health Nursing, 13*, 249–260.

Hopp, J. W., & Herring, P. (1999). Promoting health among Black American population. In R. M. Huff & M. V. Kline (Eds.), *Promoting health in multicultural populations: A handbook for practitioners* (pp. 201–221). Thousands Oaks, CA: Sage.

Huff, R. M., & Kline, M. V. (1999). *Promoting health in multicultural populations: A handbook for practitioners.* Thousands Oaks, CA: Sage.

Jackson, J. S., Torres, M., Caldwell, C. H., Neighbors, H. W., Nesse, R. M., Taylor, R. J., et al. (2004). The national survey of American life: A study of racial, ethnic, and cultural influences on mental disorders and mental health. *International Journal of Methods in Psychiatric Research, 13,* 196–207.

Joe, S. (2005, August). Prevalence and correlates of Black adolescent suicidal behavior in the United States. Paper presented at the 2005 Annual American Psychological Association Convention, Washington, DC.

Kessler, R. C., & McLeod, J. D. (1984). Sex differences in vulnerability to undesirable life events. *American Sociological Review, 49,* 620–631.

Kirkpatrick, S. M., & Cobb, A. K. (1990). Health beliefs related to diarrhea in Haitian children: Building transcultural nursing knowledge. *Journal of Transcultural Nursing, 1,* 2–12.

Kleinman, A., & Kleinman, J. (1985). Somatization: The interconnections in Chinese society among culture, depressive experiences, and the meanings of pain. In A. Kleinman & B. Good (Eds.), *Culture and depression: Studies in the anthropology and cross-cultural psychiatry of affect and disorder* (pp. 429–490). Los Angeles: University of California Press.

Laguerre, M. S. (1981). Haitian Americans. In A. Harwood (Ed.), *Ethnicity and medical care* (pp. 172–210). Cambridge, MA: Harvard University Press.

Laguerre, M. S. (1984). *American odyssey: Haitians in New York City.* Ithaca, NY: Cornell University Press.

Laurent, M. (2003). *A tribute to Haitian women – 1804 to 2004.* Retrieved May 28, 2008, from http://www.margueritelaurent.com/writings/tribute.html

Lawless, R. (1986). From invisibility into the spotlight. *Journal of Ethnic Studies, 14,* 29–70.

Lillie-Blanton, M., & Hudman, J. (2001). Untangling the web: Race/ethnicity, immigration, and the nation's health. *American Journal of Public Health, 91,* 1736–1738.

Mahalik, J. R., Burns, S. M., & Syzdek, M. (2007). Masculinity and perceived normative health behaviours as predictors of men's health behaviours. *Social Science and Medicine, 64*(11), 2201–2209.

Metayer, N., Jean-Louis, E., & Madison, A. (2004). Overcoming historical and institutional distrust: Key elements in developing and sustaining the community mobilization against HIV in the Boston Haitian community. *Ethnicity and Disease, 14,* 46–52.

Miller, N. L. (2000). Haitian ethnomedical systems and biomedical practitioners: Directions for clinicians. *Journal of Transcultural Nursing, 11,* 204–211.

Miranda, J. (2000). *Mental health outcomes for Latinos: Current knowledge base for improving mental health services.* Washington, DC: Georgetown University Medical Center.

Neuman, J. (1986). Gender, life strains, and depression. *Journal of Health and Social Behavior, 27,* 161–178.

NiCarthy, G. (2004) *Getting free: You can end abuse and take back your life.* Berkeley, CA: Seal Press.

Nicolas, G., DeSilva, A., Grey, K., & Gonzalez-Eastep, D. (2006). Using a multicultural lens to understand illnesses among Haitians living in America. *Professional Psychology: Research and Practice, 37,* 702–707.

Nicolas, G., Desilva, A. M., Prater, K., & Bronkoski, E. (2009). Empathic family stress as a sign of extended family connectedness in Haitian immigrants. *Family Process, 48* (1), 135–150.

Nicolas, G., Desilva, A., Subrebost, K., Breland-Noble, A., Gonzalez-Eastep, D., Prater, K., et al. (2007). Expression of depression by Haitian women in the U.S.: Clinical observations. *American Journal of Psychotherapy, 61*(1), 83–98.

Pan American Health Organization (PAHO). (2007). *Health in the Americas* (pp. 425–744). Washington, DC: Author.

Pape, J. W., Liautaud, B., Thomas, F., Mathurin, J. R., St. Armand, M. M., Boncy, M., et al. (1986). Risk factors associated with AIDS in Haiti. *American Journal of the Medical Sciences, 291,* 4–7.

Pedersen, P. (1988). *Handbook for developing multicultural awareness.* Alexandria, VA: American Association of Counseling and Development.

Penchansky, R., & Thomas, J. W. (1981). The concept of access: Definition and relationship to consumer satisfaction. *Medical Care, 19,* 127–140.

Pierce, W., & Elisme, E. (2001). Suffering, surviving, succeeding: Understanding and working with Haitian women. *Race, Gender and Class, 7,* 60–76.

Ponterotto, J. G., Fuertes, J. N., & Chen, E. C. (2000). Models of multicultural counseling. In S. D. Brown & R.W. Lent (Eds.), *Handbook of counseling psychology* (pp. 3–49). New York: John Wiley & Sons.

Pope-Davis, D. B., Liu, W. M., Toporek, R. L., & Brittan-Powell, C. S. (2001). What's missing from multicultural competency research: Review, introspection, and recommendations. *Cultural Diversity and Ethnic Minority Psychology, 7,* 121–138.

Portes, A., Kyle, D., & Eaton, W. W. (1992). Mental illness and help-seeking behavior among Mariel Cuban and Haitian refugees in south Florida. *Journal of Health and Social Behavior, 33,* 283–298.

Portes, A., & Rumbaut, R. G. (2001a). *Ethnicities: Children of immigrants in America.* Berkeley, Los Angeles, CA: University of California Press.

Portes, A., & Rumbaut, R. (2001b). *Legacies: The story of the immigrant second generation.* Berkeley, CA: University of California Press.

Prince, L. (2005). *Medsen fey* (leaf doctor). Retrieved September 4, 2008, from http://www.geocities.com/medsen_fey/index.html

Rhoades, J., Brown, E., & Vistnes, J. (1998). *Health insurance status of the civilian noninstitutionalized population.* Rockville, MD: Agency for Healthcare Research and Quality.

Rowlands, R. (1979). The psychopathology of the Haitian female. *International Journal of Social Psychiatry, 25,* 217–223.

Rudmin, F. (2003). Critical history of the acculturation psychology of assimilation, separation, integration, and marginalization. *Review of General Psychology, 7,* 3–37.

Sargant, W. (1967).Witch doctoring, zar, and voodoo: Their relation to modern psychiatric treatments. *Proceedings of the Royal Society of Medicine, 60,* 1055–1060.

Sue, D. W., Arredondo, P., & Davis, R. (1992). Multicultural counseling competencies and standards: A call to the profession. *Journal of Counseling and Development, 70,* 477–485.

Sue, D. W., Berner, Y., Durran, A., Feinberg, L., Pedersen, P. B., Smith, E. J., et al. (1982). Position paper: Cross-cultural counseling competencies. *The Counseling Psychologist, 10,* 45–52.

Sue, D. W., Carter, R. T., Casas, J. M., Fouad, N. A., Ivey, A. E., Jensen, M., et al. (1998). *Multicultural counseling competencies: Individual and organizational development.* Thousand Oaks, CA: Sage.

Sue, S., & Zane, N. (1987). The role of culture and cultural techniques in psychotherapy: A critique and reformulation. *American Psychologist, 42,* 37–45.

Trimble, J. E., & Fisher, C. B. (2006). *Handbook of ethical considerations in conducting research with ethnocultural populations and communities.* Thousand Oaks, CA: Sage Publications.

Turnier, L. (2000). *La Depression Chez L'Haitien Et l'Approche Clinique.* Coconut Creek, FL: Educa Vision Inc.

U.S. Department of Health and Human Services. (2001). *Mental health: Culture, race, and ethnicity—A supplement to mental health: A report of the surgeon general—Executive summary.* Rockville, MD: U.S. Department of Health and Human Services, Public Health Service, Office of the Surgeon General.

World Health Organization (WHO). (2005). *Global summary of the world AIDS epidemic.* Retrieved April 10, 2005, from http://who.int/hiv/pub/epidemiology/epiupdate/en/index.html

Zéphir, C. (1991). 'Dictator Duvalier orders the torture of journalist Yvonne Hakim Rimpel.' Haitian Women between Repression and Democracy (Enfofanm Editions). Retrieved April 10, 2008, from http://haitiforever.com/windowsonhaiti/w99351.shtml

Zephir, F. (1996). *Haitian immigrants in Black America: A sociological and sociolinguistic portrait.* Westport, CT: Bergin & Garvey.

III

The Health Effects of Self-Silencing

Introduction

Empowering Depressed Women: The Importance of a Feminist Lens

Laura S. Brown

The topic of women's depression has been a focus of my professional interests since early in my career, culminating with my service on the American Psychological Association's Task Force on Women and Depression in the late 1980s. It is also a matter that is very personal to me, and it is from the core of this personal connection that I will be commenting on the importance of feminist therapy to introduce the exciting and provocative work in this section. For feminist therapists, the personal is both political and theory generating (Brown, 1994, 2005, 2008, 2009). This notion rings especially true with me in regard to the topic of understanding and transforming depression in women, as the personal encounters with women's depression that informed my early development served as the foundation for my interests in developing feminist paradigms for personality and psychotherapy.

One woman's experience of depression constituted the emotional atmosphere of my middle childhood and early adolescence. As I have described previously (Brown, 1994, 2005), when I was 6½ years old, my mother fell into a severe postpartum depression after the birth of my youngest brother. Even after she had supposedly been successfully treated for depression, she was someone who my adult psychologist self can diagnose as dysthymic, depressed in a low-grade way for many years. She only fully emerged from that cloud around the time that I left home for university a decade later, as she began to return to the full-time paid workforce. Being the oldest child and only daughter of this family created natural stepping stones for me to the job of psychotherapist (Brown, 2005).

My experiences as my mother's daughter also lent verisimilitude to the theorizing of feminist psychologists about women's distress when I first read this work. In the early days of the second-wave white feminist movement in the United States, feminist psychologists were beginning to speak and write of the oppressive realities of women's lives and roles, and the contribution of those oppressive realities to the much higher rates of depression then seen in women (Bart, 1976; Chesler, 1972). Their descriptions were powerfully persuasive to me in establishing the credibility of feminist theory. It was as if these authors had been recording life in my family of origin, with the camera pointed at my mother.

My mother's experience of depression was prototypical of those suffered by women described by these authors. It was clear to everyone around that her life worked better, and she became happier, when she was working outside the home, an activity that was essentially proscribed for women of her age cohort, educational background, and social class. Despite her genuine desire to have children, her real joys lay in teaching and social activism, activities that a college-educated middle class woman in the 1950s and 1960s was advised to leave behind so as to follow the "motherhood mandate" (Russo, 1979) of that era. My father was not abusive, nor particularly sexist or oppressive. He was a full participant in homemaking and child rearing when not at work, and he never "babysat" his own children, but simply spent time with us when she could not. He supported and encouraged her in her efforts to find meaningful work. Her immediate social milieu was benign at worst, and actively supportive of her intellectual and political interests at best.

But the culture that surrounded my mother during the decades from her mid-20s, when I was born, through her early 40s, when she could finally become a full-time professional, prescribed roles and realities for her that were so toxic that they overpowered the smaller, minimally sexist emotional realities of her particular marriage. With the biological disruptions of pregnancy and postpartum added to the mixture, her descent into depression, while not inevitable, was eased and speeded by the social contexts in which she lived that narrowed options for women. The effects of such patriarchal social contexts on women's well-being are still omnipresent.

Failures by psychotherapists and psychotherapy researchers, then and now, to factor those sociopolitical effects into the trajectory by which women's depressions develop, mean that any interventions done without feminist consciousness will serve a depressed woman today as incompletely as my mother was served in 1959. Despite the advances in both the pharmacotherapy of depression and evidence-based psychotherapeutic and behavioral interventions, any of those treatments offered in the absence of a consciousness of the meaning of depression in women's lives are, I would argue, likely to be less effective. In the absence of feminist and multicultural lenses with which to clearly see the full experiences of depressed women, depression will be responded to by psychotherapists simply as a set of symptoms to be treated, rather than as evidence of dysfunction in the larger social milieus in which a particular woman is depressed. A feminist, multicultural paradigm of depression in women's lives adds an element of depth and aliveness to the portrait of depression that allows both the treating professional and the suffering woman to better comprehend those factors that might have contributed to, and those that might treat, her painful mood state.

A Short Tale of Disempowerment and Depression

When my mother became painfully insomniac after giving birth, the strategy my mother's physician followed was to drug her. This was standard operating procedure in 1959; he was not malevolent, simply completely immersed in the sexist and patriarchal practices that he had learned in his training as a physician, reinforced daily by the cultural context that he shared with his patient. He placed her on large doses of "tranquilizers," which functioned to simply depress her further, as they were, based on her later descriptions to me, likely some early iteration of the benzodiazepine medications. My mother did not have strong social support available, either within her own family of origin or my father's. In the days before doulas (women who serve as perinatal support persons for the laboring and recently postlabor mother), the emotional resources and support that this 32-year-old woman needed, resources that we now know to be essential to women's transition through the perinatal period with emotional well-being (Simkin, 2001), were stretched very thin.

It is also very likely that this depression brought my mother into contact with memories of physical abuse that she and her own mother had suffered at the hands of my maternal grandfather. In the late 1980s, when I reviewed the literature on women and violence, it became clear that exposure to abuse at any point in the life cycle was a risk factor for women's depression (Brown, 1990). This part of my mother's history had been thoroughly silenced in the family. It was only spoken of at the very end of her father's life when, disinhibited by strokes, he began to be physically violent again with my grandmother, who finally told the truth to her granddaughters as she sought assistance from us.

Silencing women's experiences of abuse at the hands of family members is an almost universal patriarchal reality. In the particular culture of my family, such silence is made even more powerful and oppressive through the adoption of a cultural narrative that proclaims Jewish men incapable of domestic violence (Zimberoff & Brown, 2006). No one ever did with my mother what a feminist therapist would routinely do as part of an intake process, which was to ask this depressed young woman if she had ever been a target of abuse. Consequently, no one knew what it meant that her relationships with her parents were strained, or what it might represent to her emotionally that, as her depression deepened, her two older children would at times be left in the care of a man who had abused her.

Finally, as Jack (1991) has proposed in the Silencing the Self model of women's depression, my mother's depression was aggravated by the appeal to self-sacrifice embodied in the treatment options made available to her. Her self needed to be silenced, according to the norms of the day, so that she could serve in her socially prescribed roles; the incompatibility between those roles and her needs was too much a flouting of the rules by which women of her generation were meant to live. According to my maternal aunt, the one family member who has been willing to share the details of this story with me, the psychiatrist with whom my mother finally consulted told her that she could enter individual (probably, given that it was 1959, psychoanalytic) therapy, which would be costly and lengthy, or she could check herself into an inpatient facility for something that would quickly return her to her function as a wife and mother. This was not really a choice. My mother had no internal permission to take the time and money that she needed to heal emotionally, with "selfish" being one of the worst epithets that could be hurled at a woman in that era. Selflessness, silencing her self in favor of what were constructed in the social narrative as the more valued, and allegedly conflicting, needs of her family, was the order of the day for my mother and other women like her.

I have been, and continue to be, the therapist for such women during my three decades of practice as a feminist psychotherapist. Their guilt and shame at not "snapping out of it" quickly enough, their fear that they will harm their children emotionally by being depressed, their shame at not becoming the perfect mother ideal that they had internalized, their horror of their own "selfish" desires to have the emotional claustrophobia of their lives widen for them, their very real exhaustion and the sanctions against acknowledging that it is that real-all of these forbidden realities of their experiences of depression paralyze them. In the absence of a feminist voice in therapy that supports them to heal well, and thoroughly, it would be all too simple to default to whatever is quickest. I can easily, and with grief, imagine my mother having those feelings, and making that default choice. Her struggles do not require imagining; many of them are burned into my memories of those years of our shared existence.

The quick something, electroconvulsive therapy, which was the standard of somatic treatment for depression in 1959, did get her back home and minimally functional within a few months. She could iron clothes, run the vacuum cleaner, take me on the bus to the eye doctor. It also left her a shell of herself, tired, irritable, with something intangible about herself gone, that I can remember well from my first six years of life with her. None of us in her family saw that certain "je ne sais quoi" for more than a decade. My parents were vulnerable to this appeal to go the route that was most likely to return her to her roles as homemaker and parent as quickly as possible, 30-something children of immigrants with three young children whose family system depended on everyone functioning. They had no way of knowing what the "good result" that allowed her to come home from the hospital would look like. The very real and known risks that this "therapy" would silence my mother, and dim her joie de vivre, creativity, and life force as it did, were never even entered into the equation by the experts from whom my young parents, desperate for help, sought assistance.

Feminist Visions: Necessary for Empowerment

I tell my mother's story because of how powerfully and precisely it demonstrates the dangers of simply applying therapy as usual, whatever that might be, for women struggling with depression. Doing the correct thing as prescribed in the mainstream treatment literature is, by the light of feminist therapy theory, likely to be a matter of doing half measures at best. Her story also underscores what I have come to believe is the necessity for the mental health professions of developing models for responding to women's depression that empower and give voice to, rather than disempower and silence, depressed women. Her story illustrates why women's experiences of depression must be responded to with feminist, multicultural epistemologies, in which a biopsychosocial/spiritual-existential model of distress and dysfunction becomes the lens through which each individual woman's experiences of depression are understood.

Feminist Therapy Theory: A Very Brief Overview

Feminist therapy theory, which has been developing since the early 1970s in the United States and elsewhere, is a technically integrative model of therapy that emphasizes therapist attention to issues of gender, power, and social location as a strategy for understanding how distress and dysfunction develop, are maintained, and can be ameliorated (Brown, 1994, 2005; Ballou & Brown, 2002). Multicultural models of practice have taken culture and ethnicity as their starting points for understanding human behavior, attending to the effects of discrimination, colonization, and economic oppression as factors influencing well-being and distress (Comas-Díaz, 2000, 2008). Feminist practice in the United States has become inherently multicultural over the past two decades, as feminist therapists take into account the multiple potential intersections of gender; social class; ethnic and cultural memberships; age and age cohort; spiritual or religious practice; languages spoken; experiences of colonization, both personal and familial; disability; sexual orientation; and other socially meaningful locations that contribute to identity development (Brown, 2005, 2009). Feminist therapists seek to develop egalitarian relationships with clients, in which the two collaborate in developing the goals of therapy and the process by which the client can move toward empowerment. Feminist therapists are interested in creating what Lerner (1990) described as "feminist consciousness," that is, the understanding that one's difficulties in life are not a reflection of personal deficits or failures to sufficiently strive, but rather derive from systemic forms of culturally based oppression. Development of personal power, defined in a very broad manner, is another overarching goal of feminist therapy practice (Brown, 2005, 2009).

Feminist, multicultural paradigms for distress and dysfunction assume that inherent in women's difficulties are experiences of disempowerment on one or more of these variables of body, mind, psyche, and spirit. This disempowerment can arise from many sources, and usually involves more than one risk factor. For example, childhood abuse affects the brain's capacities to return to a nonaroused resting state in times of stress and changes the reuptake of neurotransmitters at the synapse (Mueller, 2005). A feminist analysis of women's depression must take the entire biopsychosocial picture into account and invite the depressed woman to engage in strategies that directly impact mind, body, and, when possible, social reality.

Doing less than that—only focusing on the woman's intrapsychic experiences, only giving medication, and ignoring the realities of oppression and misogyny that are omnipresent in women's lives—will leave important gaps in the healing process. No one suggested to my mother that returning to paid work and engaging in social activism would treat her depression, but more than anything else, those engagements with the world were the "treatments" that finally lifted depression's veil, and that have been the wellspring of resilience for her for four decades.

Empowering women to emerge from depression, similarly, requires attention to the full range of factors influencing well-being. It also requires strategies for empowerment that are inclusive of that range. These strategies for joining with women in their movement through depression must also reflect the unique social locations and multiple, intersecting identities of each individual woman with depression. Misogyny and the oppression of women take different forms, reflecting the social realities and norms of the culture in which a particular woman lives. For a woman living in a setting where actual physical safety is constantly at risk, the feminist strategy will not look very much like psychotherapy. Norsworthy (2007) has described her work with indigenous Thai and Burmese feminists, creating healing strategies for women survivors of gender-based violence. In the groups that she has helped to create, women are offered safe havens in which to tell their truths to one another, and become more powerful because they are visible in their experiences of oppression. Her work in the Global South both is and is not like the psychotherapy that she and other feminist therapists practice in the United States. Empowerment takes many different shapes and forms, but in every instance it has as its goal the ending of women's silence about their pain and oppression.

In the absence of a feminist, multicultural theory for unpacking the multiple strands of disempowerment informing a particular woman's experience of depression, any approach to psychotherapy is less likely to be effective. The findings from empirical research on what happens when a focus on gender and empowerment is integrated into therapy as usual are striking. Add the feminist vision, empower women into voice from silence, and the outcomes of even the briefest of interventions are improved (Chandler, Worell, Johnson, Blount, & Lusk, 1999).

Handing out 20 sessions of cognitive-behavioral therapy will not address depression if it has emerged in response to workplace harassment and discrimination that is not addressed directly in the therapy. For a woman to challenge "dysfunctional cognitions" about the mistreatment not being her fault, the psychotherapist must be prepared to invite his or her client into an analysis of the function of harassment as a tool of misogyny and oppression, and support that client in placing her experience within this much larger cultural and societal context of politics and meaning. Many so-called "dysfunctional core beliefs" held by members of target groups, are representations of internalized oppression. Such core beliefs about one's worthlessness or inferiority do not spring from individual psychopathology; they are representations of social and cultural norms that are daily, if not hourly, reflected back to members of target groups via multiple avenues of media, religion, social institutions, and interpersonal relationships. These insidious traumata, as Root (1992) has named them, can be invisible or discounted when a therapist does not have a feminist theory, yet their impact on people's well-being is persistent (Sue, Bucceri, Lin, Nadal, & Torino, 2007). When a therapist has neglected to point out the power of those micro-aggressions to cement self-loathing and internalized oppression, the weekly hour of psychotherapy will have little power in the face of the other 167 weekly hours of covert and overt misogyny.

It is very unlikely that any of this integration of political and social realities into a conceptual framework for depression, and clinician responses to depression, can occur in the absence of a feminist consciousness. To consistently apply this type of analysis to a woman's experiences, a psychotherapist must come to the work equipped with a feminist theory that draws specific attention to the ways in which individual experience and misery take place in the midst of millennia of oppression, disempowerment, and silencing of members of target groups. When a therapist is attempting to practice without this lens, he or she will lack the words with which to name the distress and the vision with which to see the aspects of oppression that are deeply embedded in the psychotherapist's own culture. The self of the psychotherapist is thus to some degree silenced when a feminist analysis is absent. It can be very difficult to invite clients to name their experiences when the therapist has not yet been able to do so. Feminist therapy theory creates a sharpness of vision as to the small, yet potent, quotidian dynamics of women's oppression.

Feminist therapy theory thus argues that a therapist, to be most effective, must fold the political analysis of the role of women and other target groups in the larger milieu of patriarchal societies into his or her epistemology of women's depression. Foremost in such a psychotherapist's mind will be the necessity of raising questions, for herself or himself and the client, as to the social realities in which women's oppression, and its psychic as well as material costs, have been normalized. This normalizing of internalized oppression has occurred to the extent that the shocking statistics on women's higher rates of depression, when recited both in the popular press and in scholarly settings, have led to little or no public outcry. Higher rates of depression in women and other target groups are simply business as usual in the dominant culture; what it means to uphold that culture via the systemic silencing and disempowerment of more than half of its members is rarely foregrounded. The absence of shock, outrage, and a sense of urgency for responding to the very high rates of women's depression suggests how well integrated into the fabric of patriarchal Western cultures this debilitating silencer of women has become.

A feminist analysis of power and disempowerment defines power, not simply in the usual sense of control of other humans and/or resources, but in a manner identifying the locations, behavioral and intrapsychic, where patriarchal cultures lead people to experience powerlessness and power. Bias, stereotype, and oppression all constitute social forces that create disempowerment; they can be enacted in the larger context of society or culture and the smaller context of family and community, and intrapsychically, internalized and felt as a part of self. Feminist multicultural therapies inquire generally, theoretically, and specifically with each person, what might constitute a move toward power for a given individual in the domains where powerlessness has been experienced. A feminist, multiculturally informed model of responding to women's depression has as its goal the exposure of powerlessness as neither inevitable nor necessarily difficult to dismantle.

What If?

I try to imagine my mother as if she were a woman of 32 today, walking into my office, trudging through the emotional mire of depression, terrified about what is happening, pressured from within to get better and get over it. What would have been different if her therapist had done as feminist therapists do, asking her about abuse so that, even if she were unready to tell the story at session one to a total stranger, she would know that door to be open? What if, instead of starting with drugs, her therapist offered her somatic strategies of diet and exercise that would have cost her nothing and kept her home with her family? What if her therapist had engaged with her around the question of what it meant that, 10 years after being the first person in her family to ever graduate college, she was spending her time dusting and ironing? What if?

This fantasy has haunted me repeatedly during my career. I can see, in the lives of the depressed women who have come through my office and those of my feminist therapy colleagues, that the answers to my questions are not simple. Feminist therapy makes a difference. I cannot say if it would have made the sort of difference that my mother could have used or wanted. I say this not because of my mother's particular age cohort or values. It would be simple to identify her values as congruent with feminism. In the second half of her life she has been an activist for abused women, a campaigner for public health, a woman who, as she grows into the decade of her 80s, has an ever-increasing sense of personal power.

As a feminist therapist, I know that I cannot assume the goals and strategies that would appeal to any individual. One need not be a feminist client, either overtly or unintentionally, to benefit from the analyses of gender, power, and social location that feminist therapies bring to the psychotherapy relationship.

But I like to think that the women who I've accompanied on their journeys through depression emerged in part because what I offered them were questions about power and powerlessness, about being women, of a particular culture, social class, sexual orientation, age, and ability, who were depressed, about being women in the larger milieu in which they were daily assaulted with the micro-aggressions of sexism and misogyny. The work that follows in this volume, as well as the other small yet growing literature on the efficacy and effectiveness of feminist, multiculturally informed therapies (Brown, 2009), argues that our empirical findings support this hope.

I encourage you to read further with the depressed women in your life in mind, asking yourself two things. First, why are not the high rates of women's depression treated as an emergency? And second, how can we continually and more effectively disseminate our knowledge and our collective awareness of what creates the risk for women's depression? What follows in this section represents some valuable responses to these questions.

References

Ballou, M., & Brown, L. S. (Eds.). (2002). *Rethinking mental health and disorder: Feminist perspectives.* New York: Guilford.

Bart, P. (1976). Depression in middle-aged women. In S. Cox (Ed.), *Female psychology: The emerging self* (pp. 349–367). Chicago: Science Research Associates.

Brown, L. S. (1990). *Victimization as a risk factor for depression in women.* Proceedings of the Task Force on Women and Depression. Washington, DC: American Psychological Association.

Brown, L. S. (1994). *Subversive dialogues: Theory in feminist therapy.* New York: Basic Books.

Brown, L. S. (2005). Don't be a sheep: How this eldest daughter became a feminist therapist. *Session/Journal of Clinical Psychology, 8,* 949–964.

Brown, L. S. (2008). Feminist therapy. In J. L. Lebow (Ed.), *Twenty-first century psychotherapies* (pp. 277–308). Hoboken, NJ: John Wiley and Sons.

Brown, L. S. (2009). *Feminist therapy.* Washington, DC: American Psychological Association.

Chandler, R., Worell, J., Johnson, D., Blount, A., & Lusk, M. (1999, August). Measuring long-term outcomes of feminist counseling and psychotherapy. In J. Worell (Chair), *Measuring process and outcomes in short—and—long term feminist therapy.* Symposium presented at the annual meeting of the American Psychological Association, Boston, MA.

Chesler, P. (1972). *Women and madness.* Garden City, NY: Doubleday.

Comas-Díaz, L. (2000). An ethnopolitical approach to working with people of color. *American Psychologist, 55,* 1319–1325.

Comas-Diáz, L. (2008). Spirita Reclaiming womanist sardess into feminis. *Psychology of woman Quartely* 32.

Jack, D. C. (1991). *Silencing the self: Women and depression*. Cambridge, MA: Harvard University Press.

Lerner, G. (1990). *The creation of feminist consciousness*. New York: Oxford University Press.

Mueller, F. A. (2005). *The biological component of trauma response: A web-based survey of clinicians' training, attitudes, beliefs and practices*. Unpublished doctoral dissertation, Argosy University, Seattle.

Norsworthy, K. (2007, August). Multicultural feminist collaboration and healing from gender-based violence in Burma. In E. N. Williams (Chair), *International perspectives on feminist multicultural psychotherapy—Content and connection*. Symposium presented at the Annual Convention of the American Psychological Association, San Francisco, CA.

Root, M. P. P. (1992). Reconstructing the impact of trauma on personality. In L. S. Brown & M. Ballou (Eds.), *Personality and psychopathology: Feminist reappraisals* (pp. 229–265). New York: Guilford.

Russo, N. F. (1979). Overview: Sex roles, fertility, and the motherhood mandate. *Psychology of Women Quarterly, 4*, 7–15.

Simkin, P. (2001). *The birth partner*. Boston: Harvard Common Press.

Sue, D. W., Bucceri, J., Lin, A., Nadal, K. L., & Torino, G. C. (2007). Racial microaggressions and the Asian American experience. *Cultural Diversity and Ethnic Minority Psychology, 13*, 72–81.

Zimberoff, A. K., & Brown, L. S. (2006). Book review: "Only the goyim beat their wives, right?" *Psychology of Women Quarterly, 30*, 422–424.

15

Supporting Voice in Women Living with HIV/AIDS

Rosanna F. DeMarco

Sandra: "I endured multiple rapes...physical beatings,...unhealthy lifestyles. I got into drugs and drinking. And it came from my...need to belong somewhere. Where I didn't think I had a self or my self, a sense of self. I put myself in risky situations because I wanted to please people. I didn't say no to [unsafe] sex because I didn't want people to not like me.... I thought that that meant they liked me...and it took a long time for me to understand that that's a fallacy."

(DeMarco, Norris, & Minnich, 2004)

These words represent the voice of an African American woman living with HIV/AIDS in Boston, Massachusetts. The word "voice" is used intentionally because Sandra's words represent an active, direct, and empowered means to share her experience with others and thus to release herself from silence. She uses her voice with urgency to help other women as she had been helped over the last 10 years in support programs within her community. She decided courageously to disclose her HIV status in the most public way by being part of an HIV prevention intervention film called *Women's Voices Women's Lives*, produced to help other women of color in her community. She did this to empower all women to have the courage to move from silence to a "voice." Sandra decided to speak out in order to save others pain, stigma, and depression she came to know through homelessness, substance abuse, and eventually coinfection of HIV and hepatitis C.

This chapter discusses how Silencing the Self Theory has contributed to the creation of a gender-sensitive and culturally relevant prevention education intervention and outcome measure related to safe sex behaviors in women at risk, living with HIV/AIDS, like Sandra, in the inner city of Boston, Massachusetts. An evolving program of community-based participatory action research is described as (*1*) a systematic exploration of the complex problem of women living with HIV/AIDS in the United States; (2) the interventions used to change behavior, increase self-esteem, decrease depression in current practice, and give "voice" to women; and (3) the use of the theory of silencing the self in creating an innovative approach to HIV/AIDS prevention in African American women in the Boston community and in national and international settings.

HIV/AIDS and African American Women: Where Is Their Voice?

Poor women of color are one of the fastest growing groups of people living with HIV/AIDS (Centers for Disease Control and Prevention [CDC], 2009). The incidence of HIV is increasing particularly in women of color (77% of all women with HIV) and disproportionately among those with lower socioeconomic status. AIDS is the leading cause of death for African American women in the United States aged 25 to 44 (CDC, 2009). Though heterosexual transmission has risen for all women, there is a higher rate of HIV from heterosexual transmission among African Americans nationally. In Massachusetts, heterosexual transmission is the predominant mode of exposure for women of color specifically with partners of unknown risk and HIV status (CDC, 2009; Massachusetts Department of Public Health [MDPH], 2005).

The MDPH reports that African American women are diagnosed with HIV at levels 20 times that of Caucasian women and there are substantial increases in the proportion of African American women infected (40% in 2000 vs. 51% in 2004) (MDPH, 2005). In 2004, the majority of women living with HIV/AIDS in Massachusetts were women of color (27% African American and 24% Hispanic) and, from 1994 to 2003, the proportion of newly diagnosed AIDS cases among African American individuals increased from 25% to 35% (MDPH, 2005). This current direction of the epidemic suggests that either more women are getting tested or, more likely, their risk-taking behavior has increased related to the invisible nature of the epidemic as more people live longer and do not experience prevention intensity.

Despite these facts, women stay hidden in communities of color. They are often tortured with (1) shame because of life choices they made leading to their diagnosis, (2) ambivalence to being tested for HIV that would lead to formidable health care realities, and (3) depression from continued decreased self-esteem while they try to raise children that often have acquired the virus from them during birth.

Voice and Depression

A central theme in the context of women living with HIV/AIDS is the experience of depression and how depression plays a challenging role in gender disparities in

HIV/AIDS care and wellness trajectories. Generally, depression is one of the most common psychological experiences of people living with HIV/AIDS aligned with the following events: (1) receiving the diagnosis, (2) learning of the death of a significant other or friend with HIV, (3) disease exacerbation, (4) treatment failure, (5) HIV symptoms without AIDS, and (6) stressful life events complicated by alcohol/substance abuse (Valente, 2003).

Milan and colleagues (2005) report that elevated symptoms of depression are common among women with HIV in the United States. The annual prevalence rate for this group ranges from 20% to 60%, whereas the general population prevalence rate is 5% to 15% and the same rate for women in general is 10% to 20%. Ichovics and colleagues (2001) found that HIV-seropositive women with depressive symptoms were more likely to experience a more rapid disease progress than HIV-positive men who were not depressed even when controlling for socioeconomic status (SES), age, and substance abuse. Milan and colleagues (2005) found that when controlling for socio-demographic and clinical health factors, intimate partner conflict is a predictor of change in depressive symptoms in 761 women over a five-year period in the United States. Intimate partner conflict predicted more exacerbation of depression than bereavement, maternal role difficulty, and HIV-related social isolation in this group.

However, from the perspective of gender disparities and HIV/AIDS treatment, there is a difference between men and women and the successful use of highly active antiretroviral treatment (HAART). Men experience less depression, and lower levels of depression predict more adherence to HAART (Cook et al., 2004). Thus, men appear to have better adherence with HAART than women. Cook and colleagues (2004) diagnosed depression, using standard depression measures, in 63% of a sample of 2,000 women living with HIV. Controlling for a variety of factors, including CD4 count (the lymphocyte cell surface marker used to assess immune status and susceptibility to opportunistic infections) and viral load, age, race, substance use, and income, women treated for depression (antidepressants plus counseling or counseling alone) were more likely to report use of HAART (adherence) than those who were not treated. Cook and colleagues (2007) in a multi-state study in the United States recruited 1,710 HIV-positive women and screened them for depression using depressive symptom scores on the Center for Epidemiologic Studies Depression Scale. Crack, cocaine, heroin, and amphetamine use was self-reported at 6-month time intervals from 1996 to 2004. Controlling for virologic and immunologic indicators, socio-demographic variables, time, and study site, researchers' findings indicated that there is an interaction effect between illicit drug use and depression that acted to suppress subsequent HAART use.

From an international perspective, studies have been conducted in India, Thailand, Africa (Senegal, Uganda, South Africa), Brazil, and China specifically demonstrating a direct relationship between depression and (1) quality of life, (2) interactions with HIV medications (efavirenz or protease inhibitors),

(3) stigma, (4) test-/repeat test–seeking behaviors, (5) suicidality, and (6) low
CD4 counts (Jin et al., 2006; Kaharuza et al., 2006; Mello & Malbergier, 2006;
Olley, Seedat, Nei, & Stein, 2004; Poupard et al., 2007; Rochat et al., 2006;
Ross, Sawatphanit, Suwansujarid, & Drauker, 2007; Sahay et al., 2007; Simbayi
et al., 2007). In Africa, where two-thirds of more than 40 million people are
living with HIV/AIDS, an important South African study on those living with
HIV/AIDS demonstrated that gender (being a woman), negative life events, and
disability predicted major depression in this population (Olley et al., 2004).
Thus, at the national and international level, HIV/AIDS, gender, and depression
are highly related in a complex, interrelated matrix of prediagnosis life and
postdiagnosis realities.

The Ecological Model of HIV Prevention and
Silencing the Self

Many African American women living with HIV are poor from an SES perspective and have multiple responsibilities for dependent children and family in
addition to trying to care for their own needs. A theoretical framework and
perspective that supports multidimensional influences on behavior in the complex lives of these women is the Ecological Model. The Ecological Model comes
from the work of Bronfenbrenner (1979) and El-Bassel and colleagues (2003,
2009). This model is based on the belief that individuals, their environment, and
the processes that occur within and among these components should be viewed
as interdependent. It suggests that the behavior of individuals needs to be
considered in conjunction with their broader social contexts including the
developmental history of the individual, their psychological characteristics,
interpersonal relationships, physical environment, and culture. Behavior is a
result of knowledge, values, and beliefs of individuals as well as numerous
social influences. These social influences include things such as the context of
relationships, social support networks, and community structure. A key belief in
the model is that there are multiple levels of influence that are reciprocal and
these multiple levels must be considered to change behavior. Four levels of
reciprocal risk and protective factors that influence behavior are identified and
include four systems: (1) ontogenetic, (2) microsystem, (3) exosystem, and
(4) macrocultural (El-Bassel et al., 2003).
    The concept of silencing the self (Jack, 1991) is congruent with the Ecological
Model. How people communicate their needs and feelings and the effect of
not communicating directly is related to their psychological state (affectivity)
as described by Jack (1991) and Jack and Dill (1992). Studies report significant
relationships between self-silencing and depression using the Beck Depression
Inventory (BDI) (Ali & Toner, 2001; Ali, Oatley, & Toner, 2002; Gratch, Bassett,
& Attra, 1995; Thompson, 1995; Uebelacker, Courtnage, & Whisman, 2003).

Choosing to keep one's HIV status a secret or disclosing one's status is one of the most paralyzing dilemmas persons living with HIV/AIDS face at the family, workgroup, and intimate partner level. Disclosure is challenging when silencing one's voice would protect against intrapersonal pain. Social norms provide fertile ground for women to live up to expectations on how they should act in a formal or informal world of behaviors. Specifically, expectations of women in heterosexual intimate relationships are filled with learned and expected behaviors of pleasing others and not taking care of one's health or life in the case of HIV/AIDS. Lastly, the interaction of personal, relational, and formal/informal factors creates fertile ground for the marginalization of women and subsequent health behaviors that are not congruent with self-care.

HIV/AIDS Prevention Research and Women in the United States

Over the last five years, research has focused on the following key areas that are parallel to the theoretical framework that underpins the Ecological Model: (1) personal factors that affect positive prevention (prevention aimed at those who are already HIV positive and continue to need to prevent HIV spread and to take care of the virus load in their own bodies) such as age and education; (2) relationships and the complexity surrounding stigma, depression, substance abuse, and disclosure; (3) the benefits and barriers to social support, self-care, adherence; and (4) gender roles and the need for cultural relevance and tailoring with clinical and research work with this population (Mize, Robinson, Bocktwing, & Scheltema, 2002).

Risk-taking behaviors such as early sexual activity, multiple partners, unprotected sex, and drug and alcohol abuse/addiction greatly increase the risk for HIV infection in women and continue to be issues in positive prevention efforts (Heckman et al., 1995; Trzynka & Erlen, 2004; Wyatt, Myers, & Loeb, 2004). Race, marital status, and level of education are predictors of effective HIV prevention strategies (Crosby, Yarber, & Myerson, 2000; Lauver, Armstrong, Marks, & Schwarz, 1995; Pulerwitz, Amaro, DeJong, Gortmaker, & Rudd, 2002; Rozmus & Edgil, 1993). Three related trends are revealed in these studies: (1) African American women with lower levels of education were less likely to use HIV prevention measures than other groups surveyed, (2) older women and women of color were found to be less likely to use condoms, and (3) positive strong correlations exist between education level and AIDS-related knowledge.

Women who are premenopausal may have different biological, social, and economic issues from postmenopausal women. Women, particularly African American women, are understudied in their experiences related to HAART and normative physiological changes that occur across a pregnancy-to-menopause continuum. Since prevention of mother-to-child transmission interventions (PMTCTs) have become available, there have been significant increases in pregnancies in seropositive women (Anderson, 2004). However, there are many infected adolescents (female) who will need to face the unknown effects of HAART exposure in utero and after birth as it relates to their child-bearing considerations (Anderson, 2004). For childbearing women on HAART, there are reported irregular periods and irregular bleeding (15%). There have also been reports of anemia associated with hypermenorrhea (Hewitt, Parsa, & Gugino, 2001). HIV-positive menopausal women have been overlooked in research exploring sexual risk factors, intimate partner violence, and selected psychosocial illnesses (injection drug use, alcohol abuse, anxiety, depression, psychosis, and dementia) when childbearing may not be a worry or an issue (Clark & Bessinger, 1997; Sormanti, Wu, & El-Bassel, 2004; Zablotsky & Kennedy, 1999).

Disclosing one's HIV status has been reported to increase feelings of shame and stigma, partner violence, rejection, depression, and high-risk sexual beha-vior (Bunting, 1996; Kelly et al., 1994). Stigma, as experienced by an individual, is understood historically as the result of possessing a socially undesirable characteristic, and as highly correlated with poor self-image and withdrawal (Goffman, 1963; Moneyham, Sowell, Seals, & Demi, 2000). Withdrawal as tension reduction is part of responding to stigmatization and, thus, for persons living with HIV with strong histories of substance abuse, the temptation to fall out of recovery is profound (Schilling, El-Bassell, Schinke, Gordon, & Nichols, 1991; Sowell, Moneyham, Guillory, & Mizuno, 1999). Poor self-image is linked to increased HIV risk behaviors (Cole, 1997; Smith, Gerrard, & Gibbons, 1997; Somlai et al., 2000; Sowell et al., 1999) and decreased disease adjust-ment (Anderson, 2000), health promotion (Butler, 1995), self-advocacy (Neely-Smith & Patsdaughter, 2004), self-efficacy for negotiating safe sex (Neely-Smith & Patsdaughter, 2004), and safe sex behaviors. When women are empowered in HIV prevention efforts, they experience increased self-image, control over health care treatment decisions, self-efficacy, increased knowledge, and a positive sense of self as individuals and in relationships (Cianelli, Ferrer, & Pergallo, 2003; Norris & DeMarco, 2005). There is a relationship between low self-image, negative affectivity (depression), and lack of self-advocacy in women (DeMarco, Johnsen, Fukuda, & Deffenbaugh, 2001). From a treatment perspective, depressive symptoms are underdiagnosed and are associated with lower medication adherence, risky behaviors, and poor health outcomes (Sanzero et al., 2005)

Gender Roles and HIV/AIDS

Women's gender roles and, for some, the need to maintain connection in rela-tionships at the cost of their own health are key issues for all women living with chronic diseases but particularly for those who are seropositive (DeMarco & Johnsen, 2002, 2003; DeMarco, Lynch, & Board, 2002; DeMarco, Miller, Patsdaughter, Grindel, & Chisholm, 1998). Jack (1991, 1999) discussed the concept of silencing in the context of women's experiences with relationships. Jack supports the contention women's relationships are influenced not only by biological factors but also by psychosocial factors (Bancroft, 2002).

Self-silencing as a concept is relevant to the proposed study because heterosexual seropositive safe sex occurs in a relational context. Women living with HIV will continue to be sexually active with men. Silencing their voice during times of sexual intimacy in order to maintain connection with their partner rather than taking care of themselves with direct requests will not protect them against further strains of HIV and other sexually transmitted diseases, and will infect others (DeMarco & Johnsen, 2002, 2003; DeMarco et al., 1998, 2001, 2002; DeMarco & Norris, 2004a, 2004b; Norris & DeMarco, 2004, 2005).

HIV prevention interventions directed to women living with HIV/AIDS include studies that found women receiving social skills interventions were more likely to demonstrate direct communication and assertiveness (Wingood & DiClemente, 1996), safe and preventive sexual negotiation (Kelly et al., 1994), and more self-advocating behaviors (Harris, Kavanagh, Hetherington, & Scott, 1992). To date, the most effective HIV prevention interventions for women have been gender specific because men and women exhibit differences in a diverse range of sexual attitudes and behaviors (Mize et al., 2002). Using a meta-analysis of the effectiveness of HIV prevention for women at risk, which included women living with HIV, Mize and colleagues (2002) found that intervention studies generally improved knowledge about HIV/AIDS and increased sexual risk reduction behaviors. Findings for self-efficacy were inconsistent. These data were found across a variety of ethnicities and time frames ranging from immediately to 24 months after the intervention. The samples in the studies that were included in the analysis did not specify outcome differences across different ethnic groups or between those women at risk and those already living with HIV/AIDS.

Although many studies include African American women living with HIV, prevention studies that address only this population are less prevalent. Areas studied include psychological resourcefulness mediating the effects of social support and depression (Simoni, Montoya, Huang, & Goodry, 2005), safe sex knowledge (Whyte, Standing, & Madigan, 2004), safe sexual behavior (Whyte et al., 2004), symptom management (Miles et al., 2003), relationships between mothers and children (Feaster & Szapocznik, 2002), social support from families, and levels of psychological functioning (Smith et al., 2001).

Effective intervention programs that target women generally have focused on (1) relationship and negotiation skills with partners, (2) culturally specific topics that address the unique issues and needs of the targeted population, (3) stressors facing women such as power imbalances and sexual assertiveness, (4) peer-led approaches, and (5) randomized control research design approaches with multiple sessions (Bova & Durante, 2003; El-Bassel et al., 2003; Flaskerud, Nyamathi, & Uman, 1997; Marks, Burris, & Peterman, 1999; Pitts, Whalen, O'Keefe, & Murray, 1989; Rokeach, 1969; Weeks, Schensul, Williams, Singer, & Grier, 1995; Wingood & DiClemente, 1996).

Giving Women a Voice through Community-Based Research

I have had extensive experience and grant funding to work with community groups in the area of HIV using action research that is culturally relevant and gender sensitive. Much of this work has been with women of color, particularly in the past eight years with African American women who are HIV positive. In 1998, I joined a group of nurses who had created a nurse-led, peer-driven HIV/ AIDS prevention group for inner-city women called the Healing Our Community Collaborative (HOCC). This group has been committed to identifying key topics of concern to women (primarily women of color) and presenting one-hour talks with free lunch supported by local HIV service organizations to enhance conversation among those women willing to attend. HOCC continues to this day to provide a monthly funded series of educational programs and research projects that are nurse led and peer driven by women living with HIV/ AIDS from the inner-city community. The following describes four studies about this work and what we continue to learn about self-silencing in relation to HIV/ AIDS and prevention of these critical illnesses (DeMarco & Johnsen, 2002, 2003; DeMarco et al., 1998, 2001, 2002).

Silencing the Self Scale: Exploring Validity with African American Women

In 1998, a study was conducted to explore the validity of Jack's (1991) original Silencing the Self Scale (STSS) with women who attended our HOCC educational programs (DeMarco et al., 2001). The purpose of the study was to validate the use of the STSS with women living with HIV/AIDS. The research questions were as follows: (1) What is the range in scores on self-silencing and affectivity among women living with HIV/AIDS? and (2) What is the relationship between the measure and women's report of behaviors? The majority (10, 67%, $n = 15$) of participants were African American, ranging in age from 21 to 60 years ($M = 42$, $SD = 12.4$). Eleven of the women characterized themselves as "single," but seven women stated they had responsibility for dependent children or nonchildren at home. Only one woman was employed, while the rest were unemployed (3, 20%) or on disability (11, 73%). Most of the women (12, 80%) received their health care at what they considered major

Table 15.1 Comparison of Study Sample Means on the STSS

| STSS | M | Study Sample | | Comparison Groups |
		SD	Range	(Domestic Violence Shelter)
Externalized Self-Perception	24.00	6.64	26–8	20.30
Care as Self-Sacrifice	29.40	7.38	39–17	25.50
Silencing the Self	33.28	8.29	37–12	28.70
Divided Self	25.60	4.28	31–15	25.40
Total	102.40	15.72	133–63	99.00

medical centers in Boston, Massachusetts, while describing that the place where they got most of their support was at HIV-designated support centers (8) or at these medical care centers (5).

All of the women were living with HIV/AIDS. STSS validity was supported through a mixed-method approach of cross-sectional measures of baseline mean scores following an educational prevention program combined with individual interviews. Cronbach alpha internal consistency scores ranged from .84 to .96 on the total STSS scores and item-total correlations were .75 to .90 (DeMarco et al., 2001, 2002).

The mean STSS total score and individual subscale scores were higher for the participants ($n = 15$) than scores of women in domestic violence shelters ($n = 140$) originally measured by Jack and Dill (1992) (see Table 15.1).

Qualitative individual interview data were collected in addition to the STSS measure and were consistent with individual scoring on the STSS; that is, when women scored above the median of mean ranges from previous studies of subscale or total scale scores, interview data demonstrated examples of behaviors that describe the four subscales: Silencing the Self, Care as Self-Sacrifice, Externalized Self-Perception, and Divided Self. For example, a high subscale score that was indicative of Silencing the Self was confirmed in an interview when one of the participants talked about feeling like she was a hermit and that stigmatization related to her HIV status caused her to not tell people what she needed or felt directly and openly. This woman stated:

> I have no relationships with HIV because you get rejected a lot. So, I tend to be by myself a lot. Actually, the support from the people where I live and different organizations make it easier. Otherwise, I would be a hermit and I probably wouldn't be taking as good care of myself as I have been lately.

Another woman who had a high score on the Silencing the Self subscale stated:

> I have not found the comfort zone to discuss my HIV status with family and many of the people I socialize with. I'm going to find people in the community, a new group of people to share this with so that I can work with it. I realized how

important it is to be able to, you know, speak your mind about certain issues and to advocate through yourself when those issues aren't being addressed by my own choice.... I always surrendered all the power to the health care provider and I know that is not the way to do this right.

Although the small sample size gives us only an exploratory window into the applicability of the STSS in this group of inner-city women, these data were the first attempt to measure congruence between the measure and this group from a culturally relevant perspective. This approach to content validity was positively critiqued and reviewed by Sharts-Hopko (2002) as an innovative and legitimate way to be gender sensitive when using outcome measures with specific client groups that may have unique item responses.

Intergenerational HIV Prevention Film: Women's Voices Women's Lives

After the preceding study, we continued to offer HOCC programs to women who wanted to attend monthly meetings. We always offered a collaborative evaluation forum after each session to enhance and support peer leadership in topics or activities. African American women in the HOCC group consistently discussed the need to not just passively "take in" educational programs for their own enlightenment but the need to take community action to address "self-silencing" as it affects women within their community. The "silencing" they described related to women living with HIV who were hidden in the community and struggled with disclosure if they were seropositive or women who knew they had engaged in high-risk behaviors but were afraid to discuss these activities with anybody because they feared what HIV testing would reveal. Four African American seropositive women ranging in age from 35 to 56 years from the group suggested making a film and wanting to disclose publicly their status to help others. They wished to reach out to youth and other women in their community. In January 2002, filming began with these four women talking in a documentary style about how living with HIV changed their lives. In the film, they offer advice to viewers about risky and safer sex behavior as wisdom figures by discussing how they learned about their diagnosis, the stigma attached to them because of their status, how women silence themselves instead of advocating for safe sex, and their subsequent survivorship. The film was named by the women, *Women's Voices Women's Lives*, and is a powerful documentary, HIV prevention intervention now used nationally and internationally in numerous AIDS service organizations (DeMarco et al., 2004). It is dubbed in Vietnamese and Spanish language and curricula were created to booster the messages in the film with self-efficacy skill-building exercises.

In one of the segments of the film, the four women begin to address specifically the concept of silencing the self as an experience replete with the belief that one feels weak and unable to ask for what is needed in relationships with men. When the film is viewed by audiences to this day, the women viewers often point out that this is the segment of dialogue that makes them feel connected with all women in a common experience. In this segment, Tonia reflects on her absolute trust in a man who was fooling around with other women, but because she needed him in her life to feel good about herself, she believed the lies and half truths about his faithfulness to her:

> I believed him. Why would you think that somebody that you were in a relationship with that you have come to love, you wouldn't think that they would do anything to hurt you. I never thought he would do anything to hurt me and also I wasn't strong enough to make certain decisions for myself because I didn't want to hurt him. Never mind knowing that I was hurting myself. I didn't want to hurt him. So I put myself into a situation where I had a relationship with this man knowing later on down the line is fooling around with other girls and I wasn't strong enough that particular night to tell him to wear a condom. I wasn't strong enough to do that because I didn't want to lose him. I didn't want to lose him.

What becomes stunning in the context of Tonia's voice is that she silenced herself so much so that she literally put her life on the line so she wouldn't lose an intimate relationship in her life.

Catherine discusses the learned behavior of women and the cultural expectations that govern behaviors that really don't make much sense:

> We didn't think we had choices. We thought we had to please this guy no matter what the cost to ourselves and look where we are now. I mean come on. I don't want to see my granddaughter grow up with...with...with this sword of Damocles hanging over her. Well I can either please him or live [laugh]. I mean that is a hell of an option, don't you think?

Lastly, Quenelle connects self-esteem and the price of gaining self-worth through judgments that put women at high risk for serious illness:

> I mean everybody in the world wants love, don't you know. So because you want love are you supposed to turn around and have HIV, uh...uh...a sickness that is an incurable disease. I don't think that for love that should be anybody's price for love. And I just feel so sad that I had to go through all the things I had to go through to love myself, just to have respect for myself and not to compromise myself for someone else, to please somebody else or to make somebody else happy or to live my life as other people choose because in the end I'm the one who has to lay down with me at night. I'm the one who has to turn around and deal with the loneliness, sadness whatever it is I'm feeling. I'm the one dealing with it so why am I doing everything to please other people? Why am I trying to live up to other people's standards?

Despite all of the good intentions of each of these women to try to speak up, each of them confesses that for some reason they can't seem to do it and ultimately make the biggest sacrifice of their life—their health. Catherine states in the final portion of this segment of the film:

> Women, we are the great compromisers. Because we compromise our self respect, we compromise our health, we compromise our happiness, some cases, extreme cases we compromise our sanity. All in the name of, or maybe not all in the name of, but primarily in the name of relationships...to please him, instead of pleasing ourselves. I mean, listen, there is nothing wrong with compromise. I negotiate on a daily basis, on a regular basis and it's all good. But there got to be somethin' wrong with your thinkin' when you're willing to compromise your health, your life, actually right, your life because you are afraid of displeasing another person.

Professional and Consumer Focus Groups and Film

From April 2002 to January 2004 (when the film was officially released), 10 focus groups were held to explore the experience of those who viewed the film. The film was edited based on these data. Focus groups consisted of (1) mixed groups of men and women of color; (2) Caribbean, Cape Verdean, African American, Haitian, and Vietnamese women; (3) health care professionals involved in direct care and prevention of seropositive women in Boston; and (4) community peer educators. Data analysis indicated that viewers considered that the film contained powerful primary, secondary, and tertiary prevention messages for teens, women who are living with HIV, and health care professionals. Many commented that despite the dominance of African American warnings and images in the film, the message of poor women living in the inner city and the health disparities they experience was more sensitizing than anything else (DeMarco & Norris, 2004a, b). Health professionals suggested that the film be used specifically for women living with HIV as a way to help clients value the strength and courage of the women in the film to survive and maintain positive self-image through a directed and healthy life. In addition, the film has also been found to affect groups of all-male viewers, motivating them to be HIV tested through giving them a woman's perspective on acquiring the virus. It also sensitized them regarding what women experience when silencing themselves and deciding on how they should negotiate safe sex when their learned behavior supports women's self-silencing (DeMarco & Minnich, 2006).

Film Effects on Silencing and Safe Sex at a Woman's Harm Reduction Drop-In Center

In 2003–2004 a self-report pretest and posttest was developed to be used with the viewing of the film. The tests consisted of selected demographic questions and four scales: (1) Silencing the Self subscale, (2) safe sex behaviors, (3) safe sex intentions, and (4) safe sex attitudes. In the posttest given immediately after the film, additional questions were asked about the quality of the film and location of health care resources in viewers' community. A woman's harm reduction drop-in center in a poor neighborhood of Boston called Women Connecting and Affecting Change (Women of Color AIDS Council, Inc., WCAC) partnered with me by adopting the film as an intervention tool. Women (sex workers and homeless) who entered the drop-in center or were visited by peer educators off-site in postincarceration transition homes or community-based group homes participated in this project ($n = 131$). In all cases, the women either reported high-risk behaviors related to acquiring HIV (70%) or were HIV positive (30%). The mean age of the participants was 35 years, with 47% Caucasian, 26% African American, 12% bi- or multiracial, and 10% Latino or Hispanic. The majority of participants were single and never married (55%). In terms of education, 77% had attended high school (including obtaining a GED) or college, suggesting that despite poverty they were well educated. After establishing acceptable psychometric evidence (reliability statistics and factor analysis), findings demonstrated that mean scores were significantly higher on the pretest compared to the posttest ($n = 111$; $M = 26$ vs. 21, respectively; $SD =$ 8.3, 8.2; $p = .006$) for the Silencing the Self subscale, indicating that after watching the film, the participants reported fewer silencing behaviors. Mean scores for safe sex behaviors were significantly higher on the posttest compared to the pretest ($n = 118$; $M = 12$ vs. 13, respectively; $SD = 3.1, 2.9$; $p = .001$). This indicated that the film affected self-report of positive safe sex behaviors. In the safe sex intentions scale, one significant item indicated that the women had responded more positively after viewing the film to have a plan when they knew they would be having intercourse ($n = 90$; $M = 1.1$ vs. 1.5, respectively; $SD =$ 0.34, 50; $p = .001$). The other significant item was "I refuse to use alcohol or drugs when I am in a situation where I could be pressured to have sexual intercourse." Scores were significantly higher on the posttest compared to the pretest ($n = 127$, $M = 1.7$ vs. 1.9, respectively; $SD = 0.4, 0.3$; $p = .001$), indicating that the film may improve intentions with regard to substance use and sexual intercourse. The safe sex attitudes scale did not demonstrate any significant changes at posttesting.

The evaluation of the film yielded positive results. Eighty-nine percent of the participants ($n = 117$) reported that the film was extremely important for other women to see; 87% ($n = 115$) stated that watching the film made them want to protect themselves and others by using a condom; 28% ($n = 116$) stated that watching the film made them want to avoid sex to the greatest extreme; and 66% ($n = 116$) strongly (extremely) would recommend the film for others to view.

Since the filming in 2002 to the present, the women in the film *Women's Voices Women's Lives* have served as an advisory group. The group has been available to come to showings of the film and answer the audience's questions as well as to articulate how involvement in continued community prevention through the film increases their self-image and sense of meaning in their lives. In reflecting on their experience in making the film, each of the women describe how proud they are that their voices are being used to help others in such a profound way. At a recent International AIDS Day celebration in Boston, Massachusetts (December 2006), the women were invited to show the film and discuss the making of the film. The audience stood for five minutes to applaud them.

In the storytelling history of African American women, "naming" something means you own it. The lives of many African American women in the inner city of Boston are filled with the effects of poverty and oppression. Daily personal crises give little opportunity for reflective work or "naming" through storytelling (Dr. Sandra Young, personal communication, March 17, 2007). An exchange between African Americans in a group is coined by Young as "kitchen table talks." African American tradition supports this approach and sees conversations in groups as important and often life-saving information exchanged in a manner that everyone "at the table" could understand and act upon. According to Hill Collins (1991), expecting African American women to have skill sets that would enable them to analyze their behavior, identify their weaknesses and resource shortages, and find remedies for their problems is both unrealistic and burdensome. Such expectations can lead to intervention designs that support outsiders' negative opinions as a reality by blaming the victim. Methodologies that label behaviors or develop subtle causal connections between variables such as poverty, cognitive abilities, and survivorship choices impose negative worldviews on African American women and African Americans in general. Using intervention methods that use strengths of women to tell or write stories of their lives, what they have learned from their personal pain, and how they have moved on as survivors can help capture sensitive and relevant ways to explore positive outcomes that may be able to be sustained in everyday survivorship. Small group exchanges around issues that threaten their families and lives have proved most effective and have offered the best opportunities for long-lasting remedies. Examples of effective use of "kitchen table talks" through the use of film media are *Waiting to Exhale* and *Soul Food* (Hurston, 1990; Pinkola Estes, 1996). African American women have not been the focus of this approach perhaps because of stereotypical beliefs that reinforce that they are unable to do so (Harris, Kami, & Pollock, 2001).

Summary

Engagement in the HIV service community has allowed me to respond to community-based requests to create a prevention media project that allows African American women living with HIV to disclose their HIV status in the most public of ways to help others in their community. The film has shown promise in (1) measuring validity of silencing the self as a concept and as a measure that is sensitive to the experiences of African American women;

(2) affecting safe sex behavior, beliefs, and attitudes as well as self-advocacy in intimate relationships; and (3) used as a stimulus or focal point to enhance structured writing in a group as a way to create ethnically tailored prevention messages to seropositive women. Embedded in this work are the continued relevance of the experience of women of silencing their voice as a way to survive relationships at a variety of levels and the continued need to address self-silencing with creative prevention and research programs that are tailored to the experiences of those involved.

References

Ali, A., Oatley, K., & Toner, B. B. (2002). Life stress, self-silencing and domains of meaning in uniploar depression: An investigation of an outpatient sample of women. *Journal of Social and Clinical Psychology, 21*, 669–685.

Ali, A., & Toner, B. B. (2001). Symptoms of depression among Caribbean women and Caribbean-Canadian women: An investigation of self-silencing and domains of meaning. *Psychology of Women Quarterly, 25*, 175–180.

Anderson, E. (2000). Self-esteem and optimism in men and women infected with HIV. *Nursing Research, 49*, 262–271.

Anderson, J. R. (2004, September). *The Hopkins HIV report*. Presented at the XV International AIDS Conference: Women and HIV in the Spotlight.

Bancroft, J. (2002). Biological factors in human sexuality. *Journal of Sex Research, 39*, 15–21.

Bova, C., & Durante, A., (2003). Sexual functioning among HIV-infected women. *AIDS Patient Care and STDs, 17*, 75–83.

Bronfenbrenner, U. (1979). *The ecology of human development: Experiments by nature and design*. Cambridge, MA: Harvard University Press.

Bunting, S. M. (1996). Sources of stigma associated with women with HIV. *Advances in Nursing Science, 19*, 64–73.

Butler, M. R. (1995). Self-esteem and health promoting lifestyle as predictors of health-risk behaviors among older adolescents. *Dissertation Abstracts International, 56*, 00203.

Centers for Disease Control and Prevention. (2009). HIV/AIDS and Women Retrieved October 12, 2009, from http://www.cdc.gov/hiv/topics/women/resources/factsheets/women.htm

Cianelli, R., Ferrer, L., & Pergallo, N. (2003). A concept analysis of empowerment: Its relationship to HIV/AIDS prevention in Latina women. *Hispanic Health Care International, 2*, 6–12.

Clark, R. A., & Bessinger, R. (1997). Clinical manifestations and predictors of survival in older women infected with HIV. *Journal of Acquired Immune Deficiency Syndromes and Human Retrovirology, 15*, 341–345.

Cole, F. L. (1997). The role of self-esteem in safer sexual practices. *Journal of the Association of Nurses in AIDS Care, 8*, 64–70.

Cook, J. A., Grey, D., Burke, J., Cohen, M. H., Gurtman, A. C., Richardson, J. L., et al. (2004). Depressive symptoms and AIDS-related mortality among a multsite cohort of HIV-positive women. *American Journal of Public Health, 94*, 1133–1140.

Cook, J. A., Grey, D. D., Burke Miller, J. K., Cohen M. H., Vlahov, D., Kapadia, F., et al. (2007). Illicit drug use, depression and their association with highly active antiretroviral therapy in HIV-positive women. *Drug Alcohol Dependence, 89,* 74–81.

Crosby, R. A., Yarber, W. L., & Myerson, B. M. (2000). Prevention strategies other than male condoms employed by low-income women to prevent HIV infection. *Public Health Nursing, 17,* 53–60.

DeMarco, R., & Johnsen, C. (2002). Vulnerable populations: Women living with HIV/AIDS. In E. A. Mahoney & J. K. Shaw (Eds.), *HIV/AIDS nursing secrets.* Philadelphia: Hanely & Belfus, Inc.

DeMarco, R., & Johnsen, C. (2003). Taking action in communities: Women living with HIV lead the way. *Journal of Community Health Nursing, 20,* 51–62.

DeMarco, R., Johnsen, C., Fukuda, D., & Deffenbaugh, O. (2001). Content validity of a scale to measure silencing and affectivity among women living with HIV/AIDS. *Journal of Association of Nurses in AIDS Care (JANAC), 12,* 49–60.

DeMarco, R., Lynch, M. M., & Board, R. (2002). Mothers who silence themselves: Clinical implications for women living with HIV/AIDS and their children. *Journal of Pediatric Nursing, 17,* 89–95.

DeMarco, R., Miller, K., Patsdaughter, C., Grindel, C., & Chisholm, M. (1998). From silencing the self to action: Experiences of women living with HIV/AIDS. *Women's Health Care International, 19,* 539–552.

DeMarco, R., & Minnich, C. A. (2006). Men's experiences viewing an HIV/AIDS prevention education film by and for women. *American Journal of Men's Health, 1,* 1–7.

DeMarco, R., & Norris, A. E. (2004a). Women's voices women's lives: A web-based HIV prevention film project. J. V. M. Welie & J. Lee (Eds.), *Jesuit health sciences and the promotion of justice: An invitation to a discussion.* Milwaukee, WI: Marquette University Press.

DeMarco, R., & Norris, A. E. (2004b). Culturally relevant HIV interventions: Transcending ethnicity. *Journal of Cultural Diversity, 11,* 65–68.

DeMarco, R., Norris, A. E., & Minnich, C. A. (Co-Producers). (2004). *Women's voices women's lives.* Available from HIV Education Resources Inc., 1 Crest Street, Quincy, MA 02169.

El-Bassel, N., Caldeira, N.A., Ruglass, L.M., & Gilbert, L. (2009). Addressing the unique needs of African American women in HIV prevention. *American Journal of Public Health, 99*(6), 996–1001.

El-Bassel, N., Witte, S. S., Gilbert, L., Wu, E., Chang, M., Hill, J., et al. (2003). The efficacy of a relationship-based HIV/STD prevention program for heterosexual couples. *American Journal of Public Health, 93,* 963–969.

Feaster, D. J., & Szapocznik, J. (2002). Interdependence of stress processes among African-American family members: Influence of HIV serostatus and a new infant. *Psychology and Health, 17,* 339–363.

Flaskerud, J., Nyamathi, A., & Uman, G. (1997). Longitudinal effects of an HIV testing and counseling program for low-income Latina women. *Ethnicity and Health, 2,* 89–103.

Goffman, E. (1963). *Stigma: Notes on the management of spoiled identity.* Englewood Cliffs, NJ: Prentice Hall.

Gratch, L. B., Bassett, M. E., & Attra, S. L. (1995). The relationship of gender and ethnicity to self silencing and depression among college students. *Psychology of Women Quarterly, 19,* 509–515.

Harris, J. L., Kami, A. G., & Pollock, K. E. (2001). *Literacy in African-American communities.* Mahwah, NJ: Erlbaum.

Harris, R. M., Kavanagh, K. H., Hetherington, S. E., & Scott, D. E. (1992). Strategies for AIDS prevention: Leadership training and peer counseling for high-risk African-American women in the drug user community. *Clinical Nursing Research, 1,* 9–24.

Heckman, T. G., Kelly, J. A., Sikkema, K., Cargill, V., Solomon, L., Roffman, R., et al. (1995). HIV risk characteristics of young adult, adult, and older adult women who live in inner-city housing developments: Implications for prevention. *Journal of Women's Health, 4,* 397–406.

Hewitt, R. G., Parsa, N., & Gugino, L. (2001). The role of gender in HIV progression. *Bulletin of Experimental Treatments for AIDS.* Retrieved, October 12, 2009 from http://www.aegis.com/pubs/beta/2001/BE010406.html

Hill Collins, P. (1991). *Black feminist thought: Knowledge, consciousness, and the politics of empowerment.* New York: Routledge.

Hurston, Z. N. (1990). *Mules and men.* New York: Perennial.

Ichovics, J. R. Hamburger, M. E., Vlahov, D., Schoenbaum, E. E., Schuman, P., Boland, R. J., et al. (2001). Mortality, CD4 cell count decline, and depressive symptoms among HIV-seropositive women: Longitudinal analysis from the HIV Epidemiology Research Study. *Journal of the American Medical Association, 285,* 1466–1474.

Jack, D. C. (1991). *Silencing the self.* Cambridge, MA: Harvard University Press.

Jack, D. C. (1999). *Behind the mask.* Cambridge, MA: Harvard University Press.

Jack, D. C., & Dill, D. (1992). The Silencing the Self Scale: Schemas of intimacy associated with depression in women. *Psychology of Women Quarterly, 16,* 97–106.

Jin, H., Hampton Atkinson, J., Yu, X., Heaton, R. K., Shi, C., Marcotte, T. P., et al. (2006). Depression and suicidality in HIV/AIDS in China. *Journal of Affective Disorders, 94,* 269–275.

Kaharuza, F. M., Bunnell, R., Moss, S., Purcel, D. W., Bikaako-Kajura, W. et al. (2006). Depression and CD4 cell count among person with HIV infection in Uganda. *AIDS and Behavior, 10*(4 suppl), S105–111.

Kelly, J. A., Murphy, D. A., Washington, C. D., Wilson, T. S., Koob, J. J., Davis, D. R., et al., (1994). The effects of HIV/AIDS intervention groups for high-risk women in urban clinics. *American Journal of Public Health, 84,* 1918–1922.

Lauver, D., Armstrong, K., Marks, S., & Schwarz, S. (1995). HIV risk status and preventive behaviors among 17,619 women. *Journal of Obstetric, Gynecological, and Neonatal Nursing Clinical Studies, 24,* 33–39.

Marks, G., Burris, S., & Peterman, T. A. (1999). Reducing sexual transmission of HIV from those who know they are infected: the need for personal and collective responsibility. *AIDS, 13,* 297–306.

Massachusetts Department of Health. *Epidemiological profile FY2005.* Retrieved July 14, 2005, from http://www.mass.gov/dph/aids/research/profile2005.eppro2005.htm

Mello, V. A., & Malbergier, A. (2006). Depression and women infected with HIV. *Revista Brasileira de Psiquiatria, 28,* 10–17.

Milan, S., Icovics, J., Vlahov, D., Boland, R., Schoenbaum, E., Schuman, P et al. (2005). Interpersonal predictors of depression trajectories in women with HIV. *Journal of Consulting and Clinical Psychology, 73*, 678–688.

Miles, M. S., Holditch-Davis, D., Eron, J., Black, B. P., Pedersen, C., & Harris, D. A. (2003). An HIV self-care symptom management intervention for African-American mothers. *Nursing Research, 52*, 350–360.

Mize, S. J., Robinson, B. E., Bockting, W. O., & Scheltema, K. E. (2002). Meta-analysis of the effectiveness of HIV prevention interventions for women. *AIDS Care, 14*, 163–180.

Moneyham, L., Sowell, R., Seals, B., & Demi, A. (2000). The depressive symptoms among African-American women with HIV disease...including commentary by Boyle, J. S. *Scholarly Inquiry for Nursing Practice, 14*, 9–39, 41–46.

Neely-Smith, S. L., & Patsdaughter, C. A. (2004). The influence of self-esteem and self-silencing on self-efficacy for negotiating safer sex behaviors in urban Bahamian women. *Journal of Multicultural Nursing and Health, 10*, 15–26.

Norris, A. E., & DeMarco, R. (2004). The mechanics of conducting culturally relevant HIV prevention research with Haitian American adolescents: Lessons learned. *Journal of Multicultural Nursing and Health, 11*, 69–76.

Norris, A. E., & DeMarco, R. (2005). The experience of African-American women living with HIV creating a prevention film for teens. *Journal of the Association of Nurses in AIDS Care, 16*, 32–39.

Olley, B. O., Seedat, S., Nei, D. G., & Stein, D. J. (2004). Predictors of major depression in recently diagnosed patients with HIV/AIDS in South Africa. *AIDS Patient Care and STDs, 18*, 481–487.

Pinkola Estes, C. (1996). *Warming the stone child: Myths and stories about abandonment and the unmothered child*. New York: Lighthouse Series.

Pitts, R. E., Whalen, D. J., O'Keefe, R., & Murray, V. (1989). Black and white response to culturally targeted television commercials: A value-based approach. *Psychology and Marketing, 6*, 311–328.

Poupard, M., Ngom Gueye, N. F., Thiam, D., Ndiaye, B., Girard, P. M., Delaporte, E., et al. (2007). Quality of life and depression among HIV-infected patients receiving efavirenz-or protease inhibitor-based therapy in Senegal. *HIV Medicine, 8*, 92–95.

Pulerwitz, J., Amaro, H., DeJong, W., Gortmaker, S. L., & Rudd, R. (2002). Relationship power, condom use and HIV risk among women in the USA. *AIDS Care, 14*, 789–800.

Rochat, T. J., Richter, L. M., Doll, H. A., Buthelezi, N. P., Tomkins, A., & Stein, A. (2006). Depression among pregnant rural South African women undergoing HIV testing. *Journal of the American Medical Association, 295*, 1376–1378.

Rokeach, M. (1969). *Beliefs, attitudes, and values: A theory of organization and change*. San Francisco, CA: Jossey-Bass.

Ross, R., Sawatphanit, W., Suwansujarid, T., & Draucker, C. B. (2007). Life story of and depression in an HIV-positive pregnant Thai woman who was a former sex worker: Case study. *Archives of Psychiatric Nursing, 21*, 32–39.

Rozmus, C., & Edgil, A. E. (1993). Rural women's knowledge of and attitudes towards acquired immune deficiency syndrome. *Health Care for Women International, 14*, 301–309.

Sahay, S., Phadke, M., Brahme, R., Paralikar, V., Joshi, V., Sane, S., et al. (2007). Correlates of anxiety and depression among HIV test-seekers at a voluntary counseling and testing facility in Pune, India. *Quality of Life Research: An International Journal of Quality of Life Aspects of Treatment, Care, and Rehabilitation, 16*, 41–52.

Sanzero, L., Corless, I. B., Bunch, E. H., Kemppainen, J., Holzemer, W., Nokes, K., et al. (2005). Self-care strategies for depressive symptoms in people with HIV disease. *Journal of Advanced Nursing, 51*, 1365–2648.

Schilling, R. F., El-Bassel, N., Schinke, S. P., Gordon, K., & Nichols, S. (1991). Building skills of recovering women drug users to reduce heterosexual AIDS transmission. *Public Health Reports, 106*, 297–304.

Sharts-Hopko, N. C. (2002). Validity: What, why, how. *Journal of Association of Nurses in AIDS Care, 13*, 103–105.

Simbayi, L. C., Kalichman, S., Strebel, A., Cloete, A., Henda, N., & Mqeketo, A. (2007). Internalized stigma, discrimination, and depression among men and women living with HIV/AIDS in Cape Town, South Africa. *Social Science and Medicine, 64*, 1823–1831.

Simoni, J. M, Montoya, H. D., Huang, B., & Goodry, E. (2005). Social support and depressive symptomology among HIV-positive women: The mediating role of self-esteem and mastery. *Women-Health, 42*, 1–15.

Smith, G. E., Gerrard, M., & Gibbons, F. X. (1997). Self-esteem and the relation between risk behavior and perceptions of vulnerability to unplanned pregnancy in college women. *Health Psychology, 16*, 137–146.

Smith, L., Feaster, D. J., Prado, G., Kamin, M., Blaney, N., & Szapocznik, J. (2001). The psychosocial function of HIV+ and HIV- African-American recent mothers. *AIDS and Behavior, 5*, 219–231.

Somlai, A. M., Kelly, J. A., Heckman, T. G., Hackl, K., Runge, L., & Wright, C. (2000). Life optimism, substance use, and AIDS-specific attitudes associated with HIV risk behavior among disadvantaged inner-city women. *Journal of Women's Health and Gender-Based Medicine, 9*, 1101–1111.

Sormanti, M., Wu, E., & El-Bassel, N. (2004). Considering HIV risk and intimate partner violence among older women of color: A descriptive analysis. *Women and Health, 39*, 45–63.

Sowell, R., Seals, B., Moneyham, L., Guillory, J., & Mizuno, Y. (1999). Experiences of violence in HIV seropositive women in the south-eastern United States of America. *Journal of Advanced Nursing, 30*, 606–615.

Thompson, J. M. (1995). Silencing the self: Depressive symptomatology and close relationships. *Psychology of Women Quarterly, 19*, 337–353.

Trzynka, S. L., & Erlen, J. A. (2004). HIV disease susceptibility in women and the barriers to adherence. *MedSurg Nursing, 13*, 97–104.

Uebelacker, L. A., Courtnage, E. S., & Whisman, M. A. (2003). Correlates of depression and marital dissatisfaction: Perceptions of marital communication style. *Journal of Social and Personal Relationships, 20*, 757–769.

Valente, S. M. (2003). Depression an HIV disease. *Journal of the Association of Nurses in AIDS Care, 14*, 41–51.

Weeks, M. R., Schensul, J. J., Williams, S. S., Singer, M., & Grier, M. (1995). AIDS prevention for African-American and Latina women: Building culturally and gender-appropriate interventions. *AIDS Education and Prevention, 7*, 251–263.

Whyte, J., Standing, T., & Madigan, E. (2004). The relationship between HIV-related knowledge and safe sexual behavior in African-American women dwelling in the rural Southeast. *Journal of the Association of Nurses in AIDS Care, 15*, 51–58.

Wingood, G. M., & DiClemente, R. J. (1996). HIV sexual risk reduction interventions for women: A review. *American Journal of Preventive Medicine, 12*, 209–217.

Wyatt, G. E., Myers, H. F., & Loeb, T. B. (2004). Women, trauma, and HIV: An overview. *AIDS Behavior, 8*, 401–403.

Zablotsky, D., & Kennedy, M. (1999). Risk factors and HIV transmission to midlife and older women: Knowledge, options, and the initiation of safer sexual practices. *Journal of Acquired Immune Deficiency Syndromes, Suppl. 2*, S122–130.

16

Facilitating Women's Development through the Illness of Cancer: Depression, Self-Silencing, and Self-Care

Mary Sormanti

Women living with a life-threatening illness are confronted with a unique set of issues that affect their adaptation, many of which relate to the social expectations placed on them in their roles as partners, mothers, caregivers, and friends. Drawing upon my research with women with cancer, this chapter explores the role of self-silencing and other relational variables in women's experiences of coping with this serious illness. Chronic, life-threatening illness unfolds as a series of events (e.g., bodily, medical, relational) that affect psychosocial development by challenging such core components of a woman's well-being as identity cohesion, plans for the future, and opportunities for personal and relational growth. My research has found that self-silencing behavior in women living with cancer is related to a number of meaningful indicators of psychosocial adaptation, namely, depression, quality of life, and self-care agency (Kayser & Sormanti, 2002a; Kayser, Sormanti, & Strainchamps, 1999; Sormanti, Kayser, & Strainchamps, 1997). Accordingly, self-silencing behavior should be carefully explored during clinical work with women who are living with cancer and other serious medical conditions.

This chapter provides a brief overview of a framework for understanding the experiences of those affected by life-threatening illness, presents some of the major psychosocial sequelae associated with cancer in general as well as unique issues experienced by women diagnosed with cancer, and offers suggestions for working with women therapeutically to create positive change in their lives throughout and beyond the illness experience.

Cancer Incidence and Prevalence

Cancer, which is not a single disease but rather a term referring to more than a hundred conditions characterized by the proliferation of abnormal cells in the body, is the number two cause of death in the United States. Half of all men and one-third of all women in the United States will develop cancer in their lifetimes (American Cancer Society, 2006a). Recent incidence data from cancer registries across the world estimate that in a single year (2002), more than 5 million women were newly diagnosed with some form of cancer other than nonmelanoma skin cancer; the five-year prevalence rate for women internationally has been estimated at more than 13 million (Ferlay, Bray, Pisani, & Parkin, 2004). According to the American Cancer Society (2006b), in the United States alone more than 670,000 women were expected to be diagnosed with cancer (not including skin cancer) last year and more than 270,000 women were expected to die from their disease. Countless more children, partners, parents, friends, and colleagues of these women are also deeply affected. These numbers, while vast, only begin to convey the enormity of impact brought about by the onset of cancer. Accordingly, it elicits great fear and uncertainty despite the fact that successful treatments are currently available and considerable efforts are continually under way to advance understanding of the diseases' biological mechanisms and develop new and more effective treatments.

The Psychosocial Impact of Cancer

Generally, an individual's experience of cancer and its treatment proceeds in stages or phases that are each associated with a series of challenges, demands, and adaptive tasks that must be attended to if healthy development is to be maintained and nurtured. The first phase is the diagnosis period, which varies in length depending partly on whether and for how long an individual had physical or functional changes that raised the question of medical illness. Diagnosis is typically followed by an active treatment phase, often lasting months to years, aimed at ridding the body of the cancer or stopping the growth of abnormal cells, and a posttreatment phase, during which health and disease status are closely monitored by nursing and medical professionals. When treatment successfully eradicates or controls the cancer without significant complications, oversight by health care professionals becomes less frequent over time. When treatment is unsuccessful or life-limiting complications arise from the treatment itself, a terminal phase of the illness is also experienced. Other variables, including course of illness (e.g., progressive, constant, or relapsing), expected outcome, level of incapacitation, level of uncertainty, and family system components such as developmental phase, belief systems, and resources, have also been recognized as critical dimensions of the illness experience (Rolland, 2005).

Individuals with cancer, their families, and the professionals who attend to their psychosocial needs (e.g., social workers) are keenly aware of the myriad ways that each of these stages of illness impinges on individual and family life. Daily routines are altered, short-term and long-range plans must be reconsidered, and basic assumptions and expectations (e.g., about functional ability, sense of safety and security, the future) may be shattered. Losses are inevitable and many. Both those diagnosed with cancer and the family and friends who comprise their support networks experience a range of psychosocial sequelae that affect all areas of functioning—physical, sexual, emotional, cognitive, occupational, social/relational, and spiritual. Moreover, the accompanying psychosocial adjustment process typically continues throughout all phases of the illness experience including the period beyond active treatment (Spencer et al., 1999) and is steadily shaped by the cultural context within which it occurs. For example, culturally informed beliefs about health, illness, suffering, and healing shape people's experiences of cancer, including the ways that they interact with family members, friends, and health care professionals. Thus, a young Chinese woman in Hong Kong with newly diagnosed breast cancer is likely to be faced with a different set of family and societal expectations (e.g., about care giving and care receipt), challenges, and supports as she negotiates her illness and treatment than either a young Latina woman in the Dominican Republic or a Korean woman in New York who are faced with the same diagnoses. Each woman will benefit most from health and psychosocial services that take these cultural forces into consideration, perhaps especially when they are provided by a system that operates within or privileges a different cultural framework than hers. In the United States, although health care organizations are required by law to provide culturally competent services (Kagawa-Singer & Blackhall, 2001) and the professional literature on the value of such services is growing, there is much room for improvement in service provision to an increasingly diverse population.

Finally, although most of those diagnosed with cancer do not experience psychopathology that meets clinical criteria for mental illness, transient or periodic emotional distress is common and multiple studies indicate that clinical symptoms of depression and anxiety may be higher for this group than for the general population (Levenson, 2006; Massie, 2004; Stark et al., 2002). Research from around the world reveals prevalence rates of depression ranging from 20% to 50% among individuals with cancer (Pasquini & Biondi, 2007). A study of Japanese women and men with cancer found that approximately 41% and 19% of participants met criteria for adjustment disorder and major depression, respectively (Akizuki et al., 2003). The American Cancer Society (2007) purports that 25% of people with cancer in the United States suffer from clinical depression. Many believe that reported prevalence rates are underestimates given the overlap of depressive symptoms with common physiological symptoms of cancer such as fatigue and weight loss. Furthermore, the numbers of individuals experiencing subclinical yet burdensome symptoms of distress are also understood to be quite high. Within societies such as the United States, where women in the general population experience depression at twice the rates of their male counterparts (National Alliance on Mental Illness [NAMI], 2008), women with cancer are considered to be at even higher risk for depression.

Long-standing societal forces and contemporary shifts that have occurred (and are occurring) within and across many countries over the past two decades (e.g., advances in biomedical technologies, globalization) shape the experiences of those affected by cancer. For example, some cancers that once heralded quick and certain death are now being treated successfully, allowing many individuals with cancer to lead fulfilling, productive lives. Indeed, for many individuals life postcancer and its treatment not only reflects a return to preillness "normalcy" but also reveals a series of positive psychological and relational consequences that emerged during the illness experience (Kayser & Sormanti, 2002b; Sodergren & Hyland, 2000). Relationships with others can be strengthened, priorities and values re-appraised, and personal and familial strengths and skills recognized or developed.

These extraordinary medical and technological advances, however, also have generated significant challenges, and cancer remains a major stressor for all affected. Burdensome physical side effects and disabling conditions are commonly experienced by individuals receiving treatment for cancer. Even long-term survivorship, a primary goal for most individuals, is associated with significant "late effects" of treatment including learning disabilities, growth and fertility problems, bone and joint pain, cognitive and memory problems, cardiovascular disorders, and secondary cancers, all of which can compromise quality of life significantly. In addition, within health care systems that emphasize cost containment, a shift from inpatient to outpatient care has meant that caregiving is falling more and more into the hands of family and friends who are untrained, unsupported, and often overwhelmed not only by the medical and psychological needs of the person with cancer but also their own emotional responses to the complexities and uncertainties of cancer and its treatment. Furthermore, when family members are separated by great geographical distances, the challenges of caregiving, including family communication, health care decision making, and interactions with health care professionals, can be intensified, and the related emotional benefits such as satisfaction and greater intimacy may not be fully realized.

Finally, sociocultural conceptions of grief and death as well as the intensity and manifestations of death anxiety can be powerful forces in the illness experience. Fears of death and dying, for example, which are activated by life-threatening illness, can silence people with cancer who receive implicit and explicit messages from the world around them that their illness evokes distress in others. In the United States, cancer and those with cancer are threats to widely held and valued dominant-culture conceptions of youth, individualism, and physical agility. As a result, individuals with cancer, their families, and those in the community must work against societal forces if they are to maintain authentic, supportive relationships with one another.

Unique Issues for Women Living with Cancer

For women, in particular, the adjustments required by the many practical and emotional demands associated with cancer can be especially challenging. First, given that women across the world perform the vast majority of "unpaid care work" (i.e., activities such as cooking, cleaning, and caring for children, elders, and sick people both within one's family and in the community that are unpaid) (Budlender, 2004), a woman's diagnosis of a serious life-threatening disease such as cancer can cause major disruptions in her roles as an intimate partner, mother, daughter, or active community member. These disruptions can be the source of significant distress for many women as they struggle to maintain carefully, sometimes precariously balanced and often hard-earned schedules between paid and unpaid work that they and those around them have come to expect or have taken for granted. Moreover, a serious life-threatening illness may further complicate a woman's ability and efforts to balance allotments of time and energy for care of others (e.g., partners, children, elder parents) versus self-care activities that are perhaps now even more essential to her life and well-being (Bloom, Stewart, Johnson, Banks, & Fobair, 2001; Chris, 1992; Warner, 1986).

The challenge of being both caregiver and care recipient (i.e., cancer patient in need of medical services and psychosocial supports) at the same time can result in physical and mental health problems for women (Bloom et al., 2001; Given et al., 1993; Hackl, Somlai, Kelly, & Kalichman, 1997; Schulz et al., 1995) and can trigger a woman's re-evaluation of her roles and responsibilities, many, if not all of which, are intricately tied to her relationships with others. Within the framework of contemporary theories of women's development, which posit that (1) relationships are central to the development of a woman's sense of self (i.e., identity) and well-being (Gilligan, 1982; Jordan, 1997; Jordan, Kaplan, Miller, Stiver, & Surrey, 1991); (2) maturity and growth are dynamic, interactive processes that occur through ongoing relationships characterized by mutual recognition and response to one another's mental states and emotions (Miller, 1991); and (3) an ethic of care is fundamental to women's identities (Gilligan, 1982), such re-evaluations are especially salient. Indeed, they have been the topic of numerous academic and popular press articles, books, and films over the past 20 years. Most recently, a proliferation of personal blogs by women with cancer on the World Wide Web is further evidence of the frequency and significance of these struggles. When they occur within a culture that emphasizes and romanticizes selflessness among women—as is the case in the United States—these struggles are further exacerbated.

A second major reason that adjustment to cancer is especially daunting for women is also related to the sociocultural context in which they live and work. Because of the intense emphasis that many cultures place on women's physical appearance and continuous efforts to link physical appearance and ability with sexuality and indeed "womanhood" overall, a diagnosis of cancer can be quite damaging psychologically and relationally. When cancer or its treatment is disfiguring—either temporarily (e.g., hair loss associated with chemotherapy) or permanently (e.g., breast loss from mastectomy)–it can be experienced as a major affront to a woman's sense of self and to others' perceptions of her. Published narratives from women in the United States who have survived breast cancer and its treatment convey great distress and confusion about their experiences as cancer patients. They report that the U.S. health care system offers a "cosmetic approach to breast cancer" within a larger socio-cultural context that obscures important aspects of women's identities by overemphasizing one (i.e., sexuality) and pushes women to hide the fact that they have or have had breast cancer. Such an approach myopically views breast cancer and mastectomy as assaults on women's sexuality that must be reme-died (i.e., via breast reconstruction) if women are to be perceived and accepted as whole again (see Daton, 1997; Lorde, 1980a). This sociocultural response to a disease that predominantly affects women exacerbates the challenges of the disease and fails to recognize not only that sexuality is just one aspect of female identity but also that for many women breast "replacement" may not be the mechanism that will facilitate their healthy adjustment. Rather, other aspects of identity and daily life (e.g., spirituality, work, friendships, motherhood, physical and mental ability) may be the critical markers of a meaningful and quality life both during and after cancer treatment. Moreover, although cancer and its treatments can threaten a woman's body image and sexuality, fear of recurrence and possible death are often much more salient concerns for women with cancer (Spencer et al., 1999).

Self-Silencing and Women with Cancer

Given the sociocultural context described earlier, it could be said that women living with cancer in the United States face enormous institutionalized pressure to shape or silence their experiences in ways that maintain aspects of the tradi-tional patriarchal status quo, which privileges men through the subjugation of women. If, for example, women can continue to carry out the lion's share of unpaid care work while facing the additional demands of cancer, then changes in men's economic status and roles in the home and workplace can be minimized.

Likewise, the more often survivors of breast cancer choose breast reconstruction and breast prostheses, which "hide" (albeit not necessarily intentionally on a woman's part) the fact of their missing breast, the less the general public and the male-dominated institutions that influence it are forced to adjust their notions of sexuality and womanhood to accommodate the realities of so many women with breast cancer. This is not to suggest that women with cancer—or women in general—are primarily responsible for their historical and contemporary gender-based struggles. To do so would be akin to "blaming the victim," which only further marginalizes those who are vulnerable and fails to acknowledge their strengths. Rather, an examination of these sociocultural forces is intended to illuminate the many interrelated factors that affect women's personal experiences with cancer. It was from this foundation that my colleagues and I undertook research to explore the role that women's own self-silencing behaviors played in their lives and relationships while coping with cancer.

Description of Research

Our research sample consisted of 49 women with cancer who were identified by multidisciplinary team members at a large urban U.S. hospital. To be eligible for participation, women met several illness-related criteria. First, they had been diagnosed at least two months but not longer than three years prior to study participation. Second, they were either actively receiving treatment (e.g., chemotherapy, radiation) or were being closely monitored during the immediate posttreatment phase. Finally, all participants were mothers of at least one child aged 12 years or younger. In combination, these criteria ensured that our participants were actively dealing not only with the demands of cancer and its treatment but also with the demands related to care of a young child.

Demographically, the sample was homogeneous with regard to race/ethnicity and relationship status; all but four women were white and 84% were married. Women ranged from 23 to 48 years of age, with a mean age of 36 years ($SD = 5.6$). More than half (55%) of the sample had attained a bachelor's degree or higher. Although income information was not obtained, more than half of these women engaged in paid work outside the home. Specifically, 35% held a professional position, 18% held other positions including management or skilled labor, and 41% indicated that their occupation was homemaker/parent.

The primary aim of the research was to examine the impact of several relational variables on a woman's psychosocial adaptation to cancer. In addition to self-silencing behaviors, these included mutuality of a woman's primary partnered relationship and relationship-focused coping strategies. In general, mutuality refers to a reciprocal relationship between people or things. In our study, we used a more detailed definition conceptualized by Nancy Genero and colleagues (1992), a group of women scholars who were instrumental in the development of "Self in Relation" Theory (now commonly referred to as

Relational Theory or Relational-Cultural Theory), which served as a base for the research (for detailed descriptions of this theory, its development, and critiques, see Bot & Courbasson, 1998; Jordan, 1997; Jordan et al., 1991; Robb, 2006). This group, along with others over the ensuing years, has continued to develop their understanding of mutuality. At its foundation, their concept refers to the empathic and supportive bi-directional expression of thoughts, feelings, and activities between individuals, which incorporates elements of empathy, empowerment, and authenticity (Genero et al., 1992).

The second relational variable we examined was relationship-focused coping, which stemmed from the work of James Coyne and colleagues (1990, 1992, 1994), who examined adjustment in individuals who had lived through a heart attack and their spouses. Their work contributed significantly to the knowledge base on stress and coping associated with medical conditions by critiquing the most prominent contemporary model of the time, that developed by Lazarus and Folkman (1984). Coyne and his colleagues believed that this widely influential model, which delineated two major classifications of coping (i.e., problem focused and emotion focused), failed to account for the role of interpersonal relationships. Their subsequent research demonstrated that the coping associated with a heart attack was a dyadic process between patient and spouse. They delineated two types of relationship-focused coping: active engagement, a strategy whereby the patient actively involves the partner in his or her coping efforts, and protective buffering, a strategy marked by exclusion of one's partner in order to avoid disagreements (Coyne & Fiske, 1992). The relationship-focused coping model resonated with my and my colleagues' clinical experience with individuals and families coping with cancer, and we believed that it had applicability to women with cancer. Moreover, we suspected that it—especially protective buffering—would be closely related to self-silencing behaviors in this group.

Finally, indicators of psychosocial adaptation (i.e., our outcome variables) included quality of life, depression, and self-care agency. Quality of life was assessed with the well-known and validated Functional Assessment of Cancer Therapy Scale (Cella, Tulsky, Gray, & Sarafian, 1993), which includes 28 items covering the domains of physical, social/familial, emotional, and functional well-being as well as a domain specific to the respondent's relationship with his or her doctor. Depression was assessed with the widely known Beck Depression Inventory (Beck, Ward, Mendelson, Mock, & Erbaugh, 1961). Self-care agency, which was measured by the Exercise of Self Care Agency Scale (ESCA) (Kearney & Fleischer, 1979), reflects a woman's evaluation of her power to perform activities essential to her self-care. Although newer versions have been developed and tested with a variety of populations, the version of the ESCA we used was a 42-item 5-point Likert-type scale with established construct validity and acceptable reliability. The ESCA was originally developed to measure five subconstructs (i.e., attitude of responsibility for self, motivation to care for self, application of knowledge to self-care, valuing of health priorities, and self-esteem) posited by Kearney and Fleischer (1979).

Women completed a written questionnaire that measured each of the study variables and participated in an in-person narrative interview that explored how each woman was managing the demands of her illness (including treatment decision making and disclosure about the illness), how her significant relationships were affected, and whether and how her sense of herself had changed through her illness experience. A subsample of these women also completed the original questionnaire a second time (i.e., approximately 18 months later). These data allowed us to examine women's longer term psychosocial adjustment/well-being (i.e., whether there were any changes in levels of depression, self-care health behaviors, or quality of life) and to determine if relational factors, including self-silencing behaviors, continued to play a role.

Self-Silencing and Women's Adjustment to Cancer

The women in our research sample reported intensity levels of self-silencing cognitive schema ($X = 79.31$) similar to those reported for normative samples of undergraduate women (Jack & Dill, 1992; Remen, Chambless, & Rodebaugh, 2002) and lower than those reported for "clinical samples"—for example, mothers who abused cocaine during pregnancy and those in battered women's shelters (Jack & Dill, 1992). Moreover, the level of intensity of these self-silencing schema remained consistent at two data collection points 18 months apart, which marked a transition from active treatment to posttreatment. At Time 1, the large majority of women were receiving chemotherapy or radiation and a few were in the immediate posttreatment phase, during which they were being very closely monitored by their health care teams. At Time 2, none of the women was receiving treatment. These findings suggest that even as the demands of illness decreased with the completion of active treatment, which they did significantly, self-silencing schema were still operating. Comments from two women during active treatment who responded, respectively, to the question, "In what way(s) has your illness affected your relationship with your spouse/partner?" and an open-ended query about the ways in which their partners had helped them to cope with the illness or might have been more helpful, demonstrate an undercurrent of self-silencing schema (*emphasis mine*):

> Really, I think its put a lot of stress on him. . . . He feels that he doesn't know what to do. . . . He feels helpless, he doesn't know how to help me but I know that there's nothing he can do. I wasn't expecting him to do anything except just be there and he is most of the time but *there are times when I know he just needs a breather from me. Even though I want him there I have to realize that he has his own needs.*

> [Providing] more [support] I think is difficult for him. He could sit down and talk more in depth because he's not a very good talker like that, but he's really tired and he's got a lot of responsibility right now and *I don't want to pressure him, you*

know, because he's a person too, and there's only so much he can take.... Everything's fine. Everything right now is okay.

These narratives are consistent with at least two of the subscales that comprise the construct of self-silencing, namely, Care as Self-Sacrifice, which captures women's tendency to prioritize the needs of others over their own, and Silencing the Self, which denotes women's efforts to inhibit their own thoughts and actions as a means of avoiding conflict in the relationship. The latter woman's assertion that "everything's fine" may also be a subtle example of Jack and Dill's (1992) Divided Self subscale, which manifests as a woman's attempt to present a public self that complies with expected and gendered role demands.

Self-Silencing and Self-Care Agency

Self-silencing was related to several indicators of psychosocial adjustment for this group of women (Kayser et al., 1999). Most notably, a statistically significant negative correlation between women's self-silencing schema and self-care agency existed at both data collection points. Furthermore, self-silencing behaviors during active treatment were predictive of lower levels of self-care agency in the posttreatment phase. These data indicate that women who maintain cognitive/relationship schemas that espouse, for example, the notion of care as self-sacrifice (e.g., valuing or prioritizing care of other people's needs and desires over one's own) are less likely to engage in self-care health behaviors even during the active treatment phase of their disease, which is typically quite demanding physically and emotionally. So, activities such as attending support groups, participating in psychoeducational events and programs, using mindfulness and relaxation techniques, or maintaining preillness social connections with friends, all of which are understood to facilitate adjustment to cancer, may not be given the time or attention that could benefit these women.

Interview data further substantiated this finding and also reveal a link between self-silencing schema and a woman's sense of herself. For example, when asked to reflect on her identity, one woman responded by discussing the balance between self-care and care for others: "I'm a very family-oriented person...and I do get a lot of satisfaction doing things around the home and doing things for my children, for my husband, for other people. Probably, I would tell myself in retrospect that I spend too much time doing things for other people and not enough time doing things for myself." Despite the personal satisfaction she experienced from her unpaid care work, she recognized that it took away from self-care activities. Also, when asked to consider future changes in identity, many of the women's responses included references to taking better care of themselves, setting limits on their responsibilities for others, and struggling to convince themselves that this shift in balance between care for others and care for self did not reflect poorly on them as mothers, partners, and friends. As one woman succinctly stated: "I think it's just taking time for myself, my family, continuing to be able to set limits and say, 'No, I can't do this' and not feel like I'm a horrible person because I'm not doing 101 things all at once."

Self-Silencing, Depression, and Quality of Life

The women in our sample reported a statistically significant change in levels of depression from Time 1 ($X = 15.7$) to Time 2 ($X = 9.33$). Although self-silencing behaviors were not significantly related to either depression or quality of life at our first data collection point as we had expected, they were at 18-month follow-up (Kayser & Sormanti, 2002a). Specifically, self-silencing was positively correlated with depression and negatively correlated with quality of life; the higher a woman's levels of self-silencing, the higher her level of depression and the lower her perceived quality of life. Also, when controlling for women's education level, depression during active treatment was significantly related to self-silencing behaviors posttreatment. Although our research analyses raise additional questions (e.g., why was self-silencing significantly correlated with depression and quality of life posttreatment and not during active treatment?) and did not allow us to comment on causality (e.g., does depression during active treatment cause self-silencing behaviors posttreatment?), we do know that self-silencing is a significant correlate of psychosocial adaptation during women's experience of cancer and warrants further study.

Self-Silencing, Relationship Mutuality, and Relationship-Focused Coping

Finally, self-silencing was also associated with several other relational variables for this group of women with cancer. First, when controlling for demands of illness, self-silencing behaviors for women during the posttreatment phase were significantly correlated with their perceived levels of mutuality with their primary partners during the active phase of treatment. The higher the level of mutual exchange of feelings, thoughts, and actions a woman perceived in this relationship, the less self-silencing she engaged in. Furthermore, self-silencing behaviors during the active phase of treatment were significantly positively correlated with protective buffering coping strategies. That is, those women who reported higher levels of self-silencing also utilized coping strategies that excluded their partners from the illness experience as a means of avoiding disagreements or protecting him or her from its inherent difficulties. For example, a woman might conceal her fears about pending test results or minimize her disappointment that a partner was unable to accompany her to a medical appointment she was anxious about because she anticipates that her partner would be overwhelmed by these illness-related feelings and events. In such circumstances, a woman may utilize these or similar behavioral and cognitive strategies to cope with the stress of illness within the context of her primary partnered relationship.

At posttreatment, self-silencing was significantly correlated with both protective buffering and active engagement coping strategies. While we expected that protective buffering strategies would be associated with self-silencing given their shared theoretical/conceptual base, we were surprised by the latter finding. Given the consistent levels of self-silencing during both phases of the illness experience, it is possible that some other factor (e.g., decreased illness demands) facilitated the addition of active engagement strategies to women's coping repertoire. Further investigation is needed to illuminate the interesting associations among these relational factors and with important indicators of adjustment, including coping strategies.

Clinical Practice with Women Living with Cancer

Women with cancer have told us—through both their participation in research and their engagement with us in professional provider-recipient relationships—that living with cancer is not easy. Indeed, living with cancer can be viewed understandably as hard work (Coyle, 2006). However, women living with cancer have also shown us that they are up to the task and have demonstrated great resilience in the face of this serious life-threatening illness. Resilience, which has been described as "effective coping and adaptation in the face of major life stress" (Tedeschi & Kilmer, 2005, p. 231) and "the ability to withstand and rebound from disruptive life challenges" (Walsh, 2003, p. 1), is considered by many mental health professionals to be a dynamic process of positive adjustment to difficult circumstances that includes an interplay of forces across system levels (e.g., individual, family, community, societal). Research with women with cancer reflects this by revealing that their adjustment to the diagnosis and treatment of cancer and their related quality of life is associated with a continuum of variables. These include the level of uncertainty and extent of illness demands (McCorkle & Quint-Benoliel, 1983; Northouse, Dorris, & Charron-Moore, 1995); the meaning she or her partner has given to or derived from the illness experience (Picard, Dumont, Gagnon, & Lessard, 2005; Wenzel et al., 2002); the presence and quality of external supports available to her (Helgeson, Snyder, & Seltman, 2004); the type of coping strategies she uses (McCaul et al., 1999; Osowiecki & Compas, 1998); family and couple dynamics such as levels of mutuality, perceived satisfaction, and cohesion (Friedman et al., 1988; Kayser & Sormanti, 2002a, b; Picard et al., 2005; Sormanti et al., 1997); and prior history of psychiatric issues (Bloom et al., 1987; Penman et al., 1987). My own research, described here, also demonstrates that self-silencing behaviors can play an important role in women's quality of life and coping. All of these factors must be considered closely for women living with cancer if we as professional care providers—and they as survivors—are to better understand the risk and protective factors related to adaptation and foster the process.

What, then, can mental health professionals do to support the resilience of women with cancer within the context of their intimate relationships with family, friends, and professional care providers? Relational Theory, which has guided my research and resonated deeply with my long-standing approach to clinical work, provides meaningful direction. Accordingly, the following practice guidelines are offered as a foundation from which more specific clinical interventions can be created or shaped to meet the unique circumstances of both individual women and individual therapeutic relationships. In addition, numerous studies of psychosocial interventions for women with cancer have demonstrated effectiveness in reducing psychiatric symptoms and improving quality of life. Descriptions of many of these studies have been reviewed by the U.S.-based Institute of Medicine and should be reviewed by anyone interested in providing quality psychosocial services to this population (Hewitt, Herdman, & Holland, 2004). Meyer and Mark (1995) also conducted a meta-analysis of research examining the effects of psychosocial interventions with adults with cancer.

- Explore each woman's beliefs and expectations about her role(s) in close relationships and whether and how she expects, hopes, or anticipates that these may change throughout the illness experience. Moreover, discuss with her the known connections between certain relationship schemas (e.g., care as self-sacrifice) and important health variables (e.g., self-care behaviors, quality of life) and engage her in an ongoing discussion about the applicability of such data in her own life in general and within the current context of illness. Are their ways that she might be self-silencing or at risk for self-silencing? If so, how might she work with you and others to mitigate this situation in ways that are personally and culturally relevant and feasible to her? Be willing to share ideas based on your own practice wisdom and research knowledge, but do not undermine or preempt a woman's ability to come up with her own or privilege your ideas over hers. To do either would be a perpetuation of the myriad ways that society has silenced women's experiences and obstructed their healthy development.
- Support women's efforts to be authentic in their relationships, including those with professional providers. Although they did not use the term explicitly, Spira and Kenemore (2002) refer to it implicitly by suggesting that a critical component of women's well-being while coping with cancer is the capacity to "remain recognizable to herself . . . to continue to do many of the things they have always done as these activities often contribute to self-identity and self-esteem . . . [and] retreat from activities or relationships that are expected of them, but are not true reflections of the self" (p. 179). We can support women's authenticity by encouraging them to review their various roles, responsibilities, and relationships and determine whether changes in any of these would contribute to a more

authentic sense of self and in turn a greater sense of wellness. During stages of the illness associated with particularly high demands, authenticity may mean that women need help *accepting* more practical and emotional support from others. For many women, however, authenticity may also include *providing* ongoing care (e.g., in the form of emotional availability, empathy, understanding, and support) to partners, children, and other intimates. As professional providers, we must challenge ourselves to grapple with each woman's unfolding definition of self-care, since this is often closely intertwined with her care for others. Moreover, the "balance" between these two—to the extent that they are even separate for any given woman—is likely to be unique for each woman.

- Finally, given the importance of mutuality in women's relationships and its connections to self-silencing behaviors and health outcomes, it is imperative that we too should be mindful of our own authenticity and self-care. This mindfulness can be actualized in two ways: first, in our willingness to engage deeply with and be genuinely affected by the women with whom we work, and second, in our attention to the effects of these therapeutic relationships on our personal selves and lives and our own, sometimes shifting, conceptualizations of self-care. To do otherwise would undermine ongoing efforts at healthy adaptation to life and its challenges—both theirs and ours.

In conclusion, although cancer is hardly viewed (at least initially) as a welcomed influence in anyone's life, with adequate supports it can be an opportunity for personal and relational growth for everyone who is touched by it. In this chapter, I have summarized some of the key research findings about women's experiences living with cancer. Unequivocally, the literature supports the common-sense expectation that the introduction of a life-threatening illness into a woman's life triggers multiple challenges that reflect the cultural context(s) she lives within. My own research has shown that among these challenges is a woman's ability to grapple with both her own needs and the needs of others who are important to her while she is ill. Self-silencing schema and behaviors are integral to this process of adaptation and merit ongoing attention by practitioners and researchers alike. Until cures for women's cancers are found, it is essential that we attend to the complex psychosocial realities of the vulnerable yet strong women who will continue to be affected.

References

Akizuki, N., Akechi, T., Nakanishi, T., Yoshikawa, T., Okamura, M., Nakano, T., et al. (2003). Development of a brief screening interview for adjustment disorders and major depression in patients with cancer. *Cancer, 97,* 2605–2613.

American Cancer Society. (2007). *Depression.* Retrieved October 14, 2009, from http://www.cancer.org/docroot/MBC/content/MBC_4_1X_Cancer_and_Depression.asp?sitearea=MBC

American Cancer Society. (2006a). *Who gets cancer?* Retrieved December 10, 2006, from http://www.cancer.org/docroot/CRI/CRI_2_3x.asp?dt=72

American Cancer Society. (2006b). *Estimated new cancer cases and deaths by sex for all sites, US, 2006.* Retrieved December 10, 2006, from http://www.cancer.org/docroot/MED/content/downloads/MED_1_1x_CFF2006_Estimated_New_Cases_Deaths_by_Sex_US.asp

Beck, A. T., Ward, C. H., Mendelson, M., Mock, J., & Erbaugh, J. (1961). An inventory for measuring depression. *Archives of General Psychiatry, 4,* 561–571.

Bloom, J. R., Cook, M., Fotopolous, S., Flamer, D., Gates, C., Holland, J. C., et al. (1987). Psychological response to mastectomy: A prospective comparison study. *Cancer, 59,* 189–196.

Bloom, J. R., Stewart, S. L., Johnson, M., Banks, P., & Fobair, P. (2001). Sources of support and the physical and mental well-being of young women with breast cancer. *Social Science & Medicine, 53,* 1513–1524.

Bot, S. A., & Courbasson, C. M. (1998). Cutting the umbilical cord: A critique of the self-in-relation theory of female psychological development from psychoanalytic perspectives. *Gender and Psychoanalysis, 3,* 413–433.

Budlender, D. (2004). *Why should we care about unpaid care work?* Harare, Zimbabwe: UNIFEM.

Cella, D. F., Tulsky, D. S., Gray, G., Sarafian, B., Linn, E., Bonomi, A., Silberman, M., Yellen, S. B., Winicour, P., & Brannon, J. (1993). The Functional Assessment of Cancer Therapy Scale: Development and validation of the general measure. *Journal of Clinical Oncology, 11,* 570–579.

Chris, C. (1992). Transmission issues for women. In C. Chris & M. Pearl (Eds.), *Women, AIDS, and activism* (pp. 17–26). Boston: South End Press.

Coyle, N. (2006). The hard work of living in the face of death. *Journal of Pain and Symptom Management, 32,* 266–274.

Coyne, J. C., & Bolger, N. (1990). Doing without social support as an explanatory concept. *Journal of Social and Clinical Psychology, 9,* 148–158.

Coyne, J. C., & Fiske, V. (1992). Couples coping with chronic and catastrophic illness. In J. Akamatsu, M. A. P. Stephens, S. E. Hobfall & J. H. Crowther (Eds.), *Family health psychology.* Washington, DC: Hemisphere Publishing.

Coyne, J. C., & Smith, D. A. F. (1994). Couples coping with myocardial infarction: A contextual perspective on wives' distress. *Journal of Personality and Social Psychology, 61,* 404–412.

Daton, N. (1997). Illness and Imagery: Feminist cognition, socialization, and gender identity. In M. Crawford & R. Unger (Eds.), *In our own words: Readings on the psychology of women and gender* (pp. 95–106). New York: McGraw-Hill Companies, Inc.

Ferlay, J., Bray, F., Pisani, P., & Parkin, D. M. (2004). *GLOBOCAN 2002: Cancer incidence, mortality and prevalence worldwide IARC CancerBase* (No. 5, version 2.0). Lyon, France: IARC Press. http://www-dep.iarc.fr/

Friedman, L. C., Baer, P. E., Nelson, D., Lane, M., Smith, F., & Dworkin, J. (1988). Women with breast cancer: Perception of family functioning and adjustment to illness. *Psychosomatic Medicine, 50,* 529–540.

Genero, N. P., Miller, J. B., Surrey, J., & Baldwin, L. M. (1992). Measuring perceived mutuality in close relationships: Validation of the mutual psychological development questionnaire. *Journal of Family Psychology, 6,* 36–48.

Gilligan, C. (1982). *In a different voice: Psychological theory and women's development*. Cambridge, MA: Harvard University Press.

Given, C. W., Stommel, M., Given, B., Osuch, J., Kurtz, M. E., & Kurtz, J. C. (1993). The influence of cancer patients' symptoms and functional states on patients' depression and family caregivers' reaction and depression. *Health Psychology, 12*, 277–285.

Hackl, K. L., Somlai, A. M., Kelly, J. A., & Kalichman, S. C. (1997). Women living with HIV/AIDS: The dual challenge of being patient and caregiver. *Health & Social Work, 22*, 53–62.

Helgeson, V. S., Snyder, P., & Seltman, H. (2004). Psychological and physical adjustment to breast cancer over 4 years: Identifying distinct trajectories of change. *Health Psychology, 23*, 3–15.

Hewitt, M., Herdman, R., & Holland, J. (Eds.). (2004). *Meeting psychosocial needs of women with breast cancer*. Washington, DC: National Academies Press.

Jack, D. C., & Dill, D. (1992). The Silencing the Self Scale: Schemas of intimacy associated with depression in women. *Psychology of Women Quarterly, 16*, 97–106.

Jordan, J. V. (1997). A relational perspective for understanding women's development. In J. V. Jordan (Ed.), *Women's growth in diversity: Writings from the Stone Center* (pp. 9–24). New York: Guilford.

Jordan, J. V., Kaplan, A. G., Miller, J. B., Stiver, I. P., & J. L. Surrey, J. L. (Eds.). (1991). *Women's growth in connection: Writings from the Stone Center*. New York: Guilford.

Kagawa-Singer, M., & Blackhall, L. J. (2001). Negotiating cross-cultural issues at the end of life. *Journal of the American Medical Association, 286*, 2993–3001.

Kayser, K., & Sormanti, M. (2002a). A follow-up study of women with cancer: Their psychosocial well-being and close relationships. *Social Work in Health Care, 35*, 391–406.

Kayser, K., & Sormanti, M. (2002b). Identity and the illness experience: Issues faced by mothers with cancer. *Illness, Crisis & Loss, 10*, 10–26.

Kayser, K., Sormanti, M., & Strainchamps, E. (1999). Women coping with cancer: The influence of relationship factors on psychosocial adjustment. *Psychology of Women Quarterly, 23*, 725–739.

Kearney, B. Y., & Fleischer, B. J. (1979). Development of an instrument to measure exercise of self-care agency. *Research in Nursing & Health, 1*, 25–34.

Lazarus, R. S., & Folkman, S. (1984). *Stress, appraisal, and coping*. New York: Springer.

Levenson, J. (2006). Psychiatric issues in oncology. *Primary Psychiatry, 13*, 31–34.

Lorde, A. (1980a). *The cancer journals* (2nd ed.). San Francisco: Spinsters Ink.

Massie, M. J., (2004). Prevalence of depression in patients with cancer. *Journal of the National Cancer Institute Monograph, 32*, 57–71.

McCaul, K. D., Sandgren, A. K., King, B., O'Donnell, S., Bransstetter, A., & Foreman, G. (1999). Coping and adjustment to breast cancer. *Psycho-Oncology, 8*, 230–236.

McCorkle, R., & Quint-Benoliel, J. (1983). Symptom distress, current concerns and mood disturbance after diagnosis of life-threatening disease. *Social Science & Medicine, 17*, 431–438.

Meyer, T. J., & Mark, M. M. (1995). Effects of psychosocial interventions with adult cancer patients: A meta-analysis of randomized experiments. *Health Psychology, 14*, 101–108.

Miller, J. B. (1991). The development of women's sense of self. In J. V. Jordan, A. G. Kaplan, J. B. Miller, I. P. Stiver, & J. L. Surrey (Eds.), *Women's growth in connection: Writings from the Stone Center* (pp. 11–26). New York: Guilford.

National Alliance on Mental Illness. (2008, April). *Women and depression: What you need to know about this mental illness* (pamphlet). Arlington, VA: Author.

Northouse, L. L., Dorris, G., & Charron-Moore, C. (1995). Factors affecting couples' adjustment to recurrent breast cancer. *Social Science & Medicine, 41*, 69–76.

Osowiecki, D., & Compas, B. E. (1998). Psychological adjustment to cancer: Control beliefs and adjustment in adult cancer patients. *Cognitive Therapy & Research, 22*, 483–499.

Pasquini, M., & Biondi, M. (2007, February). Depression in cancer: A critical review. *Clinical Practice and Epidemiology in Mental Health, 3*, 2.

Penman, D. T., Bloom, J. R., Fotopolous, S., Cook, M. R., Holland, J. C., Gates, C., et al. (1987). The impact of mastectomy on self concept and social function: A combined cross-sectional and longitudinal study with comparison groups. *Women & Health, 11*, 101–130.

Picard, L., Dumont, S., Gagnon, P., & Lessard, G. (2005). Coping strategies among couples adjusting to primary breast cancer. *Journal of Psychosocial Oncology, 23*, 115–135.

Remen, A. L., Chambless, D. L., & Rodebaugh, T. L. (2002). Gender differences in the construct validity of the Silencing the Self Scale. *Psychology of Women Quarterly, 26*, 151–159.

Robb, C. (2006). *This changes everything: The relational revolution in psychology.* New York: Farrar, Straus, and Giroux.

Rolland, J. S. (2005). Chronic illness and the family life cycle. In B. Carter & M. McGoldrick (Eds.), *The expanded family life cycle: Individual, family and social perspectives* (3rd ed., pp. 492–511). Boston: Allyn & Bacon.

Schulz, R., Williamson, G. M., Knapp, J. E., Bookwaia, J., Lave, J., & Fello, M. (1995). The psychological, social, and economic impact of illness among patients with recurrent cancer. *Journal of Psychosocial Oncology, 13*, 21–45.

Sodergren, S. C., & Hyland, M. E. (2000). What are the positive consequences of illness? *Psychology and Health, 15*, 85–97.

Sormanti, M., Kayser, K., & Strainchamps, E. (1997). A relational study of women coping with cancer: A preliminary study. *Social Work in Health Care, 25*, 89–106.

Spencer, S. M., Lehman, J. M., Wynings, C., Arena, P., Carver, C. S., Antoni, M. H., et al. (1999). Concerns about breast cancer and relations to psychosocial well-being in a multiethnic sample of early-stage patients. *Health Psychology, 18*, 159–168.

Spira, M., & Kenemore, E. (2002). Cancer as life transition: A relational approach to cancer wellness in women. *Clinical Social Work Journal, 30*, 173–186.

Stark, D., Kiely, M., Smith, A., Velikova, G., House, A., & Selby P. (2002). Anxiety disorders in cancer patients: Their nature, associations, and relation to quality of life. *Journal of Clinical Oncology, 20*, 3137–3148.

Tedeschi, R. G., & Kilmer, R. P. (2005). Assessing strengths, resilience, and growth to guide clinical interventions. *Professional Psychology: Research and Practice, 36*, 230–237.

Walsh, F. (2003). Family resilience: A framework for clinical practice. *Family Process, 42,* 1–18.

Warner, R. L. (1986). Alternative strategies for measuring household division of labor: A comparison. *Journal of Family Issues, 7,* 179–195.

Wenzel, L. B., Donnelly, J. P., Fowler, J. M., Habbal, R., Taylor, T. H., Aziz, N., et al. (2002). Resilience, reflection, and residual stress in ovarian cancer survivorship: A gynecologic oncology group study. *Psycho-Oncology, 11,* 142–153.

17

Eating Disorders and Self-Silencing: A Function-Focused Approach to Treatment

Josie Geller, Suja Srikameswaran, and Stephanie Cassin

Background

Eating disorders are defined as severe disturbances in eating behavior and are characterized by a cluster of clinical features that includes low body weight, binge eating, affective and cognitive disturbances pertaining to shape and weight, and compensatory behaviors (American Psychiatric Association, 2000). Eating disorders have the greatest gender discrepancy of all psychiatric illnesses, with girls and women overrepresented, and are more prevalent in industrialized societies in which food is abundant and thinness is valued (American Psychiatric Association, 2000).

Anorexia nervosa is characterized by a refusal to maintain a minimally normal body weight for age and height.[1] Weight loss is accomplished through dieting, fasting, and excessive exercise. Despite having a low body weight, individuals with anorexia nervosa experience an intense fear of gaining weight and a disturbance in the way they experience their bodies. For example, body size may be overestimated or may become one of the primary determinants of self-evaluation. There are two subtypes of anorexia nervosa, distinguished by the presence or absence of regular binge eating and/or purging. Binge eating is defined as consuming a large amount of food within a two-hour period and experiencing a loss of control over eating, and purging refers to self-induced vomiting or use of laxatives, diuretics, or enemas for the purpose of weight loss. Individuals who do not engage in regular binge eating and/or purging behavior are diagnosed with *anorexia nervosa restricting type*, whereas those who do engage in these behaviors are diagnosed with *anorexia nervosa binge eating/purging type*.

Bulimia nervosa is characterized by repeated episodes of binge eating accompanied by use of compensatory behaviors to prevent weight gain

(American Psychiatric Association, 2000). For individuals with bulimia nervosa, body shape and weight are primary determinants of self-evaluation. Bulimia nervosa is divided into two subtypes, distinguished by the types of compensatory behaviors used. Individuals who regularly engage in self-induced vomiting or the misuse of laxatives, diuretics, or enemas are diagnosed with *bulimia nervosa purging type*, whereas those who do not engage in the aforementioned compensatory behaviors and instead use other compensatory behaviors such as fasting or excessive exercise are diagnosed with *bulimia nervosa nonpurging type*.

Etiological Perspectives on Eating Disorders

Etiological perspectives of eating disorders span a range of theoretical viewpoints including biological, feminist, psychological, developmental, and sociocultural. Biological perspectives have been criticized as being overly simplistic and deterministic because although the body itself is a physical entity, it exists within a social and cultural context (Fredrickson & Roberts, 1997). As such, our discussion focuses on three etiological perspectives that explicitly address the gender discrepancy in eating disorders, namely, the feminist, sociocultural, and self-objectification perspectives. Intersecting circles corresponding to the three perspectives are shown in Figure 17.1 to represent the overlap in ideas addressed by each of the perspectives.

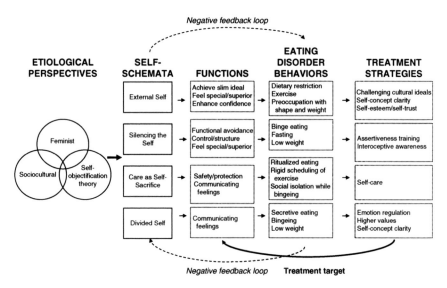

Figure 17.1 Etiological perspectives, self-schemata, functions, eating disorder behaviors, and treatment strategies.

Feminist Perspective

Feminist perspectives suggest that eating disorder thoughts and behaviors develop as a reaction to the oppression and objectification of women. The central role of beauty in female identity and in women's interpersonal relationships serves to channel women's identity concerns into preoccupation with shape and weight. These models focus on how sexist roles in patriarchal society place women in a position of diminished power in relationships, resulting in a loss of autonomy, control, and self-esteem, which creates a vulnerability to eating disorders (Frederick & Grow, 1996; Katzman & Lee, 1997; Striegel-Moore, 1993). Feminist theories also identify socialization factors that lead men and women to experience different constraints in their expression of anger (Miller, 1991).

Sociocultural Perspective

Sociocultural perspectives of eating disorders assert that societal factors, particularly as depicted by the visual media, cultivate unrealistic standards of thinness that few women can achieve (Thompson & Heinberg, 1999). The pervasiveness of thin or unrealistic female beauty ideals in the media contributes to a discrepancy between current standards of female attractiveness and the reality of women's actual bodies. This produces body dissatisfaction and contributes to extreme and/or maladaptive behaviors as attempts to meet external standards.

Self-Objectification Perspective

The self-objectification perspective posits that the pervasiveness of sexual objectification influences women to adopt an observer's perspective of their bodies as an object to be viewed and evaluated on the basis of physical appearance (Fredrickson & Roberts, 1997). Body shame and appearance anxiety intensify because the culturally prescribed ideal is impossible for most women to achieve. The habitual self-monitoring of outward appearance that accompanies self-objectification reduces the resources available for attending to inner body experiences, resulting in a diminished awareness of internal body states (Slater & Tiggeman, 2002).

Self-Silencing Perspective

Silencing the Self Theory (Jack & Dill, 1992) describes cognitive schemata that women develop in response to socialization experiences and societal expectations as described in these three etiological perspectives. According to this theory, female oppression and women's lack of power, as highlighted in feminist perspectives, may be associated with inhibiting self-expression (silencing the self) and the tendency to put the needs of others before the self (care as self-sacrifice). Similarly, the objectification of women's bodies and thin beauty ideals depicted in the visual media, as highlighted in sociocultural and self-objectification perspectives, contribute to the tendency for women to judge themselves harshly using unrealistic external standards (externalized self-perception), which contributes to a divided self and alienation from their own feelings (divided self).

Silencing the Self Schemata and Eating Disorder Behaviors

Silencing the Self Theory (Jack & Dill, 1992) asserts that the focus women place on relationships and the relation between women's self-worth and achieving and maintaining harmonious relationships make them vulnerable to suppressing feelings and prone to depression. In the past decade, eating disorder researchers have picked up on this work and explored whether eating disorder behaviors may be another means by which women cope with societal expectations and disempowering socialization experiences. This section summarizes empirical research that has addressed links among eating disorder behaviors, expressed and suppressed anger, and the silencing the self schemata.

It should be noted that a number of studies cited in this chapter were conducted in the specialized eating disorders program of a metropolitan Canadian city. To contextualize the studies that we conducted, it is important to note that Canadian eating disorder prevalence rates and gender breakdown are similar to those found in the United States (Statistics Canada, 2002), and the majority of individuals accessing specialized eating disorder treatment services identify themselves as Caucasian (e.g., Geller, 2007). Canada's health care system is publicly funded and administered, with all citizens qualifying for health coverage regardless of medical history, personal income, or standard of living. As a result, although it is likely that cultural factors such as the structure of the health care system impact access and duration of treatment services, there is no reason to believe that the cultural climate in Canada is associated with a significantly different experience of self-silencing than in other Western cultures.

In a first study conducted by our group (Geller, Cockell, Hewitt, Goldner, & Flett, 2000), we recruited clinical samples from a large Canadian tertiary eating disorders program and general psychiatry unit. We compared women with anorexia nervosa, psychiatric controls, and healthy controls on suppressed anger, as measured by the State Trait Anger Inventory (STAXI; Spielberger, 1996) and the silencing the self schemata, as measured by the Silencing the Self Scale (Jack & Dill, 1992). Women with anorexia nervosa reported higher levels of suppressed anger and higher scores on the silencing the self schemata than did the control groups on all four subscales and on suppressed, but not expressed, anger. In support of the specificity of silencing the self schemata to individuals with eating disorders, these group differences were maintained on two subscales (Care as Self-Sacrifice and Silencing the Self) after controlling for depression, self-esteem, and global assessment of functioning. This latter finding suggests that individuals with eating disorders are more likely to suppress their anger and subjugate their needs than are depressed women, and that suppressing anger and putting others' needs before one's own may play an important role in the development and maintenance of anorexia nervosa. Follow-up analyses indicated that inhibited expression of negative emotion and three of the silencing the self subscales (Care as Self-Sacrifice, Silencing the Self, and Divided Self) were significantly related to cognitive and affective components of body image dissatisfaction. This suggests that rather than experiencing anger toward an external target, the individual with anorexia nervosa may instead feel fat, and that fasting or ritualized eating and rigid scheduling of exercise may occur as a result of displaced negative feelings onto the body. Together, findings from this study suggest that women with anorexia nervosa are particularly inclined to avoid expressing thoughts and feelings when they conflict with those of others, that they give priority to others' feelings over their own, and that body dissatisfaction may reflect displaced negative feelings.

In a second study by our group examining the same constructs in a nonclinical sample of female adolescents, we found that various forms of disordered thoughts and behaviors about eating, including binge eating, purging, secretive eating, body dissatisfaction, and basing self-worth on shape and weight, were associated with suppressed anger and three of the silencing the self subscales (Silencing the Self, Externalized Self-Perception, and Divided Self) (Zaitsoff, Geller, & Srikameswaran, 2002). Similarly, in a study examining the silencing the self schemata and eating disordered behavior in an older sample of nonclinical undergraduate women, externalized self-perception was associated with preoccupation with shape and weight, both directly and indirectly through its influence on self-esteem (Ross & Wade, 2004).

Findings from these studies demonstrate that restrictive eating, bulimic behaviors, and preoccupation with shape and weight are related to suppressed anger and to the silencing the self schemata, and that this association is maintained across age and the spectrum of disordered eating. While we believe that the schemata contribute to the development of eating disorder symptoms, our clinical experience suggests that a negative feedback loop exists such that eating disorder symptoms further reinforce and perpetuate the silencing the self schemata, as depicted by the dashed arrows in Figure 17.1.

An example of this negative feedback loop includes the case of a woman who has become preoccupied with her weight and shape in response to an externalized self-perception, who then turns to magazines for guidance on how to lose weight or sculpt her body to resemble the cultural ideal. Another woman may restrict her eating as a means of self-silencing and suppressing anger, but then becomes physically fragile and emotionally numb, making it less likely that she will assert her needs or voice her opinion. Feeling overwhelmed by constantly fulfilling the needs of others, another woman might attempt to simplify and control her life by engaging in ritualistic behaviors such as calorie counting and rigid exercise routines. In the absence of gratitude from others for fulfilling their needs, she may then "reward" herself by binge eating because it provides a sense of pleasure, escape, and relief. By simplifying her own life and managing her dissatisfaction through binge eating, she is less likely to make herself a priority and set limits with others. Another example of silencing the self is the case of a patient with severe anorexia nervosa and a history of sexual abuse who presented as withdrawn and sullen, and restricted and self-harmed when she felt angry or frustrated. For her, recovery was associated with voicing her anger with her abuser and expressing herself assertively with the family members she felt had failed to protect her from the abuse. Finally, a woman may act compliant while she grows angry and hostile inside, and secretly binge eat to manage her anger and hostility. The secrecy, in turn, further promotes a divided self, making it unlikely that she will be honest and present her true self in relationships. If a woman feels unable to express her authentic self, her body may become her most effective means of communicating her emotions and distress to others. In order to disrupt this negative feedback loop, it is important to examine the functions of eating disorder symptoms as they relate to silencing the self.

Functions of Eating Disorder Symptoms

The past decade of eating disorder research has been characterized by growing interest in the functional significance of eating disorder symptomatology in the development and maintenance of the disorder (Vitousek, Watson, & Wilson, 1998). Qualitative and quantitative methodologies have been used to examine ways in which eating disorder thoughts and behaviors provide benefits and offer women an effective means of coping with difficulties, at least in the short term. This section describes functions that have been identified in the literature and relates them to the silencing the self schemata, as described in Figure 17.1. We propose that these functions mediate the relationship between silencing the self schemata and eating disorder behaviors. For example, a woman who judges herself using external standards, such as by comparing herself to cultural beauty ideals (externalized self-perception), may engage in disordered eating such as dietary restriction (eating disorder behavior) in order to achieve the slim ideal and feel special or worthy in relation to others, an important function for her. For many women, despite living with the physical and emotional costs that are associated with disordered eating, eating disorder behaviors provide a means by which they are able to negotiate and reconcile their role in a world experienced through the lens of the silencing the self schemata.

Two qualitative studies in women with eating disorders (anorexia nervosa and bulimia nervosa) involved study participants writing two letters to their eating disorder—one as a friend and one as a foe. The letters were used to identify themes corresponding to the benefits and consequences of an eating disorder (Serpell & Treasure, 2002; Serpell, Treasure, Teasdale, & Sullivan, 1999). Some themes were unique to a specific diagnosis; women with anorexia nervosa cited communicating emotions and distress (e.g., anger, frustration, sadness, loneliness, vulnerability) to others through their disorder as an important theme, whereas those with bulimia nervosa used the disorder to alleviate boredom and as a way to eat and stay slim. However, a number of benefit themes, or "functions," were common to both disorders, including feeling safe and protected, providing control and structure, looking slim and attractive (and thereby attracting attention from others), feeling special or superior, feeling confident, feeling "good" or "skilled" at something, and helping to avoid or manage emotions. Interestingly, the frequency with which the themes were mentioned differed according to diagnosis. Whereas providing control and structure and looking slim and attractive was mentioned more frequently by women with anorexia nervosa, avoiding and managing emotions such as anger was mentioned more frequently by women with bulimia nervosa.

In a recent clinical trial conducted by our group, women were specifically asked to describe the function of their eating disorder. Many of their comments reflected self-silencing, as illustrated by the following quotes:

"Purging helps get out anger and express negative feelings."

"The eating disorder is a physical way of expressing that I am feeling vulnerable and lonely. I am trying to say with my body what I have not been able to communicate with words."

"Not eating is a way of indirectly communicating with my mother that I don't want to always do what is expected of me. I am tired of the pressure, and not eating or losing weight is a way of rebelling without having to use words."

"Bingeing provides comfort and a sense of being nurtured. I am the one who looks after everyone else and bingeing is a way of looking after my needs. It's a treat. It has gotten to the point that I need to be sick in order to get time alone—otherwise, I nurture others all the time."

In line with some of these comments, in a study examining the function of disordered eating in undergraduate women, bingeing and vomiting were found to have different associations in the regulation of emotional states (Milligan & Waller, 2000). Women who binged had higher levels of anger suppression, suggesting that binge eating serves to avoid the experience of anger, whereas women who vomited had higher levels of state anger, suggesting that vomiting helps to reduce the immediate anger state.

Several other studies operationalized the benefits and costs of eating disorders and examined the relative importance of functions using decisional balance or pro/con scales. One such study that compared the responses of women with anorexia nervosa and bulimia nervosa on the Pros and Cons of Eating Disorders scale found that both groups agreed most strongly with the use of the eating disorder to stifle emotions (Gale, Holliday, Troop, Serpell, & Treasure, 2006). Another study focusing exclusively on women with anorexia nervosa found that the most important function identified for this disorder was communicating emotions such as unhappiness, distress, and anguish to others (Serpell, Teasdale, Troop, & Treasure, 2004). Supporting the negative feedback loop in our framework, this latter study found that the more a woman used her anorexia nervosa as a way of communicating emotions, the higher her drive for thinness and more severe her eating disorder symptoms. In other words, these feedback loops tend to maintain both self-silencing and disordered eating.

Finally, other researchers have examined the ability of women with eating disorders to access, identify, and express their emotions. One study comparing adolescent girls with bulimia nervosa, those with depression, and healthy controls found that girls with bulimia nervosa had more difficulty accessing and labeling their feelings and used a greater number of nonspecific emotion words (e.g., bad, awful, strange) than did the comparison groups (Sim & Zeman, 2004). A second study used a measure of attitudes and beliefs about expressive behavior and conflict over emotional expressiveness to understand the relation between eating behaviors and emotional expression. This study showed a link between dietary restriction and ambivalence about expressing anger (Quinton & Wagner, 2005). Together, these findings suggest that women with eating disorders may have difficulty identifying their feelings and that self-silencing may be a strategy that helps women manage their discomfort and ambivalence in expressing negative emotion. This reluctance to express emotion may be attributed to socialization processes in which women are taught that emotional expression is undesirable and, thus, to be avoided at all costs. Women with eating disorders may opt for the safety and protection of eating disorder behaviors to prevent anger from being expressed.

Together, these studies suggest that a critical function of eating disorder behaviors is communication and management of emotions. Possibly, some women who have developed eating disorders experienced barriers to communicating their feelings more directly growing up. They may have been raised in an environment that lacked healthy role models for communicating feelings, have a history of communication attempts being ignored or met with rejecting or unhelpful responses, or simply have learned that an emaciated body, food refusal, or bingeing and purging, are safer ways to manage or reduce distress and feel a sense of emotional or physical protection. For example, one of our patients had a father who worked long hours. She described him as having a "short fuse," being critical of others, and making derogatory remarks about women who were overweight. She wished for a close relationship with him but was afraid of his angry outbursts and disapproval. She felt that being very thin helped protect her from her father's anger and criticism.

Another illustration of the functional significance of food refusal and its relation to communication is a woman not eating a meal prepared by a family member as a passive way of communicating anger or withdrawal. In relation to our framework, this woman may be restricting her eating (eating disorder behavior) as a way of communicating her emotions (function) in order to present a compliant outer self while experiencing anger and distress inside (divided self).

Issues of emotional expression and safety are especially pertinent for women who have been sexually abused. Sexual abuse is one of several predisposing or precipitating factors cited in multifactorial models of eating disorders. For women who have been abused, eating disorder behaviors may help them in managing the cognitive and emotional sequelae of the abuse, particularly if the abuser was someone with whom they were in a relationship such as a family member, partner, or acquaintance. In the case of incest or spousal abuse, a woman may self-silence in order to avoid punishment or conflict and maintain the relationship while her inner self suffers, as described in the Silencing the Self and Divided Self subscales. In these cases, bingeing and purging behaviors may function to regulate negative emotional states related to the abuse that the woman is otherwise unable to express. Alternately, a woman may use self-starvation to transform her body from that of an attractive, voluptuous woman to that of a prepubescent girl, which communicates that she is not a sexual being, hence providing a sense of protection from being the target of future abuse (Fallon & Wonderlich, 1997).

Related to this protective function of eating disorder symptoms is the concept of functional avoidance (Cockell, Geller, & Linden, 2002). This idea was described in a study involving the development and validation of a decisional balance measure for anorexia nervosa. In this study, participants indicated the extent to which they endorsed a list of positive and negative aspects of anorexia nervosa. Although it was expected that factor analysis of their responses would produce two subscales, one for "benefits" and one for "burdens," a third subscale labeled "functional avoidance" was also identified. Functional avoidance items represented ways in which anorexia nervosa helps women avoid dealing with difficult experiences, including aversive emotions, challenges, and responsibilities, such as external expectations and pressures, and making important life decisions. For example, one woman described her reluctance to enroll in a mathematics course to complete her grade 12 requirements, as she was afraid that she would fail.

Interestingly, functional avoidance was moderately correlated with both the benefit and burden subscales, suggesting that avoiding is somewhat negatively reinforcing in the short term (benefit), while also preventing the attainment of long-term goals (burden). Subsequent research has shown that functional avoidance scores increase during the recovery process (Brown, Lockhart, & Geller, 2005), suggesting that as women's readiness for change increases, they develop insight into the complexities of their disorder and recognize that despite offering short-term relief, it prevents them from moving forward in their lives.

Most of the research on eating disorder functions has not addressed the extent to which women are aware of the utility or functional significance of their symptoms. In some cases, as in the letter-writing studies, women's awareness was implicit, as the functional themes were extracted from their own words. In other cases, however, such as in studies using independent measures of emotional expression and eating disorder behaviors, functional links were inferred by the investigators. The study on functional avoidance suggests that for some women, the recovery process is associated with a growing awareness of the functional significance of eating disorder symptoms. A final group of studies has explicitly addressed the question of awareness of functions with regard to managing and communicating emotions, and suggests that women with anorexia and bulimia nervosa may not always be conscious of this link. For instance, a lack of interoceptive awareness, or difficulty in recognizing and discriminating among internal cues such as hunger, satiety, and emotional states (Garner, Olmsted, & Polivy, 1983), has been shown to partly account for the association between suppression of negative emotions and disordered eating (Van Strien, Engels, Van Leeuwe, & Snoek, 2005). This lack of interoceptive awareness has also emerged as a strong predictor of eating disorder risk status in both cross-sectional (Leon, Fulkerson, Perry, & Cudeck, 1993) and prospective research (Leon, Fulkerson, Perry, & Early-Zald, 1995). Finally, a study comparing adolescent girls with bulimia nervosa, those with depression, and healthy controls found that girls with bulimia nervosa had the greatest difficulty identifying internal emotional states (Sim & Zeman, 2004). If a woman has difficulty labeling and expressing aversive emotions, severe food restriction or excessive food consumption may become a learned pattern of dealing with these negative and indistinct emotional states.

In summary, eating disorder symptoms provide a number of important functions in the lives of sufferers. In addition to helping women manage and communicate emotions, the latter group of studies suggests that eating disorder behaviors also serve a number of broader functions related to safety and avoidance, and that many women lack awareness of these functions due to difficulties in recognizing and discriminating internal states. It is our view that attempting to relinquish eating disorder behaviors without addressing these underlying functions can be a frustrating and self-defeating process for women and their care providers. We believe that long-lasting full recovery involves understanding the specific functions for each woman and finding alternate healthier means by which these needs can be met. In some cases, by challenging the developmental origin of the functional coping (e.g., the belief that she must conform to an unrealistically slim standard in order to be attractive and loved), the need for the coping behavior is reduced or eliminated. These are, in our view, the optimal targets of treatment.

Treatment Strategies: Helping Women Find Their Voice

A common eating disorder treatment myth is that the most rapid and effective recovery path is achieved by encouraging normal eating and weight gain as early as possible in the treatment process. In the past, traditional behavioral approaches did precisely this by having women adhere to a meal plan requiring normalized eating and/or admission to intensive treatment programs for weight gain. These interventions focused on reducing the woman's symptoms and paid little or no attention to factors maintaining the eating disorder, the woman's interest in change, or the woman's sense of autonomy in the recovery process.

Over the past several years, our eating disorder research team has focused its efforts on understanding the role of a woman's readiness for change in the recovery process from anorexia nervosa, bulimia nervosa, and eating disorder not otherwise specified, and on describing treatment relationships that promote positive outcomes. As a first step, we developed the Readiness and Motivation Interview (RMI; Geller, Cockell, & Drab, 2001; Geller & Drab, 1999) to provide a means by which women with anorexia nervosa, bulimia nervosa, and eating disorder not otherwise specified, could be engaged in conversations about their thoughts and feelings about change that would assess their readiness for change. The RMI is a semistructured, collaborative interview in which the interviewer and client work together to determine a client's readiness and motivation to change each symptom of an eating disorder. It was designed to be used in conjunction with the diagnostic questions from the Eating Disorder Examination (Cooper & Fairburn, 1987) so that both diagnostic information and motivational status could be obtained. In the RMI, interviewers use a collaborative, nonjudgmental stance to help women explore the pros and cons of their eating disorder symptoms, their readiness and motivation for change, and the extent to which change efforts are for themselves versus for others. Critical to the RMI is the interviewer's openness to the woman's experience and clear communication that the interviewer neither expects nor desires the woman to be ready to engage in change activities. As a result, for some individuals, the RMI provides women a first opportunity to talk about their ambivalence and to begin exploring and understanding the functions of their eating disorder symptoms.

Work using the RMI has shown that women's readiness for change predicts important clinical outcomes, including the decision to enroll in intensive treatment, behavioral change over time, dropout, and relapse (Geller et al., 2001; Geller, Drab-Hudson, Whisenhunt, & Srikameswaran, 2004). In some cases, changes may be made for a treatment provider or clinician. Interestingly, changing for others has been shown to be the most robust predictor of relapse, suggesting that it is important to help women make the decision to recover for themselves, as opposed to a family member, friend, or loved one.

As part of a larger study, our research group asked individuals with eating disorders how they experienced the pressure to heal when they were not yet ready for change. That is, what were their unhelpful experiences with relatives and health care professionals during the recovery process? One woman responded, "When doctors pushed me to eat things I wasn't ready for, and the ensuing lack of genuineness this created in our relationship." Another noted, "Therapists who appeared to care excessively about symptom change and push their own agenda on me, while trying to make it seem as though it were my agenda." Another commented that it was unhelpful to be told how to feel (e.g., "you should be happy about your weight gain"). Several women reported that being "guilt-tripped" into change or given an ultimatum was ineffective, and in some cases made them feel like "rebelling" through their eating disorder.

Individuals with eating disorders may attempt to change for others because they fear disapproval or criticism if they fail to meet the clinician's expectations and comply with recommendations. This fear may be well founded; our research has shown that eating disorder clinicians are poor at estimating women's readiness for change, and typically overestimate this client characteristic (Geller, 2002). Consequently, in order to present a compliant self and maintain their relationship with the clinician, women may express motivation for recovery and engage in recovery activities before they are ready to do so. Paradoxically, though well intentioned, the clinician's attitude can promote a divided self in the woman, possibly mimicking other relationships in her life and preventing her from engaging in authentic discussions about her thoughts and feelings and from understanding the functions of her eating disorder.

We believe that clinicians' stance and the nature of the relationship they form with women who have eating disorders are critical to the recovery process. Many of the principles to which we ascribe have their origins in motivational interviewing (MI; Miller & Rollnick, 2002). Central to the MI stance is maintaining a collaborative client–care provider relationship and maximizing the client's autonomy. In order to achieve this, the clinician communicates beliefs and values that foster self-acceptance, refrains from making assumptions about the woman's experience of the problem, demonstrates curiosity, and actively works to increase the woman's understanding of the problem and its function in her life.

Ten years ago, the specialized eating disorder program in which we work offered a "one size fits all" symptom reduction approach for women whose eating disorder symptoms surpassed clinical severity thresholds. Unfortunately, this model promoted a number of undesirable outcomes including disempowering, hierarchical relationships, poor therapeutic alliance, and women and care providers locked in battles about weight gain, symptom cessation, and calorie consumption. Furthermore, our research demonstrated that clients and care providers prefer a collaborative, client-centered approach to treatment and believe that such approaches produce stronger therapeutic relationships and more favorable clinical outcomes than do directive treatments (Geller, Brown, Zaitsoff, Goodrich, & Hastings, 2003).

Today, our program uses a motivational approach to help women understand the functions of their eating disorder and determine what, if anything, they want to change. We offer a menu of treatment options, tailored to client readiness. For those who are ready, we offer intensive treatment programs that provide a safe, structured environment that in addition to supporting normalized eating, also teaches women assertiveness skills, emotional expression, effective interpersonal functioning, emotion regulation, and distress tolerance. Body image groups and nutritional counseling help women better understand their internal experiences and relationships among emotional states, physiological cues, and beliefs or feelings about their bodies.

For women who are ambivalent or not ready for change, symptom reduction is not expected. Instead, we provide individual and group interventions designed to increase women's understanding of the development and maintenance of their eating disorder. These treatments include providing educational information to help challenge cultural ideals, identifying helpful and unhelpful support, and applying dialectical behavior therapy (DBT; Linehan, 1993) techniques that enhance interoceptive awareness and improve assertive communication. For example, in DBT, women learn mindfulness meditation skills to observe and identify emotions in a nonjudgmental way. Learning this skill can provide women with an alternative to bingeing, purging, and restricting, and help them develop healthier ways of addressing their emotional needs, such as talking with a trusted friend. Process-oriented group therapies increase women's self-concept clarity and interpersonal skills. Finally, community-based interventions help women improve their self-care practices and enhance their quality of life through the use of a psychosocial rehabilitation model that reduces their isolation and re-establishes supportive relationships in the community. A key feature of these treatment modalities involves helping women articulate their higher values. Women in our program, almost without exception, identify close personal relationships as one of their higher values: for example, "Being in a close relationship in which you feel accepted as you are, and in which you feel no pressure to change anything about yourself." Other women discuss the importance of self-acceptance: for example, "Coming to understand that even though you try your best, things don't always work out and asking for help is not a sign of weakness." Creativity, spontaneity, and "living in the moment" were also frequently noted. For example, "Creativity is my way of expressing myself. It is a safer way of communicating, it allows my true voice to be heard, and I feel sincere and authentic." In treatment, a woman may identify her bingeing and purging as a way in which she avoids communicating feelings to her partner. In discussion of meaningful life experiences and important personal values, she may identify honesty and emotional authenticity as important. Over time, she may recognize that in failing to tell her partner about her true feelings, she has been presenting a divided self that maintains her eating disorder and is incongruent with her value of honesty. The experience of this discrepancy may help her work with her therapist to improve her communication skills, increase her self-efficacy, and ultimately decide to make changes to her eating patterns.

In sum, our approach to treatment focuses on helping women find their voice by fostering a safe and nonjudgmental environment that promotes emotional expression. Challenging cultural ideals and providing opportunities to work on assertiveness, interoceptive awareness, the regulation of emotions, and the identification of higher values, accomplish this objective. We believe that engaging women in these activities increases their self-concept clarity and self-esteem, and allows them to address the functions of their disorder. Given that functions are critical to the development and maintenance of anorexia nervosa and bulimia nervosa, this is a critical process in helping women reduce their eating disorder behaviors and challenge their internalization of the silencing the self schemata.

Summary

Similar to women with depression, the silencing the self schemata have been shown to be highly prevalent in women with eating disorders. Research has shown that women with anorexia nervosa and bulimia nervosa are more likely than are non–eating-disordered or depressed women to suppress their anger and to endorse the Silencing the Self, Externalized Self-Perception, Divided Self, and Care as Self-Sacrifice subscales. In this chapter, we put forward a model that links etiological perspectives, the silencing the self schemata, and eating disorder behaviors, and propose that there are functions that mediate the relationship between self-schemata and disordered eating. Finally, we describe treatment strategies and suggest that the most effective interventions engage women in collaborative, nonhierarchical relationships that focus on readiness for change and address the functions of the eating disorder.

Note

1. This is defined as less than 85% of that expected or a body mass index less than 17.5 kg/m^2 (American Psychiatric Association, 2000).

References

American Psychiatric Association. (2000). *Diagnostic and statistical manual of mental disorders* (4th ed., text revision). Washington, DC: Author.

Brown, K. E., Lockhart, A. L., & Geller, J. (2005, April). *What to do when clients are ambivalent about change: Factors associated with increases in motivation.* Poster presented at the Academy for Eating Disorders 2005 International Conference, Montreal, Quebec.

Cockell, S. J., Geller, J., & Linden, W. (2002). The development of a decisional balance scale for anorexia nervosa. *European Eating Disorders Review, 10,* 359–375.

Cooper, Z., & Fairburn, C. G. (1987). The Eating Disorder Examination: A semi-structured interview for the assessment of the specific psychopathology of eating disorders. *International Journal of Eating Disorders, 6,* 1–8.

Fallon, P., & Wonderlich, S. A. (1997). Sexual abuse and other forms of trauma. In D. M. Garner & P. E. Garfinkel (Eds.), *Handbook of treatment for eating disorders* (2nd ed., pp. 394–414). New York: Guilford Press.

Frederick, C. M., & Grow, V. M. (1996). A mediational model of autonomy, self-esteem, and eating disordered attitudes and behaviours. *Psychology of Women Quarterly, 20,* 217–228.

Fredrickson, B. L., & Roberts, T. (1997). Objectification theory: Toward understanding women's lived experiences and mental health risks. *Psychology of Women Quarterly, 21,* 173–206.

Gale, C., Holliday, J., Troop, N. A., Serpell, L., & Treasure, J. (2006). The pros and cons of change in individuals with eating disorders: A broader perspective. *International Journal of Eating Disorders, 39,* 394–403.

Garner, D. M., Olmsted, M. P., & Polivy, J. (1983). Development and validation of a multidimensional eating disorder inventory for anorexia nervosa and bulimia. *International Journal of Eating Disorders, 2,* 15–34.

Geller, J. (2002). Estimating readiness for change in anorexia nervosa: Comparing clients, clinicians, and research assessors. *International Journal of Eating Disorders, 31,* 251–260.

Geller, J. (2007, June). *Providence health care annual report of the eating disorders program.* Report presented at the eating disorders program quarterly research meeting, Vancouver, British Columbia.

Geller, J., Brown, K. E., Zaitsoff, S. L., Goodrich, S., & Hastings, F. (2003). Collaborative versus directive interventions in the treatment of eating disorders: Implications for care providers. *Professional Psychology: Research and Practice, 34,* 406–413.

Geller, J., Cockell, S. J., & Drab, D. (2001). Assessing readiness for change in anorexia nervosa: The psychometric properties of the Readiness and Motivation Interview. *Psychological Assessment, 13,* 189–198.

Geller, J., Cockell, S. J., Hewitt, P. L., Goldner, E. M., & Flett, G. L. (2000). Inhibited expression of negative emotions and interpersonal orientation in anorexia nervosa. *International Journal of Eating Disorders, 28,* 8–19.

Geller, J., & Drab, D. (1999). The Readiness and Motivation Interview: A symptom-specific measure of readiness for change in the eating disorders. *European Eating Disorders Review, 7,* 259–278.

Geller, J., Drab-Hudson, D. L., Whisenhunt, B. L., & Srikameswaran, S. (2004). Readiness to change dietary restriction predicts short and long term outcomes in the eating disorders. *Eating Disorders: The Journal of Treatment and Prevention, 12,* 209–224.

Jack, D. C., & Dill, D. (1992). The Silencing the Self Scale: Schemas of intimacy associated with depression in women. *Psychology of Women Quarterly, 16,* 97–106.

Katzman, M. A. & Lee, S. (1997). Beyond body image: The integration of feminist and transcultural theories in the understanding of self starvation. *International Journal of Eating Disorders, 22,* 385–394.

Leon, G. R., Fulkerson, J. A., Perry, C. L., & Cudeck, R. (1993). Personality and behavioural vulnerabilities associated with risk status for eating disorders in adolescent girls. *Journal of Abnormal Psychology, 102,* 438–444.

Leon, G. R., Fulkerson, J. A., Perry, C. L., & Early-Zald, M. B. (1995). Prospective analysis of personality and behavioural vulnerabilities and gender influences in the later development of disordered eating. *Journal of Abnormal Psychology, 104,* 140–149.

Linehan, M. (1993). *Skills training manual for treating borderline personality disorder.* New York: Guilford Press.

Miller, J. B. (1991). The construction of anger in women and men. In J. V. Jordan, A. G. Kaplan, J. B. Miller, I. P. Stiver, & J. L. Surrey (Eds.), *Women's growth in connection* (pp. 162–180). New York: Guilford Press.

Miller, W. R., & Rollnick, S. (2002). *Motivational interviewing: Preparing people for change.* New York: Guilford Press.

Milligan, R., & Waller, G. (2000). Anger and bulimic psychopathology among nonclinical women. *International Journal of Eating Disorders, 28,* 446–450.

Quinton, S., & Wagner, H. L. (2005). Alexithymia, ambivalence over emotional expression, and eating attitudes. *Personality and Individual Differences, 38,* 1163–1173.

Ross, M., & Wade, T. D. (2004). Shape and weight concern and self-esteem as mediators of externalized self-perception, dietary restraint, and uncontrolled eating. *European Eating Disorders Review, 12,* 129–136.

Serpell, L., Teasdale, J., Troop, N. A., & Treasure, J. (2004). The development of the P-CAN, a measure to operationalize the pros and cons of anorexia nervosa. *International Journal of Eating Disorders, 36,* 416–433.

Serpell, L., & Treasure, J. (2002). Bulimia nervosa: Friend or foe? The pros and cons of bulimia nervosa. *International Journal of Eating Disorders, 32,* 164–170.

Serpell, L., Treasure, J., Teasdale, J., & Sullivan, V. (1999). Anorexia nervosa: Friend or foe? *International Journal of Eating Disorders, 25,* 177–186.

Sim, L., & Zeman, J. (2004). Emotion awareness and identification skills in adolescent girls with bulimia nervosa. *Journal of Clinical Child and Adolescent Psychology, 33,* 760–771.

Slater, A., & Tiggemann, M. (2002). A test of objectification theory in adolescent girls. *Sex Roles, 46,* 343–349.

Spielberger, C. D. (1996). *Stait-Trait Anger Expression Inventory. Professional manual.* Odessa, FL: Psychological Assessment Resources.

Statistics Canada. (2002). *Canadian Community Health Survey, cycle 1.2.* Ottawa, ON: Author.

Striegel-Moore, R. H. (1993). Etiology of binge eating: A developmental perspective. In C. J. Fairburn & G. T. Wilson (Eds.), *Binge eating: Nature, assessment, and treatment*. New York: Guilford Press.

Thompson, J. K., & Heinberg, L. J. (1999). The media's influence on body image disturbance and eating disorders: We've reviled them, now can we rehabilitate them? *Journal of Social Issues, 55*, 339–353.

Van Strien, T., Engels, R., Van Leeuwe, J., & Snoek, H. M. (2005). The Stice model of overeating: Tests in clinical and non-clinical samples. *Appetite, 45*, 205–213.

Vitousek, K., Watson, S., & Wilson, G. T. (1998). Enhancing motivation for change in treatment-resistant eating disorders. *Clinical Psychology Review, 18*, 391–420.

Zaitsoff, S. L., Geller, J., & Srikameswaran, S. (2002). Silencing the self and suppressed anger: Relationship to eating disorder symptoms in adolescent females. *European Eating Disorders Review, 10*, 51–60.

18

Self-Silencing and the Risk of Heart Disease and Death in Women: The Framingham Offspring Study

Elaine D. Eaker and Margaret Kelly-Hayes

The notion that emotions can have a direct impact on physical health has evoked speculation for centuries; a growing body of scientific evidence demonstrates that this is indeed the case. A number of studies have examined the potential etiological effect of psychological, social, and behavioral variables on cardiovascular health and disease outcomes in men and women. These variables have included such things as Type A behavior; expressions of anger; depression; social support; hostility, tension, and anxiety; and situational stress such as work stress, marital strain, aging, and personal worries (Barefoot & Schroll, 1996; De Vogli, Chandola, & Marmot, 2007; Eaker, Sullivan, Kelly-Hayes, D'Agostino, & Benjamin, 2004a; Haynes, Feinleib, & Eaker, 1982; Kawachi, Sparrow, Spiro, Vokonas, & Weiss, 1996; Kawachi, Sparrow, Vokonas, & Weiss, 1994; Osfeld & Eaker, 1985).

Since the early 1980s, the social and psychological risk factors for cardiovascular disease and decreased overall survival in women have been a focus of study (Eaker, 1998; Haynes et al., 1982; Kawachi,Sparrow et al., 1994; Kawachi et al., 1998). Promising areas for which a scientific basis for prediction is emerging include depressive symptoms, expression of anger, anxiety, hostility, and marital status related to the development of coronary heart disease, stroke, or death in women and men (Eaker et al., 2004a; Kawachi et al., 1994; 1996; Kimmel, 1999). Findings for each of these areas of risk vary by age and sex and from study to study. Currently, however, it is difficult to find a definitive consensus in the literature that concludes which specific psychosocial characteristics are clearly predictive of disease outcomes. This lack of consensus is partially due to the fact that investigation into such risk factors requires large cohorts of women, the measurement of psychosocial risk factors before the development of disease, collection of a variety of known risk factors that could explain the relationship between the psychosocial characteristics and the disease outcome, and long-term follow-up of the cohort in order to obtain enough disease or death endpoints for statistically sound results.

A well-known longitudinal cohort study that incorporates these attributes is the Framingham Heart Study. This study is significant for its groundbreaking design and the recruitment and retention of a large community cohort of both men and women who were followed and examined regularly throughout their lives starting in 1948. The Framingham Heart Study was the first to identify the major cardiovascular disease risk factors such as high blood pressure, high blood cholesterol, diabetes, smoking, obesity, and physical inactivity. This study has also contributed important information regarding risk associated with gender, age, hormones, and psychosocial characteristics. For example, Framingham was the first study to demonstrate the importance of psychosocial risk factors for heart disease in women (Eaker, Pinsky, & Castelli, 1992; Haynes & Feinleib, 1980; Haynes, Feinleib, & Kannel, 1980). During the regular biennial examination that was conducted between 1965 and 1967, an additional 300-item psychosocial questionnaire, developed by Drs. Levine and Scotch and based on the current state of knowledge regarding psychosocial risk and the development of heart disease (Haynes, Levine, Scotch, Feinleib, & Kannel, 1978), was administered to a subset of surviving cohort members. The goal was to identify various types of behavior associated with anger, situational stress, somatic strain, and personality characteristics and their impact on health and disease. In 1971, the children of the original cohort participants and the spouses of the children were enrolled into the Framingham Offspring Study ($n = 5,124$). Offspring study participants are examined every four to eight years including information on psychological risk. The purpose of this chapter is to describe research findings from the Framingham Offspring Study that explored the relationships between marriage and marital strain to the development of coronary heart disease (CHD) or death from all causes.

At the third examination cycle of the Offspring Study, from 1984 through 1987, 3,873 participants aged 18 to 77 years were examined. This data collection cycle included not only the physical and biological risk factor data but also data related to psychosocial risk factors. Subjects were mailed the self-administered psychosocial assessment forms that were collected at the scheduled clinic examination. A total of 3,682 participants (1,913 women) completed a psychosocial questionnaire, a 95% response rate. The psychosocial risk factors, including marital strain and marital status, were derived from the 300-item questionnaire administered to the parent cohort plus additional scales that were currently under investigation in the scientific area of psychological and social risk factors. From the baseline examination where the psychosocial risk factors were collected (1984–1987), participants were followed for up to 10 years to document the development of CHD or death. Participants who had CHD at baseline (prevalent cases) were excluded from these analyses and new cases (incident cases) were counted. This exclusion of prevalent cases is an important feature of longitudinal studies as it helps to ensure that the presence of disease is not the reason for the risk factors. For example, it might be the case that a strained marriage is the result of one of the spouses having heart disease. The purpose of this study is to determine if marital strain predicts the new occurrence (incidence) of coronary heart disease.

The concept that marital stress or strain may be related to CHD has existed for many years. In 1976, Medalie and Goldbourt published data from over 10,000 Israeli men demonstrating that a wife's love and support were important in reducing the risk of developing angina pectoris (Medalie & Goldbourt, 1976). More recently, a population-based prospective study of women who had been hospitalized for acute myocardial infarction or unstable angina pectoris found that marital stress was associated with a 2.9-fold risk of recurrent events (Orth-Gomer et al., 2000). In a follow-up study of the men who had participated in the Multiple Risk Factor Intervention Trial, those who divorced during the trial experienced a relative risk (RR) of 1.4 for total mortality, compared with those who remained married (Matthews & Gump, 2002). Another study found that "marital quality" was significantly related to a four-year survival in men and women with heart failure (Coyne et al., 2001). These research findings lend credence to the notion that marital status and strain or stress may be associated with the development of CHD or total mortality.

Most of these studies to date that examine marital characteristics and health outcomes have concentrated on marital feelings of happiness and satisfaction. In women, it has been found that the quality of a marriage is associated with prognosis following a heart attack (Orth-Gomer et al., 2000). A poor marriage puts a woman at increased risk of having another heart attack or subsequent complications, but only among women who already have heart disease. This leads to the question of whether the quality of a marriage might be associated with the development of new heart disease or death from all causes. When devising the new psychosocial questionnaire for the Framingham Offspring Study, we wanted to assess not only the more traditional measures of marital strain (e.g., dissatisfaction, unhappiness, and disagreements) but also aspects of interpersonal reactions to conflict that take place in marriage or marital situations. Several measures of marital strain were used to form a conceptual framework for analyses in the research study reported here: (1) marital happiness and satisfaction, (2) the amount and types of disagreements with a spouse, (3) feeling of being loved by one's spouse, and (4) self-silencing: how one reacts when in conflict with one's spouse. The first three measures reflect feelings and interactions between spouses. The fourth, self-silencing, reflects how one reacts interpersonally to stress and conflict with one's spouse and has been linked to depression in women in previous research (Jack, 1991).

Methods for the Present Analyses from the
Framingham Offspring Study

The current research was conducted under the hypothesis that marital strain in either men or women leads to the development of heart disease or premature death. Participants were categorized as currently married if they indicated that they were married or living in a marital situation at the baseline examination. All others were classified as not currently married.

Both men and women answered questions regarding their own and their spouse's feelings of marital happiness, their own marital satisfaction, whether they self-silenced during conflicts with a spouse, and whether their spouse showed his or her love for them. The marital disagreement scale was answered by both men and women and reflected the frequency (often, once in a while, or never) that the respondent and his or her spouse disagreed on 13 topics. The topics included such things as finances, leisure time, religious matters, sexual relations, in-laws, chores, drinking, and gambling. The marital dissatisfaction and disagreement scales were developed, tested, and published previously (Haynes et al., 1978). The reliability coefficients for the disagreements and satisfaction scales were .80 and .84, respectively, in the original Framingham cohort study. The marital disagreements scale was computed by summing the responses to the 13 distinct items. Each item asked about specific instances and the response options were "never disagree," "disagree once in a while," and "disagree often." The response options were scaled 0, 0.5, and 1, respectively. Thus, for the scales reflecting marital disagreements, responses were scaled between 0 and 1, with the higher score indicating more frequent disagreement or strain. Some respondents failed to provide data on some of the items. However, the extent of missing data was minimal; each item had less than 3% missing values. For everyone else, we summed the responses to the items. We coded missing items to 0 (for the people who were not missing on all items). We then dichotomized the composite scale score at the median and defined them as low and high.

We also addressed whether a person communicated with his or her spouse during conflict or chose to be quiet. The self-suppression of communication in a marital situation can be seen as a measure of "self-silencing" (Jack, 1991). The question was phrased: When you have a conflict with your spouse do you always show it, usually show it, or usually or always keep it to yourself? This question on self-silencing, as well as the question about spouses' love, have face or previous predictive validity but are not formally validated in this study.

The two outcomes of interest included the 10-year incidence of CHD and total mortality. The definition of CHD (Abbott & McGee, 1987) has been published previously; the manifestations of interest for CHD in these analyses included myocardial infarction (recognized and unrecognized), coronary insufficiency, and coronary death (both sudden and not sudden).

Known risk factors for CHD could conceivably explain any relationship observed between the psychosocial variables of interest and the disease outcomes. For example, it might be the case that women who self-silence are more likely to smoke cigarettes and it is the smoking that is the important risk factor, and not self-silencing per se. These factors were ascertained at the baseline examination (1984–1987) and included age, systolic blood pressure, body mass index (kg/m^2), current cigarette smoking, diabetes (defined as fasting blood glucose of at least 126 mg/dL or on treatment), and total cholesterol/high-density cholesterol. These risk factors were taken into account in the multivariable models predicting the 10-year incidence of CHD and death from all causes.

In addition to the physical risk factors, previous research has shown that depression is also a variable that could explain any observed relationship between self-silencing and the disease outcomes. Research has shown that self-silencing may be related to depression (Jack, 1991; Jack & Dill, 1992), and data from the Framingham Study show that depressive symptoms were directly associated with death from all causes in men and women. Compared to those in the lowest tertile of depressive symptoms, those in the highest tertile had an 88% higher risk of death during the six-year follow-up period (Wulsin et al., 2005). Other studies have shown that depression is associated with increased risk of developing coronary heart disease (Herbst, Pietrzak, Wagner, White, & Petry, 2007) and stroke (Salaycik et al., 2007). In order to ascertain whether symptoms of depression might explain any observed relationship between the risk of death and self-silencing, we additionally adjusted for symptoms of depression in the present analyses using the Center for Epidemiologic Studies Depression 20-Item Scale (Radloff, 1977). The research literature also has shown that expression or nonexpression of anger may be related to the development of coronary heart disease (Eaker et al., 2004a). Suppression of anger has also been shown to relate to depression and self-silencing (Brody, Haaga, Kirk, & Solomon, 1999). Therefore, it was important to control for suppression of anger in these analyses. We did this by including the variable "anger-in" from the Framingham Study in these analyses along with the self-silencing variable.

The relationship of the psychosocial measures to education and CHD risk factors classified at baseline were examined with Pearson correlations and t-tests for continuous and discrete variables, respectively. The 10-year age-adjusted rates and relative risks of CHD and total mortality were estimated using Cox proportional hazards regression. Each psychosocial predictor variable that reached a significance level of $p \le .10$ in the age-adjusted analyses was examined in a multivariable-adjusted Cox proportional hazards model. Relative risks for incident disease were presented relative to a one–standard deviation difference in each measure. All analyses were sex specific.

Results

The study on marital strain consisted of 1,769 men and 1,913 women, who were a mean age of 48 years ($SD = 10$; range, 18 to 77) at baseline. The causes of death for men and women, respectively, were 25% and 12% from CHD, 2.8% and 4.4% from stroke, and 35.4% and 55.4% from cancer. The analyses involving marital strain consisted of 1,493 men and 1,501 women currently married or "living in a marital situation" at the baseline examination.

Table 18.1 Demographics and Marital Strain Measures of Men and Women Married at Baseline

Total Sample	Men $n = 1,769$	Women $n = 1,912$	p value
Mean age, years	48.8	48.2	.038
Currently married, %	84.4	78.5	< .0001
Married participants	$n = 1,493$	$n = 1,501$	
Mean age, years	49.8	48.2	< .0001
Education			< .0001
12 years or less	40.8	47.0	
13–16 years	21.4	29.3	
17+ years	37.7	23.7	
Total family income			.02
$0–$9,000	19.9	24.2	
$10,000–$19,999	20.7	22.2	
$20,000–$29,999	21.5	20.4	
$30,000–$49,999	37.9	33.2	
$50,000+	0.00	0.00	
How happy is your marriage			.003
Very happy	43.4	38.9	
Happy	33.1	32.3	
Average, unhappy, very unhappy	23.5	28.8	
Marital satisfaction compared to others			< .0001
More satisfied	53.8	45.04	
As satisfied	41.0	47.3	
Less satisfied	5.2	7.7	
When you have a conflict with your spouse do you			< .001
Always show it	17.3	20.9	
Usually show it	51.5	55.8	
Usually/always keep it to yourself	31.2	23.2	
Marital disagreements scale			
Low	49.6	49.1	.79
High	50.4	50.9	
Marital disagreements (top six)			
Sex relations	9.1	7.1	.05
Family finances	6.2	8.5	.02
How to spend leisure time	6.2	8.1	.05
Bring up children	5.6	9.7	< .0001
Household chores	4.2	8.7	< .0001
Drinking	4.4	7.2	.002

Table 18.1 presents the descriptive data for the demographics and marital characteristics. The largest percentage of both men and women had a high school education or less, with more men than women having some schooling after college. Men were significantly more likely than women to report higher total family income, a happier marriage, and more marital satisfaction. Men were more likely to keep their feelings to themselves during conflict with their spouse and to report that their spouse shows their love for them very often compared to women. There were no differences between men and women regarding the level of marital disagreements. For the types of disagreements, women were more likely than men to report that they disagreed with their spouse on family finances, leisure time, bringing up children, household chores, and drinking. Men reported more disagreements on sexual relations.

Table 18.2 shows the associations between the standard risk factors for coronary heart disease, marital status, and self-silencing in women. Women who were not currently married were significantly more likely to be cigarette smokers. The only risk factor that was significantly associated with self-silencing was age. Women who said they usually or always kept their feelings to themselves when in conflict with their spouse were significantly older than women who said they always or usually showed their feelings. None of the other risk factors—systolic blood pressure, body mass index, the ratio of total to high-density cholesterol,

Table 18.2 Association between Marital Status, Self-Silencing, and Risk Factors in Married Women

Variable	*n*	Age	SBP	BMI	Total/ HDL- C	Smoker	Diabetic
			All Women (*n* = 1,913)				
			Means			Percent	
Marital status							
Currently married	1,501	48.2	122.0	25.4	4.0	27.3	2.7
Not currently married	411	48.0	120.5	25.3	4.1	37.2	2.4
p value		.67	.13	.73	.20	< .0001	.79
			Married Women (*n* = 1,501)				
When in conflict with spouse, do you:							
Always show it	302	47.3	123.0	25.8	3.9	25.9	2.7
Usually show it	805	47.7	120.8	25.2	4.0	27.4	2.5
Usually/always keep it to yourself	335	49.9	123.1	25.5	4.1	30.5	2.7
p value		.0004	.07	.21	.45	.41	.98

being a smoker, or having diabetes—were associated with the self-silencing variable. One might assume that the risk of premature death is not the result of self-silencing per se, but simply the fact of being an older woman. In fact, this was not the case.

Table 18.3 presents the multivariable relative risks for the 10-year development of heart disease or total mortality. Multivariable models predicting the 10-year incidence of CHD and total mortality controlled for the known physical risk factors of age, systolic blood pressure, body mass index (kg/m^2), current cigarette smoking, diabetes (defined as fasting blood glucose of at least 126 mg/dL or on treatment), and total cholesterol/high-density cholesterol. The beneficial relation between total mortality and being married was significant for men, but there was no relationship between marital status and survival in women. Women who reported that when in conflict with their spouse they usually or always kept their feelings to themselves (self-silencing) had over four times the risk of dying during the 10-year follow-up compared to women who always showed their feelings. Self-silencing had no effect on men's risk for developing heart disease or premature death. It should be noted that the presence of prevalent CHD was also entered into all multivariable analyses of total mortality, but this did not substantially change any of the reported results.

Table 18.3 Multivariable-Adjusted* Relative Risks** for the 10-Year Occurrence of Coronary Heart Disease and Total Mortality in Men and Women

	Coronary Heart Disease		Total Mortality	
	Men	Women	Men	Women
Event numbers/ persons at risk	126/1,680	47/1,895	175/1,769	92/1,913
All participants, RR (95%CI)				
Married versus not married	0.92 (0.51–1.65)	0.85 (0.43–1.70)	**0.54 (0.35–0.83)**[†]	1.04 (0.62–1.74)
Participants Married at Baseline				
Conflict with spouse				
Always show it (referent)				
Usually show it	0.69 (0.43, 1.10)	1.16 (0.47, 2.85)	0.79 (0.53, 1.19)	1.77 (0.76, 4.09)
Usual/always keep to self	0.89 (0.54, 1.47)	1.29 (0.48, 3.50)	0.87 (0.56, 1.36)	**4.01 (1.75, 9.20)**

* Adjusted for age, systolic blood pressure, body mass index, current cigarette smoking, diabetes (defined as fasting blood glucose of at least 126 mg/dL or on treatment), and total cholesterol/high-density cholesterol.
** Relative risk (RR) and confidence interval (CI) estimates relative to one–standard deviation change for continuous variables
[†] Bold: $p < .05$.

Secondary Analyses

To gain further insights into why self-silencing appeared to predict increased mortality in women, we further adjusted for the potential psychological mediators of depression and suppression of anger. When symptoms of depression were entered into the multivariable equation with the variable indicating self-silencing during conflict with one's spouse, women who usually or always kept the conflict to themselves had a five times greater risk of death (hazard ratio [HR] = 5.11; 95% confidence interval [CI]: 1.96–13.30), respectively, compared to women who always showed feelings during conflict. This higher hazard ratio was a result of controlling depressive symptoms in the equation. Similarly, when anger-in was included in the equation with self-silencing, the hazard ratio of self-silencing remained significant at over four times greater risk of death (HR = 4.24; 95% CI: 1.80–9.99).

Discussion

In the current research, none of the characteristics conventionally thought of as reflecting marital strain, such as one's own marital satisfaction or happiness and marital disagreements, was significantly related to the development of CHD or death from all causes in either women or men. Put into context with previous research, it seems that these characteristics are important in consideration of prognosis after a cardiovascular event, but they are unrelated to the development of CHD or mortality in people free of CHD at baseline (Medalie & Goldbourt, 1976; Orth-Gomer et al., 2000).

The most significant risk factor for reduced survival found in this particular study of marital strain was how women react during conflict with their spouse. Women who reported engaging in self-silencing (i.e., when in conflict with their spouse they "always or usually" keep the conflict to themselves) had the highest risk of death compared to women who did not report self-silencing (i.e., who "always show" their conflict with their spouse). To our knowledge, this is the first research study to demonstrate the lethal impact on women of self-silencing in intimate relationships.

The concept of self-silencing was developed by Jack (1991) and is defined as the tendency to silence one's thoughts and feelings in order to maintain safe relationships, particularly intimate relationships. In women, self-silencing thoughts and feelings can precipitate an overall self-negation through progressive devaluation of one's own thoughts and beliefs and has been found to correlate significantly with depressive symptoms in studies of various populations of women and men (Jack & Dill, 1992; Thompson, 1995) and with irritable bowel syndrome in women (Ali et al., 2000). The formal Silencing the Self Scale was published after we collected the data for the present study; however, the question regarding communication during conflict in the current study may be construed as a measure of self-silencing. The magnitude of risk for total mortality in women conveyed by this variable, after adjusting for other risk factors, is difficult to ignore (RR = 4.17; 95% CI: 1.84–9.47). In an effort to further understand this association, we included first depression and then anger-in in the multivariable model, and the association of self-silencing with mortality in women remained virtually unchanged. Therefore, there may be something inherent to the characteristic of self-silencing that is detrimental to women, independent of its known relationship to depression or suppressed anger in women. It is paradoxical that a behavior that may have developed to protect women's relationships with their spouses may ultimately be destructive to them. Self-silencing may not be a measure of marital strain. It appears to be more of an intrapersonal decision to not engage visually or verbally with one's spouse when the feeling of being in conflict is elicited. The spouse, in fact, may not even be aware that the woman is withdrawing or even feeling conflict.

Jack believes women self-silence not because they are passive and dependent but because they value relationship. She proposes that women "bite their tongues" for a variety of reasons. They may fear rejection by a partner they and their children depend on economically. Women may have had previous experiences in childhood during which their opinions were devalued or rejected. Women may have internalized the cultural belief that the woman does not challenge or conflict with the man with whom she is intimate. In addition, women may believe they are more capable of controlling their own emotions than changing the behavior of their partners. A question arises as to why self-silencing was a strong risk factor for premature death but not the development of definite heart disease in these women. While the answer is not clearly defined within this research, there are some speculative reasons that can be explored in future research. The leading cause of death in this relatively young population was, by far, cancer, for both men and women. Thus, we found that the effect of self-silencing on health outcomes in women is not limited to CHD, but is overarching and has a strong negative impact on survival, regardless of the cause of death. The physiology of this risk needs further investigation. It may also be that the smaller number of cases of heart disease in women did not allow for enough statistical power to detect a significant impact on heart disease risk. A study with a larger number of definite heart disease cases would be needed to address this question.

The present investigation of the Framingham Offspring Study substantiates the many other studies that demonstrate that married men have a survival advantage over unmarried men (Ben-Shlomo, Smith, Shipley, & Marmot, 1993; Ebrahim, Wannamethee, McCallum, Walker, & Shaper, 1995; Mendes de Leon, Appels, Otten, & Schouten, 1992; Rosengren, Wedel, & Wilhelmsen, 1989; Valkonen, 1982). A prospective study of middle-aged men in Britain, 40 to 59 years of age, found that overall there was excess mortality in men who were single or recently divorced (Ebrahim et al., 1995). A study of middle-aged Swedish men found that after adjustment for other risk factors, unmarried men had a significantly higher total mortality (Rosengren et al., 1989). The Whitehall Study also found that overall mortality was greater for all groups of unmarried men (Ben-Shlomo et al., 1993). In a study of middle-aged men in the Netherlands, unmarried men had significantly higher risk of all-cause mortality (RR = 1.7, 95% CI: 1.2–2.3) and coronary mortality (RR = 2.2, 95% CI: 1.2–4.2) than married men (Mendes de Leon et al., 1992). In a Finnish study, unmarried men had significantly higher mortality rates compared to married men (Valkonen, 1982).

The influence of marital status on longevity in women has been studied less often. The Study of Osteoporotic Fractures, a study of older (65 years and older) white women, found that married participants showed lower covariate adjusted total and cardiovascular disease (CVD) death rates compared with unmarried participants (Rutledge, Matthews, Lui, Stone, & Cauley, 2003). However, in the Finnish study reported earlier, marriage did not convey a mortality benefit for women (aged 35 to 74 years) (Valkonen, 1982). The present study, a cohort similar in age to the Finnish study, also observed that in women marital status did not appear to protect against mortality and CVD events. The lack of consistency between studies on the relation of marital status to prognosis in women may in part be a result of the age differences in the studies. Being single may be more of a detriment in older as compared to younger women.

While marital satisfaction was not related to health outcomes in either men or women, men in general reported their marriages to be happier and more satisfying than the women in the study. Our current study does not provide evidence for why this might be the case except that women were significantly more likely to report marital disagreements on a variety of issues. (Eaker, Sullivan, Kelly-Hayes, D'Agostino, & Benjamin, 2007). Previous research has indicated that for women, a high quality of dyadic interaction is particularly important for the marital satisfaction (Schmitt, Kliegel, & Shapiro, 2007). Because men in the Framingham Offspring Study were more likely to self-silence, this may have an effect on their wives' marital satisfaction.

It is interesting to note that men were actually more likely to self-silence during conflict compared to women, but also that it had no effect on their risk of death or the development of CHD. This finding also substantiates the growing research literature that indicates important gender differences in the effects of psychological and emotional factors on physical health. These differences may be a function of biology and culture and social expectations. Additionally, there are examples of gender differences regarding risk of developing heart disease and various psychosocial characteristics from the Framingham Heart Study. For example, men in occupations that are considered prestigious are significantly less likely to develop heart disease, whereas among working women the prestige of their job has no effect on their risk of heart disease (Eaker, Sullivan,

Kelly-Hayes, D'Agostino, & Benjamin, 2004b). Another example is the experience of "tension," which describes such things as "troubled by feelings of tenseness, tightness, restlessness, or inability to relax" and "often felt difficulties were piling up too much for you to handle." Increased levels of tension in men are related to the development of coronary heart disease, atrial fibrillation, and death from all causes. Tension is not a significant risk factor in women for any of these health outcomes (Eaker, Sullivan, Kelly-Hayes, D'Agostino, & Benjamin, 2005). In addition, "trait anger" in men is associated with increased risk of all-cause mortality and the development of atrial fibrillation, but not in women (Eaker et al., 2004a). Feelings of hostility are also associated with the development of atrial fibrillation in men, but not in women (Eaker et al., 2004a).

The physical mechanisms that underlie a survival advantage for married people and other psychosocial characteristics such as open communication (not self-silencing) are unknown. Some researchers have speculated that married people may have better cancer screening behaviors, risk behaviors, and access to medical care. The interaction between psychosocial factors and the body's immune function may further explain the differential survival in this study population (Gore, Kwan, Saigal, & Litwin, 2005). In addition, such characteristics as depression and other psychosocial stressors may contribute to increased platelet aggregation, inflammatory cytokine release, and vascular endothelial dysfunction, thus putting one at risk for the development of coronary heart disease (Carney et al., 2003).

The area of research that explores the differences between the sexes in regard to physical responses to stress may shed some light on the findings where men and women seem to have different psychosocial risk factors for the development of disease and death. For example, research has shown that men who care for a spouse with dementia are at higher risk for coagulation disturbances and markers for inflammation compared to women who care for a demented spouse (Mills et al., 2008). Other research has shown that women, particularly those with psychosocial stress, have higher levels of C-reactive protein, which is emerging as an important risk factor for cardiovascular disease (McDade, Hawkley, & Cacioppo, 2006). Clearly, more research is needed in order to better understand sex differences in the meaning of stressful situations and how this stress is mitigated or accentuated depending on one's sex.

There are limitations to this study. Marital status and marital strain were measured only once in the Offspring Study at the third examination. We cannot make any conclusions about how change in marital status or marital strain might affect outcomes in this population. It would be interesting, for example, to ascertain whether women who self-silence in one marriage, then divorce and remarry, self-silence in a different marriage. Another limitation involves the lack of formal validity and reliability testing for the variables that provide some of the most interesting results in this research. It is important to take this into consideration when interpreting these findings. In addition, the study cohort was predominantly white and middle-aged; the findings may not be generalizable to other ethnicities or to the elderly. Our sample in the Framingham Offspring Study, however, constitutes one of the larger datasets with prospective psychosocial data in women.

The strengths of the Framingham Offspring Study include a prospective design, inclusion of both men and women, a stable cohort, carefully assessed endpoints, and routinely ascertained information on standard risk factors. The measure of self-silencing in the Framingham Offspring Study was included in research prior to the development of the formal Silencing the Self Scale and, hence, has not been validated against the scale developed by Jack (1991; Jack & Dill, 1992). Hence, replication of our findings in other more diverse cohorts will be necessary and validation against the Silencing the Self Scale would be most useful.

Conclusion

These findings open a new avenue for psychological exploration of the impact of psychosocial risk factors on health risk, especially in women. Further development is needed for the testing of questionnaires and scales that can quickly identify women who self-silence. Because the risk behavior of self-silencing is so deleterious and can be identified, interventions should be developed and adopted by practitioners that have the possibility of preventing or reducing the effects of this damaging behavior.

References

Abbott, R. D., & McGee, D. L. (1987). The probability of developing certain cardiovascular diseases in eight years at specified values of some characteristics. In *The Framingham Study: An epidemiological investigation of cardiovascular disease, Section 37*. Bethesda, MD: National Heart, Lung, and Blood Institute.

Ali, A., Toner, B. B., Stuckless, N., Gallop, R., Diamant, N. E., Gould, M. I., et al. (2000). Emotional abuse, self-blame, and self-silencing in women with irritable bowel syndrome. *Psychosomatic Medicine, 62*, 76–82.

Barefoot, J. C., & Schroll, M. (1996). Symptoms of depression, acute myocardial infarction, and total mortality in a community sample. *Circulation, 93*, 1976–1980.

Ben-Shlomo, Y., Smith, G. D., Shipley, M., & Marmot, M. G. (1993). Magnitude and causes of mortality differences between married and unmarried men. *Journal of Epidemiological Community Health, 47*, 200–205.

Brody, C. L., Haaga, D. A., Kirk, L., & Solomon, A. (1999). Experiences of anger in people who have recovered from depression and never-depressed people. *Journal of Nervous Mental Diseases, 187*, 400–405.

Carney, R. M., Blumenthal, J. A., Catellier, D., Freedland, K. E., Berkman, L. F., Watkins, L. L., et al. (2003). Depression as a risk factor for mortality after acute myocardial infarction. *American Journal of Cardiology, 92*, 1277–1281.

Coyne, J. C., Rohrbaugh, M. J., Shoham, V., Sonnega, J. S., Nicklas, J. M., & Cranford, J. A. (2001). Prognostic importance of marital quality for survival of congestive heart failure. *American Journal of Cardiology, 88,* 526–529.

De Vogli, R., Chandola, T., & Marmot, M. G. (2007). Negative aspects of close relationships and heart disease. *Archives of Internal Medicine, 167,* 1951–1957.

Eaker, E. D. (1998). Social and psychologic aspects of coronary heart disease in women. *Cardiology Review, 6,* 182–190.

Eaker, E. D., Pinsky, J., & Castelli, W. P. (1992). Myocardial infarction and coronary death among women: Psychosocial predictors from a 20-year follow-up of women in the Framingham Study. *American Journal of Epidemiology, 135,* 854–864.

Eaker, E. D., Sullivan, L. M., Kelly-Hayes, M., D'Agostino, R. B., Sr., & Benjamin, E. J. (2004a). Anger and hostility predict the development of atrial fibrillation in men in the Framingham Offspring Study. *Circulation, 109,* 1267–1271.

Eaker, E. D., Sullivan, L. M., Kelly-Hayes, M., D'Agostino, R. B., Sr., & Benjamin, E. J. (2004b). Does job strain increase the risk for coronary heart disease or death in men and women? The Framingham Offspring Study. *American Journal of Epidemiology, 159,* 950–958.

Eaker, E. D., Sullivan, L. M., Kelly-Hayes, M., D'Agostino, R. B., Sr., & Benjamin, E. J. (2005). Tension and anxiety and the prediction of the 10-year incidence of coronary heart disease, atrial fibrillation, and total mortality: The Framingham Offspring Study. *Psychosomatic Medicine, 67,* 692–696.

Eaker, E. D., Sullivan, L. M., Kelly-Hayes, M., D'Agostino, R. B., Sr., & Benjamin, E. J. (2007). Marital status, marital strain, and risk of coronary heart disease or total mortality: The Framingham Offspring Study. *Psychosomatic Medicine, 69,* 509–513.

Ebrahim, S., Wannamethee, G., McCallum, A., Walker, M., & Shaper, A. G. (1995). Marital status, change in marital status, and mortality in middle-aged British men. *American Journal of Epidemiology, 142,* 834–842.

Gore, J. L., Kwan, L., Saigal, C. S., & Litwin, M. S. (2005). Marriage and mortality in bladder carcinoma. *Cancer, 104,* 1188–1194.

Haynes, S. G., & Feinleib, M. (1980). Women, work and coronary heart disease: Prospective findings from the Framingham heart study. *American Journal of Public Health, 70,* 133–141.

Haynes, S. G., Feinleib, M., & Eaker, E. D. (1982). Type A behavior and the ten year incidence of coronary heart disease in the Framingham Heart Study. *Activitas Nervosa Superior (Praha), Suppl 3*(Pt 1), 57–77.

Haynes, S. G., Feinleib, M., & Kannel, W. B. (1980). The relationship of psychosocial factors to coronary heart disease in the Framingham Study. III. Eight-year incidence of coronary heart disease. *American Journal of Epidemiology, 111,* 37–58.

Haynes, S. G., Levine, S., Scotch, N., Feinleib, M., & Kannel, W. B. (1978). The relationship of psychosocial factors to coronary heart disease in the Framingham study. I. Methods and risk factors. *American Journal of Epidemiology, 107,* 362–383.

Herbst, S., Pietrzak, R. H., Wagner, J., White, W. B., & Petry, N. M. (2007). Lifetime major depression is associated with coronary heart disease in older adults: results from the National Epidemiologic Survey on Alcohol and Related Conditions. *Psychosomatic Medicine, 69,* 729–734.

Jack, D. C. (1991). *Silencing the self: Women and depression*. Cambridge, MA: Harvard University Press.

Jack, D. C., & Dill, D. (1992). The Silencing the Self Scale: Schemas of intimacy associated with depression in women. *Psychology of Women Quarterly, 16*(1), 97–106.

Kawachi, I., Colditz, G. A., Ascherio, A., Rimm, E. B., Giovannucci, E., Stampfer, M. J., et al. (1994). Prospective study of phobic anxiety and risk of coronary heart disease in men. *Circulation, 89*, 1992–1997.

Kawachi, I., Sparrow, D., Kubzansky, L. D., Spiro, A., 3rd, Vokonas, P. S., & Weiss, S. T. (1998). Prospective study of a self-report type A scale and risk of coronary heart disease: test of the MMPI-2 type A scale. *Circulation, 98*, 405–412.

Kawachi, I., Sparrow, D., Spiro, A., 3rd, Vokonas, P., & Weiss, S. T. (1996). A prospective study of anger and coronary heart disease. The Normative Aging Study. *Circulation, 94*, 2090–2095.

Kawachi, I., Sparrow, D., Vokonas, P. S., & Weiss, S. T. (1994). Symptoms of anxiety and risk of coronary heart disease. The Normative Aging Study. *Circulation, 90*, 2225–2229.

Kimmel, M. (1999). Educating men and women equally. *On Campus with Women, 28*, 3.

Matthews, K. A., & Gump, B. B. (2002). Chronic work stress and marital dissolution increase risk of posttrial mortality in men from the Multiple Risk Factor Intervention Trial. *Archives of Internal Medicine, 162*, 309–315.

McDade, T. W., Hawkley, L. C., & Cacioppo, J. T. (2006). Psychosocial and behavioral predictors of inflammation in middle-aged and older adults: The Chicago health, aging, and social relations study. *Psychosomatic Medicine, 68*, 376–381.

Medalie, J. H., & Goldbourt, U. (1976). Angina pectoris among 10,000 men. II. Psychosocial and other risk factors as evidenced by a multivariate analysis of a five year incidence study. *American Journal of Medicine, 60*, 910–921.

Mendes de Leon, C. F., Appels, A. W., Otten, F. W., & Schouten, E. G. (1992). Risk of mortality and coronary heart disease by marital status in middle-aged men in The Netherlands. *International Journal of Epidemiology, 21*, 460–466.

Mills, P. J., Ancoli-Israel, S., Kanel, R. V., Mausbach, B. T., Aschbacher, K., Patterson, T. L., et al. (2008). Effects of gender and dementia severity on Alzheimer's disease caregivers' sleep and biomarkers of coagulation and inflammation. *Brain, Behavior and Immunity, 23*, 605–610.

Orth-Gomer, K., Wamala, S. P., Horsten, M., Schenck-Gustafsson, K., Schneiderman, N., & Mittleman, M. A. (2000). Marital stress worsens prognosis in women with coronary heart disease: The Stockholm Female Coronary Risk Study. *Journal of the American Medical Association, 284*, 3008–3014.

Osfeld, A. M., & Eaker, E. D. (Eds.). (1985). *Measuring psychosocial variables in epidemiologic studies of cardiovascular disease*. Washington, DC: National Institutes of Health, U.S. Department of Health and Human Services.

Radloff, L. S. (1977). The CDS-S Scale: a self-report depression scale for research in the general population. *Applied Psychological Measurement, 1*, 385–401.

Rosengren, A., Wedel, H., & Wilhelmsen, L. (1989). Marital status and mortality in middle-aged Swedish men. *American Journal of Epidemiology, 129*, 54–64.

Rutledge, T., Matthews, K., Lui, L. Y., Stone, K. L., & Cauley, J. A. (2003). Social networks and marital status predict mortality in older women: Prospective evidence from the Study of Osteoporotic Fractures (SOF). *Psychosomatic Medicine,65,* 688–694.

Salaycik, K. J., Kelly-Hayes, M., Beiser, A., Nguyen, A. H., Brady, S. M., Kase, C. S., et al. (2007). Depressive symptoms and risk of stroke: The Framingham Study. *Stroke, 38,* 16–21.

Schmitt, M., Kliegel, M., & Shapiro, A. (2007). Marital interaction in middle and old age: A predictor of marital satisfaction? *International Journal of Aging and Human Development, 65,* 283–300.

Thompson, J. M. (1995). Silencing the self: Depressive symptomatology and close relationships. *Psychology of Women Quarterly, 19,* 337–353.

Valkonen, T. (1982). Psychosocial stress and sociodemographic differentials in mortality from ischaemic heart disease in Finland. *Acta Medica Scandinavica Supplement, 660,* 152–164.

Wulsin, L. R., Evans, J. C., Vasan, R. S., Murabito, J. M., Kelly-Hayes, M., & Benjamin, E. J. (2005). Depressive symptoms, coronary heart disease, and overall mortality in the Framingham Heart Study. *Psychosomatic Medicine, 67,* 697–702.

19

Silencing the Heart: Women in Treatment for Cardiovascular Disease

Maria I. Medved

This chapter focuses on how women respond to the silencing of their hearts—quite literally. By silencing the heart I am referring to a potentially fatal cardiovascular incident such as a heart attack. Our current psychological conceptions of how women come to terms with such silencing—and the interventions designed to keep their hearts going—emerged out of the experiences of men. These conceptions, however, do not reflect the reality of women with cardiovascular disease (CVD). For women (and men) in all industrialized countries, CVD is one of the leading causes of death and disability; one out of every two women will die of a heart attack, stroke, or other cardiovascular illness.

What initially drew me to psychocardiology was the apparent imbalance between the masculine theories and models used in the field and what women with CVD were experiencing. There seemed to be a disjuncture between theory and practice, resulting in the neglect of women's perspectives and needs. Although there is increasing recognition in psychocardiology of gender differences in terms of risk, diagnosis, and treatment (see, e.g., Grace et al., 2005; Kristofferzon, Lofmark, & Carlsson, 2004), the psychological theories and models that continue to dominate the field were originally designed to capture the experiences of men, materializing out of the research tradition of the Type A personality. In 1959, Friedman and Rosenman claimed that competitive, deadline-focused, hypervigilant men—the so-called Type A personality—face a significantly increased risk of coronary heart disease. This widely disseminated research contributed to solidifying the belief that CVD is a man's disease. Ensuing epidemiological studies failed to confirm their claims and most psychologists abandoned the concept in the late 1980s (which eventually re-emerged as Denollet, Sys, and Brutsaert's [1995] Type D high hostility personality). Nevertheless, the belief that CVD is a man's disease lingers on in

415

North America. For example, it continues to be perpetuated and reflected in cardiovascular advertising directed toward physicians, where 80% of the advertisements solely depict male patients (Ahmed, Grace, Stelfox, Tomlinson, & Cheung, 2004). This influences the way the population at large thinks about CVD and the concepts researchers draw on to understand individuals with CVD, which in turn influences the treatments offered to patients and their responses to these treatments.

In this chapter, I examine how women deal with their first serious cardiovascular incident in the context of rehabilitation and recovery. However, before doing this, I will briefly outline the recovery and rehabilitation literature on gender differences in psychocardiology, highlighting a pattern of results that reveal women are at a greater disadvantage in terms of cardiac recovery than men. Drawing on Jack's (1991) idea of silencing the self, I will attempt to understand this disadvantage in terms of some of the tensions emerging out of their conflicting personal and medical needs. I draw on the voices of women to illustrate this tension, demonstrating that although the medical environment encourages women to change behaviors associated with their patriarchal socialization, inadequate recognition of this point paradoxically leads to a confirmation of the very behaviors rehabilitation providers seek to change. Finally, I will conclude with suggestions concerning recovery and rehabilitation.

Psychocardiology

A heart attack or myocardial infarction (MI) is often due to the obstruction of heart arteries by atherosclerosis (the accumulation of cholesterol, fats, and other cells), which results in decreased blood flow to the heart, causing it to lesion. Heart disease tends to occur 10 years later in women than men, mostly due to the protective effect of estrogen on the heart. In men, the first clinical symptom of CVD is frequently an MI, whereas for women it is angina (chest pain). Further, "classic" (or male) symptoms of MI include radiating pain to the arm and intense perspiration, whereas women's symptoms are more likely to include shortness of breath, fatigue, and indigestion. Even though women use the health care system more often, women delay seeking cardiac care relative to men, and when they do seek care for their symptoms, they experience a greater delay in being diagnosed and are often (mis)diagnosed with an anxiety disorder (as reviewed in Stoney, 2003). Panic attack symptoms in postmenopausal women may also be heart problems in disguise (Smoller et al., 2007). Once properly diagnosed, men and women also have unique surgical needs that are outlined in a large medical literature.

After suffering a serious cardiac incident requiring a medical intervention, anxiety is one of the most immediate and intense psychological responses of both men and women (Frasure-Smith, 1991; Moser & Dracup, 1996). Depressive symptomatology is also common in both genders with its prevalence after a cardiac event being approximately three times greater than in age-matched controls (Balzer, Kessler, McGonagle, & Swartz, 1994). Women seem to be at greater risk, reporting more anxiety (Halm & Penque, 2000) and depressive symptoms (Thomas et al., 1996) than men after a cardiac event. Beyond being an essential quality-of-life issue, psychological distress—whether anxiety, depression, or other emotional difficulties—is also a cardiac issue predictive of physical outcomes. Depression, for example, is associated with poor prognosis in individuals with an acute myocardial infarction (Lett et al., 2007) and a doubling in risk of mortality in people with CVD (Frasure-Smith & Lespérance, 2005).

Cardiac rehabilitation programs provide a crucial setting in which the reduction of depression, anxiety, anger, and other unhealthy lifestyle issues can be addressed. In general, this is accomplished by "medical surveillance," education, risk factor modification (e.g., dietary fat reduction), and psychological counseling (McGee, Hevey, & Horgan, 1999). In terms of psychological counseling, programs vary from offering nonspecific psychosocial support usually provided by nursing staff to more intensive cognitive-behavioral therapies provided by psychologists. Women are less likely to access these services because they receive fewer referrals to cardiac rehabilitation programs than men, and even if they are referred, their attendance rate is lower and their dropout rates are higher than men's (Bittner, 2000; Christain, Mandy, & Root, 1999). However, if they do manage to adhere to their rehabilitation program, they demonstrate the same (or greater) functional improvement than that of men (Brezinka & Kettel, 1995). Functional improvement refers to increased performance of everyday activities (e.g., the ability to climb stairs).

An important question, thus, is how to facilitate women's engagement with their rehabilitation activities. Barriers to women's participation are thought to include low confidence to engage in these behaviors (Thomas et al., 1996; Williams et al., 1992) and high levels of depression and anxiety (e.g., Grace et al., 2002). (Some studies frame depression and anxiety as barriers to functional rehabilitation activities, while others frame them as entities to be treated, as part of the rehabilitation itself.) Numerous psychotherapeutic interventions have been developed to increase patients' participation in heart-healthy activities and ameliorate mood and emotional disorders. One common intervention, for example, is aimed at increasing patient confidence to engage in rehabilitation recommendations under challenging conditions, that is, to persist in the face of adversity (called self-regulatory efficacy or barrier self-efficacy in social-cognitive theory, e.g., Bandura, 1997). Over the long term, though, this approach appears to be more successful for men than women (Blanchard et al., 2007).

In general, the psychosocial interventions offered in cardiac rehabilitation have a differential influence depending on the patient's gender. According to Linden's (2000) comprehensive review of the literature:

We must consider seriously the possibility that older patients (who tend to be women) benefit less from our standard treatment approaches and that treatment needs to be either specifically targeted to the psychosocial needs of older women, or that these women *may be actually better off without therapy*. (p. 449; italics added)

Why is this so? I believe that one of the fundamental reasons is that psycho-cardiology treatment—under the continued influence of the idea that CVD is primarily a man's disease—continues to revolve around the experiences and needs of men. Consequently, women are offered the same treatments as men, with the assumption that their psychological organization is essentially similar to that of men. And as we shall see, this is not the case. As King and Jenson (1994) argue, "it is unrealistic and unfair to women who undergo cardiac surgery to base their care and expectations for recovery on what has been learned from a traditionally male dominated arena of research" (p. 342). Continuing to the present, progress still needs to be made with respect to supporting women after the acute phase of their cardiac disease (Blanchard et al., 2007; Lisk & Grau, 1999; Stoney, 2003).

Much of the psychocardiological research, and by extension the findings on which the interventions are based, privileges individualistic assumptions and concepts about one's being in the world that neglect or even exclude viewing people as social and cultural beings. These assumptions and concepts mirror the psychological organization of men, who are encouraged to develop a sense of self that emphasizes distinctiveness and separation from others. However, as has often been pointed out, gender socialization in Western culture encourages women to develop a sense of self that emphasizes connections with others. For women, the development and pursuit of relationships with others is a basic and significant goal of women's way of living (Jordan, 1991). By favoring an indi-vidualistic approach, much of a woman's life (and some of a man's) is also excluded. This is not to say there is no place for individualistic concepts or that they have not added to our understanding of people with CVD, but to note that they do not capture the full picture. For women, a relational approach might be particularly important for completing the picture.

Such an approach emphasizes the interconnected social nature of individuals in relation to significant others. What is important is how relationships are estab-lished and maintained, an accomplishment that depends on cultural expectations.

Silencing the Self

One gender-specific expectation that orients women in relational behavior falls under the rubric of what Jack (1991) calls "silencing the self." According to Jack, when women believe they must negate and inhibit themselves in order to create and sustain intimacy, they "silence" their "selves." Self-silencing involves four types of beliefs and experiences. The first one is the belief that one should put the needs of others ahead of one's own. The second is that the standards and expectations of others take priority over one's own. The third implies the assumption that the expression of negative feelings can jeopardize relationships, and thus, these feelings need to be suppressed. The last one includes the experience of a divided self, which involves a compliant "outer self" that is experienced as being in conflict with a hostile "inner self."

Although some studies have found that men engage in self-silencing behaviors, they do so for different reasons (Gratch, Bassett, & Attra, 1995; Thompson, Whiffen, & Aube, 2001). Men may self-silence as an attempt to maintain power in relationships, whereas women self-silence to maintain relationships (Page, Stevens, & Galvin, 1996). This suggests that even though the behaviors may be similar, the meanings associated and attributed to self-silencing are different for men and women, reflecting their unique gendered socialization.

There are many striking points of intersection between Jack's concept of silencing the self and psychocardiological rehabilitation. Although there are many, here I will mention three: the shared focus on anger inhibition, self-care, and judging one's self by external standards. In terms of anger inhibition, if a woman has many self-silencing cognitions, she may avoid demonstrating or expressing her anger to others. In rehabilitation, patients are encouraged to express their anger because an "anger-in" style has been linked to an increased incidence of arrhythmic events (Frasure-Smith, Lespérance, & Talajic, 1995). However, if a woman is socialized to believe that anger expression could damage her relationships (and it could very well be the case that others would have difficulty dealing with it), helping her to express this emotion will be challenging.

Another point of intersection is the focus on self-care activities. Individuals who have many self-silencing beliefs think they should care for other people's needs before their own. After a serious cardiac event, adhering to one's heart-healthy activities is necessary to recover one's cardiac functioning; one needs to engage in a certain amount of self-care. Individuals, thus, are told to put their own self-care needs before others' needs, something that may be difficult for many women.

The final point of intersection is the importance of judging one's self by external standards. People who are highly self-silencing are likely to elevate the viewpoints and perspectives of others and devalue their own. This devaluation is often reinforced by the social standards in one's cultural milieu. In cardiac rehabilitation, it is important to set one's own standards, particularly regarding cardiac recovery activities, whether related to exercise, expression of anger, or other self-care activities. Women who silence their self, thus, may find it difficult to adhere to their own heart-healthy standards.

In reflecting on these three intersections, it becomes glaringly obvious that women are expected to act differently in the medical world than they might in their everyday world. In fact, they are being asked to act in ways that bring these worlds into direct disagreement with each other. Based on this observation, I argue that the opposition between rehabilitation and everyday living may partially underlie the disappointing pattern of research findings regarding women with CVD and rehabilitation, particularly involving therapeutic interventions. After a serious cardiovascular event, there is a collision between what is required to "successfully" adhere to rehabilitation recommendations and to "successfully" fulfill culturally accepted norms that saturate women's everyday lives. Clearly the space of rehabilitation, which I label as the public medical domain, and the space of the everyday world, which I label as the personal familial (familial broadly meant to denote persons in close and regular contact) domain, correspond to different needs, expectations, and requirements.

It is the personal familial domain where the majority of coping with illness occurs. Illness, whether from CVD, other diseases, or injury, presents a fundamental threat to one's self and identity. The physical loss accompanying CVD irreversibly changes one's relation with the world and thus one's sense of self (Brink, Karlson, & Hallberg, 2002). It often challenges or even shatters one's sense of security, as everything seems unstable. In times of emotional insecurity, such as after a serious cardiac event, people try to cope with uncontrollable change and instability by reverting to "known" and accepted ways of being, by seeking familiarity and avoiding novelty. As previously noted, women are encouraged to develop a sense of self highly dependent on their connections with others. To reduce a threat to one's sense of self, then, necessarily involves further immersing one's self in significant relationships such as with family members, relationships that are also newly precarious. One culturally available option is to maintain or strengthen attachments through self-silencing. In the context of being ill, the question is whether these self-silencing beliefs promote security, adjustment, and self-care.

When dealing with a distressing event, people revert to the familiar, for example, to self-silencing beliefs and behaviors. This familiarity is comforting and helps individuals emotionally and cognitively manage under duress. What often happens within the public medical domain is that women are told by their rehabilitation providers that these very self-silencing beliefs and behaviors, which are helping them cope, are potentially life-threatening. And, in fact, they are. In a study of cardiac health, self-silencing is associated with increased mortality risk in women, but not in men (Eaker, Sullivan, Kelly-Hayes, D'Agostino, & Benjamin, 2007).

The traditional space of medicine, hence, challenges the legitimacy of silencing the self in women's everyday lives, although the burden of change is placed on the individual woman to work through the details. Without support, this burden can lead to the re-enacting of the very behaviors their cardiac providers are seeking to alter.

What I would like to demonstrate in this chapter is that opposing requirements of the personal and medical spheres put women in a thorny position. It is how women experience, understand, and negotiate this position that is of interest. I will not provide a specific critique or evaluation of a particular rehabilitation program. Instead, I will examine how women navigate the terrain between their public rehabilitation space and their personal familial space by using Jack's concept of silencing the self as a framework in which to interpret locations of contradiction.

Women's Stories

The stories are drawn from interviews conducted with seven women who suffered their first serious cardiovascular event, typically an MI that required surgical intervention, within the last six months. All the women were enrolled in an inner-city cardiovascular program located in a large Canadian urban center. Health care in Canada is publicly funded and any costs associated with their rehabilitation program (and all direct medical treatment) were covered by the Canadian health insurance system. In Canada, CVD is responsible for the highest number of hospitalizations (FMCC Heart and Stroke Foundation of Canada, 2003) and the largest proportion of health care costs (Health Canada, 1998).

These women were participants in a larger study of 40 women that examined the relationship between individuals' silencing relational beliefs and their level of self-reported psychological distress as well as their performance of rehabilitation activities (Medved & Piran, under review). The results, based on a series of multiple regression analyses, indicated that beliefs concerning self-silencing are significant predictors of the experience of distress. More specifically, women who strongly endorsed many silencing beliefs were more likely to report higher levels of anxiety, depression, and holding their anger in than women who did not strongly endorse many silencing beliefs. Self-silencing beliefs were also predictive of nonadherence to recommended rehabilitation activities.

For this chapter, I was interested in capturing the often subtle meaning-making experiences associated with these quantitative findings in the interviews, focusing on how women come to terms with the conflicts between their psychological and physical needs. Before I report on the findings, it is important to note some general characteristics of the women.

The participants who contributed are different from other women who have suffered a cardiovascular event in that they have, obviously, survived their heart attack. Many women do not. Women are more likely to experience a reinfarction and are twice as likely as men to die within the first few weeks (Vaccarino, Krumholz, Yarzebski, Gore, & Goldberg, 2001). In addition, these women are currently attending a cardiovascular rehabilitation program. As mentioned earlier, women are less likely to be referred for rehabilitation and are more likely to drop out than men. This makes the women special because their medical needs are being attended to; more important, they can at least try to negotiate a balance, as difficult as it might be, between their psychological and physical needs. On the other hand, the participants appeared to fit the profile of women with CVD in that they were older and had many additional illnesses such as diabetes and arthritis (Frasure-Smith, Lespérance, Juneau, Talajic, & Bourassa, 1999; O'Callaghan, Teo, O'Riordan, Cophin, & Horgan, 1984; Schuster & Waldron, 1991).

Many women expressed a sense of uneasiness with their role as CVD patients before they even agreed to be interviewed. In contrast to my other research studies where women were willing, eager even, to participate, I found it astoundingly difficult to find female participants who were willing to involve themselves. Other researchers have encountered similar difficulties finding women with CVD (e.g., Gorkin et al., 1996) in rehabilitation programs (e.g., Conn, Taylor, & Abegle, 1991; McGee & Horgan, 1992) willing to participate in research. The women said things like, "I'm not a typical patient, I wouldn't be good for your study," "Are you sure you want me?" "I don't know if I could help you, perhaps he would be better [the man sitting across the office]." Even in these brief comments their discomfort with having CVD was palpable. Some women expressed the idea that they had not lived up to the expectations of society by having CVD—a "male disease"—and consequently experienced a sense of otherness and failure by not being a "typical" patient.

The mean age of the women who were interviewed was 66 years and all were married. One interviewed participant was black and six were white. All but two were currently retired and all reported at least a part-time work history, consisting primarily of clerical and manual work. Based on work histories and income, the women appeared to be of working to middle-class socioeconomic status. These women were part of the quantitative study mentioned earlier examining the role of self-silencing on psychological distress and self-care after a serious cardiac incident (Medved & Piran, under review); thus, they had completed the Silencing the Self Scale (STSS), the Beck Depression Inventory-II (BDI), the Spielberger State-Trait Anxiety Inventory-Y (using only the state anxiety scale—one's current experience; STAI), and the Spielberger Anger Expression Scale-2 (using the anger-in scale; STAXI). The mean scores for the 40 participants were, respectively, 88 (high range of silencing), 16 (mild range of depression), 39 (80th percentile of anxiety), and 16 (63rd percentile of anger-in). Anything over the 80th percentile is above the "normal" range for the STAI and the STAXI. While I draw on the full corpus of interviews to derive my observations, I limit my presentation to segments taken from the interviews of three women. I consider their meaning-making experiences to be exemplars. All interviews lasted approximately one hour, were conducted in private, and took place in the women's homes. The interviews were audio-taped and later transcribed. A broad interview guide was used to elicit information concerning women's experience of their cardiovascular healing in the context of their rehabilitation program and their personal lives.

Each interview was individually analyzed using narrative and discursive analytic methods (see Chase, 2005; Clandinin, 2006; Hydén & Brockmeier, 2008; Kohler Riessman, 2008; Ochs & Capps, 2001). A primary aim of narrative methodology is to capture the "whole as represented in the part," whereas an aim of discursive methods is to explore how the participant "positions" herself in the world. Once segments were selected, the entire interview was re-examined to find out how they related to statements elsewhere in the interview. Finally, the results from each participant were compared with the results from all other participants. Results and interpretations were checked by members of my research team who reviewed each step of the analysis, thus obtaining consensual validation.

To set the stage, I begin with the story of one woman, providing slightly more detail on her than the others, as I include her thoughts about communicating her experiences to the rehabilitation staff. This participant, Ms. H, a black woman, aged 72 years (STSS = 88 [high], BDI = 14 [mild], STAI = 41 [87th percentile], STAXI = 19 [83rd percentile]), is discussing her rehabilitation recommendations. Just prior to the presented segment, she mentioned she had learned some new assertiveness skills. The interviewer asks her whether there was a situation where she might want to be more assertive:

> Ms. H: Uhhh, ummm. As much as I love my grandchildren. My son is always asking me to babysit them. The rehab people said I should speak my mind because sometimes I just don't have the energy, uh, sometimes I want to do other things.
>
> Inter.: You would like to say no?
>
> Ms. H: Well, I could and he would understand. But I like looking after them. Since my operation, he has been asking me less and this really hurts me. Actually, I want to be with my grandchildren even more. I'm their grandma.

Ms. H begins by asserting that she needs to take a stand against babysitting her grandchildren—perhaps by even setting her own standards by doing what she wants—yet ends in opposition to this idea by asserting that she would like to spend more time babysitting, something that has been particularly difficult for her since her heart attack. The confrontation between her rehabilitation and personal voice illustrates the conflict many women find themselves in. On the medical side, she knows that she needs to become more assertive and take time to recuperate if she is to physically recover, citing various reasons for not wanting to babysit. Women in general tend to spend more energy on domestic activities early in their recovery than men, activities that pose a risk of further medical complications (Jenson, Suls, & Lemos, 2003). On the psychological side, she would like to spend more time with her grandchildren, an activity that is comforting, is reassuring, and solidifies her role and sense of worth as a grandmother. This example will be revisited in the section called sharing the burden.

In the next segment, this conflict is further drawn out:

> Inter.: So have you used these new assertiveness skills?
>
> Ms. H: Well, a little bit. I need to find ways to express myself clearer when something bothers me, to not hold the anger inside, to say what I mean. I need to use my assertiveness skills and my relaxation techniques.
>
> Inter.: How has that been going?
>
> Ms. H: Well I learned to breathe deeply. That's been good.
>
> Inter.: That's good. And the assertiveness skills? Have you been able to use them?
>
> Ms. H: (drawn out exhalation) That's hard. Actually, like, I feel like it just doesn't work. What a nightmare. Another thing to feel bad about. Makes me mad sometimes. It gets on my nerves. What can I do?

Ms. H lists her heart-healthy activities, but she reports them as if they were a list of duties to be accomplished. Deeply exhaling, she enacts the additional burden her rehabilitation is to her. Her lack of recovery activities (she mentions elsewhere in the interview she has not performed deep breathing outside of her rehabilitation) becomes one more thing "to feel bad about," a type of "nightmare." Fulfillment of her activities represents an additional set of external standards that she finds difficult to live up to, leading her to feel more demoralized than she already is (as she cannot even babysit as much as she would like). Concurrently, she expresses frustration in relation to her rehabilitation—that it makes her feel more nervous and tenuous than she already is. When asked, she states she has not revealed her sense of failure and frustration to the rehabilitation staff:

> Ms. H: No, not really. But it's not their fault. They're great. Just terrific. The people, the people are really caring and nice.

This participant, as most of the interviewed women, remained unfailingly polite in reference to the health care staff, aware that their continued medical treatment depended on medical personnel. Expression of their difficulties might entail a relational risk as it might be interpreted as criticism and lead to a break, however slight, with their providers. Instead, they tended to speak about how "nice" the staff were—as if this were enough in a medical setting. In the previous remark, one can sense a "divided self" response to her situation given that she is internally annoyed but externally appears calm and compliant.

Another example of the tensions emerging from the conflicting goals of the family and medical spheres are evident in the story of Ms. F, a white, 69-year-old married woman (STSS = 94 [high], BDI = 16 [mild], STAI = 43 [90th percentile], STAXI = 21 [92nd percentile]), as she discusses her desire to avoid "confrontation":

> Ms. F: When I'm angry, confrontation for me is kind of a stupid thing. I'll invent and lie rather than confront. Like, not that I'm a liar but I will make up a different story, I will circumvent it as much as I can. That way no one gets hurt.

Inter.: Has your heart attack influenced you in this way?

Ms. F: Of course, it's made me more sensitive and more likely to avoid confrontations.

Here she mentions her increased desire for interpersonal connectedness in the aftermath of her medical crisis. She appears well aware of the long tradition of cultural practices she would clash with were she to express her anger. At the same time, Ms. F is also well aware that repressing her anger is not a wise medical strategy, something reinforced in her rehabilitation:

Ms. F: I learnt that holding it [anger] in is bad. It gives you high blood pressure.

Inter.: How does that knowledge affect you?

Ms. F: Well, anger is OK, but there are healthy ways to express it such as telling the person you need to talk to them so they are ready. Don't jump to conclusions.

Inter.: Can you do that?

Ms. F: Sometimes. It's hard to do. It's difficult.

Inter.: Can you give me an example?

Ms. F: (looks away) I just can't right now but I will because I don't want to die.

In this segment, Ms. F expresses ambivalence between the cultural tradition that has cemented the thinking and behavior of women, that expression of anger is unacceptable, and her knowledge and awareness of her medical needs, that she needs to start expressing herself. These dual voices are in direct conflict. Her inability to follow through with her rehabilitation activities disturbs her to the extent that she looks away from the interviewer, seemingly ashamed that she is not able to say she has fulfilled the standards set for her in terms of cardiac self-care.

For each woman discussed so far, I have emphasized one isolatable rehabilitation issue. With Ms. H, the primary focus was on increasing self-care, and with Ms. F, the primary focus was on learning to express anger. Now with Ms. R, I present a more complicated scenario that illustrates how challenging developing individualized rehabilitation recommendations for women can become. In contrast to the previous examples, I begin with a description from an everyday life setting rather than from a rehabilitation setting. Ms. R, a white 59-year-old woman with three adult children (STSS = 90 [high], BDI = 19 [moderate], STAI = 42 [87th percentile], STAXI = 20 [92nd percentile]), discusses her relationship with her husband:

I wasn't afraid to tell him [about the heart attack]. . . . Sometimes I get more scared over his problems. . . . He was really shocked like, you know? I don't know like . . . scared. I think he was more scared than I was. Like, I am not courageous at all. But I have to be in the circumstances or to be suffering from something to really lose all control and get very fearful.

In this segment, "thick" with description of emotions, Ms. R clearly defines herself and her feelings in relation to her husband. Among other things, she explains how she tried to focus on controlling or inhibiting her emotions in order to support and engage her "more scared than her" husband. Again, what seems to be behind these activities is the cultural belief that she must put others' needs first and thus repress, or at least ignore, her negative emotions, particularly if they upset others.

At the same time, she downplays her courage and efforts because, as she points out in another part of the interview, she experiences an intense fear of death and uncontrollable bouts of crying when she is alone. Instead, with her husband at least, she puts on a brave front; she appears proud that she was not "afraid" to tell her husband she had a heart attack—as if she should have been afraid because it might upset him. The beliefs that underlie her behaviors, of course, are especially disadvantageous during the time of coping with a serious disease, a time when stating one's needs and feelings is important.

Talking about her rehabilitation, Ms. R mentions:

> Ms. R: If I need help I should ask because I've just had a heart attack.
> Inter: What do you mean, ask for help?
> Ms. R: Speak my mind, that kind of thing. And I'm really trying to deal with my depression because it suppresses my entire system. It really, really stresses me out.

Although medically vital, Ms. R has much difficulty adhering to the seemingly simple directive to ask for help, in other words no longer silencing but speaking her mind. In a way this is not surprising, as she even seemed to hesitate telling her husband she had had a heart attack. What becomes obvious in Ms. R's story is that her rehabilitation does not address the relational ways of being she is grappling with, ways that stand in clear opposition to her medical needs and which she acknowledges she would like to stop as a means to become more heart healthy.

Specifically, rehabilitation is not addressing the reasons why she might not speak her mind or express herself. Patently, there are highly gendered reasons that place women in a conundrum. One of these, for example, is the societal contradiction that women are expected to be dependent and needy, yet conversely, serve others and have no needs of their own. It appears that Ms. R is putting a lot of additional pressure on herself—for having needs of her own and being unable to do the activities she knows are essential for her health. This in turn appears to make her even more depressed and anxious than she already is. Her anxiety and depressive symptoms then make her look predominantly needy and dependent, overshadowing her strength.

Stories in Context

The stories of women in the aftermath of a first serious cardiovascular incident reveal a tension emerging out of the colliding requirements of their personal familial life and their public medical life. Although the multiple stressors the women are coping with are complex and multilayered, the tensions emerging out of the opposing requirements of these two spheres predominate. The two spheres, each representing a unique set of needs and demands, appear compartmentalized from each other. At this point, I might add that this separation has some overlap with the conflicting roles women must perform in the workplace versus the home environment.

In the personal, familial sphere of their lives, the women gave the impression that they coped with the shakiness and upheaval caused by their disease by immersing themselves in their relationships. As the dynamics of these relationships were often altered by the cardiac event, the women also had to work on re-establishing former patterns and roles that were disrupted. In attempting this, many of the participants were guided by a set of gender-specific expectations about how women should behave, that is, as outlined earlier, beliefs and expectations reflected in the concept of silencing the self (increased care of others rather than one's self, inhibition of anger, and giving even more weight to the viewpoints of others).

Simultaneously, the women seemed aware that these self-silencing beliefs resulted in ways of being that were not in their best interests, certainly not from a cardiovascular perspective. And even if they tried to ignore this awareness, through the process of rehabilitation, the risks of these beliefs, or at least the behaviors associated with them, became quite clear. On the one hand, the women knew they needed to express their anger to reduce the risk of further cardiac problems, yet on the other they wanted to avoid this because they felt more aware (or afraid) of the consequences of "confrontations"; on the one hand, they knew they needed more time and space for themselves to facilitate their recovery, yet on the other they wanted to resume their familiar roles; on the one hand, they knew they needed to develop new and healthy ways of living, yet on the other they were afraid of further changes in their lives. Challenged on their beliefs, assumptions, and behaviors in their rehabilitation, they were commonly left without personal support, facing all these conflicts and tensions completely on their own. The task was to find a way to integrate the contrasting priorities of their lives and rehabilitation programs—a task that often proved to be overwhelming.

As a consequence, their attempts to do the best they could on all fronts led to a psychological state more problematic than before. Burell and Granlund (2002) described their impression of many women in cardiac rehabilitation as "depressed, anxious, bitter, and frustrated" (p. 234). Perhaps such an observation might be explained by the seemingly impossible position women are placed in. Not surprisingly, in their struggle to plot the new behavioral, emotional, and cognitive patterns demanded by their rehabilitation regimens into their everyday lives, the women appeared resentful of the additional demands their medical treatment placed on them. None took an overtly critical stance toward these authoritarian structures that were obviously patriarchal, structures that placed the women in a seemingly unwinnable situation (once again).

At the same time, however, many of them transformed their resentment and subjectivized failure into self-blame for not trying hard enough. Perhaps we can see this even as an "appropriate" response to an individually oriented treatment that frames people as exclusively responsible for their failure or success. The women who participated in this study wanted to appear "good" and compliant with the demands of their treatment regardless of their inner sense of frustration. Given the cultural imperatives placed on women, this emerged as a divided sense of self—a sense that permeated the process of rehabilitation.

This dividedness is most blatant in mixed gender rehabilitation settings, where women not only tend to withhold their own true reactions and self-expressions but are also particularly supportive of men—at the expense of highjacking their own therapy (Burell & Granlund, 2002). In other words, although rehabilitation challenges women's self-inhibition, it certainly also confirms it.

Sharing the Burden

The question is, how can rehabilitation break this circular constellation? How can rehabilitation, while encouraging self-care, setting of personal standards, and discouraging anger inhibition, shift the silencing thoughts and behaviors of women? And how can rehabilitation do so in a way that shares the burden of change? In other words, how can rehabilitation become a site of integration rather than conflict and tension for women with cardiac difficulties? Although the constraints of this chapter do not allow for extensive technical suggestions, some recommendations can be made.

As numerous authors have pointed out, social support of women with CVD (and many other medical illnesses) is an important factor that facilitates coping; consequently, there has been much focus on interventions designed to help women develop social support systems (e.g., Lindquist et al., 2003; Rueda & Perez-Garcia, 2006; Svedlund & Danielson, 2004). The narratives of the women also illustrate that their beliefs about the acceptability of receiving support, particularly from family members, should be considered. More broadly than this, however, women's gendered thoughts, expectations, and roles in their everyday lives need to be tackled with targeted psychological interventions.

In this way, rehabilitation can help women contest individually ingrained cultural patterns of inhibition and self-negation. One strategy to help women tease apart the conflicts described is to use some techniques taken from the transtheoretical model of change (e.g., Prochaska, DiClemente, & Norcross, 1992; Prochaska & Velicer, 1997). In this kind of intersubjective intervention, reasons for change (i.e., improved cardiac health) and reasons against change (i.e., psychological comfort) are highlighted. This approach has been particularly helpful for people who are ambivalent about adopting change, and has been used in cardiovascular rehabilitation. In the context of gendered cognitions, the focus can be on exploring how self-denying beliefs might threaten women's rehabilitation progress. It is particularly essential to bring forward the character of women's experiences; that is, appropriate behaviors in cardiovascular contexts might involve altering the very ways many women cope with the stress of illness. This emphasis can help ensure that viable and shared goals are developed.

The importance of goal agreement between cardiac patients and staff was shown by Burns and Evon (2007), who pointed out that it led to enhanced levels of self-reported mood and physical health in male patients (women were not included in the study). I suspect that the collaborative development of goals may be even more essential for women given that, as Cossette, Frasure-Smith, and Lespérance (2002) argue, they are less likely to respond to advice, education, and cognitive interventions than men, and as Schneiderman and colleagues (2004) claim, women do not respond to cognitive-behavioral interventions for depression or increasing social support as well as white men in cardiovascular rehabilitation settings.

Jointly negotiating rehabilitation goals also opens participatory space for women to voice the tensions they encounter. As one example, I would like to return to Ms. H. As we saw, she tries to find her own balance between her cardiac and psychological needs. When Ms. H declares she does not want to babysit, she first brings up that the reason is that she doesn't "have the energy," followed by a second, perhaps the real one: "sometimes I want to do other things." This step appears to represent a move away from "typical" female responses and the beginning of articulating her own voice: She does not want to babysit because there are other things she would prefer to do. She appears unable, however, to sustain and expand on this voice and thus shifts back to her usual cultural position—as if not wanting to babysit is too radical a desire.

Supporting Ms. H to further develop her interests in "other things" and tying this to her cardiac activities would be an excellent point of entry for a rehabilitation intervention. In overtly addressing tensions and conflicts, as we just did for Ms. H, the tendency of women to appear as "good," accommodating patients may be mitigated. This in turn may reduce the sense of dividedness women often reported: being frustrated with demands of their rehabilitation but behaving in a culturally compliant way.

Conclusion

The stories shared by the women are reflective of their efforts to actively search for balance as they negotiate simultaneously fulfilling their psychological and physical needs after a major cardiac event while attending rehabilitation. Their stories present us with a way to make sense of the quantitative studies that demonstrate that women who are more likely to inhibit their anger, oppress themselves, and deny themselves are more likely to report decreased self-care activities as well as elevated levels of depression, anxiety, and anger-in during their rehabilitation (Medved & Piran, under review). Further, it is not inconceivable that the influence of these self-negating relational beliefs will continue over time. In women with cancer, for example, self-silencing thoughts were found to influence self-care agency even 18 months after treatment (Kayser & Sormanti, 2002).

The analysis used in this chapter was designed to reflect women's relational orientation by drawing on silencing the self theory, a theory emerging directly from the experiences of women. Such a perspective helps us to interpret the dynamics underlying women's difficulties during cardiac rehabilitation; it helps uncover a broader, fuller picture of women, or least some women, with CHD so that gender-sensitive interventions can be developed. In my view, the time has come for psychosocial cardiac rehabilitation therapies that are equally efficacious for women.

References

Ahmed, S. B., Grace, S. L., Stelfox, H. T., Tomlinson, G., & Cheung, A. M. (2004). Gender bias in cardiovascular advertisements. *Journal of Evaluation in Clinical Practice, 10*, 531–538.

Balzer, D. G., Kessler, R. C., McGonagle, K., & Swartz, M. (1994). The prevalence and distribution of major depression in a national community sample: The national comorbidity survey. *American Journal of Psychiatry, 151*, 979–986.

Bandura, A. (1997). *Self-efficacy: The exercise of control.* New York: Freeman.

Bittner, V. (2000). Heart disease in women. *Clinical Review (Spring)*, 62–66.

Blanchard, C. M., Reid, R. D., Morrin, L. I., Beaton, L. J., Pipe, A., Couneya, K. S., et al. (2007). Barrier self-efficacy and physical activity over a 12-month period in men and women who do and do not attend cardiac rehabilitation. *Rehabilitation Psychology, 52*, 65–73.

Brezinka, V., & Kettel, F. (1995). Psychosocial factors of coronary heart disease in women: A review. *Social Science Medicine, 42*, 1351–1365.

Brink, E., Karlson, B. W., & Hallberg, L. R. M. (2002). Health experiences of first-time myocardial infarction: Factors influencing women's and men's health-related quality of life after five months. *Psychology, Health, and Medicine, 7*, 5–16.

Burell, G., & Granlund, B. (2002). Women's hearts need special treatment. *International Journal of Behavioral Medicine, 9*, 228–242.

Burns, J. W., & Evon, D. (2007). Common and specific process factors in cardiac rehabilitation: Independent and interactive effects of the working alliance and self-efficacy. *Health Psychology, 26*, 684–692.

Chase, S. E. (2005). Narrative inquiry: Multiple lenses, approaches, voices. In N. K. Denzin & Y. S. Lincoln (Eds.), *Sage handbook of qualitative research* (3rd ed., pp. 651–679). Thousand Oaks, CA: Sage Publications.

Christain, A., Mandy, K., & Root, B. (1999). Comparison between men and women admitted to an inpatient rehabilitation unit after cardiac surgery. *Archives of Physical Medicine and Rehabilitation, 80*, 183–185.

Clandinin, D. J. (Ed.). (2006). *Handbook of narrative inquiry: Mapping a methodology.* Thousand Oaks, CA: Sage Publications.

Conn, V. S., Taylor, S. G., & Abegle, P. B. (1991). Myocardial infraction survivors: Age and gender differences in physical health, psychosocial state and regimen adherence. *Journal of Advanced Nursing, 16*, 1026–1034.

Cossette, S., Frasure-Smith, N., & Lespérance, F. (2002). Nursing approaches to reducing psychological distress in men and women recovering from myocardial infarction. *International Journal of Nursing Studies, 39*, 479–494.

Denollet, J., Sys, S. U., & Brutsaert, D. L. (1995). Personality and mortality after myocardial infarction. *Psychosomatic Medicine, 57*, 582–591.

Eaker, E. D., Sullivan, L. M., Helly-Hayes, M., D'Agostino, R. B., & Benjamin, E. J. (2007). Marital status, marital strain, and risk of coronary heart disease or total mortality: The Framingham Offspring study. *Psychosomatic Medicine, 69*, 509–513.

FMCC Heart and Stroke Foundation of Canada. (2003). *The growing burden of heart disease and stroke in Canada 2003.* Ottawa, Canada: Author.

Frasure-Smith, N. (1991). In-hospital symptoms of psychological stress as predictors of long-term outcome after acute myocardial infraction in men. *American Journal of Cardiology, 67*, 121–127.

Frasure-Smith, N., & Lespérance, F. (2005). Depression and coronary heart disease: Complex synergism of mind, body, and environment. *Current Directions in Psychological Science, 14*, 39–43.

Frasure-Smith, N., Lespérance, F., Juneau, M., Talajic, M., & Bourassa, M. G. (1999). Gender, depression, and one-year prognosis after myocardial infraction. *Psychosomatic Medicine, 61*, 26–37.

Frasure-Smith, N., Lespérance, F., & Talajic, M. (1995). Coronary heart disease/myocardial infarction: Depression and 18-month prognosis after myocardial infarction. *Circulation, 91*, 999–1005.

Friedman, M., & Rosenman, R. H. (1959). Association of specific overt behavior pattern with blood and cardiovascular findings – blood cholesterol level, blood clotting time, incidence of arcus senilis, and clinical coronary artery disease. *Journal of the American Medical Association, 169*, 1286–1296.

Gorkin, L., Schron, E. B., Handshaw, K., Shea, S., Kinney, M. R., Branyon, M., et al. (1996). Clinical trial enrollers vs. nonenrollers: The Cardiac Arrhythmia Suppression Trial (CAST) Recruitment and Enrollment Assessment in Clinical Trials (REACT) project. *Controlled Clinical Trials, 17*, 46–59.

Grace, S. L., Abbey, S. E., Pinto, R., Shnek, A. M., Irvine, J., & Stewart, D. E. (2005). Longitudinal course of depressive symptomatology after a cardiac event: Effects of gender and cardiac rehabilitation. *Psychosomatic Medicine, 67*, 52–58.

Grace, S. L., Abbey, S. E., Shnek, Z. M., Irvine, J., Franche, R. L., & Stewart, D. E. (2002). Cardiac rehabilitation I: Review of psychosocial factors. *General Hospital Psychiatry, 24*, 121–126.

Gratch, L. V., Bassett, M. E., & Attra, S. L. (1995). The relationship of sex and ethnicity to self-silencing and depression among college students. *Psychology of Women Quarterly, 19,* 509–515.

Halm, M. A., & Penque, S. (2000). Heart failure in women. *Prognostic Cardiovascular Nursing, 15,* 121–133.

Health Canada (1998). *Economic Burden of Illness in Canada,* Ottawa: Publications Health Canada.

Hydén, L. C., & Brockmeier, J. (Eds.). (2008). *Health, illness and culture: Broken narratives.* New York: Routledge.

Jack, D. (1991). *Silencing the self: Women and depression.* Cambridge, MA: Harvard University Press.

Jenson, M., Suls, J., & Lemos, K. (2003). A comparison of physical activity in men and women with cardiac disease: Do gender roles complicate recovery? *Women and Health, 3,* 31–47.

Jordan, J. V. (1991). The meaning of mutuality. In J. V. Jordan, A. G. Kalan, J. B. Miller, I. P. Stiver, & J. L. Surrey (Eds.), *Women's growth in connection: Writings from the Stone Center* (pp. 81–96). New York: Guilford Press.

Kayser, K., & Sormanti, M. (2002). A follow-up study of women with cancer: Their psychosocial well-being and close relationships. *Social Work, Health and Mental Health, 35,* 391–406.

King, K. M., & Jenson, L. (1994). Preserving the self: Women having cardiac surgery. *Heart and Lung, 23,* 99–105.

Kristofferzon, M. L., Lofmark, R., & Carlsson, M. (2004). Myocardial infarction: Gender differences in coping and social support. *Journal of Advanced Nursing, 44,* 360–374.

Kohler Riessman, C. (2008). *Narrative methods for the human sciences.* Thousand Oaks, CA: Sage Publications.

Lett, H. S., Blumental, J. A., Babyak, M. A., Catellier, D. J., Carney, R. M., Berkman, L. F., et al. (2007). Social support and prognosis in patients at increased psychosocial risk recovering from myocardial infarction. *Health Psychology, 26,* 418–427.

Linden, W. (2000). Psychological treatments in cardiac rehabilitation: Review of rationales and outcomes. *Journal of Psychosomatic Research, 48,* 443–454.

Lindquist, R., Dupis, G., Terrin, M. L., Hoogwerf, B., Czajkowski, S., Herd, A., et al., for the POST CABG Biobehavioural Study Investigators. (2003). Comparison of health-related quality-of-life outcomes of men and women after coronary artery bypass surgery through 1 year: Findings from the POST CAGB biobehavioural study. *American Heart Journal, 146,* 1038–1044.

Lisk, C. J., & Grau, L. (1999). Perceptions of women living with coronary heart disease: A pilot investigation. *Women and Health, 29,* 31–46.

McGee, H. M., Hevey, D., & Horgan, J. H. (1999). Psychosocial outcome assessments for use in cardiac rehabilitation service evaluation: A 10-year systematic review. *Social Science and Medicine, 48,* 1373–1393.

McGee, H. M., & Horgan J. H. (1992). Cardiac rehabilitation programmes: Are women less likely to attend? *British Medical Journal, 305,* 283–284.

Medved, M. I. & Piran, N. (under review). Self silencing in a cardiac rehabilitation program: Anxiety, depression, anger suppression, and rehabilitation adherence.

Moser, D. K., & Dracup, K. (1996). Is anxiety early after myocardial infarction associated with subsequence ischemic and arrhythmic events? *Psychosomatic Medicine, 58*, 395–401.

O'Callaghan, W., Teo, K., O'Riordan, J., Webb, H., Cophin, T., & Horgan, J. H. (1984). Comparative response of male and female patients with coronary artery disease to exercise rehabilitation. *European Heart Journal, 5*, 649–651.

Ochs, E., & Capps, L. (2001). *Living narrative: Creating lives in everyday storytelling.* Cambridge, MA: Sage.

Page, R. R., Stevens, H. B., & Galvin, S. L., (1996). Relationships between depression, self-esteem, and self-silencing behavior. *Journal of Social and Clinical Psychology, 15*, 381–396.

Prochaska, J. O., DiClemente, C. C., & Norcross, J. C. (1992). In search of how people change: Applications to additive behavior. *American Psychologist, 47*, 1102–1114.

Prochska, J. O., & Velicer, W. F. (1997). The transtheoretical model of health behavior change. *American Journal of Health Promotion, 12*, 38–48.

Rueda, B., & Perez-Garcia, A. M. (2006). Gender and social support in the context of cardiovascular disease. *Women & Health, 43*, 59–73.

Schneiderman, N., Saab, P., Catellier, D. J., Powell, L., DeBusk, R., Williams, R. B., et al. (2004). Psychosocial treatment within sex by ethnicity subgroups in the enhancing recovery in coronary heart disease clinical trial. *Psychosomatic Medicine, 66*, 475–483.

Schuster, P., & Waldron, J. (1991). Gender differences in cardiac rehabilitation patients. *Rehabilitation Nursing, 16*, 248–253.

Smoller, J. W., Pollack, M. H., Wassertheil-Smoller, S., Jackson, R. D., Oberman, A., Wong, N. D., et al. (2007). Panic attacks and risk of incident cardiovascular events among postmenopausal women in the Women's Health Initiative Observation Study. *Archives of General Psychiatry, 64*, 1153–1160.

Stoney, C. M. (2003). Gender and cardiovascular disease: A psychobiological and integrative approach. *Current Directions in Psychological Science, 12*, 129–133.

Svedlund, B., & Danielson, E. (2004). Myocardial infarction: Narrations by afflicted women and their partners of lived experiences in daily life following an acute myocardial infarction. *Journal of Clinical Nursing, 13*, 438–446.

Thomas, R. J., Houston Miller, N., Lamendola, C., Berra, K., Hedback, B., Durstine, J. L., et al. (1996). National survey on gender differences in cardiac rehabilitation programs: Patient characteristics and enrollment patters. *Journal of Cardiopulmonary Rehabilitation, 16*, 402–412.

Thompson, J. M., Whiffen, V. E., & Aube, J. A. (2001). Does self-silencing link perceptions of care from parents and partners with depressive symptoms? *Journal of Social and Personal Relationship, 18*, 503–516.

Vaccarino, V., Krumholz, H. M., Yarzebski, J., Gore, J. M., & Goldberg, R. J. (2001). Sex differences in two-year mortality after hospital discharge for myocardial infarction. *Annals of Internal Medicine, 134*, 173–181.

Williams, R. B., Barefoot, J. C., Califf, R. M., Haney, T., Saunders, W. B., Pryer, W. B., et al. (1992). Prognostic importance of social economic resources among medically treated patients with angiographically documented coronary heart disease. *Journal of the American Medical Association, 267*, 520–524.

20

Disruption of the Silenced Self: The Case of Premenstrual Syndrome

Jane M. Ussher and Janette Perz

The pathologization of premenstrual change within the annals of psychiatric nosology is now well established. Described as premenstrual syndrome (PMS) in both colloquial and research contexts and as premenstrual dysphoric disorder (PMDD) in the *Diagnostic and Statistical Manual of Mental Disorders,* fourth edition (DSM-IV; American Psychiatric Association, 2000), this conglomeration of psychological and physical symptoms has been estimated to be of the same magnitude as major depressive disorder in terms of reduction in women's quality of life and economic functioning (Halbreich, Borenstein, Pearlstein, & Kahn, 2003). Positioned as either a biomedical or a psychological disorder (Bancroft, 1993), a range of competing interventions has been proposed, with current treatments of choice being selective serotonin reuptake inhibitors (SSRIs) (Rapkin, 2003) or cognitive-behavioral therapy (CBT) (Blake, Salkovskis, Gath, Day, & Garrod, 1998). These approaches may appear diametrically opposed; however, they share one thing in common: the positioning of pre-menstrual distress as a pathology located within the woman, with the aim of treatment being to remove her "symptoms."

In contrast, we will argue that PMS is more appropriately conceptualized as a disruption in the self-silencing in which women engage in for three weeks of the month, with material, discursive, and intrapsychic factors combining to result in the premenstrual expression of anger, irritation, or feelings of sadness and depression, the most common "symptoms" of PMS. This is a disruption that leads to guilt, self-castigation, and self-pathologization on the part of women due to the positioning of negative emotional expression as inappropriate within Western discourses of femininity and the absence of empathy or support within individual relational contexts. Attributing emotional expression or distress to an embodied disorder, PMS, acts to absolve women of responsibility for breaks in self-silencing at the same time as it obviates examination of the myriad factors that may lead to premenstrual distress. Dismissing this distress as embodied illness acts to further silence women, contributing to a vicious cycle of emotional suppression followed by premenstrual eruption.

There is a growing body of research that reports a positive association between relationship strain and premenstrual symptomatology (Coughlin, 1990; Frank, Dixon, & Grosz, 1993; Ryser & Feinauer, 1992; Ussher, Perz, & Mooney-Somers, 2007; Winter, Ashton, & Moore, 1991; Wright, 1986) as well as an association between effective communication between couples and lower levels of premenstrual distress (Schwartz, 2001; Smith-Martinez, 1995; Ussher & Perz, 2008; Welthagen, 1995). This has led to the suggestion that PMS is not an individual problem but a relational issue (Ryser & Feinauer, 1992; Ussher, 2006), and that coping with PMS requires effort from both members of a couple (Rundle, 2005). In an attempt to explain the expression of premenstrual anger within relationships, it has been argued that this is the only time that some women "allow" themselves to be angry, as they can attribute anger to their hormones (McDaniel, 1988), a phenomenon described as a "redeployment" of the reproductive body to meet women's emotional needs (Elson, 2002). This implicitly suggests a calculated decision on the part of women to express anger and use PMS as an "excuse," a conclusion that is at odds with women's positioning of PMS as "loss of control," associated with distress (Ussher, 2003b, 2006). For while the majority of women described the premenstrual release of emotion as cathartic in the short term, as "getting things off my chest," this catharsis is always followed by guilt, self-criticism, and a disassociation of the woman from the behavior, through splitting the non-PMS self from the PMS self, who is "not like me." And it is the *break* in self-silencing premenstrually, the transgression from the "real me," that leads to distress as well as self-castigation.

In order to substantiate this argument, we will draw on a number of research studies we have conducted in both the United Kingdom and Australia, examining the construction and experience of PMS in groups of women who present with moderate to severe premenstrual distress. Our research is based on a mixed-methods approach, combining standardized questionnaires and in-depth narrative interviews, focusing on the positioning of premenstrual distress in women's accounts. We will draw on specific examples from the data across a range of published and unpublished studies to illustrate the arguments we will present. We will start with the foundations of our argument: an examination of levels of self-silencing in women who report PMS and the association between accounts of PMS and self-silencing. We will then examine the reasons why ruptures in self-silencing occur premenstrually and the effect of these ruptures on women's distress, and will end with two case examples drawn from the same study, which contrast accounts of PMS in relation to high or low levels of self-silencing.

Self-Silencing in Women Who Report Moderate to Severe PMS

In a recent study of 257 women who position themselves as PMS sufferers (Perz & Ussher, 2006), high levels of self-silencing and premenstrual and psychological distress were found. Levels of self-silencing among this sample, assessed by the Silencing the Self Scale (STSS) (Jack, 1991), were significantly higher than previously published levels for nonclinical populations, for example, the means for an undergraduate sample as is illustrated in Table 20.1. In particular, this PMS sample had significantly higher global, Silencing the Self, and Divided Self STSS scores than the comparison undergraduate sample. Premenstrual distress, measured in response to the item "To what extent is PMS distressing?" was high for the sample, with most participants falling within one standard deviation of the maximum response "extremely distressing." Rates of psychological distress were assessed on the Hospital Anxiety and Depression Scale (HADS; Zigmond & Snaith, 1983). While not used to formally diagnose participants, 20.8% and 40.8% of this PMS sample met the criteria for borderline and abnormal anxiety caseness, respectively. Rates for depression, while high for nonclinical samples, with 14.5% and 11.8% meeting the cut-offs for borderline and abnormal caseness, respectively, revealed 72.9% of the sample scoring in the normal range for depression.

The relationship between self-silencing and premenstrual and psychological distress was also examined, using correlational analyses (see Table 20.2). Expected findings were that all STSS subscales were positively and significantly correlated with each other and with HADS anxiety, depression, and total scores. Externalized Self-Perception, Divided Self, and global STSS scales correlated

Table 20.1 Descriptive Statistics for Silencing the Self Scale (STSS) Total and Subscales, HADS Total and Subscales, and PMS Distress

Variable	n	Mean	SD	Range	Undergraduate Sample Mean Scores (Jack & Dill, 1992)
STSS					
Externalized Self-Perception	255	18.4	5.98	6–30	18.2
Care as Self-Sacrifice	255	24.7	6.41	12–40	24.5
Silencing the Self	246	23.1	5.73	11–42	20.6
Divided Self	243	18.9	5.78	7–34	15.1
Total	241	85.2	19.43	43–144	78.4
HADS					
Anxiety	254	9.3	4.50	1–20	
Depression	253	5.4	3.83	0–17	
Total	253	14.7	7.54	1–35	
PMS Distress	255	6.8	2.32	1–10	

Table 20.2 Intercorrelations among Silencing the Self Scale (STSS) Total and Subscales, HADS Total and Subscales, and PMS Distress

	1	2	3	4	5	6	7	8
1. Externalized Self-Perception	—							
2. Care as Self-Sacrifice	.54*	—						
3. Silencing the Self	.44*	.61*	—					
4. Divided Self	.53*	.51*	.67*	—				
5. STSS total	.77*	.83*	.83*	.83*	—			
6. Anxiety subscale	.55*	.33*	.32*	.45*	.50*	—		
7. Depression subscale	.43*	.23*	.24*	.40*	.40*	.61*	—	
8. HADS total	.54*	.32*	.31*	.41*	.50*	.92*	.89*	—
9. PMS Distress	.31*	.09	.03	.21*	.20*	.26*	.28*	.30*

* $p < .001$.

positively and significantly with PMS distress, whereas these scales and Silencing the Self were negatively and significantly correlated with PMS coping. Care as Self-Sacrifice was unrelated to PMS distress. HADS depression, anxiety, and total scores were also found to significantly correlate with PMS distress. To further explore how levels of self-silencing and premenstrual distress are associated, predictive regression analyses were performed. Externalized Self-Perception [$\beta = .13$, $t(236) = 4.22$, $p < .001$], Silencing the Self [$\beta = -.10$, $t(236) = -0.2.74$, $p = .007$], and Divided Self [$\beta = .08$, $t(236) = 2.51$, $p = .013$] were found to be significant predictors of PMS distress, whereas Care as Self-Sacrifice was not [$\beta = -.02$, $t(236) = -0.49$, n.s.]. Following variable reduction, three variables were tested for exploratory predictive modeling with a stepwise multiple regression where elimination of the least significant variable from the regression model was chosen as the selection criterion. A significant regression model with all variables in the equation was identified in one step. Externalized Self-Perception, Silencing the Self, and Divided Self accounted for 14% of the variance in PMS distress [$R^2 = 0.14$; $F(3, 237) = 12.56$, $p < .001$]. Externalized Self-Perception [$t(237) = 4.34$, $p < .001$] and Divided Self [$t(237) = 2.50$, $p = .013$] made significant positive contributions, whereas Silencing the Self [$t(238) = -3.20$, $p = .002$] was a significant negative predictor.

The inverse relationship between the Silencing the Self subscale and premenstrual distress suggests that women are distressed and position their distress as PMS, partly because of their inability to self-silence premenstrually. This may explain the relatively low level of depression in this sample when compared to population norms (Zigmond & Snaith, 1983) and to women who score similarly on global self-silencing (Jack, 1991; Thompson, 1995), as women who position themselves as PMS sufferers are directing their anger outward once a month rather than internalizing it and becoming depressed. However, this is not a beneficial outcome for women, as rates of anxiety in this study were significantly higher than population norms, and women adopted a position of self-patholo-gization in relation to their anger and distress through positioning it as a disorder, PMS.

In order to understand the ways in which these patterns of self-silencing, and the relationship between self-silencing and premenstrual distress, are manifested and experienced by women, we will now turn to interview accounts. These accounts are drawn from a number of studies we have undertaken in the United Kingdom and Australia, where narrative interviews were conducted with women who positioned themselves as suffering from PMS. In order to elicit narratives, an open-ended question was asked at the beginning of the interview: "Women have different experiences in relation to PMS. Can you tell me how it is for you?" The interviewer then followed the woman's lead, asking questions of clarification as and when necessary and exploring issues of distress, coping, and communication of need or anger in relationships. The interview was thus framed as a dialogue between two people, rather than a question-and-answer situation. After transcription, the interviews were coded, line by line, thematically. Themes were grouped together and then checked for emerging patterns, for variability and consistency, for commonality across women, and for uniqueness within cases. This process follows what Stenner (1993, p. 114) has termed a "thematic decomposition," a close reading that attempts to sepa-rate a given text into coherent themes or narratives that reflect subject positions allocated to, or taken up by, a person (Davies & Harre, 1990). Pseudonyms are used in the presentation of data to ensure anonymity.

The "Real Me"—Accounts of the Silent Compliant Non-PMS Self

Drawing on both attachment theory and self-in-relation theory, Jack (1991) described self-silencing as women's propensity to engage in compulsive caretaking, please the other, and inhibit self-expression in relationships. In an attempt to achieve intimacy with their partners and meet relational needs through fulfilling the roles of "good wife" and "good mother," many women engage in self-sacrifice and silence feelings or behaviors that contradict these ideals (Carr, Gilroy, & Sherman, 1996). This leads to a self-division between an "outwardly conforming and compliant self" and an "inner self who is angry and resentful" (Jack, 1987, p. 177). Jack described this inner division as "the core dynamic of female depression" (Jack, 1991, p. 169), as it is based on women believing that they are not loved for who they are, but for how well they meet the needs of others, with the resultant silencing of desires and feelings and the use of external standards against which to judge the self leading to feelings of worthlessness and hopelessness (Duarte & Thompson, 1999).

Women who report PMS give accounts of self-silencing when they are not premenstrual and castigate themselves for breaking their outward compliance when they "have PMS" (Ussher, 2004b). The self is positioned as split between the responsible, calm, silent self who exists for three weeks of the month and the premenstrual monster who is reactive, irritable, and overwhelmed by the demands of others:

> I am like two people, my normal self and this impatient, uptight person (Helen).
> I'm just stressed and anxious—not a pleasant person to be around. It's like
> Dr. Jekyll and Mr. Hyde (Rachel).

These quotes illustrate the dramatic nature of the contrast in women's accounts: "Jekyll and Hyde" was the most common metaphor used (Ussher, 2006; Ussher & Perz, 2006), confirming the findings of the STSS analysis, where women reporting PMS score high on the Divided Self subscale. However, rather than positioning angry/irritable emotions as reflections of the "inner self," as is the case with Jack's (1991) description of the divided self in depressed women, women who report PMS position the calm, controlled, non-PMS self as the "real me" (Cosgrove & Riddle, 2003; Ussher, 2004a). The premenstrual phase of the cycle is positioned as a time when the woman is not her "normal self" because she has lost the ability to control the emotions she normally contains or represses through self-silencing. As Donna commented:

> I seem to lose the ability of self . . . of controlled self-management . . . . I don't cope
> with the challenges that life can throw at you, as well as what I normally would. I'm
> not saying that at any other time I cope really well, but I find it's harder. At other
> times, I might be able to hide my feelings. Keep things under wraps, keep my cool.
> During that time I don't seem to cope. I don't seem to be able to do that as well. I'm
> like . . . I might get upset. I might cry. I might hit out or lash out or say something, or
> revert into myself.

PMS is thus manifested by a disruption in the silenced, compliant self in the face of external demands or responsibilities. However, the outward expression of emotion is not the only signifier of PMS. Experience of a change in the *desire* to break silence or move away from a position of self-sacrifice was enough for women to pathologize themselves (Ussher, 2003b). As Helen told us, "I find that particular time of the month very difficult . . . . There's a big change in me and it makes me feel as if I'm not in control." Many women positioned one of their major premenstrual "symptoms" as a change in wanting, or being able, to provide unconditional care and support for their family premenstrually and of wishing to divest themselves of overwhelming responsibility, as Roberta describes:

> Um it's things like suddenly when I wake up one morning and I think, 'Yeah. It
> would be *really* nice not to sort of have to do *anything* . . . . I mean I, I can do what
> I've been doing for more than twenty years and I, I live with deadlines every sort of

every week of, uh, the year. Um and there's one part of me that thinks that maybe I've had enough.

Roberta is positioning the desire to attend to her own needs when she is premenstrual as a sign of internal pathology, PMS. In doing so, she is exhibiting self-policing, judging her own desires or needs in relation to the discursive constructions of women as responsible, self-renunciating, and always able to offer unlimited care and attention to others (Ussher, 2004b). Jack found that depressed women self-silenced in an attempt to emulate idealized constructions of "femininity," including "the good wife," "totally confident and self-assured," "a mother who never gets angry at her children," "give all with love and patience to my husband and children," "friendly and smiling all the time," and "slim, sexy and alluring" (Jack, 1991, p. 56). Supporting the finding of a relationship between STSS scores on Externalized Self-Perception and premenstrual distress, women's accounts of PMS center around perceived failures to live up to these same impossible ideals premenstrually, with a number of PMS/non-PMS contrasts appearing throughout the interviews: bad versus good/perfect; introversion versus extroversion; out of control versus in control; irresponsible versus responsible; failing versus coping; angry versus calm; anxious versus relaxed; sad/depressed versus happy; irrational versus rational; intolerant versus tolerant; vulnerable versus strong; irritable versus placid; and frustrated versus accepting (Perz & Ussher, 2006; Ussher, 2002b, 2004b). There is no room for transgression here—the standards of behavior underpinning the self-surveillance that results in feelings or behavior being positioned as PMS are impossibly high. Pauline, quoted next, expects herself to be "perpetually patient" and self-sacrificing. The only way she can explain transgression is through a pathological condition, PMS:

> Because of my job looking after a lady with Alzheimer's I'm perpetually being a patient person, um very understanding, not thinking about myself. But the things in those five to six days come in a bit of a *flux* and you're just [jarred] all the time.

This surveillant, judging self is most vigilant when women express anger or discontent within family relationships. This is because the expectation of care for others and the emphasis on "emotional maintenance" is invariably translated into an "ethic of responsibility," where women are positioned (and position themselves) as bearing full responsibility for maintaining relationships (O'Grady, 2005, p. 58; Jack, 1991). It has been argued that this results in women being especially prone to guilt and to a form of concern for maintaining relationships that leads to the feeling that "not upsetting people must always be given priority" (Grimshaw, 1986, p. 196). This is one explanation for why PMS is primarily an intersubjective experience, with a substantial percentage of women only positioning themselves as "PMS sufferers" when they feel that their "symptoms" impact negatively upon other people, in particular family members (Ussher, 2003a). For many women, this premenstrual break in self-silencing, where they are "cranky," "irritable," "ratty," or "demanding," is positioned as monstrous, illustrated in the example to follow, where Sharon describes herself as "devil mummy" when she isn't a "nice reasonable person" premenstrually. This reflects the judgment imposed upon women who transgress the ideals of "good mother":

> S: We have sort of like a catchword in the house, devil mummy, sort of thing you know, it's like 'you be careful because devil mummy isn't too far away and just don't do anything or don't say anything.' I'm really sorry, I try to explain it to them you know and say 'I'm really sorry, I'm *not* really in control, I'm trying but it's two people, it's like that.
>
> I: So what's the devil mummy like?
>
> S: Devil mummy she gets stroppy and angry at the least little thing like, know she'll just bite your head off for no reason, I mean I have quite a great relationship with my kids like we get on really well so um you know it's not like they're not allowed to wait for opinions about things, though we'll *argue*, but at that time of the month, I'm not gonna take it you know, the nice reasonable person that I could be isn't here anymore, you know, so they know okay 'don't bother, it's not worth it, don't push it.'

Constructions of idealized femininity also impact upon women's containment of feelings in wider society, in particular in relation to men, with many women expressing the need to contain their emotions so as not to be positioned as "weak." As Donna commented: "Men, I think, could um . . . think of you as weaker . . . and then think, and they do in here, they'll often say, 'Oh, that's Donna being emotional,' and I don't want to give them the pleasure." All of the women gave accounts of repressing or controlling their premenstrual feelings in one context but finding that they overflowed in another. The most common scenario was for premenstrual anger and irritation to be controlled in a work setting but expressed outwardly at home. As Ruth commented, "I try very hard not to snap at people in the office. I'm very conscious of doing that. So consequently I think I take it out more at home." The discursive construction of the "working woman" as professional, calm, and in control serves to provide boundaries for the outward expression of premenstrual emotion, whereas within the family situation, different rules apply, allowing women to "let go." However, many women experienced these work boundaries as a relief, as it protected them (and others) from the PMS self:

> I: Who else does it affect?
>
> M: Well it affects my husband and the children.
>
> I: Hmm.
>
> M: I don't think it affects anyone else 'cos I don't, I feel different at work. I mean I probably go to work to escape myself. I don't feel as though I take it out on my colleagues or anything like that. I just feel quite relieved to be at work really. (Mary)

Women are thus effectively policing themselves for most of the month, in order to maintain a position of equality and to avoid being positioned as the epitome of the "monstrous feminine," the abject reproductive body that is out of control (Ussher, 2006).

Cultural expectations of "appropriate" gendered behavior are policed through the privacy of intimate relationships, and the reactions of partners and family to a woman's expression of her needs, or her discontent, play a significant role in the development and maintenance of self-silencing. In describing why she doesn't tell her partner about her concerns, whether she is premenstrual or not, Celia told us:

> No, he doesn't want to know. He can't take it on board. Whether it be to do with worries I had about my sister with her bipolar, or my parents who at the moment are going through sickness, they're in their 90s and have had a stroke and falls, it worries me. I can't really discuss that at great length with him.

Celia's partner "doesn't want to know," so she represses her feelings and concerns—or at least attempts to do so, until they erupt premenstrually. The negative reactions many women receive from their male partner if they express needs or concerns premenstrually—rejection, judgment, and castigation—acts to reinforce their self-silencing. As Angela told us:

> That got to the point where I'd brought it up and said, 'Perhaps you need to have a look at some of the things you're doing as well because we both need to,' and of course I think I opened my mouth at the wrong time and that blew up into a huge argument and he just jumped on me and basically said, 'It's your shit, you go deal with it on your own, 'cause I have fucking had enough and I can't deal with this shit anymore because I'm sick of coming home and talking the same thing around and around and around and now you're blaming me,' and it's like, 'I'm not blaming you, I'm saying that there are some things that you do in response to me that add to this. It's not a blame thing,' and he just didn't want to hear it. He was just like 'Nah, your shit, get a therapist to sort it fucking out.'

Disrupting Patterns of Self-Silencing and Self-Sacrifice: Breaking Down the Divided Self

There are many complex reasons why women's anger and distress emerge premenstrually, with self-silencing being broken. There is convincing evidence from previous research that many women experience increased vulnerability and sensitivity to emotions or to external stress during the premenstrual phase of the cycle (Sabin Farrell & Slade, 1999; Ussher & Wilding, 1992), resulting from a combination of hormonal or endocrine changes (Parry, 1994), sensitivity to premenstrual increases in autonomic arousal (Kuczmierczyk & Adams, 1986; Ussher, 1987), and differential perceptions of stress premenstrually (Woods et al., 1998). Experimental research has demonstrated that dual or multiple task performance is more difficult premenstrually (Slade & Jenner, 1980), and while women can compensate with increased effort, this can result in increased levels of anxiety (Ussher & Wilding, 1991). It is thus not surprising that many women report reacting to the stresses and strains of daily life with decreased tolerance premenstrually, particularly when they carry multiple responsibilities (Ussher, 2003a). Indeed, in one study, career women with child-rearing responsibilities were found to report the highest levels of premenstrual distress (Coughlin, 1990).

In our research, women positioned PMS as the expression of otherwise repressed emotion associated with specific problems in relationships, particularly with partners or children. Without exception, when women were asked to characterize their experience of PMS, they used a "short-fuse" metaphor to describe incidents that were viewed as annoying or even as catastrophic premenstrually being tolerated or dismissed at other points in the cycle (Ussher, 2003a, 2004a). The majority of women described "losing it" or snapping in relation to domestic matters where they were normally expected to have unending patience and to take the lion's share of tasks—often in addition to undertaking paid work outside the home—as we see from Erica's account:

> *Every* morning is particularly bad in our house when I'm pre-menstrual. I've got three children. The youngest is five, seven and almost ten. Um and getting the children ready for school is just a nightmare because I, I just I mean it's, it's always quite difficult but normally, you know, I'll be saying to them, 'Come on,' you know, 'Get dressed. Get washed. Clean your teeth. Get your stuff together.' You know, 'It's nearly time to go.' When I'm pre-menstrual within minutes of the children getting up for school, I'm screaming at them and if they don't *do* what I'm asking them to do I mean it, the whole thing just escalates. I'll just, it will get *worse* and worse and worse.

Conversely, a "pressure cooker" metaphor was used to describe self-silenced emotions building up during the month and then overflowing during the premenstrual phase of the cycle, as is illustrated by Margo: "There's a few days of the month where I feel I'm not *myself*, or there's you know, anger or tension that builds up and then I release it at that point. And others around me suffer the consequences! Of that build up. Whatever it is." At the same time, women talked of expressing more deeply held grievances premenstrually, grievances they would contain during the rest of the month.

> There's things obviously in our relationship that I focus on which I feel aren't good. . . . I want to, want to face it now, whether it's, you know, him having breakfast in the morning or just about to go, I want to do it now, and that's not like me, I don't believe. (Tracey)

In an attempt to avoid this premenstrual expression of emotion, or to avoid external demands premenstrually, women reported that avoidance of others was the most effective coping mechanism they could engage in. As Nancy told us: "I withdraw. Just *totally*. Physically. Emotionally. Just sort of shut off. Shut away from other people." However, many women weren't able to withdraw due to physical constraints in their living conditions, family demands, or their own inability to negotiate time alone. For these women, premenstrual eruptions in emotion, and the negative consequences that followed, had become an unavoidable fact of their existence. This confirms previous research that reports a positive association between relationship strain and premenstrual symptomatology, as well as an association between effective communication between couples and lower levels of premenstrual distress (Ussher & Perz, 2008; Ussher et al., 2007). However, it is the *break* in self-silencing premenstrually that leads to distress, as well as to self-judgment and self-punishment.

Self-Judgment and Self-Punishment: The Consequences of Breaking Self-Silencing Premenstrually

For all of the women we interviewed, premenstrual emotions were positioned as a lack of control attributed to the body, following dominant representations of PMS in medical and self-help literature, where hormones are positioned as the cause of PMS (Ussher, 2003b; Ussher & Perz, 2006).

> I presume it's a chemical something or other is happening inside me, but I've tried various lotions and potions. It's not always exactly the same every month. But it's generally pretty horrible. And as I say I just, I think it's got to be chemical. (Ruth)

This blaming of the body may appear to function to exonerate the woman from judgments that attack her sense of self, as her transgressions are split off and projected onto a pathological condition over which she has no control. However, in addition to serving to maintain self-silencing for the rest of the month, the positioning of premenstrual emotion as PMS, and therefore as "not real," contributes further to a divided self by allowing a woman to only express herself at times when she won't be listened to or taken seriously, as the reproductive body is positioned as to blame. As the reproductive body is implicitly positioned as disordered and deviant, the outcome of this self-policing is a direct assault on the woman's corporeality—reinforcing the notion of woman as closer to nature, with subjectivity tied to the body, a body that is unruly or inferior, necessitating discipline and containment (Ussher, 2006). Michael White describes women with eating disorders as engaging in self-policing through "collaborating in the subjugation of their own lives and the objectification of their own bodies" (White, 1991, pp. 34–35). In positioning premenstrual anger, distress, or need for solitude as symptoms of an embodied disorder, PMS, the women we interviewed are doing the same.

Self-policing operates at the level of self-understanding and identity formation (Sawicki, 1998, p. 95), resulting in a feeling of being "wrong" if there is a lack of conformity to accepted modes of identity. The self-castigation women engage in for failing to meet these standards is often extreme. As Helen O'Grady comments, "when individuals perceive themselves as having failed to meet accepted norms, this can be experienced not just as a slip-up or error but as a transgression against the self - i.e. as going to the core of who one is" (2005, p. 60). For many women, a premenstrual slip-up in being "good" results in shame and guilt:

> And that's, *that's* what I find so difficult and when I'm pre-menstrual and I'm ranting and raving at everybody and getting so cross and upset about everything, *then* I start feeling guilty as well, because I *know* that the children are suffering, my husband is suffering, um because of my irritability. (Nicola)

Shame, it has been argued, results from "the distressed apprehension of the self as inadequate or diminished" (Bartky, 1990, p. 86). Premenstrually, many women experience themselves as such. Bartky goes on to argue that shame requires an audience before whom deficiencies are revealed—if not an actual audience, then an internalized one, with the capacity to judge. The women we interviewed experienced both internalized judgment and judgment on the part of others, in particular, family members:

> I shouted at my son and I felt very guilty about that. And then Leo (my partner) came in and I'd upset Liam and he then said, 'Well, why did you do that?' and by that time I was so distraught about how I was feeling about myself and how I'd been all day that I just cried. (Margaret)

This shame and guilt significantly contributes to the cycle of emotional expression followed by self-silencing as an attempt at reparation, which women who report PMS engage in. As Helen told us:

> Usually I've got a repair to make in my, my relationship with my husband because of the previous week and you know, it's difficult because you never have *time* to recover from it properly and you're back there again.

Similarly, Nicola described herself as "irritable," "bad tempered," and "needing a lot of space" and that "nobody can do anything right" when she's premenstrual, while for the remainder of the month, she is "thoughtful and considerate": "I'm back to being a nice person again. This is me. This is the person that everybody knows...the person my husband married, and, you know, everybody likes." Many of the women we interviewed reported fears of their male partners leaving them because of premenstrual behavior or emotions, leading to their renewed attempts at self-renunciation in order to repair the relationship when they were not premenstrual (Ussher et al., 2007).

However, if emotions and concerns are only expressed during the premenstrual phase of the cycle, they are easily dismissed as "just PMS," as is evident in Lisa's account of her relationship with her daughter:

> I've been upset or angry or snappy with her, she doesn't just think 'It's because she's out of order.' She will just say something like, 'Is your period due?' or something like that. And I think that's the *worst* thing *anybody* could say. You know, 'Are you getting your period? Are you getting the curse now? When's it due?' And I think that's *awful*!

This dismissal of women's emotions as PMS means that the underlying issues are not addressed, and the woman is more likely to feel guilty and to blame herself for "losing it" and then continue the cycle of repressing emotion during the rest of the cycle so as not to upset others, trying to "make up" for her premenstrual emotional state. However, when pressure builds up, she is tired or vulnerable because she's premenstrual, or she can't keep up the façade of perfection, something will act as a trigger and the cycle begins again.

However, PMS isn't simply a case of disruptions in self-silencing followed by guilt and shame. Women who are low on self-silencing also report premenstrual changes and position themselves as PMS sufferers. However, they cope with their premenstrual changes differently, being more able to articulate their needs and take time for themselves. In our current research, which is examining the differences between lesbian and heterosexual women's experience of PMS in order to interrogate the construction and experience of PMS within gendered relationships, we have found that women in lesbian relationships report lower self-silencing, more understanding on the part of partners, more ability to engage in self-care, and lower premenstrual distress (Perz & Ussher, 2009; Ussher & Perz, 2008). However, these patterns are not peculiar to women in same-sex relationships. In order to illustrate the ways in which self-silencing interacts with women's experience of premenstrual distress and coping, their positioning of the premenstrual self, and levels of anxiety and depression, two contrasting case examples are presented in the following section (Perz & Ussher, 2006).

Case Examples: Helen and Celia

Both Helen and Celia were in cohabiting heterosexual relationships, both working full time. Helen was 38 and Celia 43 years old. Helen had no children and Celia had a 2-year- old child. Table 20.3 summarizes Helen's and Celia's scores on the STSS and HADS and on levels of premenstrual distress.

Both women described their premenstrual changes similarly as being characterized by intolerance, irritation, emotional sensitivity, feeling more negative toward others, and feeling overwhelmed in the face of life's demands. Both positioned external factors as triggers for their PMS, in particular stress and

Table 20.3 Levels of PMS Distress, STSS, and HADS: Case Studies of Helen and Celia

	Helen	Celia	Undergraduate Sample (Jack & Dill, 1992)
PMS Distress	3	8	
STSS			
Externalized Self-Perception	7	20	18.2
Care as Self-Sacrifice	20	27	24.5
Silencing the Self	24	29	20.6
Divided Self	7	27	15.1
Total	58	103	78.4
HADS			
Anxiety	4	16	
Depression	1	11	

relational issues at work and home, which were described as impacting on their greater vulnerability at this time of the month. Both women reported coping by increasing self-care, taking time out to be alone, and having awareness of the reasons for their changed affect or reactivity. However, the way that these premenstrual changes were positioned by each woman and dealt with within their relationships, and the levels of distress experienced, were markedly different.

Helen scored very low on the STSS, in particular on the Divided Self and Externalized Self-Perception subscales, as well as reporting low levels of anxiety and depression, and giving an account of her PMS was in line with this. She described herself as being able to openly express her emotional experiences, her needs, and her concerns in her relationships, with no evidence of the disassociation from premenstrual emotion that characterizes many women's accounts of PMS, positioning her premenstrual emotions as valid and deserving of being taken seriously, with no concern about the negative judgments of others:

> I would never be euphemistic or anything, I would say, 'Oh I'm getting my period, I've got the shits with everything, and everything's a drama,' you know, I can vent with anyone really, but yeah, they'd either laugh or you know, be consoling, in a kind of semi-humorous way, yeah.

Helen's partner was described as nonjudgmental and accepting of her premenstrual emotional intensity: "He's come to accept that it's a complimentary thing for him and that's what he finds attractive in other people because it's not something that he experiences." She described pushing her partner to have discussions premenstrually, which she wouldn't do at other times, "because I'm feeling it's more important to me to hear him say something." While this did sometimes make him uncomfortable because he was "not expressive," he was described as being accepting, saying, "I would never have any conversations like this if it were up to me, so you know, we can bring it up, even though I don't like it." Helen said that she came from a "freaky feminist family" where she was taught not to "censor your reactions to your body," that she "quite liked" her periods, and didn't blame her body for PMS: "I wouldn't feel my body was turning against me, yeah, it's just, 'Oh poor me, I'm having a bad day.' "

Helen positioned her premenstrual desire for solitude, or for not having to engage with others at the end of a working day, as a legitimate time for recharging her batteries, allowing her to avoid engaging in "emotional labour," go with her "sooky" (emotional) feelings, or circumvent irritation that might impact on others. She described her partner and friends as being fully accepting of this behavior.

> I would, I would say openly, 'I just want to do nothing tonight.' Or you know, 'I just want to veg in front of the telly,' or, 'I just want to sit and read a book.' And I don't even mind having someone else in the house when I'm doing that, so you know if I'm living with someone, or sharing with a flatmate, I don't have a problem with the other person being there... but I make it pretty clear that I don't want to chat or I don't... you know... I don't want to do a shared activity, I want to do my own thing, yeah.

This was associated with low premenstrual distress, confirming the regression analysis, as well as low levels of depression and anxiety. There was some evidence of self-silencing, with Helen's score on the Silencing the Self subscale being slightly above previously reported nonclinical population scores, suggesting that she was, at times, keeping her feelings to herself to avoid conflict. In the interview, this was reflected in accounts of needing to be circumspect in what she says at work, in her account of not confronting her partner with "issues" when she was not premenstrual, and in her behavioral response of taking time out, or eschewing responsibility, to avoid conflict or the "emotional labour" of putting up a front premenstrually. However, as she did not pathologize her premenstrual distress or her reproductive body, the premenstrual break in self-silencing was not positioned as "out of control" and was not associated with distress.

In contrast, Celia reported high premenstrual distress, as well as depression and anxiety scores in the abnormal range, and scored well above previously reported means on all of the STSS subscales (Jack & Dill, 1992), supporting the findings of the regression analysis on the predictors of premenstrual distress. This was reflected in her interview account, which centered on a description of herself as outwardly compliant and inwardly angry, and of repressing her needs and anger in order to attend to the needs of others yet releasing these feelings in an uncontrolled way premenstrually, for which she castigated herself. She positioned herself as "childish" and "not coping" at this time of the month and said she felt frustrated and annoyed with herself for being "not together." When she isn't premenstrual, she described herself as being "able to hide my feelings. Keep things under wraps, keep my cool," whereas premenstrually she said she loses "the ability of controlled self-management," as we've seen previously, leading to conflict with her partner.

> What happens? What do I do? What's my behaviour? With my partner, Oh, yelling. And feeling very hurt...and attacked. And I might, um, leave the scene. Um, whereas I know, he's a volatile person too, and it could go one way, or...and I'm learning, because we've been together about four years now, if he says something and I react, it's very explosive. And a lot of yelling. Someone leaves who's crying, usually it's me.

Celia described herself as wanting acknowledgment of her premenstrual vulnerability from her partner, as well as care and support, but said that she doesn't get it "because men don't understand," he can't deal with her emotions, and there's "nothing he can do." However, she has never expressed these needs to her partner or talked about her PMS to him.

> I've never, ever brought up. . . . I've never, ever suggested that PMS or anything like that might be a trigger for me going off. I think it's because, um . . . I don't want to trivialise some of the issues that come up during this time by saying, 'Oh, it's just that I had PMT.'

She copes by trying to "get some time to myself" or "make a conscious decision to take things slower," without explaining why she needs to do this, or by drinking a glass of red wine and eating chocolate (which she normally doesn't allow herself to do). However, her desire for support and for recognition of her distress on the part of her partner (Ussher et al., 2007) contributes to the buildup of anger and frustration—and to the premenstrual break in her self-silencing, for which she then castigates herself. At the same time, having aware-ness that her feelings were due to PMS was described by Celia as helping her to keep things in perspective, allowing her to sometimes "modify my behaviour and check myself"—to keep her annoyance or feelings of vulnerability under control. Her premenstrual emotions were positioned as "not the reality. It's my percep-tion." Celia described herself as more distressed when she expressed her feelings premenstrually than when she managed to control them, illustrating the inverse relationship between the Silencing the Self subscale of the STSS and pre-menstrual distress.

Celia's account of lack of support from her partner, in the context of her working full time as well as caring for a 2-year-old child, suggested that she had legitimate reasons to feel angry, yet she positioned her premenstrual anger as "not real," evidence of her externalized self-perception, wherein she was judging herself by external standards of behavior for a "good" wife and mother. She is executing similar self-judgment in her description of disliking her "swollen" and "fat" premenstrual body, a positioning that is at odds with Western ideals of female attractiveness (Bordo, 1993).

These contrasting accounts of the intersubjective negotiation of PMS and of different reactions to women's outward expression of discontent stand as the most significant contrast in the interviews, reinforcing suggestions that partners play a crucial role in women's experience of premenstrual change (Jones, Theodos, Canar, Sher, & Young, 2000). Celia's experience confirms previous reports that lack of support from a partner (Schwartz, 2001) and absence of communication in relationships (Smith, 1996) are associated with higher levels of premenstrual distress. In contrast, Helen's account of open expression of her concerns and needs premenstrually and her partner's positive response confirms previous findings that women's ability to interpret emotions and handle conflict constructively is linked to lower rates of premenstrual distress (Welthagen, 1995). Helen's account of raising issues with her partner premenstrually and his admittance that this is confronting yet ultimately beneficial for the relationship also stand as confirmation of previous findings that women play a crucial role in expressing anger or initiating conflict in heterosexual relationships, leading to long-term relationship satisfaction if men are able to engage positively with the issues raised (Gottman & Krokoff, 1989). However, if anger expressed premenstrually is positioned as PMS, this can result in it being trivialized or dismissed, as was Celia's fear, thus undermining the potentially constructive role of women's outward expression of conflict. This suggests that women's premenstrual anger and distress need to be taken seriously to ensure that both the woman feels heard and the relationship has a greater chance of being experienced as satisfactory.

Material factors in Helen's and Celia's relationships may also have had a significant impact on their distress and coping. Both women adopted similar coping strategies of self-care and time-out, but it was easier for Helen, as she did not live with her partner and did not have a 2-year-old child to care for. Discursive factors, in particular, their positioning of the reproductive body, were also significant. While Helen rejected the positioning of the reproductive body as abject, Celia castigated herself for embodied changes she experienced premenstrually in a way that is reminiscent of the self-policing White has documented in women presenting with eating disorders: "the rigorous and meticulous self-surveillance, the various self-punishments of the body (mind and spirit) for...transgressions, the perpetual self-evaluations and comparisons, the various self-denials, the personal exile" (White, 1995, p. 45).

Conclusion

PMS is a complex issue, with premenstrual distress emerging as a result of a combination of material, discursive, and intrapsychic factors (Ussher, 1999,

2002a). Self-silencing is a significant factor in both the emergence of pre-menstrual distress and its positioning as PMS, a pathological disorder. Many women who take up a position of self-sacrifice and self-renunciation and who repress their needs or concerns in an attempt to be "good" report that premen-strually their own needs or concerns come to the fore. They feel overwhelmed by the normal day-to-day demands placed upon them, finding that they can't maintain the calm, compliant, coping persona they manage to inhabit for three weeks of the month. Women experience distress in relation to this change in their emotional state and level of coping, describing this distress as an embodied pathological condition, PMS, with distress exacerbated if negative emotions are outwardly expressed and responsibilities eschewed—if the idealized femi-nine position of self-silencing and self-sacrifice is effectively disrupted.

The bodily functions we understand as a sign of "illness" vary across culture and across time (Payer, 1988). The interpretation of physiological and hormonal changes as being "symptoms" of PMS, rooted in the reproductive body, cannot be understood outside of the social and historical context in which they live, influenced by the *meaning* ascribed to these changes by Western medicalized discourses and the ways in which individual women then negotiate these mean-ings (Ussher, 2003b). Premenstrual changes in state or reactivity are positioned as PMS because of hegemonic constructions of the premenstrual phase of the cycle as negative and debilitating (Parlee, 1994; Rittenhouse, 1991), which impact upon women's appraisal and negotiation of premenstrual changes in affect or sensitivity (Ussher, 2002b). In cultures where PMS does not circulate as a discursive category, women, or their families, do not attribute psychological distress to the premenstrual body and do not position premenstrual change as pathology (Chrisler, 2002). However, even within cultural contexts where PMS as a descriptor of psychological change premenstrually holds currency, women can resist a medicalized discourse, and thus resist the pathologization of the reproductive body and of their desire to express their concerns or to put their own needs first, as we have seen in the case studies in this chapter.

This conceptualization of PMS has significant implications for clinical inter-ventions with women. Women can be supported in the process of contesting PMS as an embodied pathology, allowing them to shift from a disempowering subject position, where distress is blamed on a dysfunctional reproductive body and where premenstrual changes are split off as pathology, to a position where distress is experienced as an understandable reaction to the circumstances of their lives. A women-centered therapy for PMS that we have developed (Ussher, Hunter, & Cariss, 2002), which draws on a combination of narrative and cognitive-behavioral techniques in order to break down the division between the PMS and non-PMS self, to encourage women to take ownership of pre-menstrual feelings, to reduce self-silencing and self-sacrifice, and to increase assertiveness and self-care during the whole month, has been found to result in significant reductions in anxiety and premenstrual distress. The aims of the intervention were to critically examine constructions of PMS and femininity and how these constructions impact upon women's positioning and experience of premenstrual change; to examine life stresses and relational issues that precipitate distress; and to develop coping strategies for dealing with premenstrual change and distress across the cycle, including exercise, diet, relaxation, positive thinking, and doing things one enjoys. In a randomized control trial conducted in the United Kingdom (Hunter et al., 2002), where women either were given SSRIs or took part in this psychological intervention, narrative reauthoring was found to be as effective as SSRIs in reducing premenstrual distress over a six-month period and more effective at one-year follow-up. When this therapy was converted to a self-help format and evaluated on its own or with a minimal psychological intervention (a 90-minute session with a psychologist talking through the pack), both groups reported reduced anxiety and reduced life interference from PMS postintervention. The minimal intervention group reported a broader range of improvements, including significant reductions in depression and the extent to which PMS caused distress and significant improvements in ability to cope with symptoms (Ussher & Perz, 2006).

In both studies, after taking part in this intervention, women were able to take up a position of greater equality and agency, not pathologizing themselves in relation to difficulties in relationships or in relation to life in general and moving away from a position of self-sacrifice and overresponsibility. Women reported that they still experienced premenstrual change but no longer positioned this change as an illness that was out of their control. Women were also less likely to engage in self-surveillance and self-judgment, becoming more accepting of who they were and of embodied or psychological changes that took place across the menstrual cycle. The reproductive body was repositioned as part of women's subjectivity, not as an unruly force that is other to them and feared because it is out of control. All of the women reported the effective implementation of strategies to cope with premenstrual changes in mood, sensitivity, or embodied experiences and engaging in more self-care, and reported that this resulted in a significant reduction in their "symptoms," as well as helping them to cope if they did feel distressed premenstrually. The premenstrual phase of the cycle was reframed as a time when women needed to attend to their own needs and to ask for support, rather than a time when women fail or are ill (Ussher, 2006, 2008).

The majority of women reported the development of more honest and open communication of their needs and concerns, which served to prevent the short-fuse and pressure cooker experience of repressed emotions spilling out premenstrually. Being heard in a nonjudgmental way, having their feelings validated, and receiving support in relation to their distress were reported by women to be the most positive aspects of the intervention. It was as a result of feeling validated in this way that women were able to develop more effective forms of communication with their partners and children in relation to experiences of anger, depression, or irritation across the cycle as well as in relation to premenstrual feelings of vulnerability, allowing them to feel understood rather than pathologized and dismissed: key factors that prevent sadness turning into depression (Stiver & Miller, 1988). Women were also more able to say no to unreasonable demands, to establish more egalitarian practices within the home for the sharing of responsibilities, and to express deeper concerns within relationships when they were not feeling overwhelmed premenstrually, all of which reduced premenstrual "symptoms" (Ussher, 2008; Ussher & Perz, 2006). Women reported being more confident in resisting the categorization by others of their behavior or feelings as "PMS," which had previously led to a dismissal of their needs or frustrations. Many women described being more tolerant of others premenstrually and coping better with relational issues that had caused conflict or distress, as they had learned to let go of feelings of overresponsibility and were less likely to position themselves as to blame when things were not perfect in the family. This confirms previous research that found that when women can move away from the position of self-sacrificing femininity, which leads to self-castigation for not living up to impossible ideals of perfect womanhood, and the pathologization of distress, they are more able to tolerate changes in ability to cope or ability to care for others before themselves (Mauthner, 2000; O'Grady, 2005). Disrupting the silenced self is thus beneficial for women—not just premenstrually, but throughout a woman's life.

References

American Psychiatric Association. (2000). *Diagnostic and statistical manual of mental disorders* (4th ed.). Washington, DC: American Psychological Association.

Bancroft, J. (1993). The premenstrual syndrome: A reappraisal of the concept and the evidence. *Psychological Medicine, Suppl 241*, 1–47.

Bartky, S. L. (1990). *Femininity and domination: Studies in the phenomenology of oppression.* New York: Routledge.

Blake, F., Salkovskis, P., Gath, D., Day, A., & Garrod, A. (1998). Cognitive therapy for premenstrual syndrome: A controlled trial. *Journal of Psychosomatic Research, 45*, 307–318.

Bordo, S. (1993). *Unbearable weight: Feminism, culture and the body.* Berkeley, CA: University of California Press.

Carr, J. G., Gilroy, F. D., & Sherman, M. F. (1996). Silencing the self and depression among women. *Psychology of Women Quarterly, 20*, 375–392.

Chrisler, J. C. (2002). Hormone hostages: The cultural legacy of PMS as a legal defence. In L. H. Collins & M. R. Dunlap (Eds.), *Charting a new course for feminist psychology* (pp. 238–252). Westport: Connecticut: Praeger Publishers.

Cosgrove, L., & Riddle, B. (2003). Constructions of femininity and experiences of menstrual distress. *Women & Health, 38*, 37–58.

Coughlin, P. C. (1990). Premenstrual syndrome: How marital satisfaction and role choice affect symptom severity. *Social Work, 35*, 351–355.

Davies, B., & Harre, R. (1990). Positioning: the discursive production of selves. *Journal of the Theory of Social Behaviour, 20*, 43–65.

Duarte, L. M., & Thompson, J. M. (1999). Sex-differences in self-silencing. *Psychological Reports, 85*, 145–161.

Elson, J. (2002). Menarche, menstruation, and gender identity: Retrospective accounts from women who have undergone premenopausal hysterectomy. *Sex Roles, 46*, 37–48.

Frank, B., Dixon, D. N., & Grosz, H. J. (1993). Conjoint monitoring of symptoms of premenstrual syndrome: Impact on marital satisfaction. *Journal of Counseling Psychology, 40*, 109–114.

Gottman, J. M., & Krokoff, L. J. (1989). Marital interaction and satisfaction: A longitudinal view. *Journal of Consulting & Clinical Psychology, 57*, 47–52.

Grimshaw, J. (1986). *Philosophy and feminist thinking*. Minneapolis: University of Minnesota Press.

Halbreich, U., Borenstein, J., Pearlstein, T., & Kahn, L. S. (2003). The prevalence, impairment, impact, and burden of premenstrual dysphoric disorder (PMS/PMDD). *Psychoneuroendocrinology, 28*(Supp. 3), 1–23.

Hunter, M. S., Ussher, J. M., Browne, S., Cariss, M., Jelly, R., & Katz, M. (2002). A randomised comparison of psychological (cognitive behaviour therapy), medical (fluoxetine) and combined treatment for women with premenstrual dysphoric disorder. *Journal of Psychosomatic Obstetrics and Gynaecology, 23*, 193–199.

Jack, D. C. (1987). Silencing the self: The power of social imperatives in women's depression. In R. Formanek & A. Gurian (Eds.), *Women and depression: A lifespan perspective* (pp. 161–181). New York: Springer.

Jack, D. C. (1991). *Silencing the self: Women and depression*. Cambridge MA: Harvard University Press.

Jack, D. C., & Dill, D. (1992). The Silencing the Self Scale. Schemas of intimacy with depression in women. *Psychology of Women Quarterly, 16*, 97–106.

Jones, A., Theodos, V., Canar, W. J., Sher, T. G., & Young, M. (2000). Couples and premenstrual syndrome: Partners as moderators of symptoms? In K. B. Schmaling (Ed.), *The psychology of couples and illness: Theory, research, & practice* (pp. 217–239). Washington, DC: American Psychological Association.

Kuczmierczyk, A. R., & Adams, H. E. (1986). Autonomic arousal and pain sensitivity in women with premenstrual syndrome at different phases of the menstrual cycle. *Journal of Psychosomatic Research, 30*, 421–428.

Mauthner, N. (2000). Feeling low and feeling really bad about feeling low. Women's experience of motherhood and post-partum depression. *Canadian Psychology, 40*, 143–161.

McDaniel, S. H. (1988). The interpersonal politics of premenstrual syndrome. *Family Systems Medicine, 6*, 134–149.

O'Grady, H. (2005). *Women's relationship with herself: Gender, Foucault, therapy*. London: Routledge.

Parlee, M. B. (1994). The social construction of premenstrual syndrome: A case study of scientific discourse as cultural contestation. In M. G. Winkler (Ed.), *The good body: Asceticism in contemporary culture* (pp. 91–107). New Haven, CT: Yale University Press.

Parry, B. (1994). Biological correlates of premenstrual complaints. In J. Gold, & S. K. Severino (Eds.), *Premenstrual dysphoria: Myths and realities* (pp. 47–66). London: American Psychiatric Press.

Payer, L. (1988). *Medicine and culture.* New York: Henry Holt & Company.

Perz, J., & Ussher, J. M. (2006). Women's experience of premenstrual change: A case of silencing the self. *Journal of Reproductive and Infant Psychology, 24,* 289–303.

Perz, J., & Ussher, J. M. (2009). Connectedness, communication and reciprocity in lesbian relationships: Implications for women's construction and experience of PMS. In P. Hammock & B. J. Cohler (Eds.), *Life course and sexual identity: Narrative perspectives on gay and lesbian identity* (pp. 223–250). Oxford: Oxford University Press.

Rapkin, A. (2003). A review of treatment of premenstrual syndrome and premenstrual dysphoric disorder. *Psychoneuroendocrinology, 28*(Supp. 3), 39–53.

Rittenhouse, C. A. (1991). The emergence of premenstrual syndrome as a social problem. *Social Problems, 38,* 412–425.

Rundle, R. (2005). A qualitative exploration of couples' relational experiences when one partner suffers from symptoms of PMS: A systems approach. *Dissertation Abstracts International: Section B: The Sciences and Engineering, 66,* 1185.

Ryser, R., & Feinauer, L. L. (1992). Premenstrual syndrome and the marital relationship. *American Journal of Family Therapy, 20,* 179–190.

Sabin Farrell, R., & Slade, P. (1999). Reconceptualizing pre-menstrual emotional symptoms as phasic differential responsiveness to stressors. *Journal of Reproductive and Infant Psychology, 17,* 381–390.

Sawicki, J. (1998). Feminism, Foucault and 'subjects' of power and freedom. In J. Moss (Ed.), *The later Foucault: Politics and philosophy* (pp. 93–107). London: Sage.

Schwartz, C. B. (2001). The relationship between partner social support and premenstrual symptoms. *Abstracts International: Section B: The Sciences & Engineering, 61,* 5580.

Slade, P., & Jenner, F. A. (1980). Performance tests in different phases of the menstrual cycle. *Journal of Psychosomatic Research, 24,* 5–8.

Smith, H. (1996). Anger and locus of control in young women with and without premenstrual syndrome. *Issues in Mental Health Nursing, 17,* 289–305.

Smith-Martinez, K. L. (1995). Premenstrual symptomatology and its impact on marital communication. *Abstracts International: Section B: The Sciences & Engineering, 56,* 2887.

Stenner, P. (1993). Discoursing jealousy. In E. Burman & I. Parker (Ed.), *Discourse analytic research* (pp. 114–134). London: Routledge.

Stiver, I. P., & Miller, J. B. (1988). *From depression to sadness in women's psychotherapy.* Wellesley, MA: Stone Center Working Paper Series.

Thompson, J. M. (1995). Silencing the self. Depressive symptomatology in close relationships. *Psychology of Women Quarterly, 19,* 337–353.

Ussher, J. M. (1987). *The relationship between cognitive performance and physiological change across the menstrual cycle.* Unpublished PhD thesis. London: University of London Department of Psychology.

Ussher, J. M. (1999). Premenstrual syndrome: Reconciling disciplinary divides through the adoption of a material-discursive-intrapsychic approach. In A. Kolk, M. Bekker, K. Van Vliet (Ed.), *Advances in women and health research* (pp. 47–64). Amsterdam: Tilberg University Press.

Ussher, J. M. (2002a). Premenstrual syndrome: Fact, fantasy, or fiction? In C. B. von Hofsten (Ed.), *Psychology at the turn of the millennium* (pp. 497–527). East Sussex, UK: Psychology Press.

Ussher, J. M. (2002b). Processes of appraisal and coping in the development and maintenance of premenstrual dysphoric disorder. *Journal of Community and Applied Social Psychology, 12,* 1–14.

Ussher, J. M. (2003a). The ongoing silencing of women in families: An analysis and rethinking of premenstrual syndrome and therapy. *Journal of Family Therapy, 25,* 388–405.

Ussher, J. M. (2003b). The role of premenstrual dysphoric disorder in the subjectification of women. *Journal of Medical Humanities, 24,* 131–146.

Ussher, J. M. (2004a). Blaming the body for distress: Premenstrual dysphoric disorder and the subjectification of women. In A. Potts, N. Gavey, & A. Wetherall (Eds.), Sex and the body (pp. 183–202). Palmerstone North, New Zealand: Dunmore Press.

Ussher, J. M. (2004b). Premenstrual syndrome and self-policing: Ruptures in self-silencing leading to increased self-surveillance and blaming of the body. *Social Theory & Health, 2,* 254–272.

Ussher, J. M. (2006). *Managing the monstrous feminine: Regulating the reproductive body.* London: Routledge.

Ussher, J. M. (2008). Challenging the positioning of premenstrual change as PMS: The impact of a psychological intervention on women's self-policing. *Qualitative Research in Psychology, 5,* 33–44.

Ussher, J. M., Hunter, M., & Cariss, M. (2002). A woman-centred psychological intervention for premenstrual symptoms, drawing on cognitive-behavioural and narrative therapy. *Clinical Psychology and Psychotherapy, 9,* 319–331.

Ussher, J. M., & Perz, J. (2006). Evaluating the relative efficacy of a self-help and minimal psycho-educational intervention for moderate premenstrual distress conducted from a critical realist standpoint. *Journal of Reproductive and Infant Psychology, 24,* 347–362.

Ussher, J. M., & Perz, J. (2008). Empathy, egalitarianism and emotion work in the relational negotiation of PMS: The experience of lesbian couples. *Feminism and Psychology, 18,* 87–111.

Ussher, J. M., Perz, J., & Mooney-Somers, J. (2007). The experience and positioning of affect in the context of intersubjectivity: The case of premenstrual syndrome. *International Journal of Critical Psychology, 21,* 144–165.

Ussher, J. M., & Wilding, J. M. (1991). Performance and state changes during the menstrual cycle, conceptualised within a broad band testing framework. *Social Science and Medicine, 32,* 525–534.

Ussher, J. M., & Wilding, J. M. (1992). Interactions between stress and performance during the menstrual cycle in relation to the premenstrual syndrome. *Journal of Reproductive and Infant Psychology, 10,* 83–101.

Welthagen, N. (1995). *The influence of premenstrual symptoms on marital communication*. Unpublished PhD thesis, University of Pretoria.

White, M. (1991). Deconstruction and therapy. *Dulwich Centre Newsletter (Adelaide)*, 21–40.

White, M. (1995). *Re-authoring lives: Interviews and essays*. Adelaide, South Australia: Dulwich Centre Publications.

Winter, E. J., Ashton, D. J., & Moore, D. L. (1991). Dispelling myths: a study of PMS and relationship satisfaction. *The Nurse Practitioner, 16*, 37–40.

Woods, N. F., Lentz, M. J., Mitchell, E. S., Heitkemper, M., Shaver, J., & Henker, R. (1998). Perceived stress, physiologic stress arousal, and premenstrual symptoms: Group differences and intra-individual patterns. *Research in Nursing and Health, 21*, 511–523.

Wright, S. E. (1986). Premenstrual syndrome (PMS) and perceived marital inequity. *Dissertation Abstracts International, 46*, 3879.

Zigmond, A. S., & Snaith, R. P. (1983). The Hospital Anxiety and Depression Scale. *Acta Psychiatrica Scandinavica, 67*, 361–370.

21

"I Wasn't Being True to Myself": Women's Narratives of Postpartum Depression

Natasha S. Mauthner

I suppose if you look back to my mother I was thinking that, you know, once I have a baby then I'm no longer the businesswoman, I'm you know the person who should always be there with the hugs and does the ironing. And I was almost pushing the rest of me out of the way saying, 'Okay, I had those skills but those are not useful in what I'm doing now,' you know. I wanted to revel in being at home and doing the housework and this, that, and the other but I wasn't really being true to myself.

Sonya is one of many women I interviewed in Britain and the United States in the 1990s about their experiences of motherhood and postpartum depression. I begin this chapter with her words by way of illustrating a theme that recurs in these women's narratives and that is central to this book. Women spoke about a conflict between their expectations and their experiences of motherhood, which they sought to "resolve" by denying aspects of themselves and their identities that did not conform to their ideals. They could see no way of enacting or voicing their thoughts and feelings within interpersonal and cultural contexts that, as they perceived it, rigidly prescribe what a "good mother" ought to think, feel, and do and condemn mothers who fall short of these ideals. This move into silence, or as Dana Jack (1991, 1999) terms it, "silencing the self," protected mothers from what they experienced as a cultural and interpersonal invalidation and dismissal of their feelings. However, this move was also highly costly because it was linked to their depression. As Sonya further explained, "I'm imposing standards...that are much, much too high and I was trying to fulfil them and making myself feel ill."

The aim of this chapter is to discuss the contrasting ways in which postpartum depression has been understood and theorized and to highlight how particular conceptualizations are tied to the theoretical and methodological approaches that are used. I begin the chapter by providing an overview of cross-cultural, medical, social, and feminist perspectives on postpartum depression. This field of research has traditionally been dominated by medical and quantitative approaches that neglect women's perspectives and portray them as passive "victims" of their individual biology, psychology, or social context. A smaller body of social science and feminist work, mostly of a qualitative nature, has drawn attention to the insights women have into their depression and how their narratives can give us access to particular interpretations of their experiences. Until very recently, this work had developed mostly *in parallel to* the dominant medical tradition, and indeed has been marginalized by it. But as I discuss further in the following section, a detectable shift is taking place whereby mainstream medical researchers are beginning to acknowledge the value of qualitative studies and recognize that they provide particular, distinctive, and important understandings of postpartum depression (e.g., Boath & Henshaw, 2001; Oates et al., 2004).

In the second part of the chapter, I briefly discuss two qualitative studies I conducted in the 1990s in Britain and the United States and highlight my use of feminist relational theory and methodology. The third part of the chapter draws on these studies, and on the narratives of 35 women, to outline a "relational" perspective on postpartum depression. My discussion suggests that depression is linked to the processes through which mothers negotiate cultural norms, standards, and expectations of motherhood. More specifically, I argue that these women are engaged in active struggles in which they are trying to conform to culturally derived and interpersonally upheld expectations of motherhood, but in doing so feel disconnected from parts of themselves, from other people, and from the surrounding culture. Their sense of disconnection results in a silencing of the self and ultimately in feelings of depression. The chapter concludes by discussing the implications of this approach for the prevention and treatment of postpartum depression.

Theories of Postpartum Depression

Cross-Cultural Perspectives on Postpartum Depression

Before reviewing dominant theories of postpartum depression, it is worth highlighting a growing strand of research that is concerned with its cross-cultural manifestation and that is relevant to this chapter given the international scope of this book. Cross-cultural interest in postpartum depression began with the work of anthropologists who carried out ethnographic studies of childbirth in other societies and found little evidence of postpartum depression in countries such as India, China, Jamaica, Mexico, and Kenya. Anthropologists have argued that postpartum depression is therefore a culture-bound syndrome restricted to Western industrialized societies (Chrisler & Johnston-Robledo, 2002; Stern & Kruckman, 1983). The absence of depression following childbirth has been attributed to adherence to certain "postpartum rituals" within more "traditional" societies. These rituals include a confinement period of rest and care for the mother, practical and emotional support from other women, and social recognition of the mother's new status.

Other, more recent studies, however, suggest that unhappiness following childbirth *is* found across cultures and that prevalence rates are similar across countries, but that there may be cross-cultural variations in how it is expressed, labeled, interpreted, and treated. Over the past two decades, the instrument most frequently used internationally for research into postpartum depression has been the Edinburgh Postnatal Depression Scale (EPDS; Cox, Holden, & Sagovsky, 1987). The EPDS has been translated into many languages and has been found to be an acceptable, reliable, and valid screening instrument for postpartum depression in other cultures. Cross-cultural studies find that postpartum depression is an experience that women in all cultures experience (Goldbort, 2006) and that prevalence rates of postpartum depression in Western nations such as Europe, the United States, and Australia are remarkably similar to those found in many other countries including Taiwan (Huang & Mathers, 2001), Lebanon (Chaaya et al., 2002), Turkey (Inandi et al., 2002), Iran (Mazhari & Nakhaee, 2007), Japan (Yamashita, Yoshida, Nakano, & Tashiro, 2000), China (Lee et al., 1998), Chile (Jadresic, Araya, & Jara, 1995), Asia, and South America (Affonso, De, Horowitz, & Mayberry, 2000).

Furthermore, despite differences in cultural contexts and health and postnatal care systems, the risk factors for postpartum depression also share similar themes cross-culturally with one notable exception. The sex of the infant—and specifically having a female child—is a greater risk factor for postpartum depression in China, Turkey, and India, where male children are more highly valued than female offspring (Goldbort, 2006; Rodrigues, Patel, Jaswal, & Souza, 2003). Despite the similarities in prevalence and risk factors across cultures, there appear to be important cultural differences in how postpartum depression is interpreted and treated. Non-Western cultures tend to attribute it to social causes rather than biological origins (Dennis & Chung-Lee, 2006; Edge, Baker, & Rogers, 2004; Goldbort, 2006; Kim & Buist, 2005) and are more likely to adopt treatments not based on a Western model (Stewart & Jambunathan, 1996).

These findings are supported by a large-scale psychiatric transcultural study of postpartum depression involving 11 countries (France, Ireland, Italy, Sweden, the United States, Uganda, the United Kingdom, Japan, Portugal, Austria, and Switzerland), which constitutes one of the most significant recent contributions to cross-cultural understandings of postpartum depression. The primary aim of the study was to develop, translate, and validate research instruments and measures for use in international, cross-cultural research on postpartum depression (Asten, Marks, Oates, & TCS-PND Group, 2004). As part of this project, Oates and colleagues (2004) conducted a qualitative study of the experience, expression, and attributions of postpartum depression across these countries. Their research confirms that "morbid unhappiness" was a common phenomenon following childbirth in all cultures, and that the signs and symptoms described were compatible with a diagnosis of postpartum depression. As was the case in the studies mentioned earlier, the participants viewed the causes and remedies as lying in the psychosocial domain, emphasizing family relationships and social support. A need for intervention by health professionals was not universally recognized.

Cross-cultural studies highlight a central, enduring, and unanswered question concerning whether postpartum depression should be understood as a biological or cultural phenomenon. This tension is reflected in the two dominant theories of postpartum depression: the medical model and social science perspectives on postpartum depression.

The Medical Model of Postpartum Depression

The medical model of postpartum depression dominates academic, professional, and lay understandings. Here, postpartum depression is conceptualized as a medical condition—a "disease" or "illness"—considered to be biological or hormonal in origin (Hendrick, Altschuler, & Suri,1998). Its onset is within the first four weeks after childbirth and it is said to affect approximately 1 mother in 10 with symptoms typically lasting 2 to 6 months (Cooper, Campbell, Day, Kennerley, & Bond, 1988; O'Hara, 1997). It is differentiated from the milder "postnatal blues" believed to affect 50% to 80% of mothers in the first days after the birth (Stein, 1982; York, 1990), and from the more serious "puerperal psychosis" said to affect 1 to 2 mothers per 1,000 (Kendell, 1985). Medical and psychiatric research efforts have been devoted to describing, predicting, preventing, and treating postpartum depression (e.g., Cox & Holden, 1994). For example, researchers have endeavored to uncover the underlying factors correlated with postpartum depression, including biological variables (e.g., hormones, other biochemicals, genetic factors), psychological characteristics (e.g., personality traits, self-esteem, previous psychiatric history, family history, attitudes toward children, deficiencies in self-control, attribution style, social skills), a range of social variables (e.g., unplanned pregnancy, method of feeding the baby, type of delivery, obstetric complications, infant temperament, previous experience with babies, marital relationship, social support, stressful life events, employment status), and sociodemographic characteristics (e.g., social class, age, ethnicity, education, income, parity) (O'Hara & Zekoski, 1998).

Taken together, the results of these studies are inconclusive and contradictory (Hendrick et al., 1998; Llewellyn, Stowe, & Nemeroff, 1997; Romito, 1989; Small, Brown, Lumley, & Astbury, 1994; Stowe & Nemeroff, 1995; Wisner, Parry, & Piontek, 2002). Typically, a given factor—for example, whether postpartum depression is associated with the birth of a first or subsequent child—might be positively associated with postpartum depression in one study, negatively in another, and not at all in a third (see Green, 1990). The most consistent findings are that postpartum depression is linked to the quality of the marital relationship (Boyce & Hickey, 2005; Everingham, Heading, & Connor, 2006; Mauthner, 1998; Rodrigues et al., 2003), previous history of depression (including past postpartum depression), family psychiatric history, limited social support, and the occurrence of stressful life events other than childbirth, such as death in the family, illness, moving, or child-related stresses (Cooper & Murray, 1998; O'Hara, Schlechte, Lewis, & Varner, 1991; O'Hara & Swain, 1996; Swendsen & Mazure, 2000; Wilson et al., 1996; Wisner & Stowe, 1997).

An important limitation of these studies is the lack of attention paid to mothers' accounts of their experiences of postpartum depression. Taking women's own words and perspectives as primary sources of knowledge about their experiences goes against a tradition in medicine, psychiatry, and experimental psychology in which "subjectivity" and qualitative research have been marginalized. Similarly, research on postpartum depression has been characterized by a belief among many that being depressed renders women incapable of meaningful insights into the experience or trustworthy accounts of their feelings (Small et al., 1994). This methodological devaluation of women's perspectives has in turn shaped emerging clinical theories of postpartum depression. By excluding women's narratives, subjectivity, and agency, these theories inevitably fall into deterministic arguments in which biological, personality, and social factors are seen to act upon and within essentially passive women. The most obvious example of this is the notion that women who are depressed are victims of their hormones (e.g., Dalton, 1971, 1989). Postpartum depression is also seen as the result of "dysfunctional" personalities or relationships (e.g., Boyce, 1994). Through this individualistic approach, postpartum depression comes to be viewed as a pathological condition rooted in deficiencies pertaining to the individual mother, rather than as the product of a complex interplay of individual, interpersonal, and sociocultural factors, in which individual women subjectively and actively interpret and negotiate what is happening to them.

However, an important shift appears to be taking place whereby researchers from medical and psychiatric backgrounds are acknowledging the limitations of quantitative approaches and recognizing the distinctive contributions of qualitative methods and "lay" or subjective perspectives (e.g., Buston, Parry-Jones, Livingston, Bogan, & Wood, 1998; Entwistle, Renfrew, Yearly, Forrester, & Lamont, 1998). Boath and Henshaw (2001), for example, criticize systematic reviews of treatment approaches for postpartum depression because of their focus on randomized controlled trials to the exclusion of other study designs, including more qualitative approaches such as observational studies. The aim of their research was to identify and critically review *all* published studies of the treatment of postpartum depression, including those that would be excluded from systematic reviews because of their stringent inclusion criteria.

The transcultural study of postpartum depression mentioned earlier provides another excellent example of this shift toward qualitative research. The research team, which included medical anthropologists, explain why the inclusion of qualitative methods—focus groups and interviews with mothers, fathers, grand-mothers, and health professionals—was essential to achieving the aims and objectives of the study and to overcoming the limitations of quantitative approaches:

> In order to avoid the assumptions of cross-cultural equivalence inherent in quantitative research instruments and the questionnaire method, it was felt that qualitative methods were the appropriate way to explore and gain understanding of the attitudes and beliefs of women and those involved in caring for them and making suggestions for the systems of their care. (Oates et al., 2004, p. s11)

> A further aim of the study was to be better informed about appropriate services to meet the needs of women with postnatal depression. Qualitative research methods are particularly appropriate in identifying dimensions of care and treatment that matter to health care recipients, and those that influence health care decision-making and treatment. (Oates et al., 2004, p. s11)

This shift is significant because it legitimizes the use of qualitative research and brings into the mainstream over two decades' worth of qualitative social scientific research on postpartum depression that has largely been marginalized by clinical researchers.

Social Science Perspectives on Postpartum Depression

Social science perspectives on postpartum depression have developed largely as a critique of the medical model and in particular its failure to consider women's perspectives on their experiences of motherhood and depression (Littlewood & McHugh, 2003; Mauthner, 2002; Rodrigues et al., 2003). These studies explore women's narratives, experiences, and perceptions of their depression, in parti-cular, its time of onset and duration; its perceived contributing factors; its consequences for women, their children, and their families; women's views of professional support as well as other sources of support; and the recovery process (Beck, 1992, 1993; Everingham et al., 2006; McIntosh, 1993; Morgan, Matthey, Barnett, & Richardson, 1997; Nahas & Amasheh, 1999; Nahas, Hillege, & Amasheh, 1999; Small et al., 1994; Stewart & Jambunathan, 1996; Wood, Thomas, Droppleman, & Meighan, 1997).

An important strand of this work is feminist analyses of postpartum depres-sion (Berggren-Clive, 1998; Chrisler & Johnston-Robledo, 2002; Lee, 1997;

Mauthner, 2002; Nicolson, 1998; Oakley, 1980; Romito, 1990; Stoppard, 2000; Taylor, 1996), many of which are rooted within broader feminist critiques of medicine and psychiatry, gendered "psychopathologies," and gendered parenting structures and ideologies (e.g., Stoppard, 1997, 1998; Ussher, 1991). Like social science perspectives, feminist accounts of postpartum depression challenge medical theories' view of women's depression as an individual, often biological, problem that leaves the broader social, political, and cultural contexts unexamined. They also take issue with the notion that postpartum depression is treated as a disease with clear symptoms and characteristics. They argue that postpartum depression is a category elaborated by the medical and psychiatric professions to describe a cluster of signs and symptoms and in this sense it is a medical and social construct.

My characterization of a particular group of scholars as feminist is based on their use of gender as an analytic tool in understanding postpartum depression. Feminist approaches share an emphasis on women's gendered subjectivities and on the inequalities women face in public and domestic spheres—inequalities that researchers believe lie at the root of depression. However, there are also divisions within feminist thinking about postpartum depression. One strand of research is dominated by a structural approach in which postpartum depression is seen as a normal and understandable response to the oppressive conditions of motherhood within Western societies, including the devaluation of motherhood and caregiving, the medicalization of childbirth, inadequate provision of childcare, limited parental leave, problematic re-entry into the labor market for mothers, and difficulties combining motherhood with paid work (e.g., Lewis & Nicolson, 1998; Nicolson, 1998; Oakley, 1980; Romito, 1990). This tradition of work has tended to emphasize the losses associated with motherhood, which are seen as responsible for postpartum depression. According to proponents of this theory, becoming a mother entails a loss of self, occupational status, identity, autonomy, physical integrity, time, sexuality, and male company. A mother also loses her established relationship with her partner because the division of domestic tasks tends to become more pronounced along gender lines after the birth of a child. Postpartum depression is therefore seen by some feminist thinkers as a form of bereavement—it is a grief response to these losses and, above all, to the mothers' lost identity. This feminist understanding reflects a broader strand of feminist thinking on motherhood that accentuates its negative side and focuses on the oppressive aspects of its role, including gender inequalities within the workplace and within society more generally.

A different strand of feminist research explores not only the structural and material conditions of women's lives but also cultural attitudes toward femininity, motherhood, and postpartum depression. These scholars argue that structural approaches are overly deterministic and neglect women's agency and the ways in which they actively negotiate the social and cultural contexts within which they live (Chrisler & Johnston-Robledo, 2002; Lafrance, 2009).

Berggren-Clive (1998), for example, argues that postpartum depression is directly related to the stresses inherent in the transition to motherhood and the intrapsychic conflicts imposed by the myths of motherhood. Stoppard (2000) espouses a "material-discursive" theory of depression that she applies to postpartum depression as well as depression occurring at other times in women's lives. Her theory has three key concepts: subjectivity, gender, and embodiment. She argues that postpartum depression can be understood as follows:

> A set of experiences arising at the intersection of women's lives and their bodies. These experiences are socially constructed in relation to cultural meanings of marriage and motherhood and socially produced by the practices of being a wife and a mother. These meanings and practices are both shaped and regulated by discourses of femininity, as well as by structural conditions characterizing the societal context within which women live their lives as wives and mothers. (Stoppard, 2000, p. 140)

Also located within this second strand of feminist research is the relational theory of postpartum depression put forward in this chapter in which individual beliefs, ideals, and aspirations; interpersonal dynamics; cultural scripts of motherhood; and material conditions of mothers' lives—all of which are gendered—intersect in complex ways, leading to a silencing of the self and resulting in depression.

Feminists also have different views on how women's feelings come to be labeled as postpartum depression. Some argue that women are unwilling and passive victims of psychiatric labeling and that labels are a form of medical and social control and should be abandoned (Nicolson, 1986; Oakley, 1986; Romito, 1989). Others observe that many women embrace the label "postpartum depression" and are active participants in the medicalization of their experiences (Mauthner, 2002; Stoppard, 2000; Taylor, 1996). These scholars have explored why women self-label, and some argue that women's appropriation of this psychiatric label can be viewed as a form of resistance to gender roles, norms, and expectations (Lafrance, 2009; Mauthner, 2002; Taylor, 1996).

While feminist work has done an excellent job of mapping the cultural and structural restrictions on women's lives, there is still a need to explore the different ways in which individual women deal with the ideologies, meanings, practices, and social conditions of motherhood. The tendency within some feminist work to assume that social structures and cultural discourses affect women in a uniform way, and to present women's responses to motherhood as homogenous and universally negative, leaves unanswered the question of why some women become depressed and others do not (Mauthner, 1999). In practice, women vary in their emotional reactions to motherhood. Moreover, individual women experience a range of conflicting feelings about being mothers. Feelings of frustration, distress, and depression can exist alongside feelings of joy, reward, and fulfilment. Motherhood may bring with it losses, changes, and constraints, but it also brings positive changes, not least a new child. As many writers have argued, motherhood is above all an experience of ambivalence (Hollway & Featherstone, 1997; O'Reilly, 2004; Parker, 1995; Pillemer & Luescher, 2004; Rich, 1986).

The Research Projects: Qualitative Studies of Postpartum Depression in the United Kingdom and the United States

Research Questions

This chapter draws on two qualitative studies of postpartum depression conducted in Britain and the United States during the 1990s in which I sought to use women's own narratives as the starting point for my own understanding of postpartum depression. I was interested in finding out what the mothers themselves had to say about motherhood, their emotional and psychological responses, their feelings of depression, and how these connected to other aspects of their lives—in particular, their interpersonal relationships and expectations of motherhood. How did they experience, view, and make sense of their depression? What did they think were the reasons for their depression? I was also interested in understanding the *processes* through which women become depressed. In particular, I felt that existing research, with its emphasis on identifying a fixed set of "variables" or "factors" that characterize a typical woman with postpartum depression, simplified and reduced women's experiences to a set of categories, and that in an effort to fit women into these "boxes," much of the complexity and diversity of their lives and experiences was overlooked. I wanted to understand the complex, changing, and variable circumstances, relationships, and social contexts within which the women became depressed and recovered from depression. I was also interested not only in those aspects of women's lives that they had in common but also, and perhaps more important, in the differences among them.

Methodological Features

In prioritizing women's own accounts of their experiences, my research follows in the footsteps of a long tradition of feminist research that seeks to use women's narratives of their experiences as starting points for understanding and theorizing their lives (Du Bois, 1983; Edwards, 1990; Gilligan, 1982; Henwood & Pidgeon, 1995). Qualitative and feminist scholars have also been influential in highlighting the critical role played by researchers in shaping the research process and product. Central to qualitative and feminist research are the notion of reflexivity and the call on researchers to reflect upon and understand their own personal, political, and intellectual biographies and the role these play in theorizing research data and creating knowledge (Harding, 1992; Maynard, 1994; Stanley & Wise, 1993). My research is rooted within a postfoundational tradition and commitment to reflexive practices and ways of coming to know and understand the social world (see Mauthner, 2002; Mauthner & Doucet, 1998, 2008). In practice, this entails identifying, articulating, and taking account of the range of personal, interpersonal, institutional, pragmatic, emotional, theoretical, epistemological, and ontological influences on our research, for example, during data analysis and the interpretation stages of research (see Mauthner & Doucet, 2003).

Theoretical Perspectives

My research has been informed by several bodies of scholarship, including feminist conceptualizations of motherhood and mental health; sociological accounts of parenthood; and relational theory, which has been described as "one of the most influential strands of feminist psychology today" (Wilkinson, 1996, p. 13). Theories of "normal" development implicitly or explicitly contain within them theories of "psychopathology." Within classical theories, psychological problems are generally seen to arise when a person fails to separate from others and become an independent and autonomous human being. Women with psychological problems have tended to be seen as too "dependent" and insufficiently individuated and autonomous (Jack, 1991). From a relational perspective, psychological problems result from a sense of "disconnection" from oneself, other people, and the surrounding world. The experience of disconnection occurs when, for different reasons, a person cannot participate in a responsive relationship, the surrounding relational context is unresponsive, or a person feels her or his experience does not resonate with cultural norms and expectations (Kaplan, 1984; Steiner-Adair, 1990; Stiver & Miller, 1988; Willard, 1988). For example, a recurring theme within relational writings concerns the sense of disconnection girls and women experience when they come under pressure to conform to cultural standards and norms of femininity and womanhood (Brown & Gilligan, 1992; Jack, 1991; Stiver & Miller, 1988; Taylor, Gilligan, & Sullivan, 1995).

A relational approach opened up a space for me to theorize postpartum depression as a relational problem involving individual, interpersonal, and cultural "disconnections." Depressed women cannot see their experiences of motherhood reflected in other mothers or in cultural representations of motherhood. Their sense of difference and deviance leaves them feeling cut off from the world and unable to confide their emotions in other people. This dual emphasis on the cultural context and personal relationships constitutes the core of this relational understanding of postpartum depression. Women's depression, I suggest, is intimately linked to cultural ideas of femininity and motherhood, to gendered divisions and expectations of parenthood, and to broader societal conditions that reinforce this gendered division of roles and responsibilities. I also argue that it is within the context of women's interpersonal relationships that these cultural and gendered norms and expectations take on meaning and define women's understandings of motherhood (Mauthner, 2002).

Research Methods

My British study included face-to-face interviews with 40 women, 18 of whom self-diagnosed as having had postpartum depression (15 of which had also been diagnosed as such by a health professional). In the United States, I met 17 women who had experienced postpartum depression (and been diagnosed as such by a health care professional). I heard their narratives within the context of a post-partum depression self-help group, which I attended regularly over 6 months, and conducted additional in-depth interviews with a few of them. This paper draws on the narratives of the British and North American women who experienced postpartum depression, all of whom were living with a male partner at the time I met them. These women were diverse in terms of their age; educational, socioeconomic, and ethnic backgrounds; nationality; religious beliefs; number of children; and employment status. I used a range of methods to analyze the narratives, including the "voice-centered relational method" and thematic ana-lyses (for more details see Mauthner, 2002; Mauthner & Doucet, 1998, 2003).

Women's Narratives of Postpartum Depression

Trying to Be the Perfect Mother: Conflicting Expectations and Experiences of Motherhood

One of the common threads to emerge from women's narratives in both Britain and the United States is their search for perfection. Women who had always set high standards for themselves said they continued to do so when they became mothers. They expected perfection from themselves and from their children. Their compulsion to be "perfect" mothers must be understood within the con-text of a culture that simultaneously idealizes and devalues motherhood. Motherhood is assumed to be women's destiny and primary identity. Getting it right, as a mother, defines a woman in a way that no other identity does. This idealization of motherhood, combined with the high value placed on paid work in societies such as Britain and the United States, compelled these women to justify devoting time to the unpaid work of motherhood. Being a mother was not enough—they had to be perfect and exceptional mothers.

Women had different ideas about what it meant to be a perfect mother. The first-time mothers, for example, had very romanticized images of motherhood.

They painted soft portraits of serene mothers gazing at peaceful, beautiful babies. They pictured themselves with calm babies who fed every four hours and slept much of the time. The women who became depressed after a second or third baby knew from experience the reality of motherhood. They realized that looking after a young baby is hard work, both physically and emotionally. Their difficulties arose because, for different reasons, they were struggling to cope with the arrival of a new child and yet had firm expectations that they should be able to cope. Frances, who became depressed after her third child was born, explains:

> I'm my own worse enemy in a way because . . . I'm quite independent . . . and . . . I just like to think and show people that I can cope, and perhaps I couldn't at the time . . . but I didn't want to show it to anyone. . . . I thought . . . 'I've gone through two other children,' and I wasn't going to let myself down by admitting the fact that I couldn't cope.

There were also differences among the first-time mothers' ideals. For some, breast-feeding was the essence of being a good mother; for others, it was having a "natural" labor free of drugs and interventions, bonding with their child from birth, giving up paid work to look after their children, or "doing it all" by working outside the home *and* caring for their families. Each woman's depression centered around the specific aspects of motherhood that were most important to her and each mother was left feeling inadequate when she failed to live up to her ideal. Celia, mother of two daughters, explains:

> One of the reasons I felt so down was because I had to admit to myself that I was not an earth mother, and no matter how much I wanted to be the sort of parent that stayed at home, perhaps I had to accept the fact that I would be happier going to work. . . . I think it was a sort of conflict really. . . . I wanted to feel very content at home but I couldn't . . . and my feeling deep down was that I was failing as a mother if I couldn't cope with being at home.

Postpartum depression, I suggest, is neither about women's ideals and experiences of motherhood nor about the actual choices and decisions they make. Rather, it arises out of the discrepancy they experience between the mother they want to be and the mother they feel they are. It is a response to the distress created when there is an incongruity between expectations and realities of motherhood, when what women think they *should* feel is different from the reality (see also Beck, 2002; Berggren-Clive, 1998; Morgan et al., 1997; Nahas et al., 1999). Postpartum depression occurs when mothers cannot live up to the culturally derived but unrealistic standards they set for themselves, and rather than let go of their standards, they try to change themselves to fit their ideals.

The Moral Dimension of Postpartum Depression

During the depression, then, the women found it difficult to let go of their images and ideals of motherhood. They tried to live up to these because, in their eyes, failure to do so meant that they were "bad" mothers. Indeed, throughout their depression they criticized themselves relentlessly on moral grounds. As Sonya explains:

> I used to think 'The kitchen floor is dirty, therefore I'm a terrible person'... you know, you're *crucifying* yourself all the time..... When you're in the illness, everything is the end of the world – it's black and white, good and bad. 'You were bad, you didn't do the cooking right, you didn't socialise enough, you didn't make enough witty, sparkling conversation'.... As soon as someone's gone, you're saying to yourself, 'You're bad, you're bad, you didn't do this, you didn't do that.'

Mothers (rather than fathers) tend to be held socially responsible for any faults or failings in the home or in children, and this weighed heavily on these women and operated as a powerful source of pressure to conform to cultural norms and standards. To some extent, this pressure and accompanying feelings of guilt are a universal feature of motherhood within Western societies. Feelings of guilt are exacerbated, however, when women are depressed, making it difficult for them to see themselves as anything but bad mothers.

Other scholars have similarly noted the moral and condemnatory dimension of depression. Most notably, in an article on depression, or what he termed "melancholia," Freud (1995, p. 157) noted that "dissatisfaction with the self on moral grounds is far the most outstanding feature." More recently, in her studies of depression, Jack (1991) has detected the presence of an internalized moral voice of the culture within women's accounts. She termed the voice the "Over-Eye" because of its surveillant, vigilant, and moral quality. The Over-Eye, she notes, carries a patriarchal flavor both in its collective viewpoint about what is good and right for a woman and in its willingness to condemn her feelings when they depart from what is expected, as well as from cultural standards, norms, and imperatives.

Jack also elucidates an inner division and two-voice dialogue in women's narratives of depression between this moral voice and "the voice of the 'I'" that speaks from experience and knows from observation. Depression, she notes, is associated with an inability to believe and legitimate the voice of the "I" and act on its values. Jack's analysis echoes the inner dialogue and struggle that the women with postpartum depression spoke of. While the mothers were trying to conform to cultural standards and expectations of motherhood, they were simultaneously questioning and resisting the very norms they were struggling to fulfill. Sandra's account of her difficulties combining paid work with motherhood provides a good illustration.

Four months after her daughter's birth, Sandra returned to her full-time job as a district nurse against her wishes, under her husband's pressure and for financial reasons. Despite returning to work, she still felt she should be like the "mums [who] stayed at home," who "bake and clean," and "cooked and ironed and looked after the home." She attempted to fulfill the demands of being a full-time mother while being in full-time employment. Although a part of her believed she should be able to "achieve everything," another part, based on her actual mothering experiences, told her that "to a degree *it's impossible* practically to do that." "I'd set myself these goals which were *impossible*," she continues. "I couldn't work out how you were supposed to deal with the baby and do everything else as well, which you can't." She says:

> It tends to be the mothers who are at home that seem to go everywhere with the kids, go swimming, go to ballet classes, do this, do that . . . and that's what I feel I should be doing. I should be sewing and baking and cooking and going swimming with her and I mean . . . that's cloud cuckoo land. I'm not very good at sewing anyway. I don't particularly like baking.

In attempting to resolve this conflict with herself as well as with her husband, Sandra felt she had no other choice but to "make myself" carry on and do everything, even though she realized that this was contributing to her depression:

> I think I'd almost got into the way of thinking, 'Well yes, I ought to be better, I ought to try harder'. . . which is what happened when I got depressed. . . . I felt so guilty. . . . I felt I should have done better and it was all my fault.

Although Sandra questioned her culturally derived norms and standards for herself, she felt compelled to fulfill them in part because they were reinforced by her husband's expectations and by her perceptions of other mothers.

Cultural Narratives of Motherhood

As we can see from Sandra's narrative, the moral standards the mothers used to judge their behavior and feelings came from at least two sources: the cultural context in which they lived and their interpersonal relationships. The cultural context is one in which strong normative prescriptions about "the right way" to be a "good" mother still prevail (Choi, Henshaw, Baker, & Tree, 2005; Warner, 2005), while at the same time mothers are told that there is no *one* right way to mother a child (Marshall, 1991; Phoenix & Woollett, 1991). What characterized the mothers I spoke to, however, was that they picked up on the idea that there is only one right way to be a good mother and constructed notions of "good" mothering in highly rigid and monolithic ways. They attempted to conform to these norms for fear of being seen to be lacking and inadequate. They feared that by expressing their difficulties and negative or ambivalent emotions, they would be judged "bad" mothers, have their children taken away, and possibly be institutionalized.

The differing meanings of motherhood for individual women reflect the variation, and sometimes contradiction, in cultural narratives of motherhood. This is particularly apparent in the dilemma many women face about whether and how to combine motherhood with paid employment (Hays,

1996). Anglo-American societies are becoming increasingly work centered and are governed by a culture of self. David Karp calls the United States in particular a "me, myself, and I" society, arguing that we are living in "the age or narcissism" (Karp, 1996, p. 175). This self-interested, competitive world places little value on care work and can leave women (and men) feeling devalued in their roles as caregivers. Limited family-friendly and parental leave policies, especially in the United States, reinforce this devaluation of parenting work. Yet society still portrays motherhood as the epitome of womanhood, as something to which all women should aspire (Douglas & Michaels, 2004). Child care is seen as primarily women's responsibility, and any psychological, emotional, or social problems in a child are invariably blamed on inadequate mothering. Restricted family and structural supports, such as day care and maternity benefits in particular, reinforce cultural notions of the importance of full-time motherhood. These conflicting messages can leave women feeling confused about how best to fulfill their parental responsibilities. These mixed messages might be seen as offering men and women a variety of parenting models rather than a single right way to be a parent. Indeed, as Marshall (1991) comments, there is a growing discourse of flexibility in child care and parenting. Child care manuals suggest that "women can mother in many varied and satisfactory ways and that there is not *one* right way within the context of a loving and caring relationship" (Marshall, 1991, p. 73). Each mother knows what is best for her and her child.

The women I spoke to, however, drew selectively on cultural models. They did not embrace the notion that different women find their own individual, but equally valid, ways of mothering. Instead, they elaborated rigid and prescriptive ideals. This was partly because, as Marshall points out, alongside an explicit endorsement of flexibility lies an implicit right way of doing things, a set of moral standards to be followed rigidly. Pregnancy, childbirth, and motherhood are areas of women's lives that have traditionally been dominated by the views of a host of so-called experts—so much so that women themselves find it difficult to develop their own views and use these as a guide to parenting. Indeed, women who have experienced postpartum depression describe losing their own voices to those of others—health care professionals, family members, and friends—telling them how they should feel, think, and behave as mothers. Although they question these voices because they seem out of tune with the day-to-day reality of their lives as mothers, they nevertheless feel under pressure and compelled to conform to them.

The Interpersonal Context

The ways in which individual mothers interpreted, negotiated, and experienced social norms of motherhood depended in part on their interpersonal relationships, for these were sites where cultural prescriptions could be reinforced in overt and covert ways. Their relationships with other mothers with young children, for example, were particularly important because cultural notions of motherhood took on meaning and became concrete for the women through a process of "checking out" their feelings and comparing their experiences with those of other mothers (Mauthner, 1995).

Relationships with partners, family, friends, and health professionals were equally important. Some women felt that their male partners reinforced their sense of failure and inadequacy because they felt they received little emotional or practical support, and felt their partners silenced and rejected them when they attempted to disclose their feelings. Those who described very positive relationships with partners who were described as supportive, helpful, and understanding nevertheless found it difficult to talk about their feelings because they felt this was a sign of weakness and an admission of failure as a mother. Celia explains:

> My husband is very supportive... but on the whole, I don't think he ever realised my true feelings about it all, because I was so good at creating this impression of coping, and I didn't really express how I really felt.

Irrespective of the quality of her relationship with her husband, each mother described withdrawing from him as she did from other people (see also Everingham et al., 2006). They felt a profound sense of isolation from others and alienation from themselves. As Jack has described it, they "silenced the self" (1991) and felt unable and unwilling to disclose their feelings to partners, relatives, friends, or health professionals. This social withdrawal and isolation characterized all of their experiences of postpartum depression (Mauthner, 1998) and has been found repeatedly in studies of women experiencing depression following childbirth in diverse cultural settings (Berggren-Clive, 1998; Brown & Lumley, 2000; Chan & Levy, 2004; Chan, Levy, Chung, & Lee, 2002; Edge et al., 2004; Edhborg, Friberg, Lundh, & Widstrom, 2005; McIntosh, 1993; Morgan et al., 1997; Nahas et al., 1999; Nahas & Amashah, 1999; Rodrigues et al., 2003; Small, Johnston, & Orr, 1997; Tammentie, Paavilainen, Astedt-Kurki, & Tarkka, 2004; Thome, 2003; Whitton, Warner, & Appleby, 1996; Wood et al., 1997).

Journeys to Recovery

Women's journeys to recovery involved some kind of resolution or acceptance of their difficulties and internal conflicts, in whichever way individual mothers felt was best for them, their children, and their families (see also Berggren-Clive, 1998). It was not simply that they embraced or rejected cultural ideas and different mothers resolved the conflict in different ways. In all cases recovery was marked by their ability to accept themselves and their children for whom they were (see also Breen, 1975; Lafrance, 2009; Willard, 1988). They were able to let go of their standards, come to terms with what they saw as their "imperfections," abandon their condemnatory attitude toward themselves, and acknowledge their strengths and positive characteristics. Louise and Dona explain:

> I remember just crying my eyes out, 'cos I realised I loved Seamus so much . . . even though he'd upset me. And . . . from that day on, I felt I just started to accept the way he was, rather than fighting against it all the time – saying 'You shouldn't be like this, you should be quiet, you shouldn't be crying.' I just started, for some reason, accepting the way he was and saying, well, he was just Seamus, that's just the way he was and I was just gonna make the best of it. And I feel that by accepting it, that did help me to sort of overcome the feelings that I got about him.

> I think probably for me the biggest thing I've changed was just that it's okay to feel certain things. And I think, again, a lot of this was just the way I was brought up and the way that I've learned to cope is that everything that ever concerned me or that I was scared, frightened, or whatever about, stayed inside, so that now what I'm able to do is kind of say, 'Okay, this is bothering me.'

Implications for the Prevention and Treatment of Postpartum Depression

Many of the women I spoke to were receiving readily available pharmacological treatments for their depression. Indeed, within both the United States and the United Kingdom, antidepressants tend to be the treatment of preference for postpartum depression (Dennis & Chung-Lee, 2006; Logsdon, Wisner, Hanusa, & Phillips, 2003; Wisner et al., 1997, 2002). Yet the efficacy and safety of such treatments has not been clearly established (Boath & Henshaw, 2001; Dennis & Stewart, 2004). Even the psychiatric profession is becoming increasingly concerned about the overprescription of drugs to pregnant and breast-feeding women, the long-term effects of such drugs on children, and the fact that many health plans in the United States continue to pay for medication but not psychotherapy (Boath & Henshaw, 2001).

Among the women I interviewed, "talking therapies" were by far the preferred treatment option (see also Oates et al., 2004; Small et al., 1994). Many were seeking these alternative forms of treatment but found them difficult to locate, access, or afford. Those that were successful found this type of support through a health professional or therapist who had some understanding or knowledge of postpartum depression. Indeed, a number of studies have shown that various types of talking treatments with health visitors, child health clinic nurses, and individual or group psychotherapists are effective in reducing levels of depression and increasing rates of recovery (Cooper & Murray, 1997; Gerrard et al., 1993; Holden, Sagovsky, & Cox, 1989; Morris, 1987; O'Hara, 2000; Seeley, Murray, & Cooper, 1996; Wickberg & Hwang, 1996).

For many of the women I spoke to, it was through talking to another mother, finding that their experiences resonated with other women, and realizing that they were not alone in their feelings that the women began to recover (see also Berggren-Clive, 1998; McIntosh, 1993; Tammentie et al., 2004; Ugarriza, 2004), partly because these relationships allowed them to openly voice and question the very ideals of motherhood they had struggled to fulfill (Mauthner, 1995, 2002). Some women found it particularly helpful to talk to other mothers within the context of a postpartum depression support group. The group gave them permission to discuss feelings of ambivalence toward mother-hood, the *realities* of day-to-day life with small children, the gendered nature of cultural expectations of parenthood, and the importance of setting realistic and "good enough" mothering ideals. Indeed, other studies have similarly found that attending a support group is a common treatment preference (Beck, 1992, 1993; Berggren-Clive, 1998; Holopainen, 2002; Nahas et al., 1999; Templeton, Velleman, Persaud, & Milner, 2003; Ugarriza, 2004). Studies suggest that these groups can significantly improve women's mood and mental health (Eastwood, 1995; Foyster, 1995; Jones, Watts, & Romain, 1995; May, 1995) by providing mothers with a network of "like women," a safe environment to express their feelings without fear of condemnation, and an opportunity to give and receive advice. In their Australian study, Morgan and colleagues (1997) found significant improvements in women's levels of depression when they attended weekly sessions of a postpartum depression group. In a Canadian study, Dennis (2003) found that telephone-based peer support among mothers identified as high risk for postpartum depression was effective in decreasing depressive symptomatology among new mothers. One of the key implications highlighted by my research on both sides of the Atlantic and supported by these other studies is the importance of providing nonjudgmental forums in which women can *talk* about their feelings of motherhood and depression to sympa-thetic others. Prenatal and postnatal support groups in particular can potentially play a vital preventive role by providing access both to support networks with other women and to well-informed health professionals who can offer support themselves or refer women to other relevant health care providers (see Mauthner, 2002).

My studies also highlight interesting cultural differences between the British and North American women's perceptions of the causes and appropriate treat-ment of postpartum depression. Although both groups expressed confusion and ambivalence about the biochemical origins of their feelings, the benefits of medication, and the value of a medical approach to postpartum depression more generally, overall the North American women were much more committed to a medical explanation of their distress. Although they talked about difficulties in their relationships and oppressive cultural expectations of mothers and gen-erally pointed to other problems in their lives at the time of their depression, most were convinced that the underlying cause of their depression was hormonal. They were also more likely to advocate pharmacological solutions, which they saw as playing an important role alongside talking treatments. Indeed, many more American than British women were on medication and believed in its efficacy; they were also on a greater number of different types of medication and for longer periods of time. These differences raise interesting questions concerning the extent to which emotional problems are medicalized within different cultures. This theme was highlighted in the transcultural study of postpartum depression discussed earlier, where researchers found that of the 11 countries included in the research, the United States was the only one where women identified antidepressants as a suitable remedy for postpartum depression. The other countries placed greater treatment preference on having someone to talk to and on the importance of acceptance, understanding, and social support from within family and social networks (Oates et al., 2004). Interestingly, health professionals across all the centers and countries included in the study also recognized the importance of, and increased need for, talking therapies for women with postpartum depression.

References

Affonso, D. D., De, A. K., Horowitz, J. A. & Mayberry, L. J. (2000). An international study exploring levels of postpartum depression symptomatology. *Journal of Psychosomatic Research, 49*, 207–216.

Asten, P., Marks, M. N., Oates, M. R., & the TCS-PND Group. (2004). Aims, measures, study sites and participant samples of the Transcultural Study of Postnatal Depression. *British Journal of Psychiatry, 184*(suppl. 46), s3–s9.

Beck, C. T. (1992). The lived experience of postpartum depression: A phenomenological study. *Nursing Research, 41*, 166–170.

Beck, C. T. (1993). Teetering on the edge: A substantive theory of postpartum depression. *Nursing Research, 42*, 42–48.

Beck, C. T. (2002). Postpartum depression: A metasynthesis. *Qualitative Health Research, 12*, 453–472.

Berggren-Clive, K. (1998). Out of the darkness and into the light: Women's experiences with depression after childbirth. *Canadian Journal of Community Mental Health, 17*, 103–120.

Boath, E., & Henshaw, C. (2001). The treatment of postnatal depression: A comprehensive literature review. *Journal of Reproductive and Infant Psychology, 19*, 215.

Boyce, P. (1994). Personality dysfunction, marital problems and postpartum depression. In J. Cox & J. Holden (Eds.), *Perinatal psychiatry: Use and misuse of the Edinburgh Postnatal Depression Scale* (pp. 82–102). London: Gaskell.

Boyce, P., & Hickey, A. (2005). Psychosocial risk factors to major depression after childbirth. *Social Psychiatry & Psychiatric Epidemiology, 40*, 605–612.

Breen, D. (1975). *The birth of a first child.* London: Tavistock.

Brown L. M., & Gilligan, C. (1992). *Meeting at the crossroads: Women's psychology and girls' development.* Cambridge, MA: Harvard University Press.

Brown, S., & Lumley, J. (2000). Physical health problems after childbirth and maternal depression at six to seven months postpartum. *BJOG: An International Journal of Obstetrics & Gynaecology, 107*, 1194–1201.

Buston, K., Parry-Jones, W., Livingston, M., Bogan, A., & Wood, S. (1998). Qualitative research. *British Journal of Psychiatry, 172*, 197–199.

Chaaya, M., Campbell, O. M. R., El Kak, F., Shaar, D., Harb, H., & Kaddour, A. (2002). Postpartum depression: Prevalence and determinants in Lebanon. *Archives of Women's Mental Health, 5*, 65–72.

Chan, S., & Levy, V. (2004). Postnatal depression: A qualitative study of the experiences of a group of Hong Kong Chinese women. *Journal of Clinical Nursing, 13*, 120–123.

Chan, S. W., Levy, V., Chung, T. K., & Lee, D. (2002). A qualitative study of the experiences of a group of Hong Kong Chinese women diagnosed with postnatal depression. *Journal of Advanced Nursing, 39*, 571–579.

Choi, P., Henshaw, C., Baker, S., & Tree, J. (2005). Supermum, superwife, supereverything: Performing femininity in the transition to motherhood. *Journal of Reproductive and Infant Psychology, 23*, 167–180.

Chrisler, J. C., & Johnston-Robledo, I. (2002). Raging hormones? Feminist perspectives on premenstrual syndrome and postpartum depression. In M. B. Ballou & L. S. Brown (Eds.), *Rethinking mental health and disorder: Feminist perspectives* (pp. 174–197). New York: Guilford Press.

Cooper, P. J., Campbell, E. A., Day, A., Kennerley, H., & Bond, A. (1988). Non-psychotic psychiatric disorder after childbirth. A prospective study of prevalence, incidence, course and nature. *British Journal of Psychiatry, 152*, 799–806.

Cooper, P. J., & Murray, L. (1997). The impact of psychological treatments of postnatal depression on maternal mood and infant development. In L. Murray & P. J. Cooper (Eds.), *Postpartum depression and child development* (pp. 201–220). London: Guilford Press.

Cooper, P. J., & Murray, L. (1998). Postpartum depression. *British Medical Journal, 316*, 1884–1886.

Cox, J., & Holden, J. (Eds.). (1994). *Perinatal psychiatry: Use and misuse of the Edinburgh Postnatal Depression Scale.* London: Gaskell.

Cox, J. L., Holden, J. M., & Sagovsky, R. (1987). Detection of postnatal depression: Development of the 10-item Edinburgh Postnatal Depression Scale. *British Journal of Psychiatry, 150*, 782–786.

Dalton, K. (1971). Prospective study into puerperal depression. *British Journal of Psychiatry, 118*, 689–692.

Dalton, K. (1989). *Depression after childbirth: How to recognize and treat postnatal depression.* Oxford: Oxford University Press.

Dennis, C. L. (2003). The effect of peer support on postpartum depression: A pilot randomized controlled trial. *Canadian Journal of Psychiatry, 48*, 115–124.

Dennis, C. L., & Chung-Lee, L. (2006). Barriers and maternal treatment preferences: A qualitative systematic review. *Birth, 33*, 323–331.

Dennis, C. L., & Stewart, D. E. (2004). Treatment of postpartum depression, part 1: A critical review of biological interventions. *Journal of Clinical Psychiatry, 65*, 1242–1251.

Douglas, S., & Michaels, M. (2004). *The mommy myth: The idealization of motherhood and how it has undermined women.* New York: Free Press.

Du Bois, B. (1983). Passionate scholarship: Notes on values, knowing and method in feminist social science. In G. Bowles & R. D. Klein (Eds.), *Theories of women's Studies*. London: Routledge and Kegan Paul.

Eastwood, P. (1995). Promoting peer group support with postnatally depressed women. *Health Visitor, 68*, 148–150.

Edge, D., Baker, D., & Rogers, A. (2004). Perinatal depression among black Caribbean women. *Health and Social Care in the Community, 12*, 430–438.

Edhborg, M., Friberg, M., Lundh, W., & Widstrom, A. M. (2005). "Struggling with life:" Narratives from women with signs of postpartum depression. *Scandinavian Journal of Public Health, 33*, 261–267.

Edwards, R. (1990). Connecting method & epistemology: A white woman interviewing black women. *Women's Studies International Forum, 13*, 77–90.

Entwistle, V. A., Renfrew, M. J., Yearly, S., Forrester, J., & Lamont, T. (1998). Lay perspectives: Advantages for health research. *British Medical Journal, 316*, 463–466.

Everingham, C. R., Heading, G., & Connor, L. (2006). Couples' experiences of postnatal depression: A framing analysis of cultural identity, gender and communication. *Social Science & Medicine, 62*, 1745–1756.

Foyster, L. (1995). Supporting mothers: An inter-disciplinary approach. *Health Visitor, 68*, 151–152.

Freud, S. (1995). Mourning and melancholia. In E. Jones (Ed.), *Collected papers, volume IV: Papers on metapsychology. Papers on applied psycho-analysis*. London: Hogarth Press.

Gerrard, J., Holden, J. M., Elliott, S. A., McKenzie, P., McKenzie, J., & Cox, J. L. (1993). A trainer's perspective of an innovative programme teaching health visitors about the detection, treatment and prevention of postnatal depression. *Journal of Advanced Nursing, 18*, 1825–1832.

Gilligan, C. (1982). *In a different voice: Psychological theory and women's development*. Cambridge, MA: Harvard University Press.

Goldbort, J. (2006). Transcultural analysis of postpartum depression. *American Journal of Maternal Child Nursing, 31*, 121–126.

Green, J. M. (1990). Who is unhappy after childbirth? Antenatal and intrapartum correlates from a prospective study. *Journal of Reproductive and Infant Psychology, 16*, 175–183.

Harding, S. (1992). *Whose science? Whose knowledge?* Milton Keynes, UK: Open University Press.

Hays, S. (1996). *The cultural contradictions of motherhood*. New Haven, CT: Yale University Press.

Hendrick, V., Altschuler, L. L., & Suri, R. (1998). Hormonal changes in the postpartum and implications for postpartum depression. *Psychosomatics, 39*, 93–101.

Henwood, K., & Pidgeon, N. (1995). Remaking the link: Qualitative research and feminist standpoint theory. *Feminism and Psychology, 5*, 7–30.

Holden, J. M., Sagovsky, R., & Cox, J. L. (1989). Counselling in a general practice setting: Controlled study of health visitor intervention in treatment of postnatal depression. *British Medical Journal, 298*, 223–226.

Hollway, W., & Featherstone, B. (1997). *Mothering and ambivalence*. London, New York: Routledge.

Holopainen, D. (2002). The experience of seeking help for postnatal depression. *Australian Journal of Advanced Nursing, 19*, 39–44.

Huang, Y. C., & Mathers, N. (2001). Postnatal depression – biological or cultural? A comparative study of postnatal women in the UK and Taiwan. *Journal of Advanced Nursing, 33*, 279–287.

Inandi, T., Elci, O. M., Ozturk, A., Egri, M., Polat, A., & Sahin, T. K. (2002). Risk factors for depression in the postnatal first year, in Eastern Turkey. *International Journal of Epidemiology, 31*, 1201–1207.

Jack, D. C. (1991). *Silencing the self: Women and depression.* Cambridge, MA: Harvard University Press.

Jack, D. C. (1999). Silencing the self: Inner dialogues and outer realities. In T. E. Joiner & J. C. Coyne (Eds.), *The interactional nature of depression: Advances in interpersonal approaches* (pp. 221–246). Washington, DC: American Psychological Association.

Jadresic, E., Araya, R., & Jara, C. (1995). Validation of the Edinburgh Postnatal Depression Scale (EPDS) in Chilean postpartum women. *Journal of Psychosomatic Obstetrics and Gynecology, 16*, 187–191.

Jones, A., Watts, T., & Romain, S. (1995). Postnatal depression: Facilitating peer group support. *Health Visitor, 68*, 153.

Kaplan, A. G. (1984). *The 'self-in-relation': implications for depression in women. Work in progress, No. 14.* Wellesley, MA: Stone Center Working Paper Series.

Karp, D. A. (1996). *Speaking of sadness: Depression, disconnection, and the meanings of illness.* New York, Oxford: Oxford University Press.

Kendell, R. E. (1985). Emotional and physical factors in the genesis of puerperal mental disorders. *Journal of Psychosomatic Research, 29*, 3–11.

Kim, J., & Buist, A. (2005). Postnatal depression: A Korean perspective. *Australasian Psychiatry, 13*, 68–71.

Lafrance, M. N. (2009). *Women and depression.* London, New York: Routledge.

Lee, C. (1997). Social context, depression, and the transition to motherhood. *British Journal of Health Psychology, 2*, 93–108.

Lee, D. T., Yip, S. K., Chiu, H. F., Leung, T. Y., Chan, K. P., Chau, I. O., et al. (1998). Detecting postnatal depression in Chinese women: Validation of the Chinese version of the Edinburgh Postnatal Depression Scale. *British Journal of Psychiatry, 172*, 433–437.

Lewis, S. E., & Nicolson, P. (1998). Talking about early motherhood: recognizing loss and reconstructing depression. *Journal of Reproductive and Infant Psychology, 16*, 177–197.

Littlewood, J., & McHugh, N. (2003). *Maternal distress and postnatal depression: The myth of Madonna.* London: Macmillan.

Llewellyn, A. M., Stowe, Z. N., & Nemeroff, C. B. (1997). Depression during pregnancy and the puerperium. *Journal of Clinical Psychiatry, 58*, 26–32.

Logsdon, M. C., Wisner, K., Hanusa, B. H., & Phillips, A. (2003). Role functioning and symptom remission in women with postpartum depression after antidepressant treatment. *Archives of Psychiatric Nursing, 17*, 276–283.

Marshall, H. (1991). The social construction of motherhood: An analysis of childcare and parenting manuals. In A. Phoenix, A. Woollett, and E. Lloyd (Eds.), *Motherhood: Meanings, practices and ideologies* (pp. 66–85). London: Sage.

Mauthner, N. S. (1995). Postnatal depression: The significance of social contacts between mothers. *Women's Studies International Forum, 18*, 311–323.

Mauthner, N. S. (1998). Re-assessing the importance and role of the marital relationship in postnatal depression: Methodological and theoretical implications. *Journal of Reproductive and Infant Psychology, 16*, 157–175.

Mauthner, N. S. (1999). 'Feeling low and feeling really bad about feeling low': Women's experiences of motherhood and postpartum depression. *Canadian Psychology, 40*, 143–161.

Mauthner, N. S. (2002). *The darkest days of my life: Stories of postpartum depression.* Cambridge, MA: Harvard University Press.

Mauthner, N., & Doucet, A. (2003). Reflexive accounts and accounts of reflexivity in qualitative data analysis. *Sociology, 37*, 413–431.

Mauthner, N. S., & Doucet, A. (1998). Reflections on a voice-centred relational method: Analysing maternal and domestic voices. In J. Ribbens & R. Edwards (Eds.), *Feminist dilemmas in qualitative research: Public knowledge and private lives* (pp. 119–146). London: Sage.

Mauthner, N. S., & Doucet, A. (2008). 'Knowledge once divided can be hard to put together again': an epistemological critique of collaborative and team-based research practices. *Sociology, 42*, 955–969.

May, A. (1995). A multidisciplinary approach to postnatal depression. *Health Visitor, 68*, 146–147.

Maynard, M. (1994). Methods, practice and epistemology. In M. Maynard & J. Purvis (Eds.), *Researching women's lives from a feminist perspective* (pp. 10–26). London: Taylor and Francis.

Mazhari, S., & Nakhaee, N. (2007). Validation of the Edinburgh Postnatal Scale in an Iranian sample. *Archives of Women's Mental Health, 10*, 293–297.

McIntosh, J. (1993). Postpartum depression: Women's help-seeking behaviour and perceptions of cause. *Journal of Advanced Nursing, 18*, 178–184.

Morgan, M., Matthey, S., Barnett, B., & Richardson, C. (1997). A group programme for postnatally distressed women and their partners. *Journal of Advanced Nursing, 26*, 913–920.

Morris, J. B. (1987). Group psychotherapy for prolonged postnatal depression. *British Journal of Medical Psychology, 60*, 279–281.

Nahas, V., & Amasheh, N. (1999). Culture care meanings and experiences of postpartum depression among Jordanian Australian women: A transcultural study. *Journal of Transcultural Nursing, 10*, 37–45.

Nahas, V., Hillege, S., & Amasheh, N. (1999). Postpartum depression: The lived experiences of Middle Eastern migrant women in Australia. *Journal of Nurse-Midwifery, 44*, 65–74.

Nicolson, P. (1986). Developing a feminist approach to depression following childbirth. In S. Wilkinson (Ed.), *Feminist social psychology: Developing theory and practice.* Milton Keynes, UK: Open University Press.

Nicolson, P. (1998). *Post-natal depression: Psychology, science and the transition to motherhood.* London: Routledge.

Oakley, A. (1980). *Women confined: Towards a sociology of childbirth.* Oxford: Martin Robertson.

Oakley, A. (1986). *Telling the truth about Jerusalem*. Oxford: Blackwell.

Oates, M. R., Cox, J. L., Neema, S., Asten, P., Glangeaud-Freudenthal, N., & Figueiredo, B. (2004). Postnatal depression across countries and cultures: A qualitative study. *British Journal of Psychiatry, 184* (Suppl. 46), s10–16.

O'Hara, M. (1997). The nature of postpartum depressive disorders. In L. Murray & P. J. Cooper (Eds.), *Postpartum depression and child development* (pp. 3–31). London: Guilford Press.

O'Hara, M. (2000). *Long-term outcome of interpersonal psychotherapy for postpartum depression*. Proceedings of the Marce Society Biennial Conference 2000, Manchester, UK.

O'Hara, M. W., Schlechte, J. A., Lewis, D. A., & Varner, M. W. (1991). Controlled prospective study of postpartum mood disorders: psychological, environmental, and hormonal variables. *Journal of Abnormal Psychology, 100,* 63–73.

O'Hara, M. W., & Swain, O. M. (1996). Rates and risk of postpartum depression a meta-analysis. *International Review of Psychiatry, 8,* 37–54.

O'Hara, M. W., & Zekoski, E. M. (1998). Postpartum depression: A comprehensive review. In R. Kumar & I. F. Bockington (Eds.), *Motherhood and mental illness 2: Causes and consequences* (pp. 17–63). London: Wright.

O'Reilly, A. (Ed.). (2004). *From motherhood to mothering*. Albany, NY: State University of New York Press.

Parker, R. (1995). *Torn in two: The experience of maternal ambivalence*. London: Virago.

Phoenix, A., & Woollett, A. (1991). Motherhood: Social construction, politics and psychology. In A. Phoenix, A. Woollett, & E. Lloyd (Eds.), *Motherhood: Meanings, practices and ideologies* (pp. 13–27). London: Sage.

Pillemer, K., & Luescher, K. (Eds.). (2004). *Intergenerational ambivalences: New perspectives on parent-child relations in later life. Contemporary perspectives in family research volume 4*. Oxford: Elsevier.

Rich, A. (1986). *Of woman born: Motherhood as experience and institution*. London: Virago.

Rodrigues, M., Patel, V., Jaswal, S., & Souza, N. D. (2003). Listening to mothers: Qualitative studies on motherhood and depression from Goa, India. *Social Science and Medicine, 57,* 1797–1806.

Romito, P. (1989). Unhappiness after childbirth. In I. Chalmers, M. Enkin, & M. J. N. C. Keirse (Eds.), *Effective care in pregnancy and childbirth* (Vol. 2, pp. 221–227). Oxford: Oxford University Press.

Romito, P. (1990). *La naissance du premier enfant: Etude psycho-sociale de L'experience de la maternite et de la depression postpartum*. Lausanne, Switzerland: Delachaux and Niestle.

Seeley, S., Murray, L., & Cooper, P. J. (1996). The outcome for mothers and babies of health visitor intervention. *Health Visitor, 69,* 135–138.

Small, R., Brown, S., Lumley, J., & Astbury, J. (1994). Missing voices: What women say and do about depression after childbirth. *Journal of Reproductive and Infant Psychology, 12,* 89–103.

Small, R., Johnston, V., & Orr, A. (1997). Depression after childbirth: The views of medical students and women compared. *Birth, 24,* 109–115.

Stanley, L., & Wise, S. (1993). *Breaking out again: Feminist consciousness and feminist research*. London: Routledge and Kegan Paul.

Stein, G. (1982). The maternity blues. In I. F. Brockington & R. Kumar (Eds.), *Motherhood and mental illness* (pp. 119–150). London: Academic Press.

Steiner-Adair, C. (1990). The body politic. In C. Gilligan, N. P. Lyons, & T. J. Hanmer (Eds.), *Making connections: The relational worlds of adolescent girls at Emma Willard School* (pp. 162–182). Cambridge, MA: Harvard University Press.

Stern, G., & Kruckman, L. (1983). Multidisciplinary perspectives on postpartum depression: An anthropological critique. *Social Science and Medicine, 17*, 1027–1041.

Stewart, S., & Jambunathan, J. (1996). Hmong women and postpartum depression. *Health Care for Women International, 17*, 319–330.

Stiver, I. P., & Miller, J. B. (1988). *From depression to sadness in women's psychotherapy. Work in progress, No. 36*. Wellesley, MA: Stone Center Working Paper Series.

Stoppard, J. (1997). Women's bodies, women's lives and depression: Toward a reconciliation of material and discursive accounts. In J. M. Ushher (Ed.), *Body talk: The material and discursive regulation of sexuality, madness and reproduction*. London: Routledge.

Stoppard, J. (1998). Dis-ordering depression in women: Toward a materialist-discursive account. *Theory and Psychology, 8*, 79–99.

Stoppard, J. (2000). *Understanding depression: Feminist constructionist approaches*. London, New York: Routledge.

Stowe, Z. N., & Nemeroff, C. B. (1995). Women at risk of postpartum-onset major depression. *American Journal of Obstetrics and Gynecology, 173*, 639–645.

Swendsen, J. D., & Mazure, C. M. (2000). Life stress as a risk factor for postpartum depression: Current research and methodological issues. *Clinical Psychology: Science and Practice, 7*, 17–31.

Tammentie, T., Paavilainen, E., Astedt-Kurki, P., & Tarkka, M. T. (2004). Family dynamics of postnatally depressed mothers: Discrepancy between expectations and reality. *Journal of Clinical Nursing, 13*, 65–74.

Taylor, J. M., Gilligan, C., & Sullivan, A. (1995). *Between voice and silence: Women and girls, race and relationships*. Cambridge, MA: Harvard University Press.

Taylor, V. (1996). *Rock-a-by baby: Feminism, self-help, and postpartum depression*. New York, London: Routledge.

Templeton, L., Velleman, R., Persaud, A., & Milner, P. (2003). The experiences of postnatal depression in women from black and minority ethnic communities in Wiltshire, UK. *Ethnicity & Health, 8*, 207–221.

Thome, M. (2003). Severe postpartum distress in Icelandic mothers with difficult infants: A follow-up study on their health care. *Scandinavian Journal of Caring Sciences, 17*, 104–112.

Ugarriza, D. N. (2004). Group therapy and its barriers for women suffering from postpartum depression. *Archives of Psychiatric Nursing, 18*, 39–48.

Ussher, J. M. (1991). *Women's madness: Misogyny or mental illness?* Hemel Hempstead, UK: Harverster Wheatsheaf.

Warner, J. (2005). *Perfect madness: Motherhood in the age of anxiety*. New York: Riverhead.

Whitton, A., Warner, R., & Appleby, L. (1996). The pathway to care in post-natal depression: Women's attitudes to post-natal depression and its treatment. *British Journal of General Practice, 46*, 427–428.

Wickberg, B., & Hwang, C. P. (1996). Counselling of postnatal depression: A controlled study on a population based Swedish sample. *Journal of Affective Disorders, 39*, 209–216.

Wilkinson, S. (1996). *Feminist social psychologies: International perspectives.* Buckingham, UK: Open University Press.

Willard, A. (1988). Cultural scripts of mothering. In C. Gilligan, J. V. Ward, & J. M. Taylor (Eds.), *Mapping the moral domain: A contribution of women's thinking to psychological theory and education* (pp. 225–243). Cambridge, MA: Harvard University Press.

Wilson, L. M., Reid, A. J., Midmer, D. K., Biringer, A., Carroll, J. C., & Stewart, D. E. (1996). Antenatal psychosocial risk factors associated with adverse postpartum family outcomes. *Canadian Medical Association Journal, 154*, 785–799.

Wisner, K. L., Parry, B., & Piontek, C. M. (2002). Postpartum depression. *New England Journal of Medicine, 347*, 194–199.

Wisner, K. L., & Stowe, Z. N. (1997). Psychobiology of postpartum mood disorders. *Seminars in Reproductive Endocrinology, 15*, 77–89.

Wood, A. F., Thomas, S. P., Droppleman, P. G., & Meighan, M. (1997). The downward spiral of postpartum depression. *MCN: The American Journal of Maternal/Child Nursing, 22*, 308–317.

Yamashita, H., Yoshida, K., Nakano, H., & Tashiro, N. (2000). Postnatal depression in Japanese women: Detecting the early onset of postnatal depression by closely monitoring the postpartum mood. *Journal of Affective Disorders, 58*, 145–154.

York, R. (1990). Pattern of postpartum blues. *Journal of Reproductive and Infant Psychology, 8*, 67–73.

22

Seeking Safety with Undesirable Outcomes: Women's Self-Silencing in Abusive Intimate Relationships and Implications for Health Care

Stephanie J. Woods

Women who are abused by male intimate partners experience a wide range of serious physical and mental health symptoms for which they seek health care. The effects of trauma, violence, and self-silencing may compromise a woman's relationships with health care practitioners, which could negatively impact the woman's health. In this chapter, I describe the physical and mental health consequences of women experiencing intimate male partner violence. Then, based on the literature and my own research, women's self-silencing within intimate relationships and the associations between silencing, physical and mental health symptoms, and health care utilization will be discussed. Ways in which intimately abused women relate to self and others will be examined. Lastly, implications for health care professionals who care for women who have experienced trauma, violence, and self-silencing will be addressed.

Violence against Women Is a Worldwide Problem

Violence against women by an intimate partner is a global social and health problem, occurring in both developing and industrialized countries, "in all cultures, and at every level of society without exception" (World Health Organization [WHO], 2002, p. 15). In their World Report on Violence and Health, the WHO (2002) cited the findings of Heise, Ellsberg, and Gottemoeller (1999) that 10% to 69% of women in 48 population-based surveys around the world reported physical violence by an intimate partner at some point in their lives. Similar lifetime prevalence rates were reported by the WHO (2005) in their 10-country study of 24,000 urban and rural women; that is, 15% to 71% of these women experienced physical and/or sexual violence by male intimate partners. Further, 30% to 56% of this sample reported experiencing both physical and sexual violence, and 20% to 75% of the women experienced emotional abuse by a partner including threats, insults, humiliation, and intimidation (WHO, 2005). Summarizing the findings of several researchers, the WHO (2002) noted that worldwide, there were consistent events that triggered the violence against women by an intimate partner. These included arguing, questioning or disobeying the man, not adequately caring for the house or children, refusing to have sex, and the man's suspicion of his partner's fidelity. Women were particularly vulnerable to intimate abuse in societies with distinct inequalities between men and women and rigid cultural norms and gender roles (WHO, 2002).

Intimate Partner Violence in the United States

Epidemiological surveys show that one in three American women will have experienced physical, emotional, or sexual abuse by a family member or intimate partner at some point during her life (The Commonwealth Fund, 1999; Plichta & Falik, 2001; Tjaden & Thoennes, 2000). Intimate partner violence (IPV), or domestic violence, may take a variety of forms, including physical violence, emotional abuse, sexual violence, threats of violence, and risk of homicide of women by men within an intimate relationship (Parker, McFarlane, Soeken, Silva, & Reel, 1999; Woods, Wineman, et al., 2005). Physical violence may involve hitting, kicking, punching, slapping, choking, and assaulting with a weapon (Saltzman, Fanslow, McMahon, & Shelley, 2002). Emotional or psychological abuse consists of criticisms, insults, belittlement, isolation, and shaming (Basile & Saltzman, 2002). Sexual violence is any forced or unwanted sexual activity including partner rape (Basile & Saltzman, 2002). Threats of violence include threats or gestures of harm to the woman or her loved ones, pets, property, and things the woman cares about (Saltzman et al., 2002). Often a woman will experience multiple forms of violence, for example, a woman who is being physically abused may also experience emotional abuse or threats of violence. Although there is variability across women in frequency, severity, and the length of time over which abuse occurs, a single violent episode is meaningful, as described later.

Physical and Mental Health Consequences of IPV for Women

Intimate partner violence has been shown to have both acute and long-term effects on the physical health of women (Campbell, 2002; Campbell et al., 2002;

Coker et al., 2002; Garcia-Moreno, Watts, Jansen, Ellsberg, & Heise, 2003; Woods, Hall, Campbell, & Angott, 2008). For instance, Campbell and colleagues (2002), in a multisite case-control study of 2005 HMO enrollees, found that intimately abused women compared to nonabused women experienced more (1) gynecological problems, including sexually transmitted diseases, urinary tract and vaginal infections, and painful sexual intercourse; (2) central nervous system problems such as neuromuscular symptoms, back pain, headaches, and seizures; and (3) chronic stress-related health problems such as hypertension and increased susceptibility to viral and bacterial infections. Women who have been out of the abusive relationship almost seven years experienced similar symptom patterns of physiological distress, neuromuscular symptoms, and chronic pain (Wineman, Woods, & Zupancic, 2004).

Even more fundamentally, alterations in neuroendocrine and immune function have been reported in research with women experiencing intimate abuse and posttraumatic stress disorder symptomatology (Gill, Vythilingam, & Page, 2008; Woods, Page, & Alexander, 2003; Woods, Page, Hall, & Alexander, 2008; Woods, Page, et al., 2005; Woods, Wineman, et al., 2005). More generally, research is beginning to demonstrate that the quality of social contacts and intimate relationships, such as good friendships and marriage, affects immune and endocrine function (Kiecolt-Glaser & Newton, 2001; Taylor et al., 2006). Findings of effects on neuroendocrine and immune functioning are important because they may help provide a deeper understanding of the interaction and integration of physiological pathways and emotional responses to trauma and violence and their effects on health.

Research on battered women also supports IPV as a significant risk factor for psychological/emotional health problems, including depression (Cascardi, O'Leary, & Schlee, 1999; Dienemann et al., 2000), substance abuse (Curry, 1998; Walton-Moss et al., 2003), and posttraumatic stress disorder (Bennice, Resick, Mechanic, & Astin, 2003; Wineman et al., 2004; Woods, 2000). Much of my own work has focused on posttraumatic stress disorder (PTSD) in women who have experienced intimate male partner violence. Part of the diagnostic criteria for PTSD is exposure to a traumatic event(s). Traumatic events, as described by the American Psychiatric Association (2000), involve experiencing, witnessing, or being confronted with an event that involves threat, harm, or death of oneself or others, and responses of "fear, helplessness, or horror" to these events. PTSD is characterized by symptoms of re-experiencing the trauma, avoidance and numbing, and hyperarousal.

A woman involved in an ongoing intimately abusive relationship is subject to chronic threat and injury/harm as a result of the frequency and/or intensity of intentional violent acts. The abused woman is also exposed to repetitive acute episodes of physical, emotional, and/or sexual violence. In a meta-analysis of 11 studies, Golding (1999) reported that 31% to 84.4% of women who experienced IPV met criteria for a diagnosis of PTSD (weighted mean prevalence = 63.8%).

All types of IPV—physical, emotional, and sexual abuse; threats of violence; and risk of homicide—have been found to predict PTSD in women (Wineman et al., 2004; Woods, Hall, Campbell, & Angott, 2008). Further, more frequent and severe intimate violence was associated with more severe PTSD symptoms.

It is important to note that many women experiencing intimate partner violence have also suffered significant physical, emotional, and sexual abuse, as well as neglect, as a child (Tjaden & Thoennes, 2000; Whitfield, Anda, Dube, & Felitti, 2003). Heim and Nemeroff (2001) noted that exposure to such early adverse events is a major risk factor for mental health problems, including development of depression and PTSD (DeBellis & Putnam, 1994; Goenjian et al., 1996; Shea, Walsh, MacMillan, & Steiner, 2005). Empirical evidence documents that exposure to childhood trauma may increase vulnerability to future stress and result in long-term neurobiological changes in stress response (Follette, Polusny, Bechtle, & Naugle, 1996; Friedman, Jalowiec, McHugo, Wang, & McDonagh, 2007; Heim, Newport, Bonsall, Miller, & Nemeroff, 2001; Resnick, Yehuda, Pitman, & Foy, 1995; Yehuda & Flory, 2007). This evidence suggests that there may be some women in intimately abusive relationships who are at more extreme risk of developing serious physical and mental health problems because of the effects of abuse experienced during their early developmental years. It is also unknown what effects exposure to early adverse or traumatic events, and the possible neurobiological changes that may occur, have on sensitivity to the prevailing sociocultural norms of silencing and the ways in which women connect with self and others.

Silencing Within an Intimate Relationship

The social-psychological context within which intimate partner violence occurs is important to consider. Violence or the threat of violence against women by men generally occurs within a context of intimacy, coercion, and intimidation and is a powerful means of subordinating women and maintaining social control (Dobash, Dobash, Cavanaugh, & Lewis, 1998; Humphreys & Campbell, 2004). Dobash and Dobash (1988) reported that men use violence against women "to silence them, to win arguments, to express dissatisfaction, to deter future behavior and to merely demonstrate dominance" (p. 57). A society structured along gender lines, with its unequal power relationships, fosters self-silencing and furthers the disconnection between a woman's authentic thoughts and feelings and what is publicly shown. Intimate partner violence results in severe silencing and lack of connection within a woman's self, her immediate relationships, and society (Landenburger, 1988; Miller, 1988; Pearlman & Courtois, 2005).

Miller and Stiver (1997) stated that "an inner sense of connection to others is *the* central organizing feature of women's development" (p. 16). That is, a woman's sense of self-esteem and well-being are connected to the quality of the human attachments she forms and her inner sense of connection with others

(Brown & Gilligan, 1992; Jack, 1991; Jordan, 1990). Women often silence themselves in relationships rather than risk negative interpersonal outcomes such as isolation, rejection, conflict, or violence (Belenky, Clinchy, Goldberg, & Tarule, 1986; Thompson, Whiffen, & Aube, 2001). For example, Belenky and colleagues found that women who experienced violence in their childhood homes often learned to maintain silence and keep secret the abusive events in their current home life. Yet this self-silencing comes with a price. Women who were silent were unable to see themselves participating in the give and take or exchange with others (Belenky et al., 1986).

One psychological mechanism through which silencing may occur is shaming. Shame is a painful feeling of being flawed, inadequate, or worthless as a person and is often imposed through ridicule, criticism, control, judgment, rage, and power-over behaviors by significant others. Shaming may originally stem from external sources, but over time can become internalized. Shaming is a powerful means of socializing and subordinating, keeping people from expressing their authentic reality, and thus it serves to disconnect, isolate, and silence individuals (Hartling, Rosen, Walker, & Jordan, 2000). Miller (1988) asserted that a terrifying sense of isolation results when a woman's thoughts, feelings, and actions are unacceptable in important relationships. Strategies of disconnection from the relationship with self and others are often used for protection or to ensure safety of thoughts and feelings that are not welcome or accepted (Briere, 2002; Jack, 1991; Jordan, 2003). Thompson and colleagues (2001) found in their research that women with critical and intolerant intimate partners tended to silence their thoughts and feelings, judge themselves by external standards, and disconnect from their feelings. They posited that a woman's disconnection within herself, which may have originally been meant as self-protective, was associated with increased depressive symptomatology.

A clear association between self-silencing and depression has been found in research with both women and men (Carr, Gilroy, & Sherman, 1996; Duarte & Thompson, 1999; Hart & Thompson, 1996). Cramer, Gallant, and Langlois (2005) found that depression in female undergraduates was predicted by higher self-silencing, higher self-concealment, and lower self-esteem (depression in male undergraduates was predicted by higher self-silencing and self-concealment only). Besser, Flett, and Davis (2003) reported a strong positive correlation between silencing the self and both depression and loneliness in men and women in their third year of undergraduate psychology, regardless of their current intimate relationship status. Besser and colleagues also found that higher levels of self-criticism were related to more silencing the self and postulated that persons who were highly sensitive to external feedback may use self-silencing as a means of protection or a way to sustain or improve relationships.

Although self-silencing may be used as a strategy of self-protection and as a way to sustain relationships, it comes with other costs. Women experiencing silencing will never know or feel the freedom of truly sharing their everyday authentic feelings or experiences or the meanings they carry. They cannot speak of their joys and victories nor their sorrows and suffering. And they will not know the acceptance, compassion, and nurturance that can accompany authenticity in relationship with self and others.

A series of studies I have conducted are described in the following section. First, I discuss women's self-silencing within intimate relationships and the relationships between silencing and mental health symptoms. Next, I describe the lasting physical and mental health consequences for women who have left an intimately abusive relationship and their health care utilization. Finally, I examine the severity of physical and mental health symptoms intimately abused women are experiencing and the ways they connect or relate to self and others.

Self-Silencing, PTSD, and Depression in Abused, Postabused, and Nonabused Women

The initial study examined differences on self-silencing in intimate relationships between abused, postabused, and nonabused women and the relationships between IPV, silencing the self (Silencing the Self Scale and subscales of Externalized Self-Perception, Care as Self-Sacrifice, Silencing the Self, and Divided Self; Jack, 1991), depression (Beck & Steer, 1993) and PTSD symptomatology (Horowitz, Wilner, & Alvarez, 1979; Saunders, Arata, & Kilpatrick, 1990) in women (Woods, 1997).

An ethnically diverse purposive group of 160 women (53 currently abused, 55 postabused who had been out of the abusive relationship at least two years, and 52 nonabused women) was recruited through bulletin board postings and pamphlets placed in shelters, clinical and community agencies, and newspapers. The average age of women in this study was 33.9 years ($SD = 11.7$) with a range of 18 to 67. Forty percent of the women were high school graduates and 46% had completed college. There were no differences between women in the three groups on age and race/ethnicity. The postabused and nonabused women had more formal education and higher income than the abused women. The average length of abusive relationship for the abused and postabused women was 7.5 years. The average length of time out of the abusive relationship for postabused women was 9.19 years. Almost three-quarters of abused women experienced PTSD symptoms and moderate depression. Approximately half to two-thirds of the postabused women continued to experience PTSD symptoms and mild depression, even though they had been out of the abusive relationship an average of 9 years.

What Differences Exist on Self-Silencing Between Abused, Postabused, and Nonabused Women?

The abused, postabused, and nonabused women differed significantly on the total Silencing the Self Scale [STSS; $M = 105.49, 87.19,$ and 65.67, respectively;

$F = 38.40$ (2, 157), $p < .001$]. Abused women [$M = 21.86$; $F = 27.26$ (2, 157), $p < .001$] had significantly higher levels of externalized self-perception than women who had left the intimately abusive relationship ($M = 17.87$) and nonabused women ($M = 13.21$), indicating that abused women more strongly judged themselves by external standards. Additionally, post hoc analysis indicated that postabused women experienced significantly more externalized self-perception than nonabused women.

Women were asked to identify external standards they felt they do not meet as part of the STSS measure. The standards women, as a whole, identified centered around issues of respect for self, relationships, autonomy, appearance/attractiveness and caring for home and family, and "being good enough." The women's "words" included "I'm not pretty," "I'm not attractive," "I'm overweight and not thin enough to be in public," "I'm not as intelligent as others," "I can't relate to other people well enough," "I'm not able to live up to my husband's standards of how the house should be kept up," "I can't cook or clean good enough," "I'm not a good enough mother, friend, or companion," and "I don't feel worth loving." It is interesting to note that the external standards that women in my study named as not meeting are strikingly similar to those identified in Jack's (1991) research, which was completed almost a decade earlier and in a different geographical location in the United States.

While these words were representative of all the women in this sample, several postabused women spoke of their goals and potential: "I want to make things good for my kids," "I want to take care of myself emotionally," "I want to go to school and get good grades," "I want to have a job title that my son can look up to," "I want to put myself first," "I want to achieve the goals I have set for myself," and "I want to be independent and responsible for my life." Overall, even though nonabused women in this sample showed less tendency to judge themselves by external standards, one nonabused woman echoed the sentiments of abused and postabused women when she said, "I do not do as much for family members as I should."

Abused women [$M = 27.14$; $F = 7.45$ (2, 157), $p < .001$] had higher levels of care as self-sacrifice in their interpersonal relationships than women who had left the intimately abusive relationship ($M = 23.60$) and those who had never been abused ($M = 21.72$). Post hoc analysis showed that postabused and non-abused women did not differ on care as self-sacrifice (Woods, 1997). This finding shows that abused women believe more strongly that putting others' needs before their own is essential and to do otherwise is selfish. A major theme identified in Gilligan's (1982) work was the commonly held belief that women should devote themselves to the care and protection of others "while remaining selfless." Societal images of intimacy and circumstances needed in order to be loved are introduced in early childhood, are repeated throughout adolescence and adulthood, and provide the groundwork for a woman to adapt and put the needs of others, including her partner, ahead of her own. An abused woman in this sample stated, "I think too much of others...more than I do for myself." A postabused woman wrote, "I need to be all things to all people." The contradictory positions within the patriarchal definitions of feminine love, that is, sacrifice the self or sacrifice the other, help keep women in unhealthy relationships and contribute to further self-negation (Jack, 1991). Yet, several postabused women seemed to be working at discovering their voices in relation to demands for self-sacrifice. They wrote, "I need to have more consideration for myself," "I need to set my limits/boundaries," and "I need to stick to my decisions."

Abused women [$M = 30.10$; $F = 24.53$ (2, 157), $p < .001$] had significantly higher levels on the Silencing the Self subscale in their interpersonal relationships than women who had left the intimately abusive relationship ($M = 24.86$) and nonabused women ($M = 18.31$), indicating that abused women inhibited voice or self-expression as a means of preserving relationship and decreasing conflict. The postabused women experienced significantly more silencing than nonabused women. Abused women noted that, "By keeping my feelings in, people won't get hurt" and "I bury my feelings." Several postabused women wrote, "I feel I do not give enough attention to my husband and children" and "I need to make him happy." These findings are congruent with the literature that women often silence themselves to avoid violence or rejection, please others, promote harmony in intimate relationships, and avoid attracting a partner's criticism and ridicule (Belenky et al., 1986; Jack, 1991; Thompson et al., 2001). Rose, Campbell, and Kub (1997) identified subordinating, which includes a woman's active self-silencing within her intimate relationships, as a primary means of caring for, and protecting the self in their research with an urban community sample of battered women.

Abused women [$M = 27.41$; $F = 62.99$ (2, 157), $p < .001$] had higher levels of the divided self in their interpersonal relationships than both women who had left the intimately abusive relationship ($M = 20.46$) and nonabused women ($M = 13.47$), indicating that abused women experienced more disconnection or inner split within self and in relationships (Woods, 1997). Post hoc analysis indicated that postabused women had higher levels of the divided self than nonabused women. The findings from this study support previous research that intimately abused women disconnect from their feelings and thoughts to meet their partner's needs, avoid violence, and/or maintain the relationship (Jack, 1991; Landenburger, 1988; Thompson et al., 2001). Thompson and colleagues (2001) found that women in an intimate relationship with a critical and intolerant partner had higher scores on the STSS Divided Self subscale and tended to present a compliant façade while hiding their true feelings, including anger. Abused women in the current study had stated, "I lose my sense of who I am" and "I can't feel as comfortable as I should around my partner." A postabused woman noted, "I need to be able to tell others my true feelings." These results also provide evidence for the paradox identified by Brown and Gilligan

(1992) and Miller (1991) that speaks to girls and women needing to withhold considerable portions of their authentic selves out of the relationship in order to be allowed in, or keep, the relationships.

Chronic disconnection and isolation are major sources of suffering and pain within many contexts (Jordan, 2003). Support for the association between isolation, pain, and disconnection in women who have experienced intimate abuse was given by a woman in the postabused context. This postabused woman was in prison and had heard of my study through her social worker and expressed a desire to participate in the research. I instructed the social worker on the research protocol including obtaining written informed consent. The social worker administered the study questionnaire to the woman, who, after completing it, hand wrote her story on the back of the questionnaire booklet. This woman had been married for 20 years when her abusive partner, stating God had revealed to him that the sin and rebellion of family friends was preventing him from accomplishing the redemption of the world, killed that family: the father, mother, and their three daughters. Despite a long history of physical, emotional, and sexual abuse resulting in severe injuries, including a ruptured spleen and damaged ear drums, this woman was judged "a principal party in the planning and commission of the crime." She wrote "'normal' life before prison was no contact with the outside world. He got the mail, he answered the phone, he controlled all the money . . . he kept the keys. He kept a loaded gun by the bed and often carried it on his person. I experienced more freedom as a maximum security inmate than I had known in 20 years of marriage."

> What Relationships Exist Between Intimate
> Partner Violence, Silencing the Self, Depression,
> and PTSD Symptomatology?

Women experiencing more frequent and severe intimate partner violence tended to have higher beliefs in societal norms and gender-specific socialization as delineated within the silencing the self construct. Higher beliefs in the self-silencing construct were associated with higher levels of depression in all the women as shown by a Pearson r correlation of .68, $p < .001$. Each of the STSS subscales was also significantly associated with depression, with correlations ranging from .53 to .70, $p < .001$. These findings indicate that women who tended to judge themselves by external standards used silencing as a means of preserving relationship and avoiding conflict and had more disconnection with self and in relationships experienced more severe depression.

Self-silencing within the woman's intimate relationship was also associated with higher levels of PTSD symptomatology in all the women as shown by a Pearson r correlation of .52, $p < .001$. Each of the STSS subscales was significantly associated with PTSD, with correlations ranging from .48 to .61, $p < .001$. Ways of sustaining and maintaining intimate relationships as defined by the silencing the self construct was also examined as a mediator of IPV and PTSD (Woods & Isenberg, 2001). A series of regression equations as outlined by Baron and Kenny (1986) were completed to test for mediation. The relationship between intimate partner violence and PTSD was partially mediated by self-silencing. This finding demonstrates that women who had more voice and connection with their authentic self, and within their interpersonal relationships, experienced less severe PTSD symptomatology than women who had higher levels of self-silencing and disconnection with self and in relationships.

The Lasting Physical and Mental Health Consequences of IPV

In the next study, I looked at long-term physical and mental health consequences for women who had left an intimately abusive relationship and their health care utilization. The participants consisted of 50 ethnically diverse women, average age of 37 years ($SD = 11$), who had been in their abusive relationship 10.13 years ($SD = 7.58$). These women experienced similar levels of self-silencing within their current intimate relationship as the postabused women described in the research earlier. Silencing was also associated with increased depression and PTSD symptoms (Clair & Woods, 2001). Slightly more than half of these postabused women met criteria for the diagnosis of PTSD (Woods & Wineman, 2004), and none of the women had recovered their preabused physical health state even though they had been out of the abusive relationship an average of 6.7 years ($SD = 6.41$).

The postabused women had averaged 11 visits to a health care professional during the years when they were in an active abusive relationship and averaged 9 visits during the past year (Clair & Woods, 2001). Seventy percent of the postabused women were never asked if they were being physically, emotionally, or sexually harmed by an intimate partner. Of the 12 women asked about intimate abuse, only 2 women identified receiving any direct help from the health care professional. When asked what they "had wished health care workers would have done to help," several women said that identifying options, giving information, and finding someplace safe would have been helpful. One woman said health care workers could "talk one-on-one with me" and another stated "anything would have been helpful." In response to the question one woman wrote, "to realize that abuse is not acceptable nor is it necessary."

How Intimately Abused Women Relate to Self, Others, and Health Care Practitioners

Lifton (1993) asserted that if someone is exposed to violence and trauma, that person internalizes a sense of worthlessness, thereby affecting not only identity, esteem, and voice but also the help they receive from others. I am currently examining several areas including severity of physical and mental health symptoms in intimately abused women and the ways they connect or relate to self and others. In this study, 157 ethnically diverse women currently experiencing intimate partner violence have entered into a two-year project investigating longitudinal relationships and trajectories of change among IPV, childhood maltreatment, resilience, posttraumatic stress disorder (Foa, Riggs, Dancu, & Rothbaum, 1993), depression (Briere, 1995), physical health, diurnal adrenocortical hormones, and immune function. The women were recruited through bulletin board postings, pamphlets, and weekly visits by the research team to three crisis battered women's shelters and community agencies providing domestic violence services in a midwestern state. All women have access to the services offered by the domestic violence agencies. Additional interventions are not part of the current study. The mean age of the women is 33.7 years ($SD = 9.52$) and they have been in the abusive relationship an average of 5.35 years ($SD = 6.7$). At least three-quarters of the women have a high school education or partial college or technical training. Most women meet diagnostic criteria for PTSD and about half of the sample are experiencing clinically significant depression. A substantial proportion of the women report physical health symptoms falling into four major areas: neuromuscular, stress, sleep, and gynecological symptoms. At entry into this study, IPV has been found to be predictive of more frequent physical health symptoms and more severe depressive and posttraumatic stress symptoms (Woods, Hall, et al., 2008; Woods, Page, et al., 2008). More than three-quarters (76.4%) of the women have sought health care treatment at least once during the previous nine months for physical health symptoms.

Beliefs about safety, trust, esteem, intimacy, and control are profoundly affected by violence and trauma (Pearlman, 2003). Each of these beliefs or cognitive schemas is important in developing and maintaining relationship with self and others and was assessed in these study participants using the Trauma and Attachment Belief Scale (Pearlman, 2003). There were significant associations between both PTSD and depression and each of the schemas of safety, trust, esteem, intimacy, and control. Women with more severe PTSD and depressive symptoms had greater struggles with a sense of safety for self and others, were more likely to distrust others, had greater disruption to their self-esteem or sense of self-worth, experienced increased difficulty with feeling connected to self or emotional closeness with others, and were likely to believe that they could not control thoughts, feelings, and actions because of fear, dissociation, intrusive memories, or feelings of helplessness (Woods, Page, et al., 2008).

These findings have serious implications for women seeking health care and for practitioners providing care. Women's attempts at obtaining professional help may be compromised by the effects of silencing, trauma, and their beliefs about connecting to self and others that have been, at least in part, a result of their lifetime experiences. The next section addresses implications of self-silencing, trauma, and relationship beliefs for health care professionals caring for abused women.

Implications for Health Care Professionals

Findings from research provide in-depth insights as to what might be most helpful for health care professionals in caring for women who have been steeped in the prevailing sociocultural scripts of self-silencing and self-sacrifice and who have experienced abuse in intimate relationships. Women exposed to violence or trauma often experience physical and mental health issues that provide multiple entry points into the healing professions. However, the varied characteristics of silencing, trauma and violence, and beliefs about relationships with self and others may compromise a woman's ability to speak openly about her experience in health care settings. And this could have dire consequences for a woman's health.

There is a rawness and a vulnerability to finding one's voice—and connecting to self and others—particularly after experiencing violence in deeply personal and intimate relationships. This vulnerability is further intensified if the woman is experiencing any posttraumatic stress or depressive symptoms as a result of the abuse. The shame and stigma associated with abuse may be heightened because these same concerns and issues are also attached to experiences of mental health symptoms.

Discovering voice, connecting with self, and learning to express one's thoughts and feelings are interwoven processes that need to be honored, encouraged, and allowed. Often women have not been taught how to identify or name a need or want and may need assistance and support in finding the words to describe their thoughts and feelings. Further, women have been frequently shamed or humiliated in all types of settings for having, and expressing, their authentic thoughts, feelings, or meanings of experiences.

Seeking health care can be intimidating and overwhelming even for persons with a sense of self and voice. The extent to which self-silencing occurs in all women is an issue, as withholding information affects the health care received and could negatively impact overall health. Yet, women who have experienced a lifetime of silencing and abuse within intimate relationships, who struggle with a personal sense of safety and worth and a mistrust of others, and who are disconnected from their authentic self, present a challenge for practitioners. Health care practitioners can help stay connected to women through patience, compassion, and respect, and by using words that help convey their effort at trying to understanding what the woman may need (Pearlman, 2003).

Green and Kimerling (2004) noted that persons who experience trauma, and who have or are experiencing PTSD, may be more likely to seek health care treatment in primary care settings than secondary or tertiary settings. Primary care settings provide a unique and important opportunity for early identification and possibly prevention of violence against women. Despite all the empirical support about the harmful effects of IPV, the knowledge of injury prevention with early intervention, and the number of different training programs available, many health care practitioners still do not routinely screen for intimate abuse. Incorporating simple questions into each routine assessment with women such as "Is anyone hurting you?" or "Are you safe at home?" can assist both the practitioner and the woman in identifying harmful situations and open up discussion for how best to proceed. Generally, an immediate need is safety. Practitioners can assist women to develop strategies that address their safety needs (and that of their children). They can assist in developing an exit plan, provide a list of community and legal resources in the area, or make referrals to other helping professionals and local domestic violence agencies.

Practitioners in all care settings may need to assist the woman to be visible as she attempts to describe her experiences and her health needs. They may need to recognize when she is not fully present or connected to herself or the other. Short responses to practitioner questions, agitation or jumpiness, and lack of eye contact may all be signals to the healer that the woman may be feeling shame or is struggling to find words that accurately describe what she is thinking or feeling. Gentle questions, encouragement, and possibly an occasional prodding query may help the woman gain a sense of comfort and safety and assist her in identifying more fully her health needs. Safety and trust will also need to be established. All the sophisticated medical technology and empirically based physical and mental health interventions will not be effective if a safe, trusted connection between the practitioner and the woman does not exist.

Human relationships provide a context for a large amount of self-silencing and violence in the world; relationships are also the essential context for healing the effects of self-silencing and violence (Briere & Scott, 2006; Miller & Stiver, 1997; Pearlman & Courtois, 2005). Within a health care context of mutual empathy, women can experience their own pain, authenticity, and vulnerability and experiment with their own voice without fear or worry. Connection, responsiveness, engagement, acceptance, and safety within the professional healing relationship offer support for the client's vulnerability and pain and assist in fostering the courage needed to move toward connection and relinquish strategies of disconnection (Hartling et al., 2000; Jordan, 2003). For those who have experienced trauma and abuse, this is often a slow process. Encouraging openness and connection goes against lifelong learning and dangerous vulnerability arises (Briere, 2002). Women, particularly those who have experienced violence, often wonder that if they risk using their voice, will they be heard? Will they be accepted? Will they be blamed or stigmatized? Will they be dismissed or humiliated? Will they be safe? Will they be shamed?

Jordan (1989) noted the importance of both the speaker and the listener in creating authentic dialogue and engagement. Honoring emotional openness and rewarding trust with compassion, care, and respect are vital to enhance growth-fostering relationships (Jordan, 2003). A woman may be sharing details of abuse and violent experiences for the first time, and the often-associated intense feelings of shame, anger, agitation, and embarrassment may be present (Briere & Scott, 2006). The woman may be especially sensitive to nuances in the practitioner's voice and body language and may fear stigmatization. Practitioners need to be aware of any issues, biases, or feelings that may arise within themselves and their influences on how they view the woman, what and how they hear her story or symptoms, and the care provided.

Even though a woman's encounters with physicians, nurses, and staff may be brief, they can have powerful positive or negative effects. Mutual empathy, caring, therapeutic nurturance, and engagement within the health care context require that health care professionals or healers be able to bear their own vulnerability, stay present when listening to painful stories and feelings, and identify and empathize with their own experiences of disconnection and shame (Briere, 2002; Hartling et al., 2000; Jordan, 2003). It also requires the ability to tolerate uncertainty (Jordan, 2003). If the health care professional or healer adopts the traditional image of "all-knowing," uses "power-over" strategies, is distant, or becomes disengaged within the health care context, these behaviors reinforce the dominant sociocultural patterns that often created the need to develop chronic personal and societal disconnection (Jordan, 2003; Walker 2002). Boundaries are also important: Jordan (2003) posited that if healers could think of the boundary line as a place of meeting, then they can state their limits rather than create and enforce an armored dividing line.

Finally, sociocultural influences affect the woman's process of healing. Women are generally socialized to express feelings such as sadness, fear, or helplessness directly, but are often taught to diminish or avoid stronger emotions such as anger, which presents issues within any health care context (Renzetti & Curran, 2002). Practitioners in all types of health care settings who are aware of the impact of societal beliefs and gender-specific socializations can encourage and support a full range of thoughts and feelings within the healing relationship (Briere & Scott, 2006). Authenticity, compassion and empathy, respect, and commitment in the health care relationship are essential for promoting health and healing for women who have experienced intimate violence (Walker, 2002).

Summary

Women who have experienced intimate violence tend to judge themselves by external standards, inhibit voice or self-expression as a means of preserving relationships and decreasing conflict, and experience disconnection or inner split within the self and in relationships. The studies described in this chapter offer support for the silencing the self construct and underscore the influence of societal and gender-specific norms and expectations for sustaining intimate relationships for abused and postabused women.

Women abused by intimate male partners experience serious physical and mental health symptoms, including depression and PTSD, for which they seek health care. However, the varied effects of self-silencing, trauma and violence, and beliefs about self in relationships may compromise a woman's relationships with practitioners in all health care settings. Health care practitioners need to be aware that a woman who has experienced trauma and violence often does not have full voice when trying to express her needs or experiences, which could adversely impact the woman's health.

References

American Psychiatric Association (APA). (2000). *Diagnostic and statistical manual of mental disorders* (4th ed., text revision). Washington, DC: American Psychiatric Association.

Baron, R. M., & Kenny, D. (1986). The moderator-mediator variable distinction in social psychological research: Conceptual, strategic, and statistical considerations. *Journal of Personality and Social Psychology, 51*, 1173–1182.

Basile, K. C., & Saltzman, L. E. (2002). *Sexual violence surveillance: Uniform definitions and recommended data elements.* Atlanta, GA: National Center for Injury Prevention and Control, Centers for Disease Control and Prevention.

Beck, A. T., & Steer, R. A. (1993). *Beck Depression Inventory manual.* San Antonio, TX: The Psychological Corporation.

Belenky, M. F., Clinchy, B. M., Goldberg, N. R., & Tarule, J. M. (1986). *Women's ways of knowing.* New York: Basic Books.

Bennice, J. A., Resick, P. A., Mechanic, M., & Astin, M. (2003). The relative effects of intimate partner physical and sexual violence on post-traumatic stress disorder symptomatology. *Violence and Victims, 18*, 87–94.

Besser, A., Flett, G. L., & Davis, R. A. (2003). Self-criticism, dependency, silencing the self, and loneliness: A test of a mediational model. *Personality and Individual Differences, 35*, 1735–1752.

Briere, J. (1995). *Trauma Symptom Inventory professional manual.* Odessa, FL: Psychological Assessment Resources.

Briere, J. (2002). Treating adult survivors of severe childhood abuse and neglect: Further development of an integrated model. In J. E. B. Myers, L. Berliner, J. Briere, C. T. Hendrix, T. Reid, & C. Jenny (Eds.), *The APSAC handbook on child maltreatment* (2nd ed., pp. 1–26). Newbury Park, CA: Sage Publications.

Briere, J., & Scott, C. (2006). *Principles of trauma therapy: A guide to symptoms, evaluations, and treatment.* Thousand Oaks, CA: Sage Publications.

Brown, L. M., & Gilligan, C. (1992). *Meeting at the crossroads.* New York: Ballantine.

Campbell, J.C. (2002). Health consequences of intimate partner violence. *Lancet, 359*, 1331–1336.

Campbell, J. C., Jones, A. S., Dienemann, J., Kub, J., Schollenberger, J., O'Campo, P., et al. (2002). Intimate partner violence and physical health consequences. *Archives Internal Medicine, 162,* 1157–1163.

Carr, J. G., Gilroy, F. D., & Sherman, M. F. (1996). Silencing the self and depression among women: The moderating role of race. *Psychology of Women Quarterly, 20,* 375–392.

Cascardi, M., O'Leary, K. D., & Schlee, K. A. (1999). Co-occurrence and correlates of posttraumatic stress disorder and major depression in physically abused women. *Journal of Family Violence, 14,* 227–249.

Clair, D., & Woods, S. J. (2001). *Post-battered woman's use of and experiences with health care.* Paper presented as part of a symposium on Trauma Across the Lifespan at the 25th Annual Midwest Nursing Research Society Conference, Cleveland, OH.

Coker, A. L., Davis, K. E., Arias, I., Desai, S., Sanderson, M., & Brandt, H. M. (2002). Physical and mental health effects of intimate partner violence for men and women. *American Journal Preventive Medicine, 23,* 260–268.

The Commonwealth Fund. (1999). *Violence and abuse.* New York: The Commonwealth Fund.

Cramer, K. M., Gallant, M. D., & Langlois, M. W. (2005). Self-silencing and depression in women and men: Comparative structural equation models. *Personality and Individual Differences, 39,* 581–592.

Curry, M. A. (1998). The interrelationships between abuse, substance use, and psychosocial stress during pregnancy. *Journal of Obstetric, Gynecologic, and Neonatal Nursing, 27,* 692–699.

DeBellis, M. D., & Putnam, F. W. (1994). The psychobiology of childhood maltreatment. *Child Adolescence Psychiatric Clinics of North America, 3,* 663–677.

Dienemann, J., Boyle, E., Baker, D., Resnick, W., Weiderhorn, N., & Campbell, J. (2000). Intimate partner abuse among women diagnosed with depression. *Issues in Mental Health Nursing, 21,* 499–513.

Dobash, R. E., & Dobash, R. P. (1988). Research as social action: The struggle for battered women. In K. Yllo & M. Bograd (Eds.), *Feminist perspectives on wife abuse* (pp. 51–74). Newbury Park, CA: Sage.

Dobash, R. P., Dobash, R. E., Cavanaugh, K., & Lewis, R. (1998). Separate and intersecting realities: A comparison of men's and women's accounts of violence against women. *Violence Against Women, 4,* 382–414.

Duarte, L., & Thompson, J. (1999). Sex differences in self-silencing. *Psychological Reports, 85,* 145–161.

Foa, E. B., Riggs, D. S., Dancu, C. V., & Rothbaum, B. O. (1993). Reliability and validity of a brief instrument for assessing post-traumatic stress disorder. *Journal of Traumatic Stress, 6,* 459–473.

Follette, V. M., Polusny, M. A., Bechtle, A. E., & Naugle, A. E. (1996). Cumulative trauma: The impact of child sexual abuse, adult sexual assault and spouse abuse. *Journal of Traumatic Stress, 9,* 25–35.

Friedman, M. J., Jalowiec, J., McHugo, G., Wang, S., & McDonagh, A. (2007). Adult sexual abuse is associated with elevated neurohormone levels among women with PTSD due to childhood sexual abuse. *Journal of Traumatic Stress, 20,* 611–617.

Garcia-Moreno, C., Watts, C., Jansen, H., Ellsberg, M. C., & Heise, L. (2003). Responding to violence against women: WHO's multicountry study on women's health and domestic violence. *Health & Human Rights, 6*, 113–129.

Gill, J., Vythilingam, M., & Page, G. G. (2008). Low cortisol, high DHEA-S, and high levels of stimulated TNF α and IL-6 in women with PTSD. *Journal of Traumatic Stress, 21*, 530–539.

Gilligan, C. (1982). *In a different voice*. Cambridge, MA: Harvard University Press.

Goenjian, A. K., Yehuda, R., Pynoos, R. S., Steinberg, A. M., Tashjian, M., Yang, R.K. et al. (1996). Basal cortisol and dexamethasone suppression of cortisol and MHPG among adolescents after the 1988 earthquake in Armenia. *American Journal of Psychiatry, 153*, 929–934.

Golding, J. M. (1999). Intimate partner violence as a risk factor for mental disorders: A meta-analysis. *Journal of Family Violence, 14*, 99–132.

Green, B. L., & Kimerling, R. (2004). Trauma, posttraumatic stress disorder, and health status. In P. P. Schnurr & B. L. Green (Eds.), *Trauma and health: Physical health consequences of exposure to extreme stress* (pp. 13–42). Washington, DC: American Psychological Association.

Hart, I. B., & Thompson, J. M. (1996). Gender role characteristics and depressive symptomatology among adolescents. *Journal of Early Adolescence, 16*, 407–426.

Hartling, L. M., Rosen, W., Walker, M., & Jordan, J. V. (2000). *Shame and humiliation: From isolation to relational transformation. Work in progress, No. 88*. Wellesley, MA: Stone Center Working Paper Series.

Heim, C., & Nemeroff, C. B. (2001). The role of childhood trauma in the neurobiology of mood and anxiety disorders: Preclinical and clinical studies. *Biological Psychiatry, 49*, 1023–1039.

Heim, C., Newport, D. J., Bonsall, R., Miller, A. H., & Nemeroff, C. B. (2001). Altered pituitary-adrenal axis responses to provocative challenge tests in adult survivors of childhood abuse. *American Journal of Psychiatry, 158*, 575–581.

Heise, L. L., Ellsberg, M., & Gottemoeller, M. (1999). *Ending violence against women: Population Reports Series L, No.11*. Baltimore, MD: Johns Hopkins University School of Public Health, Center for Communications Programs.

Horowitz, M. J., Wilner, N., & Alvarez, W. (1979). Impact of event scale: A measure of subjective stress. *Psychosomatic Medicine, 41*, 209–218.

Humphreys, J., & Campbell, J. C. (2004). *Family violence and nursing practice*. Philadelphia: Lippincott.

Jack, D. C. (1991). *Silencing the self: Women and depression*. Cambridge, MA: Harvard University Press.

Jordan, J. V. (1989). *Relational development: Therapeutic implications of empathy and shame. Work in progress, No. 39*. Wellesley, MA: Stone Center Working Paper Series.

Jordan, J. V. (1990). *Courage in connection: Conflict, compassion, creativity. Work in progress, No. 45*. Wellesley, MA: Stone Center Working Paper Series.

Jordan, J. V. (2003). *Valuing vulnerability: New definitions of courage. Work in progress, No. 102*. Wellesley, MA: Stone Center Working Paper Series.

Kiecolt-Glaser, J. K., & Newton, T. (2001). Marriage and health: His and hers. *Psychological Bulletin, 127*, 472–503.

Landenburger, K. M. (1988). Conflicting realities of women in abusive relationships. *Communicating Nursing Research, 21*, 15–20.

Lifton, R. J. (1993). From Hiroshima to the Nazi doctors: The evidence of psychoformative approaches to understanding traumatic stress syndromes. In J. P. Wilson & B. Raphael (Eds.), *International handbook of traumatic stress syndromes* (pp. 11–23). New York: Plenum Press.

Miller, J. B. (1988). *Connections, disconnections, and violations. Work in progress, No. 33.* Wellesley, MA: Stone Center Working Paper Series.

Miller, J. B. (1991). The development of women's sense of self. In J. V. Jordan, A. G. Kaplan, J. B. Miller, I. P. Stiver, & J. L. Surrey (Eds.), *In women's growth in connection* (pp. 11–26). New York: Guilford.

Miller, J. B., & Stiver, I. (1997). *The healing connection: How women form relationships in therapy and in life.* Boston: Beacon Press.

Parker, B., McFarlane, J., Soeken, K., Silva, C., & Reel, S. (1999). Testing an intervention to prevent further abuse to pregnant women. *Research in Nursing and Health, 22*, 59–66.

Pearlman, L. A. (2003). *Trauma and Attachment Belief Scale.* Los Angeles: Western Psychological Services.

Pearlman, L. A., & Courtois, C. A. (2005). Clinical applications of the attachment framework: Relational treatment of complex trauma. *Journal of Traumatic Stress, 18*, 449–459.

Plichta, S. B., & Falik, M. (2001). Prevalence of violence and its implications for women's health. *Women's Health Issues, 11*, 244–258.

Renzetti, C. M., & Curran, D. J. (2002). *Women, men, and society* (5th ed.). Boston: Allyn & Bacon.

Resnick, H. S., Yehuda, R., Pitman, R. K., & Foy, D. W. (1995). Effect of previous trauma on acute phase cortisol level following rape. *American Journal of Psychiatry, 152*, 1675–1677.

Rose, L., Campbell, J. C., & Kub, J. (1997). *The role of social support and family on women's responses to battering over time.* Paper presented at the meeting of the Nursing Network on Violence Against Women International, Charleston, WV.

Saltzman L. E., Fanslow J. L., McMahon P. M., & Shelley, G. A. (2002). *Intimate partner violence surveillance: uniform definitions and recommended data elements, version 1.0.* Atlanta, GA: Centers for Disease Control and Prevention, National Center for Injury Prevention and Control.

Saunders, B. E., Arata, C. M., & Kilpatrick, D. G. (1990). Development of a crime-related post-traumatic stress disorder scale for women within the symptom checklist-90-revised. *Journal of Traumatic Stress, 3*, 439–448.

Shea, A., Walsh, C., MacMillan, H., & Steiner, M. (2005). Child maltreatment and HPA axis dysregulation: Relationship to major depression and post traumatic stress disorder in females. *Psychoneuroendocrinology, 30*, 162–178.

Taylor, S. E., Gonzaga, G. C., Klein, L. C., Hu, P., Greendale, G. A., & Seeman, T. E. (2006). Relation of oxytocin to psychological stress responses and hypothalamic-pituitary-adrenocortical axis activity in older women. *Psychosomatic Medicine, 68,* 238–245.

Thompson, J. M., Whiffen, V. E., & Aube, J. A. (2001). Does self-silencing link perceptions of care from parents and partners with depressive symptoms? *Journal of Social and Personal Relationships, 18,* 503–516.

Tjaden, P., & Thoennes, N. (2000). *Extent, nature, and consequences of intimate partner violence.* Findings from the National Violence Against Women Survey No. NCJ 1818671. Washington, DC: U.S. Department of Justice.

Walker, M. (2002). *How therapy helps when the culture hurts. Work in progress, No. 95.* Wellesley, MA: Stone Center Working Paper Series.

Walton-Moss, B., Morrison, C., Yeo, R., Woodruff, K., Woods, A., Campbell, J. C., et al. (2003). Interrelationships of violence and psychiatric symptoms in women with substance use disorders. *Journal of Addictions Nursing, 14,* 193–200.

Whitfield, C. I., Anda, R. E., Dube, S. R., & Felitti, V. J. (2003). Violent childhood experiences and the risk of intimate partner violence in adults: Assessment in a large health maintenance organization. *Journal of Interpersonal Violence, 18,* 166–185.

Wineman, N. M., Woods, S. J., & Zupancic, M. (2004). *Intimate partner violence as a predictor of post-traumatic stress disorder symptom severity in women.* Paper presented at Sigma Theta Tau International's 15th International Nursing Research Congress: Dublin, Ireland.

Woods, A. B., Page, G. G., O'Campo, P., Pugh, L. C., Ford, D., & Campbell, J. C. (2005). The mediation effect of posttraumatic stress disorder on the relationship of intimate partner violence and IFN-y levels. *American Journal of Community Psychology, 36,* 159–175.

Woods, S. J. (1997). *Predictors of traumatic stress in battered women: A test and explication of The Roy Adaptation Model.* Unpublished doctoral dissertation, Wayne State University, Detroit, Michigan.

Woods, S. J. (2000). Prevalence and patterns of post-traumatic stress in abused and post-abused women. *Issues in Mental Health Nursing, 21,* 309–324.

Woods, S. J., Hall, R. J., Campbell, J. C., & Angott, D. M. (2008). Physical health and posttraumatic stress disorder symptoms in women experiencing intimate partner violence. *Journal of Midwifery and Women's Health, 53,* 538–546.

Woods, S. J., & Isenberg, M. A. (2001). Adaptation as a mediator of intimate abuse and traumatic stress in battered women. *Nursing Science Quarterly, 14,* 215–221.

Woods, S. J., Page, G. G., & Alexander, T. S. (2003). *Symptoms of PTSD, WBC counts, and diurnal cortisol circadian patterns in intimately abused women.* Poster presented at the Psychoneuroimmunology Research Society 10th International Annual Meeting, Amelia Island, FL.

Woods, S. J., Page, G. G., Hall, R. J., & Alexander, T. S. (2008). *PTSD, cortisol, immune function with battering over time.* Unpublished raw data (R01 NR009286).

Woods, S. J., & Wineman, N. M. (2004). Trauma, posttraumatic stress disorder symptom clusters, and physical health symptoms in postabused women. *Archives of Psychiatric Nursing, 18,* 26–34.

Woods, S. J., Wineman, N. M., Page, G. G., Hall, R. J., Alexander, T. S., & Campbell, J. C. (2005). Predicting immune status in women with PTSD and childhood and adult violence. *Advances in Nursing Science, 28,* 332–345.

World Health Organization (WHO). (2002). *World report on violence and health: Summary.* Geneva: World Health Organization.

World Health Organization (WHO). (2005). *WHO Multi-country study on women's health and domestic violence against women: Summary report of initial results on prevalence, health outcomes and women's responses.* Geneva: World Health Organization.

Yehuda, R., & Flory, J. D. (2007). Differentiating biological correlates of risk, PTSD, and resilience following trauma exposure. *Journal of Traumatic Stress, 20,* 435–447.

Commentary: Self-Silencing and Women's Depression

Janet M. Stoppard

The chapters in this collection provide ample evidence of the promise of formulations drawing on the self-silencing construct for understanding women's depression. The self-silencing construct provides a lens through which to make sense of women's experiences, currently labeled as depressive symptoms. Locating self-silencing within a relational framework helps to understand how women's depression may arise from disruptions in women's ongoing connections with others or failed attempts to sustain such connections (Jack, 1991; 1999a). As the research presented in this volume attests, there is now accumulating evidence that self-silencing is one outcome of life experiences known to increase risk of depression among women. Indeed, the extent to which a woman engages in self-silencing may signal the presence of depressogenic conditions in her life. More generally, self-silencing among women may serve as a marker for depression-inducing conditions that form a backdrop to many women's lives (see Astbury, this volume).

The potential utility of the self-silencing construct for understanding women's depression and, in turn, for ameliorating the problem of women's depression depends, however, on the validity of this construct. Further, the usefulness of the self-silencing construct for understanding women's depression rests on, and is delimited by, the manner in which concepts that underpin its meaning are understood. Chief among these concepts are depression, social context, and gender. In what follows, I offer some comments on limitations inherent in current conceptualizations of self-silencing, depression, social context, and gender. These limitations are ones that, in my view, would need to be overcome before the potential of self-silencing as an approach to understanding and responding to women's depression can be more fully realized.

Limitations of the Self-Silencing Construct

The Silencing the Self Scale (STSS) and other measures (see Smolak, this volume) to assess the self-silencing construct provide valuable research tools for investigating the role of psychological factors in women's depression. The promise of findings based in the self-silencing construct is likely, however, to be attenuated if research remains at the level of individual psychology. Transforming the self-silencing construct into a score (or scores) on a questionnaire has the effect of channeling understanding in directions that preclude consideration of social and cultural influences that shape women's lives and prefigure their lived experience. When self-silencing is conceived as a psychological variable, a characteristic of individual women, one danger is that individuals who self-silence may be judged as having a deficient self, a defect best remedied by means of interventions intended to modify an individual's cognitions or beliefs. Such "individualistic technologies of change" (Marecek, 2006, p. 299) risk becoming victim blaming, or may be interpreted as such by recipients, if the social context in which self-silencing arises is not given equal attention.

It is instructive here to consider findings of earlier attempts to explain women's higher prevalence of depression compared to men's in terms of cognitive vulnerability factors posited by cognitive-behavioral theories of depression (e.g., dysfunctional attitudes, self-defeating thoughts, ruminative self-focused coping). Among women, measures of such cognitive vulnerabilities have been found to be positively correlated with scores on depressive symptom measures (Hankin & Abramson, 2001; Nolen-Hoeksema, Larson, & Grayson, 1999). One interpretation of such findings has been that higher rates of depression among women can be explained by their tendency to have cognitive attributes that render them more vulnerable to becoming depressed. However, when the empirical underpinnings of this assumption were questioned, it turned out that women were no more likely than men (and less likely in many cases) to evidence the forms of depression vulnerability posited by cognitive-behavioral theories (Miller & Kirsch,1987; Stoppard, 1989). Findings that men score as high as, or higher than, women on measures of self-silencing and the various reformulations proposed to retain the gendered character of this construct (see Smolak, this volume) are reminiscent of earlier efforts to ground explanations for women's depression in cognitive vulnerability factors.

Rather than seeking refinements to the psychometric properties of measures such as the STSS and pursuing explanations for unpredicted findings they yield, there needs to be a shift away from conceptions of self-silencing as a feature of individual psychology. A more fruitful line of inquiry would be to explore how women's sense of self (or identity) is constituted and constrained discursively by discourses of femininity circulating in the culture in which they live. Among other things, such inquiries would aim to explicate the social meaning of activities currently associated with the figure of the "good" woman. Conceptions of self-silencing reflected in the content of measures such as the STSS are themselves rooted in assumptions about what it means to be a "good" woman. To what extent are such assumptions culturally and historically specific and so likely to render the experiences of some women invisible?

Limitations of the Depression Construct

Adherence to medicalized conceptions of depression as depressive disorder, defined according to diagnostic criteria contained in the *Diagnostic and Statistical Manual of Mental Disorders* (DSM), also sets limits on the scope of inquiries into women's depression. Treating the major depressive disorder (MDD) category as prototypical of depression ignores evidence that *atypical depression* is diagnosed more frequently among women, while MDD is more commonly diagnosed among men (Hamilton, 1995). Moreover, mixed anxiety and depression, more common among women, is not included as a diagnostic category in the DSM. What these examples illustrate is that the DSM, a cornerstone of research on depression, excludes aspects of the depressive experiences of women in its formulation of the diagnostic category of depression.

Whether operationalized as responses on symptom questionnaires or mapped by diagnostic criteria, aspects of women's depressive experiences remain unexplored. For instance, in a study of older women's experiences of being depressed, Guptill (2005) found little correspondence between how women described their experiences and the symptoms they endorsed on a version of the Center for Epidemiologic Studies Depression (CES-D) scale modified for older adults that included items corresponding to diagnostic criteria for MDD. A prominent aspect of how these older women described their experience of being depressed was loneliness, stemming particularly from feeling socially cut off or alienated as a result of existing on the margins of society. At the same time, depressed mood and loss of interest or pleasure in previously enjoyed activities, key symptoms of MDD, were endorsed by few women on the CES-D scale. Of relevance here are Marecek's (2006) reminders that "depression is a cultural category arising in a particular time and place" (p. 284) and that "the diagnostic category of depression encompasses just a small fraction of the total field of depressive suffering" (p. 285).

Understanding the Conditions That Promote
Self-Silencing and Depression

Although studies exploring links between self-silencing and depressive experiences in individual women are an important step on the way to understanding women's depression, research focused on depressed women contributes little to explaining how they became depressed. How is self-silencing implicated in the process of becoming depressed? Is self-silencing a precursor to becoming depressed, an aspect of depressive experiences, or a consequence of being depressed? Do similar conditions lead to both self-silencing and depression, or do different conditions lead to self-silencing and depression?

In her groundbreaking study that resulted in the formulation of self-silencing as a way of understanding women's depression, Dana Jack (1991) drew attention to the everyday lives of women struggling to sustain an intimate relationship under conditions in which their efforts were ultimately unsuccessful. According to Jack, the women who participated in her study became depressed when they realized that in the process of sacrificing their own needs in service of those of their relational partners, they had lost themselves or, to use Jack's terms, they had "silenced the self." The self that is silenced is the "authentic self," one that, in Jack's account, is relational.

For Jack, the source of self-silencing lies in conditions characterized by "specific forms of unequal, negative intimate relationships as well as larger social structures that demean an individual's sense of self-worth" (1996, p. 15). This aspect of Jack's theorizing points to the need to go beyond a narrow focus on self-silencing as an attribute of individual psychology to include the social context in which women's everyday lives are embedded. A shift to more psychosocial approaches to understanding women's depression, however, raises the issue of how to conceptualize "social context." Researchers have drawn on a variety of strategies in this regard, from ones that focus on more micro aspects of social life (e.g., stressful life events) that affect individual women to use of more macro indicators of conditions in society that are structured along gender lines and have an impact on large numbers of women (e.g., income inequalities).

Social Context as Local Conditions

When social context is conceptualized at the micro level by focusing on the local conditions of people's lives, research by British sociologist George Brown and colleagues (Brown & Harris, 1989) has made an important contribution to understanding how events arising in the context of women's everyday lives can lead to their becoming depressed. A key finding, now replicated with several different samples of women in studies conducted since the 1970s (see Brown & Harris, 1989), is that onset of depressive disorder can be predicted with a relatively high degree of certainty from knowledge of events occurring in women's lives during the 6 to 12 months before they became depressed. To assess events in women's lives, Brown and colleagues collected information from individual women using a structured interview called the Life Events and Difficulties Schedule (LEDS) (Brown, 1989). The LEDS enables the degree of personal threat implied by an event to be rated in the context of a woman's ongoing life situation. Personal threat is defined in terms of important losses and disappointments (e.g., death of a close relative), including threats to a valued role (such as being a mother), and loss of a cherished idea (e.g., trust in the good character of a spouse).

More recently, Brown, Harris, and Hepworth (1995) have explored the social meaning of events that may provoke depression in the women who experience them. Two aspects of events, the degree to which they involve, or imply, humiliation and/or entrapment, have been found to characterize events that provoke depression onset. Humiliating events are ones that render a woman devalued in relation to herself or others, such as failure or rejection in an important relationship. Entrapping events are those that signify the persistence or worsening of an already stressful situation. Brown and colleagues (1995) summarized their findings in the following way: "Probably equally significant to being humiliated and devalued is what is symbolized by such atypical events in terms of the woman's life as a whole – in particular, the experience of being confirmed as marginal and unwanted" (p. 19).

Clear parallels are apparent between Brown and colleagues' identification of events in women's lives that lead to feelings of being marginalized and unwanted as a cause of becoming depressed and Jack's characterization of social conditions that "demean an individual's sense of self-worth" as a source of self-silencing. An interesting direction for future inquiry would be to combine Brown and colleagues' methodology for mapping the meaning of events in women's lives with assessment of self-silencing to explore how self-silencing is implicated in the experience of life events that lead to feelings of being marginal and unwanted.

Social Context as Structural Conditions

When social context has been conceptualized in more macro terms, structural conditions reflected in indicators such as poverty and income inequality have been included in models for prediction of risk of depression. Women (especially women of color and single-parent women) are overrepresented among the poor, and these economic indicators have been found to be strongly associated with risk of depression among women in the United States (Belle & Doucet, 2003). Structural conditions that lead to or exacerbate income and other inequalities between women and men also shape the circumstances of individual women's lives by governing the allocation of social and material resources that may help to offset the negative impact of stressful life events.

Astbury (this volume) argues that "risk factors" for women's depression "might more accurately be conceptualized as proxy variables for a range of rights violations." She presents a convincing case for reframing risk factors for women's depression (among which she includes gender-based violence, life events resulting in humiliation and entrapment, and unfair treatment in the workplace) as instances of violations of women's human rights. Astbury's analysis repositions women's depression and the overrepresentation of women among the depressed as arising from, and evidence of, social injustices sustained by women, rooted in conditions that disadvantage women economically, politically, and socially. The kind of analysis developed by Astbury is in keeping with approaches that point to the importance of so-called "determinants of health" in understanding the health of populations (Evans, Barer, & Marmor, 1994). Not only is gender a determinant of health, which includes mental health, but also each of the determinants—key ones being income, education, and employment—is gendered (Stoppard, 2004). A more fully contextualized understanding of women's lives needs to attend not only to the local contexts that constitute the particular circumstances of individual women's lives but also to the more distal conditions that shape these circumstances. In essence, both micro and macro approaches to conceptualizing "social context" are needed to better understand links between self-silencing and women's depression.

Limitations in Conceptualizing Gender

A typical strategy for addressing gender in research is in terms of "sex of subject" by recording whether participants are female or male. This strategy is quite limited, however, because gender is conflated with biological sex, and other important aspects of gender are ignored. When gender is treated only as an individual characteristic (as female or male), structural and symbolic aspects of gender are overlooked (Stoppard, 2000).

Gender has also been conceptualized structurally in terms of the division of labor in society, where women do most of the work involved in caring for family members, a central aspect of which is child care. The lives of women who combine family caregiving with paid employment (usually outside the home) have been depicted as involving a double day or second shift (Lorber, 1994). The gendered division of labor is reflected in society in the substantial ways in which the everyday experiences of most women differ from those of most men. For instance, knowing that a woman is a mother of young children already provides some information about what her everyday activities are likely to involve—and also how her daily life will differ from that of a father with young children at home.

When gender is characterized solely as an individual characteristic, a woman's involvement in family caregiving is likely to be attributed to her psychological nature as someone oriented toward relationships because of her feminine personality traits. Overlooked here are structural conditions in society that operate to maintain prevailing gender relations: women generally earn less than men (because of pay and employment inequities); good-quality, affordable child care is lacking; and jobs are typically not structured in ways that take family needs into account. Given these structural conditions, it is hardly surprising that women continue to have primary responsibility for child care and other activities in the home.

The third, symbolic aspect of gender is most often overlooked, or obscured in use of individualizing concepts such as "gender stereotypes" or "sex role attitudes." Rather than being restricted to the level of individual beliefs, symbolic aspects of gender operate at the cultural level and are reflected in widely shared beliefs about what it means to be a woman (or a man). Cultural "discourses of femininity" portray the "good" woman as someone whose activities ideally are oriented toward relationships and caring for family members (especially children) (Jack, 1991; Lafrance, 2009; Ussher, 1991). Such discourses both dovetail with and provide support for family and societal arrangements in which women do much of the work of caring while placing the needs of others ahead of their own. When women put their own needs first or make self-care a priority, they risk being seen as selfish, something that a good woman must strive to avoid.

The importance of attending to the symbolic aspect of gender is highlighted by Lafrance's (2009) study of women's experiences of recovery from being depressed. For the women in Lafrance's study, overcoming depression involved a process of resisting the culturally endorsed ideal of the good woman while struggling to sustain the legitimacy of an identity in which they put their own needs first. Self-care was central to their well-being but threatening to their identities as women. The process of recovery from being depressed was one marked by a form of resistance in which women struggled to position themselves within a cultural context that celebrates the good woman identity and condemns women's (and especially mothers') attention to their own needs as selfish. Findings such as those by Lafrance point to the importance of understanding the role played by self-silencing in maintaining the good woman ideal as a mainspring of women's identity and how disruption of the silenced self is implicated in resistance to this culturally endorsed ideal (see Ussher & Perz, this volume).

Concluding Comments

A fuller understanding of the links between self-silencing, gender, and depression means moving beyond a limited conception of gender as an individual characteristic and also addressing social context in ways that extend beyond the particular circumstances of individual women's lives to include structural conditions that shape all women's lives. Attention also needs to be given to strategies for assessing depressive experiences that are not confined to symptoms on self-report questionnaires or diagnostic criteria for MDD in the *DSM*.

Consideration also needs to be given to methodological issues in research on self-silencing and women's depression. While use of measures such as the STSS fits well with the requirements of quantitative methodologies and the need for numerical data, the contribution that qualitative research approaches can make to understanding women's experiences of being depressed and overcoming such experiences should not be overlooked (see Jack, 1999b; Lafrance & Stoppard, 2006; Stoppard & McMullen, 2003). The research by Dana Jack, described in her book *Silencing the Self: Women and Depression* (1991), was original not least because it resulted in identification of self-silencing as a way of understanding women's depression. Her research was also groundbreaking because she had the courage to employ a qualitative methodology at a time when use of such approaches was both highly unusual and devalued within psychology. Regardless of the methodology used, researchers should aim to follow Jack's lead by carrying her innovative work forward in ways that honor attention to women's experiences without individualizing and pathologizing women's depressive suffering.

Acknowledgment

The author thanks Michelle N. Lafrance for her constructive feedback on an earlier draft of this commentary.

References

Belle, D., & Doucet, J. (2003). Poverty, inequality, and discrimination as sources of depression among U.S. women. *Psychology of Women Quarterly, 27*, 101–113.

Brown, G. W. (1989). Life events and measurement. In G. W. Brown & T. O. Harris (Eds.), *Life events and illness* (pp. 3–45). London: Unwin Hyman.

Brown, G. W., & Harris, T. O. (1989). Depression. In G. W. Brown & T. O. Harris (Eds.), *Life events and illness* (pp. 49–93). London: Unwin Hyman.

Brown, G. W., Harris, T. O., & Hepworth C. (1995). Loss, humiliation and entrapment among women developing depression: A patient and non-patient comparison. *Psychological Medicine, 25*, 7–21.

Evans, R., Barer, M., & Marmor, T. (Eds.). (1994). *Why are some people healthy and others not? The determinants of health of populations.* New York: Aldine de Gruyter.

Guptill, A. M. (2005). *Understanding depression in older women: A qualitative study.* PhD dissertation, University of New Brunswick (Canada), Canada. Retrieved December 4, 2008, from Dissertations & Theses @ University of New Brunswick database. (Publication No. AAT NR35746).

Hamilton, J. A. (1995). Sex and gender as critical variables in psychotropic drug research. In C. V. Willies, P. P. Rieker, M. M. Kramer, & B. S. Brown (Eds.), *Mental health, racism, and sexism* (pp. 297–349). Pittsburgh, PA: University of Pittsburgh Press.

Hankin, B. J., & Abramson, L. Y. (2001). Development of gender differences in depression: An elaborated cognitive vulnerability-transactional stress theory. *Psychological Bulletin, 127*, 773–796.

Jack, D. C. (1991). *Silencing the self: Women and depression.* Cambridge, MA: Harvard University Press.

Jack, D. C. (1996, August). *Silencing the self: Theory and new findings*. Paper presented at the meeting of the American Psychological Association, Toronto, Canada.

Jack, D. C. (1999a). Silencing the self: Inner dialogues and outer realities. In T. E. Joiner & J. C. Coyne (Eds.), *The interactional nature of depression: Advances in interpersonal approaches* (pp. 221–240). Washington, DC: American Psychological Association.

Jack, D. C. (1999b). Ways of listening to depressed women in qualitative research: Interview techniques and analysis. *Canadian Psychology, 40*, 91–101.

Lafrance, M. N. (2009). *Women and depression: Recovery and resistance*. London: Routledge.

Lafrance, M. N., & Stoppard, J. M. (2006). Constructing a non-depressed self: Women's accounts of recovery from depression. *Feminism & Psychology, 16*, 307–325.

Lorber, J. (1994). *Paradoxes of gender*. New Haven, CT: Yale University Press.

Marecek, J. (2006). Social suffering, gender, and women's depression. In C. L. Keyes & S. H. Goodman (Eds.), *Women and depression: A handbook for the social, behavioral and biomedical sciences* (pp. 283–308). Cambridge: Cambridge University Press.

Miller, S. M., & Kirsch, N. (1987). Sex differences in cognitive coping with stress. In R. C. Barnett, L. Biener, & G. K. Baruch (Eds.), *Gender and stress* (pp. 278–307). New York: Free Press.

Nolen-Hoeksema, S., Larson, J., & Grayson, C. (1999). Explaining the gender difference in depressive symptoms. *Journal of Personality and Social Psychology, 77*, 1061–1072.

Stoppard, J. M. (1989). An evaluation of the adequacy of cognitive/behavioural theories for understanding depression in women. *Canadian Psychology, 30*, 39–47.

Stoppard, J. M. (2000). *Understanding depression: Feminist social constructionist approaches*. London: Routledge.

Stoppard, J. M. (2004). Social explanations of depression: A gendered social determinants model. In J. Ruggieri & W. Yu (Eds.), *Determinants of health: An Atlantic perspective* (pp. 69–84). Fredericton, New Brunswick, Canada: Policy Studies Centre, University of New Brunswick.

Stoppard, J. M., & McMullen, L. M. (Eds). (2003). *Situating sadness: Women and depression in social context*. New York: New York University Press.

Ussher, J. M. (1991). *Women's madness: Misogyny or mental illness?* Hemel Hempstead, UK: Harvester Wheatsheaf.

Appendix A: The Silencing the Self Scale

By Dana Crowley Jack

Please circle the number that best describes how you feel about each of the statements listed below. If you are not currently in an intimate relationship, please indicate how you felt and acted in your previous intimate relationships.

Strongly disagree	Somewhat disagree	Neither agree nor disagree	Somewhat agree	Strongly agree

*1. I think it is best to put myself first because no one else will look out for me.

1	2	3	4	5

2. I don't speak my feelings in an intimate relationship when I know they will cause disagreement.

1	2	3	4	5

3. Caring means putting the other person's needs in front of my own.

1	2	3	4	5

4. Considering my needs to be as important as those of the people I love is selfish.

1	2	3	4	5

5. I find it is harder to be myself when I am in a close relationship than when I am on my own.

1	2	3	4	5

6. I tend to judge myself by how I think other people see me.

1	2	3	4	5

7. I feel dissatisfied with myself because I should be able to do all the things people are supposed to be able to do these days.

1	2	3	4	5

(continued)

(Continued)

	Strongly disagree	Somewhat disagree	Neither agree nor disagree	Somewhat agree	Strongly agree

*8. When my partner's needs and feelings conflict with my own, I always state mine clearly.

    1   2   3   4   5

9. In a close relationship, my responsibility is to make the other person happy.

    1   2   3   4   5

10. Caring means choosing to do what the other person wants, even when I want to do something different.

    1   2   3   4   5

*11. In order to feel good about myself, I need to feel independent and self-sufficient.

    1   2   3   4   5

12. One of the worst things I can do is to be selfish.

    1   2   3   4   5

13. I feel I have to act in a certain way to please my partner.

    1   2   3   4   5

14. Instead of risking confrontations in close relationships, I would rather not rock the boat.

    1   2   3   4   5

*15. I speak my feelings with my partner, even when it leads to problems or disagreements.

    1   2   3   4   5

16. Often I look happy enough on the outside, but inwardly I feel angry and rebellious.

    1   2   3   4   5

17. In order for my partner to love me, I cannot reveal certain things about myself to him/her.

    1   2   3   4   5

18. When my partner's needs or opinions conflict with mine, rather than asserting my own point of view I usually end up agreeing with him/her.

    1   2   3   4   5

19. When I am in a close relationship I lose my sense of who I am.

    1   2   3   4   5

20. When it looks as though certain of my needs can't be met in a relationship, I usually realize that they weren't very important anyway.

    1   2   3   4   5

*21. My partner loves and appreciates me for who I am.

    1   2   3   4   5

(continued)

Strongly disagree	Somewhat disagree	Neither agree nor disagree	Somewhat agree	Strongly agree

22. Doing things just for myself is selfish.

    1   2   3   4   5

23. When I make decisions, other people's thoughts and opinions influence me more than my own thoughts and opinions.

    1   2   3   4   5

24. I rarely express my anger at those close to me.

    1   2   3   4   5

25. I feel that my partner does not know my real self.

    1   2   3   4   5

26. I think it's better to keep my feelings to myself when they do conflict with my partner's.

    1   2   3   4   5

27. I often feel responsible for other people's feelings.

    1   2   3   4   5

28. I find it hard to know what I think and feel because I spend a lot of time thinking about how other people are feeling.

    1   2   3   4   5

29. In a close relationship I don't usually care what we do, as long as the other person is happy.

    1   2   3   4   5

30. I try to bury my feelings when I think they will cause trouble in my close relationship(s).

    1   2   3   4   5

31. I never seem to measure up to the standards I set for myself.

    1   2   3   4   5

If you answered the last question with a 4 or 5, please list up to three standards you feel you don't measure up to.

1.

2.

3.

4.

* Items with an asterisk are reverse-scored.

Index

Note: Page numbers followed by "*f*" and "*t*" denote figures and tables, respectively.

CPSIA information can be obtained at www.ICGtesting.com
Printed in the USA
BVOW03s0842160714

359342BV00002B/45/P

9 780199 932023